Cousins and Strangers

The publisher gratefully acknowledges the generous contribution provided by the Program for Cultural Cooperation between Spain's Ministry of Culture and United States' Universities, which helped support the publication of this book.

The publisher gratefully acknowledges the contribution provided by the General Book Endowment Fund of the Associates of the University of California Press, which is supported by generous gifts from individuals.

Cousins and Strangers

*Spanish Immigrants in Buenos Aires,
1850–1930*

JOSE C. MOYA

University of California Press

BERKELEY   LOS ANGELES   LONDON

University of California Press
Berkeley and Los Angeles, California

University of California Press, Ltd.
London, England

© 1998 by
The Regents of the University of California

Library of Congress Cataloging-in-Publication Data

Moya, Jose C., 1952–
    Cousins and strangers : Spanish immigrants in Buenos Aires,
  1850–1930 / Jose C. Moya.
        p.   cm.
    Includes bibliographical references and index.
    ISBN 978-0-520-21526-9 (pbk. : alk. paper)
    1. Spaniards—Argentina—Buenos Aires—History.   2. Immigrants—
  Argentina—Buenos Aires—History.   3. Spain—Emigration and
  immigration—History.   4. Argentina—Emigration and immigration—
  History.   5. Spaniards—Cultural assimilation—Argentina—Buenos
  Aires.   6. Social adjustment—Argentina—Buenos Aires.   7. Buenos
  Aires (Argentina)—Ethnic relations.   I. Title.
  F3001.9.S7M6   1997
  982'.00461—dc20
                                                                96-26731
                                                                    CIP

Printed in the United States of America

08   07
9   8   7   6   5

For Paula, Cristina, and Sebastián

Contents

Illustrations

Maps

Figures

Tables

Acknowledgments

Support from various institutions during the past decade made this study possible. A Doherty Foundation Fellowship from Princeton University and a Fulbright Fellowship allowed me to spend two years in Buenos Aires conducting research for a dissertation that—to the exasperation of friends and family—became an endless search for the gist of the immigration experience at a time when such searches were increasingly tagged as universalizing and essentialist by many an advocate of specificity and constructionism. A Marion Johnson Fellowship from Rutgers University allowed me to complete the dissertation. A grant from the Del Amo Foundation made possible a postdoctoral research trip to Spain in 1989. Invitations to conferences in Galicia and Asturias by my Spanish colleagues Xavier Castro and Nicolás Sánchez-Albornoz provided opportunities for further research escapades. Since 1990, yearly research grants from the Academic Senate of the University of California and occasional ones from the Latin American Studies Center at UCLA have supported this project. And the University of California Press demonstrated boundless patience as I delayed the publication of this book almost five years with further research and perpetual revisions and additions.

The personnel in scores of libraries, archives, immigrant associations, parishes, and town halls in Spain, Argentina, and the United States offered crucial assistance, often overcoming institutional inefficiency or rigidity with an ample dosage of goodwill and ingenuity. The immigrants and returnees who welcomed me into their homes on both sides of the Atlantic were, similarly, too numerous to thank individually here. The forty or so who put up with my intrusive tape recorder are recognized—though not properly thanked—in the notes. My even more numerous coworkers during fifteen years of toiling in factories inoculated me against the airy academic notion that reality and common sense are "bourgeois inventions." This social history of immigrants and workers benefited much from that unorthodox—and at the time, unwanted—training.

Fellow historians have consistently made me glad that I switched trades. In Buenos Aires, I was fortunate to enjoy the camaraderie and cooperation of Alicia Bernasconi, María and Fernando Devoto, Luigi Favero, Alejandro Fernández, Carlos Mayo, Mario Nascimbene, Carlos Newland, Antonio Pérez-Prado, Eduardo Saguier, Carina Silberstein, and Ruth Seefeld. They trashed the myth of Porteño pedantry and are much to blame for my incurable infatuation with their city. At Rutgers University, Robert Alexander, Gwendolyn Hall, and Mark Wasserman offered valuable advice during the early stages of this project; my eternal mentor, Sam Baily, became the force behind it and a source of unending inspiration as both scholar and friend; and Virginia Yans-McLaughlin freely shared with me her almost intuitive understanding of immigration. At UCLA, the late Bradford Burns, Bob Burr, James Lockhart, Eric Monkkonen, Jan Reiff, Bill Summerhill, Albion Urdank, and Mary Yeager read more advanced versions of the manuscript and offered the type of counsel that makes one proud to have scholars like these as colleagues. My doctoral students Nathaniel Acker, Nuri Alexander, Christine Ehrick, Maria Ana Quaglino, Reinaldo Roman, Judith Sweeney, and Ericka Verba did likewise, confirming—one more time—that they are "students" only in the sense that we all are—or should be. Outside my alma mater and my home institution, Jim Baer, Dain Borges, and Birgit Sonesson read chapters of the manuscript and made helpful suggestions; Ida Altman, Jeremy Adelman, Stephanie Bower, William Douglass, Louisa Hoberman, Ronald Newton, Walter Nugent, David Rock, and Kristin Ruggiero read it in its entirety and offered subtle and priceless criticism. Despite the generous and wise advice of these friends and colleagues, I managed to leave in plenty of blunders and awkward prose for Rose Anne White and Sarah K. Myers to struggle with. The book is the better for their efforts, and whatever flaws remain should be read as evidence of my endurable folly.

As with most immigrants, my greatest debt is to my family: my late mother, Marta Hajje, who introduced me to—as she used to say and as I still believe—the pleasures of the mind; my father and emotional sustainer, Edmundo; my life companion and great love, Paula Soler Moya, who also became my forebearing editor and aesthetic guru; my *bella figlia* and soul mate, Cristina; and my son, Sebastián, whose wit and humor buoy us all.

Introduction

During the era of mass transoceanic migrations, between the midnine-teenth-century and the Great Depression, more than 4 million Spaniards came to the New World. Their major destination was Argentina, especially Buenos Aires, where a third of those who settled in the country stayed.[1] According to Argentine statistics, 2,070,874 Spaniards entered the country between 1857 and 1930. Some returned after stays of varying lengths, others went back and forth, but more than half (54 percent) remained permanently. Even the net immigration surpassed that of all the conquistadors and settlers who came to Spanish America during the entire colonial period.[2] In fact, by the eve of World War I there were more Spaniards in the city of Buenos Aires (306,000) than there had been in all of the Spanish colonies at any given time before the Wars of Independence. More Spaniards lived in the Argentine capital then than in any Spanish city except Madrid and Barcelona. They formed one of the largest immigrant urban communities in the world and helped turn Buenos Aires into the second largest city on the Atlantic seaboard (after New York City) and the largest south of the equator. Yet, although volumes on the conquistadors fill shelves, not one scholarly book has been written about the experiences of these more recent and numerous newcomers to Buenos Aires.[3]

Several factors account for this neglect. An obvious one is that the immigrants' experiences, though intensely and intriguingly human, included no mythical conquests of empires, no brave and bloody battles. And if they lacked the mantle of masculine bravura and heroism that could have dazzled traditional, and predominantly male, historians, they also lacked the aura of "otherness" or subjugation that could have attracted more progressive Western scholars. North Americans and western Europeans, for instance, have penned forty-one volumes on the Yanomami (all published) but only two on Spaniards in postindependence Latin America (both on Mexico and both unpublished).[4]

A related reason for this scholarly oblivion is the fact that although Spaniards formed the fifth largest numerical group of European emigrants, relatively few headed for the United States or other eventually "developed" countries where social history first appeared and flourished. Although European emigration to the United States (32.6 million between 1820 and 1930) outnumbered that to Argentina (6.5 million) by a ratio of 5 to 1, studies on the former surpass those on the latter by a ratio of 26 to 1. The Argentine inflow exceeded Canada's and almost doubled Australia's. But Argentine immigration studies amount to 16 percent of Canada's and 42 percent of Australia's. Similar figures could be found among the sending countries. Spain's exodus quadrupled that of Sweden, but studies of Spanish emigration amount to only two-thirds of Sweden's.[5] Clearly, "historical significance" forms an arbitrary concept defined less by the number of people affected than by economic power and academic resources.

The development of immigration history may have also been retarded in both Spain and Argentina by the repressive atmosphere of right-wing dictatorships, by the fact that when these fell the scholarly revival concentrated—quite naturally—on political issues, and by a strong orthodox Marxist tradition that favored the study of class and labor over immigration and ethnicity.

Yet the lack of attention to Spanish immigration on the part of Argentine historians cannot be fully attributed to these factors. It is true that Italian arrivals, at 45 percent of the total Argentine inflow, surpassed the Spaniards, who made up one-third of the total. But studies on the former by Argentine professional and amateur historians (44) quadruple those on the Spaniards (11). The Spanish inflow, in turn, was ten times greater than the German and Jewish ones and dwarfed Welsh immigration. But studies of Germans in Argentina by Argentines (23) more than double works on Spaniards; those on Jews (156) are fourteen times more numerous; and those on the Welsh (13) surpass them.[6]

Here too, the Spanish immigrants were not "other" enough. They were, to use the apt title of Charlotte Erickson's compilation of letters from English immigrants in nineteenth-century North America—"Invisible Immigrants."[7] As the title of this book suggests and its last chapter illustrates, ambivalence consistently marked the host country's attitudes toward the Spaniards. They represented the "charter group," the bestowers of the original culture, "cousins" but also "uncultured" new arrivals, foreigners, "strangers." It is precisely this ambiguous attitude, however, that makes their study an ideal vantage point from which to examine the process by which notions of alterity are formed. Their "dual personality," after all, manifested not some static essence but a historical construction in a constant process of definition. This also makes their study relevant to that of similarly situated immigrant groups such as the Portuguese in Brazil, the British in the United States, and the French in Quebec.

Invisible or not, the Spaniards in Argentina were, above all, immigrants. As the rest of this book demonstrates, in terms of their immigration and adaptation patterns, their experiences resembled—and of course diverged from—those of other newcomers in Argentina and elsewhere in the world. This study, therefore, aims not simply to illuminate the history of a key but previously unstudied group. It also attempts to contribute to a better understanding of the immigration experience in general. In order to do so, it searches not for ad hoc explanations of the process but for recurrent and recognizable immigration and adaptation patterns; compares them to those of other immigrant groups throughout the world; and inserts empirical findings and theoretical insights within the general scholarly literature on immigration. The text, and particularly the notes, contain a thorough overview of this literature. Only this comparative approach, I believe, can advance the field toward more general, inductive theories.

Although not among my original intentions, the book also offers some insights into the historical formation of modern Argentina as it examines the transformation of Buenos Aires' social ecology, spatial and occupational mobility, women's work, the formation of its class structure, and the evolution of a nationalist discourse. Given the prominent role of the capital, where one-third of Argentines lived, these findings are inescapably relevant for an understanding of the country.

The book's organization reflects both the immigration-adaptation process as it unfolds and the study's principal assumptions and analytical framework. There are scholarly works that concentrate on the migration side of the process, that study it as a demographic phenomenon and analyze the determinants of population movements. Others focus on the adaptation side, examining how the newcomers form neighborhoods in the host city, their occupations and mobility, institutions, and so forth. A basic assumption of this book, however, is that one cannot be understood without the other; or, at least, that adaptation cannot be understood without reference to the Old World background.[8] The presumption that one can represents little more than an unfortunate legacy of North American "exceptionalism," of the notion that the new country's superiority and the assimilating power of its environment made pre-arrival traits more or less irrelevant. Most histories of immigrant communities continue to pick up the story only after the arrivals step off the vessel. But since at least the 1970s, the best in the field have rejected this environmentalist approach and the notion that immigrants are blank slates to be colored by North American culture. Political disillusionment with this culture in U.S. academic circles during that decade at times led some to dismiss the assimilationist melting-pot concept and replace it with a pluralistic paradigm that stressed the continuities of pre-arrival ways. As the trend matured, a more balanced approach began to emphasize the complex interplay between the premigration heritage and the host environment, between continuity and change.[9]

The notion that adaptation was shaped by the interplay between pre-arrival traits and the host environment formed an a priori position of this study. My findings have proved it correct but have also shown that immigration patterns themselves were an important explanatory variable; that the way people came (in terms of auspices, numbers, rhythm and timing of the flow, and so forth) would greatly influence the way they adapted to the host city.

Another assumption reinforced by early findings is that the nation-state may provide the best unit of analysis for studying emigration or immigration policy but a poor one for examining the actual process. Spanish emigration, after all, was not a national phenomenon but part of a global one that took more than 50 million Europeans across the Atlantic during the period. On the other extreme, emigration originated not in a nation (indeed, for much of the period most of the peninsula did not participate) but in particular localities and villages. Traditional wisdom notwithstanding, the vantage point for studying the process lies not in the middle but in the extremes or, more precisely, in the meeting of the extremes: of global forces and local conditions, of the world and the village.

The analytical framework of this study is, therefore, macro-micro and dialectical. It examines how the interaction between macrostructural forces and microsocial networks shaped emigration and adaptation patterns. It also examines how this interaction formed early molds that themselves became independent variables which would partially explain subsequent developments. Initial empirical findings demonstrating the importance of these early molds encouraged me to push back the starting date of this study to 1850 from the originally planned 1880–1930 period (the conventional time span of most studies of southern and eastern European emigration, since the bulk of the flow took place during this period). The effort proved worthwhile because it allowed a more accurate examination of continuity and change, showing that key features of the mature immigrant community originated in patterns set in its infancy rather than in contemporary events.[10]

Another dialectical aspect of this study centers on its combination of quantitative and qualitative analysis. The former relies on linked databases with information on more than 60,000 individuals culled from a variety of manuscript sources in Buenos Aires and various Iberian localities; the latter, on anything from the ethnic and working-class press to interviews, poetry, plays, and jokes (for more on sources, see the appendix). This methodological combination tries to prevent the partial or even erroneous conclusions that relying on only one type of documentary evidence can lead to. It also aims to uncover past social realities and perceptions, and the relationship between the two, rather than just to analyze texts and public discourse—as in much intellectual and cultural history. This does not represent a purely materialistic approach, but it does assume that social realities are more than mere cultural constructions forged ex nihilo and that at times the latter can actually dim or misrepresent the former.

A different sort of assumption in this book relates to the connection between structures and individual agency. Perhaps the most distinguishing characteristic of recent studies of immigration lies in their homocentric nature. They have questioned deterministic theories that portray immigrants as helpless pawns moved from one place to another to satisfy the needs of impersonal world systems or classes. Instead, these studies have elevated the status of the immigrants to that of active participants in the process. They present emigration as the accumulation of thousands of personal decisions taken in the face of other options. After all, only a minority of people faced with similar circumstances chose to emigrate. This study finds itself in full accord with this trend. Yet, as time went along, I became less interested in stressing the immigrants' role as volitional actors in the drama and more intrigued by how structural parameters limited and shaped that volition; by the intersection and tension between individual agency and larger historical forces. It became increasingly apparent that emigration represented more than the sum of personal decisions. Departures did not peak in Spain when they did simply because people decided to leave.

The first chapter of the book examines precisely the larger context within which these decisions were taken. It tries to explain why Spain became a country of emigrants when it did, not by listing personal motives, not by resorting to the "push" of ills that existed well before the outflow began, but by revealing the global forces that spread the phenomenon throughout Europe in a recognizable pattern. It also tries to ascertain the relationship between rural impoverishment and emigration by comparing the areas that sent their inhabitants overseas with those that did not and by comparing those who left with those who stayed behind.

The second chapter explains how the same global forces that made Spain—and other European countries—exporters of people turned Argentina into a country of immigrants. It is shorter than the others because it merely provides the broader Argentine context and leaves specific aspects of the host city to the pertinent places in the second part of the book.

Chapter 3 shifts from the macrostructural context of population movement to its microsocial mechanisms and examines how the interaction of the two created particular emigration patterns. Whereas the previous two chapters set the larger stage and explain emigration *a grosso modo*, this one uncovers its internal workings. It does so with a microhistorical approach that focuses not on Spain, or even its regions, but on specific towns, villages, and kinship networks. At the same time it ties local trends to the larger forces previously examined to explain why people left some areas and not others; why those who left headed for certain destinations and not others; how the departures from various localities differed from one another in terms of social background and position within the family structure; and how emigration "fever" spread from a few original foci to the rest of the peninsula.

Whereas the first three chapters center on the migration aspects of the process, the next three deal with adaptation. The term is here defined as the process by which newcomers adjusted to their new environment, settled in the host city, found jobs and ways to improve their material conditions, and developed an organized community. The term assimilation, on the other hand, is rather murky. It often includes these themes but has a wider meaning relating to the adoption of new loyalties, identities and cultures.[11] It is also a longer-term process that goes beyond the second and subsequent generations and whose outcome or end is in no way predetermined. I examine the issue in the last sections of the last two chapters. But because this book covers only the pre-1930 period and the immigrant generation its focus will be on adaptation, on process rather than outcome.

The same dialectical macro-micro framework used to examine migration (expanded to include Buenos Aires' physical and class structures among the first set, and the immigrants' social networks and cultural background among the second) also provided the best approach for analyzing the lives of the newcomers in their adopted city. Chapter 4 examines how this interaction (plus migration patterns themselves) influenced the residential choices of the Spaniards in Buenos Aires. Although it finds the Chicago school model and the concept of chain migration limiting in themselves, it combines the two to analyze the changes and continuities in the city's social ecology, the issues of spatial centralization and segregation, how immigrants formed neighborhoods, why they settled where they did, the relationship between occupational and geographical mobility, and why home-ownership rates varied among the arrivals.

Chapter 5 describes Buenos Aires' labor market, the Spanish community's occupational distribution, and how it differed from that of other nationalities. It then compares the occupational status of the different Iberian ethnic and hometown groups, looking at pre-arrival traits, emigration patterns, and what I termed invisible skills to explain divergences in it. Linking data on Buenos Aires' immigrants with that on their parents in Spain, it measures the degree of transatlantic social continuity. It also evaluates the role of gender, marital status, length of residence in the country, and age in terms of occupation; and it employs various methods and sources to measure socioeconomic mobility.

Chapter 6 examines the formation and function of community organizations, from the first ones to appear in 1852 to the huge institutional structure of the twentieth century, which included everything from the two largest mutual-aid societies in Latin America and the largest private bank on the continent to a plethora of hometown associations. It also analyzes the sources of contention in the community (class, regionalism and ethnonationalism, and conflict ideologies, particularly anarchism) and the mechanisms that attenuated those conflicts.

The last chapter shifts the focus from adaptation to an intellectual history of the continuities and changes in the host society's attitudes toward the Spaniards and in the latter's actions and responses. It employs the same macro-micro framework but translates it so that general Western ideological trends and local conditions form the two elements of analysis. It demonstrates how the interplay between the two shaped the definition of Spaniards' dual personality as "cousins and strangers."

Although this book deals with Spanish immigration to Buenos Aires in general, its micro-macro approach demanded that some villages and towns be chosen for more intensive study. Because no single locality could be representative of a country as varied as Spain, the method followed consisted in selecting as wide and dissimilar a variety as possible. The towns and villages chosen for analysis do indeed cover a wide spectrum in many respects. The four major ethnic groups in the peninsula and in Buenos Aires are represented: Galicians, Basques, Catalans, and Castilians. The sample includes areas of early, middle, and late emigration; cities and hamlets; industrial, proto-industrial, and administrative towns; agricultural and fishing villages; localities on the coast and in the interior; and various types of economies. In other words, the issue of representativeness was resolved in a way by having as many "unrepresentative" cases as feasible.

The localities are in six areas listed below (see also Map 1). Populations in 1900—and, where applicable, areas in square kilometers—are in parentheses, and numbers of immigrants in the sample are in brackets:

1. Ferrol (32,794) [714], a port town in the Galician province of La Coruña, had some shipbuilding, a canning industry, and a long tradition of emigration.

2. The county of Corcubión [618], also in the province of La Coruña, some seventy kilometers west of Ferrol on the European continent's northwestern corner, includes the coastal municipalities of Corcubión (1,551; 7.6), Finisterre (4,708; 29.6), Cee (4,060; 55.2), Mugía (6,542; 120.6), and Camariñas (4,153; 51.8); and the interior municipalities of Dumbria (3,526; 120.2), Vimianzo (8,637; 186.9), and Zas (5,621; 132). This was a rural area, with fishing and maritime villages on the coast and agricultural ones in the interior. As in most of Galicia, handkerchief-sized plots dotted the landscape. Each municipality had a main village of 500 to 1,400 inhabitants, with the rest of the population dispersed in dozens of smaller units throughout the area.

3. The neighboring municipalities of Caldas de Reyes (7,505; 65.4) [497] and Cuntis (5,866; 79) [342] and, immediately to the south, the three adjacent municipalities of Cambados (8,520; 23.5) [117], Rivadumia (3,057; 19.6) [206], and Meis (3,740; 51.8) [73], all in the Galician province of Pontevedra, just north of Portugal. This was also a zone of *minifundios* (small farms) and dispersed settlements, often with a main valley village surrounded by miles of green, rolling hills and scores of brownstone hamlets.

4. The village of Val de San Lorenzo (1,720; 62.1) [128] in the so-called Maragato district of the interior province of León. The zone formed part of the large, semiarid, cereal-producing plateau of Old Castile. Wool

Regions:
1. Andalucía
2. Aragon
3. Asturias
4. Basque Country
5. Catalonia
6. Estremadura
7. Galicia
8. León
9. Levant
10. New Castile
11. Old Castile

Map 1. Regions and provinces of Spain. Regions: 1) Andalusia; 2) Aragon; 3) Asturias; 4) Basque Country; 5) Catalonia; 6) Estremadura; 7) Galicia; 8) León; 9) Levant; 10) New Castile; 11) Old Castile.

washing and weaving, and the trade of muleteers, furnished the other main source of income in the village. This is an area of late emigration, as most of the Argentine-bound villagers left after 1900.

5. The coastal town of Mataró (19,704) [97], in the northeastern province of Barcelona. In an area often called "the Manchester of Spain," this was a growing and prosperous manufacturing town (except at times of industrial crisis) with a long tradition of emigration to the River Plate.

6. The province of Navarre (307,669) [3,120], in northern Spain. Navarre includes the administrative city of Pamplona (made famous outside Spain by Ernest Hemingway and the annual running of the bulls); four towns with more than 6,000 inhabitants (Corella, Estella, Tafalla, and Tudela); and hundreds of smaller population centers. The province was chosen, in part, because of its contrasts. Ethnically and linguistically, its northern Pyrenean valleys form Basque bastions, and the southern lands, along the Ebro River, are quasi-Castilian. Likewise, the north was characterized by farmsteads and dispersed settlements; the south, by concentrated population centers, similar to Mediterranean agrotowns.

Discussing all of these towns and villages in every chapter would run the manuscript into the thousands of pages. I have, thus, used them selectively, to examine the micro-scale aspects of migration and their interaction with macro-scale forces and to compare the contrasting or similar patterns that this interplay produced.

PART 1

MIGRATION

1 Five Global Revolutions
*The Macrostructural Dimensions
of Emigration in Spain*

Late in 1882 Lázaro Carrau, the Argentine vice consul in Mataró, an industrial town of 20,000 on the Catalan coast twenty-nine kilometers north of Barcelona, sent a dispatch to Buenos Aires' Ministry of Foreign Relations with the following information: "The strikes and labor unrest that have driven 5,000 workers into public charity push hundreds across the ocean, attracted by the flourishing economy of the River Plate."[1] The central question in the next three chapters is a simple one: Why did these Mataronese and 2 million other Spaniards migrate to Argentina between the midnineteenth century and the first decades of the twentieth?

To vice consul Carrau the answer was as simple as the question: adverse conditions in Spain and auspicious ones in the River Plate. Unknown to him, this minor official explained migration in the manner that scholars would employ for a century and that many still do. The very simplicity and directness of this "push-pull" scheme, sometimes elaborated into a theory, provides, at the very least, a useful heuristic device.[2] It has, however, one basic flaw. We could find a myriad of places in which labor unrest, famine, wars, starvation, and a whole array of "push" factors never led to emigration and in which fertile, empty lands, flourishing economies, high wages, and other "pull" factors never enticed immigration. In other words, push and pull conditions have concurred in countless areas and countries of the world from time immemorial to the present, yet mass transoceanic migration occurred only during a particular historical epoch: from the midnineteenth century to the Great Depression of 1930. Close to 60 million Europeans (and 10 million Asians[3]) left their native continents during this period. No population movement of that magnitude had ever occurred before. None has occurred since.[4] Clearly, then, the explanatory value of an ex post facto list of the most conspicuous ills of sending socie-

ties and of the most obvious attractions of receiving areas is limited, because one could easily compile similar lists for periods and places where
no migration took place.

Our main question may thus be simple. The answer is not. The conspicuous and the obvious do not always explain. The strikes and labor unrest that the vice consul in Mataró saw as causes, as push factors, represented only symptoms of something bigger, symptoms of the expansion of
a world system of which mass migration was both a part and a conse-
quence.[5]

In general terms, five concurrent and interrelated trends, often referred
to as revolutions, can explain why the massive displacement of people occurred between the midnineteenth century and the Great Depression.
Spanish emigration to Argentina was part of, and can only be understood
in the context of, these world trends.

THE DEMOGRAPHIC REVOLUTION

What has been referred to as the "Malthusian devil," the "vital revolution," and, more often, the "demographic revolution" formed one of these
trends. The overall picture of European demographic cycles that K. F.
Helleiner presented in his 1967 survey has not been sharply altered by
numerous recent studies: depression in the fifteenth century; some recov-
ery in the sixteenth; reverses in the seventeenth; and growth from the
second half of the eighteenth on.[6] It is to this last stage that the term
revolution has been applied. Even though the continent lost some 40 million of its natives through emigration, its population grew from 140 million in 1750 to 429 million in 1900, and its share of the world's inhabitants increased from 17 percent to 25 percent.[7] What recent studies have
shown is that growth before this last stage was not only slow (around 0.2
percent per year) but intermittent (periods of high growth rarely lasted
more than two decades). The demographic revolution implied not only
high growth rates (more than 1 percent per year in the nineteenth century) but also, for the first time in the continent's history, continuous, un-
broken expansion virtually unchecked by decimating plagues or—as long
as the Pax Britannica endured—devastating wars. As one scholar put it,
Europe broke out of the demographic system of *l'ancien régime.*[8] In a
sense, mass emigration and declining fertility replaced plagues and wars
as the checks in this emerging system.[9]

The broad demographic cycles in Spain resembled those in Europe as a
whole and had a direct impact on the magnitude and regional composition

of emigration.[10] The population increase of the sixteenth century particularly affected the central plateau, formed by Castile and León, and neighboring Estremadura and Andalusia (see Map 1). Although other factors played a role, it is significant that even though this area contained fewer than 70 percent of the country's inhabitants, it supplied 91 percent of the Spanish settlers—and 97 percent of the women—in the Americas during the first century of colonization.[11] The revival of population growth in the eighteenth and nineteenth centuries, however, replaced, in the words of Catalan historian Jaime Vicens Vives, "a centripetal demographic tendency with a centrifugal one"; that is, the periphery of the peninsula—particularly the northern periphery—supplanted the central plateau as the fastest growing area in the country. At times almost synchronically, at others with a lag, the northern coastal zones (Galicia, Asturias, Santander, the Basque country, and Catalonia) began in the late eighteenth century to replace Castile, Estremadura, and Andalusia as the main source of settlers in the Spanish empire. In his study of Bourbon Mexico, David Brading found that "most immigrants came from the mountainous seaboard of northern Spain"; and Susan Socolow, in her prosopographical study of Buenos Aires merchants during the late colonial period, reached a similar conclusion.[12]

By the middle of the nineteenth century, when emigration from Spain resumed, the trend was firmly established. My analysis of all the manuscript returns of the unpublished Buenos Aires census of 1855 shows that, by that date, more than 80 percent of the Spaniards in the city came from the northern Atlantic, Cantabrian, and Mediterranean coastal areas (see Table 1 and Map 1).

Overpopulated Galicia, the "Ireland of Spain,"[13] where, as the local proverb went, "Children are the wealth of the poor," provided by itself almost four-tenths of the newcomers, a proportion that would grow as high as 54 percent in the decades to come. *Gallego* had already become a generic—and often demeaning—term for all Spaniards in Argentina. At about midcentury, when Juan Manuel de Rosas asked the musician Francisco Gambin, "Are you *gallego?*" he responded, "No, sir, I am a native of Cádiz." The dictator impatiently replied, "Well, *gallego* from Cádiz."[14]

Basques, many of whom were fleeing the devastation of the Carlist Wars, followed in numeric importance and accounted for about one-quarter of the Spaniards in the city, a proportion that would decline by the end of the century. During these early years the Basques were attracted by opportunities in the nascent sheep-raising industry and in the *saladeros* (meat-salting plants), where they were replacing the Irish as butchers. To a Scot visiting a Buenos Aires slaughterhouse in 1865, "This

Table 1   Regional population in Spain and regional origins of Spaniards in Buenos Aires, selected years (in percentages; less than .5 = 0)

Region	Spain	Buenos Aires		
	1857	1855	1878–1884	1900–1910
Galicia	11	38	54	48
Basque country	5	25	17	7
Catalonia	12	12	9	9
(Non-Castilian speakers, cumulative)	(28)	(75)	(80)	(64)
Asturias	3	4	5	7
Santander	1	3	2	2
(Northern periphery, cumulative)	(32)	(82)	(87)	(73)
Andalusia	19	12	4	8
Levant	12	1	2	2
Canary Islands	1	4	1	1
(All periphery, cumulative)	(64)	(99)	(94)	(84)
Old Castile	9	0	3	7
New Castile	10	1	1	3
León	6	0	1	3
Estremadura	5	0	0	0
Aragón	6	0	1	3
(Central Spain)	(36)	(1)	(6)	(16)
Number	15,464,340	4,191	2,761	12,508

SOURCES: For Spain, Junta General de Estadística, *Censo de la población de España según el recuento verificado el 21 de mayo de 1857* (Madrid: Imprenta Nacional, 1857).

(*continued on next page*)

Table 1 (continued)

For Buenos Aires in 1855, municipal manuscript census returns. I took all the cases, rather than a sample, of Spaniards living in the city, except for a section of sixteen blocks that was missing. In addition to the 4,191 in the table there were 1,184 cases of Spaniards for whom the variable "place of birth" (usually recording the region, province, or town of birth) was either not recorded or not legible. Unless the sixteen missing blocks and/or the unknown cases included a disproportionate number from a particular regional group—a remote probability—the reliability of the figures should be close to that of a statistical universe.

For Buenos Aires, 1878–1884, the source is a list of the province of birth of all the Spaniards treated in the Spanish Hospital of Buenos Aires during those years, from *Memorias de la Sociedad Española de Beneficencia* (Buenos Aires, 1879–1885). At the time this was the only Spanish hospital or clinic in the city. The only factor that could distort the representativeness of the figures, then, would be for a particular regional group to have a greater or lesser tendency to use the hospital or to become ill, a highly unlikely tendency.

For Buenos Aires, 1900–1910, the sources are the membership forms for all of the Spaniards who became members of the Asociación Española de Socorros Mutuos de Buenos Aires during that decade. I stopped at 1910 because after that date the growth of regional associations would have slanted the sample against those regional groups that had developed their own mutual-aid societies. Nevertheless, although the association was at the time by far the dominant one in the Spanish community and open to all Spaniards, it is still possible that some groups could have had a greater associative tendency than others, tilting the sample.

I used Argentine sources instead of Spanish emigration statistics because the latter start only in 1882 and include the provincial origins of emigrants to Argentina only for 1885–1895 and after World War I. Even for those years, the official figures for Basque emigration are, by their own account, totally unreliable due to heavy Basque departure from the port of Bordeaux. Emigration from provinces near other foreign ports, such as Marseille, Lisbon, or Gibraltar, was probably also undercounted.

robust, resistant, and industrious race . . . with their blue berets and naked legs and feet covered by dry blood" resembled "Scottish highlanders after a battle."[15] Catalans, "the Jews of Spain," mostly from the province of Barcelona and the Balearic Islands, represented a little more than one-tenth of the Iberian-born population in the city. The fact, then, that Spanish—that is, Castilian—was not the native tongue of three-quarters of the "Spaniards" in the city (see Table 1) points to the relevance of assessing regional origins. Perhaps the tendency of observers to compare these groups with non-Spaniards was not altogether fortuitous.

It was not a coincidence either that these regions showed the first, second, and third highest population density, respectively, in the Spanish census of 1857. Perhaps as significant, on the other end of the scale, the twenty Spanish provinces (of a total of forty-nine) with the lowest population densities represented the birthplaces of a mere twenty Spanish immigrants in midnineteenth-century Buenos Aires, even though together they contained more than 5 million inhabitants.

This correlation of provincial population density with rates of emigration led the Catalan demographer Jordi Nadal to conclude that "the demographic excess has been the principal cause of the phenomenon."[16] Yet the demographic development of the country as a whole does not coincide with the timing of the emigration flow. The rate of population growth was highest in the first half of the nineteenth century, outpacing or at least keeping pace with the general western European rate, in contrast to Italy and Portugal.[17] Yet Spain's emigration reached a peak at a relatively late date, resembling the pattern of Mediterranean and eastern European rather than western European emigration. In fact, as Figure 1 shows, in the case of Argentina, Spanish immigration reached massive proportions only in the first decade of the twentieth century, later than Italian immigration.

Many scholars have commented on the questionable nature of early Spanish censuses, and this may explain the difference between the timing of demographic expansion and emigration.[18] But it may also be that Spain, like Russia on the other end of the continent, presents the not too common pattern of early population growth but late emigration.[19] What makes Spain's pattern more intriguing is that, unlike Russians, Spaniards were not only the first Europeans to cross the Atlantic but also one of only four national groups present at the genesis of modern transoceanic emigration in the eighteenth century, particularly its second half. The other three were the British, mostly English and Scotch-Irish heading for their North American colonies; the Germans, mostly Palatines and other southwesterners from the Upper Rhine sharing the same destination; and the Portuguese, mostly northeasterners from Entre Douro and Minho attracted by Brazilian gold.[20]

The pattern of Spain and Russia indicates that demographic expansion by itself does not lead to mass migration. The fact that after the interruption of the eighteenth-century transatlantic movement caused by the Napoleonic Wars, Britain and Germany rejoined the flow with soaring vigor but Spain and Portugal did not, suggests that the tardy development of the other four revolutions on the Iberian Peninsula can explain the paradox wherein the first Europeans to migrate to the New World were also among the last to join the nineteenth-century exodus in a massive way.

THE LIBERAL REVOLUTION

Moses' demand to the pharaohs illustrates a basic point about emigration: in order for it to happen, rulers have to let people go. The spread of liberalism as the dominant European ideology facilitated this basic prerequisite

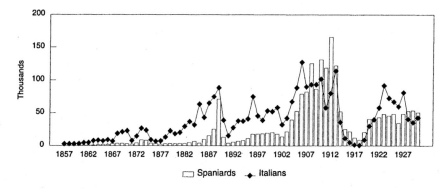

Figure 1. Spanish and Italian emigration to Argentina, 1857–1930. Data are from Argentine official statistics.

in the nineteenth century to a degree unknown in the mercantilist past or in the socialist and "quasi-liberal" future.[21]

The mercantilist view of population was akin to contemporary bullionism and can be conveniently summarized in two often quoted statements, one by a Prussian minister—"No nation can have too many inhabitants"—the other by the marquis de Vauban—"By the number of their subjects is measured the grandeur of kings." Because the wealth of kingdoms could be measured in grams of metals and thousands of inhabitants, it followed that the Crown should do its utmost to prevent the flight of both specie and subjects.

Several developments in the late eighteenth century began to challenge this view. One was the demographic revolution and the interpretation of it by what could be called the pessimist classical economists. Among these were Gianmaria Ortes, David Ricardo, and the man whose name would become a synonym for overpopulation crisis, Robert Malthus.[22] Their labyrinthine essays conveyed a straightforward message: population increased faster (geometrically in Malthus' famous argument) than did the means of subsistence, and this imbalance would eventually have catastrophic effects. The message found a particularly receptive ear in countless municipal administrators who had experienced the threats of overpopulation firsthand. The earliest advocacy of free emigration originated not from royal dignitaries but from these minor local officials.[23]

A different sort of challenge to emigration restrictions ensued from "optimist" classical economists, such as Adam Smith. Although they devoted much more ink to the free movement of merchandise, support for the free movement of people was implicit in their writings. The "invisible hand" that naturally and efficiently moved goods and capital could logically do the same for labor. From a different perspective—that of the general welfare instead of economic laissez faire—Utilitarian philosophers, such as Jeremy Bentham and John Stuart Mill, agreed. Most importantly, as we should soon see, other liberals went farther and, as good heirs of the Enlightenment, transformed freedom of movement from a matter of economic policy or social utility into a question of philosophical principle, of personal, inalienable rights.

As the nineteenth century progressed, one European country after another extended this right, and this time the trend spread in roughly the same geographical pattern as mass emigration itself: from Britain to Germany, to Scandinavia, and to southern and eastern Europe.[24]

The partial revocation of bans on emigration came to Spain later than to northwestern Europe and, as had been the case in other places, thanks to the goading and insistence of local authorities. In 1853, after years of petitions from local officials, a royal decree lifted the prohibition on emigration to the newly independent republics of the Americas for Canary Islanders.[25] The stated purpose of the decree—"to give a convenient outlet to the surplus population of the Islands, surplus, that, far from being an element of prosperity, serves to delay progress"—clearly forfeited a mercantilist tenet. In 1857 the Crown extended this right to the rest of its subjects, and two decades later the liberal constituent Cortes enshrined it in the Constitution of 1869.

During the rest of the mass-migration period restrictions mostly targeted potential military conscripts.[26] Males between the ages of eighteen and twenty-three had to leave a deposit of 6,000 reales de vellón (£60, about four times the ship fare to Buenos Aires in the midnineteenth century) or find substitutes to serve in their places before departing. Bans on departures, however, have historically proved less efficient for this particular sex and age group. Even in modern police states, where the efficiency of emigration controls dwarfs that of nineteenth-century Spain, thousands of male adolescents have surmounted legal barriers by using anything from rafts and inner tubes to homemade tunnels, airplane wheels, and even pole vaults and kites. Spanish youths did not have to reach those levels of ingenuity. They simply had to circumvent or bribe low-paid port officials or leave from foreign ports—an easy task for those who lived close to international borders. For instance, of the 160 draft-age males listed as residing in the Americas in a local 1864 census of the Navarrese municipality of Baztán, in the Pyrenean piedmont, I found only 36 (22 percent) who had bothered to leave the required deposit or to find a substitute.[27] Although this represents only one verifiable case, qualitative contemporary sources often listed draft evasion as a main cause of emigration and agreed with my quantitative evidence that prohibitions did little to inhibit the flight of determined draft dodgers.[28] Indeed, the cleavage between legal controls and actual routine was conspicuous enough for an 1889 Madrid comedy to use as a farcical ploy a twenty-two-year-old youngster emigrating with the papers of a sixty-year-old man and vice versa.[29]

Despite the swelling tide of liberalism, mercantilist views on population continued to color the thinking of key sectors in Spanish society for most of the mass-emigration period. In 1881, for example, an advocate of the southern landed aristocracy still maintained that "the more populous a country, the richer it is," described emigration as a national calamity, and urged the government to promote internal migration to regions with labor shortages.[30] In that same year, a newspaper editor from Madrid published a booklet which asserted that "population is the wealth, the strength, the standard by which one nation is ranked above others" and proposed an obligatory program of primary-school indoctrination about the evils of emigration.[31] At the start of the twentieth century, two Galician physicians expressed the contemporary tendency to associate social problems with epidemics when they ascribed tuberculosis, leprosy, and syphilis to emigration.[32] And as the mass exodus neared its end, Wenceslao Fernández-Flórez's 1930 novel *Luz de luna* condemned the "tragic flow, full of tears and blood . . . that empties Spain."[33]

The tenor of many contemporary titles on emigration sounded equally mournful—*Adios a la patria* (Farewell to the Motherland), *Hijos que se ausentan* (Sons [and Daughters] Who Depart), *La zafra de carne* (The Harvest of Flesh), *La peregrinación de los vencidos* (The Wandering of the Vanquished)[34]—or insulting—*El tacaño Salomón* (Solomon the Miser), Benito Pérez Galdós's thespian lampoon of Spaniards in Buenos Aires.[35] Other anti-emigration writers simply relied on the unimaginative but popular *El problema de la emigración*, sometimes followed by a more execrative subtitle like "and the crimes committed in it."[36] Whatever the titles, the writings of the contemporary political and literary elite exposed a strong anti-emigration bias. Of the twenty-seven pre-1930 Spanish books on the subject that I located and examined, eighteen clearly condemned emigration as a drain on the nation's labor supply and/or a threat to its morals—a fear exacerbated by the departure of married men and by the increasing departure of single women by the early years of the twentieth century.[37]

Female "morality," after all, had been a constant concern of emigration foes. In an 1873 play, for example, the tobacco smoking and dissoluteness of a female character was recurrently explained with, "Well, you see, [she was] raised in America."[38] A decade later, a more sanctimonious Navarrese complained about "girls" who "left home pure and chaste, laborious and Christian and come back, when and if they return, licentious and unbridled, indolent and irreligious. The body unwilling for rustic work or even hard domestic tasks; the soul possessed by a ravenous desire for dazzling diversions; the fancy flying after unfeasible ambitions."[39] Some anti-emigration writers again relied on the impact of titles: *Ebano blanco* (White Ebony);[40] or the less equivocal *Carne importada (Costumbres de Buenos Aires): Primera parte de la trata de blancas* (Imported Flesh [Customs of Buenos Aires]: First part of White Slavery).[41] Others relied on fictitious characters. In a comedy playing in Oviedo in 1913, when Pepa, an illiterate peasant in her fifties, tells the parish priest that her daughter is going "pa Guenos Aires," the priest responds with displeasure: "Uhf! To Buenos Aires. . . . Ah, Buenos Aires! Of so many women the perdition. . . . That's where they go to get a man when they have lost all hope here . . . and then there without their parents' supervision . . . you can imagine."[42] At about the same time the government echoed the concern when it established a "Royal Patronage for the Suppression of White Slavery"[43] and when its Consejo Superior de Emigración, in blatantly misogynous language, concluded that "the sex most chastised by the demoralization [of emigration] is the feminine one. Its characteristic weakness, inferior education, mental indigence, causes, in summary, of a physiological nature, combined with material ambition, give women an instinctual tendency to prostitute themselves. . . . Emigration and prostitution: Both affairs appear intimately connected."[44]

Yet despite their overwhelming pragmatic and moral apprehensions, few foes of emigration dared to propose legal bans on it. The same advocate of southern landed interests who in 1881 affirmed the mercantilist tenet, "The more populous a country, the richer it is" and who urged all sorts of legislation to cure the emigration malady acquiesced to the dominant liberal discourse of the day when he diplomatically added "but without denying the individual the right to be the final arbiter of what is best for him."[45] The newspaper editor who in the 1880s advocated primary-school indoctrination to prevent emigration also wrote: "No, it is not licit to ban emigration nor to reproach those who have the drive to cross the ocean in search of opportunities denied by the obscure villages where their ancestors' bones rest. How can we censure them! Isn't that innate drive, after all, the origin of human knowledge, wealth and progress?"[46] And a Madrid legislator who, in a 1910 speech, attributed many of the country's economic problems to emigration, went on to defend "the paramount human liberty, the one that deserves the most respect, that of movement," adding, "The door has to remain open."[47]

This negative attitude toward emigration, combined with the assertion of the individual's right to emigrate, also appears in contemporary creative literature.[48] The Asturian playwright who condemned sinful Buenos Aires through the character of the priest and who in the prologue to his 1913 play wrote, "He who forever abandons his nation does it more harm than he who takes his own life because the latter leaves everything to his country and the former deprives it of his person and some of his goods," also claimed that it would be "absurd for the government to abuse the force of law and drown individual liberty or repress economic freedom."[49] And the popular Galician bard Manuel Curros Enríquez, who depicted immigrant steamers as "perfidious slaveships," said of the emigrant:

> Non o culpo, ¡coitado!, no o axo,
> non pido pragas nin castigo pra el,
> nin de que é dono de coller me esquezo
> pra onde lle conviñer.
> ¡Que aquél que deica seu natal curruncho
> e fóra dos seus eidos pon os pés,
> cando troca o seguro polo incerto,
> motivos ha de ter![50]

> Careful! I neither blame nor judge him,
> I don't wish him ill or seek his punishment,
> nor do I forget that he is free to go
> wherever it suits his interests.
> That he who leaves his native hearth
> and faraway from his haunts plants his feet,
> when he trades the secure for the uncertain,
> plenty of motives must he have!

Liberalism had freed a genie that could not easily revert to the bottle. What as late as the first half of the nineteenth century was taken for granted, the state's prerogative to prohibit the departure of its citizens, had now become preposterous, anathema to the accepted wisdom and "political correctness" of the day. The dominant liberal elites, particularly those who opposed emigration, found themselves hostage to their own discourse. Indeed, the rhetoric of individual liberty had become so ingrained in the official political culture that royal decrees intended to curb emigration dutifully repeated the right of citizens to go where they would, and deputies who introduced restrictive legislation in Parliament sessions outdid each other in their elocutionary defense of "sacred freedoms."[51] To do otherwise would betray Spain's separation from the "civilized countries of the Continent," would confirm the fear of Spanish liberals that, as the French claimed, "Africa begins in the Pyrenees." Moreover, the ambivalence of many liberal opponents of emigration went beyond the issue of freedom. As the previous quotations about aspiration and drive suggest, in a land with a scarcity of entrepreneurs, the figure of the emigrant epitomized for many personal initiative, restlessness, and ambition, indeed, the quintessence of classical liberalism.

If the liberal dogmas, ideals, and apprehensions of the modernizing elite prevented restrictive legislation, so did the emerging world view of the masses. As the nineteenth century progressed, elements of liberalism deeply penetrated popular culture. For the majority, freedom remained a grand abstraction; freedom of speech, of finite use for villagers of few words; political freedom, of even less use in a realm dominated by clientism and caciques, or corrupt political bosses; but freedom of movement, the right to go where one pleased, seemed completely tangible and was put to use by more than 4 million Spaniards. At this level, the concept of individual liberty rooted itself in popular public morality. When I asked an emigrant from a small Galician village if the draft or other restrictive laws had posed an obstacle, his definition of personal liberty was less elegant but more palpable than that of the Madrileño legislator mentioned above: "What damned law was going to stop me?" Freedom of movement had now become part of both natural law and masculine bravado.[52] And when Spanish nationalists denounced emigration as the unpatriotic abandonment of the motherland, the Andalusian and Galician popular wit responded with the following rhymes questioning the motherland's motherliness:

Adios España querida
tierra donde yo nací
para el rico madre eres
y madrasta para mí

Farewell, dear Spain,
land where I was born.
For the rich you are a mother
and a stepmother for me.

¡Vámonos a Buenos Aires,
miña cariña de rosa,
vámonos a Buenos Aires,
qu-esta terra non é nosa![53]

Let's go to Buenos Aires,
my darling rose,
let's go to Buenos Aires—
this land is not ours!

The liberal revolution, then, proved instrumental to emigration by rooting the concept of freedom of movement in both official and popular culture. It proved equally instrumental by uprooting many other things. If liberalism brought greater liberty for the common folk, it also brought greater amounts of those ingredients inherent to social freedom and conducive to migration: change, competition, disruption, insecurity, and inequality. However anachronistic, mercantilism in the nineteenth century served to protect Spain from changes, challenges, and dislocations. It protected inefficient farmers from external competition, outmoded rural artisans from factory-made wares, unproductive peasants from ambitious neighbors, autarkic villages from the imperatives of market forces. As the century progressed, however, a barrage of liberal measures, from support for free trade to attacks on entails, mortmain, and municipal commons, lifted much of this protection. The liberal revolution was, thus, intimately related to the transition from the static, seignorial agricultural system to a more dynamic, capitalist one. In Spain this relationship was, as we shall now see, a particularly strong one.

THE AGRICULTURAL REVOLUTION

In some European countries the transition from subsistence to commercial agriculture resulted in a remarkable increase in efficiency and productivity. In England, where this revolution first took place in the eighteenth century, it was associated with "improving landlords," who introduced the drill planting, horse hoeing, and crop rotation that made the multiplication of yields possible, and with the "enclosure movement," which signaled the disappearance of communal lands.[54] Increased productivity meant that fewer farmers were able to feed more people, and the disappearance of commons ruined those yeomen who could not afford to become "improving landlords." Both trends, together with the demographic revolution, created a surplus rural population that became the major source of migrants and emigrants. In France, the demise of the seignorial agricultural system came about through a revolution from below, which bolstered a large and secure middle class of peasant farmers. This, combined with the lowest demographic growth in Europe, gave the country the lowest emigration rate in the Continent (an annual average of 0.2 per thousand population during the 1860–1910 period).[55]

In Spain, unlike France, the demise of the seignorial agricultural system was accomplished relatively late and by a liberal revolution from above.[56] Unlike England, the transition to commercial agriculture did not signal dramatic improvements in technology and efficiency. But, as in England, it brought about—aided by demographic pressure—disruption in much of rural Spain, the reduction of communal lands, and a stimulus to population movements.

Physiocratic ministers of the Bourbon kings had made some efforts to rationalize agriculture during the second half of the eighteenth century, but the first serious attack on the seignorial system came after the First Carlist War (1833–1840). Ecclesiastical disentailment, begun by the progressive government of Mendizábal in 1836, acquired such an impetus that in less than eight years more than three-quarters of the Church's lands had been sold off.[57] The next major liberal attack on the old system came from 1855 on and at the expense not only of the clergy but also of civil corporations, including municipal commons. All together, one-quarter of the country's territory had been transferred from corporate to private hands by the end of the century.[58]

Catholic conservatives, not surprisingly, blamed ecclesiastical and civil disentailment for depriving the peasantry of the usufruct of Church lands and village commons and for the ensuing army of beggars that roamed the country. That large numbers of peasants joined their cause and opposed bourgeois reforms suggests that they may have had a point, and many modern scholars concur.[59] Contemporary observers often attributed mass emigration to this agrarian misery. When at the beginning of the twentieth century a writer summarized the opinions of seventeen so-called experts on the subject, he found that twelve pointed to rural destitution as the principal cause of emigration.[60]

Empirical evidence, however, weighs against this contemporary consensus on the nexus between rural penury and emigration. After the middle of the nineteenth century, when the effects of disentailment had reached a peak, the most affected, impoverished and latifundista regions of the country (Estremadura, western Andalusia, and most of the Castilian plateau) provided a puny portion of the Spanish immigrants in Buenos Aires (2 percent in 1855 and 3 percent in 1878–1884), even though they comprised 22 percent of the national population. Inversely, the Basque country, the richest and most equitable rural region of Spain, contained less than 4 percent of its population in 1877 but provided 25 percent of its emigrants in 1855 and 17 percent in 1878–1884. And the two Galician Atlantic provinces, where disentailment had expelled few peasants from the land, furnished between 37 percent and 51 percent of the Spanish emigrants, even though they accounted for only 5 percent of the national population.[61]

This inverse relationship between rural poverty and emigration can also be observed at a more confined territorial level. For example, Andalusia, a land of latifundia and destitute, landless laborers, was the birthplace of about one-tenth of the Spaniards in Buenos Aires during the nineteenth century. However, a closer look reveals that the bulk of them (89 percent) originated from either cities or more prosperous rural areas of widespread landownership.[62]

A probe into the other geographical extreme of the country and the more limited scope of a single province produces similar results. The northern Navarrese mountains not only enclosed the most fertile valleys in the province but also enjoyed one of the most democratic land-tenure systems in the country. Middle-sized granges with sturdy Basque farmhouses dotted the dales, and this part of the province relishes the distinction of being the one area in Spain to retain its municipal commons intact until this day.[63] As a modern scholar put it, "All Spain had opposed disentailment, but only [northern] Navarra opposed it with success."[64] A traveler in the 1880s termed the tenure system *comunismo* and observed that "it calls the attention of the tourist to see no beggars. . . . The well-being is so general that if one of those swarms of paupers that cause pity and shame in the forsaken places of Old Castile, between Avila and Burgos, would suddenly appear in these valleys, the alarmed inhabitants would, even though they are not pusillanimous in war, flee in horror."[65] Yet it was precisely in these relatively prosperous rural valleys, rather than in the more arid and less egalitarian south of the province, that emigration attained massive proportions in the nineteenth century. As early as the middle of the century, emigration per capita had reached levels surpassed in Europe only by some famine-struck Irish counties.[66] And during the rest of the century these northern valleys provided 87 percent of the rural Navarrese immigrants in Buenos Aires, even though they only contained 51 percent of Navarre's rural population.

But if impoverished and/or inegalitarian rural areas did not produce a large number of emigrants, what took place within the relatively better off and more democratic areas that did? Can we find the link between poverty and emigration here? That is, were poor and landless peasants more likely to emigrate than their more fortunate neighbors? Because no published material or aggregate data exist that would allow us to answer this question, I collected and analyzed manuscript census data from three rural Spanish zones of emigration. The initial results suggested that the better off, rather than the poor, made up the bulk of the exodus. For example, in Zas, a rural municipal district in the Galician province of La Coruña, 70 percent of those who had emigrated by 1897 were literate, in comparison with only 29 percent of those who stayed behind. This, however, misrepresented reality because the nonimmigrant population contained a much larger number of women and older people, whose literacy rates were substantially lower than that of young men—the main emigrant group. After controlling for gender and age by comparing the cohort of fifteen-to-forty-year-old men, the gap dropped sharply but nevertheless remained: 70 percent of the emigrants but only 57 percent of those who stayed behind were literate.[67] The pattern repeated itself in the two other rural areas (five hamlets in the municipal district of Corcubión, La Coruña, and the village of Val de San Lorenzo, León): even after accounting for distortions created by age and gender differences, literate peasants were more likely to emigrate than illiterate ones.[68]

If, instead of literacy, we use occupation and landownership as a measure of socioeconomic background, the results are even more explicit. When compared with their more prosperous neighbors, the landless and poor in the village of Val de San Lorenzo were twice as likely to stay home: only 12 percent of the village landless laborers emigrated, but 23 percent of the landed peasants and 27 percent of the larger proprietors did. A similar breakdown is difficult to make for the municipal district of Zas because, despite having five times as many inhabitants as Val de San Lorenzo, it was much more rustic, with its population of mostly small farmers disseminated through more than a hundred tiny villages. Yet it is significant that members of the small group of merchant-artisans were three times as likely to emigrate as was the peasant population in the late nineteenth century. The social structure of the handful of agricultural villages encircling the maritime town of Corcubión was, if anything, more horizontal. But even in this rather flat milieu, the relatively more skilled were more likely to leave. One-quarter of the peasant households but two-thirds of the artisan-peasant ones (those that included a carpentry shop) had at least one of its members overseas in 1905.

The proclivity of nineteenth-century reformers, politicians, journalists, diplomats, and poets (and of present-day pundits) to blame rural impoverishment for pushing people to abandon their homes and loved ones echoed a mix of genuine sympathy and phony commiseration for, as John Denham put it, "those who groan beneath the weight of want." On a more cerebral plane, it reflected the ostensible logic of the push-pull concept. Indeed, the link between adversity and emigration seems so inherently rational that when in 1884 a perplexed Argentine consul in Cádiz tried to explain why *"in spite* of good crops and a relative well-being among the local working-classes, emigration to Argentina is increasing," he resurrected a decade-old push factor: "the drought of 1873."[69] He probably could not even conceive of replacing "in spite" with "because" in his report. Yet, in spite of our emotional and intellectual leaning, ascribing emigration to relative prosperity is actually more accurate than blaming real or putative ills and adversities. As I have shown, whatever the method and lens of analysis—national, regional, provincial, municipal, parochial—the evidence consistently reveals that the exodus originated not from the most impoverished and inegalitarian areas but from the relatively better off and more economically democratic ones and, within these areas, not among the poorer peasants but among their more fortunate neighbors.[70] My intent has not been to demonstrate that the liberal agricultural revolution did not engender poverty—it clearly did—but to show that the link between the transition to capitalist agriculture and emigration lies elsewhere, because the communities and people it pauperized rarely emigrated. ~~made poor~~

Penury for many, after all, represented just one of the ingredients in the Pandora's box of capitalist agriculture. Among the other ingredients were dislocation, insecurity, dissatisfaction, opportunities, and ambition, all inseparable siblings of emigration. Surely, as revisionist medievalists have stressed for decades, the precapitalist rural world was not a motionless one. But at least by comparison, the more autarkic agriculture of *l'ancien régime* offered both a level of Spartan security, broken only by occasional famines, and a lack of opportunities for all except a few enterprising landlords. The sociocultural corollary of this was a relatively stationary rural milieu and a rather static worldview. Commercial agriculture consistently undermined both. It disrupted the stillness of the countryside by introducing absolute property rights (which turned land into a commodity and subverted the security of the customary tenancies and emphyteutic lands of the seignorial past), fluctuation (in land value, demand, prices, national or world supply), acquisitiveness (from the increasingly greedy rural bourgeoisie, who often coveted the lands of their less enterprising, or rapacious, neighbors), and competition (anywhere from the next-door neighbors to the faraway lands to which many would emigrate). And it subverted peasant satisfaction with the modest safety of subsistence agriculture by fostering concepts of ownership and social motion, usually idealized as progress or betterment.

In Galicia, for example, between the late nineteenth century and the mid-1920s emigration in part obeyed the peasantry's dissatisfaction with the mere usufruct of *foros* (quasi-emphyteutic, fixed-rent leases that could be inherited through three generations) and their desire for the "perfect property" of direct ownership. Thousands of peasants fulfilled their desires thanks to money made in the Americas. Indeed, the redemption of *foros* trailed closely the inflow of remittances, which by the early 1900s reached 50 million pesetas annually. Many were even buying out leases in Galicia while still in Buenos Aires.[71]

Emigration also seemed the perfect expression of motion as betterment in rural Navarre. Three-quarters of the 812 northern Navarrese emigrants who expressed a motive for leaving in nineteenth-century notarial records listed *mejorar fortuna*, which has the dual connotation of "improving one's fortune" and "increasing one's wealth."[72] With fruitful lands and access to them for the majority, these people were among both the contemporary world's most fortunate and its most footloose inhabitants. *Mejorar fortuna* did not mean fleeing the ills of fortune but seeking the promise of it. Contemporary observers and modern scholars have blamed the practice of primogeniture in these regions for excluding younger siblings from the farm and forcing them to emigrate.[73] But primogeniture excluded the younger progeny from ownership, not from the farm. The census lists show that the spacious Basque farmhouses often included younger brothers and sisters, with or without their spouses and children.[74] The preservation of municipal commons, which covered 80 percent of the land, further facilitated the livelihood of noninheritors. The belief in movement as progress, however, truly looms in the cases of would-be inheritors who preferred departure to property. My analysis of the 1897 census list for the Baztán Valley in northern Navarre shows that 28 percent (62 out of 219) of all emigrants were firstborns from farm-owning families. Many of them heeded the local proverb "Kanpoak ikusi ta etxera geros (Go see foreign lands, but return home)." Many others simply chose the potential riches of the pampas over the security of ownership in Pyrenean valleys. Of twenty-four emigrant eldest sons of farm owners whom I was able to trace throughout their lives, fifteen died in Argentina. Ambition, not necessity, had moved them.

Necessity, no doubt, moved many. What contemporary observers described as "swarms of vagabonds roaming the peninsula" obviously

roamed out of necessity. Some of the most impoverished Galician and Asturian peasants sojourned to the Castilian wheat plains for generations before and during the overseas emigration period.[75] In the Leonese village of
Val de San Lorenzo, those who could not afford the transatlantic passage
often walked or rode a mule to Asturian mines.[76] Poorer peasants from
the Galician village of Zas labored in Portuguese fields and swept the
streets of Madrid rather than those of Buenos Aires.[77] But for those who
"crossed the puddle," the popular metaphor for emigrating overseas, the
disruption and opportunity of capitalist agriculture proved more causal
than did its poverty. Despite omnipresent pitiful images of rural emigrants in contemporary literature, most of these people confronted the imperatives of capitalism with diligence and vigor.

THE INDUSTRIAL REVOLUTION

Like the other three revolutions I have discussed so far, the industrial
revolution was not one of those ten-days-that-shook-the-world upheavals.
Prolonged and lingering, it nevertheless changed the world in a more radical and revolutionary way than did any—perhaps all—radical political
revolt.

Despite its momentousness, its takeoff in the late eighteenth century
was rather modest and affected only textile production, specifically cotton;
its greatest invention, besides Watt's steam engine, was the humble spin-
ning jenny. As the nineteenth century progressed, the escalating use of
coal, iron, and heavier machinery exposed its repercussions. Toward the
end of the century steel and electricity propelled production to new
heights. By this time industrialization had spread from its English cradle
to most countries in the North Atlantic, and farther, drastically changing
the world.

A mobile labor force was a sine qua non of the industrial revolution.
Industrialization fed on the surplus rural labor released by demographic
swelling and commercial agriculture and in turn encouraged further
population movement by both displacing and attracting rural artisans. Its
relationship to urbanization and internal migration is evident. Its link to
the overseas exodus is less obvious but no less direct. With some exceptions, such as the Irish case, the industrial revolution and emigration
spread together over the European map: from England to Germany, to
Scandinavia, to southern and eastern Europe, and, hurdling much of the
Eurasian landmass, to Japan.[78]

Spain's first attempts to industrialize started at the same time as England's and were also based on cotton-textile production for colonial consumption. Unlike England's, these first steps proved clumsy ones and, given the limitation of the national market, halted with the loss of the empire. The next, and this time sustainable, spurt came in the 1840s, with the rebirth—and increased mechanization—of the Catalan textile sector.[79] Ironically, capitalist agriculture, which in England supplied much of the money for manufacturing ventures, had drained the country of capital by steering resources into the acquisition of disentailed lands.[80] Thus financing was provided, again ironically, by returning expatriates from the ex-colonies whose downfall had previously ruined the industry and by fortunes made in Cuba.[81] The other regional industrial focus developed some decades later, with the expansion of Basque metallurgy and shipping. By the first decades of the twentieth century this region had surpassed Catalonia as Spain's foremost industrial area.

The relationship between the spread of industrialization and emigration in the European continent is also partly noticeable in the Iberian Peninsula. Not only did Catalonia and the Basque region join the overseas exodus relatively early, but their emigration rates declined earlier than did those in other areas of the peninsula (a pattern observable in other European countries, Italy being one of the best known examples). My data on Spaniards in Buenos Aires around the middle of the nineteenth century indicate that even in those cases in which the early streams originated in nonindustrialized areas, such as Galicia and Andalusia, most immigrants departed from larger towns where some proto-industrialization was already taking place.[82]

The regional disequilibrium in industrial development similarly affected the occupational background and skills of the emigrants. Jaime Vicens Vives maintained that whereas Galicia exported "unskilled labor exclusively," Catalonia and the Basque region "also sent technicians and even factory owners and businessmen."[83] Spanish statistics tend to support his statement. In the first decade of this century, 45 percent of the overseas passengers with occupations departing from the Basque provinces were listed as industrialists and artisans, 20 percent as businessmen, and 17 percent as professionals. The comparable figures for Catalonia were 15 percent, 20 percent, and 5 percent; and for underdeveloped Galicia, the main source of emigrants for the last two centuries, they dropped sharply, to 2 percent, 6 percent, and 1 percent.[84]

The industrialization of these two areas also affected the rest of the country. Without the hindrance of internal customs barriers, the wares of their factories displaced many of the artisan or homespun industries throughout the peninsula. The rapid development of a Catalan wool industry in the midnineteenth century, for example, dealt "a crippling blow to thousands of small looms all over Spain."[85] As in most places, early mechanization was accompanied by the proletarianization of artisans and a deterioration of their living conditions.[86] As was the case with the commercialization of agriculture, the demand for labor in these industrial centers also served to encourage internal migration and to weaken the traditional ties of rural folk to their birthplaces. As early as 1877 more than one-quarter of Barcelona's inhabitants were not Catalan, and many of those who were had come from the rural interior of the region.[87] Bilbao had a similar impact on the people of the Cantabric.

Although in a sense internal migration to industrial centers and emigration overseas were parts of the same process of population dislocation and shifting that accompanied the development of capitalism, the relative timing and causation of the two is difficult to pinpoint.[88] It has been argued, for example, that the pull of national industrial centers successfully competed with the attraction of the New World and actually lowered rates of emigration.[89] But then why did the spread of emigration follow industrialization so closely? One would be tempted to conclude that the disruption caused by the early stages of industrialization (when along with capitalist agriculture and demographic acceleration, it displaced more people that it could absorb) encouraged emigration but that as the process matured, it acted as a check on it.

Overall, this seems to have been the pattern, but the process was not always that linear. In the case of England, for instance, Brinley Thomas argued that periods of high internal migration (and high rates of domestic investment) and of high emigration (and high capital export) occurred in cyclical intervals over a long time span.[90] In Spain, a country that exported little capital, these cycles of internal and transoceanic movement were not as visible, although, as the vice consul in Mataró reported, periods of disinvestment in industrial areas often caused upsurges in emigration.

Some of my data also show that: 1) industrialized areas that attracted internal migrants at the same time sent natives overseas;[91] 2) these areas often served as stepping stones in stage migration, that is, many immigrants from rural zones in Buenos Aires had previously resided (as indicated by the birthplaces of their children) in industrial towns; and 3) there was also a sort of delayed stage migration, that is, members of one generation migrated from the countryside (or from nonindustrial towns) to the industrial center, and their grown-up children emigrated from the industrial town where they had been born to Argentina. It is difficult to calculate exactly what percentage of the total emigration from industrial zones was made up of these types of movements. But regarding the third type, the case of Mataró may be illustrative: 47 percent of the parents of Mataronese immigrants in Buenos Aires had migrated to Mataró before their children were born. Of those, roughly half had come from the surrounding rural districts; one-quarter, from other places in Catalonia; and the remaining one-fourth, from other parts of Spain. As I demonstrate in chapter 3, this type of short- and long-range internal mobility facilitated overseas emigration in more than one way.

Industrialization spurred migration not only by attracting and displacing labor but also by creating new demands and desires, particularly among the young. In 1912, for example, a Galician priest detected the origins of Atlantic crossings in the acquisitiveness of youngsters who coveted patent-leather boots, leisure suits, flamboyant cravats, and other consumer articles.[92] In the same vein, a fictitious Asturian parish priest in a 1913 play blamed the exodus on the younger generation's craving for factory-made shoes and garments instead of homespun espadrilles and blouses; for watches, jewelry, and combs instead of the folksy rosaries, scapularies, and shawls; and for new gadgets such as guns, phonographs, and bicycles. The easiest way to acquire these, it seemed, was to make money overseas, where, the youngsters thought, "they leash dogs with sausages."[93] And another product of the industrial revolution, the photograph, carried those illusions and yearnings across the ocean, as an immigrant observed:

> Every time one of these aristocrats of the duster and the broom [Spanish servants in Argentina] takes a picture in her Sunday best ('tailleur' dress, stockings, patent leather bootees), she immediately sends a copy home. The photograph passes from house to house throughout the village, and in every one enthusiastic comments are made, inferring from those seignorial attires an enviable well-being. If there is a young maid in the house, a desire awakens in her to leave for Argentina, and that night the meek bumpkin dreams of faraway lands, of palaces and gold, of fortune and happiness. The most determined decide to take the trip.[94]

The combination of the four revolutions described thus far created, over the course of the nineteenth century, a situation in which population movements and outflows were almost inevitable. However, another element was needed to make mass transoceanic emigration a reality: an inexpensive way to transport not photographs and dreams but masses of people across the ocean.

THE TRANSPORTATION REVOLUTION

Improvements in transportation were usually designed to move goods rather than people. But as people began to move en masse they, from the perspective of ship owners, became cargo. By the first half of the nineteenth century emigrants to North America had become one more article of freight used as a profitable way to fill up ships only partially loaded with English wares on their way west but fully loaded with bulky Canadian timber, Virginian tobacco and Southern cotton on their way back. Emigration was thus intimately related to trade. As Marcus Lee Hansen, the pioneer historian of the movement, once put it, "Large-scale peasant emigration was possible only when the European demand for American products was so steady as to insure an adequate supply of vessels and when the tentacles of trade pushed inland to facilitate transportation on land."[95]

The trade of the industrial revolution, rather than trade in general, promoted improvements in transportation. As long as specie and spices furnished the main articles of exchange, galleons, the sextant, and the marine chronometer sufficed. As heavy and bulky items with limited value per weight or mass (such as coal, iron, machinery, timber, cotton, or wheat) became the main commodities of trade, advancements in the means of transporting them became a necessity; and the technological and innovative capacities that the industrial revolution unleashed made them possible. From the midnineteenth century on, steamships increasingly replaced sailing vessels, the screw propeller supplanted the cumbersome paddle wheel, and iron (and later steel) hulls superseded wooden ones.[96] Meanwhile, the sequential introduction of the double-expansion, triple-expansion, steam-turbine, and diesel marine engines kept cutting down fuel consumption and pushing up speed.[97]

Like the three previous trends, the transportation revolution was a late development in Spain. Technologically, the country did not possess the capacity to participate in it. Spain's transoceanic trade, one of the major driving forces behind transportation improvements elsewhere, had dwindled (after a short-lived renaissance in the late eighteenth century) with the loss of its overseas colonies. Not surprisingly, most of Spain's emigrants were transported to their destinations by British, German, or French ship companies.[98] Before the 1870s small Spanish maritime entrepreneurs had controlled much of the trade, but as emigration and opportunities for profits increased, the giant emigrant shipping firms stepped in.[99] Hamburg-Amerikanische Packetfahrt A.G. became a household word in thousands of Iberian villages as *la amburguesa;*[100] Koninklijke Lloyd and Nord-westdeutsche Lloyd became *las loids;* and the Royal Mail Steam Packet received the rather unfortunate translation of *la mala real* (the real bad) or, shorter and better, *la mala*. Spanish companies improved their standing after the turn of the century but only came to dominate the trade again during World War I, when the shipping of competing, nonneutral nations was disrupted. No matter what the nationality of the liners, the larger ships and the faster, safer, and more frequent crossings facilitated the emigration of Spaniards as much as that of other Europeans.[101] To a Spanish poet writing in 1915, "the waters" did not separate his nation and Argentina anymore, thanks to:

> Los grandes vapores, dulces mensajeros
> de paz y progreso, de dicha y de calma,
> nos ligan, nos juntan, nos traen y nos llevan,
> rompiendo y saltando las olas atlánticas.[102]

> The great steamers, sweet messengers
> of peace and progress, of joy and calm,
> link us, unite us, bring us and take us,
> breaking and jumping the Atlantic waves.

What occurred with the fares on the *dulce mensajeros* fares is less clear. Historian J. D. Gould asserts that in Europe as a whole, "transatlantic fares altered very little, in the trend, after about 1830."[103] Yet an analysis of the lowest advertised fares from Galicia to Buenos Aires by two major companies (see Figure 2) shows not only yearly but also long-term fluctuations. Taking the whole period, from 1850 to the outbreak of World War II, Figure 3 shows that the displacement of Spanish vessels by foreign steamers in the early 1870s raised fares, in constant currency, during the last three decades of the nineteenth century by about a third.[104] The improved technology and greater competition, however, eventually slashed prices to levels lower than those of the 1850s during the first two decades of the twentieth century. But they shot up again to all-time peaks after the mid-1920s.

The real cost of transatlantic transportation, however, dropped more than what fares in constant money indicate. For instance, in the 1860s Galician-owned vessels charged an average of forty-two gold pesos for a trip to the River Plate, which took some sixty-one days. At the time, unskilled laborers in Buenos Aires earned about one gold peso a day and worked six days a week. If we add to the fare the cost of unearned wages during the fifty-two workdays lost during the ocean crossing, the real cost of the trip for the immigrant laborer rises to ninety-six gold pesos. In the

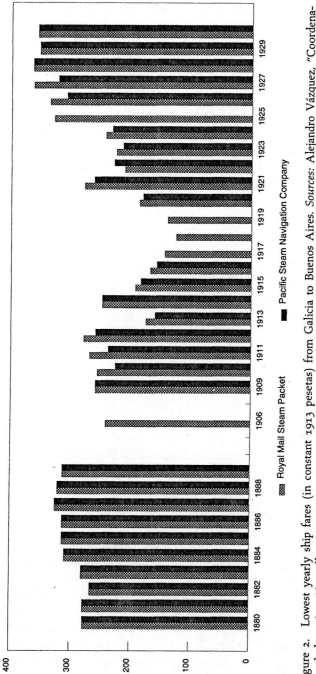

Figure 2. Lowest yearly ship fares (in constant 1913 pesetas) from Galicia to Buenos Aires. *Sources:* Alejandro Vázquez, "Coordenadas de la emigración gallega a América, 1850–1930: Un estudio comparativo" (paper presented at IV Coloquio de Metodología Aplicada, Poio, Spain, June 26–28, 1989), 13; and idem, "Alguns aspectos do transporte da emigración galega a América, 1850–1930," *V Xornadas de Historia de Galicia* (Orense, Spain) (1990):117–34.

Royal Mail Steam Packet ■ Pacific Steam Navigation Company

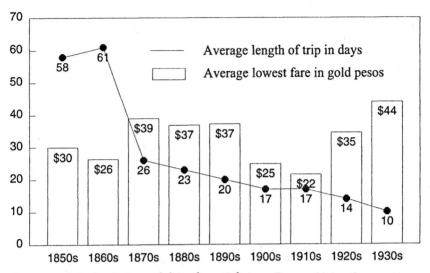

Figure 3. Length of trips and fares from Galicia to Buenos Aires, 1850s–1930s. *Sources:* See Figure 2. Vázquez gives the fares in constant 1913 pesetas; I converted them to gold pesos.

next decade, British-owned steamers raised the fare for the same trip to sixty-two gold pesos but shortened its duration to twenty-six days (twenty-two workdays).[105] Thus, in spite of the higher prices exacted by the British companies, the true cost of the trip for a Gallego laborer had dropped by 12 percent, from ninety-six gold pesos in the 1860s to eighty-five in the 1870s. For skilled workers, whose wages tripled those of day laborers, faster journeys represented even greater savings (see columns B and C in Table 2).

It is likely that this formula exaggerates the value of unearned wages during the trip and thus the drop in the real cost of transportation. After all, the passengers not only earned no money on the ship but also spent none on room and board. Yet, even if we assume that once in Buenos Aires these basic necessities consumed three-quarters of wages (a rather high estimate, because the rest would cover not only discretionary income, savings, and remittances but also essentials like clothing, furniture, debt payments, and so forth), days at sea continued to represent lost real earnings. Calculating these losses at only one-quarter of wages still shows that faster crossings reduced the real cost of the Atlantic voyage to a much greater degree than shifts in passenger fares would indicate (in Table 2, compare column A with columns D and E). And the reduction tran-

Table 2 Trends in the passenger fares from Galicia to Argentina (column A) and in the real costs of the trips, calculated as fare plus value of unearned income during the ocean crossing (columns B–E), 1850s–1930s[a] (cost in 1850s = 100)

	A	B	C	D	E
Decade	Fares	Fare plus lost wages for a day laborer	Fare plus lost wages for a skilled worker	Fare plus ¼ lost wages for a day laborer	Fare plus ¼ lost wages for a skilled worker
1850s	100	100	100	100	100
1860s	88	99	102	93	98
1870s	130	76	58	104	81
1880s	123	66	37	96	65
1890s	124	56	29	92	59
1900s	83	48	29	66	46
1910s	72	46	25	59	40
1920s	115	66	35	92	60
1930s	147	73	36	112	72

SOURCES: For fares, see Figure 2 (Vázquez gives the fares in constant 1913 pesetas; I changed them to gold pesos to facilitate the calculation of columns B to E, which include Buenos Aires wages in that currency). For 1850–1870 wages, María Sáenz Quesada, *El estado rebelde: Buenos Aires entre 1850–1860* (Buenos Aires: Editorial de Belgrano, 1982), 210; and sundry examples gathered from newspaper advertisements and municipal manuscript ledgers in the archives of Instituto Histórico de la Ciudad de Buenos Aires, División Archivo Historico. For post-1870 wages, Guy Bourdé, *Urbanisation et immigration en Amérique Latine, Buenos Aires, XIXe et XXe siècles* (Paris: Aubier, 1974), 242–48; Roberto Cortés Conde, *El progreso argentino, 1800–1914* (Buenos Aires: Editorial Sudamericana, 1979), 211–39; James Scobie, *Buenos Aires: Plaza to Suburb, 1870–1910* (New York: Oxford University Press, 1974), 266; Guido Di Tella and Manuel Zymelman, *Las etapas del desarrollo económico argentino* (Buenos Aires: Editorial Universitaria de Buenos Aires, 1967), 317, 328, 341, 369, 399.

[a] The "real" cost of the trip in column B is calculated as follows: (price of fare) plus (6/7 of days spent on sea; that is, lost working days because Sundays did not count) times (average daily wage for an unskilled laborer in Buenos Aires during the given decade). The calculation for column C is the same, except that wages for skilled workers are used. Columns D and E offer an alternative way of calculating the true cost of the trip: the same formulas are used as for columns B and C, respectively, but the number of working days lost on the ocean crossing are multiplied by 1/4 of the unearned daily wages. The rationale here is that loss of potential wages during the trip was offset by the fact that during the journey the passengers spent little or nothing on room and board, which would become necessary expenditures once they arrived in Buenos Aires. The loss of potential earnings was thus conservatively calculated at 1/4 of wages; that is, the proportion that would be either saved or spent on items other than rent and food, such as light and durable consumer goods, insurance, debt payments, recreation, and so forth.

scended the purely monetary. Most ocean crossings in sailing ships were not the odysseys of sea novels—but neither were they leisure cruises. If, as the English poet-satirist Samuel Butler put it, "Nothing makes a man or woman look so saintly as seasickness," the steadier steamers definitely reduced the number of godly faces. The psychological effects probably equaled the physiological ones. By reducing the trip from two months to two weeks, steamers facilitated the emigration of those earthy country and town folks who concurred with that other famous English wit, Dr. Johnson; namely, that "being in a ship is being in jail, with the chance of being drowned."

The transportation revolution that carried millions across the waves moved even larger numbers across the land. As late as the middle of the eighteenth century, Spain could have been described as "some nine million people in a country without roads," where the existing untended trails dated mostly to Roman and Medieval times.[106] The next hundred years, particularly the 1840s, saw the first significant infrastructural improvement in more than fifteen centuries: a network of thirty-to-sixty-foot-wide royal roads, usually built on a limestone foundation and paved with gravel or slabs.[107] According to historian David Ringrose, this system proved to be costly, inadequate for the transportation requirements of the Spanish interior, and a primary cause of its stagnation.[108] But whatever its cost or deficiencies for the hauling of freight, the expanding network of wider, macadamized roads, bridges, and stagecoach companies spiraled the mobility of people. Between 1775 and 1850 the speed of journeys tripled, fares fell by one-half to two-thirds, and passengers proliferated from fewer than 2,000 to some 825,000 a year.[109] And the expansion of royal roads continued in the second half of the century, from 5,100 kilometers in 1850 to 35,400 in 1900, and to 43,200 by 1910.[110] Of particular significance for migration, this expansion connected the ports of La Coruña and Vigo to the Galician, Leonese, and Old Castilian hinterland (which by 1900 supplied more than half of the Spanish emigrants to Argentina), and it consisted of roads for wheeled traffic (obviously, horseback riding to the port was a poor option: few Spanish peasants owned horses, and those who did would either have to sell the animal in the port city before setting sail or have someone take it back to their hometown).

The importance of paved roads and horse-drawn carriages for internal and overseas travel was eventually dwarfed by "iron roads" and the "iron horse." The first train in Spain appeared in 1848, twenty-three years after its English birth. This twenty-eight-kilometer-long line connected Barcelona with Mataró, the town with which this chapter began, and in part owed its existence to emigration, because rich Mataronese returnees from the Americas were among its backers.[111] In turn, it modestly eased further Mataronese emigration by dropping traveling time to the port of Barcelona from three hours by stagecoach to one hour (in both cases including stops) and cutting third-class fares from fourteen to six reales, less than the eight-real daily wage of local unskilled laborers.[112]

The relationship between trains and emigration was neither automatic nor immediate. In maritime towns like Mataró, a three-hour carriage ride to the port most likely never deterred anyone from crossing the ocean. In the interior, the political centralism of the day tended to direct lines toward Madrid rather than toward seaports. The first long-distance line, which connected Madrid with Valencia and Alicante, ran through provinces with few overseas emigrants and did little to change that. On the other hand, Galicia, the area with the highest real and potential emigration, was the last Spanish region to get the railroad.[113]

Eventually, however, the train did enlarge the pool of prospective emigrants by making it easier for the hinterland to participate. By the early 1880s, the emigration ports of La Coruña and Vigo had been connected to the rest of Galicia, León, and the north in general. By 1900 the Spanish railroad system had basically reached its modern extension: 11,039 kilometers of rails linked much of the country to all of the main ports and carried 23.4 million passengers a year, at an average commercial speed of thirty-eight kilometers per hour. Two decades later only 405 kilometers of rail had been added, trains rode only five kilometers per hour faster, but riders almost tripled, to 61 million a year.[114]

Turn-of-the-century popular verses trolled the massive, multiclass nature of train travel:

La gente mas elevada
va en primera acomodada.
En los coches de segunda
la gente mediana abunda.
En los asientos de tercera
va la gente bullanguera.[115]

The most elevated people
go comfortably in first class.
In second-class coaches
the middling kind abound.
On third-class seats
ride the rowdy crowd.

The third-class fare of 0.045 pesetas per kilometer plus 25 percent tax meant that prospective "rowdy emigrants" from, say, Madrid would spend 38.5 pesetas for the 685-kilometer trip to the port of Barcelona, the equivalent of nineteen days of a common laborer's wages, eleven days of a carpenter's, and one-fifth of the ship fare to Buenos Aires. Others, like the emigrants from the village of Val de San Lorenzo in León, combined the oldest forms of locomotion with the newest: a 9-kilometer walk or donkey ride to Astorga and a 425-kilometer train trip to the Galician port of Vigo. Compared with the pretrain days of 1850, traveling to the port by 1900 had become more than half as expensive, five times faster, and also much safer;[116] the trains, along with the rural guard, reduced a feature of travel in Spain that was immortalized in Goya's drawings: highway robbery.

Together with safety, affordability, and speed, the railroad offered emigrants a greater choice of embarkation points and the chance to circumvent the monopolistic practices of shipping firms.[117] More and more they began to depart not from the closest seaport but from the one that offered the best services and fares. For example, in the midnineteenth century almost all Navarrese emigrants departed from the neighboring ports of Pasajes (San Sebastián's port), Bayonne, or Bordeaux, but by the early twentieth century more than half were taking advantage of fare wars on the Mediterranean routes and riding the train to Barcelona for embarkation to the River Plate. This greater internal mobility made price fixing by steamship companies more difficult, because emigrants could ride to ports serviced by other independent companies. In the years before World War I, for instance, the Spanish emigration commission noticed how attempts by ship companies to fix prices on the Cantabrian and North Atlantic ports backfired, because they led thousands of emigrants to travel to southern and foreign ports.[118]

Taking people to the port and across the ocean was not the only way in which the transportation revolution fueled emigration. The same steamers and trains that carried millions to the Americas carried the American grain, the British manufactures, and the Catalan textiles that competed with millions of peasant and artisan producers and induced many of them to emigrate or send their children overseas as a way to confront the new challenges. The railroad companies, which by 1900 employed 100,000 people, were the first to lure many future emigrants from their native villages. For instance, brothers Esteban, Julian, and Francisco Pueyo, from Tafalla, Navarre, migrated to Catalonia in the mid-1890s to work on the last section of the southern Zaragoza–Barcelona railway, the same line they later rode to embark for Buenos Aires in the early 1900s.[119] If some people moved to work on the railroad, others moved when it made their jobs obsolete. A nineteenth-century Navarrese tune put it this way:

> Cocheros y carreteros,
> ya podéis tocar a luto,
> que ya se ha secado el arbol
> que solía daros fruto.[120]

> Coachmen and cart drivers,
> you can begin to mourn
> that the tree has withered,
> the one that used to bear you fruit.

Indeed, some of the Pueyo brothers' older relatives had departed for Buenos Aires two decades earlier, when the *matapobres* (the "poor-people-killer" as the train was christened by those it ruined) withered the tree that used to bear them fruit, a mule-and-carriage service to Pamplona.

CONCLUSION

Contemporary Spanish observers ascribed the massive exodus from their country to a myriad of so-called causes: agrarian backwardness and poverty, lack of industry and economic stagnation, political corruption, abusive taxes, the demoralization of society, the machinations of shipping companies and their agents, bad harvests, floods, rural inheritance practices, labor unrest, the spirit of adventure, and so on. Some modern scholars have taken a similar approach. The author of one of the few articles on Spanish immigration in Argentina, for example, assigned two major causes to it: "indigence" and the "spirit of adventure that is identifiable with the very nature of Spaniards."[121] At certain times and places, of course, there was some relationship between bad harvests, floods, labor unrest, high taxes, and so forth and the escalation of emigration. But the immense majority of crop failures, floods, strikes, tax increases, and other banes of human existence have never led to emigration. The same is true of industrial backwardness, economic stagnation, and indigence. Indeed, as I have showed, emigration was tied not to lack of industry but to the unsettling effects of early industrialization, not to socioeconomic stillness but to change, transition, and disruption, and the flow was thinnest in the poorest areas and among the poorer folks. The spirit of adventure is of even less etiological value because one can simply—and arbitrarily—identify this nebulous concept with "the very nature" of those groups that have emigrated and deny it to those that have not.

Producing an ad hoc list of national maladies and camouflaging them into push factors would have been both facile and sterile. After all, I could have compiled an unending list of such push factors for Cuenca, a province that sent as many people overseas as did Inner Mongolia. So instead of listing ex post facto causes or searching for what are at best immediate causes, I have examined how the five key trends in the early phases of capitalist modernization (demographic expansion, liberalism, the commercialization of agriculture, industrialization, and advances in transportation) created in Spain a migration-prone situation—perhaps a situation in which emigration was all but inevitable. If mass migration was caused by something, that something was not backwardness but modernization, a process that engendered poverty for many, opportunities for others, and change, competition, disruption, and motion for a greater number. Indeed, movement and flux—of capital, goods, services, technologies, ideas, and peoples—became the mark of modernization, and as it spread so did overseas emigration. The fact then that, with the probable exception of demographic expansion, the key trends in the modernization process unfolded later in Spain than in much of Europe explains, *a grosso modo*, why the first Europeans to cross the Atlantic were among the last to join the nineteenth-century exodus en masse.

To come back to where I began, the strikes and labor unrest that the Argentine vice consul in Mataró saw as causing emigration were no more than symptoms of a developing capitalism and at best immediate causes. The macrotrends examined in this chapter, not the strikes of one year or the unemployment of the next, explain why Spain became a country of emigrants when it did. This answers only the first part of our main question, however. The second part is why Argentina became a country of immigrants.

2   Argentina Becomes
a Country of Immigrants

The pull factor observed by the vice consul in Mataró—Argentina's flourishing economy in the early 1880s—was also, at best, an immediate cause that can explain yearly fluctuations in immigration but not the long-term phenomenon. After all, dozens of countries with occasional flourishing economies received few if any immigrants while Argentina welcomed thousands, not only during prosperous years but also during its worst economic depressions. At any rate, both its often flourishing economy and its immigration were the outcome of the country's insertion into the world capitalist system and the effect on it of the five global revolutions discussed in chapter 1.

The European demographic revolution affected both Argentina's economic growth and immigration in elemental ways. The proliferating population of the Old World, in particular the spiraling urban proportion that did not grow its own food, generated the demand for temperate-zone foodstuffs that allowed Argentina's integration into the Atlantic trade system. And this expanding market for food on one side of the Atlantic synchronically created a market for labor on the other, because even though Argentina had the pampas, one of the three finest farm belts on the planet,[1] it lacked the farmers. At the time of its political emancipation in 1810, the new country of a million square miles, the size of continental Europe, held fewer than half a million souls, about one-half the population of Barcelona Province, one-quarter that of tiny, mountainous Switzerland, or one-fifth that of even tinier London. In the increasingly interrelated world of the nineteenth century, Argentina seemed destined to act as both breadbasket and receptacle for Europe's multiplying millions.

Indeed, at the most primary level Argentine immigration formed part of a demographic-ecological phenomenon. The surplus population of Eu-

Table 3   Destination of European overseas emigrants, ca. 1820–1932

	Year data begin	Number	Percentage of total	Cumulative percentage
United States	1820	32,564,000	57.9	57.9
Canada	1821	5,073,000	9.0	67.0
Argentina	1840	6,501,000	11.6	78.5
Brazil	1821	4,361,000	7.8	86.3
Uruguay	1836	713,000	1.3	87.6
Australia	1840	3,443,000	6.1	93.7
New Zealand	1840	588,000	1.0	94.7
South Africa	1840	731,000	1.3	96.0
Cuba	1880	1,394,000	2.5	98.5
Mexico	1880	270,000	0.5	99.0
Algeria	1893	150,000	0.3	99.3
Chile	1850	90,000	0.2	99.4
Venezuela	1832	70,000	0.1	99.5
Puerto Rico	1880	62,000	0.1	99.7
Brit. W. Indies	1835	60,000	0.1	99.8
Hawaii	1907	40,000	0.1	99.8
Zimbabwe	1890	30,000	0.1	99.9
Peru	1850	30,000	0.1	99.9
Paraguay	1882	21,000	0.0	100.0
New Caledonia	1879	12,000	0.0	100.0
Total		56,183,000		

SOURCES: For the United States (including Hawaii), a computer database I compiled for the Ellis Island Project (Rutgers University) using U.S. official statistics. For Canada through Mexico, I began with figures on intercontinental migration in A.M. Carr-Saunders, *World Population: Past Growth and Present Trends* (London, 1936), 49, and then deducted the portion made up by non-European migration (usually Chinese, Japanese, or East Indian), preferably using receiving-country statistics in Imre Ferenczi and Walter F. Willcox, *International Migrations*, vol. 1 (New York, 1929). Because this volume covers the period up to 1924, I extrapolated the data on non-European immigration between 1924 and 1932. Argentine official statistics begin in 1857, but I was able to extend the starting date back to 1840 by using manuscript passenger lists in Argentina, Archivo General de la Nación, Sala X, 36.8.17–36.8.40. Statistics for Australia, New Zea-

(continued on next page)

Table 3 (*continued*)

land, and South Africa begin in 1861, 1851, and 1881, respectively; the figures from 1840 to those years are based on British and German emigration data, at the time the two principal emigrant groups to Oceania and South Africa. Similarly, Cuban and Mexican official statistics begin in 1901 and 1911; the figures from 1880 to those dates are based on Spanish and Italian emigration statistics, at the time the principal European emigrants to Cuba and Mexico. Algeria represents a unique, or exaggerated, case of seasonal movements and sojourning. Some 4.1 million Europeans (84 percent of them French and 15 percent, Spaniards) entered the colony between 1893 and 1924, but 98 percent of them left. Although the figures for the other countries represent gross rather than net immigration, using the same in the case of Algeria would have been misleading and distorting. I thus computed Algeria's immigration as net immigration times 166 percent, roughly the gross–net ratio for most other countries. The figures for Chile were computed from Ferenczi and Willcox, *International Migrations*, 582–84; and Carlos Díaz and Fredy Cancino, *Italianos en Chile* (Santiago: Ediciones Documentos, 1988), 54–57, 76, 118. The figures for Venezuela were computed from Adela Pellegrino, *Historia de la inmigración en Venezuela siglos XIX y XX* (Caracas: Academia Nacional de Ciencias Económicas, 1989), vol. 1, 74, 80, 134, 162, 164, 168. The figures for Puerto Rico were based on Spanish emigration statistics times 110 percent; those for Peru, from data and estimates in Mario E. del Río, *La inmigración y su desarrollo en el Perú* (Lima, 1929), 112–15, 161, and Wilfredo Kapsoli et al., *Primer seminario sobre poblaciones inmigrantes* (Lima: Consejo Nacional de Ciencias y Tecnología, 1987), vol. 1, 34, 39; those for Paraguay, from Ferenczi and Willcox, *International Migrations*, 559–62, and Paraguay, Ministerio de Relaciones Exteriores, *Datos estadísticos sobre el movimiento de inmigración en el Paraguay desde 1882 hasta 1908* (Asunción, 1908), 8–9; and those for the British West Indies, Zimbabwe, and New Caledonia, from Ferenczi and Willcox, *International Migrations*.

rope's "Malthusian devil" did not simply head for countries with flourishing economies but for particular geographies. As Table 3 shows, 96 percent of the 56 million Europeans who left their continent in the century after the end of the Napoleonic Wars settled in four particular regions: North America (in particular the area north of the Mason-Dixon Line, south of the Canadian Laurentian Shield, and east of the Rocky Mountains), where 67 percent of the total settled; the River Plate (formed by eastern Argentina, Uruguay, and southern Brazil), which attracted more than 20 percent of the total; Australasia, with 7 percent; and, in smaller numbers, South Africa. These regions comprise the bulk of the non-European temperate zone and have warm-to-cool climates with an annual precipitation of 50 to 150 centimeters, thinly spread aboriginal populations, some of the world's best pasture and wheat-producing lands, immense cattle and sheep herds, consistent surplus production of cereals, and, with the exception of South Africa, largely Caucasian populations.[2] So while the destinations of Europeans may have ranged from Algeria to Zimbabwe, more than nineteen out of twenty settled in what Alfred Crosby aptly called Neo-Europes, and their movement formed part of what the same author termed ecological imperialism, a migration-invasion of Old World fauna (humans included) and flora.[3] In Argentina, European settlers pushed the Pampa Indians out of the grasslands that bear their name and the Araucanians out of Patagonia; by the outbreak of World War I, they and their second- and third-generation descendants constituted four-fifths of the national population. European cattle, sheep, goats, asses, pigs, rabbits, dogs, cats, chickens, bees, and rats drove back the native Patagonian rabbits, guanacos, and rheas. The Castilian wild artichoke supplanted local needlegrasses in such a way that an amazed Charles Darwin wrote in the 1830s, "I doubt whether any case is in record of an invasion on so grand a scale of one plant over the aborigines."[4] Hundreds of other European weeds continued to encroach, until by the 1920s only one-quarter of the pampas' wild herbage was indigenous. By then Old World wheat, barley, flax, and alfalfa blanketed the grasslands, and European bacteria, parasites, and pathogens had become an integral component of the country's epidemiological history. From this perspective, Argentine immigration seems indeed the outcome of powerful biogeographical and demographic global forces, part of an inevitable flow of Old World organisms, from *Homo sapiens* to microbes, that came to transform and form the national biotas of the Neo-Europes.

Compared with the substantiality of biology, climate, geography and demography, politics may seem truly superstructural, almost immaterial, in explaining why Argentina became a country of immigrants. Yet politics, and thus human agency, played a role. To begin with, European ecological invasion was originally tied to politico-military conquest. Closer to our topic, the mercantilist politics of the Spanish Crown for centuries hindered immigration to the River Plate viceroyalty by, on the one hand, restricting departures from Spain and, on the other, prohibiting the entry of non-Spaniards into the colonies.[5] The liberal revolution, as we saw in chapter 1, eradicated the former hindrance in Spain during the second half of the nineteenth century. On the other side of the Atlantic, the same revolution, this time in the form of a movement toward political independence, eradicated the latter hindrance in Argentina during the second decade of the same century.

Patriot leaders, from the moderate José de San Martín to the Jacobinic Mariano Moreno, expressed the need to "break the destructive dams that prevent foreigners from settling our vast, deserted land."[6] Even before the formal declaration of independence, the Provisional Junta, theoretically ruling in the name of Ferdinand VII (the Spanish monarch deposed by the Napoleonic invasion of the Iberian Peninsula), decreed in 1810 that "the English, Portuguese, and other foreigners not at war with Argentina [which presumably excluded Ferdinand's subjects] can freely settle in the country, will have all the rights of citizens, and the government will protect those engaged in the arts and the cultivation of the land."[7] By the 1820s the welcome mat had been extended to even the ex-colonial rulers, although persistent Hispanophobia made the official welcome questionable. The necessity to populate the country through immigration became a top item on the liberal agenda of the new republic's leaders, a necessity best expressed in the famous dictum of Juan Bautista Alberdi, "Gobernar es poblar" (To govern is to populate).

To populate, however, involved more than a quantitative process. It meant, for Alberdi and his generation, doing so with "people of better quality," with "the civilized races of Europe," for "who would not a thousand times rather have his sister or daughter marry an English cobbler than an Araucanian chieftain? In America all that is not European is barbaric."[8] Only "the influx of masses with deep-rooted habits of order and industry," not "books of philosophy," could bring the "life-giving spirit of European civilization," a spirit that would "get rid of the primitive element of our popular masses."[9] Domingo Sarmiento, the other leading liberal ideologist of the nineteenth century and future president of Argentina (1868–1874), feuded long and bitterly with Alberdi but concurred with him and with the liberal "Generation of 1837" in general that only mass immigration could "drown in waves of industry the Creole rabble, inept, uncivil, and coarse, that stops our attempt to civilize the nation."[10]

The government's attempt began soon after the birth of the nation. A law of August 2, 1821, authorized the state to arrange for the transportation of "industrious European families" to settle the country.[11] A decree of September 22, 1822, granted one square league of land to those brave souls willing to settle in the Patagonia beyond the Indian frontier.[12] Two months later another decree exempted immigrants from military service. Two years later Bernardino Rivadavia, the leading liberal of the decade, created a Comisión de Emigración, which set up quarters in London and tried to entice English, Scottish, and other northern European immigrants with offers of free passage, free land, and start-up money.[13] The 1830s and 1840s, however, witnessed a decline in official immigration schemes as the conservative and xenophobic Juan Manuel de Rosas, governor of Buenos Aires and de facto ruler of the country from 1829 to 1852, abolished the immigration commission and abandoned Rivadavia's dreams of turning the pampas into a Jeffersonian society of Anglo-Saxon yeomen.[14]

After this nativist interim, the liberal elite that overthrew Rosas resumed Rivadavia's efforts with greater energy. The Constitution of 1853,

which lasted until 1949, gave foreigners all "the civil rights of citizenship" and the federal government a mandate to "foment European immigration."[15] To comply with this constitutional directive, the government
funded an immigration committee founded in 1856 by a group of Buenos
Aires businessmen; the committee was nationalized in 1862 and evolved
into a department under several ministries.[16] Between 1864 and 1889 this
department appointed dozens of immigration and propaganda agents in
several European cities and maintained in Buenos Aires the Hotel de Inmigrantes, the Argentine equivalent of Ellis Island, which provided newcomers with free food, medical attention, lodging for five days, employment information, and, at times, free transportation to the interior for
harvest workers. Mostly during the 1860s and 1870s, provincial governments created agricultural colonies that allotted the immigrant farmer a
thirty-to-forty-hectare land parcel, animals, seeds, and implements. By
1880 there were 695 of these colonies with 53,000 farms in the provinces
of Santa Fe, Córdoba, and Entre Ríos.[17] Official involvement in immigration reached a peak in the late 1880s, when the government tried its hand
at what it misleadingly called—in order, one would guess, not to conflict
with its liberal principles—*inmigración subsidiaria*, which was not really
subsidiary but subsidized: between 1888 and 1890, Argentine immigration agents dispensed 133,428 free passages to Buenos Aires in several
European countries.[18]

Were the Argentine ruling classes' racist disdain for their native population and the resulting, deliberate policies and programs to Europeanize
the country key factors in explaining why Argentina became a country of
immigrants? I do not think so. The political elite in the United States, for
example, disdained the immigrants instead of the native population, but
the United States attracted seven times as many immigrants as did Argentina. On the other hand, the Peruvian elite scorned their country's Indians and *cholos* (a local term for dark-skinned mestizos), if anything with
greater intensity than did their Argentine counterparts and, in order to
"civilize" their Andean nation with European blood, created dozens of
immigration commissions, published and distributed immigrants' guides,
contracted propaganda and emigration agents in Europe, offered would-be
immigrants free ship passage, free lodging in Lima, free train transportation to the interior, and free land (fenced, with tools, seeds, oxen, and access to water).[19] And yet, for all the racist attitudes and official efforts of
its ruling class, Peru attracted in one hundred years fewer European immigrants than did Argentina in one month and fewer than did the United

States in one week.[20] Peru was no isolated case. Gran Colombia, Costa Rica, Nicaragua, Honduras, and Guatemala engaged in similar pursuits.[21] Again, in spite of their political elites' desiderata and efforts to whiten the population, all of these countries put together received fewer European immigrants in a century of national history than did one Argentine province in a month. Clearly, the racism, prejudices, visions, and ambitions of the Western Hemisphere's national political elites did little or nothing to determine whether their countries would become nations of immigrants.

The Argentine leaders' racial attitudes, therefore, seem more relevant to the country's elite intellectual history than to its demographic formation. And their official schemes to foster immigration reveal more about the nation's political and institutional history than about its immigration. The commission established by Rivadavia, for example, tells us more about his generation's Anglophilia than about the settlement of the pampas. After all, it brought fewer than a thousand British colonists, and fewer than a tenth stayed.[22] The xenophobic Rosas abolished the commission and never lilted about immigration's civilizing influence, but as he imposed order and as sheep raising boomed, more people came during his rule than during that of liberal Rivadavia.[23] The political leadership that followed Rosas persistently coveted Anglo-Saxon yeomen and Teutonic *bauers* but, for reasons that had little to do with political desires, received Italian *contadini* and Spanish *labradores* instead. The government's experiment with "subsidiary" immigration in the 1888–1890 period probably offers the perfect example of the gap between political effort and nonpolitical realities. The free passages brought thousands of people who left on the spur of the moment, with no clear plans, no connections in Argentina, and no way to handle the economic downturn of the following year. The subsidized passages left the country with a debt of 3 million gold pesos and, according to the Immigration Department's hypocritical gripe, "an army of spiritless bums."[24]

Official schemes obviously attracted official and semiofficial attention. Ministries, commissions, committees, lawyers, political figures and their foes, the press, and others produced documents, treatises, reports, theses, speeches, denunciations, news columns, and essays. The subsidized immigration of the late 1880s, for instance, gave fodder in the following decades to dozens of studies and more than twenty doctoral dissertations that repetitiously weighed the pros and cons of "artificial" immigration.[25] This abundance of references and records has misled many a historian into exaggerating the import of governmental policy and official institutions.[26]

Some have even presented the Argentine flow as "artificial or official," compared with the "spontaneous or natural immigration" in the United States.[27] Yet despite the abundance of contemporary records and the attention of modern scholars, fewer than 2 percent of the 6.5 million immigrants who arrived in Argentina between 1840 and 1930 did so with government-paid fares. Obviously, no one wrote an official report or a dissertation about the millions of parents, uncles, spouses, and common folks who paid for 98 percent of the fares and sent millions of remittances and letters home that became, in the words of Italian parliamentarian Enrico Ferri, "a call and a gospel." Perhaps Ferri was right when he described "the mail stamp" as "the most powerful Argentine immigration agent."[28]

The Argentine government did take direct and indirect measures to aid "the mail stamp" that proved more important than its awkward attempts to bring immigrants at any cost. One measure consisted simply of opening the country's gates. When the principal host nations, including Argentina, began to restrict entries from the 1920s on, the period of mass transoceanic migration came to an end. Other measures consisted of those political decisions that led to the formation of a national institutional infrastructure in the 1862–1880 period. These two decades saw the founding of a national treasury, army, custom office, capital, bureaucracy, and postal, educational, and legal systems. National consolidation, in turn, proved essential for immigration, because it promoted social order, personal and property security, Argentina's insertion into the world market, and its own version of the agricultural revolution.

From the early days of the republic, national leaders perceived the bond between agricultural and demographic development. Its first civilian president, Rivadavia, tried to foster both with his plan to grant public lands to immigrants in emphytheusis. But conditions in the aftermath of emancipation proved propitious for neither. Recurrent civil strife and caudillo struggles in the countryside prevented planting and repelled settlers. Under the circumstances, only rustic ranching, which required little capital or labor input and exploited the natural resources of the pampas, thrived. Relatively few, seminomadic gauchos herded and hunted wild or semitamed cattle and horses on huge, unfenced estancias for their hide and tallow. In this primitive pastoralism, roaming cattle impeded crop farming and ambitious cattlemen obstructed agricultural colonization projects, viewing them as antithetical to their interests or, at best, costly pipe dreams of liberal ideologues. Yet, indirectly and in the long run, rudimentary ranching facilitated immigration by allowing national capital accumulation at a time when other activities were not viable, by providing government revenues and thus aiding political stability, and by creating the first sustained links with the international economy.[29]

The pastoral economy also became more complex and labor intensive as the nineteenth century progressed. In the decades after independence, meat-salting plants introduced factory methods such as wage levels, division of labor, and large-scale production on one site. These *saladeros* grew in number and size for much of the century to supply the Western Hemisphere's slave markets with jerked beef that apparently not even the slum dwellers of Manchester would eat. With no European demand for its main product, however, the industry all but collapsed with the abolition of slavery in Cuba and Brazil during the late 1880s.

Another quadruped, scorned in the equestrian culture of the pampas, provided the second step in the transformation of Argentina's pastoral economy. A country in which beef abounded to such an extent that, as late as the 1860s, the carcasses of more than 60 percent of the slaughtered cattle ended up as carrion for dogs and vultures, in which even the must humble gaucho considered shepherding undignified and mutton unpalatable, and where a sheep was worth little more than an egg, seemed an unlikely place for a flourishing ovine industry.[30] Yet by 1865 a visiting Briton already felt that "the oil springs of Pennsylvania are outdone and the gold fields of California and Australia eclipsed, by the sheep-farming business of Buenos Aires."[31] Sheep multiplied, from 6 million around the middle of the century to 23 million in 1864, to a high of 74 million by 1895, when they outnumbered humans eighteen to one, giving Argentina the second largest flock on earth.[32] To supply the increasing demand from the garment and carpet factories of Belgium and France (Australia supplied England's), owners gradually replaced the rough-fleeced merinos (actually mixed and degenerated descendants of sixteenth-century Spanish merinos) with imported, long-wool Rambouillets, and annual wool exports rose from an average of 6,000 tons in the 1840s to 120,000 tons four decades later.[33] Another imported variety, the Lincoln, provided the tender meat that enabled stock raisers to export 56,000 tons of frozen lamb by the end of the century.[34] The sheep-business boom would have been impossible without the inflow of other European breeds: Irish, Scottish, and Basque shepherds. Sheep farming was three times as labor intensive as cattle grazing, and the pampas' native plainsmen had neither the cultural inclination nor, given the abundance of wild cattle free for the taking, the material necessity to shepherd. Not surprisingly, sheep tending became so

much an immigrants' occupation that an Irish minstrel in the pampas had
to set the record straight with the following tune:

> Usted pensar que los gringos
> no saber nada más que
> cuidar ovejas en campaña.
> Pero usted se equivoca,
> porque ellos saben también
> tomar mate y chupar caña.[35]

> You thinking [sic] that immigrants
> don't knowing [sic] anything but
> tend sheep in countryside.
> But you are wrong
> because they also know how to
> drink mate and guzzle booze.

The third and final phase in the evolution of Argentina's pastoral economy, cattle breeding and beef export, had been retarded by the abundant
Creole livestock itself—because its stringy flesh appealed little to the European palate—by the expansion of sheep raising on the pampas that absorbed grazing lands and by the difficulty of shipping fresh beef across
the Atlantic. Argentine estancieros, the national army, and new marine
technology overcame those obstacles after the 1880s. Ranchers embraced
the practice of importing and breeding pedigreed animals with such enthusiasm that by 1900 the high-grade-beef Shorthorns and Herefords outnumbered all other strains in the national stock.[36] Eight years later, Creole
cattle accounted for only 8 percent of the stock in Buenos Aires Province.[37] The military conquest of Patagonia from the Araucanian Indians in
1879–1880 allowed sheep raising to move south to cheaper and more arid
lands, whose hard weeds tasted good enough for the notoriously undis-
criminating herbivores and freed up much of the pampas for cattle grazing. Steamers allowed the transportation of cattle on the hoof, and after
the turn of the century refrigerated ships permitted the massive export of
frozen and, later, chilled beef. By the early twentieth century the 25 million head outnumbered humans five to one, and Argentina had replaced
the United States as the major supplier of the British market. The additional element which made this possible was a steady influx of immigrants. Unlike the cattle hunting and herding of the postindependence
decades, where one gaucho could care for two thousand head, the new
cattle-beef economy required armies of laborers to erect the barbed-wire
fences that prevented unwanted mixing of thoroughbred animals, to plant
the alfalfa that fattened the livestock in a way the pampas' wild grasses

could never do, to milk cows in the mushrooming *tambos* (dairy farms, usually Basque owned), and to build the wells, windmills, water pumps, and other devices of the modern estancia. Cattle barons, who a generation earlier had opposed immigration, now welcomed it with as much enthusiasm as the arrival of Brahma bulls.

The fences that checked the promiscuity of prize bulls also made possible the last stage in Argentina's agricultural revolution, agricultural now in the strict sense of the word and revolutionary in any sense. Cultivated land increased about fiftyfold, from a half million hectares in 1870 to 24.5 million hectares in 1914.[38] As late as the first date, the country still imported most of its cereals; by the second date, it had turned into a veritable breadbasket, the world's largest producer of corn and linseed and the second largest exporter of wheat.[39] If the pampas provided the rich, deep topsoil for this cereal boom, Europe provided the *brazos* (literally "arms," and a pseudonym for immigrants often found in the writings and speeches of the country's rural oligarchy). Indeed, Argentina's agropastoral economy had steadily evolved toward more labor-intensive forms: from hunting feral cattle and horses for their hides (pre-1810), to herding and slaughtering semitamed animals for the *saladeros* (circa 1810 to 1890), to sheep raising (post-1840), and finally to cattle breeding and crop farming (post-1880). This tendency both fed on and induced immigration, which increased with each stage (see Table 4). Moreover, the agricultural revolution on the pampas made possible the even more labor-intensive commercial and industrial economy of the urban centers, where 53 percent of the Argentine population resided by 1914.[40]

Perhaps the industrial revolution, at least in Bertrand Russell's definition of it as a process "to make instruments to make other instruments, to make still other instruments 'ad infinitum,'"[41] never took place in Argentina. But if a capital-goods industry never developed, manufacturing certainly did. The number of manufacturing establishments increased from fewer than 3,000 in 1853 to 23,300 in 1895 and to 48,800 in 1914.[42] Between the last two dates, capital investment in constant money augmented fivefold, horsepower consumption expanded 12,000 percent, and the number of industrial workers grew from 180,000 to 410,000.[43] A few *frigoríficos* (meat-packing plants) formed the strongest single sector in terms of capital investment.[44] Thousands of small workshops that fabricated all sorts of light consumer articles, from socks and shoes to hats and umbrellas, and from safety pins and cradles to coffins and nails,[45] formed the main source of opportunities and employment for immigrants within the secondary sector of the economy. European arrivals owned between two-

Table 4 Immigration to Argentina, 1857–1930

Period	Entries	Departures	Net immigration	Percentage who remained in Argentina
1857–1860	20,000	8,900	11,100	55.5
1861–1870	159,570	82,976	76,594	48.0
1871–1880	260,885	175,763	85,122	32.6
1881–1890	841,122	203,455	637,667	75.8
1891–1900	648,326	328,444	319,882	49.3
1901–1910	1,746,104	643,881	1,120,322	63.1
1911–1920	1,204,919	935,825	269,094	22.3
1921–1930	1,397,415	519,445	877,970	62.8
Total	6,278,341	2,898,689	3,379,652	53.8

SOURCE: Guy Bourdé, *Urbanisation et immigration en Amérique Latine: Buenos Aires (XIX et XX siècles)* (Paris: Aubier, 1974), 163.

NOTE: Figures do not include an estimated 1,290,000 immigrants who entered Argentina through Montevideo between 1857 and 1930 and 839,000 who departed, leaving a net number of 451,000 (Bourd, *Urbanisation et immigration*, 162).

thirds and four-fifths of all industrial establishments in the country during the period and furnished from one-half to two-thirds of the workers (a proportion that was higher in Buenos Aires).[46] To the exasperation of rural oligarchs, these shops, together with the budding retail commercial sector, provided plenty of alternatives to planting alfalfa and stretching fences on their estancias. This was particularly important for Spaniards, whose tendency to settle in towns surpassed that of all other immigrant groups.[47] Iberian folk tunes such as the following were inspired by the attraction of this expanding urban economy more than by the fertility of the pampas:

> Buenos Aires, boa terra,
> boa terra pode ser,
> que leva a fror de Galicia,
> e non a deixa volver[48]

> Buenos Aires, good land,
> good land it must be,
> that takes the flower of Galicia,
> and does not let it return.

If the growth of light industry in Argentina offered newcomers jobs and opportunities, the surge of heavy industry on the other side of the Atlantic allowed the international division of labor on which Argentina's agropastoral and general progress rested. The demand for machine belts and lubricants during the takeoff of the industrial revolution in England, for instance, permitted the hide and tallow exports on which Argentina relied for the first half of the nineteenth century. The industrialization of woolen manufacturing on the European continent around the middle of the century propelled Buenos Aires' sheep-raising boom. Early in the twentieth century, the demand from industrial producers of oil paints, printers' ink, and linen enabled Argentina to become the world's largest grower of flax. By then linseed accounted for one-tenth of the country's exports. And, of course, increased demographic concentration in urban industrial centers concomitantly enlarged the demand for temperate-climate foodstuffs.

Industrialization also generated the revolution in transport and technology that steered Argentina into its "golden age." The conquest of Patagonia, and thus the releasing of pampa lands for cattle grazing and crop farming, would have been impossible without the telegraph or the Remington repeating rifle. The export of standing cattle and grain became profitable only when the larger and faster steamers replaced the old sailers. Without refrigerated ships and canning methods the pampas would have never become a synonym for beef in the European mind. And without the replacement of the horse cart by the "iron horse" Argentina would have resembled more a basket case than a breadbasket. The lack of viable transportation, after all, had long constrained crop farming. Cereal, unlike cattle, does not move by itself. The Buenos Aires pampa, unlike the Great Plains, has no navigable rivers or canals. The traditional and slow horse carts could only carry two tons at a time. Hauling the production levels of the first decade of the twentieth century would have required an unthinkable 5 million annual horse-cart trips and a no less preposterous bottleneck on the grasslands. Thus large-scale cereal farming became possible in Argentina, unlike the Mississippi-drained North American prairies, only after a railroad boom had blanketed the pampas with a fan-shaped web of tracks converging on the port city of Buenos Aires. The national railway system, about 70 percent of it British owned, expanded from 2,500 kilometers in 1880 to 9,400 kilometers in 1890, and to 33,500 kilometers in 1914, when the country boasted the seventh longest system in the world.[49] By then, the trains carried 10 million tons of cereal annually, 72 million passengers, and even 5 million tons of the previously trotting cattle.[50]

Another critical transportation improvement related to disembarkation. Not without irony for a city whose inhabitants call themselves Porteños, Buenos Aires had a shallow mud bank instead of a natural port. The Río de la Plata and its feeder rivers emptied a constant current of silt onto the estuary's shores. A French visitor in 1830 called the process of disembarking in the city "barbarous" and "a national shame."[51] Two decades later, a British traveler described his landing as surely a worse ordeal than that of the Spanish discoverers because in the intervening centuries "a mass of petrified mud has piled on the shore forming veritable rocks and forcing boats to search blindly for a safe course."[52] For much of the nineteenth century both passenger ships and freighters had to anchor eight or ten kilometers from the riverbank and transfer people and freight to smaller boats, which in turn would ferry the cargo to high-wheeled horsecarts one and a half kilometers inland. As late as 1880, a 500-ton ship required 100 days to unload its cargo. Under these circumstances, it is difficult to exaggerate the importance of the construction of a mammoth artificial deep-water port in the 1890s that allowed transatlantic steamers to offload directly onto the docks and cut those 100 days to 10.[53] Hydraulic discharging machinery on the four basins, a dock for repairs, grain elevators, a steam-driven flour mill, and wharves made it, according to an English visitor, "a splendidly equipped harbour."[54] The old waterfront facilities could not have handled a fraction of the 30,000 ships, half a million passengers, and 18 million tons of cargo that went through the port of Buenos Aires in 1910.

The five global revolutions that transformed Europe as the nineteenth century progressed also formed modern Argentina. They made Europe, including Spain, a continent of emigrants and Argentina a land of immigrants. The demographic explosion that generated a surplus of labor in Europe also created the demand for temperate-climate foodstuffs that spurred Argentina's agropastoral growth, which in turn created a demand for immigrant labor. Moreover, as Argentine exports competed with European peasant producers they often promoted an emigration-prone situation. Similarly, liberalism lifted mercantilist restraints (such as the British Corn Laws on one side of the Atlantic and the Spanish colonial monopoly on the other), the sort of stagnant security that these restraints provided, and the restrictions on the departure and arrival of people on both sides of the Atlantic. The agricultural revolution that displaced peasants in the Old World demanded agricultural workers in the peasantless but fertile plains of the New World. The industrial revolution that displaced artisans in the Old World increased the demand for Argentine commodities and thus the Argentine demand for European labor. It also fueled British capital accumulation and the investments and loans that proved essential for railroad construction in both Argentina and Spain. The railroads that took emigrants from the European hinterlands to the departing ports, and from Buenos Aires to the Argentine provinces, also took the pampas' cereal to Buenos Aires. The steamers that made mass emigration possible also allowed profitable transportation of the bulky or heavy commodities with low value per mass or weight that made up Argentina's exports. The improved deepwater port at Buenos Aires facilitated disembarkation of people as much as embarkation of goods.

To go back to the consular dispatch with which I began chapter 1, the push of unemployment in Spain and the pull of an economic upswing in Buenos Aires, which the Argentine vice consul in Mataró identified as the causes of emigration, could at best explain fluctuations in the flow. Clearly, the flow itself formed part of a global movement and obeyed mighty forces, which went from the primariness of physical and demographic ecology, through the materiality of economics and technology, to the elusiveness of political philosophy.

3 Weaving the Net

Microsocial Dimensions
of Spanish Emigration to Argentina

The five revolutions—and macrostructural trends in general—can, and do, explain why Spain became a country of emigrants and Argentina a land of immigrants. But they alone do not explain why the displaced Mataronese workers whom the vice consul saw depart headed for Argentina. First of all, staying in their own town presented an alternative. This, in fact, was what most of the town's inhabitants did. But even after they decided to look for greener pastures elsewhere, why not cross the Mediterranean instead of the Atlantic and seek fortune in Algeria, as most of the emigrants from Levant—the region immediately to the south—were doing?[1] Or why not follow the footsteps of emigrants from the neighboring provinces of Castellón and Huesca, and even fellow Catalans from the Balearic Islands, and just cross the frontier into France, where the language would sound less foreign than the Castilian of Buenos Aires?[2] One could argue that rural Algeria or southern France offered limited prospects to the inhabitants of industrial Mataró, but then why not imitate most other Europeans and head for North America? Ship fares to the United States were lower, factory jobs more abundant, and wages higher.[3] If an ex-Spanish colony was what they longed for, the two jewels of the old empire, Mexico and Peru, offered free transportation and land at the time, as did Venezuela and Paraguay. Australia, New Zealand, South Africa, Brazil (which also granted free passages and land), and the Spanish Caribbean colonies could have presented other possible destinations.[4] In other words, geographical proximity, language similarities, the cost of transportation, wage differentials, ex-colonial status, and the offerings of host governments were all variables that would seem to have steered the Mataronese to destinations other than Argentina.

The mere presence of a vice consul in this town can perhaps give us a clue to understanding the otherwise difficult-to-explain preference of its inhabitants for Argentina. Were we to use the number of consular offices as a yardstick of international standing, we would decidedly include Argentina as one of the great global powers of the second half of the nineteenth century. Sprinkled over the European map, one could find these offices not only in commercial centers like Genoa, Marseilles, and Cádiz but also in places as obscure as Albenga, Carril, and San Lucas de Berramenda; in Spain alone there were thirty-five at the time. The consuls in Marseilles or Liverpool did just what ordinary consuls do: they informed the Ministry of Foreign Relations of the political and economic situation of the country, the state of Argentine trade relations, the prices of the country's exporting commodities, and so forth. What could a vice consul do in Carril or Mataró?

Although according to diplomatic regulations the duties of these consuls mirrored those of London or Paris, in reality they functioned as little more than propaganda agents. Once in a while they had to defend the claims to exemption from the Spanish draft of the Argentine-born sons of returned emigrants, but their principal assignment was to inform the townspeople of the benefits offered by Argentina as a country of immigration and to controvert negative rumors or local press reports on the conditions of immigrants in that country. They distributed booklets, maps, and pamphlets or gave out personal information on Argentina, and the more active ones visited nearby villages and work centers. Even though Spanish law prohibited consuls from doing so, some acted as emigration agents, receiving a commission from ship companies for every person they embarked, or associated themselves with these agents or *ganchos* (hooks), as they were called in Spain.[5]

But to conclude that the Mataronese chose Argentina because there was a vice consul in the town would be misleading. A reverse argument would be more accurate: there was a vice consul in the town because the Mataronese had previously emigrated to Argentina. And, in fact, they had.

Emigration from Mataró to Buenos Aires dated back at least to the middle of the eighteenth century and was originally related to transatlantic trade.[6] Some of the early arrivals, like Salvador Bausili, who landed in about 1750, had previously moved to Cádiz—then the only Spanish port allowed to trade with the Indies—where they owned, or served in, mercantile houses.[7] In the last quarter of the century the advent of industrialization in Mataró and the town's manufacturing of cotton socks and taffeta trimmings for the colonial market intensified relations with the Americas.[8] Meanwhile, the Bourbons' Comercio Libre decree of 1778 authorized direct trade between several ports in the peninsula (including Barcelona) and in the colonies (including Buenos Aires). Together with the industrial revolution, this expedited the overseas movement of Catalan products and people and the departure of Mataronese from a nearby port. Some of these emigrants are known to every Argentine schoolchild. Domingo Matheu, who reached Buenos Aires in 1793, served as a lieutenant in the Catalan battalion formed to defend the city against the British invasions of 1806–1807 and later became part of the first independent government of the republic. His *paisano* (fellow townsman) Juan Larrea, who came seven years later, fought against the British in the same battalion with the rank of captain and later became president of the General Assembly of 1813 and founder of the republic's navy.[9] The majority, though, shared the fate of Juan Riera, an illiterate widower who simply added to "the number who lived faithfully a hidden life, and rest in unvisited tombs," as George Elliot (in *Middlemarch*) artfully depicted history's forgotten many. Whether famous patriots or obscure folks, by the outbreak of the independence movement in 1810, the Mataronese, numbering about fifty, formed a significant nucleus in the Spanish colony of the city.

Conditions after emancipation were anything but propitious for immigration in general; obviously, they were less so for *peninsulares* (the common colonial American term for natives of the Iberian Peninsula). Resentment against them peaked in the second decade of the nineteenth century, when the newly independent government prohibited associations of more than three Spaniards, forbade them from marrying Argentine women, confiscated many of their properties, encumbered many with forced loans, and jailed or executed the most intransigent loyalists.[10] Argentine authorities denied Spanish ships entry to national ports well into the 1830s. On the other side of the Atlantic, the Spanish Crown prohibited the emigration of its subjects to the newly independent countries, a ban that was lifted only in 1857.

Yet some Mataronese kept on coming. Esteban Sebilla, an illiterate youth of twenty-five, arrived in 1815, probably with the assistance of a neighbor. At least ten more arrived between 1829 and 1853. I was only able to identify twelve Mataronese in the Buenos Aires manuscript census returns of 1855. But the returns indicated the hometown of only about a third of the Spaniards in the city. Certainly, many of the more than five hundred Catalans in Buenos Aires whose hometowns were not listed came from Mataró.

Of as much importance as numbers for later immigration, this group included an inordinate proportion of enterprising and successful individuals, the prototype of the pioneer in the migration chain. Five of the twelve people identified owned property, a ratio ten times higher than that of the Spanish population as a whole. Jaime Mayol, for example, arrived in 1837, and some twenty years later his thriving wholesale business allowed him to have four maids, a clear sign of upper-class status. Antoni Cuyas Sampere arrived in 1826 and in the following decades tried his hand at piracy, the slave trade, manufacturing, finances, and politics.[11] He became wealthy enough to act as banker to Justo José de Urquiza, Entre Ríos's strongman, and influential enough to convince the caudillo to exempt Spaniards from compulsory military service in that province. The 1855 census shows him running a soap factory in Buenos Aires and living next door to three *paisanos.* Clearly, the war and chaos that completely halted all official relations between Spain and Argentina weakened but did not sever the informal linkages between Mataró and Buenos Aires.

After the midnineteenth century, official relations between the two countries recuperated. In 1859 "Her Catholic Majesty, Queen of the Spains Dona Isabel II recognize[d] the Argentine Republic or Confederation as a free, sovereign and independent nation." After some hard-fought revisions to stress Argentina's jus soli concept of citizenship, representatives of both countries signed and sealed the treaty in Madrid in 1863.[12] A decade later the Argentine Ministry of Foreign Relations appointed Lázaro Carrau—with whose report we began the first chapter—vice consul in Mataró.

Yet the real clue to understanding Mataronese emigration to Argentina lay not in the protocol and formality of that appointment but in the less formal reality it concealed. If one takes a closer look at the obscure places served by the Argentine foreign-service corps, it becomes clear that most were assigned to towns in emigration zones. And if one scrutinizes the consulates, odd and unconventional consuls appear. Indeed, the Argentine vice consul at Mataró was neither a diplomat nor an Argentine. Sr. Carrau was a Mataró druggist with personal and commercial overseas relations, married to the daughter of Josep Riera Canals, an *americano,* or successful returnee who maintained business and family connections with Buenos Aires.[13] Carrau's "colleagues" also proved more *americano* than diplomat.[14] The "dignitary" who succeeded him in the post was none other than Antoni Cuyas Sampere, the old Mataronese pirate and soap manufacturer from Buenos Aires, who, besides "diplomat," now added "historian" to his curriculum vitae with the publication of *Apuntes históricos sobre la provincia de Entre Ríos de la República Argentina.*[15] The next vice consul, Don Ignacio Mayol, was very likely related to Jaime Mayol—the emigrant who appears in the Buenos Aires 1855 census with a wholesale business and four maids—and perhaps a returnee himself. The formal titles notwithstanding—and they usually loved the flags, stamps, and other paraphernalia that went with them—these consuls were, at least in the smaller towns, more a part of the immigrants' social network of information and/or assistance/exploitation than of the Argentine foreign service.[16] It was precisely the existence of these networks that steered the Mataronese to Argentina rather than to nearby Algeria, Catalan-speaking southern France, the higher wages of North America, or the offers of free passage by ex-colonial Mexico and Peru. That the consular offices only supported the existing informal immigrant networks is indicated by the fact that in the few cases in which these offices were created in provinces that lacked social linkages with Buenos Aires, like Valladolid and Córdoba, the results in terms of attracting immigrants proved disappointing.[17]

The capacity of the immigrant social networks to maintain a continuous movement of people between Mataró and Buenos Aires was restricted not only by the chaos and Hispanophobia of postindependence Argentina but also by the structure of the immigrant transportation routes. From 1840 to at least 1860, only four ship routes carried emigrants from Europe to the River Plate. One, out of Liverpool, especially active during the potato famine of the 1840s, ferried the Irish in English ships. Out of Bayonne and Bordeaux, with stops in Pasajes (San Sebastián's port), French vessels carried Basques from both sides of the Pyrenees. A few Spanish brigs and polacres transported Galicians out of five ports in the provinces of Pontevedra and La Coruña. And Genoa served as the port of departure for Ligurian emigrants. I examined all of the Argentine passenger lists from 1840 to 1860 and, except for a corvette with sixteen passengers that came in 1849, did not find a single vessel out of Barcelona (the international port closest to Mataró) with more than eight passengers aboard.[18] As late as 1878 the Argentine consul in Barcelona still complained that many emigrants had to go to Marseilles or Bordeaux to reach the River Plate and that the majority, thus, headed for Cuba. For obvious geographical reasons, ships from the first three routes could not stop in Barcelona. But in the 1880s the use of larger and faster carriers and more frequent ocean crossings enabled steamships from the Genoa route to make stops in Barcelona. Only then did emigration from Mataró pick up and did Argentina replace the Spanish Caribbean as the main destination.[19] In other words, only the interaction of the information and assistance emanating from family and friends in Argentina with macrostructural factors (such as ship routes, the technological improvements in transportation, the disruptions created by industrialization and laissez-faire policies, and the Argentine transformations discussed in the previous chapters) could actually sustain a significant emigration stream from Mataró to Buenos Aires.

The interaction of global and local forces also created a distinct pattern of migration. Movement from Mataró to Buenos Aires resembled much of nineteenth-century migration in that it flowed from a smaller population center to a larger one. But unlike the norm, it flowed from a more to a less industrially developed place, from the heart of what was often called the Spanish Manchester to the mostly administrative-commercial capital of an agropastoral country. This situation made Mataró a town of both in-migration and emigration. In some cases it attracted and expatriated the same people. For example, six of the twenty-one persons who left Mataró for Buenos Aires in 1910 were nonnatives who had previously moved to the town.[20] In other cases this stepping-stone migration became intergenerational. Twenty of the fathers and nineteen of the mothers of the forty-three Mataronese immigrants in Buenos Aires whose parentage I was able to trace were nonnatives of Mataró. That is, in almost half of the cases one generation had migrated from rural areas or small towns to Mataró, and the next generation had emigrated overseas. Still others combined and compounded these moves. At about the turn of the century, for example, Antonio Salvador moved from his native village in the province of Castellón to Mataró, where he worked as a blacksmith.[21] There he met and married Catalina Villanueva, like himself a rural migrant, from the province of Teruel, a weaver at a local textile factory. In 1904 the couple had their first child, and two years later moved to Barcelona, where their second daughter was born. The next step took these Aragonese rural migrants and their Catalan-born daughters across the Atlantic to Buenos Aires, where their third daughter, Rosario, was born in 1910. Then, sometime before 1920, the family returned to Spain and resettled in Mataró, the hometown of their first daughter and a place where their third daughter had thirty-two compatriots.[22]

Another trait of the Mataronese pattern of emigration referred to its size, rhythm, and timing. I searched through almost 100,000 records of members of six immigrant associations in Buenos Aires, including two Catalan societies, and was able to find only 102 Mataronese immigrants. In contrast, I found more than 700 from Pamplona, a town only slightly larger than Mataró, and more than 250 from Ribadumia, a collection of villages with a population one-eighth that of Mataró, both in regions where voluntary associations were less common than in Catalonia. The sources on the other side of the Atlantic yielded similar results. I perused seven Mataró newspapers published at intervals between 1864 and 1915 and found a profusion of articles on municipal politics, industrial production, labor friction, and the activities of workers' and bourgeois' associations but surprisingly few on emigration, most of which dealt with it at the national, rather than local, level.[23] The 1900 municipal *padrón* (manuscript census) tallied only 209 absentee residents in a population of 18,765, or 1.1 percent of the total. The 1920 *padrón* yielded an even smaller figure: 166 absentees in a population of 23,726, or 0.7 percent of the total. Similar documents in five other Spanish municipal districts that I studied (Corcubión, Finisterre, and Zas in La Coruña; Val de San Lorenzo, in León; and the Baztán Valley, in Navarre) produced absentee-to-resident ratios that ranged from 2.2 to 35 times higher than those of Mataró. Not only was the Mataronese flow moderate in volume, it also began early (around the mid-1700s), stretched over a period of almost two centuries (instead of concentrating in just a few decades), and declined earlier than in other parts of Spain (ceasing before the Spanish Civil War). Unlike other Spaniards, the Mataronese did not participate in the sizable movements to oil-rich Venezuela in the 1950s or to northern Europe in the 1960s and 1970s. From a town of both in-migration and emigration, Mataró became, after the Civil War, a town of in-migration only (mostly southern Spaniards) and of immigration from the 1980s on (mostly Africans and Latin Americans).

The combination of deeply established transoceanic microsocial connections with a developing industrial economy on the sending side affected not only the size, rhythm, and duration of the emigration stream but also its quality. Without a moribund or declining economy shoving them out and with solid social networks providing information and support, the Mataronese could afford to be selective in their emigration. When compared with other Spaniards departing for Argentina, the Mataronese contingent included a remarkably high proportion of skilled workers, merchants, and better-off folks and a much lower proportion of poor and unskilled laborers (see Table 5). As the Argentine consul in Barcelona put it, "The push for Catalans is the desire to make fortunes rather than the need to placate hunger."[24]

In turn, who emigrated and the means by which they did so affected how the group adapted to the host country, as I detail in the following chapters. The fact that the Mataronese arrived with certain skills and in small-to-moderate numbers over a long period instead of concentrated in large bunches and a short time span meant that the existing networks of support in Buenos Aires were never overtaxed or overwhelmed. Those al-

Table 5   Comparison of the skill levels of emigrants to Argentina from Mataró (1909–1910), the Baztán Valley (1909), and Spain as a whole (1915)

Emigrants from	Percentage of unskilled and semiskilled workers	Percentage of artisans and skilled workers	Percentage of merchants and nonmanual workers	Number
Mataró	37	40	23	35
Baztán	85	11	4	46
Spain	92	4	4	9,447

SOURCES: For Mataró, "Bajas de Domicilio, 1908–1916," a bound volume in the municipal archive. Despite the dates in the title, 1909 and 1910 seem to be the only years in which the town clerk actually registered everyone who moved out of the town. I used Baztán for a comparison because it was the only other municipality for which I was able to find comparable data in "Estadística de emigración, año 1909," two loose manuscript leaves in the municipal archive at Elizondo. The figures for Spain are computed from data in Consejo Superior de Emigración, *La emigración española transoceánica, 1911–1915* (Madrid, 1916), 50–53, which contains information on the occupation of emigrants to the main countries of destination only for 1915.

ready in the city could help their slowly arriving *paisanos* with greater efficacy and resources than if they had disembarked more abruptly, and probably also with a more agreeable disposition than if they had come as a crowd instead of as company. At least three-quarters of the 102 Mataronese whom I found in Buenos Aires either lived in nuclear families or had relatives in the city, but there were none of the extended kinship groups with dozens of "uncles," "cousins," and other hangers-on so common among the immigrants from most of the sixteen other Spanish localities I examined. In terms of residency, they spread more evenly throughout the city's districts than did the other groups; and in terms of occupation, they proved better able to reach higher positions and avoid menial and low-paying jobs.

The Mataronese case is obviously not representative of Spanish emigration as a whole. Indeed, if anything, it demonstrates the inadequacy of the very concept of "Spanish emigration as a whole," for when it comes to understanding the process of emigration, national aggregates come perilously close to being meaningless. On the other hand, local singularity may pose a greater epistemological dilemma: if every village and town constitutes a unique case, a general understanding of the process becomes all but impossible. I am convinced, however, that what I discovered in

Mataró was particular, not unique. It represents not an anomaly but a type of emigration likely to appear wherever the following circumstances combine: the sending area's economy both suffers the fluctuations and uncertainties natural to capitalism and enjoys long-term growth and greater industrial maturity than does the destination; the destination is a newer, expanding (sometimes rapidly) economy, like that described in chapter 2; old, deeply rooted family and microsocial connections link the sending and receiving localities; and trade and transportation routes also connect the two localities, or nearby ones, although these routes, as in our case, can be ruptured or disrupted for even decades.

OTHER EXAMPLES OF THE "MATARÓ TYPE" OF EMIGRATION: FERROL AND BILBAO

Analysis of emigration from the towns of Ferrol (Franco's birthplace, which recently lost its epithet "del Caudillo") and Bilbao corroborates the argument that Mataró represents a type rather than a local oddity. Like Mataró and other urban centers on the northern periphery of the peninsula, these towns took little part in the mostly Andalusian and Estremaduran conquest of the Indies;[25] began their overseas exodus by way of Cádiz during the first half of the eighteenth century; and dilated that exodus only after the so-called Bourbon Reforms ended the Cádiz—Veracruz—Lima monopoly on imperial trade. In one of the earlier reforms, in 1767, the Crown inaugurated the Carrera de Buenos Aires, a mail-packet service between that city and La Coruña, the port across the estuary from Ferrol, which carried, in addition to letters, freight and an annual average of twenty-five passengers to the River Plate.[26] In 1788, and after decades of petitions, the Crown finally granted Ferrol and Bilbao direct access to the Americas.[27] As the century turned, trade and emigration formed a thick stream between these towns and Buenos Aires, one that was soon thinned by the succession of the War of the Third Coalition (which included British invasions of Buenos Aires in 1806 and 1807), the Napoleonic invasion of the Iberian Peninsula (1807–1814), the related Argentine War of Independence (1810–1816) and the decades of civil war and turmoil that followed.

Yet, as Figures 4 and 5 illustrate, war and chaos did not sever the links between these towns and Buenos Aires. During the decades when macrostructural conditions obstructed emigration, the microsocial networks became inactive but not inert, the chain became dormant but did not die. When all formal political, economic, and diplomatic relations between

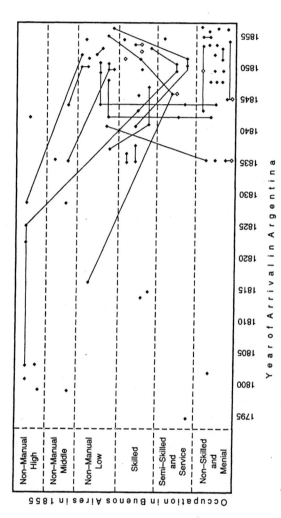

Symbols: ◆ Male ◇ Female; Lines between symbols indicate kinship link

Figure 4. Year of arrival, occupation, and kinship links of immigrants from Ferrol in Buenos Aires, 1795–1855. Not all of the 112 Ferrolean immigrants in the manuscript census returns are listed, only the 112 residing in the major areas of Spanish settlement in Buenos Aires (the wards of Catedral Sud, Monserrat, San Telmo, and Concepción). The returns indicate the relationship of the inhabitants of the house to the head of the household but give only paternal surnames, not paternal and maternal surnames as is the common Spanish practice. Many of the immigrants who appear in the figure with no kinship links were probably related to each other through their mothers or through marriage. The figures do not include either those immigrants who had resided in Buenos Aires but had died or moved by 1855 or those who listed their province, region, or country, not their hometown, as their birthplace on the census returns.

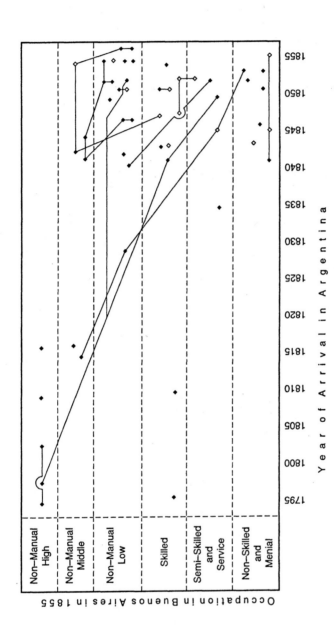

Y e a r   o f   A r r i v a l   i n   A r g e n t i n a

Symbols: ◆ Male ◇ Female;   Lines between symbols indicate kinship link

Figure 5. Year of arrival, occupation, and kinship links of immigrants from Bilbao in Buenos Aires, 1795–1855. Not all of the 75 Bilbaoan immigrants in the manuscript census returns are listed, only the 52 residing in the major areas of Spanish settlement in Buenos Aires (the wards of Catedral Sud, Monserrat, San Telmo, and Concepción). See note to Figure 4 for an explanation of other limitations in the sources.

Spain and Argentina ceased, Bilbainos and Ferrolanos on both sides of the Atlantic maintained their informal transoceanic ties, during the worst years probably just through the memory of each other.[28] As general conditions improved and communication channels reopened, information, then assistance, and eventually people began to cross the Atlantic again. The somnolent chain actually awoke earlier in Bilbao and Ferrol than in Mataró due to these towns' location along the transportation routes mentioned before.

If family memories kept the chain alive, so did family money. Indeed, Figures 4 and 5 illustrate the relevance for emigration of both Menander's adage, "It is not easy to find the relatives of a poor man," and its flip side. In all cases in which a newcomer came to join a relative from whom he or she had been separated for more than thirty years, that relative occupied a high occupational status. That is, the prosperity of immigrants determined how long the connections with their Old World kin could survive during periods of interruption in communications. The economic success of immigrants from Bilbao, Ferrol, and Mataró, not simply their family remembrances, prevented the dormant chain from falling into an endless sleep, as happened in more than one case.[29]

The figures also show two other aspects of this type of emigration. The first is that family members, rather than emigration agents or labor contractors, constituted the principal sponsors of newcomers even during this early period—contrary to John and Leatrice Macdonald's scheme of chain migration, in which the arrival of unrelated males through the auspices of *padroni* (labor bosses) supposedly characterizes the early stages of the flow.[30] A second interesting insight is that although, not surprisingly, males predominated, women at times acted as middle links in the chain. A common pattern in this respect was for a young woman to join an uncle's family and then, after a few years of working as a seamstress or servant, to facilitate the coming of her younger siblings or parents.[31]

There are two additional important points that the figures do not show. One is that links in the networks transcended direct blood and/or village ties. At least seven of the immigrants who appear with no family links over time were actually assisted in their trip by Argentine in-laws rather than by direct relatives or townfolks. The Gómez brothers from Ferrol, for instance, came to live with the Argentine widow of their uncle and their Argentine-born cousins. This shows both the strength and resilience of primary linkages across the ocean. Bonds could survive the death of blood or *paisano* relations. In other words, the chain kept on functioning long after the original link was gone. The second point is precisely the inadequacy of the metaphor of chain migration. I have kept lines indicating kinship links to a minimum for legibility, and thus, graphically, the figures may sometimes give the impression of chains. But were I to draw a line between all of the immigrants who were related, the figure would definitely resemble more a web than a chain. Moreover, the person who assisted the newly arrived in his or her movement was in some cases not the closest kin.[32]

Overall, then, Ferrol and Bilbao exhibit the principal traits of the Mataronese pattern of emigration: a flow that begins in the eighteenth century and, after a disruption but not a complete rupture during the turmoil of the early decades of the nineteenth, continues in a protracted and moderate fashion till the 1920s, declining earlier than in other parts of Spain; the towns of origin, more industrialized than the host one, experience concurrent in-migration and emigration and play a role as way stations for stepping-stone emigration, including its delayed variety, in which one generation moves to the town and the next, overseas; cyclical business uncertainties at home, opportunities for occupational independence in the younger American economies, and, above all, long, traditional, deeply rooted family connections—rather than a waning home economy—provide the stimulus for crossing the ocean; and, as I demonstrate in the next chapters, an easier adaptation in the host country, facilitated by this pattern of stretched-out, moderate-sized emigration.

THE ANTITHESIS OF THE MATARÓ PATTERN: AGENTS AND BUNCHES

In another, less common, type of emigration, people recruited by impersonal government, private, or semiofficial agents, arrived in a sudden gush. Whereas spontaneity distinguishes the Mataronese type of emigration, artificiality marks the latter. In a typology of emigration (excluding slave trades, which, in a conceptually questionable manner, have at times been lumped with voluntary movements) they could occupy opposite poles.

The emigration of Malagueños to Argentina in the late 1880s provides a distinct example of this artificially induced type of movement. During most of the 1880s the Argentine consul in the province of Málaga reported that no emigrants had left for the River Plate; and Spanish official publications confirmed this by showing that between 1885—when emigration statistics discriminating province of origin began—and 1888 not a single resident of Málaga had gone to Argentina. Then suddenly, in 1889, 10,141 Malagueños appeared in Spanish records as having left for Argentina. The Argentine government, in a effort to increase the labor supply for the nation's rapidly growing economy, had decided to try subsidized immigration and, in order to counteract what it perceived as a dangerous concentration of Italians in the country, distributed the free passages in Spain, France, and northern Europe. The sudden upsurge in Málaga's exodus followed the distribution by emigration agents of 10,400 free passages in the province's countryside. Yet in the following years, as the free passages ceased, so did emigration.[33] The early 1890s witnessed a sharp depression in much of Latin America, but the abysmal failure of the Argentine authorities to sustain the emigration stream from Málaga had less to do with the economic downturn, or the cessation of free fares, than with the lack of an established network of relatives and friends in Buenos Aires. Although Malagueños had resided in the city since colonial times, their emigration, as noted before and for reasons that are not clear, had dwindled by the 1880s. At any rate, most of the early comers had originated from the city of Málaga and thus were unlikely to be related to the new arrivals, most of whom were peasants. That the lack of immigrant networks of support, not the economic slump, caused the abrupt end of emigration from Málaga becomes obvious if we compare this case with that of Pontevedra, a province tied to Argentina by an old and thick mesh of microsocial threads (see Table 6). Thousands kept on coming from Pontevedra, even during the depression.[34]

In the absence of immigrant social networks, artificial efforts to foment immigration can even have counterproductive effects, as exemplified by the 1833 and 1836 expeditions from the Canary Islands organized by semiofficial agents of the Argentine government and by private profiteers. Many of the necessary macroconditions were present: on one side, a population-hungry country with vast open spaces and increasing ties to the world economy; on the other, overpopulated islands (emigration often starts in small islands) experiencing the boom-bust cycles of commercial export agriculture (at the time, a crumbled wine-export economy was being replaced by cochineal production—which in turn would become obsolete with the appearance of synthetic dyes a few decades later). The agents had advanced passages to about 200 families with the condition that once in the new land they would repay the money, something that proved a taxing burden despite the Argentine government's extension of the payment deadline from four to fourteen months and eventually to three years.[35] Lacking the support of previously established kin and *paisanos* and pressed by the government (perhaps forced; the documents are not explicit on this), the Canary Islanders found themselves with little alter-

Table 6   Emigration to Argentina from Málaga and Pontevedra, 1886–1895

	1886	1887	1888	1889	1890	1891	1892	1893	1894	1895
Málaga	0	0	0	0	10,141	189	9	61	3	15
Pontevedra	2,552	1,672	3,294	5,094	5,940	2,340	717	1,573	2,274	2,863

SOURCE: Spain, Dirección General del Instituto Geográfico y Estadístico, *Estadística de la emigración e inmigración de España, 1882 a 1890* (Madrid, 1891), 68–71.

native other than to contract themselves to Argentine employers, who then deducted part of their wages in order to repay the government for the ship fares. In these exploitative arrangements, employers (including some patrician families, such as the Sáenz Valientes and the Viamontes) deducted one-third of the salary and held undisputed control over the labor of people who had become, at least de facto, bonded servants.[36] Others were even less fortunate, being forcefully conscripted into road-building crews or the local militias. I tried to trace the 156 individuals on the passenger list of the 1836 expedition and found at least 11 (the identity of some with common Christian names and patronymics—the sources did not include maternal surnames—could not be verified) in the records of the city's poorhouse, graveyards (killed by typhus, tuberculosis, or scarlet fever), and insane asylum.[37]

This first adverse immigration experience not only failed to form a group of pioneers who could later call friends and relatives—the common genesis of chain migration in the cases of Mataró, Ferrol, and Bilbao—but also originated an unfavorable image of Argentina in the Canary Islands. The importance of immigrant networks, after all, transcended direct sponsorship. The letters sent home, the bragging of returnees, and the tales of successful sons generated a cultural climate in villages of origin that stimulated emigration. For example, Ramón Mayo, a Galician immigrant at about the turn of the century, wrote in his diary that he had come to Buenos Aires to join an uncle but also reminisced about the epic tales of adventurous and successful emigrants his mother had once told him as bedtime stories.[38] Clearly, this subjective world of tales and heroes, and the dreams it engendered, prompted Ramón's emigration as much as did the assistance of his relative. The inauspicious Canarian scheme, instead of creating well-established "uncles" and bedtime tales of triumph, had the apparent opposite effect of keeping the islanders away from Argentina. Although the Canary Islands were one of Spain's main nuclei of emigration, providing as much as 15 percent of transatlantic crossings, they made up less than 2 percent of the stream to Argentina; and whereas most other Iberian regional groups preferred Argentina as a destination, Canarians relegated it to almost last choice. About 80 percent of them headed for Cuba, the remainder selected Puerto Rico, Venezuela, and often even Uruguay and Brazil, over Argentina.[39]

The fact that exploitative immigration schemes usually afflicted localities without primary social ties to the host country probably indicates that they were more difficult to impose on people with more knowledge and connections. For example, in September 1852 José Zambriano, the Spanish consul in Buenos Aires, received complaints about the arrival of a brig from the port of Carril in the Galician province of Pontevedra with 159 immigrants on board who had been contracted by the infamous Llavallol agents.[40] The consul reported to the Spanish Ministry of Foreign Relations in Madrid that the immigrants had arrived illegally, without passports, and decried the indecent and unhygienic housing arrangement: a grimy warehouse in the Barracas district of Buenos Aires with "no privacy for the sexes" and no sanitary facilities. Yet on his inspection trip he found no one there. The immigrants had abandoned the warehouse and had gone to live with relatives and friends; many broke the original contracts that tied them to a particular employer for two years and went to work with townsfolk; and others did not even pay the agents for the fare. One of the agents complained that it proved more difficult to control these arrivals than to prevent domestic cattle from going wild in the open pampas. Indeed, the contracted immigrants had gone feral.

Not only did emigration induced artificially by government and private agents often result in fiascos, it was also less common than official sources would lead us to believe. I found hundreds of folios concerning the Canarian expeditions in Argentine archives, but documents on the forty-times-more-numerous spontaneous Galician flow were remarkably rare.[41] Similarly, on the other side of the Atlantic, the journals of the Spanish government's Consejo Superior de Emigración for the year 1909 carried more articles (six) about Colombia, and the emigration of Spaniards to Santa Marta through the auspices of abusive agents of the Great Northern Central Railway and banana plantations, than about Argentina (four). But actual emigrants to Argentina, unlike official articles about them, outnumbered those headed for Colombia by 1,243 to 1, and Spanish residents in Buenos Aires outnumbered those in Santa Marta by 3,750 to 1.[42] Despite this exaggerated attention to recruited immigration, the practice seems to have been limited mostly to poorer areas with no tradition of spontaneous emigration, like rural Andalusia, and to less desirable destinations, like the tropical plantations, mines, or construction sites of Hawaii, Louisiana, Colombia, and Panama. In Argentina, no more than 2 to 3 percent of all Spanish arrivals came through impersonal recruitment schemes.

EMIGRATION AS BOTH A FAMILY AFFAIR AND A BUSINESS ENTERPRISE: THE BAZTÁN VALLEY, NAVARRE

Spontaneous movements organized solely on the basis of affective ties and impersonal recruitments by agents clearly occupy the poles in a typology of voluntary emigration according to sponsorship. But emigration from most localities occupies the less distinct medial space. In these cases primary ties and less intimate arrangements coexist, and emigration appears as both a family affair and a business enterprise.

Figure 6 illustrates the family-affair side of emigration from the Baztán Valley, in the Navarrese Pyrenees, to the River Plate and the capacity of these affairs to reproduce themselves exponentially. The movement of this particular family group from Arizkun (a cluster of hamlets on the northern edge of the valley with 276 households and 1,630 inhabitants in 1855) had an apparently unpromising start in 1838, when Juan Garchitorena Goyeneche, a twenty-two-year-old quarrier, left for Montevideo on a French vessel out of Bayonne.[43] Two years later his brother Martín and two cousins followed. But in the ensuing years a protracted Argentine siege of Montevideo—which earned the city the sobriquet Troy of the River Plate—the scourge of the Uruguayan Guerra Grande (1839–1851), and the French and English blockades of Buenos Aires seemed to have terminated the incipient chain. After midcentury, however, as calm returned to Argentina but eluded Uruguay, some of the Garchitorena kin joined the thousands who fled across the river to booming Buenos Aires, and the family's transatlantic flow revived, shifting its course to the western shores of the estuary.[44] In the next two decades the number of people moving swelled as the original trunk ramified, developing forward branches with younger relatives and new generations and lateral ones with in-laws and increasingly distant relatives. By the 1860s the tree included scores of nephews of the in-laws of the cousins of the Garchitorena Goyeneche brothers, many of whom would eventually become trunks themselves. Graphically, thus, chain migration came to resemble more an overlapping succession of forks than a linear sequence of links. This tendency to branch out allowed the process to spread and multiply with a self-generating force that Figure 6 can only suggest.[45]

If kinship provided the organizing principle and the force behind the flow, business interests expedited it. These interests included ship builders, owners, captains, and companies from Bayonne and other French towns that, at the time, dominated the Basque emigrant trade on both sides of the Pyrenees. As steamers replaced sailing vessels during the 1870s, the larger port of Bordeaux supplanted Bayonne as the main exit point, and huge German, English, and French (non-Basque) steamship companies elbowed out the independent shipbuilders and captains from the increasingly massive and lucrative trade.[46]

Although the actual transportation across the ocean became a global trade dominated by multinational capital, other aspects of the emigration business remained parochial affairs. About two dozen agents, innkeepers, lenders, notaries, and other petty entrepreneurs in the Baztán Valley sold the passages, on commission, to almost all of the people listed in Figure 6; advanced the fare to two-thirds of them; transferred the remittances from family members already settled in Argentina that paid for the rest of the tickets; prepared the paperwork for the trip; and provided other services, such as transportation to the port and collection of loans and inheritances in Europe and the Americas. They even played the role of matchmakers, marrying villagers on different sides of the Atlantic by power of attorney and facilitating other arrangements, as the following 1854 notarial record indicates: "Jaime Maripericena, resident in Buenos Aires, remits eleven gold ounces to Francisco Garaicoechea, primary-school teacher in Lecároz, in order that his niece María Copena, resident of Ascain [France], could marry the aforementioned teacher."[47] Esteban Fort, an emigration agent from Elizondo, a village of 1,200 and the administrative center of the valley, had sold Jaime his ticket to Buenos Aires, lent him and his nephew money for their fares, and transferred the dowry for his niece. Although official and private foes of emigration constantly denounced these agents for seizing the lands peasants placed as collateral for passage loans, about two thousand notarial records covering four decades do not include a single instance of farm-confiscation in this corner of Spain.

At this level the business of emigration, its vilification by the Spanish government notwithstanding, represented not an alien and impersonal element but a more formal aspect of the microsocial networks, not the antipode of kinship-organized emigration but something which at times was difficult to differentiate.[48] Esteban Fort was also, after all, Jaime Maripericena's maternal great-uncle. Esteban's oldest son, Matías Fort Añescar,

Figure 6. Ramification of the "chain": Emigration of a family group from the village of Arizkun, Navarre, to Argentina, 1838–1870.

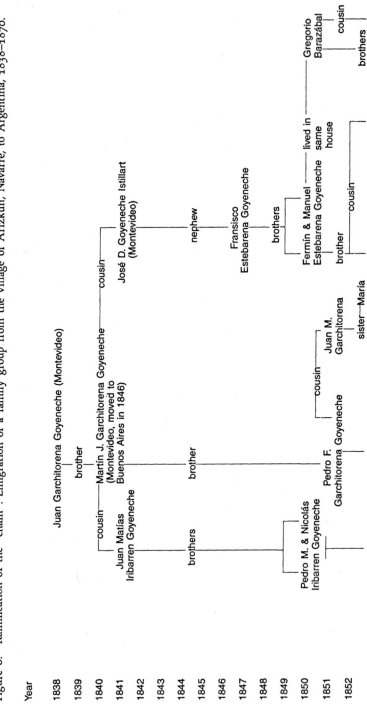

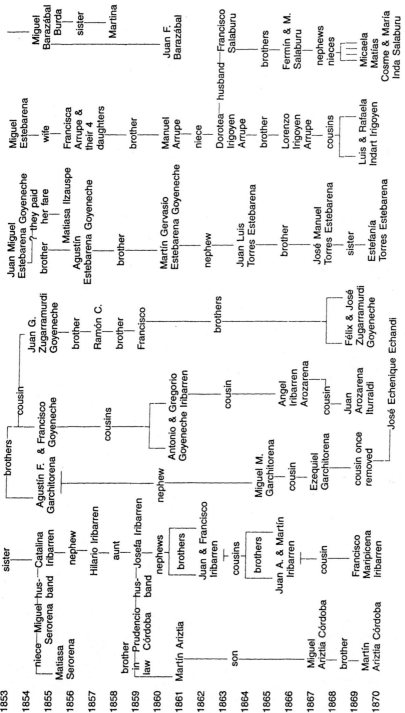

Sources: Municipal *padrones* of the Baztán Valley for 1846, 1853, and 1864; Buenos Aires, 1855 census returns; notarial records transcribed in C. Idoate Ezquieta, *Emigración navarra del Valle de Baztán en el siglo XIX: Inventario de documentos* (Pamplona, 1987).

went to Mexico in 1846 and three years later recruited sixteen youths to work in that country. But the establishment they went to work for was owned by a fellow townsman, and Matías' "customers" included at least six cousins. Matías' younger brother Ezequiel headed for Cuba in 1851 to start a line of the family business that recruited no more than six immigrants, half of whom were relatives. The failure had to do with the success of youngest brother, Martín, who, with perfect timing, headed for Buenos Aires that same year, right when Argentina was becoming the favorite destination of the Navarrese. Martín became so successful that in 1854, at the age of twenty-five, he took over the family business. His father became his agent for one year and then retired to run his local inn.[49] Matías came back from Mexico, became an agent for his brother, and later moved, with his Mexican wife, to Buenos Aires to replace Martín as the family's representative there. Having a permanent post in the Argentine capital allowed the Fort brothers to provide services (such as issuing powers of attorney and appointment, collecting inheritances and debts, or searching for lost relatives) with greater speed than could their competitors. It also allowed a new policy of discounts in which immigrants received reductions of 5 to 15 percent if they paid the fare sooner than the normal one-year term. From 1854, when Martín took over the business, to his death in 1876, the Fort brothers and their agents issued more than 240 passages to the River Plate. Yet even in this, the most formal of emigration agencies in the valley, no fewer than a fifth of the customers were first-degree relatives of the Fort brothers or their agents. Were we to count more distant kin and friends, the line between family and business affairs would become even more nebulous.

This, plus the business' dependance on reputation and trust within the local community, clearly deterred shady operations. Contrary to the vituperative claims of Spanish nationalists and emigration foes, most of these local agents were neither the cause of the exodus nor crooked and perfidious swindlers out to dupe naive peasants. Studies in other parts of the world support this conclusion.[50]

THE VILLAGE AND THE WORLD: DESTINATIONS FROM
THE BAZTÁN VALLEY, NAVARRE AND CORCUBIÓN COUNTY,
LA CORUÑA

The case of the Fort brothers shows not only the overlapping of primary and institutional auspices in emigration but also the variety of destinations, which the following notarial record further illustrates:

Elizondo, December 26, 1848

Julián Zozaya, ex-resident of Havana, and Ignacio Eliceche, ex-resident of Mexico, testify that Pedro Oteiza [who had lived in Cuba], legal resident of Ciga [a village in the valley], is single, since he wishes to marry María Francisca Larralde, widow of Clemente Ezpeleta, who died in Buenos Aires during the war of Montevideo.[51] [These procedures tried to prevent a sort of transatlantic bigamy, in which people who were already married overseas took local wives.]

Quantitative analysis confirms what anecdotal evidence suggests. Figure 7, covering the emigration of 2,180 individuals over a period of two centuries, shows how, in a manner resembling that of multinational corporations, this rural valley of fewer than nine thousand souls not only established branch colonies in six countries but also adapted to macrohistorical shifts by diverting the flow from some branches to others over time. In the decades before the demise of the Spanish Empire, the thickest stream ran toward Mexico, whose new heights in silver output had turned it into the jewel of the Crown; the rest of the current radiated to Venezuela, then experiencing a cacao-export boom, and to Cuba. But as the most violent wars of emancipation in the Western Hemisphere ravaged the first two colonies (600,000 died in Mexico's fight for independence and 100,000 in Venezuela's), many of the Baztanese living there fled to Cuba: between 1820 and 1839 the island colony received more than four-fifths of all overseas emigrants from the Baztán Valley. Toward the end of this period, however, some began to go to the River Plate, and by the 1840s more than half of all Baztanese emigrants streamed to the expanding pastoral economy of its eastern bank. After midcentury the now more peaceful and prosperous western bank lured more than three-quarters of them, and it remained their favorite destination until the 1930s.[52] As the nineteenth century drew to its end, the current to Mexico (where dictator Porfirio Díaz's formula of *pan o palo* [bread or the club] had reestablished political order and economic growth) revived, and a stream emerged to the sheep-raising zones of California's Central Valley, which thickened steadily and became the most copious one after World War II, when the Golden State's economic acceleration made Argentina's erratic performance seem like decline.[53]

The Baztanese clearly shifted direction in response to changing conditions in the host countries, but this does not mean that, as in the push-pull model, they were mechanically drawn by the strongest magnet around. For example, the United States experienced some of its most spectacular

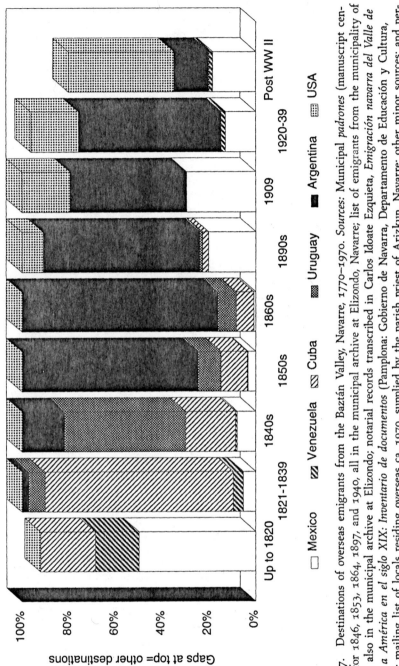

Figure 7. Destinations of overseas emigrants from the Baztán Valley, Navarre, 1770–1970. *Sources:* Municipal *padrones* (manuscript censuses) for 1846, 1853, 1864, 1897, and 1940, all in the municipal archive at Elizondo, Navarre; list of emigrants from the municipality of Baztán, also in the municipal archive at Elizondo; notarial records transcribed in Carlos Idoate Ezquieta, *Emigración navarra del Valle de Baztán a América en el siglo XIX: Inventario de documentos* (Pamplona: Gobierno de Navarra, Departamento de Educación y Cultura, [1987]); mailing list of locals residing overseas ca. 1970, supplied by the parish priest of Arizkun, Navarre; other minor sources; and personal interviews.

growth after the Civil War, but no one from the Baztán Valley went there then. When, decades later, they did go, they eluded the great immigrant magnets in the Northeast and Midwest. A coffee-driven boom and government-paid passages made Brazil the most popular destination for Spanish emigrants during the 1890s (and the third most popular over the whole mass-emigration period), but, apparently, no one from the valley migrated there in two centuries of exodus. Another dark liquid made Venezuela the top choice for southern European emigrants, including Spaniards, during the 1950s, but the Baztanese abstained from its oil bonanza and petrodollars. A decade later, millions of Spaniards took the train to the industrial towns of France, Germany, The Netherlands, and Switzerland, and again the Baztanese, a stone's throw away from the border, failed to follow their compatriots.

If the pull of economic prosperity cannot fully explain the destination choices of the Baztanese, neither can the previous presence of relatives and friends alone. It is true that the case of Mexico provides a perfect example of the dormant-chain phenomenon, of how primary linkages across the Atlantic survived the impact of decades of disruption and revived emigration once structural conditions improved. But primary ties did not always prove so resilient. The stream to Venezuela did not endure the shock of the Wars of Independence and the ensuing civil strife; it simply perished—in part because the country's economic recuperation came later and less forcefully than did Mexico's. More intriguing, the movements to Cuba and Uruguay also waned and expired, not because of any external shock but simply because other destinations proved more alluring. In other cases the chain did not perish but was stillborn when the successful emigration of a few failed to incite even an initial flow. For example, three Aycinena brothers from the hamlet of Berroeta in the Baztán Valley moved to Guatemala from Mexico City late in the eighteenth century, engaging in trade and amassing the largest fortune in the colony. Their serendipity seemed confirmed by the ownership of several haciendas, a title of marquis from Charles III, the foundation of a beneficence institution in their native valley, and a son and grandson who later became presidents of the Guatemalan Republic. Yet these model pioneer emigrants failed to initiate a flow of their relatives or townsfolk to Guatemala. Similarly, Baztanese in late-colonial Peru included some prominent merchants and the most prominent citizen in the viceroyalty—Viceroy Agustín de Jáuregui y Aróstegui, but the Old World kin of those who stayed after independence preferred to wait for their relatives to die and collect the inheritances rather than join them in Peru.[54]

Destinations were thus determined by a delicate combination of micro-social connections and (auspicious) structural conditions. Guatemala and Peru clearly lacked the latter; the booming economies of the postbellum United States, 1890s Brazil, and 1950s Venezuela lacked the former. Argentina from the midnineteenth century to its post-Perón quagmire, California since the late nineteenth century, and Mexico since the Porfiriato, with an interim during the revolution, achieved the right combination. Over the centuries, travelers and adventurers from the Baztán Valley ranged from Manitoba to Tierra del Fuego, to mythical El Dorado, where leader Pedro de Ursúa, from the village of Arizkun, found a violent death in 1559 instead of gold.[55] But only in fertile soils did the roaming of wanderers turn into long-term, sustainable migration. These El Dorados were not necessarily the most golden places; they were the ones that better accommodated the background of the Baztanese. The valley enclosed the principal center of livestock (ovine and bovine) raising in Navarre and a zone of disseminated settlement rather than large villages. Its inhabitants, therefore, seemed well equipped, both in practical and cultural terms, for the pastoral economies and solitary expanses of the New World's grasslands. Unlike most of their compatriots in the United States, Argentina, and Mexico, they originally settled not in New York or Florida but in California (with smaller numbers in Idaho and Nevada), not so much in the Argentine capital but on the pampas of Buenos Aires Province, not only in Mexico City but also on the ranches of Durango and the north.

Thus destinations, at least initially, resulted not simply from the capricious wandering of townsfolk but also from a certain compatibility between sending and receiving areas. Later, however, the original shepherds and cattle hands both moved into other endeavors and attracted kin and friends who did not intend to work in pastoral activities. For example, a few Baztanese opened up three brick ovens on the outskirts of Buenos Aires around midnineteenth century, and in the ensuing years some forty newcomers from the valley bypassed the road to the sheep farms of the pampas; half of them eventually even abandoned brick making and moved into more general activities. Something similar must have happened in Mexico with bread instead of bricks. Of the sixty-one Baztanese residents in that country who received the valley's parish newsletter around the 1970s, almost one-third (nineteen) were bakers.

Data on the destinations of emigrants from Corcubión, a Galician county on the northwestern tip of the Iberian Peninsula made up of coastal fishing villages and inland agricultural settlements, is less abundant but does suggest patterns similar to those of the Baztán Valley. As in the

Table 7   Destination of overseas emigrants from three municipalities in
Corcubión County, La Coruña, in selected years, 1887–1930 (in percentages)

	Finisterre		Corcubión		Zas	
	1887	1897	1905	1930	1897	1924
Argentina	93	85	65	81	40	83
Cuba	4	5	22	13	52	10
Brazil	0	1	9	1	2	2
Uruguay	1	2	0	0	7	3
United States	1	4	4	5	0	2
Others	0	2	0	0	0	0
Number[a]	290	246	117	107	60	902

SOURCES: Municipal *padrones* for the given years.
[a] Includes all the inhabitants listed as residing overseas the year the censuses were taken, not just the ones who left that year.

latter case, Argentina was the favorite destination from at least the 1880s to 1930 (see Table 7). But, unlike the pastoral Baztanese, these Galicians did not settle on the sheep- and cattle-raising pampas. Instead, they concentrated in La Boca and Barracas, Buenos Aires' old shipping areas along the Riachuelo River, because the first to come were sailors from the maritime villages of the county.[56] An important merchant marine port in Patagonia, Río Gallegos, provided an area of secondary settlement. Unlike the Baztanese, these Galicians skirted Mexico in favor of the port cities of Havana, Santiago de Cuba, and Santos (São Paulo's harbor). Some headed for the United States and settled not on the sheep ranges of the West but in Brooklyn, where a few ship-boiler workers had previously landed. Sometime in the 1940s a new destination emerged when Benigno Lago, an immigrant from Corcubión who had made a small fortune in Patagonian coastal shipping during the 1920s, moved to Peru and started an even more successful fishing and fish-flour business.[57] Local lore asserted he was the richest man in Peru, and his bronze statue in the village's plaza seemed to corroborate the fable. Thus, in the two decades after World War II, scores of townfolk followed Benigno to Callao and Chimbote, at the time two of the largest fishing ports in the world thanks to an extended boom in Peru's fish-processing industry.

Here too, choice of destination clearly reflected some affinity between the area of settlement and the background of the emigrants. It responded to more than the haphazard roamings of sailors or the mechanical pull of economic forces. Individual Corcubionese seamen settled in Guayaquil, Mexico City, Valparaíso, New Orleans, and other urban areas, and no one followed them. On the other hand, plenty of prosperous, attractive economies, including bustling ports, never pulled any of these Galician globetrotters, just as the immense sheep ranges of New Zealand and Australia never attracted Baztanese shepherds.[58] Only a felicitous, at times even fortuitous, combination of local social networks and larger trends, of wandering adventurers and welcoming soils, produced sustainable, long-term migration. The combination was neither inevitable nor purely capricious. It contained, as we have seen, an element of predictability.

The relative weight of the combination's components, however, varied through time. In the initial stages of the process the auspicious structural condition, the suitability of the host land to the newcomers' background and abilities, was particularly important. The lack of fertile soils or of a sheltering harbor could turn a few meandering shepherds or mariners into no more than that. Yet, as the number of arrivals increased, the flow gained an internal, self-propelling momentum, related in large part, as Figure 6 illustrates, to the tendency of kinship-based movements to branch out. At this stage, many whose skills did not particularly fit the features of the host area that originally attracted the pioneers headed in the same direction in response to the call of family, friends, and friends-of-friends. For example, by the second decade of the twentieth century more than 55 percent of the immigrants from Corcubión County residing in the harbor areas of Buenos Aires came from the agricultural villages of the county's interior. These peasants did not work in, nor were they attracted by, the neighborhood's nautical enterprises. They simply trailed acquaintances who, in turn, had followed those sailors from the county's coastal villages who had settled there two or three generations before.

This capacity of well-established primary networks to sustain by themselves an incoming stream helps explain the fact, normally overlooked in economic studies of migration, that immigrants kept on arriving even during the host country's worst depressions and during the sending country's most prosperous times, when the movement had become an irrational choice from a material perspective.[59]

Yet even the most extensive web of microsocial networks cannot support a continuous movement if adverse macrostructural conditions persist for too long. Many traditional and sturdy emigration currents have withered or halted in the face of restrictive legislation or quotas, prolonged disruption of transportation routes, endemic political instability and economic decline in the host country, or lasting prosperity at home. Others have shifted direction.

When brothers Victor and Luis Insua Papín, sailors from Finisterre, moved to Buenos Aires's La Boca district in 1950, they were following a family tradition that went back to 1846, when the grandfather of their great-grandfather had gone there to work as a caulker.[60] None of the intervening four generations had failed to send at least two siblings as permanent or temporary emigrants. But despite this tradition, younger brothers José and Joaquín headed for Venezuela two years later, at the insistence of their father, who maintained that, for sailing (in the merchant marine), Argentina was still the place but that, for prospering, Venezuela held the key to the future. (The two brothers in Argentina became self-employed ship mechanics; the ones in Venezuela, grocers). During the 1950s an increasing number of the Insuas' kin and townsfolk concurred with the patriarch's interpretation and made oil-rich Venezuela their favorite destination. A decade later the rupture with tradition proved sharper. For the first time in seven generations no one went to Argentina, a country increasingly paralyzed by an enigmatic, politico-economic malaise. Instead, they headed to unfamiliar places with strong currencies like Switzerland, West Germany, and Sweden.[61] This proved to be the last generation of emigrants. The economic miracle of the 1980s finally turned Spain from a country of emigrants into one of immigrants, with the arrival of increasing numbers of Latin Americans, Africans, Filipinos, and eastern Europeans.

The Argentine connection, however, did not die. It is present in the local practice of drinking mate, a brew called Paraguayan or Jesuit tea in English, that is virtually unknown outside the River Plate region;[62] just as it is present in the Baztán Valley in the *zikiro batu*, despite its Basque name, a style of barbecuing beef on vertical stakes that came straight from the pampas, which, in turn, made the Basque versions of handball their own. It lives on in the local folklore, in town nomenclature (the streets, taverns, and cafés named after New World places), in the old "mansions" built by returnees when Argentina was rich, in the "tourists" and their Argentine-born children who come to the fishing town during Southern Hemisphere winters. Indeed, the transatlantic social networks have been reinvigorated since the late 1970s by a new and somewhat ironic role: to assist a reverse flow, in which young second-and third-generation Hispano-Argentines cross the "puddle" eastward in search of dreams very similar to those of their grandparents.

OF PARENTS AND OFFSPRING: DIFFERING EMIGRATION PATTERNS IN GALICIA AND NAVARRE

Local particularities and their interaction with larger forces determined not only where people went but also who went, as the following two poems suggest. Both were written in 1880, the first in Euskara (the Basque language) by an obscure poetaster as an entry in a Navarrese literary contest with the theme, "The sweetness and excellence of the rural life in our mountains, counterpoising it to the miseries and degradations that emigration to America offers";[63] the second in Galician by that language's foremost poetess, Rosalia de Castro.[64] Both declaim the sorrows of emigration, but notice the difference in who, within the family unit, is supposedly afflicted.

¡Amerika! ¿zenbat dira?
!Zenbat! zugaz zurturik,
Irten beren erritikan,
Gurasoak lagarik,
Usterikan biurtzea
Diruz oso beterik.
¿Eta zenbat itzul dira?
Ez joan ziran erdirik
Ez, egiyaz, an ill dira,
Lagun bat gabetanik
Urrun dagon beren Ama
Maiteaz oroiturik
Beragandik iges egin
Barkaziyoa biyotez
Jainkoari eskarik

Este vaise y aquél vaise,
e todos, todos se van.
Galicia, sin homes quedas
que te poidan traballar.
Tés, en cambio, orfos e orfas
e campos de soledad,
e nais que non teñen fillos
e fillos que non tén pais.
E tés corazóns que sufren
longas ausencias mortás,
viudas de vivos e mortos
que ninguén consolará

America! How many?
How many! lured by you
have left their hometown,
abandoning their parents,
hoping to come back
loaded with gold.
And how many have returned?
Not even half of those who left.
No, there they have perished
without a friend,
remembering their mother
who is far away,
crying for having forsaken her,
with broken hearts
imploring God's mercy.

This one goes and that one goes
and all, all go.
Galicia, you stay without men
who could till your soil.
You have, however, orphans
and fields of solitude
and mothers without children
and children without fathers.
And you have hearts that suffer
long, deadly partings,
widows of the living and the dead
whom no one will console.

Both poems lament the plight of parents, particularly mothers separated from their emigrant children, but only the Galician verse wails about "orphans . . . children without fathers . . . [and] widows of the living." This expresses more than Rosalia de Castro's superior lyrical imagination. In the fishing village of Finisterre, wives of overseas emigrants offered religious services for their safe return and sang the following hymn:

Miña Virxiña de Monte
que miras sempre para o mar
facede que os emigrados
volvan sans o seu fogar.[65]

My little Virgin from Monte
who is always facing the sea,
make the emigrants
come back safe to their homes.

Popular sarcasm christened such services "masses of widows."[66]

Quantitative analysis substantiates the intimations of poems and folk sarcasm. The data in Table 8 confirm the essence, if not the maudlin laments, of the Navarrese rhymes: the unmarried offspring of Baztanese families did indeed comprise the bulk of those who left home for the New World; from the 1840s to the 1920s they accounted for 85 to 98 percent of all overseas emigrants from the valley. Moreover, the bard's failure to recite about "orphans and widows of the living" reflected a social reality, not his inability to come up with a felicitous phrase. Fathers and husbands rarely emigrated. At no time during a century of exodus did they account for more than a small fraction of the departures. By the same token, the data on the Galician municipalities included in Table 8 faithfully reflect the reality that Rosalia de Castro described poetically. The young offspring of Galician families left in large numbers, but so did husbands and fathers, who presumably but not always, left home temporarily. They comprised the majority of emigrants from Finisterre (54 percent) and Corcubión (65 percent) around the turn of the century and a plurality from Corcubión (26 percent) and Zas (25 percent) in the 1920s.[67]

What could account for this marked difference in the departure of Navarrese and Galician husbands? Maritime towns dominated the municipal districts of Finisterre and Corcubión. But the proverbial lax morals of sailors could not explain the preponderance of married men in the exodus, for when I separated the coastal towns from the surrounding agricultural villages, the pattern remained unaltered. What is more, the rural municipal district of Zas lies dozens of kilometers inland, and fathers there were ten times more likely to emigrate than were those from the Baztán Valley, which is about the same distance from the coast. It is true that Spanish ethnic stereotypes often characterized Galician peasants as prone to natural unions and Navarrese ones as austere Catholics, righteous to a fault. A Galician lawyer and priest who wrote a book about emigration from that region in 1902, told a visiting English woman that "fifty percent of the young men who emigrate from Galicia to South America are illegitimate children, and youths who go to hide their dishonour beyond the sea."[68] Yet my analysis of the 1,432 baptismal records for Finisterre between 1885 and 1900 (a time span concurrent with the data in Table 8) shows only 64 bastard births (4.47 percent of the total) in this supposedly promiscuous region.[69] A similar examination of the Arizkun parish in the heart of the supposedly straitlaced Navarrese highlands reveals 19 illegitimate births (3.75 percent of the total of 507), including 7 "fatherless infants" and 3 who were surreptitiously left at the portal of the parish church. The gap between the two rates of illegitimacy seems to me any-

Table 8   Position in the family unit of overseas emigrants from the Baztán Valley, Navarre, and from three municipalities in Corcubión County, La Coruña, in selected years (in percentages; less than .5 = 0)

	Baztán Valley				Finis terre	Corcubión		Zas
	1847–1864	1890s	1909	1920s	1890s	ca. 1905	1920s	1920s
Husband	5	3	2	2	54	65	26	25
Wife	0	0	2	0	1	0	4	4
Offspring	85	93	96	98	43	31	60	55
Other kin	10	4	0	0	2	4	10	16
Number	236	79	43	55	246	110	107	74
Male	94	83	84	82	93	93	83	97
Married	6	4	9	2	55	68	38	27
Mean age	25	21	22	22	31	33	32	27

NOTE: The municipal *padrones* from which the data were drawn may undercount households that emigrated in toto and left no relatives behind who could list them as *vecinos*, or legal residents of the municipality (thereby underestimating the number of women residing overseas). I found families from these villages listed in Buenos Aires sources, such as census returns and voluntary-association records, that were not listed as absent in the Spanish *padrones*. But because few emigrants completely severed their links with their hometowns, those cases do not seem to be common. The *padrones* often listed natives who had been absent for more than two decades, indicating the persistence of links. I also corroborated the reliability of the *padrones* by contrasting them with a different type of source: a municipal manuscript listing all the emigrants who left Baztán 1909 (the only list of its kind that I was able to locate). The results, in the third column, coincided with the *padrones*'. At any rate, because the sources for all of the villages are identical, whatever bias they may contain does not distort comparisons. Some *padrones* have disappeared, and others do not include the place where the absentees resided, and the dates used here reflect these limitations.

thing but significant and suggests that the disparate participation of husbands in the emigration of northern Navarre and the Galician villages is not likely to have its origins in diverging ethnic attitudes toward marriage and parenthood.

The Baztán Valley, and the Basque country in general, possessed distinguishing material, not moral, attributes that perhaps can explain the contrast in the composition of emigrants. Unlike the other localities in Table 8, primogeniture (actually, a local transformation of it that permitted parents to choose the inheritor) allowed the bequest of undivided rustic property. Mostly thanks to this, and to emigration itself, this zone of the country avoided both the *minifundios* of Galicia and the latifundia of Andalusia. Middle-sized farms clearly made it more viable, and attractive, for the head of the household to stay home.

The peculiar way in which precapitalist practices survived the agricultural revolution in Navarre also affected the composition of the emigrant group. As in other parts of Spain, agropastoral capitalism in northern Navarre continually encroached on autarkic agriculture, thanks to the urbanization and industrialization of the Basque country, to the strategic position of the area along the Bayonne–Madrid route, to the ensuing contraband, and to remittances of emigrant money from Argentina, Mexico, and, later, California. But the most pernicious effects of market agriculture were softened here by ready access to municipal commons that still covered more than four-fifths of the Baztán Valley. As a result, when I explored the composition of emigrants from nonpropertied families, the proportion of fathers rose slightly (6 percent, in comparison with 3 percent for the farm-owning families) but still paled in comparison with the figures for the other villages examined.[70]

For Galicians, on the other hand, the combination of greater demographic pressure and lack of primogeniture spawned a multitude of uneconomic handkerchief plots rather than middle-sized farms. This *minifundismo* was aggravated by related practices. Bequeathing to all offspring obviously split farms into smaller units; inheriting from different sides of the family also scattered an individual's property into insulated, tiny plots. Public authorities often attempted to consolidate isolated parcels by encouraging peasants to exchange them with neighbors. But years of subdivision had forged a bewildering puzzle, and these efforts usually yielded epidemics of litigation instead of larger farms. And the no-less-endemic use of stone fences did more to hinder the use of plow animals than to fence off legal disputes.

It is true that even Lilliputian Galician farms could normally sustain the family (thanks mostly to New World arrivals like the potato and maize and Old World staples like the milk cow). *Gallego* peasants were not pushed across the ocean by hunger, as the regional bards regularly voiced,[71] and those who left were not the truly needy (see chapter 1). But hunger and plenty are poles of a continuum, and along that spectrum *gallego minifundistas* placed farther on the side of penury than did northern Navarrese farmers. The fact that Navarrese emigrants usually listed "improving their fortune" as their motive for departure but their Galician counterparts most often used "seeking sustenance" seems more than formulary.[72] These people had enough resources to afford the seeking but often not enough to be fastidious about who would do so. Many families (by the 1920s, the majority) did wait for their children to grow and then sent them overseas. But others could not—or would not—wait, so the father left instead. The tiny plot and the lack of commons could do little to retain him. Significantly, and contrary to the case of most emigrants, older emigrants tended to be less, not more, literate than their cohorts who stayed home.[73] Movement for many of them had become more an acceptance of defeat than a symbol of progress.[74]

It is unlikely, however, that economic necessity alone can explain the huge difference in the participation of fathers in the emigration of the two regions. The fact that propertied Galician fathers were three to six times more likely to emigrate than were their landless Navarrese counterparts cannot be attributed solely to the small size of Galician farms and to the beneficial effects of Navarrese communal lands.

Northern Navarrese do indeed demonstrate an idiosyncratic cultural attachment to their *echea* (a concept that includes both home and house, household and dwelling) that defies purely materialistic explanations.[75] Actual living space in these massive Basque farmhouses is not as ample as it seems at first sight because animals occupy the lower floor. Yet their architecture and landscape give them the appearance of cozy chateaus that not even the most untamed wanderer would like to leave. In the 1840s a British visitor made the same observation and compared them to "the Chalets of Switzerland."[76] The importance of this visual image in keeping fathers at home cannot be proved but should not be discarded. Similarly, the local belief that a medieval king bestowed universal *hidalguía* (nobility) to the valley's inhabitants may be a legend and meaningless when it comes to actual social status. But the myth has become "history" for the Baztanese and has fostered a communal pride and loyalty that they express in their conventional reference to their birthplace as "the very noble and very loyal Valley and University [in the archaic sense of a corporate entity] of the Baztán." The resulting coats of arms on the houses may be dubious as marks of nobility but serve to solidify the identification of the physical structure with the patriarchal family. Indeed, each farmhouse is identified by a family name, and when natives list their birthplace they refer not only to the village or hamlet but also to the name of the *echea*.[77] The ability of northern Navarrese fathers to stay home clearly originated in the particular set of material circumstances that I have discussed. But the ensuing cultural sense, and definition, of domesticity must have enforced the tendency to do so, even among those heads of household who did not own a farmhouse.

Galicians also showed a strong attachment to their birthplace. *Morriña* (the Galician word for homesickness) was repeated so often in the diaspora that it became part of the Spanish language. Yet whereas Basques usually named their specific house and village as their birthplace, Galicians more often referred to the largest neighboring town. For example, of eighty-nine Galician immigrants who, in Buenos Aires' sources, listed Vimianzo as their hometown, only twenty-two were actual natives of the town; the rest had been born in one of the surrounding, smaller villages.[78] Anecdotal evidence points in the same direction. A returnee from the town of Corcubión, remembering his stay in Buenos Aires in the 1920s, said, "I met this guy from Vimianzo there. . . . Well, he claimed he was from Vimianzo, but he must have been from one of the *aldeas* [smaller villages]."[79] In a similar vein, a Galician immigrant in Buenos Aires interjected, when he heard a friend claim to be from Santiago, "Si, Santiago de la puta de tu abuela" ["Yes, Santiago of the whore of your grandmother," which in Spanish rhymes with Santiago de Compostela].[80] Indeed, deflating the assertion of others to urban or semiurban birth became a staple of Galician immigrant humor. Apparently, *morriña* did not translate into the proud, personal identification with village or house of birth that characterized Basque heads of family.

The profusion of "widows of the living and children who have no father" in the Galician countryside clearly originated in the particular development of the agricultural economy that I described. But material reality eventually engendered autonomous cultural preferences, or at least more accepted norms of behavior in Galician male society—norms that could explain the apparently humorous denial of the *aldea* of birth; or why fathers who could afford a servant for their children kept leaving for Buenos Aires; or why old-timers in Zas still talked with admiration about the exploits of Don Manolo, a prosperous man who returned from overseas every two years to "make a child" and ended up making a dozen; or why, in nearby Bayo, a villager described a father whom he rarely saw as "daring, a worldly man" but asserted that his married uncle never emigrated because "he amounted to little; he was too homey." "Too homey" did not imply here the ideal of patriarchal security in a large, revered farmhouse that it did in Navarre, but a lack of drive, perhaps even unfulfilled paternal duty. Dominant mores in both places cherished the concept of "the man of the house," but in Galicia this coexisted with the accepted notion of "the man who leaves the house in search of sustenance."

In his memoirs one emigrant recalled that "Finisterre was poor, very poor. As a child, I walked barefoot for a long time, and so did many others. Clothes full of patches; the majority of Finisterrans lived in those conditions . . . well, not me so much because I had my father in America and he always sent something."[81] Another Finisterran, an expatriated journalist in Cuba, titled a section of an article on emigration, "Man Is a Natural Emigrant," alluding to Argonauts, Celtic warriors, crusaders, and conquistadors to prove his point.[82] Apparently, the rite of emigration in Galicia both conformed to the public notion of paternal duty (so long as emigration did not become permanent abandonment) and reaffirmed a certain definition of masculinity: man, not only as provider but also as wanderer, explorer, adventurer. The endless references to "the adventurous spirit of the Celtic race" in contemporary Galician writings suggest that emigration did indeed validate an ethnic definition of manhood.[83]

It is obvious that both material and cultural factors played a role in the different participation of Galician and Basque fathers in the overseas exodus. What seems relevant is not to appraise the relative importance of each but to underscore how a global, and apparently uniform, force, in this case the agricultural revolution, yielded distinct fruits in different soils and that the significant soil here is not the nation-state but more circumscribed spaces. The interaction between the world trend toward agricultural capitalism described in chapter 1 and local particularities (such as land-inheritance and -tenure practices and levels of demographic pressure and of communal ownership) determined not only the number but also the composition of emigrants from different parts of the Spanish countryside. Moreover, this interaction also produced, or reinforced, new variables—in the case I have described, cultural ones like normative definitions of domesticity, paternal duty, and manhood; variables that proved equally important in determining who emigrated. This level of macro-micro analysis can also elucidate how emigration "fever" spread over the Iberian Peninsula.

EMIGRATION FEVER: THE DIFFUSION OF INFORMATION

In the 1770s the famed lexicographer Samuel Johnson defined emigration from the Scottish Highlands as an epidemical fever.[84] A century later and a thousand miles away, a Florentine wit mocked Italian politicians and "rhetorical writers" for their monotonous abuse of "the cliché 'the plague of emigration,'" which those "more erudite, but more myopic than a mole, elongate into: 'the plague of emigration to faraway America.'"[85] Around the same period, an "erudite" Asturian elongated the cliché in a different way: "the plague of emigration that takes away, as Saint Matthew said, 'the salt of the earth.'"[86] Scores of Spanish officials, journalists, dramatists, and authors omitted the biblical reference and simply used the common phrase "la fiebre de la emigración," or, less often, "la fiebre de la Argentina" (the fever of Argentina). In a similar vein, nineteenth-century Finns spoke of "American fever,"[87] as did the Swedes next door,[88] the Irish spoke of the "contagion" of emigration,[89] and the Poles—in the early 1890s—of "Brazilian fever."[90] Moving southeast, one finds the fever metaphor in Hungary, Bohemia, Slovakia, and Croatia.[91]

Why this prevalence of fever motifs in so many places, languages, and times? That they turned into clichés begs the question. Such idiomatic expressions develop not accidentally but precisely because they describe real or perceived traits in social phenomena. In this case, they could have been employed by anti-emigration writers to denounce the exodus as a malady of the social body. But the fact that these writers usually preferred more drastic metaphors (such as the cancer or evil of emigration, hemorrhage, white slavery, flesh trade) and that the fever image was also used by the defenders of emigration suggests a different intention. What the variations of the theme (fever, epidemic, plague, contagion) share, and what I believe contemporaries wanted to express by using them, is the tendency of emigration to spread sociogeographically in a manner resembling that of an infectious disease.

Empirical analysis at various geographical levels confirms what the metaphors suggest: that, at its crux, emigration embodies a process of diffusion, not of germs but of information, concepts, and behaviors.[92] At the national level, Figure 8 and Map 2 show that until the 1860s Spanish emigration was basically limited to a dozen provinces that, with less than 30 percent of the national population, furnished 95 percent of the exodus. Two of them (La Coruña and Pontevedra) provided two-thirds, even though they contained only 6 percent of Spain's inhabitants. Actually, Figure 8 shows that during the middle decades of the nineteenth century the geographical origins of the arrivals were somewhat more confined than they had been half a century earlier, when the imperial, ecclesiastical, and military bureaucracies had recruited people from a larger number of places in the peninsula. After independence, however, the Iberian provinces that continued the American stream were not those from which a few individual colonial administrators, priests and soldiers had come but those in which a chain of spontaneous, private migration based on family and *paisano* networks and transatlantic trade had formed.

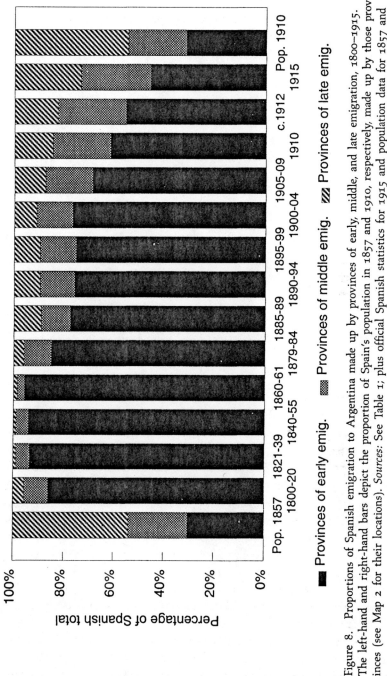

Figure 8. Proportions of Spanish emigration to Argentina made up by provinces of early, middle, and late emigration, 1800–1915. The left-hand and right-hand bars depict the proportion of Spain's population in 1857 and 1910, respectively, made up by those provinces (see Map 2 for their locations). *Sources:* See Table 1; plus official Spanish statistics for 1915 and population data for 1857 and 1910.

■ Provinces of early emig.　▦ Provinces of middle emig.　▨ Provinces of late emig.

Map 2. Spanish provinces of early, middle, and late emigration.

From these early foci, emigration fever slowly spread, first to a group of adjacent provinces and eventually all over the peninsula. At the outbreak of World War I the group of adjacent provinces, with 23 percent of the national population, provided 28 percent of the emigrants, a large increase from the 4 percent of the midnineteenth century; and the area made up of the twenty-six provinces that joined the crossings last provided 26 percent of the emigrants, still a smaller proportion than its 46 percent share of the national population, but a far cry from the puny 1 percent this area had furnished fifty years before.

The same process of original concentration and subsequent diffusion can be detected at the regional level. Ever since the late colonial period Galicians have constituted the principal Iberian ethnic group in Argentina. Yet for much of the nineteenth century, to speak of "Galician" emigration was no less misleading than to speak of "Spanish" emigration, for only the two Atlantic provinces, La Coruña and Pontevedra, participated

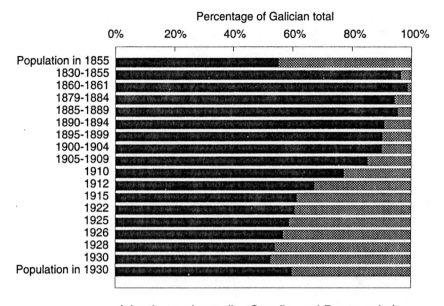

Figure 9. Proportions of total Galician emigration to Argentina made up by the two Atlantic and the two interior provinces, 1830–1930. The top bar (population in 1855) and the bottom bar (population in 1930) provide the measure of overparticipation or underparticipation. *Sources:* See Figure 8.

in it (see Figure 9). The interior province of Orense, with a population of 372,000, or 21 percent of the region's total, accounted for the grand total of 1 individual in the 2,000-strong Galician community of Buenos Aires in 1855, exactly the same number it provided to the Galician contingent of 682 that entered Argentina in 1860. The other non-Atlantic province, Lugo, accounted for only 24 and 8 individuals in the respective years, and as Map 3B shows, most of them came from the port of Ribadeo in the northeastern corner of the province. Indeed, the maps show that origins were more restricted also at the regional level in the midnineteenth century than they had been in the late colonial period[93] and that even within the provinces of La Coruña and Pontevedra emigration was limited to a few towns and villages.

As was the case at the national level, here too the "contagion" disseminated, and the interior provinces slowly but steadily increased their participation. By the late 1920s their relative emigration had surpassed that

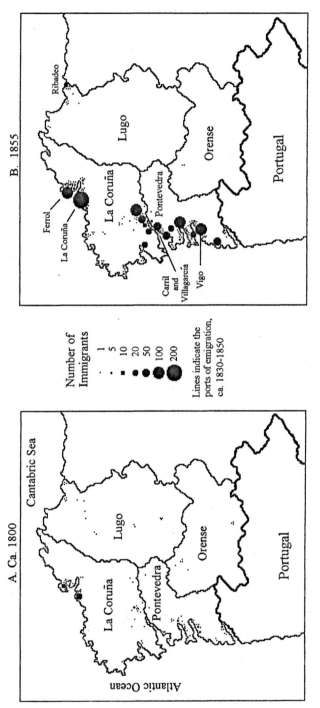

Map 3. Local origins of Galician immigrants in Buenos Aires, ca. 1800 (A) and 1855 (B).

of the Atlantic provinces, for they contained 40 percent of the Galician population but supplied 47 percent of the Galician emigrants to Argentina.

Moving to the other extreme of the country and to the county level, Figure 10 shows how Navarrese emigration to Argentina was originally restricted to the northern county of Pamplona, which contained 36 percent of the province's population in 1857 but supplied 91 percent of the departures. In the next decades, first the adjacent northern county of Aoiz, and then the three other counties steadily increased their participation in the exodus. By the 1920s these latecomers were providing a proportionally larger number of emigrants than was the county in which the stream originated.

The further down one moves in the geographical scale, the more meaningful the process of diffusion becomes. Map 4A indicates the distribution of the Navarrese population in 1877, from the province's capital to its tiniest hamlet. The following map indicates the place of origin of more than 300 Navarrese who arrived in Argentina between 1830 and 1859 and shows the huge difference between the distribution of these emigrants and that of the general population. Actually, the map shows that emigration was even more concentrated than the county figures in Figure 10 indicated. It was not Pamplona County in general that provided 91 percent of the Navarrese exodus during this period but only two restricted areas of the county: the city of Pamplona and the northern valleys. The next four maps depict how the "epidemic" spread from these two foci—first to the rest of the county, then to the other Pyrenean valleys in the county of Aoiz, and later to the larger towns in the south of the province—and how its axis shifted southward. Here also the county figures are misleading. By the post–World War I period the northern counties of Pamplona and Aoiz still provided half of the emigrants, but most of them now came from the southern edges of the counties. Indeed, a comparison of this 1916–1930 map with the 1830–1859 one demonstrates a reversal of origins: latecomers from the southern half of the province had replaced the northern pioneers as the principal sustainers of the stream.

This consistent pattern of diffusion undermines, perhaps demolishes, the push-pull interpretation of migration. It would be ludicrous to argue that poverty, lack of opportunities, military conscription, political corruption and the myriad other ills encompassed in the term "push factors" affected only the one-tenth of the Iberian Peninsula that for most of the nineteenth century supplied more than nine-tenths of the exodus; that these push factors later spread in an amazingly uniform pattern from

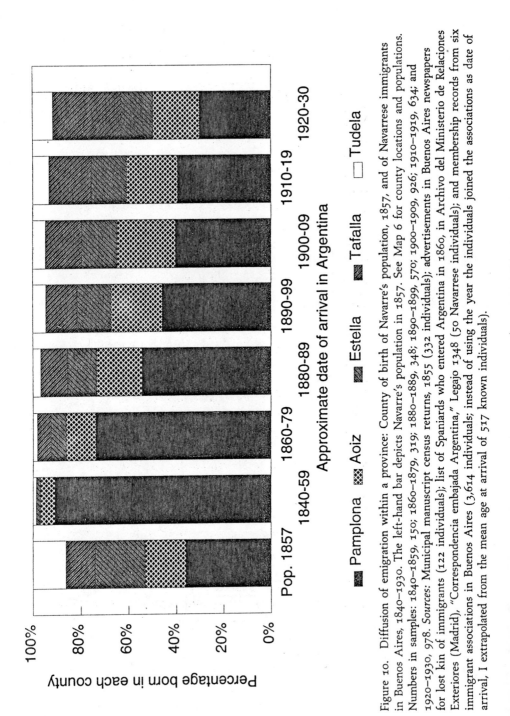

Figure 10. Diffusion of emigration within a province: County of birth of Navarre's population, 1857, and of Navarrese immigrants in Buenos Aires, 1840–1930. The left-hand bar depicts Navarre's population in 1857. See Map 6 for county locations and populations. Numbers in samples: 1840–1859, 150; 1860–1879, 319; 1880–1889, 348; 1890–1899, 570; 1900–1909, 926; 1910–1919, 634; and 1920–1930, 978. *Sources:* Municipal manuscript census returns, 1855 (332 individuals); advertisements in Buenos Aires newspapers for lost kin of immigrants (122 individuals); list of Spaniards who entered Argentina in 1860, in Archivo del Ministerio de Relaciones Exteriores (Madrid), "Correspondencia embajada Argentina," Legajo 1348 (50 Navarrese individuals); and membership records from six immigrant associations in Buenos Aires (3,614 individuals; instead of using the year the individuals joined the associations as date of arrival, I extrapolated from the mean age at arrival of 517 known individuals).

hamlet to hamlet, from county to county, from province to province, to previously happy lands; and that eventually they disappeared from the original areas of emigration to concentrate their affliction on the originally satisfied nonemigrating areas. Historical reality, not simply lack of logic, militates against such a scenario. The original provinces of emigration shown on Map 2 included the richest ones in the peninsula; the coastal belt of Pontevedra and La Coruña that dominated the Galician flow during the nineteenth century (see Map 3) formed the most developed zone of the region; and the northern valleys where Navarrese emigration began (Map 4B) enclosed some of the province's most fertile land, most democratic land-tenure system, and what a French 1868 tourist guidebook called "one of the richest territories of Navarre."[94]

What the communities of early emigration had in common was not a monopoly of poverty and push factors but a strategic location along information and transport channels. All were on the seaboard, in small islands, or in plains and valleys no more than twenty-five miles inland. By and large, then, emigration fever disseminated from periphery to center.

Proximity to the coast was not enough, however. The four coastal provinces of the Levant (Murcia, Alicante, Valencia, and Castellón), with 12 percent of the peninsula's population, provided less than 1 percent of the flow to Argentina as late as 1900 (in part because much of the emigration here crossed the Mediterranean, to Algeria, instead of the Atlantic). Likewise, the Andalusian coastal provinces of Huelva, Granada, and Almería provided 1, 7, and 0 emigrants to the 5,700-strong Spanish community of Buenos Aires in 1855. On the other hand, the area surrounding the transatlantic ports of Cádiz, Puerto de Santa María, and Gibraltar provided the bulk of early Andalusian emigration. Most other areas of early emigration surrounded the other ports (La Coruña, Ferrol, Vigo, Gijón, Santander, Bilbao, and Barcelona) that the Bourbons' free-trade reforms had opened up to American commerce during the last quarter of the eighteenth century.

Yet distance from international ports was less important than was access to information, whatever the route. For example, the maritime municipalities of Corcubión and Finisterre are 50 kilometers farther from the port of La Coruña (a total distance of 120 kilometers) than is the inland municipality of Zas, in the same county, but the exodus from them began and took force some two generations before that from Zas because news about the New World entered through other sources. One was the numerous Catalan fishermen and merchants who from the late eighteenth century on introduced new fishing methods, founded the sardine-salting

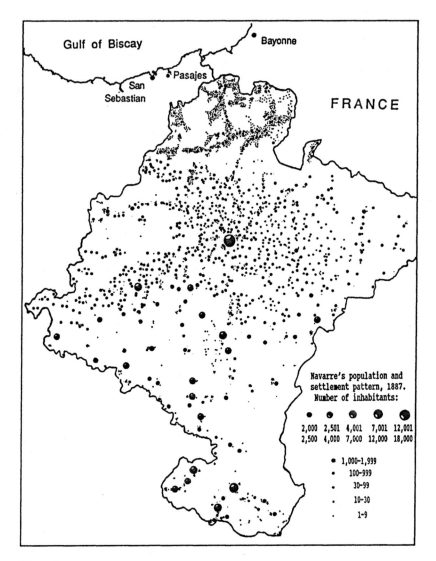

Map 4A
Settlement patterns of Navarre's population in 1877 (A) and local origins of
Navarrese immigrants in Buenos Aires, 1840–1930 (B–F). Maps B–F show the
local origins of 3,614 Navarrese immigrants in Buenos Aires whose specific
birthplace I was able to identify, not total emigration from Navarre. *Sources:*
See Figure 10.

1840–1859

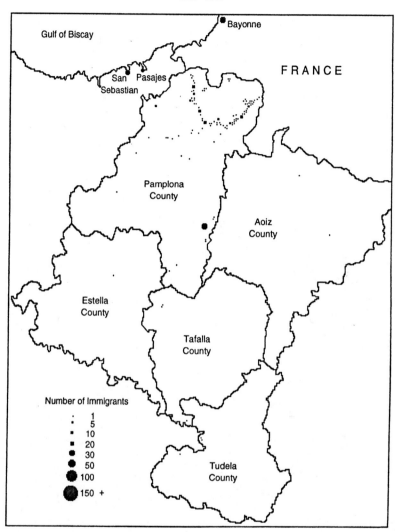

Map 4B

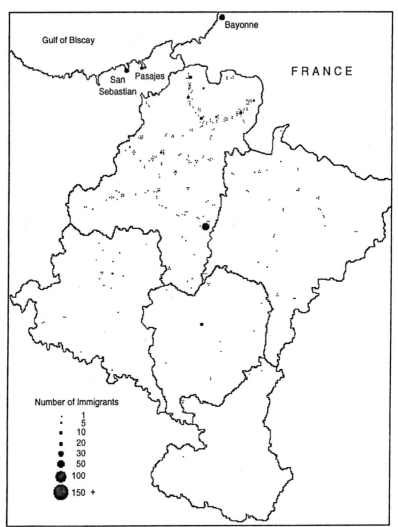

Number of Immigrants

	1
	5
	10
	20
	30
	50
	100
	150 +

Map 4C

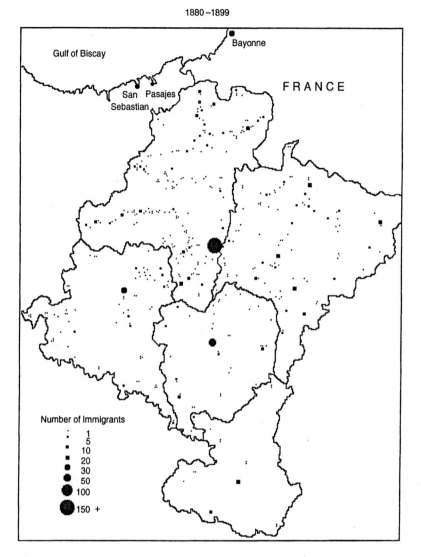

1880–1899

Gulf of Biscay

Bayonne

FRANCE

San Pasajes
Sebastian

Number of Immigrants

·   1
·   5
■ 10
 20
 30
 50
 100
150 +

Map 4D

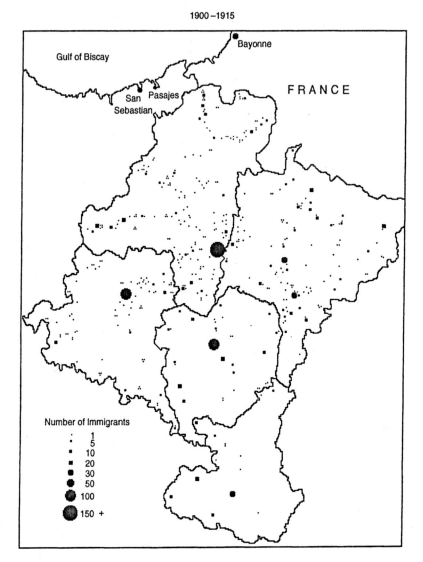

1900–1915

Gulf of Biscay

Bayonne

FRANCE

San Pasajes
Sebastian

Number of Immigrants

·   1
·   5
■   10
■   20
●   30
●   50
●   100
●   150 +

Map 4E

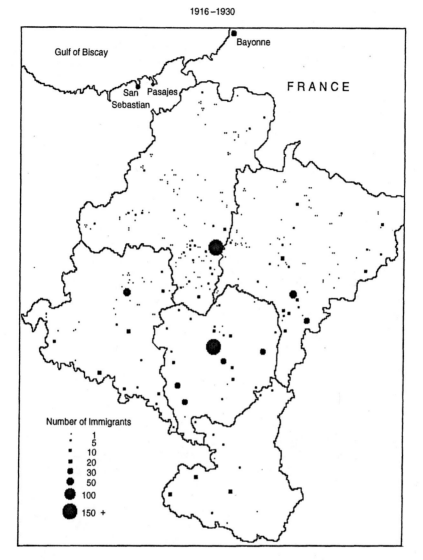

1916–1930

Bayonne

Gulf of Biscay

San   Pasajes
Sebastian

FRANCE

Number of Immigrants
·   1
    5
■   10
   20
   30
●   50
  100

  150 +

Map 4F

industry, and linked the area, through trade, to Barcelona, the Mediterranean, and the Americas.[95] The local inhabitants who became sailors in Catalan vessels and other merchant marines also provided plenty of tales about the lands across the ocean. So did local fishermen, whose boats at times sailed as far north as La Coruña and as far south as Villa García, a minor port on the Galician lower *rías* (fjords) but an important one in terms of emigration to Argentina. Yet another possible source of information were ships seeking refuge from storms, and later coal, which occasionally anchored outside the shallow harbors of Finisterre and Corcubión.

Information did not always enter directly from the sea. In the northern Navarrese valleys of pioneer emigration it came through the Pyrenees. Although some dwellers of these valleys had been going to the Indies since the sixteenth century, few, if any, had settled in the southern fringes of the Spanish Empire (see Figure 10). The surge of emigration to the River Plate in the 1840s therefore represented not the continuation of a late-colonial flow interrupted by the War of Independence and its aftermath— as had been the case in Mataró, Ferrol, and Bilbao—but a new movement related to French Basque emigration. The original source of the French stream is not clear, but information about Argentina probably first arrived there in the form of government propaganda. I found fiscal records from 1826 in the Argentine national archive that included a letter and receipts from a Monsieur Loreilhe, "emigration commissioner of Buenos Aires in Burdeos." The slips detailed more than 2,000 francs for printing 600 brochures of thirty-six pages, posters, newspaper advertisements, and 10,000 leaflets. Bitter at the Argentine government's decision to discharge him, Monsieur Loreilhe bragged about the 50 subagents he had employed and claimed that the 1,500 prospective emigrants he planned to send were not the "effeminate and feeble scum" that the new commissioners were picking from the streets of Paris but "moral and robust Basque farmers."[96]

These recruitment efforts bore little immediate fruit, due to the chaotic and violent situation in Argentina at the time. But they sowed seeds that germinated a decade later when Juan Manuel de Rosas, the "Restorer of the Laws," imposed some order in the country, sheep raising expanded in the pampas, and French Basque shepherds began to arrive.

Navarrese emigration to Argentina began, therefore, in the northern valleys because information about the River Plate originally entered from across the border. The channels were numerous. The road from Pamplona to Bayonne, the principal port of departure for Montevideo and Buenos Aires, crossed the region. Exports of wool and hides and imports of sugar, cacao, spices, salted and fresh fish, and textiles tied the two sides commercially.[97] Local muleteers carried not only these commodities but also information. The Pyrenees aided the muleteers by leaving the Aragonese heights behind, tapering toward the coast, and becoming easily surmountable.[98] The many mountain trails and passes also provided perfect grounds for what a local writer called "the sport of an adventurous race," and an English visitor "their bane: the all-corrupting habit of smuggling."[99] The omnipresent *kontrebandistak*, in turn, developed elaborate webs that included innkeepers, corrupt border patrols, and merchants; webs that carried information and smuggled not only liquor or tobacco but also people.[100] Similarly, by the 1840s French Basque ship owners had created a network of emigration agents and subagents on both sides of the border, which included an increasing number of their Spanish "cousins." A common culture and language fostered cross-border deals, and so did social and kinship ties. The manuscript census for Baztán Valley in 1847 listed 120 people (about 2 percent of the 7,400 inhabitants) as absent in France and 94 French-born individuals as living in the various villages of the municipality. About 7 percent of the marriages around that time involved partners from across the border. Foreigners in official statistics, these people were neighbors and relatives to each other. Finally, the dispersed settlement pattern of the region allowed the easy dissemination of information across the frontier and throughout the valleys.

Information about Argentina spread from the borderlands to the rest of the province through many of the same mechanisms by which it crossed the border (trade routes, mule drivers and ambulatory salesmen, itinerant workers, emigration agents, and so forth); through some new mechanisms (bureaucrats, schoolteachers, soldiers and draftees relocated by the Spanish state, or students sent to the provincial capital for their secondary education); and through modified ones (internal, instead of cross-border, migration).

But how intense was internal migration in Navarre among the generation previous to the emigrant one? What forms did it take? And how was it related to overseas emigration and the diffusion of information? To answer such questions it is not enough to find from aggregate sources, such as published censuses, that internal population shifts occurred. After all, the people who moved internally may not be related to those who later emigrated. What one needs is information on the mobility patterns of the parents of people who actually emigrated. I found such data for 562 Navarrese men who became members of Laurak-Bat, Buenos Aires' main Basque association, during the first three decades of the twentieth century, thanks to the fact that the enrollment forms included the name and birthplace of the members' parents. The data gathered show intense internal mobility among the parents of Navarrese immigrants in Buenos Aires: 40 percent of the fathers and 44 percent of the mothers had been internal migrants; that is, they were not natives of their offspring's hometown. Intraprovincial mobility predominated, but longer distance, or interprovincial, mobility was also significant, accounting for 15 percent of all moves. From the perspective of the emigrating sons, the majority (60 percent) had at least one parent born outside his hometown, and more than one-tenth (11 percent) had at least one parent born outside his native province. Because it is unlikely that the migrating parents left no relatives in their birthplaces, one could say that about four-tenths of that generation had kin in other villages and towns and that six-tenths of the next generation did. If anything, this is a conservative estimate. It does not, after all, take into account the mobility that may have occurred in the previous generation (that is, the grandparents of the immigrants in Buenos Aires) or mobility by in-laws and other relatives.

Whatever its exact degree, this mobility clearly expanded the Old World social space of the majority of Navarrese emigrants beyond geographical constraints. That is, their family ties in Spain were not restricted to their native localities, or even to a radius of ten or so kilometers from their hometown but radiated out to more distant places, where uncles, aunts, cousins, and so on resided.

These long-distance linkages acted in the nineteenth century as a sort of *Homo sapiens* wireless telegraph, relaying information from the New World to the locality of immediate origin and from there, through visits and letters, to the other Iberian localities where relatives, and relatives of relatives, lived. This contained an inherent capacity for exponential expansion similar, and related to, the branching out of kinship-based emigration that I previously examined and illustrated in Figure 6. There the networks attracted people increasingly distant, in time and kinship, from the original immigrant: nephews and grandnephews, in-laws, cousins of cousins, offshoots who later became trunks, ramifying the process and giving it a self-generated tendency to multiply. The same could, and did, happen with localities. Indeed, given the high degree of internal mobility, the ramification of kinship emigration often included a component of geographical expansion and ramification. After all, the cousins who followed the overseas emigrants had at least a 40 percent chance of living in other localities, and so did the cousins of those cousins, theoretically ad infinitum. More than half of the people in the kinship chain illustrated in Figure 6, for example, were not natives of Arizkun, the birthplace of the pioneer immigrants in it. The disseminating power of such a process makes obvious the preponderance of fever motifs across so many places and times.

The contagion of emigration spread over the map much like an ink blot on paper. But often the ink left seemingly capricious blanks (see Map 4). In many cases these were simply empty lands. But in other cases, even in zones of diffuse settlement like northern Navarre, the epidemic leaped over inhabited valleys and passed over villages and towns. Long-distance kinship linkages, unshackled from geographical restrictions, were often behind these enigmatic gaps. For example, Fermín Irazoqui, a youngster of twenty-one as the nineteenth century reached its midpoint, was born and raised in Aoiz, a village thirty kilometers east of Pamplona with little knowledge of Argentina at the time.[101] Fermín's father, however, was a cart driver from Lecaroz, a hamlet in the heart of the Baztán Valley, the zone of pioneer Navarrese emigration in the Pyrenean piedmont. In 1852 Fermín went to join his Baztanese paternal uncles in Argentina. Over the next decade two of Fermín's maternal relatives from his native village of Aoiz and four from another community eight kilometers to the south, where his mother's family apparently originated, followed him. Kinship-based, rather than spatially based, linkages hurdled some forty kilometers of land, leaving a large blank on the map and a new, isolated focus of infestation. From then on, news of Argentina would disperse northward from Aoiz until it met the stronger epidemic that was spreading south from the Baztán Valley and filled in the blank. It also spread southward into previously uninfested lands. Given the significant degree of interprovincial, or long-distance, mobility, the same vaulting process could take place over four hundred instead of forty kilometers.

Internal migration may have at times curbed the overseas stream by offering alternatives to it. Women, in particular, often preferred Spanish destinations to American ones. The 1897 Baztán Valley manuscript census, for example, listed seventy-nine absentees overseas, only 16 percent of whom were female, and ninety-seven absentees in the rest of Spain, 57 percent female. Other areas also exhibited this gender gap.[102] At another level, however, internal movements clearly fostered overseas emigration by loosening traditional ties to the soil and by abetting the propagation of information about overseas opportunities.

Internal movement was not restricted to Navarre. Because the membership forms of other Spanish associations in Argentina did not contain information on immigrants' parents, I used Spanish baptismal records and, more efficiently, civil birth registries, available since 1870, to trace the parents of immigrants from seven localities in different regions of the peninsula. The results, in Table 9, expose an overall mobility similar to that in Navarre: 41 percent of the fathers of the immigrants and 39 percent of their mothers were not natives of their offsprings' hometown; 55 percent of the immigrants had at least one migrant parent; and intraprovincial mobility accounted for three-quarters of all moves. These proportions were much higher for urban immigrants than for those from small rural villages, however. Significantly, the two communities with the lowest proportion of migrants in their population, Vimianzo and Val de San Lorenzo, contracted emigration fever two or three generations later than the other localities in the table did.

Whether across frontiers or within them, information—in an age without radio, television, telephones, and fax machines—disseminated mostly through word of mouth: the stories of muleteers, coach drivers, itinerant workers, and traveling salesmen; the boasting of returnees and emigration agents; the American letters that passed from house to house and were read aloud by the local schoolteacher or a literate friend or kin; family visits and letters from one Spanish town to another; gossip in taverns and churches; bedtime tales of adventurous emigrants; and folk songs such as these:

> Ameiriketara joan nintzan
> xentimorik gabe
> andik etorri nintzan
> maitia bost milloien jabe
> txin, txin, txin, txin,
> diruaren otsa,
> aretxek ematen dit
> maitia biotzian poza.[103]

> Teño de ir a Buenos Aires
> Anque sea por un ano,
> Anque no traiga diñeiro,
> Traigo o aire americano[104]

> I left for the Americas
> without a cent
> and I returned, darling,
> with five million.
> Tlin, tlin, tlin, tlin,
> the sound of money,
> that is, darling,
> what cheers my heart.

> I have to go to Buenos Aires
> even if for just a year,

Table 9 Birthplace of the parents of Spanish immigrants from seven Iberian localities living in Buenos Aires ca. 1900–1930, as an indicator of internal migration in the previous generation (in percentages)

Birthplace of immigrant	N	Non-migrant Same as offspring	Short-distance migrants Surrounding district	Rest of province	Long-distance migrants Rest of region	Rest of Spain	Total
Father's birthplace							
Finisterre	34	59	32	3	0	6	100
Corcubión	40	50	10	20	13	8	100
Vimianzo	22	73	23	0	5	0	100
Val de San Lorenzo	72	93	3	4	0	0	100
Pamplona	92	35	8	35	2	21	100
Tafalla	94	59	26	12	0	4	100
Mataró	39	54	23	8	5	10	100
All	393	59	16	15	3	8	100
Mother's birthplace							
Finisterre	34	68	24	0	0	9	100
Corcubión	40	63	15	8	3	13	100
Vimianzo	20	80	20	0	0	0	100
Val de San Lorenzo	74	95	0	4	1	0	100
Pamplona	97	33	13	47	3	3	100
Tafalla	94	62	11	26	0	2	100
Mataró	38	53	21	8	3	16	100
All	397	61	12	20	2	5	100

SOURCES: The list of immigrants in Buenos Aires was compiled from membership records of various Spanish voluntary associations in that city. I later linked the immigrants to their parents using baptismal records in the respective parishes and, more efficiently, local civil birth registries, available since 1871.

NOTE: Description of the localities: Finisterre, a fishing village in the Galician province of La Coruña, located at the northwestern tip of the European continent (thus the name); Corcubión, twenty-four kilometers to the south, a maritime town of about 1,500 in 1900 and the administrative center of the county; Vimianzo, an agricultural area located in the same county some sixty-four kilometers inland; Val de San Lorenzo, an agricultural village of about 1,700 in the province of León; Pamplona, the capital of Navarre; Tafalla, a town of about 6,000 in the same province some sixty-four kilometers south of Pamplona; Mataró, a Catalan industrial town of about 20,000 inhabitants thirty-two kilometers from Barcelona.

even if I bring no money,
I'll bring American airs.

The same process that disseminated information about the Americas
augmented it. People became not simply aware of the lands across the
ocean but also, and more importantly, increasingly knowledgeable about
where to go, how to get there, whom to go to for assistance, where to stay,
how to find a job, and so on. Through this process, Buenos Aires became
more familiar to millions of Spaniards than Madrid, or even their own
provincial capitals.[105] It became less threatening and mysterious without
losing its mystique. Eventually, even people who had never been there
could describe particular neighborhoods, streets, and sights, at times in
amazing detail.

As awareness of, and familiarity with, far-away places spread and increased, so did the idea and the practice of emigration. It evolved in stages,
from an unknown concept to a far-fetched idea, to a pioneer venture, to a
common practice, and, in some places, to expected behavior, a habit. Indeed, contemporaries used the term fever not only to convey its tendency
to spread geographically but also its psychological thrust, as when Ortega
Munilla wrote in 1881: "Emigration is a dream, a delirium, a fever that
medicine can study,"[106] or when an anonymous Basque poet employed the
term to explain his own departure:

Gazte nintzen oraiño,
Aski errana da,
Adin hartan gutiño
Gauza pisatzen da;
Aditu nuieneko
Montebiden fama,
Herriaren uzteko
Lotzen-zaut su-lama.[107]

I was still a boy then.
That says enough.
At that age
one ponders little;
Since I heard of
Montevideo's fame,
a fever possessed me
to abandon the village.

A Galician emigrant expressed the same idea in a novel suggestively titled
La sugestión de America, in which he wrote of an arrival in Buenos Aires:
"He had gone there out of suggestion. It was there that everyone went. He
would have felt perplexed if someone had asked him why he had emi-

grated to the great metropolis."[108] Others coined a new term, *emigromania.*[109]

This process of diffusion and suggestion, accomplished basically by the primary, microsocial networks of humble folks, by kin and friends, and by friends of friends, made the movement of 70 million people across the oceans possible in the nineteenth and early twentieth centuries. Most of these people may have been responding to larger historical forces over which they had limited control, but in the process they became active participants. Their tales and boasting, their gossip and songs made possible the population movements that changed and shaped the world. It was a bloodless revolution from below that involved a much greater number of peasants and workers than did all political revolutions put together.

The power of this popular, microsocial revolution, however, came from its interaction with the macrostructural revolutions I described in chapter 1. Macadamized roads, trains, steamers, and other innovations of the transportation revolution allowed ordinary people to carry information farther, faster, and in denser flows. The expanding apparatus of the liberal state improved the mail system and relocated schoolteachers, bureaucrats, national guards, and draftees, facilitating the spread of news across the peninsula. The agricultural and industrial revolutions took peasants to markets and salesmen to villages, connected countryside and towns, and increased internal mobility, which, as we saw, fostered the geographical spread of overseas emigration.

In light of this, the paradox that the first Europeans to cross the Atlantic were also among the last to cross it en masse acquires new dimensions. The late development of the macrostructural revolutions in Spain retarded, as we saw in chapter 1, the intensity of the transatlantic movement. It also stalled its extension. Tardy modernization slowed down communication within the peninsula, delaying the spread of emigration fever from the original foci and thus keeping down its overall volume and turning Spain into a nation of late emigration.[110]

In addition, the country's geographical shape, topography, and settlement patterns exacerbated the retarding effects of late modernization. The square, massive shape of the peninsula, unlike the elongated form of the Italian one, meant that information had to travel long distances to reach the hinterland from the coast. The Iberian topography, which made Spain Europe's most mountainous country except for Switzerland, further retarded the flow of information toward the central plateau. The nucleated settlement pattern of central and southern Spain, together with the tardy and incomplete development of the country's infrastructure, added another impediment. News about opportunities overseas could only spread with difficulty when population nuclei were separated by dozens of kilometers of empty land, parched plateaus, impassable sierras, and bad roads. The ink blot not only left blanks but spread in slow motion once it reached physical impediments. Thus, for much of the nineteenth century, emigration continued to be restricted to places like Mataró, which already had a century-old traditional link with Buenos Aires, to the Galician littoral, where people walked to the ports, and to towns and villages in the northern periphery, where the dispersed settlement pattern facilitated the diffusion of primary information.

The contrast with Ireland, a country, like Spain, of late modernization but also a densely populated island dominated by an accessible central plain, where the few mountains cluster on the coast and do not impede communications and where few people lived more than eighty kilometers from a port, is illuminating. There the contagion spread from Ulster with greater speed than the infamous potato famine, to cover the whole island in a few decades.[111] As the nineteenth century passed its midpoint, even the four counties least affected by emigration, with 21 percent of the country's population, supplied 11 percent of the overseas flow (see Figure 11). The least emigratory half of the island provided 34 percent of the Atlantic-crossing contingent. Around the same time, the 21 Spanish provinces least affected by emigration, with 36 percent of the country's population, supplied no one to the Argentine stream. The least emigratory half of the peninsula provided less than 1 percent of the exodus, and as late as 1900 it still furnished less than 7 percent of those who sailed for the River Plate. The fact that for so long so much of the peninsula did not participate made Spain a country of late emigration.

Yet in this country of late emigration the intensity of the transoceanic current from the Navarrese northern valleys or the Galician Atlantic coast surpassed that of most Irish counties as early as the midnineteenth century. Most of the Cantabrian seaboard began to ship large numbers of people to the Americas a generation before Scandinavia and other areas of so-called old emigration did. On the other hand, the Andalusian hinterland joined the flow as late as the Greek mainland, the Portuguese interior, Sicily, and other southern and eastern European regions of "new" emigration. The New Castilian plateau joined even later and with less force.

This reiterates the limits of national-level analysis and the inevitability of a global-local approach. The move of northern Navarrese shepherds to

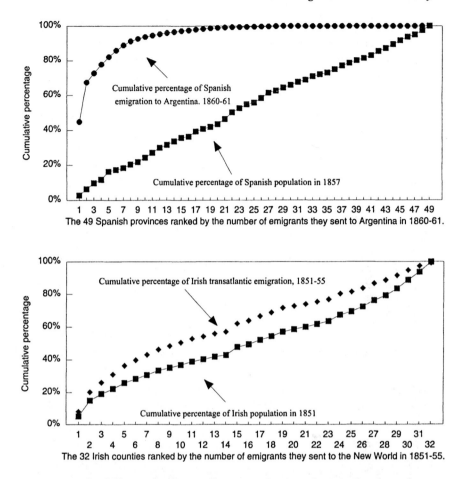

Figure 11. The diffusion factor: Cumulative population and emigration from the forty-nine Spanish provinces and the thirty-two Irish counties around the midnineteenth century. The wider the gap between the lines, the greater the spatial concentration of emigration; the smaller the gap, the greater the spatial dispersion. For example, the two Spanish provinces with the highest emigration rates contained 6 percent of the country's population and provided 67 percent of the emigrants; the two Irish counties with the highest emigration rates contained 15 percent of the country's population and provided 20 percent of the emigrants.

the pampas in the midnineteenth century had, after all, more in common with the move of Irish shepherds from Wexford and Westmeath counties to the same place during the same time than with the abrupt and late tide of Andalusian peasants to the city of Buenos Aires in the years before World War I.[112] The latter shared more with the contemporary Sicilian rush to New York than with the old, protracted, moderate flows of skilled workers from industrial Mataró, Bilbao, and Ferrol to Buenos Aires. These resembled, in timing, rhythm, and composition, the long-established streams from Ulster and the English Midlands to North America rather than the agent-sponsored movements from the Canary Islands and Málaga to Argentina—which, in turn, were more akin to the recruitment of Andalusians, Portuguese, and Japanese in Hawaii than to the rest of Spanish emigration to the River Plate.[113] The nation-state may provide the perfect unit of analysis for studying emigration and immigration policy but a flawed one for examining the actual process. Here, traditional wisdom to the contrary, the vantage point is not the middle but the extremes or, more precisely, the meeting and interaction of the extremes: of global revolutions and local particularities, of international capitalism and kinship networks, of the world and the village.

Moreover, the macro-micro approach employed here has uncovered not an infinity of unique local cases but particular local patterns. It has revealed not the epistemological nightmare (and aridity) of limitless variety but the intellectual challenge (and richness) of finite diversity. It is true that the peculiarities of Mataró, the Baztán Valley, or Corcubión impeded a generalized characterization of Spanish emigration. Yet these localities represent types of emigration rather than singular instances, types that are likely to appear respectively in English industrial towns, Irish pastoral valleys, and Ligurian fishing villages, for instance. Indeed, by exposing the universal nature of local patterns, this approach may, in the end, bring us closer to a general understanding of population movement than will any, presumably broader, national-level perspective.

This dialectical macro-micro approach (expanded to include Buenos Aires' physical and class structures among the first set and the immigrants' social networks and cultural background among the second) also provides the best framework for analyzing the lives of the newcomers in their adopted city. Furthermore, as I demonstrate in the following chapters, the patterns of emigration, produced by the interaction of global and local forces, in turn produced particular patterns of adaptation. That is, how and when people came greatly influenced where they settled, how they made a living, and how well they fared in the new land.

PART 2

ADAPTATION IN THE NEW LAND

4   Settling in the City

As Argentina celebrated the centennial of its liberation from Spain in 1910, a peaceful army of Spaniards, 131,000 strong, disembarked on its shores. Legions like these dwarfed the sum of all expeditions the ex-metropolis had sent during three centuries of colonial rule and made Buenos Aires the third largest Spanish city after Madrid and Barcelona. Among the new conquistadors were Juan Díaz Novo and Francisco Lema, two youngsters from Corcubión County, on the northwestern tip of the Iberian Peninsula.[1] The two expeditionists had in common more than their county of birth and the year of their departure. They were both eighteen years old, single, following in the footsteps of at least three generations of emigrants rather than breaking new paths, had embarked from the port of La Coruña, and had stayed in the same inn while awaiting the departure of their English steamer.

There were some differences also. Juan was born in Corcubión, a coastal village of 1,600 and the administrative center of the county, to a local merchant and a school teacher; Francisco, in Vimianzo, a rural village of 1,200 in the interior of the county, to small peasant-proprietors. Juan spoke Galician and Castilian and wrote florid Spanish prose for his townsfolk's magazine in Buenos Aires. Francisco spoke little Castilian and could barely scratch his name. Once off the boat, Juan settled with his uncle's family in an apartment house on Belgrano Street, three blocks south of the city's center; Francisco, with his cousins in a tenement across Plaza Almirante Brown, in La Boca district on Buenos Aires' southern fringe.

This chapter aims to explain how the interaction of kinship links, birthplace, social class, and Buenos Aires' ecology determined the residential patterns of Juan, Francisco and their compatriots in the Argentine capital.

THEORETICAL BACKGROUND

The residential patterns of immigrants in New World cities have long attracted the attention of observers. On their tours of the Americas, fin-de-siècle European intellectuals rarely failed to comment on the settlements formed by their less "enlightened" countrymen, usually with more embarrassment than pride.[2] During the same period, progressive reformers made immigrant enclaves and housing a favorite topic in their diatribes.[3] But it was the post–World War I urban sociologists of the Chicago school, particularly William I. Thomas, Robert E. Park, Louis Wirth, and Ernest Burgess, who first analyzed the subject in a systematic way.[4]

Two primal notions, Ferdinand Töennies' famous *Gemeinschaft-Gesellschaft* dichotomy (translated into rural-urban, primary-secondary) and the idea of ecological succession (drawn from the biological sciences), provided the backbone for the two basic concepts in the Chicago school's ethnic-urban studies. The ghetto—significantly, the title of Wirth's magnum opus—formed the first of these two concepts. In its spatial dimensions the ghetto represented a segregated, compact, and relatively closed area of first settlement in the central, low-rent, decaying, industrial wards of the city. In its social component, the awkward and largely unsuccessful attempts of the peasants to replicate the Old World's *Gemeinschaft* left a vacuum characterized by disorganization (Thomas' term), marginality (Park's term), or demoralization (used by both Thomas and Park).[5] This identification of immigrant enclaves with rootlessness later received a more lyrical treatment in the pioneer urban histories of Oscar Handlin.[6]

The second concept was decentralization or outward movement (also referred to as invasion and succession). In its spatial dimension this meant that members of the immigrant group, particularly the second and third generations, would inevitably move on from the initial enclave in the core to areas of second settlement on the semiperiphery of the city and later to the suburbs, to be replaced at each stage by newcomers (see Figure 12 for the most specific representation of this thesis, Burgess' concentric-zone model). Thus, Irish neighborhoods, *Kleindeutschlands*, and Swede Towns transmuted into Little Italies, Polonias, or Jewish ghettoes and these would eventually turn into Black slums or Puerto Rican barrios. The social implication of this spatial movement was, of course, a linear movement from lower-class and immigrant culture (the central ghetto), to working-class and mixed culture (the semiperipheral areas), and finally to middle-class and the North American mainstream (the suburbs)—in a word, assimilation.

Figure 12. Burgess' concentric-zone model of urban structure and growth.

Zone	Characteristics
1	The inner core or Central Business District. It concentrates the political, commercial and high cultural life of the city. Mostly non-residential.
2	The Zone of Transition receives the "invasion" of small business and factories unable to compete successfully for space in zone 1. It includes the first-settlement immigrant ghettos with their dilapidated tenements, rooming houses, vice businesses, social disorganization and crime.
3	The Zone of Independent Workingmen's homes is an area of second-settlement characterized by multiple-family housing (mostly two-family dwellings) and "invading" immigrants, in large part second-generation, escaping from the ghettos' deterioration.
4	The Zone of Better Residences includes one-family homes, comfortable apartment buildings, and financial, commercial and recreational services for the residents, who are middle-class, native-born and often the married children of second-generation working-class parents from zone 3.
5	The Commuters' Zone includes upper-middle and upper class suburbs with larger homes and receives the most successful residents from zone 4.

Source: Ernest W. Burgess, "The Growth of the City: An Introduction to a Research Project," *Publications of the American Sociological Society* 18 (1924): 88-89.

The Chicago school's model of immigrant urban settlement, then, includes two related but distinct dimensions: spatial and social. For more than two decades its social dimension has received numerous attacks.[7] Most social scientists no longer describe immigrant neighborhoods as foci of anomie and social pathology but as places where the newcomers, making use of their premigratory culture and skills, responded intelligently and rather successfully to new challenges. Others go farther and maintain that movement to the suburbs did not represent a symbolic rite of passage into middle America, that ethnic culture persisted there.[8]

Revisionism regarding the spatial aspects of the central-ghetto-to-suburb model has been more subdued, perhaps due to the obvious disappearance of turn-of-the-century ethnic enclaves from the North American urban landscape.[9] To be sure, the replacement of the term ghetto with "settlement" in the literature involves more than abstract semantics or a euphemism. Unlike the homogeneous, closed environment implicit in ghetto, the word settlement implies a more open ambience where immigrants interacted with the rest of society and other ethnic groups and in which back-and-forth spatial mobility was common.[10] Other researchers have questioned—often implicitly—one or another minor element of the model.[11] Nevertheless, in spatial terms the Chicago school model has stood the test of time in North American academia.[12] It has also been widely upheld in Argentine and Latin American urban studies.[13]

The concept of chain migration offers a different, though not opposing, approach to the question of immigrant settlement.[14] It emphasizes how the village, kinship, and social linkages of the immigrants influenced choice of residence in the host city. This approach, mostly used by historians, has never been presented as an alternative or challenge to the Chicago school model for two basic reasons.[15] First, unlike the Chicago sociological paradigm, it does not present a comprehensive model of urban ecology, and it offers little or no insight into the evolution of cities. Second, again unlike the Chicago model, which is primarily class based, it is basically "class blind." It assumes that immigrants belonged to one class: the peasantry in the Old World or its equivalent in the New, the urban lower class. As the title of a well-known book illustrates, immigrants in the host country were perceived as "urban villagers."[16]

My intent here is not to impose North American paradigms and approaches on a South American city (although, as geographer Charles Sargent pointed out, "in its physical growth, . . . Buenos Aires by 1930 had considerably more in common with a city such as Chicago than with most other Latin American cities").[17] The Chicago sociological model and the chain-migration concept simply offer the theoretical possibility of integrating urban ecology and immigrant networks, socioeconomic class and ethnic culture, macrostructural and microsocial variables, in the analysis of settlement patterns in Buenos Aires. They also present an opportunity to place the case of the Spaniards in Buenos Aires in the wider framework of general immigration-urban studies and, hopefully, to contribute to this corpus with new perspectives from "the South."

The first section of this chapter briefly describes the noticeable persistences from the colonial past and the less conspicuous changes affecting Buenos Aires during the midnineteenth century. The second section outlines the Spanish settlements and the ethnic ecology of Buenos Aires during the same period, examines the issue of segregation or clustering and the question of spatial centralization, and analyzes intra-Spanish class and local patterns. The rest of the chapter repeats the format but for a later time period. Section three describes the spatial and infrastructural metamorphosis of Buenos Aires into a belle-epoque grand metropolis and the less conspicuous continuities from the past. Section four, the longest in the chapter, examines the changes and continuities in the Spanish residential patterns discussed in the second section.

THE GRAN ALDEA DURING THE MIDNINETEENTH CENTURY

The Buenos Aires encountered by the ancestors of Juan Díaz Novo and Francisco Lema around the middle of the nineteenth century apparently did not differ much from the colonial town of 1800. Beginning with the landing, the ritual for disembarkation had not changed in half a century: vessels anchored some ten kilometers from the mud bank that passed for a port; passengers transferred to smaller boats that took them closer to shore and then jumped onto high-wheeled horse carts that carried them a kilometer to a broken-down wooden pier. A former British chargé d'affaires at Buenos Aires recalled in 1852 that "the wild and savage appearance of the tawny drivers of these carts, half naked, shouting and screaming and jostling one another, and flogging their miserable jaded beasts through the water . . . is enough to startle a stranger on his first arrival, and induce him to doubt whether he be really landing in a Christian country."[18] Two decades earlier a French youngster had also complained about the "coarse and impertinent" cart drivers who showered arrivals with obscenities and xenophobic epithets ("*gringo, carcamán, godo* or *sarraceno*") if they dared to question the abusive treatment or the exorbitant prices.[19] And to Benito Hortelano, a Madrileño printer who arrived on New Year's Day, 1850, the vociferous amphibious horse-cart drivers "resembled more wild boars than persons."[20]

The "tawny" drivers, the scores of mulatto washerwomen on the riverbank, and the black guards standing at the end of the pier (who, cloaked from head to toe in the bright red of Rosas' Confederacy, frightened Hortelano) bore witness to another continuity from the viceregal past: the survival of the colonial mestizo and black populace in a town that by the end of the century would be overwhelmingly white. Indeed, some quarters were still solidly black, with a significant proportion of African-born former slaves.[21]

As newcomers reached the shores, the unimpressive, flat urban landscape supplied further evidence that the Argentine capital—its 91,000 inhabitants notwithstanding—was still a *gran aldea*,[22] an overgrown village.

To a Scottish traveler in 1848, "The appearance of Buenos Ayres on land-ing [was] anything but prepossessing; the filthy and dilapidated look of the houses, which are only a single story high, tempts one to inquire whether they have owners or occupiers."[23] The next year, a North Ameri-can approaching the city from the opposite direction (the pampas instead of the River Plate), described it in similar words: "From a distance, the ap-pearance of Buenos Ayres is by no means prepossessing, and possesses none of the picturesque beauty of Santiago, Lima, Rio de Janeiro, or, in-deed, the great majority of the South American capitals."[24] Around the same time, the French visitor Xavier Marmier found "not a single build-ing of quality in the city with the exception of governor Rosas' home," described most dwellings as little better than shacks, and compared streets to sewers.[25] And in 1855 the Chilean writer Benjamín Vicuña Mackenna depicted the city's general aspect as "pleasant but not beautiful, much less awesome, as in Mexico, even though they share the same type of architec-ture, since the blocks are small, the houses only one story high, low and cramped, the streets narrow, and the sidewalks high and garnished with bungling and useless posts."[26] To a Chilean, the gridiron layout typical of Spanish American colonial towns seemed too common to mention. But Old World visitors rarely failed to notice the "chessboard" formed by straight streets intersecting at right angles every 137 meters, some, among them Charles Darwin, commending its "perfect regularity" and others condemning its dullness or monotony.[27]

As in 1800, the pampa encroached on the town. Less than twenty blocks from the central Plaza de la Victoria (today's Plaza de Mayo), one could find pastures, corrals, vegetable plots, the huts of the gauchos, and the rather plain country homes of the rich.

Yet under this curtain of continuities, a visitor from 1800 would have certainly detected change: the "odd" patronymics among the country-home owners (Brittain, Gowland, Horne, Stegmann, Dowhall, Billing-hurst); the name of the "decent" hotel (Albergo di Genova) where Benito Hortelano and his companions sought refuge after spending their first night at a Basque inn that turned out to be a whorehouse; the equally "ex-otic" signs of the neighboring stores (*botería alemana, agencia Liverpool, fonda francesa, hotel de Provence, café italiano*). Beyond the facade of ar-chitectural continuities, the Spanish immigrants were indeed coming to a very different town. They no longer landed in an outpost of empire where they made up the only significant nonnative group, monopolized trans-atlantic trade, dominated the city's commerce, and controlled the state bureaucracy. Buenos Aires was now the capital of an independent, and still somewhat hostile, country. Foreigners accounted for 36 percent of the city's denizens, but Spaniards made up only 18 percent of the foreign-born population. As the surnames of country-home owners suggested, British merchants had elbowed their way into the Iberians' old international trade monopoly. The store signs revealed the presence of other foreigners in local commerce. And Creoles now controlled the government and its bureaucracy.

The physical aspect of the *gran aldea* also began to change soon after the downfall of the xenophobic regime of Juan Manuel de Rosas in 1852. The new ruling liberal elite would now attempt to fulfill its obsession to "civilize" the country and Europeanize the town. In the building boom that followed, the colonial style was abandoned as fit only for "savages and moors." "Down with estancia architecture," would exclaim Domingo Sarmiento, one of the most enthusiastic proponents of "progress" and a future president of the republic. The Francophile elite fancied Parisian Second Empire architectural styles but, because most constructors and masons were Ligurians, they had to settle for Italian neo-Renaissance.[28]

Changes also occurred in the use of materials. Quicklime, marble, and slate replaced adobe and pantiles in house construction. Hardened dirt gave way to paving stones. Even the wooden number plates on buildings were replaced with French porcelain ones. In the search for comfort the "bungling and useless posts" described by Vicuña Mackenna, a reminder of Buenos Aires' equestrian ambience, were torn down by city ordinance in 1858. In the previous two years the town's inhabitants were awed by two miracles of progress: gas lighting, which replaced horse tallow in the lampposts of the city's center, and the first train, that mysterious horseless carriage that led gauchos to kneel in astonishment when they first glimpsed it.[29]

SPANISH SETTLEMENT IN THE GRAN ALDEA

The Argentine Wars of Independence and the ensuing civil strife, as we saw in previous chapters, severed all formal relations between the new republic and the old metropolis but not the kinship and *paisano* ties between Spaniards in Buenos Aires and their localities of origin. During the most difficult years, personal memories and family loyalties kept the links alive. As the turmoil subsided, the dormant chains revived and began to carry information, assistance, and people (in that order) across the Atlantic again. With the addition of a few new streams, the revived crossings swelled the Spanish community in Buenos Aires to 5,800 by 1855—more than twice as large as it had been at any time during the colonial period.[30]

These emigration patterns also helped to configure settlement patterns. Many of the late-eighteenth-century arrivals from Spain, who were tied, as we saw, to the Bourbons' imperial reforms and free-trade decrees, had settled in what was then the administrative and commercial hub of the city: the central plaza and the zone immediately to the south.[31] The reawakened chains thus tended to carry newcomers there, even though the imperial administration was gone, the succeeding republican bureaucracy did not represent a source of employment for them, and the commercial axis of the city was already shifting—albeit slowly—toward the northern side of the central plaza. More than half of the Spaniards in the city, but less than one-quarter of the rest of the population, lived in this area, which ran roughly nine blocks from Cangallo Street (now Teniente General Perón) on the north to Chile Street on the south and nine blocks from the riverbank in the east to Lima Street on the west (see Maps 5 and 6).[32]

Unlike in the colonial past, however, Spaniards now encountered a host of non-Iberian neighbors. They shared much of the western part of this zone with the French, the southern one with the Italians, and the northern one with the English. On the southwestern corner it bordered the black neighborhood of Monserrat, but Spaniards intermingled (spatially) with its residents to a much lesser degree than they did with their European immigrant neighbors.

Those who came as part of new streams, with few or no connections to the downtown merchants of the late colonial period (as we saw was the case with the northern Navarrese), were more likely to settle in other areas, particularly those tied to the postindependence expansion of the pampas' pastoral economy. Barracas al Norte, along the small Riachuelo River on the eastern end of town, was one of these. A Swedish sailor described it in 1852 as a suburb of wide, unpaved streets and no sidewalks, dominated by hide, wool, and mane warehouses (*barracas*; hence the name) and by slaughterhouses and which emitted a disagreeable odor that the many gardens and flowers could not neutralize.[33] He also noticed the large number of Basque immigrants, and so did the Chilean Vicuña Mackenna, the Frenchman Marmier, and the Scot MacCann.[34] Not counting those born north of the Pyrenees, however, Galicians slightly outnumbered their Basque compatriots here. Overall, 9 percent of the Spaniards in the city but only 3 percent of non-Spaniards lived in Barracas.

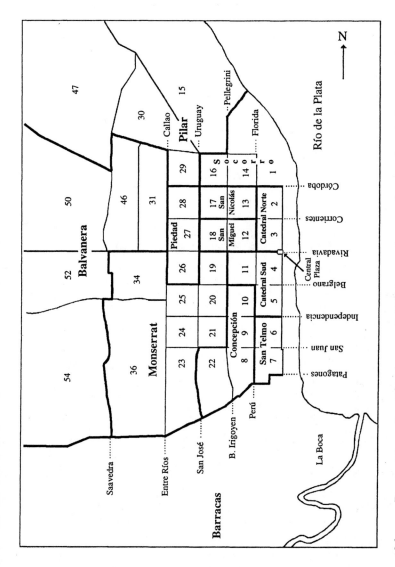

Map 5. Buenos Aires, 1855. The city was divided into twelve *juzgados* (wards), which are named on the map and delimited by thick lines. With the exception of the *juzgado* of Barracas, which included La Boca, on the southern edge of the city, the *juzgados* were subdivided into *cuarteles* (smaller units, usually four blocks by four blocks), which are numbered on the map. The principal thoroughfares are shown as dotted lines.

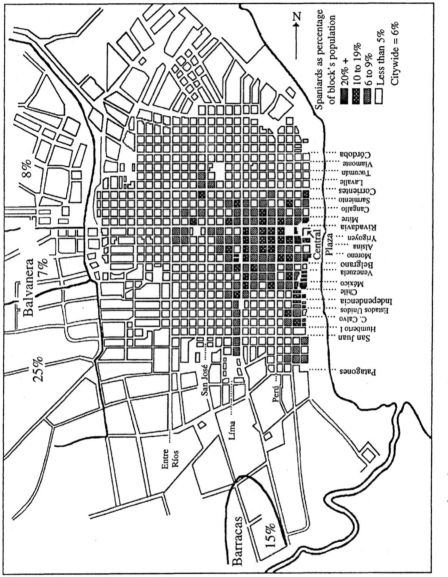

Map 6. Residential concentrations of Spaniards in Buenos Aires, 1855. Note that in peripheral areas, information is available by precinct (delimited by thick lines) rather than by block.

The third area of Spanish concentration, the three outer precincts (*cuarteles*) of the Balvanera ward (*juzgado*), on the western outskirts of the city, was the least important. Only 5 percent of Buenos Aires' Spaniards, and 3 percent of non-Spaniards, lived here. Dairy farms and Basque-owned brick ovens provided the major source of employment, and most "Spaniards" spoke Euskara, particularly its Navarrese dialect, rather than Castilian.

Although Spaniards concentrated in these areas, they did not dominate them numerically. Indeed, there were only six blocks in the entire city in which they accounted for more than one-fifth of the population (see Map 6). Even the most concentrated block, an atypical one with three large Basque boardinghouses, was only 42 percent Spanish (68 percent if their Argentine-born children are included). Moreover, the boundaries of immigrant enclaves tended to overlap. For example, the Spanish-Italian ratio for the whole city was 52; that is, there were 52 Spaniards for every 100 Italians in 1855. In the precinct immediately south of the central plaza (an area of concentrated Spanish settlement; see Maps 5 and 6), the ratio was 239. However, as one moved south along the riverbank toward the Italian enclave of La Boca, the ratio dropped, precinct by precinct, to 107, 34, and 21. This shows that even in their respective enclaves the two groups shared space with each other and that the mixing increased as one reached equidistance from the two enclaves. Indexes of dissimilarity (I_D; see Table 10) confirm the high level of residential mixing between Spaniards and Italians and an even higher level between Spaniards and the French.

In terms of separation from the rest of the population, the indexes of segregation (I_S) in Table 10 show that Italians were less segregated from the rest of the population than Spaniards, who in turn were less segregated than the French. Because values below 25 at the ward level are generally taken as an indication of little segregation, the indexes also suggest fairly even spatial dispersion for the first two groups and moderate segregation for the French. Moreover, even at the precinct and city-block level the indexes of segregation of the three groups remained lower than those of several other migrant groups in New and Old World cities computed at the ward level.

Indeed, the data in Table 11 clearly place Buenos Aires as one of the least ethnically segregated immigrant cities in the world at the time. Newcomers here dispersed more evenly than did so-called old immigrants in U.S. cities and Celtic Britons in English cities—who in turn were less segregated than future migrants (such as southern and eastern Europeans around the turn of the century, black Americans after the Great Depres-

Table 10 Indexes of residential dissimilarity and segregation for Spaniards, Italians, and the French in Buenos Aires, 1855, measured by three areal units

	By ward	By precinct	By city block
	Index of dissimilarity		
Spaniards and Italians	20.4	24.6	35.2
Spaniards and French	18.9	22.4	31.3
French and Italians	28.8	34.4	43.8
	Index of segregation		
Spaniards	17.2	22.8	30.0
Italians	14.9	18.4	26.6
French	27.5	33.0	42.9
Number of units =	12	36	368

SOURCE: Municipal manuscript census returns, 1855.

NOTE: The index of dissimilarity (I_D) represents the percentage of a given group that would have to move in order to achieve complete desegregation vis à vis another group—called index of segregation, or I_S, if the other group is the rest of the population. The values range from 0, complete integration, to 100, complete segregation, with values below 25 or 30 at the ward level generally taken as an indication of little segregation. To give a simple example, if all blacks lived in the "Southside" and all whites in the "Northside," then 100 percent of blacks or 100 percent of whites (or equivalent combinations, say 50 percent of blacks and 50 percent of whites) would have to move in order to accomplish complete integration, thus an index of 100. It is, nevertheless, hypothetically possible to have an index of 0 and still complete actual segregation. For instance, half of the blacks and half of the whites may live in the "Southside" and half in the "Northside," showing a 0 index of dissimilarity, yet blacks may be totally segregated in the western corners of both zones. Theoretically the problem could go on ad infinitum. Both populations may be equally distributed among the city's districts, but all blacks may live in only a few totally segregated blocks within each district, or equally distributed among all blocks and totally segregated in some buildings within each block, and so on. In practical terms we may never encounter such an extreme, but this shows the importance of the measuring areal unit; in general, smaller units produce higher segregation indexes. I thus computed it for the three main immigrant groups in Buenos Aires on the bases of wards or *juzgados* (12 units), precinct or *cuartel* (36 units), and city blocks (the 368 that were platted) to eliminate the possibility that high segregation in small areas could result in misleadingly low indexes.

The size of the population does not affect the index. But small numbers can obviously make the index irrelevant (e.g., the segregation index of, say, ten Eskimos in a city of 10 million).

The formula for the index of dissimilarity is: $I_D = \frac{1}{2} \Sigma \mid X_i\text{-}Y_i \mid$ where X_i represents the proportion of all members of any particular group residing in any areal unit i, and Y_i represents the proportion of all members of the group with which the first group is being compared (or the rest of the population for the I_S) that resides in that areal unit.

For a discussion of the dissimilarity index, see O. Duncan and B. Duncan, "A Methodo-

(continued on next page)

Table 10 (*continued*)

logical Analysis of Segregation Indexes," *American Sociological Review* 20 (April 1955):210–17, who originated it; Nathan Kantrowitz, "The Index of Dissimilarity: A Measurement of Residential Segregation for Historical Analysis," *Historical Methods Newsletter* 7 (September 1974):285–89; and M. J. White, "Segregation and Diversity Measures in Population Distribution," *Population Index* 52 (1986):198–221, who concludes that the I_D remains the best measurement of spatial segregation available. Not only does it have more than 95 percent correlation with other indexes, but its widespread use by sociologists, geographers, and—to a lesser degree—historians facilitates comparisons.

sion, and South Asians and West Indians in England after the 1960s) would be.[35]

The evidence from midnineteenth-century Buenos Aires thus contradicts the concept of ghetto, with much more force than that of North American revisionist works. Clearly, the settlements of Spaniards and other immigrants in the city at the time were the very opposite of homogeneous and impermeable.

On the surface, residential intermixing by class in Buenos Aires seemed to be even more pronounced than its spatial blend of nationalities. The manuscript census schedules for 1855 list peons, stevedores, and washerwomen as neighbors of such distinguished citizens as future presidents Bartolomé Mitre and Domingo Sarmiento and showed that mansions shared city blocks with dilapidated tenements. This conformed to the widespread view of preindustrial "walking cities" as relatively integrated places.[36] Yet as I went over the schedules for the entire city, some documents appeared to list a disproportionate number of laborers and illiterates; even the handwriting of the census takers (local boys who registered their own blocks at a penny per person) seemed to betray lower-class status. The occasional proximity of future presidents and present paupers camouflaged a reality of class segregation.

To measure this reality, I calculated the index of dissimilarity between the literate and illiterate inhabitants of the city. The result (38.2 at the precinct level) indicates significant class segregation, more—at this particular time—than that based on nativity (compare with Table 10).[37] Indeed, because the census takers listed infants as illiterates, this index includes literate parents living with their young children as instances of integration and thus underestimates class segregation. In the case of Spaniards, for whom I can separate minors, literate Spaniards were 25 percent more segregated from their illiterate compatriots than all Spaniards were from the rest of the population.

Table 11 Comparison of immigrant segregation in Buenos Aires and other world cities, ca. midnineteenth century

Group	City	Year	City's total population (000s)	Number of wards	Average population of the ward (000s)	Group's percentage of city's total population	Group's index of segregation
Italians	Buenos Aires	1855	88	12	7	11	14.9
Germans	St. Louis	1860	161	10	16	43	16.0ᵃ
Spaniards	Buenos Aires	1855	88	12	7	6	17.2
English	New York	1855	623	22	8ᵇ	4	20.0
Irish	St. Louis	1860	161	10	16	22	21.0ᵃ
English	St. Louis	1860	161	10	16	5	24.0ᵃ
Irish	Philadelphia	1860	565	24	24	17	25.1
Irish	Boston	1855	160	12	13	29	26.0
French	Buenos Aires	1855	88	12	7	7	27.5
Irish	Detroit	1853	30	8	4	20	27.9
French Canadians	Toronto	1852	30	7	4	2	29.4ᶜ
Irish	New York	1855	630	19	8ᵇ	28	31.0
Welsh	Liverpool	1871	493	16	31	4	33.9
Irish	Philadelphia	1850	409	27	15	18	35.0
Germans	Philadelphia	1860	566	24	24	8	35.3
Scots	Liverpool	1871	493	16	31	4	36.0

Germans	New York	1855	623	22	8[b]	15	36.0
English	Buenos Aires	1855	88	12	7	2	36.6
Irish	Liverpool	1871	493	16	31	16	37.9
Germans	Boston	1855	160	12	13	2	38.6
Irish	Cardiff	1871	40	3	13	9	44.0
Germans	Milwaukee	1860	45	9	5	35	44.1
Irish	Buffalo	1855	72	13	6	18	45.3[d]
Irish	Milwaukee	1860	45	9	5	7	52.7
Blacks	Philadelphia	1850	409	27	15	5	53.0
Germans	Buffalo	1855	72	13	5	39	59.0[d]

SOURCES: Except where noted, the sources for the other cities are: Boston: Stanley Lieberson, *Ethnic Patterns in American Cities* (New York: Free Press of Glencoe, 1963), 78 for indexes, and Peter R. Knights, *The Plain People of Boston, 1830–1860: A Study in City Growth* (New York: Oxford University Press, 1971), 17, 34, 36 for the rest; Buenos Aires: manuscript census returns (people listed in the military, ecclesiastical, maritime, and institutional portions of the census were not counted because they simply lived where the respective institutions were, with no residential choice involved—at any rate, using these parts of the census never altered the I_s by more than a whole number); Cardiff: Richard Dennis, *English Industrial Cities of the Nineteenth Century: A Social Geography* (Cambridge, England: Cambridge University Press, 1984), 224 for the index, and William Rees, *Cardiff: A History of the City* (Cardiff: Corporation of the City of Cardiff, 1969), 298, 320 for the rest; Detroit: calculated from data in JoEllen Vinyard, *The Irish on the Urban Frontier: Nineteenth Century Detroit, 1850–1880* (New York: Arno Press, 1976), 98–100; Liverpool: Colin G. Pooley. "The Residential Segregation of Migrant Communities in Mid-Victorian Liverpool," *Transactions, Institute of British Geographers*, n. s., 2 (1977):366, 372; Milwaukee: Kathleen N. Conzen, *Immigrant Milwaukee, 1836–1860: Accommodation and Community in a Frontier City* (Cambridge, Mass.: Harvard University Press, 1976), 14, 130; New York Germans: Stanley Nadel, *Little Germany: Ethnicity, Religion, and Class in New York City. 1845–80* (Urbana: University of Illinois Press, 1990), 182, gives indexes for Germans of 28.9 in 1855, 31.4 in 1865, and 27.2 in 1875; Philadelphia 1850: Carolyn Adams et al., *Philadelphia: Neighborhoods, Divisions, and Conflict in a Postindustrial City* (Philadelphia: Temple University, 1991), 9–10; Philadelphia 1860: Lesley Ann Kawaguchi, "The Making of Philadelphia's German-America: Ethnic Group and Community Development, 1830–1883" (Ph.D. diss., University of California, Los Angeles, 1983), 188, 193, and Alan N. Burstein, "Immigrants and Residential Mobility: The Irish and Germans in Philadelphia, 1850–1880," in *Philadelphia: Work, Space, Family, and Group Experience in the 19th Century*, ed. Theodore Hershberg (New York: Oxford University Press, 1981), 180.

(continued on next page)

Table 11 (continued)

NOTE: Because smaller measuring units usually generate higher indexes, and vice versa, the gap between Buenos Aires and those cities with significantly more populous wards (St. Louis, Philadelphia, Boston, Liverpool, and Cardiff) is probably wider than the values indicate.

[a]Index and percentage based on a sample of heads of families (Fredrick A. Hodes, "The Urbanization of St. Louis: A Study in Urban Residential Patterns in the Nineteenth Century" [Ph.D. diss., Saint Louis University, 1973], 36, 40).

[b]Index based on fourteen sample electoral districts from wards 4, 5, 9, and 10, with a total population of 110,846 and an average population of 7,918 (Kenneth A. Scherzer, The Unbounded Community: Neighborhood Life and Social Structure in New York City, 1830–1875 (Durham, N.C.: Duke University Press, 1992), 54, 59, 214. I used Scherzer's indexes because the measuring areal unit is more comparable in size to Buenos Aires' wards. The indexes for the whole city, using the twenty-two wards with an average size of 28,315, are: English, 9.8; Irish, 17.7; and Germans, 30.1. Computed from data in Robert Ernst, Immigrant Life in New York City, 1825–1863 (New York: Columbia University Press, 1949), 193–94.

[c]Index of dissimilarity of French Canadians from the English-born population. Their I_s is not given by Warren E. Kalbach, Historical and Generational Perspectives of Ethnic Residential Segregation in Toronto, Canada: 1851–1971, Research Paper no. 118 (Toronto: University of Toronto Centre for Urban and Community Studies, 1980), 13.

[d]Index and percentage based on heads of family and computed against native-born instead of I_s (Laurence A. Glasco, Ethnicity and Social Structure: Irish, Germans and Native-Born of Buffalo, N.Y., 1850–1860 (New York: Arno Press, 1980), 20, 60, and 66.

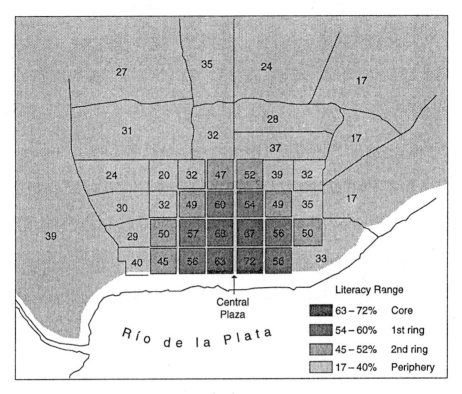

Map 7. Literacy rates in Buenos Aires, by district, 1855.

My analysis of the general population's literacy for every precinct (usually an area of four by four blocks) not only shows significant segregation but also a citywide pattern analogous to Burgess' concentric-zones layout in a perfectly inverse way. That is, whereas in the Burgess model the socioeconomic status of inhabitants increased from ring to ring as one moved outward from the city core, in midcentury Buenos Aires it steadily declined (see Map 7). Again, the registration of infants as illiterates if anything underestimates the gap from ring to ring.

If occupation and wages are added to literacy as measures of social status, the results confirm the residential centralization of the better-off groups. As Table 12 shows, among the Spanish born, clerks earned twice as much as did unskilled laborers, were three times as literate, and were five times as likely to live in the downtown area.[38] Domestic servants, who typically lived in the houses of those who could afford them, were the only lower-status workers to concentrate in the central quarters.

Table 12 Zones of residence of all Spaniards, Spanish clerks, unskilled laborers, and servants in Buenos Aires, 1855 (in percentages)

Zone	All Spaniards	Clerks	Unskilled laborers	Servants
Core	29	56	11	46
First ring	27	20	15	30
Second ring	14	10	10	9
Periphery	30	14	64	15
Total	100	100	100	100
Number	5,310	427	1,042	332
Percent literate	56	96	32	46
Average monthly wages in pesos	–	800	400	390

SOURCES: Municipal manuscript census returns, 1855; average wages computed from a list of salaries in Estado de Buenos Aires, *Rejistro [sic] estadístico correspondiente al semestre 1⁰ de 1855 segunda época*, nos. 5 and 6 (Buenos Aires: Imprenta Porteña, 1855), 60.

NOTE: Core = precincts 3, 4, 11, and 12; first ring = precincts 2, 5, 10, 13, 18, and 19; second ring = 6, 9, 14, 17, 20, 26, and 27; periphery = all other precincts.

Although Burgess' concentric-zones layout refers to the city as a whole, his disciples applied it to particular ethnic groups and detected the same pattern of increasing socioeconomic status with increasing distance from the core.[39] Again, 1850s Buenos Aires inverts the model. Within each major immigrant group the literacy rate declined as distance from the center of the city increased. Moreover, those nationalities with higher literacy rates also showed the highest rate of centralization: 72 percent of the English, 61 percent of the French, 56 percent of Spaniards, and 41 percent of Italians were literate; in the same rank, 44 percent of the English, 41 percent of the French, 29 percent of Spaniards, and 16 percent of Italians lived in the four central precincts. Tellingly, when a contemporary observer ranked the immigrant groups in terms of socioeconomic status, he ranked them in precisely the same order.[40]

North American historians debate whether their midnineteenth-century "walking cities" already mirrored Burgess' concentric-zones layout or still reflected its inverse.[41] For contemporary Buenos Aires the latter was clearly the case. The privileged few obviously could not dominate numerically the densely populated central quarters, nor could the less fortunate majority be totally relegated to the outskirts. Some class intermixing was physically unavoidable. Nonetheless, class spatial differentiation not only marked the city but also formed a centripetency where the better off, not simply the rich, gravitated toward the core in a remarkably concentric pattern. A central-enclave-to-suburb move at this time would have represented downward mobility.

Settlement Patterns of Spanish Regional Groups

As in other aspects of the migration experience, the interaction between regional origin and socioeconomic status always proved to be a better predictor of residential patterns than did the combination of nationality and class. Moreover, the emigration patterns of the group, not necessarily the level of development in their region of origin, would often determine their socioeconomic success and consequent residential centralization.

Andalusia, for example, was, if anything, one of the most backward regions of the Iberian Peninsula characterized by unproductive latifundia and a landless, impoverished peasantry. Yet Andalusians in Buenos Aires exhibited the highest literacy rate among Spanish regional groups, the lowest concentration in low-skilled occupations, and the highest concentration in skilled, high nonmanual, and professional jobs. They had a virtual monopoly on distinctive "Andalusian" occupations, such as actors, guitar makers, and comedians, and on less colorful ones, such as watchmakers. Predictably, they were also the most centralized Iberian regional group: 47 percent lived in the city's four central precincts.

Ironically, the relatively high status of Andalusian immigrants was the indirect product of the feature often blamed for the region's impoverishment: latifundia and the resulting nucleated, Mediterranean-type, rural settlements. Regions characterized by large estates have customarily displayed low emigration rates, particularly in the nineteenth century.[42] Some scholars have argued that the peasantry there was more prone to seek a solution to their grievances in millenarian rebellions rather than overseas departures.[43] Whatever the merits of such an explanation, latifundia and the resulting concentrated rural settlements in Andalusia clearly inhibited the diffusion of information that, as we saw in the last chapter, preceded and accompanied the spread of emigration fever. In preindustrial times, news and new behaviors could not disseminate easily where totally uninhabited expanses and faulty roads (or none at all) separated population centers. In a vicious cycle, the dependence of the landless peasantry on prepaid passages or overseas remittances for their fare further retarded the formation of transatlantic information and assistance networks. Vaguely aware of the lands across the ocean and even less informed about how to get there, the Andalusian peasantry stayed home for much of the nineteenth century. For many the choice between rebellion and departure was simply not there at the time. Therefore, the majority of Andalusians in Buenos Aires originated in areas along the main channels of information with well-established American connections: cities with transatlantic ports or those near them, particularly Cádiz, El Puerto de Santa María, Gibraltar, and Málaga.

This emigration pattern explains their settlement choice. The retarded and meager exodus of the peasantry and the resulting urban background of the arrivals led to a relatively high occupational status, which in turn led to residential centralization. So did the fact that they came through resurrected chains that had lain dormant during the postindependence chaos but dated back to the late eighteenth century, when Cádiz was the main commercial link between the metropolis and the River Plate viceroyalty. As shown in chapter 3, in the dormant chains the previous success of immigrants determined how long transatlantic family ties could survive without actual physical contact. Most Andalusians in the 1850s thus arrived under the auspices of rich and aged "uncles," crafty old merchants who had weathered the anti-Spanish storm of independence and had preserved the riches imperial mercantilism once made possible. This ex-colonial mercantile elite had settled in what was then the city's commercial hub, the precincts just south of the central plaza, and their newly arriving "nephews" and "nieces" naturally followed them there.

Andalusians were also one of the few Spanish groups in Buenos Aires for whom Castilian was a native tongue. It is possible that this, along with their proverbial loquaciousness, may in part account for their centralized settlement pattern, because it could procure them jobs in the city's commerce as salespersons. Yet the other Castilian-speaking regional group, the Canary Islanders, were the least centralized group—only 7 percent, as opposed to 47 percent of the Andalusians, lived in the four central precincts. Again, migration patterns provide the principal explanation. The Canary archipelago was not significantly less developed than Andalusia. In fact, around the middle of the century it had enjoyed an economic boom based on the export of cochineal that, according to a contemporary historian, had benefited all social classes.[44] But the *canarios* had few previous kinship ties in Argentina. Most had come, as we saw in the previous chapter, under the auspices of unsuccessful and, as it turned out, highly exploitative colonization schemes in the 1830s. Many of those in Buenos Aires in

1855 appear on an 1836 list of immigrants who had not been able to re-imburse the Argentine government for the passages it had advanced.[45] If there was a group in the city that fit the old stereotype of immigrants as wretched refuse, the islanders were surely it. They had the lowest literacy rate, highest concentration in menial occupations, and highest incidence of widowhood of all regional groups. Some ended up in the poorhouse or the insane asylum. Their condition influenced their settlement. A disproportionate number lived in the northeastern ward near the Recoleta cloisters (the poorest in the city), where they once had sought refuge—ironically, the most select part of town today. Others roamed the farm areas on the periphery, where they had served as de facto indentured servants. As was the case with the Andalusians, however, those with better jobs tended to live in the central quarters.

Settlement Patterns of Hometown Groups

This pattern of inter- and intragroup residential separation found at the national and regional level was also present at the more confined level of town or village of origin. As Table 13A shows, immigrants from Bilbao were more literate and skilled, richer, and more likely to employ domestic servants than were immigrants from Ferrol, a town of about the same size (18,000) but less commercially and industrially significant and in a less developed region of Spain. The latter, in turn, ranked much higher on the same indicators than did the newcomers from the Baztán Valley in northern Navarre, one of the richest and most egalitarian zones in the peninsula but basically agropastoral in nature. The transferability of skills was thus more important in this rank than was the relative prosperity of the locality of origin. Some immigrants from the Baztán Valley, for instance, would eventually amass great fortunes in sheep and cattle raising. But this Old World skill was of limited immediate value in the urban milieu and of little long-term value for those who stayed there. Whatever the origin of their inequalities, Table 13B shows how the local groups with higher socioeconomic status were more residentially centralized, and Table 13C displays how within each of the three groups the better-off members were more centralized.

Map 8 illustrates this interaction between local origin and socioeconomic status in the settlement patterns of immigrants from Ferrol. These newcomers did not form a single nucleus but clustered together neverthe-less: only 1 of the 112 identified Ferroleans in the city lived more than four blocks away from a *paisano,* and only 5 lived more than two blocks

Table 13 Socioeconomic status and place of residence in Buenos Aires, in 1855, of immigrants from Bilbao, Ferrol, and the Baztán Valley (in percentages)

A. Indicators of socioeconomic status

	N	Literate	Unskilled	Low non-manual	Medium and high nonmanual	Has servants
Bilbao	75	75	13	34	15	12
Ferrol	112	55	33	24	8	2
Baztán	81	23	66	12	2	0

B. Area of residence

	Core	First ring	Second ring	Periphery
Bilbao	43	25	13	19
Ferrol	41	8	19	32
Baztán	16	16	0	68

C. Intragroup segregation[a]

	Bilbao		Ferrol		Baztán	
	Literate	*Illiterate*	*Literate*	*Illiterate*	*Literate*	*Illiterate*
Center	46	33	50	30	37	10
First ring	26 (72)	22 (55)	11 (61)	4 (34)	32 (69)	11 (21)
Second ring	14 (86)	11 (66)	18 (79)	20 (54)	0 (69)	0 (21)
Periphery	14	34	21	46	31	79

SOURCE: Municipal manuscript census returns, 1855. See table 12 for precincts included in each zone.

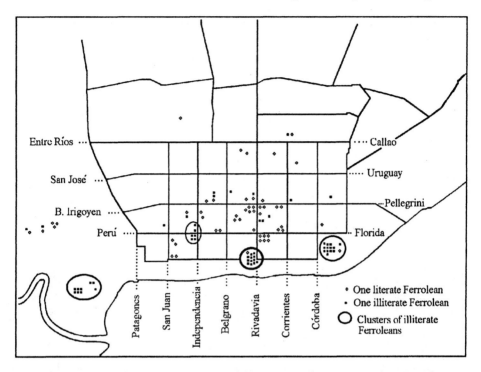

Map 8. Social-class segregation (as measured by literacy) of immigrants from Ferrol, Galicia, residing in Buenos Aires in 1855.

away. At the same time, however, the map depicts a significant level of intragroup class segregation. Thirty-six of the 50 illiterate Ferroleans lived in four clearly defined clusters (three being poor peripheral zones and the other, a central lower-class strip on the riverbank inhabited by a polyglot mélange of sailors, peons, washerwomen, and prostitutes). Only 3 of their 62 literate *paisanos* resided here. These settlement patterns suggest not the traditional, class-blind migration chain of North American and Australian historiography but a series of class-divided ones.[46]

Even in its traditional form, the concept of chain migration clearly enhances our capacity to predict. After all, if all we knew about prospective Spanish immigrants was their nationality, we could only say that there was a 5 percent chance that they would settle in any one of four specific blocks in the city; if we knew that they were from Ferrol, the chances would zoom to 31 percent. However, if we also knew that the prospective Ferrolean immigrants could not read or write, the chances would zoom again, to 66 percent. In other words, integrating social class into the chain-

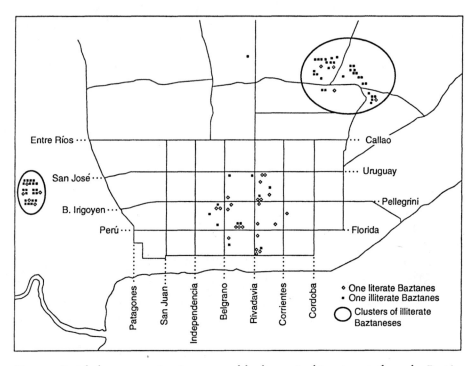

Map 9.   Social-class segregation (as measured by literacy) of immigrants from the Baztán Valley, Navarre, residing in Buenos Aires in 1855.

migration concept doubled our capacity to predict specifically where prospective emigrants would settle.

Map 9 shows the same general clustering and intragroup class segregation among the immigrants from the Baztán Valley. It also indicates the importance of immigration patterns in residential choice. As with the other groups, illiterate Baztanese were more likely to reside in the periphery than were their literate townsfolk. Yet unlike the flows from Ferrol and Bilbao, which dated back to the late colonial period, the flow from Baztán went back only to the 1830s and the emergence of sheep raising on the pampas. They therefore lacked the ties to the spatially centralized merchant elite of colonial times, with the result that literate Baztanese were less likely to reside in the central quarters than were the literate immigrants from Ferrol and Bilbao. Indeed, only two of the eighty-one identifiable Baztanese in the city lived in the main Spanish neighborhood on the southern edge of the central plaza. Also, if we compare this map with

Map 8, we can see that although illiterate immigrants from both the Baztán Valley and Ferrol were overrepresented on the periphery, the two groups resided in different sections of that zone. That is, their shared low status concentrated them in poorer areas of the city, but within these areas they were totally segregated from each other, solely on the basis of Old World ties and the chain-migration process.

Indeed, although the combination of socioeconomic status and local origin clearly represented the most powerful predictor of residential choice, when the variables were separated, the latter always proved a better predictor than the former. This is due in part to the fact that the hometown variable implicitly included information about the level and type of skills of the immigrants, the resulting occupational status, and thus their residential choice. However, the predictive capacity of the hometown variable went beyond its implication of social class. In a sense, the whole process also created a new variable that was to affect future settlement: the existence of a network of already established influential kin and paisanos.

The case of the Durañona family from Bilbao serves as an illustration. Ramón, a seventy-two-year-old widowed ex-merchant who had come to Buenos Aires in 1797, lived off his rents with his servant on Victoria Street (now H. Yrigoyen), three blocks south of the central plaza. Forty-seven years later, passenger records list his relative Martín coming via Montevideo, but Martín does not appear in the city's census schedules for 1855. In 1849 Casimiro (another relative) arrived, followed a year later by Antonio (Ramón's nephew) and his wife. Antonio's good grammar and mathematical skills landed him a job in the store of an old Bilbaoan friend of his uncle two blocks from the latter's residence. Illiterate, Casimiro lacked the preparation for a job in commerce. But he was given a job as an attendant in the Bilbaoan-owned jai alai court around the corner. It is probable that literate Antonio would have found a similar job and lived in a similar area had he not been from Bilbao. If illiterate Casimiro, on the other hand, had been born in the Baztán Valley instead of Bilbao, his chances of working in a handball court in the center of town instead of at a brick oven or slaughterhouse on the city's fringe would have been less than one in ten. In a sense, Casimiro possessed an invisible skill that assisted him in his adaptation to the host city: the social network created by his economically successful predecessors in the chain. As was the case in general, patterns set early in the process became independent variables in determining future settlement, sometimes even in the face of rapid change.

FROM GRAN ALDEA TO GRAND METROPOLIS

A Spanish immigrant in early-twentieth-century Buenos Aires reproached the pomposity of a chant he heard students intoning on their way home from the university as an example of Porteño vanity:

> Calle Esparta su virtud,
> su grandeza calle Roma.
> ¡Silencio! Que al mundo asoma . . .
> la gran capital del Sud.[47]

> Let Sparta silence her virtue,
> let Rome hush her grandeur.
> Silence! That on the world arises . . .
> the great capital of the South.

The lines may have been pompous, but the students had a point. "The great capital of the South" did arise on the world urban scene with amazing vigor and speed. In the 1850s Mexico City and Rio de Janeiro had twice as many inhabitants as did Buenos Aires; and Salvador da Bahia, Lima, Santiago (Chile), and Havana surpassed it.[48] By 1890 the Argentine capital exceeded all other Latin American cities in population. On the Atlantic seaboard of the midnineteenth century, no fewer than eighteen cities, from Bristol to Boston and Baltimore to Bordeaux, surpassed Buenos Aires in population.[49] By 1914 only New York did. It was then, as proud Porteños put it, the second largest "Latin" city in the world—after Paris—and the largest of any kind south of the equator (see Table 14).

Constant geographical expansion accompanied this demographic ascent.[50] An Italian physician who visited Buenos Aires every three years between 1854 and 1863 claimed that continual growth made a painting of the city "true today, inexact tomorrow, false next year."[51] And this only heralded the urban onslaught on the pampas. Georges Clemenceau observed in 1910 that the lack of natural obstacles, the rise in value of central building plots, and perpetual speculation combined to push the urban edge ever farther into the grasslands.[52] The city now sprawled over some 125 square kilometers and more than 4,700 platted blocks, a far cry from the 14 square kilometers and 400 blocks of 1850.[53] The Catalan economist Federico Rahola remembered "riding the tram through sixty-five kilometers of perfectly paved and urbanized streets" in 1905; only in London had he seen such distances.[54] The French prime minister agreed that "one of the peculiarities of Buenos Aires is that you can see no end to it".[55] And, on his 1929 visit, Le Corbusier went further and recommended a legal ban to halt the incessant expansion of the city.[56]

Table 14 Total and Spanish-born population, Buenos Aires, 1855–1936

	Total population			Spaniards	
Year	Number	Percentage of population born abroad	Number	Percentage of total population	Percentage of population born abroad
1855	91,395	36	5,792	6.3	17.6
1869	177,787	52	14,609	8.2	15.9
1887	433,373	53	39,562	9.1	17.3
1895	663,854	52	80,352	12.1	23.3
1904	950,891	45	105,206	11.1	24.6
1909	1,231,698	46	174,291	14.2	31.1
1914	1,575,814	51	306,850	19.5	38.5
1936	2,415,142	36	324,650	13.4	37.3

SOURCES: Estado de Buenos Aires, *Rejistro [sic] estadístico correspondiente al semestre 1º de 1855 segunda época*, nos. 5 and 6 (Buenos Aires: Imprenta Porteña, 1855); Buenos Aires, Dirección General de Estadística Municipal, *Censo general de población, edificación, comercio e industrias de la ciudad de Buenos Aires, 1887*, 2 vols. (Buenos Aires: Compañía Sud-Americana de Billetes de Banco, 1889); idem, *Censo general de población, edificación, comercio e industrias de la ciudad de Buenos Aires, 1904* (Buenos Aires: Compañía Sud-Americana de Billetes de Banco, 1906); idem, *Censo general de población, edificación, comercio e industrias de la ciudad de Buenos Aires, 1909*, 3 vols. (Buenos Aires: Compañía Sud-Americana de Billetes de Banco, 1910); Buenos Aires, Comisión Técnica Encargada de Realizar el Cuarto Censo General, *Cuarto censo general, 1936*, 4 vols. (Buenos Aires: Talleres Gráficos de Guillermo Kraft, 1938); Argentina, Superintendente del Censo, *Primer censo de la República Argentina, 1869* (Buenos Aires: Impr. del Porvenir, 1872); Argentina, Comisión Directiva del Censo, *Segundo censo de la República Argentina, 1895*, 3 vols. (Buenos Aires: Taller Tip. de la Penitenciaria Nacional, 1898); and Argentina, Comisión Nacional del Censo, *Tercer censo nacional, 1914*, 10 vols. (Buenos Aires: Talleres Gráficos de L. J. Rosso, 1916–1919).

Infrastructural development kept abreast of spatial expansion. Even a reserved Scottish reverend could not fail to notice on his 1906 return, "[W]hat a marvelous change had taken place in the harbour of Buenos Aires since 1881!"[57] The construction of a deepwater port in the mid-1890s had eliminated the colorful disembarkation ritual remembered by so many travelers. "Now," added the Caledonian pastor, "steamers and sailing ships are berthed alongside wharves as good as any in the old country." By 1910, 15,000 ships and 9 million tons of cargo—about three times the freight of 1895—entered a harbor wrung by human artifice and tenacity from an uncooperative river that daily deposited its own cargo of silt. Only constant dredging kept the then twelfth busiest port in the world from reverting into a mud bank.

Before extracting the River Plate's silt, the municipality began to tap its more obvious resource. Water, ironically, had been traditionally a scarce and expensive commodity next to the world's second widest estuary.[58] Turn-of-the-century Porteños still remembered how their parents kept potable water "locked, like a precious liquid."[59] Well water was brackish and often contaminated by the seepage of privies.[60] Those who could afford to, built cisterns under their courtyards to collect the rain that fell on their roofs. The rest depended on the muddy liquid taken by itinerant water carriers from the river's edge. In 1870, however, the municipal authorities, spurred by an outbreak of cholera that killed 15,000 inhabitants, ordered the construction of a water system that pumped thirteen liters per capita per day—a significant increase from the estimated two liters of 1852.[61] In the following decades the extension of the pipelines, mightier pumps, and the construction of a two-hectare waterworks multiplied that volume, absolutely and in comparison with other cities (see Table 15). In 1880 Buenos Aires' per capita water consumption amounted to only 13 percent of London's; by 1900 it equaled it; by 1920 it doubled it and reached two-thirds the level of water-guzzling North American cities.[62] Civic authorities proudly equated the "degree of culture and progress of a city" with "the amount of water consumed by each of its inhabitants," and extolled the water pipes as "the veins of a living organism."[63]

As the veins expanded, so did the arteries. As late as 1880 a North American woman missionary could complain about the lack of natural or artificial drainage that made even paved streets an impassable slush during the rainy season.[64] Just a decade later, however, an English resident regarded the "famous drainage" as the greatest public work in the city, surpassing the opening of the celebrated Avenida de Mayo and other "monumental records of edile imbecility";[65] and a Spanish visitor referred to the sewer system as "reputedly, one of foremost in the world."[66] By the end of World War I, about 4,000 kilometers of sewer lines covered the entire Federal District.

Municipal water and sewers changed the city in many ways. Wells, cisterns, and ambulatory water carriers eventually became no more than memories. So did the washerwomen of the riverbank. Photographs of 1888 still show the strand covered with hanging sheets and kneeling women—by then mostly white—scrubbing clothes on the puddles left in the stony

Table 15 Consumption of running water in Buenos Aires, in comparison with other world cities, 1870–1923

| | | | Buenos Aires' per capita daily consumption as a percentage of that in other world cities | | | |
Year	Piped water use (000s of m³)	Liters per capita per day	London	Paris	New York	Boston
1870	880	13	–	–	4	3
1875	1,303	17	–	–	–	–
1880	1,749	17	13	9	6	–
1885	4,128	29	24	–	–	–
1890	9,352	49	39	20	13	–
1895	30,855	130	97	–	–	35
1900	39,673	133	102	–	–	–
1905	48,512	131	106	–	33	–
1910	62,126	130	–	95	–	–
1915	90,823	155	–	–	–	–
1920	158,685	258	195	–	63	67
1923	201,040	307	–	–	–	–

SOURCES: Buenos Aires, Dirección General de Estadística Municipal, *Anuario Estadístico de la Ciudad de Buenos Aires*, 1891 (first date of publication), 1895, 1900, 1905, 1910, and 1915–1923 (a summary volume). London's figures computed from data on population and water use in London, Metropolitan Water Board, *London's Water Supply, 1903–1953* (London: Staples Press, 1953), 100–3, 140–41, 358; Paris', from Laure Beaumont-Maillet, *L'Eau à Paris* (Paris: Hazan, 1991), 194, 199, 221, and Colin Dyer, *Population and Society in Twentieth Century France* (New York: Holmes & Meier, 1978), 9; New York's, from data on population and use in Charles H. Weidner, *Water for a City: A History of New York City's Problem from the Beginning to the Delaware River System* (New Brunswick, N.J.: Rutgers University Press, 1974), 54, 58, 164, 280–83; Boston's, from Fern L. Nesson, *Great Waters: A History of Boston's Water Supply* (Hanover, N.H., and London: University Press of New England, 1983), 10, 18, 44.

riverbed by the receding tide.[67] Over the next decade commercial steam cleaners, water spigots at home, and public laundries, together with the construction of the port, eliminated what the magazine *Caras y Caretas* then called "one of the most typical and picturesque aspects of Buenos Aires' physiognomy."[68] Water trucks assisted an army of Galician and

Neapolitan sweepers in keeping the streets clean. Municipal water made hosing the sidewalks a Porteño habit that endures until this day. In contrast to the French visitor who compared them to sewers in 1850, early-twentieth-century travelers found Buenos Aires' streets as "swept and washed as the floors of a salon."[69]

Running water was not the only element to improve municipal sanitation. The disappearance of the horse tram in 1910 helped the street sweepers in a different way, and so did the increasing replacement of dirt roads with cobblestones, granite, concrete, or asphalt. The introduction in 1902 of the septic tank represented an antiseptic blessing for privies in the city's outer environs.[70] Municipal trash collection expanded steadily from the 1870s, ending the practice of dumping private garbage on vacant lots or the public thoroughfare and helping to turn dozens of foul dumps into some of Buenos Aires' most beautiful plazas and gardens.[71] A related municipal service began in 1887, when the police, "fearing that the alarming procreation of stray dogs would turn the city into a second Constantinople," decided to poison them.[72] Dogs' foes seem to have fared no better. A Spanish resident in 1910 noted with surprise and dismay the lack of cats in the city, which he attributed to the scarcity of rats and the rushed pace of family life.[73] Together, these municipal services must have had an impressive effect. In 1852 an English squire, offended by the stench of carcasses on the streets, muttered "Buenos Ayres! What a misnomer!"[74] Four decades later his compatriot May Crommelin exclaimed, "'Good Airs!' Such is, literally translated, the rightful name of this great town."[75] By then most other visitors echoed this opinion.[76]

Combined with the other services, the expansion or popularization of running potable water, bathtubs, sinks, toilets, and free public baths contributed to another persistent observation by visitors: the tidy and healthy appearance of the population. A sociologist from the University of Wisconsin found Porteños "as tall as New Yorkers . . . clean, ruddy and vigorous."[77] In more absolute terms, the Mexican José Vasconcelos described them as "a new and healthy race; a beautiful race of tall robust lads and splendid, firmly slender women, of a vim and luxuriance found in no other place."[78] A Catalan economist noted that not even the working class would wear the soiled blouses common among the proletariat of Barcelona and Paris, which gave the city a "bourgeois air."[79] And the Valencian novelist Blasco Ibáñez went further and ventured an explanation for the tidy aspect of the population: "The first influence Argentina exercises on certain immigrants is to teach them to wash and dress cleanly."[80] The decline of infectious diseases, death rates, and infant mortality corroborate the visitors' observations.[81] By 1910 Buenos Aires' death rate was below that of New York, Paris, or Vienna.[82] Its infant-mortality rate of 8.8 per hundred live births compared favorably with London's 11.0, Berlin's 15.4, Madrid's 21.0, St. Petersburg's 28.9, and Cairo's 37.6.[83] Among major cities, only those in Scandinavia showed lower rates than Buenos Aires.

Early-twentieth-century visitors and immigrants were more dazzled by Buenos Aires' profusion of public lighting than by the low mortality rates of its public. After its introduction in 1881, electricity steadily began to supplant gas in street lamps, just as gas had elbowed out oil and tallow candles earlier. By 1910 a correspondent from "the City of Lights," no less, would admit that "the abundance of electric bulbs" made the streets of Buenos Aires "very well lit, much more so than our Parisian streets."[84] That same year a Madrileño globetrotter felt that no other city in the world spent so much electric energy on street lights and that Argentines suffered from "illumination mania.[85] And four years later an Englishman concurred, remarking that "the electric bulb is to Buenos Ayres as the seaweed or the limpet to a rocky shore. Except along Broadway, no New Yorker ever looks on such prodigality of electric lamps. . . . No wonder the electricians love Buenos Ayres!"[86]

Public transportation had an unpromising beginning in 1852 with the introduction of the omnibus, a glorified urban version of the stagecoach that proved "an exotic plant of impossible acclimatization" to Buenos Aires' infamous potholes.[87] The railroad, introduced five years later, was pivotal to Argentine economic development but less momentous to urban transportation because the terminals were outside the city's central districts and the stops far apart.[88] Not without its irony in "the age of machines," the horse tram routed the iron horse when it came to moving city dwellers. Introduced in 1869, horse trams carried 2.3 million passengers just a year later and more than 100 million by the end of the century (see Table 16). Mechanical innovation eventually prevailed over animal power with the appearance in 1898 of the electric streetcar. In 1905 two Scottish missionaries on their way to Bolivia observed that "electric tramways cross each other at almost every corner and everyone rides even for very short distances."[89] Five years later, *The Times* labeled it "one of the most remarkable tramway systems in the world . . . three times the mileage of London's!";[90] a tourist guidebook referred to Buenos Aires as "the City of Tramways";[91] and a rather fastidious English tourist could muster only one complaint against them: "the tram-men's disconcerting habit of going on strike."[92] This labor "habit" apparently could not curb Porteños' riding habit—as contemporaries termed the measure of per capita usage.

Table 16 Public transportation in Buenos Aires, 1870–1930

Number of passengers by mode of transportation (in 000s).

Year	Total population (in 000s)	Railroad	Horse tram	Electric streetcar	Subway	Bus	Total	Number of rides per capita	Kilometers of streetcar lines
1870	187	1,100	2,376	–	–	–	3,476	19	30
1875	214	n.a.	13,744	–	–	–	13,744	64	126
1880	287	n.a.	13,617	–	–	–	13,617	47	–
1885	395[a]	3,632	27,236	–	–	–	30,868	78	150
1890	527	6,478	56,141	–	–	–	62,619	119	247
1895	650	n.a.	84,992	–[b]	–	–	84,992	131	383
1900	816	11,348	100,605	22,282	–	–	134,235	165	450
1905	1,014	15,030	54,487	114,455	–	–	183,972	181	483
1910	1,307	21,788	142	323,648	–[c]	–	345,578	264	647
1915	1,563	33,576[d]	–[e]	352,353	30,548	–	416,477	266	801
1920	1,629	43,285	–	479,412	41,323	–[f]	564,020	346	809
1925	1,914	84,163	–	601,220	62,235	99,041	846,659	442	837
1930	2,254	106,285	–	542,362	75,256	372,787	1,096,690	486	844

SOURCES: Population data from N. Besio Moreno, *Buenos Aires* (Buenos Aires, 1939), 429–31; other data from various volumes of Buenos Aires, Dirección General de Estadística Municipal, *Anuario estadístico de la ciudad de Buenos Aires, 1891–1923*, and of the *Revista de economía argentina, 1924–1932*.

a. The numbers are for 1887, not 1885.
b. Service began in 1898.
c. Service began in 1913.
d. Numbers include suburban passengers after 1915.
e. Service ended in 1913.
f. Service began in 1922.

With 246 rides per person that year, they proved more mobile than English, German, or Austrian urbanites, though still less so than North Americans.[93] The appearance of the subway in 1913, only six years after its New York debut, helped them catch up. In less than two years the *subte* was moving 30 million people annually. In 1930 it carried 75 million. That year, with the help of the recently introduced bus, public transit hauled more than a billion people, making the "Parisians of the South" the most mobile people on earth—with the exception of the Parisians themselves.[94]

As mass transit expanded, so did individual modes of transportation. In 1905 a Catalan traveler observed that "few cities in the world surpass Buenos Aires in the abundance of cabs, despite the vastness of its tramway network."[95] There were then 3,320 of these horse-drawn carriages for hire, a number that peaked to just over 4,000 in 1916.[96] After that the machine again displaced the beast. The 9 automobiles introduced in 1903 multiplied to 20,000 within twenty years, half of them taxicabs.[97] These shared Buenos Aires' thoroughfares with a diminishing number of carriages (1,700 in 1923) and a poorly recorded, but increasing, number of bicycles, motorcycles, bicycles with motors, and other hybrids.[98]

The radial expansion and infrastructural development of the city allowed and encouraged the hallmark of urban modernization: spatial specialization. The mass-transit system facilitated the separation of home and work. The extension of municipal water, sewer, drainage, garbage collection, paving, and lighting lured many to previously undesirable residential neighborhoods. The construction of the deepwater port shifted shipping facilities and related commercial activities north of the central plaza, accentuating the nonresidential character of the area.

In addition to the commercial-residential division in land use, business areas themselves became increasingly differentiated. A financial district, christened La City in a bout of Anglophilia or grandiosity, came to occupy an area of three by four blocks just north of the central Plaza de Mayo. To a supercilious Spanish visitor the rows of banks and the frenzied pace could not impress anyone who had seen Cannon Street and the original "City," but they could easily awe "the humble Gallego or the Genoese laborer."[99] Just west of this area, the tramless Florida assured its position as the city's premier luxury shopping street, compared, depending on the nationality of the visitor, with the Rue de la Paix, Bond Street, Fifth Avenue, Via Veneto, or the Carrera de San Jerónimo.[100] Travelers described it as a Vanity Fair, where Lalique, Brindau, Tiffany's and Harrod's branches, elite clubs, art nouveau furniture stores, jewelers, furriers, luxury-car dealers and, to the surprise of a Londoner, no less luxurious bootblack's saloons elbowed out "shops devoted to the more sober necessities of life." Despite the increasing vogue of Avenida de Mayo and Callao Street, it was still here that genteel ladies engaged in the new habit of "shoping" [sic], the gilded youth flirted, and poor immigrant families in their Sunday best window shopped. Farther west, an entertainment district took shape along Cuyo and Corrientes streets. It included anything from the grand opera house (the Teatro Colón) to "cinematograph shows for men only, which for indecency cannot be outdone in Port Said or Havana."[101] Some ten blocks westward, around the Plaza Once, wholesale and cheaper retail outfits colored the area. And continuing a trend already visible in the 1860s, the search for more and cheaper land and municipal regulations pushed industries, particularly of the "unhealthy, dangerous, and annoying" type, into the southern and southwestern districts of the city. Tanneries, sawmills, breweries, distilleries, brick factories, ironworks, and warehouses concentrated in La Boca, Barracas, and San Cristóbal Sud (districts 2, 3, and 4 on Map 10C); the municipal dump occupied the adjacent Barrio de las Ranas (Neighborhood of the Frogs); and slaughterhouses and meat-packing plants moved farther west to the aptly named Mataderos and Nueva Chicago in census district 1.

Differentiation also increased in residential space. As the rustic cattle barons and modest local elite of the midnineteenth century turned into the world-class oligarchy that gave rise to the French expression *riche comme un argentine*, an exclusive, upper-class quarter developed in Barrio Norte (in the northern half of census district 20 and the eastern part of district 19). A Spanish immigrant novelist poignantly depicted the beaux arts mansions there as "suggestresses of dreams in the minds of the needy in this their 'Redeeming City'."[102] Whether the needy also became more spatially isolated is difficult to determine.[103] Clearly, they were too numerous to concentrate in any one place; but the southern districts, particularly neighborhoods to which polluting and unhealthy industries had moved, contained a disproportionate number of them. At the bottom of the pyramid, scavengers scratched a living from the municipal dump in the Barrio de las Ranas (in district 2) and shared it with a group of petty entrepreneurs—many of them recent Spanish arrivals—who "made a handy profit by fattening herds of pigs on such leftovers."[104] Working- and lower-middle class neighborhoods appeared throughout the Federal District with the expansion of the streetcar, often surrounding older and higher-class population nuclei that had formed when the more expensive railroad pro-

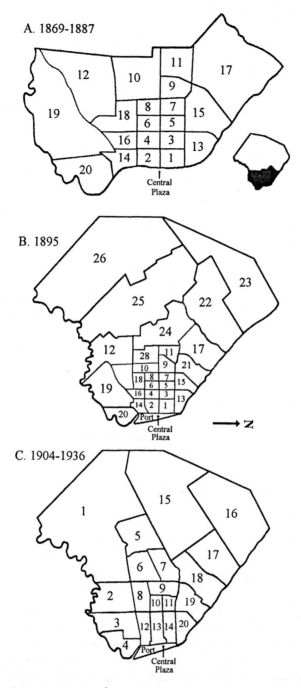

A. 1869-1887

11
12
10
9
17
8 7
19 18 15
6 5
16 4 3
13
14 2 1
20
↑
Central
Plaza

B. 1895

26
25
23
24
22
12
28 11
10 9 17
18 8 7 21
19 6 5 15
16 4 3
14 2 1 13
20 Port ↑
Central
Plaza

→ N

C. 1904-1936

1
15
16
5
6 7
17
9 18
2 8
10 11 19
3 12 13 14 20
4 Port ↑
Central
Plaza

Map 10. Census districts in Buenos Aires,
1869–1936.

vided the only link to the central city.[105] Ethnically, the first decades of the twentieth century witnessed the formation of the most homogeneous and isolated immigrant enclaves in the city: the Jewish "ghetto" in districts 9 and 11, and the Middle Eastern one in district 18.

The spectacular metamorphosis of the compact, pedestrian town of 1850 into the sprawling centennial city of 1910 concealed, however, important continuities from the past. The grand metropolis—no less than the *gran aldea*—was essentially an entrepôt between the wealth of the pampas and the markets of Europe. The secondary sector of the economy did expand, but most of it remained either artisanal or small scale. Despite the concentration of hazardous manufacturing plants in the southern districts, spatially disseminated family workshops and small factories continued to dominate the industrial geography of the city into the twentieth century. In 1909 the average number of workers per industrial establishment (eleven) was less than half that of New York (twenty-six) and less than a third of Chicago's (thirty-seven).[106] The relative absence of gargantuan plants and heavy industrial zones in turn precluded, or at least did not foster, the spatial concentration of large numbers of factory laborers and the formation of vast industrial neighborhoods.[107] The composition of immigration represented a different sort of continuity. Although some new groups appeared (for example, Jews and Middle Easterners after the turn of the century and Poles in the 1920s), Italians and Spaniards combined continued to provide more than three-quarters of the arrivals, as they had since the midnineteenth century. This lack of a sharp division between old and new waves, characteristic of North American immigration, fostered stability in the sociospatial structure of the city.

SPANISH RESIDENTIAL PATTERNS
IN THE GRAND METROPOLIS

The demographic ascent of Buenos Aires was outpaced, in relative terms, by that of its Spanish community. Six thousand strong in 1855, it swelled to 105,000 half a century later, and its proportion of the city's total population increased from 6 percent to 11 percent (see Table 14). In the next decade the immigration waves that carried Juan Díaz Novo and Francisco Lema to the River Plate tripled the number to 307,000 by 1914—a figure that represented one out of every five Porteños and the largest concentration of Spaniards in the world outside Madrid or Barcelona. They had also gained ground on the largest immigrant community in the city. In 1887 there had been only 29 Spaniards for every 100 Italians in Buenos Aires; by the outbreak of World War I they had reached parity (98).[108]

As the number of Spaniards in Buenos Aires soared, their spatial distribution remained remarkably stable. Using location quotients (LQ), Map 11 shows that between 1887 and 1930 the area just south and west of the central plaza (which became census district 13 after 1904) continually had the highest concentration of Spaniards in the city (this area, as shown on Map 6, had also been the principal Spanish enclave in the midnineteenth century). The concentration of Spanish immigrant institutions and businesses added to the Iberian color of the area. All along, this core was flanked on the south and the north by districts in which Spaniards were less concentrated but still overrepresented. This made Spaniards, again through out the whole period, one of Buenos Aires' two most spatially centralized nationalities (along with the French) and, on the average, twice as centralized as Argentines and Italians (see Table 17).[109]

Did the implication of the Spaniard's continuous spatial centralization change over time? In the pedestrian city of the midnineteenth century, as we saw, geographical centralization was positively related to higher social status. By the first decade of this century, however, Buenos Aires had developed many of the necessary conditions to fit Burgess' model of central-city poverty and flight to the suburbs: a heterogeneous population in terms of class, ethnicity, and family composition; continual immigration; expansive suburbs with public services; an efficient transportation system that linked periphery and center; hazardous or polluting factories; and increased spatial differentiation (both between and within residential and business zones). The consistent vituperation of the central-districts *conventillos* by fin-de-siècle social reformers and literati reinforced the impression of growing inner-city decay. Like North American progressives, they vied for the most lurid portrayal of the tenements' crowding, lack of sanitation, and deteriorating morality, often raising the specters of social anarchy, promiscuity, and incest.[110] In less dramatic language, modern scholars tend to agree. Sargent, for example, maintained that "by 1900 . . . Buenos Aires had shifted from a traditional pre-industrial city to its reciprocal in terms of income segregation, the Burgess concentric model."[111] Historian James Scobie referred to "the newest arrivals [settling] in the 'deteriorating' (from a residential viewpoint) downtown core, many of them undoubtedly in conventillos, which accords with models and studies of United States immigration."[112] Many other North American and Argentine scholars have made the same claim.[113]

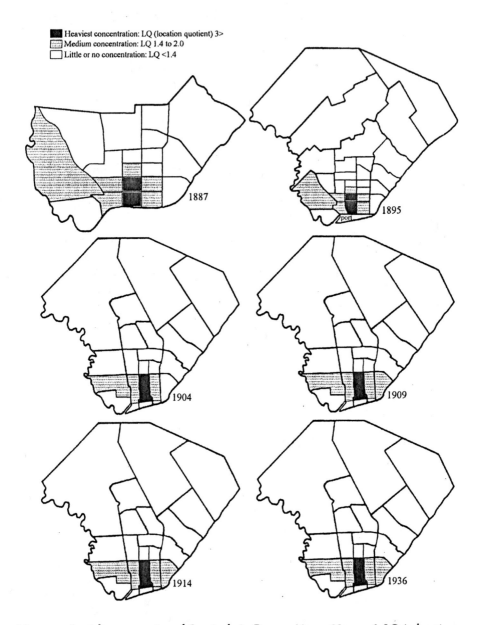

Map 11. Spatial concentration of Spaniards in Buenos Aires, 1887–1936. LQ is location quotient, or the ratio between the percentage of all Spaniards residing in a given district of Buenos Aires and the percentage of the rest of the population residing in that district. An LQ of 1 indicates that the two groups are equally represented in the district; an LQ of more than 1 indicates that Spaniards are overrepresented; an LQ of less than 1, that Spaniards are underrepresented.

Table 17   Residential centralization of principal national groups in Buenos Aires, 1855–1936 (percentages of each group residing in the central zone; highest value for each year is in boldface, second highest underlined.)

Year	Total population	Non-Spaniards	Argentines	Spaniards	Italians	French	Germans	English
1855	28	27	–	<u>39</u>	27	**53**	–	–
1887	30	28	27	<u>47</u>	24	**52**	43	35
1895	20	18	17	33	15	<u>33</u>	30	22
1904	34	31	30	**51**	29	<u>50</u>	42	35
1909	27	24	23	<u>41</u>	22	**42**	34	34
1914	22	19	18	35	17	**39**	32	<u>36</u>
1936	16		14	26	11	<u>30</u>	30	**43**

SOURCES: Estado de Buenos Aires, *Rejistro [sic] estadístico del Estado de Buenos Aires, correspondiente al semestre 1⁰ de 1855*, segunda época, nos. 5 and 6 (Buenos Aires: Imprenta Porteña, 1855), 40, for the total population, and the municipal manuscript census returns for the various nationalities; Buenos Aires, Dirección General de Estadística Municipal, *Censo general de población, edificación, comercio e industrias de la ciudad de Buenos Aires, 1887* (Buenos Aires: Compañía Sud-Americana de Billetes de Banco, 1889), vol. 2, 60–66, includes only people more than six years old; Argentina, Comisión Directiva del Censo, *Segundo censo de la República Argentina, 1895* (Buenos Aires: Taller Tip. de la Penitenciaria Nacional, 1898), vol. 3, 15; Buenos Aires, Dirección General de Estadística Municipal, *Censo general de población, edificación, comercio e industrias de la ciudad de Buenos Aires, 1904* (Buenos Aires: Compañía Sud-Americana de Billetes de Banco, 1906), 79–88; idem, *Censo general de población, edificación, comercio e industrias de la ciudad de Buenos Aires, 1909* (Buenos Aires: Compañía Sud-Americana de Billetes de Banco, 1910), vol. 1, 3–17; Argentina, Comisión Nacional del Censo, *Tercer censo nacional, 1914* (Buenos Aires: Talleres Gráficos de L. J. Rosso, 1916–1919), vol. 2, 129–48; and Buenos Aires, Comisión Técnica Encargada de Realizar el Cuarto Censo General, *Cuarto censo general, 1936* (Buenos Aires: Talleres Gráficos de Guillermo Kraft, 1938), vol. 2, 130–71.

NOTE: The central zone comprised *cuarteles* 3, 4, 11, 12, 18, and 19 in 1855; districts 1–7 in 1887; districts 1–7 and 29 in 1895; and districts 10–14 and 20 from 1904 through 1936. Because the district boundaries changed, only the figures for the latter period are comparable.

Yet my analysis of the available data points to much greater continuity in the city's sociospatial structure and questions this scholarly consensus. Map 12 shows that in 1887 the literacy rate of the city's wards continued to declined with distance from the center, as it had in 1855. The same was true in 1895 (see Map 13). Again as in the midnineteenth century, the more literate national groups were more centralized, and within each group the literate were more centralized than their less-educated compatriots. The early-twentieth-century censuses do not provide data on liter-

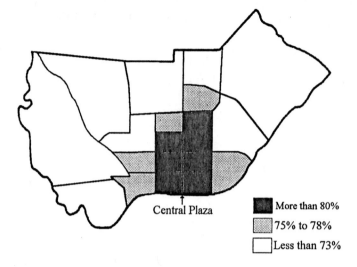

Map 12. Literacy rates in Buenos Aires, by district, 1887.

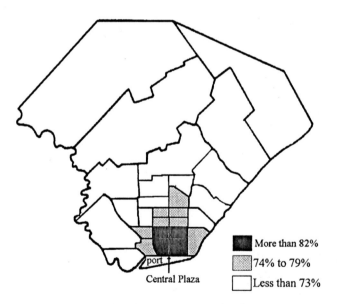

Map 13. Literacy rates in Buenos Aires, by district, 1895.

Table 18   Selected measures of living conditions, by zone, in Buenos Aires, 1904 (in percentages, except persons per room)

	Persons per room	School-age children illiterate and not in school	Population not vaccinated	Houses with no sewer system	Houses with no running water	Rental houses with no baths
Center	1.6	9.4	5.2	1.6	0.7	8.8
Semiperiphery	2.3	12.4	7.4	53.5	21.4	37.9
Periphery	2.1	14.2	9.1	99.2	83.6	74.1

SOURCE: Calculated from data in Buenos Aires, Dirección General de Estadística Municipal, *Censo general de población, edificación, comercio e industrias de la ciudad de Buenos Aires, 1904* (Buenos Aires: Compañía Sud-Americana de Billetes de Banco, 1906), cxi, 7–16, 76–77, 121–22, and 131.

NOTE: The center comprised districts 10–14 and 20; the semiperiphery, districts 3, 4, 8, 9, and 19; the periphery, districts 1, 2, 5–7, and 15–18.

acy by ward, but employing six alternative indicators relating to health care, child illiteracy and school attendance, sanitary conditions, and crowding,[114] Table 18 shows that living conditions declined centripetally in 1904. Using an even wider number of proxies for social well-being or status, Table 19, Map 14, and Map 15 demonstrate the same correlation between better status and centralization in 1909, 1914, and even as late as 1936.

Published censuses and statistical annuals do not include other indicators. But using alternative sources from the records of mutual-aid societies, I compiled a sample of 3,555 Spanish residents in 1910 and 1912 that permits an analysis of occupational status and place of residence. The results (depicted on Map 16) corroborate those from the other indicators. The average occupational status of the inhabitants peaked in the central districts, dropped in the next ring, and hit bottom on the outskirts and in the oligarchical Barrio Norte (district 20) because of the large number of servants. The other exception to the concentric pattern (the high rank of a northwestern belt formed by districts 5, 7, and 18) reveals the improving conditions of the city's north side.[115] Still, proximity to the center, rather than latitude, persisted as the best single predictor of zonal quality.

The most direct test of the hypothesis that the upwardly mobile left the core for the outskirts is a cross-tabulation of occupational and resi-

Table 19 Social-welfare indicators for Buenos Aires' twenty wards, 1909 (ranked on the mean rank of all indicators)

Ward	Houses with a sewer system		Houses with running water		Deaths per thousand inhabitants		Deaths due to infectious diseases per thousand inhabitants		Inhabitants vaccinated		School-age children not attending school		School-age children illiterate	
	Percentage	Rank	Percentage	Rank	Number	Rank	Number	Rank	Percentage	Rank	Percentage	Rank	Percentage	Rank
14	100	1	100	1	11.2	8	0.6	1	97.1	2	19.5	5	12.1	1
20	100	1	100	1	9.0	3	0.7	3	97.9	1	22.9	6	17.0	6
10	100	1	100	1	7.4	1	0.7	2	97.1	3	24.2	10	18.2	8
13	100	1	100	1	8.8	2	0.8	5	91.3	12	19.4	4	13.4	3
12	100	1	100	1	10.4	5	0.8	7	92.4	11	18.5	2	16.9	5
11	100	1	100	1	9.4	4	0.7	4	86.8	17	19.1	3	15.1	4
19	79	10	83	10	27.0	18	1.0	11	93.3	10	16.1	1	12.6	2
4	100	1	100	1	11.0	6	1.0	9	95.9	5	26.5	16	19.2	11
9	100	1	100	1	20.8	17	0.8	6	88.9	14	23.4	9	18.1	7
3	100	1	100	1	31.3	19	1.0	10	96.5	4	23.2	8	19.7	12
8	36	11	70	11	11.1	7	1.1	13	95.0	6	25.3	14	21.8	14
16	0	15	32	13	15.6	15	1.6	18	94.1	7	24.3	11	19.0	10
7	7	14	27	15	15.1	14	1.2	15	85.9	19	23.0	7	18.2	9

18	11	12	18	17	11.5	10	1.1	14	90.0	13	25.5	15	22.6	16
6	9	13	28	14	11.3	9	1.0	12	88.7	15	27.8	17	22.1	15
15	0	15	0	20	14.3	13	0.9	8	93.6	8	32.2	20	30.1	20
5	0	15	42	12	17.5	16	1.3	16	87.3	16	24.5	12	23.3	18
17	0	15	23	16	12.0	12	1.7	19	85.5	20	24.6	13	21.1	13
1	0	15	5	19	11.5	11	1.3	17	86.3	18	29.1	18	29.6	19
2	0	15	12	18	31.4	20	1.9	20	93.6	9	29.8	19	23.0	17

SOURCE: Buenos Aires, Dirección General de Estadística Municipal, *Censo general de población, edificación, comercio e industrias de la ciudad de Buenos Aires, 1909* (Buenos Aires: Compañía Sud-Americana de Billetes de Banco, 1910), Vol. 1, 63–86, 102–4, 180–82; vol. 2, 88.

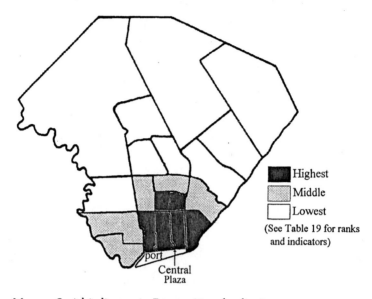

Highest
Middle
Lowest
(See Table 19 for ranks
and indicators)

port

Central
Plaza

Map 14. Social indicators in Buenos Aires, by district, 1909.

dential mobility among central-city residents—an examination never attempted by its proponents because published statistics do not permit it. Using members' registers from a Catalan mutual-aid society, I was able to trace 180 adult males living in the center (districts 10–14 and 20) in 1898 through a fourteen-year interim and a group of 375 from 1912 to 1919. The results (see Table 20) show a high frequency of spatial mobility: 92 percent of those in the first sample and 82 percent of those in the second had changed addresses in the respective periods. Yet, contrary to the invasion-succession postulate, these peripatetic Catalans preferred to move within the inner wards: three out of four moves between 1898 and 1912, and four out of five between 1912 and 1919, did not cross the central-city boundaries. Moreover, only 16 percent of the upwardly mobile, but 26 percent of the occupationally stagnant and 36 percent of those who went down the job ladder, moved into the outer districts. Outward relocation in the first decade of the twentieth century was more often a sign of failure than a flight from ghetto to suburb. In the next decade, as transport, municipal services, and prospects for home ownership improved in the outer districts, moving there became more neutral (see the bottom of Table 20). But there was still no positive correlation between economic success and outward mobility.

Several factors account for this preservation of the inner city's high

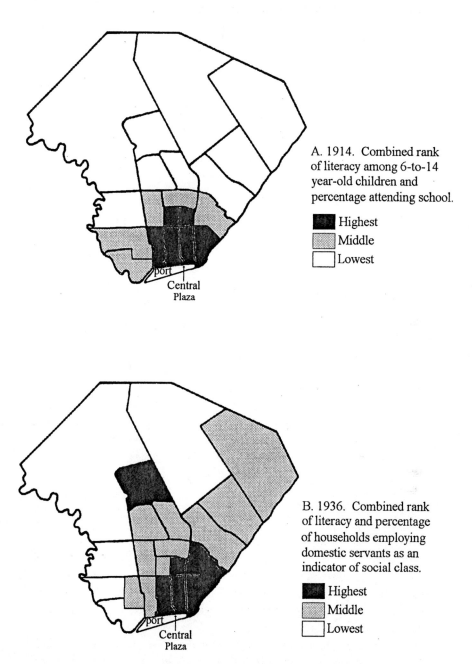

A. 1914. Combined rank of literacy among 6-to-14 year-old children and percentage attending school.

■ Highest
▨ Middle
□ Lowest

port
Central
Plaza

B. 1936. Combined rank of literacy and percentage of households employing domestic servants as an indicator of social class.

■ Highest
▨ Middle
□ Lowest

port
Central
Plaza

Map 15. Social indicators in Buenos Aires, by district, 1914 and 1936.

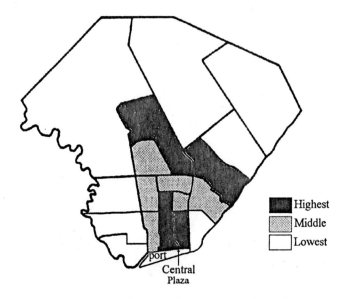

Map 16.   Occupational status of 3,555 Spaniards residing in
Buenos Aires, 1910–1912, by district. Values assigned to occupational categories: unskilled, 1; semiskilled, 2; skilled, 3; low nonmanual, 4; middle nonmanual, 5; low professional, 6; high nonmanual, 7; and high professional, 8. The occupational status of
the district was then defined as the mean job-category value of
the individuals residing there. *Sources:* Membership applications
of the Asociación Española de Socorros Mutuos de Buenos Aires,
1910 (2,086 applicants with jobs); and the membership register of
the Montepío de Monserrat for 1912 (1,409 names).

status. The continuing role of the Argentine capital as a fundamentally
commercial and administrative center facilitated the retention in the urban core of a "clean" economic base grounded in the tertiary sector. Furthermore, the limited spatial concentration of heavy industry inhibited
the formation of large industrial-workers' ghettoes in general, and the
southwestern shift of polluting or vexatious factories kept the existing
ones away from the city center. The fact that the infrastructural improvements and services described in the previous section originated in and
were normally superior in the core fostered the preservation of its status.
And the continuity in the national make up of Argentine immigration
discouraged the abandonment of neighborhoods by older groups in the
face of incursions by ethnically and socially different newcomers. What
took place in Buenos Aires then was—as in most European cities—con-

Table 20 Relationships between occupational and residential mobility among Catalan immigrants living in the central wards of Buenos Aires, 1898–1912 and 1912–1919 (in percentages)

Type of job mobility	N	Did not move	Moved within the same ward	Moved to a bordering ward	Moved toward the center of the city	Moved toward the periphery	Moved long distance but with no centric direction	Total
Type of residential mobility between 1898 and 1912								
Upward	83	11	27	32	0	13	17	100
None or lateral	159	9	21	40	0	19	11	100
Downward	22	0	32	27	4	23	14	100
All	264	9	24	36	.4	18	12	99.4
Type of residential mobility between 1912 and 1919								
Upward	75	16	37	25	4	11	7	100
None or lateral	641	23	26	25	4	11	11	100
Downward	36	25	14	31	7	12	11	100
All	752	23	26	25	4	11	11	100

SOURCES: Membership registers of Montepío de Monserrat (a Catalan mutual-aid society in Buenos Aires) for 1898, 1912, and 1919.

tinual, but moderate and normal, outward population movement as the city expanded in that direction, not outward flight, as in the invasion-succession phenomenon of many U.S. cities.[116] The two types of movements are different not only in size but also in their socioeconomic and even psychosocial implications. Outward movement in the River Plate metropolis simply lacked the collective psychosis associated with the North American stampedes of frightened people fleeing from the "dangerous" inner city. In this light, the "inner-city problem" seems to be the result of specific historical developments rather than an inevitable stage in urban modernization, as some geographers suspect.[117]

What could explain the basic contradiction between these findings and what appears to be a scholarly consensus on the transformation of Buenos Aires' ecology? One explanation may be the common overestimation of outward movement through the logically faulty assumption that the decline in the percentage of an expanding city's population residing in a statically defined center automatically proves such movement and that, again under an unproved axiom, this represents an exodus of the better off.[118] Another may be the tendency to identify, almost routinely, tenements with the city center. Scobie, for example, maintained that "the number of slum [*conventillo*] dwellers declined as one moved away from the downtown core and virtually disappeared at a distance of forty blocks from the plaza."[119] But this is true only in so far as the number of dwellers of any type declined as one moved away from the core. The very source he used shows that the proportion of inhabitants living in *conventillos* in the four central districts was actually lower than in semiperipheral districts and that central tenements were more likely to have running water, sewer, and baths.[120] A third reason for the contradiction may be the common supposition that the overrepresentation of natives—many of whom were second-generation immigrants—on the periphery and the inverse "concentration" of some late-emigration groups, such as Middle Easterners, in the center, is evidence of ecological succession. That argument disregards the following facts: natives had always been overrepresented on the periphery, even in 1855 when the dynamics of invasion and succession could not yet have developed; this signaled at the time not their upward mobility but their relative poverty; the recently arrived Middle Easterners, despite a visible downtown slum, actually concentrated in peripheral wards; and the early-arriving French, whose emigration peaked and declined the earliest, were also the most centralized nativity group in the city.[121]

Yet the principal root of the discrepancy may relate to the nature of qualitative sources. The emphasis of turn-of-the-century observers on central-city tenements and poverty may well reveal more about the observers than about the social ecology of the city. Those who wrote about immigrant poverty were not the poor but upper- and middle-class—and usually native-born—reformers, essayists, and literati who normally resided and worked in the central districts. Peripheral poverty did not greatly affect their daily lives and thus could be safely ignored or even idealized. Fin-de-siècle memorialists, for example, often depicted the suburbs (*arrabales*) nostalgically as the habitat of vanishing gauchos, horsemounted beggars (who in the best of native equestrian ideals literally looked down on the donor), and colorful, drum-beating blacks.[122] Later, with the evident ethnic transformation of the city, the outskirts began to be portrayed—still in picturesque terms—as home to the *compadrito* (a blend of lower-class dandy and tough and an urban counterpart of the gaucho in Argentine cultural mythology), the *cafficho* (pimp), Lunfardo (the "cool" argot of the demimonde), and that supreme Porteño icon, the tango.[123]

Poverty in the central city, on the other hand, could not easily be ignored or "folklorized." Those who wrote encountered it daily, near their houses and offices, on their way to the publisher or the bank, on their spouses' trips to church or to Florida Street's Lalique's and Tiffany's. It represented anything from an aesthetic eyesore to a threat to their personal safety. At times it grated on their nerves and brought visions of social upheaval led by degenerate foreigners and anarchists, often considered synonymous terms. Thus physical proximity and xenophobia (the central city had always contained a greater proportion of foreigners) clearly influenced where in the city contemporary observers detected—and recorded—poverty.

The much observed, studied, and castigated central-city tenement was likely to appear as the embodiment of housing blight to later generations of researchers. These students, in turn, tended to quote, not surprisingly, from the most vivid and grim contemporary descriptions of central tenements.[124] A similar process occurs with visual images, the paramount "evidence" of a positivist age. Contemporary photographers understandably tilted their lenses toward the visible (because of their central location and size), dramatic, and photogenic *conventillos* rather than toward the thousands of poor, plain little houses of the sprawling periphery, leaving a slanted record of lower-class housing in the city. The recurrent reproduction of the most graphic and dramatic images from this surviving corpus in later publications in turn reinforced the original biased association of residential deterioration with the inner city.[125] Scobie admitted that "the large number of inhabitants [per building] also gave the conventillo visibility in contemporary sources—a visibility not shared by other housing for non-elite groups. Such visibility substantially facilitates examination of the conventillo."[126]

Yet the bulk of the working class in turn-of-the-century Buenos Aires resided not in the tiny *conventillo* rooms with the five children, garbage, excrement, cats, dogs, and rats usually portrayed by reformers but in small, unattractive two- or three-room houses on the periphery. Poverty in Buenos Aires, as in most other places, was less dramatic, plainer, and more insipid than the Dickensian descriptions of the well-to-do. At its peak in 1887, only one-quarter of the city's total population lived in *conventillos* of any kind, and the proportion dropped to 14 percent by 1904 and to 9 percent by 1919.[127]

The abundance of qualitative sources on central-city tenements—and their reproduction by historians—thus served to obscure the facts that central propinquity continued to be an indicator of zonal value and social well-being (in terms of sanitary facilities, availability of health care, condition of the housing stock, and land and property values) and that the poor (as measured by rates of literacy, school attendance, mortality, and occupation) continued to be overrepresented in peripheral wards rather than in central ones.[128]

Home Ownership and Housing Strategies

The spatial centralization of the Spaniards, however, greatly affected the way they adapted to the city's housing market. As Table 21 shows, they consistently exhibited lower rates of home ownership than all the other principal immigrant groups in the city. The higher rates of the British, German, and French immigrants probably reflected their concentration in higher-paying, nonmanual occupations (clerks, merchants, professionals, and so forth). In a sample from the manuscript schedules of the 1895 national census that I collected, 50 percent of the British, 44 percent of Germans, and 32 percent of the French appeared in the nonmanual categories—in comparison to only 26 percent of Spaniards and 23 percent of Italians. The significantly better jobs of the northwestern Europeans more than compensated for the fact that they also concentrated in the inner wards of the city, where real estate was less affordable (see Table 17).

The explanation for why home-ownership rates were lower for Spaniards than for Italians is more elusive. Part of it may be that although the latter appeared slightly less represented than the former in the nonmanual occupations, they were more skilled within the manual-labor categories. Of the 2,116 Italian manual workers in the above-mentioned sample, 46 percent were better-paid artisans, as compared with only 31 percent of the 2,488 Spaniards. Italians were also older. In 1904, for instance, 67 percent of them versus only 56 percent of Spaniards were more than thirty years old. Because it is unlikely that they left their country at a significantly older age, and considering the earlier timing of the Italian immigration flow (see Figure 13), this maturity evidences a greater proportion of long-time residents who, even if they earned no more than Spaniards, had

Table 21   Home ownership among immigrants in Buenos Aires

Group	Total population of each group				Percentage owning real estate			
	1887	1895	1904	1909	1887	1895	1904	1909
Germans	3,900	5,297	5,169	7,444	12.5	10.4	12.8	14.1
British	4,160	6,838	5,400	7,113	13.7	8.1	11.3	12.1
French	20,031	33,185	27,574	25,751	9.9	7.6	15.0	19.0
Italians	138,166	181,693	228,556	277,041	9.5	9.2	12.6	14.5
Spaniards	39,562	80,352	105,206	174,291	7.5	4.8	8.2	8.2

SOURCES: Buenos Aires, Dirección General de Estadística Municipal, *Censo general de población, edificación, comercio e industrias de la ciudad de Buenos Aires, 1887* (Buenos Aires: Compañía Sud-Americana de Billetes de Banco, 1889), vol. 2, 35–36, 142; Argentina, Comisión Directiva del Censo, *Segundo censo de la República Argentina, 1895* (Buenos Aires: Taller Tip. de la Penitenciaria Nacional, 1898), vol. 3, 16; Buenos Aires, Dirección General de Estadística Municipal, *Censo general de población, edificación, comercio e industrias de la ciudad de Buenos Aires, 1904* (Buenos Aires: Compañía Sud-Americana de Billetes de Banco, 1906), 82–89; and idem, *Censo general de población, edificación, comercio e industrias de la ciudad de Buenos Aires, 1909* (Buenos Aires: Compañía Sud-Americana de Billetes de Banco, 1910), vol. 1, 17, 101.
NOTE: The figures are computed from population censuses and indicate the percentage of each group (including children, which produces misleadingly low proportions) who owned real estate, whatever the number of units. The 1904 census also includes a building census that records not the number of individuals from a given nationality who own property but the number of properties owned by members of that nationality, which is obviously higher than the former unless not a single individual from that group owns more than one house. The number of x-owned properties as a percentage of the total x population in the city in 1904 is as follows: Germans, 20.3; British, 17.7; French, 17.4; Italians, 16.1; and Spaniards, 9.3, which indicates the relative absence of multiproperty owners among the last group.

had more years in which to save. It also indicates concentration in the age range most prone to home ownership. Two other demographic traits—the lower celibacy of Italians (23 percent single in 1904, in contrast to 35 percent of Spaniards) and their higher fertility (464 children per every 100 married women, compared with 397 for Spaniards)—encouraged home buying.[129] Culturally, the ideal of home ownership seems also to have been particularly intense among Italians.[130] In Buenos Aires they had higher ownership rates than did the much more affluent British. Similarly, in Tampa, Florida, they received lower average wages than did Spanish immigrants there, but their rate of home ownership was much higher.[131]

History and geography (in the form of immigration and settlement

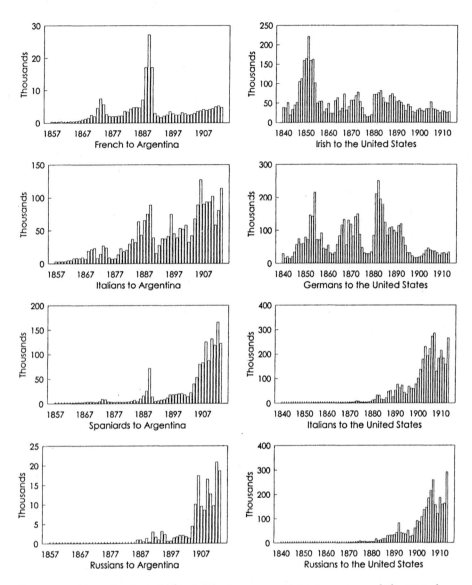

Figure 13. Year of arrival of principal emigrant groups in Argentina and the United States. *Source:* Imre Ferenczi and Walter Willcox, *International Migrations* (New York: National Bureau of Economic Research, 1929), 377–94, 543–46.

patterns), however, matched—and at times surpassed—the explanatory force of economic, demographic, or cultural determinants regarding the different ownership rates in the two groups. Because of their early linkages to colonial merchants, who traditionally resided near the central plaza, Spaniards had concentrated from the very beginning in the center, where the land values were the highest in the city and, thus, the possibilities of ownership the lowest. Once set, this pattern of relative centralization persisted for almost a century (as shown on Maps 6 and 10). On the other hand, because their early ties to Ligurian cabotage sailors (who had, in the most natural of fashions, settled in La Boca) and to Piedmontese vegetable gardeners, Italians, again from the start, had been overrepresented on the periphery, which had the lowest land values and thus the highest possibilities of ownership in the city. It is telling that in 1887 there were more Spanish home owners in the Italian neighborhood of La Boca than in the Spanish quarters south of the central plaza, where the price of land was nineteen times higher.[132] That year the Spaniards' ownership rate (7.5 percent) amounted to only 79 percent of the Italians' (9.5 percent). But had their distribution among the city's districts been the same as the Italians', their ownership rate would have been 10.7 percent, or 113 percent of the latter's.[133] In other words, only the Spaniards' concentration in less affordable districts prevented them from surpassing the overall home-ownership rate of the Italians in that particular year.

The relative weight of the different variables changed over time, however. In 1887, recent waves from Lombardy, Veneto, the Piedmont, and Liguria had actually saddled the Italian community in Buenos Aires with a higher proportion of fresh arrivals than that in the Spanish community.[134] Of all the Italians who had settled in Argentina in the previous three decades, six-tenths had done so in the preceding quinquennium, as opposed to only one-third of the Spaniards. By the time of the next municipal censuses (1904 and 1909), however, the northern Italians of the 1880s had become old-timers, while a veritable tidal wave from the Iberian Peninsula (which carried 1 million people to the River Plate in the decade before World War I) swiftly swelled the Spanish community. By then the economic and demographic variables spawned by longer residency (greater saving capacity, higher average age, higher nuptiality and fertility rates) and/or cultural preferences had replaced residential patterns as the principal explanation for the gap in home ownership. Had the Spaniards' geographical distribution in 1904 been the same as the Italians', the gap in home ownership between the two groups would have dropped by little more than one-quarter; and in 1909, by just one-tenth, with the remaining variance clearly attributable to the above-mentioned factors.[135] The decreasing significance of geographical distribution also reflects a narrowing gap between central and peripheral land prices. In 1887, for example, land values in the district just south of the central plaza were 26 times higher than in the suburb of Palermo (district 19); in 1904 they were only 2.5 times as expensive; and five years later, 1.6 times.[136]

Overall, the expansion of public transit, municipal services, and credit pushed the fringe of the urban periphery and boosted home buying among all groups during the first third of this century. Spanish writer José María Salaverría, who lived in Buenos Aires for three years around 1910, attributed the "plot-buying frenzy" to the outlook of an aspiring immigrant "mass who even if they lack the money, gorge on credit . . . and have the audacity to think in millions." What he termed "the psychology of advertisement" reflected the rush. In European cities pawnshops normally announced, "Money advanced on wages or jewels," and people resorted to them in case of extreme need. In Buenos Aires, lenders trumpeted, "Money available, ANY SUM! from 10,000 to 100,000,000, for mortgages. Long terms! Borrowers set the installments!" and multitudes dashed to them, not to cover basic needs, or even to procure a home, but to speculate. In no other place did the Shakespearean admonition about borrowers and lenders fall on such deaf ears.[137] The picturesque, and apparently efficient, selling techniques of ubiquitous auctioneers likely abetted the spread of home buying on the periphery. They included free Sunday trips to the sites for the whole family plus a traditional barbecue, drinks on the house—literally—a band, and dancing under a circus tent. So, perhaps, did the appeal to ethnic loyalties and rivalries. An advertisement in *La Prensa* (October 5, 1909, p. 22, and subsequent issues) announced plot auctions in a new suburban development called Villa España, praising the Spanish community for their response and urging them on: "There is great competition among buyers! Who will beat the record? The French, Argentines and Italians are taking a good share!"

Whether in search of a home or not, Spaniards moved often within the city. Table 20 shows that only 9 percent of those traceable through the fourteen-year span and 23 percent of those who were traceable through the seven-year-period had remained at the same address. Moving around town proved three to seven times more common than "moving up in the world," but no clear connection between permanency and upward occupational mobility appeared. In the 1898–1912 sample the successful tended to stay put more often, but that reversed in the 1912–1919 group. The table refers only to Catalans, but additional data from the membership application forms, ledgers, and medical records of the main Spanish and Galician mutual-aid societies in the city point in the same direction.[138] Of 183 Spanish immigrants who were traceable through an average span of six years and a period covering the first three decades of this century, only 16 percent retained the same address—a level of mobility that conforms to what historians have found in contemporary North American cities.[139] Age, marital status, and gender—rather than occupational mobility—proved the best predictors of residential trends, with young, single males being the least-rooted group.

Centrifugal displacement in search of home ownership was not, however, the principal type of residential movement. Only 15 percent of all those who moved did so toward the periphery. Almost as many (13 percent) marched in the other direction. The rest (72 percent) moved within or to a bordering ward with no centric direction. Indeed, most movers did not go very far. The majority (55 percent) did not move more than twenty blocks away, and almost one-fifth stayed within a five-block radius. Whatever the direction or distance, everywhere in the city residential mobility appeared as the norm and permanency as the exception.

This residential transiency, traditionally construed as a negative mark of social uprootedness and economic—or even moral—instability, is now perceived by most urban historians as normal for the period and perhaps even an indication of opportunities.[140] Thus the fact that for the spatially centralized Spaniards much of the shifting took place within the inner wards and was accompanied by upward occupational mobility undermines Scobie's dichotomous description of downtown Buenos Aires as "the home of the powerful . . . and the newly arrived laborer . . . typified by the conventillo and the palacio."[141] Central Buenos Aires was never "Manhattanized."[142] It was always more than a citadel of oligarchs and a dumping ground for the indigent. Merchants, literate and ambitious clerks, frugal shopkeepers, well-read printers, and the middling groups in general also concentrated here. The presence of a few prolific literati could not have elevated the area's literacy rate to the city's highest. Octogenarian plutocrats could not have dropped its mortality rate to the city's lowest. Likewise, the housing stock was not limited to the attention-grabbing "conventillos and palacios."

Indeed, housing options in the central city ran a wide gamut between, and below, tenements and mansions.[143] The range in rents was the broadest in the city.[144] Underneath most tenements one could find seedy boardinghouses, taverns, and pensions. The poorhouse, insane asylum, jail, and roofless streets (the inner wards had not a single bridge or overpass) ranked even lower. The tenements themselves were not as unvarying as they were portrayed. At that time, working-class rental housing may have had a similar appearance everywhere—whether alleys in London, "Cholo courts" in Los Angeles, *cortiços* in Rio de Janeiro, or *conventillos* in Buenos Aires, a rectangular open space was flanked on one or both sides by rows of rooms.[145] But just as New York had "rear" and "new-law" tenements, Rio, *estalegens* as well as *cortiços*, and Seville *corrales de vecinos* and *casas de vecinos*, Buenos Aires had *conventillos* and *casas de inquilinato*.[146] Census takers (who never clearly defined the infamous *conventillo*) often grouped the two types, and the second term could at times act as no more than an euphemism. But real differences in degree and, to many of its dwellers, in kind, existed. The *casas de inquilinato* normally had larger rooms, a greater number of them per family, better sanitary and physical conditions, and a more pleasing—or at least less offensive—aspect. As iron, steel, and concrete became the universal building materials in the central wards of belle-epoque Buenos Aires and as its edifices grew taller ("aiming to catch New York's skyscrapers," as a hyperbolic contemporary put it), the number of middle-class apartment buildings increased.[147] Single-family homes, or row houses, occupied a wide belt below and above the middle. Upscale apartments followed, and the beaux art chateaus of the aristocratic plutocracy, palatial by world standards, occupied the pyramid's tip.

A handful of Spanish inner-city residents came close to that apex, and some of their descendants reached it. A somewhat larger number ended up in poorhouses or in prisons; about a quarter in run-down pensions and more-or-less wretched tenements, and some of them responded by joining and directing rent strikes—the best known of which took place in 1907.[148] One out of ten, and a larger portion of heads of households, was able to buy a home in the central wards.[149] The bulk just rented modest but un-Dickensian dwellings, including single-family houses, and moved about a great deal, searching for larger, cheaper, or better quarters closer to work, family or friends.

This range of central residential options made buying a small house on the outskirts (particularly in the poorer southwest, where the prospects were the greatest) a less unequivocally attractive strategy and adds a new angle to the Spaniards' relative lack of home ownership. How much of this lack was due to their geographical concentration in the least affordable parts of town, their late-immigration pattern, and the resulting economic and demographic variables previously discussed, and how much to their personal and cultural preferences? How many simply elected to spend their hard-earned pesos on land back home, or in buying a corner grocery store from the ubiquitous "uncle," or in turning their sons into accountants and their daughters into schoolteachers? Home ownership, as many scholars have found—and perhaps many immigrants always knew—does not necessarily indicate economic prosperity or a wise venture. Several U.S. historians have noted that home ownership was lower among middle-class native white Americans than among working-class immigrants.[150] According to Stephan Thernstrom, "in Newbury Port, Massachusetts, Irish immigrants were acquiring homes at the expense of their children's education."[151] Writing about nearby Boston, Daniel Luria agreed that home ownership represented a bad investment which adversely affected occupational mobility;[152] an assessment expressed in fiction long before (1906) in that classic indictment of early-twentieth-century urban plight: Upton Sinclair's *The Jungle.*

For many immigrants, like Sinclair's Rudkiss from Lithuania, the home-ownership ideal must have been so potent that the Sicilian proverb "As little as it is, so long as it is mine," rather than financial expediency, could have acted as the guiding principle.[153] For them, Buenos Aires was not a bad place to be. Its proportion of owner-occupied homes (36 percent in 1909) fell one point short of the United States' but more than tripled that in Britain (10 percent).[154] But to turn the proverb into a universal proprietary fetish is to underestimate the immigrants' diversity.

Thousands of Spanish residents of the inner wards perhaps did not buy a peripheral house not because they could not afford the monthly payments but because they preferred renting in the core to owning in the outskirts. In return for the lack of "a house to call one's own," they got running water, sewer facilities, baths, a wide selection of rental housing, asphalted streets, better transportation, garbage collection and street cleaning, less-crowded quarters (measured in inhabitants per room rather than per hectare), better educational opportunities for their children, and proximity to the community's main service-providing institutions (the Spanish hospital and mutual-aid societies). Less essential, but for homesick immigrants no less important, they had easier access to their national arts and pastimes: the zarzuelas (Spanish operettas, which in 1910 offered 1,317 performances and attracted 1.4 million spectators); the visiting Spanish drama and comedy companies (with 1,500 performances and an audience of 1.5 million); the *pelota* (jai alai) courts on Belgrano Street; the Spanish *romerías* (religious feasts but de facto festivals for drinking, dancing, and courtship); the sumptuous Club Español; and hundreds of regional or village-based social organizations that provided camaraderie and Old World gossip.

Then there were, of course, the daily chats in the cafés of, and nightly promenades along, their cherished Avenida de Mayo.[155] To Clemenceau the tree-lined, elegant avenue resembled London's Oxford Street;[156] to most Porteños, the Champs Elysée. But Spanish immigrants, the majority of whom had seen Madrid only on postcards, would swear by all the saints—or more blasphemous variants—that it was Buenos Aires' rendition of La Gran Vía. Their argument had dubious architectural merit, but their presence made the difference: the avenue came to be popularly known as "la calle de los españoles." A stroll along this sumptuous boulevard—even today, after years of decay and tawdry facades have defiled its magnificent art nouveau and art deco structures—will provide a sharp clue as to the kind of attraction the city's center must have had for the Iberian immigrants.[157]

Segregation

Many of the same factors that preserved the status of central areas also deterred high levels of ethnic residential differentiation. Indeed, compared with other multi-ethnic cities, Buenos Aires continued to show, just as it had in the midnineteenth century, one of the lowest average indexes of segregation in the world. As Table 22 demonstrates, mean segregation in Buenos Aires around 1910 only reached one-half to three-quarters the level that it did in U.S. cities.

Part of this gap can be explained by what North American sociologists have termed the social-distance hypothesis, which presents ethnic residential differentiation as a function of the sociocultural distance (irrespective of socioeconomic disparity) between a given ethnic group and the dominant culture; i.e., that of the charter group.[158] The data in Table 23 strongly support the hypothesis. In Toronto, London, and eleven U.S. cities, the Anglo-Protestant immigrants had the lowest indexes of segregation, followed by the Catholic but English-speaking Irish, with Germans and Scandinavians not far behind. After a huge gap came Polish and Italian Catholics and Russian Jews, whose spatial segregation at the time surpassed that of black Americans.[159] Correspondingly, in Buenos Aires, Montreal, and Rio de Janeiro the Latin-Catholic nationalities exhibited the

Table 22   Residential segregation in Buenos Aires, in comparison with other multi-ethnic cities, ca. 1910

Ranked by the mean index of segregation of the three most numerous foreign-born groups		Ranked by the mean index of segregation of the ten most numerous foreign-born groups	
Toronto	6.3	Buenos Aires	24.1
Buenos Aires	16.9	Paris	28.9
Paris[a]	19.0	Toronto	30.1
Rio de Janeiro[b]	31.7	Boston	33.6
Philadelphia	34.1	Cleveland	35.4
Cincinnati	34.2	Columbus	35.6
Cleveland	34.6	St. Louis	35.8
Columbus	35.0	Syracuse	36.5
St. Louis	35.8	Pittsburgh	37.3
London[c]	38.0	Cincinnati	38.5
Pittsburgh	40.6	New York City	38.8
Chicago	42.3	Philadelphia	39.7
Montreal	42.5	Montreal	40.1
Boston	44.2	Chicago	40.6
New York City	43.1	Rio de Janeiro	40.7
Syracuse	44.3	Buffalo	41.2
Buffalo	52.0	London	41.7
South African cities[d]	57.8		

SOURCES AND METHODS: Buenos Aires' indexes and mean computed from raw data in Buenos Aires, Dirección General de Estadística Municipal, *Censo general de población, edificación, comercio e industrias de la ciudad de Buenos Aires, 1909* (Buenos Aires: Compañía Sud-Americana de Billetes de Banco, 1910), vol. 1, 3–17; Toronto's and Montreal's indexes and means computed from raw data in Canada, Census and Statistics Office, *Fifth Census of Canada, 1911* (Ottawa: C.H. Parmelee, 1912), vol. 2, 402–4 and 414–16; New York's indexes and mean computed from raw data in United States, Department of Commerce and Labor, Bureau of the Census, *Thirteenth Census of the United States Taken in the Year 1910* (Washington, D.C.: Government Printing Office, 1912), vol. 3, 253; for the other U.S. cities, I calculated the averages from the indexes in Stanley Lieberson, *Ethnic Patterns in American Cities* (New York: Free Press of Glencoe, 1963), 209–18, and determined the larger groups from United States, *Thirteenth Census of the United States*, vol. 2, 512, 890, and 1128, and vol. 3, 252–53, 260, 426–28, 605, and 609.

Because Lieberson computed the indexes of dissimilarity between each group and native whites (instead of the rest of the population), I computed the indexes for Buenos Aires, Rio de Janeiro, London, and the Canadian cities between each group and the native population to make them as comparable as possible. Using the rest of the population instead of natives for Buenos Aires, the mean index for the top three immigrant groups would have been 17.5 instead of 16.9 and for the top ten groups, 23.5 instead of 24.1. That is, using the different

(*continued on next page*)

Table 22 *(continued)*

methods did not alter the indexes much and would not have altered the ranks at all. I also computed the index versus the rest of the population instead of native whites for sixteen immigrant groups in New York, Philadelphia, and Boston; the results diverged, on the average, only 2.3 points from those of Lieberson. The same inspection for the top ten groups in Montreal produced an average divergence of 3.2 points.

[a]For 1896, an average computed from indexes in Philip E. Ogden, *Foreigners in Paris: Residential Segregation in the Nineteenth and Twentieth Centuries* (London: University of London, Department of Geography, 1977), 22.

[b]For 1920, computed from raw data in Brazil, Directoria Geral de Estatistica, *Recenseamento do Brazil, 1920* (Rio de Janeiro: Typ. da Estatistica, 1922–1930). Unfortunately, the census does not specify nativity by ward for São Paulo, a city with a larger immigrant population than Rio.

[c]Includes Irish (I_s 20.9) and Scots (I_s 21.6) as "foreign-born." The mean goes up dramatically because the third most numerous group, Russian Jews, had an I_s of 71.4. Computed from raw data in *Census of England and Wales, 1911: County of London, Areas, Families or Separate Occupiers and Population* (London: His Majesty's Stationery Office, 1914), 217–32.

[d]Calculated as the mean of the median index of dissimilarity between whites and blacks, whites and mulattoes, and mulattoes and blacks for all South African towns with a population of more than 2,000 in 1911, from indexes in A. J. Christopher, "Segregation Levels in South African Cities, 1911–1985," *International Journal of African Historical Studies* 25, 3 (1992):561–82. With the apartheid policies of the 1950s, the level of segregation increased dramatically, and by 1985 it had reached a mean index for all groups (whites, blacks, coloreds, and Asians) of 91.0, close to complete residential separation.

lowest segregation, followed by Austrian or Irish Catholics, then mostly Protestant Germans and English, and far behind by Ashkenazi Jews and Muslims or Maronites from the Ottoman Empire.[160]

The social-distance hypothesis cannot, however, explain the entire gap. When I calculated the mean segregation index on the basis of the ten most numerous immigrant groups in each city, four of the ten in Buenos Aires were neither Latin nor Catholic, and six of the ten in U.S. cities were either Nordic, Protestant, or English-speaking. The results still showed Buenos Aires as significantly less segregated. The English segregation index in Buenos Aires was less than half that of Italians in the United States. Lutheran Germans were less segregated in Catholic Buenos Aires than in eight of the twelve Protestant North American cities listed in Table 22.

Differing timing and rhythm of arrival, in addition to distance from Anglo-Protestant or Hispano-Catholic culture, accounts for part of the gap. As Figure 13 shows, immigration not only began later and was less massive (notice that the scale of the graphs varies) in Argentina than in the United States but it was also less divided into early and late waves. The French stream to the River Plate did peak earlier than the others, and the Spanish and Russian movements did take off rather late, but there was less of the sharp split between old and new currents that characterized

Table 23 The effect of "social distance" on ethnic residential segregation in Latin-Catholic and Anglo-Protestant cities, ca. 1910: Index of segregation from native population

Latin-Catholic cities

Cultural type	Buenos Aires (1909) Group	I^s	Montreal (1911) Group	I^s	Rio de Janeiro (1920) Group	I^s
Latin-Catholic	Italians	7.9	French	15.9	Portuguese	24.7
	French	21.3	Italians	24.3	Spaniards	31.1
	Spaniards	21.4	Belgians	30.8	Italians	39.4
Non-Latin Catholic	Austrians	22.0	Irish	39.6		
Anglo/Germanic Protestant	Germans	24.8	English	37.6	Germans	36.6
	English	29.4	Scots	42.1	English	49.3
Jewish, Muslim, Maronite	Russians	49.6	Syrians	48.0	Turks	47.5
	Turks	50.0	Russians	62.8	Russians	52.8

Anglo-Protestant cities

Cultural type	Mean of 11 U.S. Cities[a] (1910) Group	I^s	Toronto (1911) Group	I^s	London (1911) Group	I^s
Anglo-Protestant	English/ Welsh	17.8	Scots	3.2	Scots	21.6
	Scots	21.6	English	7.7		
English-speaking Catholic	Irish	25.5	Irish	7.8	Irish	20.9
Protestant non-British	Germans	26.7	Germans	13.0	Germans	26.3
	Swedes	32.7	Swedes	18.7		
Southern and eastern Europe/ Jewish, Catholic or Orthodox	Poles[b]	57.0	Italians	40.5	Italians	46.1
	Russians	57.2	Rumanians	65.9	Poles	69.8
	Italians	58.9	Russians	66.7	Russians	71.4

(continued on next page)

Table 23 *(continued)*

SOURCES: See the notes and sources for Table 22.

ªThe segregation index represents the average of each immigrant group in the eleven U.S. cities listed in Table 22, except for Scots, who were not among the top ten groups in Chicago or New York City, and for Swedes, who were not among the top ten in St. Louis, Philadelphia, Columbus, or Cincinnati.

ᵇPoles are not listed in the 1910 census and are not included in Lieberson's tables for 1920, so I used his data for 1930 but also calculated the Polish I$_s$ for Chicago in 1920 to check for variance: it was 51.2.

North American immigration (compare the two columns of graphs in Figure 13). The high segregation indexes for U.S. cities around 1910 in part obeyed the recency and abruptness of southern and eastern European immigration and the socioeconomic distance (not only sociocultural) from natives and old settlers that this entailed.[161] The native and old-stock middle and even working classes did not just flee from the sudden invasions of poor foreign peasants who spoke strange tongues, prayed in peculiar ways, and even paraded "bizarre" statues in public. They also barred the newcomers from particular neighborhoods by procedures that ranged from market mechanisms and informal discrimination of the no-Irish-or-dogs variety to institutionalized bigotry in the form of municipal zoning laws or restrictive housing covenants (legal contracts that prohibited owners from selling or renting to specified ethnic groups, outlawed by the U.S. Supreme Court in 1948).[162] On the other hand, the more parallel arrival time of immigrants in Argentina deterred the formation of wide socioeconomic gulfs between them and the resulting high spatial separation. The greater continuity in the composition of the flow (predominantly Italo-Hispanic all along) further discouraged residential flight. The native-born middle class (made up primarily of second- and third-generation Argentines) was less likely to flee from waves of new arrivals who resembled their parents or grandparents or to bar them from their neighborhoods with discriminatory zoning laws and housing covenants.[163]

If anything, Figure 13 underplays the difference between the two host countries, for it misleadingly depicts Spanish emigration to Argentina as being as belated as that of Italians and Russians to the United States. In comparison with the hundreds of thousands who landed in the decade before World War I, the thousands who came in the midnineteenth century barely appear on the graphs, giving them a similar outline. But if we remove the early-twentieth-century peaks and show nineteenth-century immigration in cumulative form (see Figure 14), a different pattern emerges. The Spanish current now appears significantly earlier than does that of the two other groups. These early arrivals may not make a visual impression on a graph that covers the whole mass-migration period, but it is impossible to overestimate their importance. In 1855 the 5,800 Spaniards in Buenos Aires already accounted for 6 percent of the city's inhabitants. By contrast, in the same year the 968 Italians in New York City made up 0.01 percent of the city's population, and the 116 Russians represented an even more infinitesimal proportion.[164] This lack of old, established communities and the abruptness of the immigrants' arrival accounts for part of the huge gap in the segregation indexes of southern and eastern Europeans in North American cities on the one hand and the Spaniards in Buenos Aires on the other. The high segregation of Russians and Middle Easterners in Buenos Aires, groups that truly resembled North American "new" immigrants in that they not only arrived late but few preceded them in the city during the nineteenth century, confirms the importance of long-settled communities in the residential adaptation of later arrivals.

The cultural, linguistic, and religious breach between these last two groups and the host city was no doubt a factor in their residential isolation, but again the social-distance hypothesis has its limits. After all, Spaniards—the charter group in Argentina—were consistently and considerably more segregated, both from the rest of the population and from Argentines, than Italians were; in most census years they were also more segregated than the French; and on occasions even more than the British (see Table 24).

The fact that the immigration of Italians peaked earlier than did that of Spaniards (Figures 13 and 14) could partially account for their greater residential dispersion.[165] Yet the Italians were already the least segregated Europeans in 1855 and always displayed a lower index of segregation than did the French, who arrived even earlier. In other words, from the beginning and regardless of relative time of arrival, Italians showed a greater capacity or willingness to intersperse among the native population. For instance, in 1855 they outnumbered Spaniards two to one in the city as a whole but four to one in the black areas of Monserrat—which may explain why the most acrid lyrics in Afro-Argentine carnival songs were often reserved for the "apolitanos [Neapolitans] / usurpers, / who every job / take from the poor."[166]

This difference sprung in part from the nature of the major settlement zones of the two groups and the way they originally reached the city. Most of the early Spanish arrivals of the midnineteenth century came, as we saw, through the auspices of the old colonial merchant community of

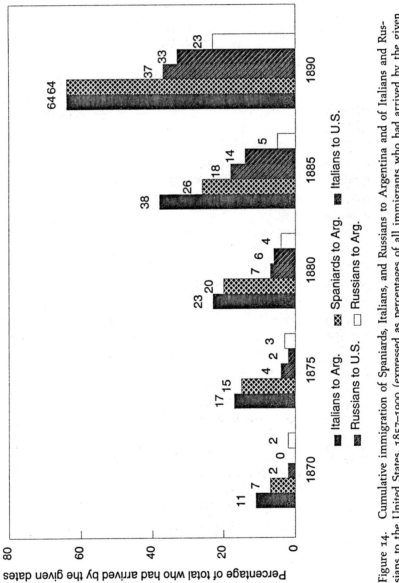

Figure 14. Cumulative immigration of Spaniards, Italians, and Russians to Argentina and of Italians and Russians to the United States, 1857–1900 (expressed as percentages of all immigrants who had arrived by the given dates). *Source:* Database compiled from Argentine and U.S. official statistics.

Table 24 Indexes of residential segregation for the principal immigrant groups in Buenos Aires, 1855–1936

Group	1855	1887	1895	1904	1909	1914	1936
Between each group and the rest of the population							
Spaniards	17.2	28.7	24.4	24.7	21.7	18.7	14.7
Italians	14.9	15.7	12.1	10.6	11.5	11.2	12.2
French	27.5	24.8	19.9	19.6	19.3	19.7	19.3
Jews[a]	–	–	57.8	45.9	47.5	–	40.3
Turks[b]	–	–	–	–	49.0	33.1	29.3
Between each group and the native-born							
Spaniards	21.0	28.2	25.3	21.4	19.1	14.4	
Italians	16.5	9.9	7.7	7.9	7.7	10.4	
French	32.1	26.8	21.9	21.5	22.3	20.2	
Jews	–	–	–	49.0	–	37.5	
Turks	–	–	–	50.0	34.1	30.0	

SOURCES: Municipal manuscript census returns, 1855; Buenos Aires, Dirección General de Estadística Municipal, *Censo general de población, edificación, comercio e industrias de la ciudad de Buenos Aires, 1887* (Buenos Aires: Compañía Sud-Americana de Billetes de Banco, 1889), vol. 2, 60–66; Argentina, Comisión Directiva del Censo, *Segundo censo de la República Argentina, 1895* (Buenos Aires: Taller Tip. de la Penitenciaria Nacional, 1898), vol. 3, 15; Buenos Aires, Dirección General de Estadística Municipal, *Censo general de población, edificación, comercio e industrias de la ciudad de Buenos Aires, 1904* (Buenos Aires: Compañía Sud-Americana de Billetes de Banco, 1906), 79–88; idem, *Censo general de población, edificación, comercio e industrias de la ciudad de Buenos Aires, 1909* (Buenos Aires: Compañía Sud-Americana de Billetes de Banco, 1910), vol. 1, 3–17; Argentina, Comisión Nacional del Censo, *Tercer censo nacional, 1914* (Buenos Aires: Talleres Gráficos de L. J. Rosso, 1916–1919), vol. 2, 129–48; and Buenos Aires, Comisión Técnica Encargada de Realizar el Cuarto Censo General, *Cuarto censo general, 1936* (Buenos Aires: Talleres Gráficos de Guillermo Kraft, 1938), vol. 2, 130–71 for nativity and vol. 3, 295–99 for religion (Jews). Because of changes in the city's census districts, the data are entirely comparable only from 1904 on. The computations for 1887 are, moreover, based on the population aged six and over, a fact that may have raised the indexes because many of the immigrants' Argentine-born children are excluded.

[a]The source for Jews, Eugene F. Sofer, *From Pale to Pampa: A Social History of the Jews of Buenos Aires* (New York: Holmes & Meier, 1982), 87, includes Argentine-born Jews. To see whether this altered the indexes significantly and using data from the 1909 and 1936 municipal censuses, I computed the index for the foreign-born only (who accounted for 80 percent of the 16,500 Jews in the city in 1909 and 39 percent of the 120,177 in 1936). The indexes went up only one to two points when the Argentine-born were excluded.

[b]Immigrants from the Ottoman Empire, mostly Sirio-Lebanese and Armenians.

the city and thus settled primarily in the central areas, which were inhabited by this mercantile class. The major ties of the early Italians arrivals, on the other hand, were to the Genoese sailors' colony in the peripheral vicinity of La Boca. The central area had a greater potential for growth in that it offered a wider range of residential and occupational choices, and as time went on, the Spanish settlement there both became more concentrated and expanded spatially to the south. The settlement in La Boca, an area of wooden buildings that already by 1887 showed the highest illiteracy rate of any district in the city and the third highest concentration of *conventillo* dwellers, offered more limited residential and occupational perspectives, and from very early on Italians began spreading into San Telmo, San Nicolás, and almost every other district of the city.[167]

Clearly then, levels of segregation resulted from factors other than the usual, and critical, foursome of sociological studies: sociocultural distance, including degree of assimilation or discrimination; socioeconomic class; length of residence; and the so-called pluralist hypothesis, which views segregation as a function of the ethnic group's desire to preserve its culture.[168] History, often disregarded by sociologists, also played an important role. As was the case with residential centralization, the patterns of spatial distribution set in the early formative period shaped the mature communities and displayed a remarkable degree of continuity.

Intra-Spanish Residential Patterns

The influence of early configurations and historical development on later residential patterns proved no less crucial at the intra-Spanish level. As Table 25 indicates, of all the Iberian regional groups in Buenos Aires in 1910, Galicians showed the greatest proclivity to mix residentially with other Spaniards, just as they had in the midnineteenth century. Inversely, the stereotypically Spanish Andalusians were particularly segregated, less prone to intermingle with their compatriots than the presumably un-Spanish (or anti-Spanish) Catalans and Basques. That had been exactly the case half a century earlier. An entire peninsula, different languages and cultures, and an even wider economic gap separated Galicians and Catalans in the Old World. Yet in 1910 Buenos Aires the two groups constituted the most spatially united pair among the twenty-eight possible combinations. Again, they had also sported the lowest index of mutual segregation in 1855. Clearly, early settlement patterns, rather than socioeconomic or cultural proximity, accounted for the overall interspersion of

Table 25 Residential segregation between Spanish regional groups in Buenos Aires, 1855 and 1910: Indexes of residential dissimilarity between each pair (the higher the index number the more segregated the groups are from each other)

1855

	Galicians	Basques	Catalans	Andalusians	Asturians
Galicians	–				
Basques	16.2	–			
Catalans	15.5	21.9	–		
Andalusians	19.4	25.4	23.6	–	
Asturians	27.8	26.0	34.5	30.6	–
Canary Islanders	17.5	30.8	27.7	32.1	38.6

1910

	Galicians	Basques	Catalans	Andalusians	Asturians	Leonese	New Castilians
Galicians	–						
Basques	20.9	–					
Catalans	12.8	30.4	–				
Andalusians	18.4	28.0	28.7	–			
Asturians	15.6	22.8	19.8	24.8	–		
Leonese	17.6	20.1	25.8	23.7	18.0	–	
New Castilians	19.1	24.2	27.2	23.4	21.1	24.9	–
Old Castilians	20.5	22.6	22.3	23.8	21.3	27.3	13.9

SOURCES: Municipal manuscript census returns, 1855; and membership records of 1,547 Spaniards who joined the Asociación Española de Socorros Mutuos de Buenos Aires in 1910.
NOTE: For an explanation of the segregation index, see Table 10.

Galicians, for the greater spatial aloofness of Andalusians, and for the residential propinquity of Galicians and Catalans.

Something similar took place at the provincial level. Among Galician immigrants in Buenos Aires in 1910, those from the coastal provinces of La Coruña and Pontevedra mixed spatially with each other to a much

Table 26 Residential segregation between Galician provincial groups in Buenos Aires, 1910: Indexes of residential dissimilarity between each pair

	La Coruña	Pontevedra	Lugo
La Coruña	–		
Pontevedra	15.5	–	
Lugo	28.6	21.2	–
Orense	22.4	21.2	19.3

SOURCE: Membership application forms of the 659 Galicians who joined the Asociación Española de Socorros Mutuos de Buenos Aires in 1910.

greater degree than with their fellow *gallegos* from the interior provinces of Lugo and Orense, who in turn showed a high degree of mutual integration (see Table 26). A corresponding analysis cannot be made for the midnineteenth century precisely because although there were more than 2,300 *gallegos* in the city then, fewer than a score originated from the interior provinces, from which emigration took off more than a generation later (see Figure 9). The provinces were more or less equidistant in the Old World. The fact that their denizens in the New World host city were not reflects their disparate emigration patterns. That is, those who came at the same time were more likely to settle in the same place.

Descending on the geographical scale to the intraprovincial level, Table 27 shows the residential differentiation among immigrants from the five counties of Navarre living in Buenos Aires around 1920. Unlike the Galician provinces, these counties were not equidistant, either geographically (see Map 4) or socioculturally. The northern counties—particularly the Pyrenean valleys—formed then Euskara-speaking bastions of dispersed farmsteads and hamlets, communal lands, widespread ownership, and an agropastoral tradition. As one moved south the Basque language became less audible, settlements more nucleated, land tenure more unequal, and pastoralism less common. By the time one reached the Ebro Valley on the south, the larger commercial vineyards and the omnipresent Castilian made this area more akin to the Rioja region than to northern Navarre. Yet geographical distance between the Navarrese in Buenos Aires poorly reflected their geographical and sociocultural distance back home. For instance, immigrants from Estella mixed less with their next-door neighbors

Table 27 Residential segregation between immigrants from the various counties of Navarre living in Buenos Aires, ca. 1920: Indexes of residential dissimilarity between each pair

	Pamplona	Aoiz	Estella	Tafalla	Mean index
Pamplona	–				13.7
Aoiz	10.7	–			15.2
Estella	10.6	11.9	–		16.1
Tafalla	12.7	18.1	17.1	–	18.3
Tudela	21.0	19.9	24.9	25.3	22.8

SOURCE: Membership records of various immigrant associations in Buenos Aires for 1,202 Navarrese who joined between 1919 and 1921.

from Tafalla than with the more distant Aoizians, and newcomers from the southernmost county (Tudela) mixed less with the arrivals from the adjacent county (Tafalla) than with those from the spatially and culturally more distant northern counties. The tempo of emigration seemed a stronger predictor. As we saw in the previous chapter, the Navarrese stream to the River Plate originated in Pamplona County and from there spread consecutively to Aoiz, Estella, Tafalla, and Tudela (see Map 4 and Figure 10). The mean segregation indexes of the Navarrese in Buenos Aires from one another went from low to high exactly in that order.

The molding force of initial arrangements on latter residential formations proved, if anything, more potent at the microlevel of specific Iberian localities. For example, newcomers from the town of Ferrol who lived in Buenos Aires during the first three decades of the twentieth century were the fourth most centralized residents among the Spanish hometown groups I examined (see Table 28). This resulted in part from the Ferroleans' urban background and the corollary occupational makeup (they had the fourth lowest concentration in unskilled jobs, the third highest in skilled ones, and the fourth highest in nonmanual occupations among the seventeen groups in the sample). Yet their centralization was also the outcome of residential distribution patterns fashioned in the early days of the community. In 1855, 65 percent of the Ferroleans in the city had resided in the central precincts that later became districts 12, 13, and 14; by the end of World War I, 56 percent of them lived there. And the degree of

Table 28 Ward of residence in Buenos Aires of immigrants from seventeen Spanish villages and towns, 1902–1930 (in percentages)[a]

Village or town	N	Ward[b]																			
		1	2	3	4	5	6	7	8	9	10	11	12	13	14	15	16	17	18	19	20
Caldas	424	1	6	9	4	1	2	1	1	5	2	2	23	27	8	1	1	0	3	2	1
Cambados	114	1	1	8	0	1	0	3	3	4	3	0	22	34	11	1	1	4	4	1	2
Ribadumia	54	0	2	4	2	13	0	0	6	4	2	0	9	30	22	0	0	2	2	0	4
Cuntis	160	1	3	8	2	1	1	3	4	4	6	3	14	28	8	0	0	3	6	4	4
Ferrol	414	1	3	9	3	4	2	1	4	2	3	2	19	24	10	0	1	1	2	2	5
Finisterre	72	0	3	29	19	6	1	1	0	7	0	1	14	6	6	0	0	0	0	0	7
Corcubión	87	1	3	7	9	0	1	1	6	3	3	8	14	29	8	0	1	2	0	1	1
Mugía	64	2	17	9	9	2	3	2	14	2	3	2	11	8	6	0	0	0	6	3	2
Camariñas	45	0	7	2	38	0	0	0	2	2	0	0	4	16	9	0	0	0	0	18	2
Vimianzo	96	4	8	17	13	0	1	1	19	2	4	1	5	7	2	0	2	0	3	13	0
Pamplona	378	3	3	4	1	5	3	1	6	5	6	2	8	25	12	2	2	1	3	2	4
Aoiz	56	0	2	11	4	2	7	5	2	4	2	20	9	20	4	5	5	0	0	0	0
Lumbier	90	3	1	0	0	4	9	1	1	7	0	1	3	36	23	0	1	1	0	7	1
Estella	110	2	2	5	2	0	4	1	1	6	6	1	9	26	23	3	4	0	3	2	1
Tafalla	242	3	3	5	2	1	3	2	8	7	5	2	16	19	8	8	0	0	4	1	3
Val de San Lorenzo	96	5	2	6	0	0	5	2	5	2	0	1	0	3	7	5	2	0	0	15	7
Mataró	64	8	5	6	0	3	2	2	6	8	13	0	6	11	11	0	13	3	3	2	0

Total, sample	2,566	2	4	8	4	2	2	1	5	4	3	2	14	23	10	2	1	1	4	3	3
All Spaniards in Buenos Aires	173,290	3	5	11	3	3	4	3	5	6	3	3	9	13	8	3	2	5	5	5	
All non-Spaniards in Buenos Aires	1,222,738	4	4	7	6	4	5	4	7	6	4	3	5	4	4	4	4	9	6	3	

SOURCES: Membership records of six immigrant voluntary associations in Buenos Aires; for all Spaniards and non-Spaniards, Buenos Aires, Dirección General de Estadística Municipal, *Censo general de población, edificación, comercio e industrias de la ciudad de Buenos Aires, 1909* (Buenos Aires: Compañía Sud-Americana de Billetes de Banco, 1910), vol. 1, 3–17.

NOTE: Caldas, Cambados, Ribadumia, and Cuntis are in the Galician province of Pontevedra; Ferrol, Finisterre, Corcubión, Mugía, Camariñas, and Vimianzo are in the Galician province of La Coruña (the last five of these, in the county of Corcubión); Pamplona is the capital of the province of Navarre, and Aoiz, Lumbier, Estella, and Tafalla are towns in that province; Val de San Lorenzo is a village in the province of León; Mataró is in the province of Barcelona.

[a]Not all rows add up to 100 because of rounding and because less than 0.5 was listed as 0.

[b]The two wards with the heaviest concentrations of immigrants from each village or town are in boldface type. For the location of the wards, see Map 10C.

continuity surpassed what the two figures suggest. After all, in the latter period twenty Ferroleans lived in neighborhoods where their predecessors could not have lived simply because they did not exist in the midnineteenth century. If we exclude that score and actually compare the same area of the city (that is, the area that was built and inhabited in both 1855 and 1920), the proportion of all Ferroleans residing in what became districts 12–14 during the two periods is amazingly similar: 64 and 63 percent, respectively.[169]

This contradicts the notion (perhaps accurate in most U.S. cities) that old immigrant groups were the most decentralized because they had had more time to move out of the core areas of first settlement. The Ferroleans were among the most centralized Iberian townspeople precisely because of their early arrival, the residential patterns formed then, and the durability of these molds. Moreover, the persistence of these microlevel patterns both derived from and helped to shape the city's macrostructure. Ferroleans stayed around and kept settling in the central wards partly because the inner city preserved its status. In turn, their residential behavior, combined with that of many other hometown groups (Iberian or not), fostered this type of ecological stability in the face of rapid spatial and infrastructural expansion.

The settlement of immigrants from Val de San Lorenzo—a village of 1,700 at the turn of the century, with a mixed economy based on subsistence and commercial cereal farming, mule pack hauling and trading, and wool weaving—offers a telling analogy. Like the Ferroleans, the Valense in Buenos Aires were underrepresented in menial, unskilled occupations and overrepresented in nonmanual and mercantile positions, due apparently to their previous commercial experience and the relative complexity of the economy of their native village in comparison with other places of similar size. Even so, they were the least spatially centralized of the seventeen groups in Table 28 and the last to arrive in Argentina. According to the village historian, the first emigrant to the River Plate departed in 1864. But the data I have collected—both in the village and Buenos Aires—indicate that they did not begin to arrive in significant numbers until after the turn of the century.[170]

Their late arrival, plus the way they adapted their premigration skills to the host city's labor market, influenced the Valense's lodging choices.[171] By the time they arrived in Buenos Aires, opportunities for artisan weavers and muleteers had long waned in the face of textile mills and railroads, so many of them ingeniously put their previous experience to use and became itinerant milkmen. But the trade was then so dominated by earlier arrivals from the western Pyrenees that the Valense had little choice but to search for delivery routes not fully exploited by their Basque competitors. Such lines were not likely to run through the old Spanish areas of the central city, with their well-established, densely populated, and thus more profitable neighborhoods. Nor were they likely to cross the southern and midwestern districts, where the Basque presence dated back to the 1840s. By default, the routes were apt to be in the rapidly expanding northern districts along the River Plate.

Within these geographical limits the specific niche originated rather arbitrarily. Around 1900, Benito Ares, a Valense pioneer in Buenos Aires, began to experiment with what turned out to be a lucrative delivery route close to the city's botanical gardens in the district of Palermo (part of wards 18 and 19). Some years later he founded in the same area a "Milk, Chocolate, and Ice Cream Store." The transition from itinerant milkman to store owner became a model of upward mobility for his townsfolk, and Palermo a favorite destination. By the early 1920s more than half (58 percent) of the Valense in the city lived in this district, a place that held fewer than a tenth of Buenos Aires' Spaniards.

The case of the Valense again contradicts the notion that latecomers or the recently arrived originally concentrated in the inner city. Their spatial decentralization and uncommon choice of neighborhood sprang precisely from the recency of their immigration and the lack of binding ties to the past. Unlike arrivals from most other towns in Table 28, these latecomers did not encounter the magnetic pull of a traditional, nineteenth-century enclave in the heavily Spanish central districts. They were also the only group in the sample that began to arrive when Palermo and the northern periphery were already developed. Their residential behavior suggests one of the ways in which the urban periphery could grow without invasion-succession movements. Many moved there straight from European towns, not from downtown Buenos Aires.[172]

Some even headed directly for the satellite colonies that developed early on beyond the city limits. For example, a Valense immigrant recalled his 1911 arrival in the town of Santos Lugares, two kilometers west of the Federal District: "I was told immediately that there were daily reunions of *paisanos* in the house of Lorenzo Andrés. There I was received as if I were an envoy. A shower of questions relating to the village fell on me. It was as if we were in the native village. How fortunate it is to arrive in a foreign land and find one's self among one's people with so much camaraderie and fraternity!"[173] These satellite colonies, common to many groups,[174] did not resemble therefore areas of second settlement in the North American sense of the term; that is, places where the more established and successful immigrants moved after having "made it" in the city. Back-and-forth flows linked these colonies to both Europe and Buenos Aires. If anything, the more successful tended to gravitate toward the capital city. An immigrant from Val de San Lorenzo explained that a common strategy among her *paisano* dairy-store owners consisted in opening an establishment in the province or in peripheral areas of the city, where the rent or price for it was cheaper and the competition weaker, and to move centripetally if, and as, the business prospered.[175]

Other qualitative and quantitative evidence points in the same direction. For example, Carmen Urtasún, the daughter of an immigrant from Peralta, Navarre, related how her family had moved to Villa Ballester (the townspeople satellite colony in the province of Buenos Aires) but had eventually returned to the city when the father's business became prosperous.[176] An analysis of applications for membership in the main Spanish mutual-aid society in Buenos Aires suggests that the Urtasúns' case was not uncommon. Between 1908 and 1910 the transfer papers of members who came from other Spanish mutual-aid societies in South America were kept in their files, allowing me to differentiate between the 201 migrants from the satellite towns in the province of Buenos Aires and the 5,032 members who had joined in the city. The data indicate that immigrants who settled in the city were more skilled than those who settled in the province. Despite this, those who came from the province were twice as likely to own their own businesses as were their compatriots in the Federal District and, on the average, ten years older. This suggests a migration of older people into—or back to—the city after having "made it" in the province.[177]

The town of Mataró, whose transatlantic stream moved in a rhythm almost antithetical to that of Val de San Lorenzo, offers added insights into the effect of emigration patterns on residential distribution. As we saw in the previous chapter, the literacy and skill level of the emigrants from this Catalan industrial center greatly surpassed the Spanish average. That background carried on into the New World, making them the most literate and skilled of the seventeen groups in the sample. Such socioeconomic makeup in turn facilitated their residential concentration in the better areas of the central city and the northern suburb of Belgrano (ward 16). But their residential idiosyncrasy lay in dispersion rather than concentration in any particular ward, and it reflected their distended rhythm of immigration (see the first section of chapter 3). The arrival of scattered individuals over a long time period dating back to the eighteenth century deterred residential agglomeration and made the Matarones by far the most evenly distributed of all the groups in Table 28. It probably also deterred other forms of agglomeration. Unlike the Valense, the Ferroleans, and at least eleven other groups in the sample, the Matarones never formed a hometown association in Buenos Aires. And the diversity of their surnames and the tales of old immigrants indicate that extended kinship groups were as rare. The pattern of arrival—perhaps aided by their presumably more capitalist cultural background—turned the Mataronese into the least communal of the groups and the closest thing to the liberal image of immigrants as self-reliant free spirits and individualistic trailblazers.

By contrast, immigrants from the county of Corcubión, in the northwestern tip of the peninsula, seemed to belong to one large, interrelated clan.[178] Whereas the sample of 68 immigrants from Mataró included 57 different patronymics—or 1.2 persons per surname—the sample of 696 immigrants from the county of Corcubión included 95 different patronymics—or 7.3 persons per surname. Francisco Lema, the immigrant from the village of Vimianzo with whom I began this chapter, shared his last name with no fewer than 98 other newcomers from the county.[179] After Lema, Francisco's mutual-aid society application form stated *sin segundo* (without a second). But not everyone was that honest. Because a single surname—in Spain, though not in Argentina—denoted unknown or unacknowledged paternity, the immigrants—even many who appear in baptismal certificates with just a matronymic because of their illegitimate birth—commonly used two surnames in their community affairs.[180] The practice—and the dishonesty—exposes a veritable appellative web among the Corcubionese. Two doors down from Francisco's tenement room were three Lema Trillo brothers (either his cousins or legitimate half-brothers), followed up the hall by five Blanco Trillo siblings living with an older Trillo Lema woman—apparently their mother. In the same linear block one could find two Blanco Domínguezes, three Domínguez Blancos, two Trillo Domínguezes, four Casais Blancos, and one Domínguez Casais. Along the Plaza Brown the combinations continued: Blanco Martínez, Martínez Domínguez, Martínez Lema, and an honest Martínez X. Indeed, just four last names (Lema, Blanco, Domínguez, and Martínez) in various combinations sufficed to provide paternal and maternal surnames to 78 Corcubionese residents of southern Buenos Aires. And their communalism extended beyond primary ties to secondary associations. Unlike the Mataronese, they founded two native-place societies in Buenos Aires, which by the 1920s had more than 800 dues-paying members, and their own monthly magazines.

Corcubionese solidarity also found a spatial expression. Their residential agglomeration doubled that of the Mataronese. More than one-third concentrated, of all places, on a few blocks in the Italian enclave of La Boca (ward 4 and the southern part of 3).[181] Unlike the Valense, this odd choice sprang not from recency of arrival and lack of ties to old established settlements. On the contrary, it was the outcome of a long tradition dating back at least to the midnineteenth century, when a group of sailors from the main maritime villages of the county (Corcubión and Finisterre) settled—not unnaturally—in the shipping quarters along La Boca ("mouth") of the Riachuelo River (see chapter 3). Others followed, and by the end of the century more than a hundred Corcubionese resided in the area (based on the occurrence of local patronyms, since the manuscript schedules of the 1895 Argentine census only indicate country of birth).

But then why did Francisco Lema, the son of peasants from the interior village of Vimianzo, reside in maritime La Boca while his *paisano* Juan Díaz Novo, from a maritime merchant family in the coastal village of Corcubión, reside in downtown Buenos Aires?

The answer to the first half of the question lies partially in the ramification and diffusion processes analyzed in the first chapter. Over time, emigration fever tended to branch out from the pioneer families to ever-more-distant kin (the cousin-of-a-cousin phenomenon) and—in a related process—to spread from the original foci to neighboring localities. By the twentieth century many from Corcubión County reached La Boca pulled by the self-propelling momentum of this process rather than by the area's nautical activities. Indeed, by the end of World War I the majority (55 percent) were, like Francisco, peasants from the agricultural villages of the county's interior who simply trailed the "grandchildren of the cousins of the cousins" of the coastal towns' sailors who had originally settled the area three generations earlier.

The answer to the second half of the question lies in a combination of Old and New World developments. In 1851, according to a local enumeration, the municipality of Corcubión had 1,324 inhabitants, of whom 230 were "men of the sea." Half a century later (1905) a municipal manuscript census (which I transferred into an electronic data set) listed 1,608 residents but only 62 sailors or fishermen. The town may have not reached even the lowest official definition of urban (more than 2,000 inhabitants), but its economy had gone beyond that of a fishing village. The expansion of the sardine-salting industry, of the coal-supplying business for passing steamers, of local and regional commerce, and—as administrative head of the county—of the state bureaucracy made Corcubión's social structure quasi-urban by the early decades of the twentieth century. While the town developed, on the other side of the Atlantic, La Boca declined. The completion of Buenos Aires' deepwater port and northern harbor in the last decade of the nineteenth century put an end to the southern district's previous maritime prosperity. With the transoceanic traffic gone and the city's south-side shipping relegated to cabotage, the area lost its economic sway. It turned increasingly into a lower-class ward, hardly the place to attract the offspring of merchants, schoolteachers, scribes, clerks, tradesmen, and bureaucrats from Corcubión County's developing main town. Of twenty-eight immigrants from the town whose parents belonged to this petite bourgeoisie, twenty-four had settled in the central city and only one in La Boca. On the other hand, of the sixty-two immigrants from the county whose parents were peasants, rural laborers, sailors or fishermen, sixteen had settled downtown and twenty-three in La Boca.

Francisco Lema and Juan Díaz Novo may have come from the same Galician county, at the same age, on the same year and boat, and belonged to the same native-place association in Buenos Aires, but they belonged to different worlds. Below the Corcubionese close-knit communalism and appellative web lay fissures along lines of specific native-place, social class, gender, marital status, and even kinship (see Table 29). For those born in the town of Corcubión the chances of living in central Buenos Aires were two out of three; for those born in Vimianzo, they did not reach one out of five. Immigrants from the whole county employed in menial jobs were three times more likely to live in La Boca than in the central wards; the inverse was true for those in the middle- and upper-white-collar class. As in the midnineteenth century, the invisible skill or who-you-know-factor played a role: unskilled laborers from the town of Corcubión were still twice as likely to live in the downtown area as were unskilled laborers from Vimianzo. Moreover, intervillage differentiation could appear within the same city district or even within a few city blocks. As Map 17 illustrates, immigrants from Vimianzo clustered on the west side of Plaza Brown in La Boca; those from Camariñas, on the south side; and those from Finisterre, on the north side. In a way, the Corcubionese recreated in the microcosm of a few city blocks the settlement patterns of their Galician county, transmuting Old World villages and hamlets into New World buildings and blocks.[182] The conspicuous and extended kinship web

Table 29   Occupational, demographic, and residential disparities among immigrants from Corcubión County (La Coruña) in Buenos Aires, 1900–1930 (in percentages)

Municipality	N	Unskilled and menial	Skilled	Male	Single	Residents of the city center[a]
Corcubión	87	14	33	65	43	63
Finisterre	72	17	21	65	40	34
Mugía	66	21	22	82	58	32
Camariñas	45	33	6	92	62	30
Vimianzo	96	41	16	78	58	19

SOURCES: Membership application forms for the Asociación Española de Socorros Mutuos de Buenos Aires, 1900–1930; and membership registers plus medical records from the Centro Gallego de Buenos Aires, 1907–1930. The original sample shrank by more than a quarter because the latter association's registers did not include the address of the members. I thus had to check the member's medical records for the information, but many were lost. This made the numbers for the three other municipalities in Corcubión County (Cee, Dumbria, and Zas) too small for the above analysis.

a. Wards 10–14 and 20.

could equally obscure internal divisions. The recurrence of surnames may give the impression of an interrelated clan—and historians a headache when trying to reconstruct kinship ties. But natives can pinpoint the specific local origin of patronyms, differentiate various branches of families, and draw the line at which people with the same surnames cease to be "related"—a line that is highly class conscious. As we saw was the case with Ferroleans and northern Navarrese in the midnineteenth century, the Corcubionese migration chain was not class blind.

In general terms, and as was also the case in the midnineteenth century, no single regional, provincial, or village group completely dominated a district, or even a few blocks, in Buenos Aires. People from different Iberian localities and from different European countries sharing the same linear city block represented the norm rather than the exception.[183] Even the heavily Corcubionese blocks shown on Map 17 housed residents from at least six other Iberian localities and lay, after all, in the heart of a traditional Ligurian vicinity. Concomitantly, the mononucleated native-place enclave, as Table 28 revealed, hardly appeared in Buenos Aires. Immigrants from a given Spanish locality rarely, if ever, formed a single cluster

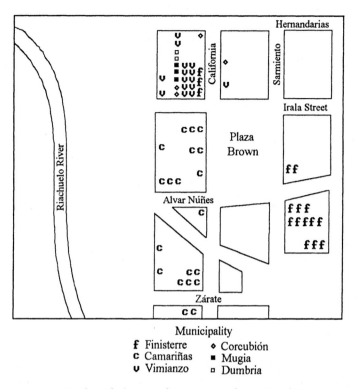

Map 17. Residential clusters of immigrants from Corcubión County, Galicia, in the La Boca neighborhood of Buenos Aires, ca. 1910.

of a few blocks where the majority concentrated and where they represented the only significant group.

Although the concept of an Argentine melting pot has received its share of scholarly attacks, these residential trends, along with the comparatively low ethnic-segregation level of the city, must have fostered contact and blending with other groups.[184] Of the 600 membership application forms for the main Spanish mutual-aid society in Buenos Aires around 1920 for which I recorded the name, birthplace, and local address of the sponsors, 185 of the latter were neighbors rather than kin or townsfolk of the applicants. New World spatial propinquity rather than Old World ties also explained the presence in Corcubión County's association of members with "typically Galician" surnames, such as Jones, Ivanissevich, Braghini, and Von der Becke, or of advertisements by La Boca Italian merchants in the association's monthly magazine, or why so many of the *paisanos'* American offspring married, as the parents put it with no great pleasure, *pichones de italianos* (second-generation Italians or, literally, Italian fledglings). Residential proximity and mixing clearly promoted "Argentinization" or, more precisely, assimilation into an eclectic and undefined but rapidly forming Porteño culture.

Other aspects of residential distribution nourished ethnic preservation. Spatial mixing with fellow Spaniards from other towns and regions advanced a national identity that may be construed as an indispensable step from parochialism to "Argentinism" but that can also be interpreted as slowing down that process. Indeed, as I will later discuss, Iberian localism could have coexisted with broader and newly gained Spanish (or ethnonationalist, such as Basque or Catalan) patriotism to present a more formidable barrier against Argentinization. By the same token, the scarcity of mononucleated native-place enclaves did not imply either that the townsfolk were evenly distributed among the general population or that they were isolated from one another. The majority usually resided in two or three identifiable clusters, and even those who appeared as dispersed often had at least one neighbor from the same hometown. Of the 2,566 individuals in Table 28, only 231 (or 9 percent) lived more than five blocks away from a fellow villager.[185]

At any rate, the transportation developments described above had done much to free the villagers' urban communities from the restraints of a physical neighborhood. For example, thirty city blocks separated Manuel Cordero of Val de San Lorenzo from his *paisana* María Navedo in 1922, but they came together in matrimony two years later. Sixteen city blocks, in turn, separated them from Francisco Andrés, but they belonged to the same village association, and their Argentine-born daughter subsequently married his Argentine-born son. What, then, were the territorial limits of their social space? A radius of sixteen blocks, of thirty blocks, of a few wards? Did it include the town of Santos Lugares, eleven kilometers from the main enclave in Palermo, where many of their *paisanos* and relatives lived? In the first decades of this century railroads, electric tramways, subways, buses, and telephones made such questions less relevant than they seem.

Changes and continuities in the ecology and infrastructure of Buenos Aires, therefore, continuously interacted with the socioaffective linkages and ideals of the newcomers to influence the community's spatial development. Yet by the midnineteenth century this interaction had already created certain molds that became key variables in shaping the future. Given the absence in Buenos Aires of imposed locational forces, such as institutionalized bigotry, restrictive zoning laws, and discriminatory housing covenants, these early molds and the social networks of the immigrants acted as the epoxy in the maintenance of cohesive Spanish settlements.

Most Argentine urban studies—most ecological approaches, for that matter—have consistently underestimated these forces, stressing only external ones such as the labor and housing market and the transportation system. Obviously, then, the Spaniards and the different Iberian groups should have spread throughout the city in the same manner as the rest of the population. But they did not. On the other hand, the class-blind chain-migration concept also fails to explain adequately the residential patterns of the Spaniards. That is, significant intravillage class segregation should not have existed. But it did. The Chicago school model yielded equally faulty results. The concentric zones proved to be the inverse; the outward movement or ghetto-to-suburb thesis, of limited applicability; and the invasion-succession phenomenon, nonexistent during this period.[186] Frail when separated, the insights from the ecological studies of Chicago school sociology and those from the chain-migration studies of social history magnified their exegetic strength when united. The combination provided an appropriate framework to explain the complex, and not always lucid, interplay between class and culture, emigration patterns and residential arrangements, the urban ecology and kinship networks.

Individual agency usually existed within the confines of this process. Had we asked Francisco Lema why he lived across Plaza Brown in 1920, his answer would have likely been: "because cousins Modesto and Celestino lived there." That was true, but far from the whole picture. He also lived there because of binding ties almost a century old; because over time the mechanisms of kinship ramification and spatial diffusion carried "Argentine fever" from the coastal strip of pioneer emigration to his hinterland village; and because that area in La Boca had declined, becoming not only a Corcubionese enclave but also a male enclave, a neighborhood of poor, illiterate, single young men of peasant background like himself—an urban ecological process that in turn derived from large external forces, such as Argentina's position in the international division of labor and Buenos Aires' role as entrepôt. Immigrants were not simply pawns at the mercy of impersonal forces; rather, they were willful agents normally within the restraints of structures and the bonds of the past. To paraphrase Ortega y Gasset, Francisco Lema was "himself and his circumstances," even if some of the circumstances were not obvious to him. It is in the interplay between these macrotrends and the microlinkages of villagers and kin, and in the molds produced by it along the way, that we find the best insight into why this illiterate laborer from Vimianzo lived across Plaza Brown and why thousands of his compatriots lived where they did.

The same synergetic process—dynamic and not always visible to either participant or observer—determined how (and how successfully) the newcomers made a living in the city that one of them called "a promise, a career, even a religion."[187]

5 Making a Living and "Making America"

In the middle of a hot January night in 1869, José María Rojas, an ex-secretary of the Argentine treasury, got out of bed to open the door of his old Buenos Aires mansion for his Basque maid. She was coming back from a ball to which a prosperous *paisano* shoemaker had taken her in a carriage. He had also favored her with a gift of an ounce of gold. "How can one expect her to sweep and wash the dishes after this," Don José complained in a personal letter to ex-governor Juan Manuel de Rosas, then in exile in Southampton, England, "the effects of that dance are already noticeable in her."[1]

If Don José's Buenos Aires did not yet embody the classic three-class society, neither did it typify a dual one of haves and have-nots, or *gente decente* and *gente de pueblo*. As his gripes betray, transatlantic waves had begun to erode the traditional "respectable" and "commonfolk" dichotomy of the colonial past. Uppity and ambitious arrivals strove to vulgarize balls, carriages, and doubloons—customary appurtenances of the better classes. In a sense, the prosperous Basque shoemaker had become a "non-decent have." Many of Don José's friends had probably waned into "decent have-nots" whose wealth consisted of a long string of patrician surnames, the titles of don and doña, and an octogenarian ex-slave, the remnants of a golden past. Falling patricians and a greater number of rising plebeians nourished an urban middle stratum of shopkeepers, clerks, merchants, accountants, and so on, which at the time of Don José's letter comprised a fifth of the city's working population and a quarter of the Spanish community.

A two-class model, then, whether based on a cultural *gente decente*–*gente de pueblo* dichotomy or on a materialistic have–have-not dialectic, does not accurately describe the social structure of either the city or the immigrant community.[2] Less reductionist classifications able to show degrees, not just poles, better suit the questions raised in this chapter: what was the nature of the labor market in Buenos Aires and the occupational distribution of the Spanish community within it in the decades following 1850, and how did this change with the rapid modernization of the turn of the century? How did Spaniards fare economically in comparison with other groups in the city? What variables (e.g., regional, local, and social origins, gender, age, and marital status) explain intra-Spanish differences in occupational status? And how often and to what extent did Spanish immigrants improve their economic situation?

A classification appropriate to both my questions and the empirical data is the one developed in 1976 by Mark Szuchman and Eugene Sofer precisely with Argentine urban centers and immigrant populations in mind.[3] Based on eight occupational categories (see Table 30), it offers a reasonable alternative to the extreme aggregation of a dichotomy and to the paralyzing atomization of unclassified occupations (the various data sets for this chapter—not counting those from Spanish sources—contained 48,684 individuals and 410 distinct job descriptions). Moreover, the classification offers the added advantage of familiarity and comparability because it resembles that used by Stephan Thernstrom in his landmark study of Boston—which in turn derives from one devised by the statistician Alba M. Edwards in the 1930s and used in most North American mobility studies ever since.[4] Needless to say, and as I shall point out, this, or any other, classificatory scheme, has clear limitations.

SPANISH OCCUPATIONAL STRUCTURE IN THE SECOND HALF OF THE NINETEENTH CENTURY

Using this vertical stratification scheme, Table 30 shows the occupational structure of the Spanish colony in 1855. Unskilled and menial workers, representing 30 percent of all employed Spaniards, occupied the bottom rung. Day laborers, peons, and porters working in the city's harbor and warehouses and in proto-industrial establishments, such as brickyards, mills, slaughterhouses, tanneries, and furniture, soap, and candle factories, accounted for 68 percent of this category. The rest were maids, washerwomen, ironers, wet nurses, and other domestic servants, 58 percent of them female. Children under the age of fourteen accounted for a fifth of the servants, and the contemporary labor shortage apparently reached this sector, judging by the abundance of classified advertisements like the following—both from 1855: "A fourteen-year-old servant named María

Table 30 Occupational distribution of Spanish immigrants in Buenos Aires, 1855, 1869, and 1895 (in percentages)

Year	N	Unskilled and menial	Semiskilled and service	Skilled	Low nonmanual	Middle nonmanual	Low professional	High nonmanual	High professional
1855	4,566	30.1	16.0	22.2	22.7	2.7	1.7	4.2	0.4
1869	1,795	31.7	16.1	23.4	22.1	2.3	1.4	2.5	0.4
1895	3,317	35.1	15.6	23.3	18.4	5.6	1.4	0.4	0.2

SOURCES: Manuscript schedules for Buenos Aires' 1855 census (a statistical universe of all Spaniards in the city), for the first national census of 1869 (a 1 in seven random sample of all the Spaniards in the city), and for the second national census of 1895 (a sample from wards 2, 3 and 19). The 1895 sample was gathered primarily to compare Spaniards with other groups then and may not be totally comparable with the other two because the three wards may not be representative of the city as a whole. Indeed, the increase in 1895 in the unskilled category and the decrease in the low and high nonmanual ones reflects some preponderance in the sample of working-class neighborhoods versus districts with large commercial establishments. Nevertheless, the marked continuity in the overall distribution suggests that the 1895 sample cannot be that unrepresentative.

Castro, white and pox-marked, has run away from her employers' home. The girl is already contracted, the police have been notified, and whoever hides her will be penalized"; and "A 50-peso [the equivalent of a week's wage for a servant] reward to whoever returns a lost eleven-year-old mestizo boy [*chinito*] named Reyes Pizarro to his employers at 185 Santa Clara Street."[5] The advertisements became so common that the newspaper developed an icon of a boy with a stick and bundle on his shoulder to head the column. Further down the respectability scale, a lumpen class occupied the fringes of the Porteño social structure, but, at the time, it was still heavily black and mestizo. Although Spanish newspapers constantly denounced white-slavery rings and the indigence of their conationals in Argentina, the manuscript schedules list only two prostitutes and three beggars among the 5,700 Spaniards in the city, figures so paltry that they must reflect more than just the normal tendency of censuses to undercount the marginal.

Semiskilled and service occupations formed the next category on the ladder and employed 16 percent of Spaniards. It included people like watchmen, gardeners, muleteers, sailors, waiters, cooks, and apprentices. The line separating them from the bottom category was often a thin one. Cooks, for example, particularly if female, did not have significantly higher status or income than other servants. On the other hand, there could be a considerable difference between the occupations within this category and even within the same occupation. For an economist, the distinction between a waiter in one of the city's best hotels and one in a cheap billiard hall may be irrelevant, but for the individual immigrant it represented a huge gap. Unfortunately, sources do not always allow such differentiations. Another methodological problem absent from the first category that appears in this and other rungs refers to qualitative changes in the same occupation over time. The tasks of a peon or day laborer did not change in any substantial way between 1850 and 1930. A barber, on the other hand, was also a tooth puller and a phlebotomist in the nineteenth century but just a haircutter in the twentieth century. I tried to rank such occupations differently at different periods, but—fortunately, in terms of methodological complications—this never altered the overall distributions among categories by more than 0.5 percent.

Skilled laborers constituted the next level and the top rung of manual workers. Twenty-two percent of Spaniards belonged to this category, and a cumulative 68 percent to the broader manual classification.[6] At the time, carpenters, masons, smiths, tanners, shoemakers, seamstresses, and bakers—that is, people with crafts that formed part of many rural arrivals' premigratory traditions—dominated this category. Those with skills that only urban immigrants usually possessed—such as machinists, watchmakers, typographers—comprised just a tenth of the artisans. Other eventually numerous skilled workers such as gas fitters, plumbers, electricians and mechanics, were still either a novelty or yet to come. Midnineteenth-century artisans, whether self-employed or not, usually lived and toiled in the same place, with the room facing the street serving as shop and the interior ones as living quarters—although on occasion the same room served both purposes. In addition to the existence of a large body of independent artisans and the inclusion of board in the remuneration, other preindustrial traits included intimate relationships with employers and the ownership of working tools. None of the Spanish craftsmen in the city worked in establishments that employed more than eight people, and ownership of tool sets made it possible for many of them to become independent workers, shop owners, or even small manufacturers. Although it may seem contradictory, some of the early workers' demands in the city included the refusal to use "one's own tools," presumably to save them from wear and tear.[7]

The low nonmanual category, to which 23 percent of Spaniards belonged, comprised a variety of small proprietors (e.g., grocers, innkeepers, clothing-store owners, hardware dealers) and employees (e.g., clerks, salesmen, bank tellers, office workers). Increasingly dominated by foreigners, this category still accommodated young men from "decent" native families, as raconteur Lucio V. López reminisced in 1882: "And what clerks! What salesmen, those of the stores then! How far indeed are the French and Spanish storekeepers of today from possessing the lineage, the social virtues, of that gilded youth, native born, last descendants of the aristocratic retailers that were colonial."[8] In terms of income, many low nonmanual workers could earn less than long-established artisans. But the significance of this category transcended the purely economic. It entailed a social dimension crucial for the throngs of lower-middle-class newcomers from Iberian provincial towns who, armed with introductory letters and a bourgeois demeanor, aspired to procure a position in the city's commercial or financial houses. Their disdainful refusal to toil in manual tasks would earn them the title of *señoritos* (little lords or effete misfits)—half mocking, half envious—from their rougher compatriots.[9] The phenomenon was not exclusive to Spaniards. Among Italians a similar group, baptized *spostati* by detractors, appeared;[10] and the more pragmatic Germans, instead of a label, developed a caustic piece of advice for the young, middle-class arrivals who felt themselves too good for a manual job: *Umlernen* (retrain yourself).[11] In a similar vein, the aspiration to be occupationally independent, to be one's own boss, found an outlet in this category, in the thousands of small retail shops of Buenos Aires that catered to the social ideals of immigrants as much as to the demands of the market.

The remaining four categories—middle nonmanual, low professional, high nonmanual, and high professional—made up less than a tenth of all Spaniards in Buenos Aires in 1855. The first two groups formed something resembling an upper middle class: midsized merchants and manufacturers, ship captains, pharmacists, music teachers, journalists. The last two categories (wholesale and international merchants, large landowners, stock brokers, and professionals, such as doctors and lawyers) fashioned the immigrant upper crust. Some of its members were also part of the local elite. The merchant Marcos Muñoa, president of the Sala Española de Comercio, belonged to several patrician societies and reputedly owned the most sumptuous mansion in Buenos Aires.[12] The Ferrolean Vicente Monjan, appeared in the directory of the Comisión de Hacendados, the forerunner of the Sociedad Rural (the association of Argentina's rural oligarchy). The Basque businessman Vicente Casares was already a bona fide Porteño Brahmin and founder of an illustrious Argentine lineage: by the first decades of the next century, sixteen of his descendants appeared on the rolls of the aristocratic Jockey Club.[13] Others had not yet reached those heights but apparently had begun the climb. Carlos Noel's modest sweets shop on Defensa Street later became one of the country's major industrial establishments, and his grandson would serve as president of the Union Industrial Argentina and as mayor of Buenos Aires.[14] Antonio Llambias, a cigar maker who rolled tobacco leaves in the front room of his home on Victoria Street (now H. Yrigoyen), would enjoy a similar distinction, with his grandson Joaquín becoming mayor in 1916. And Ramón Santamarina, still a poor *gallego* boy at midcentury, became the largest landowner in a country of large landowners by the end of the century, marrying his daughter to the son of President Nicolás Avellaneda.[15]

The occupational distribution of Buenos Aires' Spaniards retained the same profile for the rest of the nineteenth century (see Table 30). The only noticeable change—the decline in the high nonmanual category—resulted from the fact that many of the colonial wholesale merchants, alive in 1855, were dead by the next census years (1869 and 1895) and their businesses in the hands of their Argentine-born descendants or British and German competitors. The loss of manuscript schedules for subsequent Argentine censuses and the lack of appropriate alternative sources makes it impossible to determine whether such distributional constancy persisted into the twentieth century.[16]

In comparison with Argentines and with the total population, Table 31 shows Spaniards underrepresented on the extremes of the occupational spectrum and overrepresented in the middle in 1854 and 1869, respectively. Spanish immigrants, along with the other newcomers, had began to forge a three- (or multi-) class structure out of a traditional two-class society. Because foreigners constituted more than half of Buenos Aires' inhabitants and about three-quarters of the working population, their more layered social arrangement was destined to overwhelm the old dual structure, which had its roots in the colonial chasm between the white elite and the mostly colored populace. This process was further facilitated by the fact that the southeastern fringe of the old Spanish Empire—lacking sedentary Indians, mines, and a plantation economy—had developed, to begin with, less rigid and less polarized social structures than did the Mexican and Peruvian core or the slave societies of the Caribbean.

EVOLUTION OF THE SOCIAL STRUCTURE
AND LABOR MARKET IN BUENOS AIRES

The formation of a multitiered structure did not prevent—perhaps even aided—the consolidation of the economic, social, and political position of the old stock native upper class. The enormous profits that the wealth of the pampas and the growing export economy made possible turned what at midcentury had been a modestly rich elite with a rather provincial outlook into the opulent and cosmopolitan oligarchy of the belle epoque. Descendants of late-eighteenth-century northern Spanish merchants on their paternal side and of sixteenth-century conquistadors and settlers on their maternal side, and infused with the blood of some early immigrant parvenus, families like the Anchorenas, Alvears, Alzagas, Martínez de Hoz, Sáenz Valientes, Unzués, Williams, Zuberbühlers, and others had formed by the end of the nineteenth century an agropastoral plutocracy imbued with the idea of pedigree and impermeable to the foreign-born nouveau riche.

In the 1850s it had been possible for a printer from Madrid, like Benito Hortelano, or a Basque physician, like Toribio Ayerza, to gain access to the local elite. By the end of the century, unless the newcomers possessed titles of nobility or intellectual renown the doors to the world of the gilded caste were not likely to open, no matter how pecuniarily successful

Table 31 Occupational distribution of Spaniards and Argentines, 1854, and of Spaniards and the total population in Buenos Aires, 1869 (in percentages)

Group	Unskilled and menial	Semiskilled and service	Skilled	Low and middle nonmanual	Low professional	High nonmanual	High professional
				1854			
Spaniards	20.5	6.2	26.0	45.2	0.7	0.,	0.7
Argentines	25.0	11.3	20.5	35.8	1.9	3.4	2.1
				1869			
Spaniards	31.7	16.1	24.5	24.8	1.4	1.0	0.4
All	29.3	25.8	22.1	17.0	2.9	2.2	0.6

SOURCES: For 1854, computed from a list of occupations for 532 Argentines and 146 Spaniards from Karl F. Graeber, "Buenos Aires: A Social and Economic History of a Traditional American City on the Verge of Change, 1810–1855" (Ph.D. diss. University of California, Los Angeles, 1977), 143–46; for all inhabitants in 1869, computed from a list of the various occupations in the city of Buenos Aires and the number of people employed in each in Argentina, Superintendente del Censo, *Primer censo de la República Argentina, 1869* (Buenos Aires: Imprenta del Porvenir, 1872), 64–75; for Spaniards in 1869, manuscript schedules for the first national census. The figures for the two years are not comparable because Graeber's sample comes from a few districts rather than the entire city. Also, the figures for Spaniards in 1869 and those in Table 30 do not coincide because some occupations had to be categorized differently to make them comparable with published census data. All artisans had to be placed in the "Skilled" category, even if they owned a store or a shop, and all merchants in the "Low and middle nonmanual" category because the published census did not distinguish between employed and proprietor artisans or between small and large merchants.

they became. Some would actually try to exploit the Argentine elite's penchant for titles. The Italian consular agent in San Fernando, a small town in the middle of the pampas, became *cavaliero* [*sic*]; the vice consuls in Santa Fe and Córdoba went further and turned into *condes;* and the Austro-Hungarian representative in Buenos Aires toppled them with *príncipe.* Spaniards loved to ridicule such pretensions in others but were not immune to them. Don Francisco de Otín y Mesia, their government's business agent in Buenos Aires in the 1880s, exhibited a string of ten titles of nobility, including some outlandish ones, such as Knight of the Rose of Brazil and the Polar Star of Sweden and Commendatary of the Order of the White Elephant of Siam. But by the turn of the century, the days when the Argentine ruling class could be awed by spurious titles, the continental manners of mediocre French artists, the accounting practices of Liverpool merchants, or the eloquence of a Madrileño printer, were over.

The ossification of the native upper crust had a more limited impact on the arrivals than did the growth of a native middle class of recent immigrant origins. After all, even during the more accessible early period no more than a twentieth of the immigrant population could reasonably have aspired to join the ranks of the local elite. Unlike the largely nonwhite, marginalized, and poorly educated native popular sectors of the midnineteenth century, the new breed of second- and third-generation Argentines posed stiff competition for newcomers. They were as white as the arrivals, usually taller—thanks to the beef and milk of the prodigal pampas—better schooled, and proud denizens of a grand world-class metropolis. As demographic Europeanization proceeded, the city became, by default rather than design, less pigmentocratic. As commerce, the educational system, the media, and so forth expanded, it became more culturally bourgeois. Consequently, arrivals with "a good appearance" and "a good education" (Latin American euphemisms for Caucasian looks and bourgeois manners) as their sole skills lost some of their previous edge. Already by 1895 natives outranked the European born not only on the top tiers of the occupational structure but in the intermediate ones as well (see Table 32). By the third national census, in 1914, the gap had widened. The foreign born were now heavily overrepresented in the unskilled and menial category and among manual laborers in general. The historic trend found histrionic expression in numerous post–World War I plays and farces in which middle-class, Argentine-born characters repudiated the coarse deportment and lowly positions of their Spanish, Italian, and Jewish parents.[17]

A development that eased the competition encountered by European ar-

Table 32 Occupational distribution of natives and immigrants in Buenos Aires, 1895 and 1914 (in percentages)

Group	Unskilled and menial	Semiskilled and service	Skilled	Low and middle nonmanual	Low professional	High nonmanual	High professional
				1895			
Natives	25.9	11.7	27.0	26.4	5.2	2.6	1.1
Immigrants	30.1	13.3	30.1	23.4	2.3	0.6	0.2
				1914			
Natives	11.7	11.5	25.1	37.2	69.9	4.9	2.8
Immigrants	26.1	12.7	29.6	26.2	2.4	2.4	0.5

SOURCES: For 1895, a sample of 7,361 foreigners and 1,562 Argentines living in districts 2, 3, and 19, drawn from the manuscript schedules for the second national census; for 1914, computed from data in Argentina, Comisión Nacional del Censo, *Tercer censo nacional, 1914* (Buenos Aires: Talleres Gráficos de L. J. Rosso, 1916–1919), vol. 4, 201–12. The figures are comparable within each year, and so are the gaps between natives and foreigners across the two periods. However, the overall occupational distribution of the two periods is not necessarily comparable because the three districts in the 1895 sample may not be representative of the entire city.

rivals from the native middle class was the increased role of the state as employer. It is true that given the low rates of naturalization of the immigrants,[18] and the resulting lack of connections with the political machinery, the state bureaucracy did not prove to be a rich fountain of opportunities for the Spanish born or for foreigners in general. At times the growth of the public sector could even have negative effects on immigrants. The expansion of the mostly native municipal police force,[19] for example, eliminated what in the midnineteenth century had been an important source of employment for Galicians, service as watchmen. But, on the whole, by providing an alternative source of employment for the native middle classes, both the rising second generations and the old-stock déclassé, the federal and municipal bureaucracies eased competition in the private tertiary sector for the newcomers.

For the masses of working-class arrivals the escalating proletarianization of the labor force had a greater and more direct impact than did the hardening of the native upper crust or even the emergence of a second- and third-generation native middle class. The turn-of-the-century increase in large manufacturing and service enterprises, in labor unions, and in the number of strikes by skilled workers attest to this change.[20] Its impact was threefold. First, the spread of capitalist impersonal work relationships heightened class consciousness among both skilled and unskilled laborers. Second, new modes of production and mechanization displaced some artisans or downgraded the level of skill of their particular craft. For example, tobacco cutting, an important craft in the mid-1800s, had completely disappeared by 1914 because of the introduction of shredders. Similarly, the skills required from tailors and dressmakers decreased with the spread of cutting, sewing, and pressing machines; with new modes of production like the task system (where the tailor only made a specific part of the garment) and contracting (usually entailing female and child piecework in sweatshops or at home); and with new consumer practices (the acceptance of, if not preference for, ready-made, mass-produced clothing). Third, the development of large manufacturing and service enterprises often meant shrinking opportunities for occupational independence: the self-employed Basque muleteers of the 1850s were eventually replaced by the *gallego* conductors of the British-owned railroad and trolley companies; ambulant watermen were run out of business by water-bottling factories and underground pipes; carriage drivers, by the bus and subway companies; candle makers, by electric-light monopolies; blood letters, by hospitals and clinics, and so on.

Due to Argentina's retarded industrialization, however, the deskilling of labor and the proletarianization of workers came later, at a slower pace, and in a less drastic manner than the transitions described by historians like E. P. Thompson for the English working class and Harry Braverman for the North American one.[21]

In regard to the first process, the proportion of low-skilled laborers in Buenos Aires' workforce actually declined from 55 percent in 1869 to 34 percent in 1914, while that of skilled workers rose from 22 to 28 percent (see Table 33).[22] By comparison, during the same period the proportion of low-skilled laborers in New York City also declined, but much more modestly, from 56 to 48 percent, while that of skilled workers dropped precipitously, from 24 to 13 percent. In both cities the expansion of the tertiary economy augmented the share of the white-collar categories in the labor force at the expense of the nonmanual sector. Focusing on this sector may thus make the contrast between the top two cities of the Atlantic basin sharper and more accurate. In 1870 artisans and skilled workers accounted for about 30 percent of all manual toilers in both cities. By 1910–1914 that proportion had gone down to 21 percent in New York and up to 46 percent in Buenos Aires. There was no sign in the southern metropolis at the time of the large-scale (sub)standardization of manual labor then taking place in the northern industrial milieu of mass production, assembly lines, and "scientific management," something that reflected—not without its irony—the very backwardness of Argentine industry. Although mechanization had advanced much in the River Plate by the early years of the twentieth century, automation had not. The latter development usually lowers the skills required from the labor force, the former not always does. A machinist, after all, is, if anything, more skilled than a smith; and, whether one does it in a factory or not, running a lathe demands greater dexterity than jerking a hand saw.

Argentina's "backwardness" also checked the process of proletarianization. Although the average number of workers per manufacturing shop in the city almost doubled, from six in 1887 to eleven in 1909, that level of concentration still represented less than half of New York City's mean of twenty-six and less than a third of Chicago's thirty-seven. This inhibited the development of Taylorism (a principal source of deskilling in Braverman's account) and reflected the retarded formation of monopoly capitalism.[23] In a sense, the Jeffersonian society of modest yeomen that Argentina's liberal ideologues once envisioned and latifundia impeded found its expression in Buenos Aires rather than the pampas, in a Porteño "economic democracy" dominated by thousands of "industrial magnates" who were little more than penny capitalists and hyperbolic artisans. This diffu-

Table 33   Composition of the labor force of Buenos Aires and of New York City, ca. 1870 and ca. 1910 (in percentages)

Year	Unskilled and menial	Semiskilled and service	Skilled	Low and middle nonmanual	Low professional	High nonmanual	High professional
				Buenos Aires			
1869	29.3	25.8	22.1	17.0	2.9	2.2	0.6
1914	21.3	12.3	28.1	29.9	3.9	3.2	1.3
				New York			
1870	31.6	24.8	24.0	16.0	1.5	1.1	1.0
1910	23.0	25.3	13.2	30.0	5.2	2.1	1.2

SOURCES: For Buenos Aires, computed from Argentina, Superintendente del Censo, Primer censo de la República Argentina, 1869 (Buenos Aires: Impr. del Porvenir, 1872), 64–75, and from Argentina, Comisión Nacional del Censo, Tercer censo nacional, 1914 (Buenos Aires: Talleres Gráficos de L. J. Rosso, 1916–1919), vol. 4, 201–12; for New York, computed from United States, Secretary of the Interior, Ninth Census, 1870: The Statistics of the Population of the United States (Washington, D.C.: Government Printing Office, 1872), vol. 1, 793, and from United States, Department of Commerce and Labor, Bureau of the Census, Thirteenth Census of the United States Taken in the Year 1910 (Washington, D.C.: Government Printing Office, 1914), vol. 4, 180–92.

sion of ownership may have represented an outmoded and economically inefficient legacy from the preindustrial past, but it also bolstered (and stemmed from) the immigrants' desire to be their own bosses. Independent occupations did not disappear, they went through a sort of metamorphosis. So if free-spirited muleteers were no more, no-less-autonomous truck drivers emerged. Independent watermen became an anachronism, but independent plumbers did not. The demand for the candle maker's product became limited in secular society, but the need for the electrician's services increased. And as blood letters and leeches disappeared, a type of ambulatory nurse who provided a variety of house-to-house services emerged. The cultural ideal of independence was so strong that even today, after the development of monopoly capitalism and gigantic state apparatuses, the one-person or family enterprise permeates the general Porteño scape. So ubiquitous are these petty entrepreneurs that Argentines had to coin a word to describe the phenomenon: *cuentapropismo* (one's-own-ism).

The evolution of the Argentine urban economy thus seems to have charted a middle course between monopoly industrial capitalism and agrarian nonindustrial growth. Automation and mass production did not reach a point where unskilled toilers became the principal demand of the labor market. At the same time the manufacturing, commercial, and financial sectors of the economy (though ultimately resting on the agro-export realm) developed to a degree that required the infusion of a significant number of skilled and literate workers. This middle course probably offered more opportunities for occupational mobility and independence than did either extreme.[24] Moreover, it affected not only the adaptation of immigrants but also the type of prospective emigrants. Argentina, for instance, attracted a larger share of skilled and literate Italian immigrants than did the more developed United States (the other main destination for Italians) and by, the same token, attracted a larger proportion of skilled and literate Spanish immigrants than did less-developed Cuba (the other main destination for Spaniards).[25]

Greater opportunities for newcomers to Buenos Aires when compared with more-developed industrial cities resulted not only from the structure of the labor market but also from the nature of the competition. North American cities had larger, older, and better-established sectors of native-born and old-immigrant skilled and white-collar workers, who posed a more formidable competition for the newly arrived.[26] On top of this, a more nativist middle class plus shop-oriented and xenophobic trade unions (contrasted to the more political, internationalist, and open unionism of

Buenos Aires) further restricted opportunities for newcomers to North—as compared with South—America.

SPANIARDS AND THEIR "COMPETITION"

If Buenos Aires offered a relatively high level of opportunities and a weaker competition, how successful were Spaniards in taking advantage of them in comparison to others? As we saw, in 1854 and 1869 they had been more successful than Argentines and than the general population in securing a niche in the skilled and low- and middle-nonmanual categories and less successful in reaching the top of the occupational spectrum, tradi- tionally the preserve of the native elite. At the time, however, Argentines and the "general population" included a large number of ex-slaves and their descendants, seminomadic gauchos, and poor *chinos* (the contempo- rary term for persons of partial Indian descent), who were exploited and despised by the white *gente decente*. By the end of the century the Por- teño mestizo lower classes had declined in relative, and probably in abso- lute, terms, due to decimation in wars, limited migration from the interior Indian provinces, and the cataract of European blood.[27] In the interval, a more competitive immigrant and second-generation class of skilled and white-collar workers had taken shape. By the 1895 census, therefore, Spaniards were underrepresented not only at the top but also in the mid- dle of the occupational ladder and when compared with both the rest of the foreign-born population and Argentines (see Table 34).

Luckily for the Spanish arrivals, the new Creoles soon developed the taste for positions in the public bureaucracy that had characterized the old Creoles, leaving many opportunities open in the expanding private terti- ary sector. So although Spaniards were proportionately outnumbered in the middle class as a whole by the native born, they were still, by 1909, more than twice as likely to own a commercial enterprise as were the lat- ter, even after controlling for possible gender and age distortions.[28]

In terms of comparisons with other immigrant groups, published cen- suses do not list the occupations of the different nationalities, but a sample of 8,906 individuals I gathered from the 1895 manuscript returns shows Spaniards far behind the British, Germans, and the French in occupational status (see Table 34).[29] The contrast with Italians was less conclusive, be- cause Spaniards appeared slightly more concentrated in white-collar occu- pations but also in low-skilled ones. Other data point in the same direc- tion. The 1887 municipal census shows the British and Germans four times as likely as Spaniards to own an import-export business; the French,

Table 34 Occupational distribution of the major nativity groups in Buenos Aires, 1895 (in percentages)

Group	N	Unskilled and menial	Semiskilled	Skilled	Low nonmanual	Middle nonmanual	Low professional	High nonmanual	High professional
Spaniards	3,317	35.1	15.6	23.3	18.4	5.6	1.4	0.4	0.2
Italians	2,756	28.9	12.6	35.3	13.2	7.1	2.3	0.4	0.2
French	815	19.9	11.8	36.0	16.2	11.5	3.2	1.3	0.1
Germans	222	12.2	6.3	37.4	20.7	12.6	7.2	3.2	0.5
British	234	9.0	3.4	37.6	38.0	5.1	5.1	1.7	0.0
Argentines	1,562	25.9	11.7	27.0	21.6	4.8	5.2	2.6	1.2

SOURCE: Manuscript schedules for the second national census, 1895.

NOTE: Percentages were computed from a sample of every employed adult from a heavily Spanish ward (2) and from two wards (3 and 19) with a mix of nationalities, which explains why Spaniards outnumber Italians in the sample when the reverse was true in the city. The sample may also be biased toward working-class neighborhoods.

twice as likely; and Italians, one-third as likely.[30] Similarly, in 1909 one-fifth of the adult males of each of the three northern European groups owned a commercial enterprise, compared with only 7.7 percent of Spaniards and 7.3 percent of Italians.[31] Throughout the period the English, German, and French residents exhibited a higher literacy rate than Spaniards, who in turn, showed higher rates than Italians. Luckily for the Mediterranean immigrants, the Anglo, Teutonic, and Gallic newcomers never constituted more than a fourth of the foreign residents in the city, a proportion that actually declined by the early twentieth century, when they were in part replaced by less threatening, at least in the short run, Middle Easterners and eastern European Jews.[32] From a low of half of all foreigners in the city in 1855, Spaniards and Italians together increased their proportion to two-thirds by 1869, and between 1887 and 1936 accounted for seven- to eight-tenths of the foreign born.

Iberians would thus find in the immigrants from the neighboring Mediterranean peninsula their main, if not their toughest, competition for jobs and resources. In certain respects, Spaniards had some advantages over Italians: knowledge of the official language of the country; a higher literacy rate (56 versus 41 percent in 1855, 79 versus 61 percent in 1887, 74 versus 64 percent in 1914, 88 versus 80 percent in 1936); and a smaller percentage of unskilled newcomers (77 percent of Spaniards with occupations but 89 percent of Italians who entered Argentina between 1876 and 1895 were listed as rural or urban laborers).[33] These advantages, however, were not decisive or permanent. The Castilian of other Iberian linguistic groups, at least of those from a rural background in their region of origin, did not surpass by much the Italians' *cocoliche* (a derogatory term for the broken Castilian spoken by Italian "greenhorns"). The gap in the literacy rate of the two groups narrowed in the twentieth century, and so did the level of skill of newcomers. In fact, during the years before World War I the proportion of unskilled newcomers reversed. In 1909, for example, 78 percent of the Spanish arrivals and 68 percent of the Italians were listed as unskilled workers.

Both groups tried to make the most of their premigratory baggage. Spaniards seem to have done better in commerce, where language skills and literacy gave them an edge. A contemporary Italian observer commented that Spaniards "formed the endless army of clerks and salesmen in the stores of Buenos Aires, jobs for which they show special aptitudes thanks to their eloquence and good manners; and from this army, the shrewdest, most active, and intelligent go on to become great merchants."[34] Census data tend to support this assessment. In 1887, for instance, Spaniards were twice as likely to work in the city's commerce as were Italians and three times as likely to own a medium-sized or large commercial enterprise;[35] and my sample from the 1895 census returns shows them heavily overrepresented among store clerks. The other activities in which, according to the Italian observer, Spaniards proved particularly successful—journalism, bookstores, education, and the cigarette and clothing industries—also showed the effect of premigration traits: knowledge of the language and of two traditional Spanish industries.[36] Italians, on the other hand, seem to have fared better in manufacturing and handicrafts, where the strong industrial tradition of northern Italy provided some advantage.[37]

The sharpest and most intriguing contrast between the two groups relates to their participation in domestic service. As Table 35 shows, Spaniards were the nativity group in Buenos Aires most concentrated in this sector (with the exception of the small Irish minority), and Italians were among the least concentrated. Contemporaries' observations point in the same direction. Lino Palacios, the creator of a popular comic strip about a *gallega* servant ("Ramona"), remembered in an interview that "in the beginning [ca. 1860s] most servants were Creole girls from the provinces. The estancieros brought these *chinitas* as they used to call them, from the countryside. Then came the *aluvión español* [Spanish flood], and all maids were Spanish, *gallegas*. Italians rarely worked in the house, only outside, washerwomen and things like that. The *gallego* was the classic manservant."[38]

The reason for such concentration is not clear. It lies not in gender divisions, for Spaniards of both sexes were overrepresented. Nor could it be found in a celibacy rate which exceeded that of most other immigrants, because the concentration persisted after controlling for marital status and age (see bottom of Table 35). In addition to lower nuptiality, the Spanish women in the sample also married later than did the Italians (a mean age of 26.3 versus 22.5), those who were married had been so for a shorter period (a mean of 10.7 years versus 15.3 years) and had fewer children (a mean of 2.9 versus 4.0). Yet, again, even when controlling for all this, the gap persisted. Linguistic explanations do not advance us much. Spanish speakers from the city or province of Buenos Aires, after all, placed at the bottom when it came to work in domestic service. Germanic-language-speaking women clustered in the sector to a higher degree than did their Romance-language-speaking sisters. Among Spaniards, the proclivity of

Table 35 Employed males and females engaged in domestic service in Buenos Aires, by nativity, 1895

Males			Females		
Birthplace	Percent-age	N	Birthplace	Percentage	N
Spain	39.8	397	Ireland	91.7	12
France	24.6	187	Spain	88.0	266
Argentina (except Buenos Aires)	22.6	234	Argentina (except Buenos Aires)	82.4	245
Austria	18.2	22	England	80.6	31
Italy	15.5	766	Germany	75.0	36
England	11.4	44	France	68.6	169
Buenos Aires Province	10.3	445	Italy	64.9	313
Buenos Aires City	7.0	383	Buenos Aires Province	61.1	450
Germany	4.5	66	Buenos Aires City	47.9	211
All	17.5	2,774	All	68.3	1,906

Controlling for marital status and age
(single or widowed aged twelve to forty only)

Spain	48.6	208	Ireland	100.0	9
Argentina (except Buenos Aires)	41.1	112	Spain	90.7	172
			England	90.5	21
France	36.8	68	Argentina (except Buenos Aires)	88.5	183
Austria	33.3	12			
England	25.0	16	France	74.1	85
Italy	19.0	289	Buenos Aires Province	68.7	313
Germany	14.3	14	Italy	68.6	140
Buenos Aires Province	13.3	241	Germany	66.7	18
Buenos Aires City	9.3	215	Buenos Aires City	49.6	137
All	23.7	1,267	All	73.4	1,180

SOURCE: A sample of the 1895 national census schedules for Buenos Aires' district 15, kindly provided to me by Stephanie Bower of Indiana University Southeast. The sample, drawn from an upper-class neighborhood (Barrio Norte) and limited to those who filled out their own household forms, is selective rather than representative by design (Professor Bower's purpose was to study the provincial elite living in the city). The proportion of servants in the labor force therefore is much higher than in the city as a whole. This should not affect the data's reliability for comparisons between groups.

Galicians and Basques to hire themselves out as servants far surpassed that of their Castilian-speaking compatriots.[39] Social class seems an equally unconvincing—or at least incomplete—explanation. Northern Europeans relatively outnumbered Italians as domestics despite their higher general occupational status. And compared with Spaniards, Italian women's avoidance of domestic service came at the expense of concentration in other unskilled and menial jobs more than through the holding of higher positions.

The answer probably lies in a combination of employers' prejudices, employees' ethnocultural preferences, and the groups' economic situation. The Porteño gilded classes deemed French or English servants (and, in a belle-epoque fad, Japanese butlers) a mark of status.[40] On the other side, the higher-than-average economic position of northern European immigrants allowed more of them to eschew domestic service, counterbalancing—though not voiding—the effects of employers' preference. So French nationals concentrated in domestic service to a lesser degree than did Spaniards, not because employers preferred the latter (they did not) but because the French could better avoid it. The two ultramontane neighbors of the French, however, occupied a roughly similar economic position in Buenos Aires, making employers' biases in their case a potentially more determining force. Some evidence indicates that Argentine employers did prefer, after the French themselves, the latter's trans-Pyrenean neighbors to those from across the Alps. Of the 245 households in the sample that employed Spanish servants, 62 percent were headed by native Argentines; of the 214 that employed Italians, only 47 percent were. This did not relate to affordability. The average economic position of people who employed Spanish domestics somewhat surpassed that of those who employed Italians. Moreover, Italians were more dependent on their own *paesani* for domestic employment. Thirty percent of the households employing Italian servants were headed by an Italian. In comparison, only 7 percent of the households employing Spanish servants were headed by a Spaniard.

The other side of the equation must have been the immigrants' own biases. An examination of the classified advertisements that appeared in Buenos Aires' leading newspaper on two random days in 1910 showed that Italians were less likely than Spaniards to offer themselves for hire as servants, particularly women and for live-in arrangements.[41] The pattern went beyond the River Plate. From Buffalo to Brooklyn, Toronto to Tampa, and San Francisco to São Paulo, Italians, especially women, shunned domestic service with a constancy unknown to most of their neighbors (with the possible exception of Jews), even those who were better off financially.[42] Of all the twenty-six groups or places all over the world listed in Table 41 (see page 248), the Italian diaspora's engagement in domestic service ranked by far the lowest. Clearly, unless some maniacal Italophobia plagued all corners of the hemisphere, this had to reflect the newcomers' choices. Domestic service did not rank high in the Spaniards' prestige scale either, but, at least for some regional groups, its stigma seems to have been less intense. Many considered it more acceptable and respectable than factory work.[43] Interestingly, the Iberian groups with the greater propinquity for domestic service (Basques, Galicians, and Asturians) shared a rural background of widespread peasant proprietorship and female participation in farming, among themselves and with the two groups in North America with the largest relative number of domestics (Swedes and the Irish). Does this indicate a transplanted bias of farm maidens who once perceived indoor work around the house as preferable to tilling and carried such values to the new land? Whatever the answer, the decision to work in domestic service was culturally informed rather than simply imposed by external demand, the nature of the city's labor market, and the communities' demographic structure.

IMAGING THE GALLEGA MAID: DOMESTIC SERVICE, ETHNICITY, AND SEXUALITY

Don José's letter at the beginning of this chapter illustrated a common lament of the Porteño bourgeoisie about the indolence and insolence of their increasingly Spanish domestic servants.[44] Such grumbles were by no means restricted to Argentina. Throughout the nineteenth century, they appeared with monotonous consistency anywhere from France to Japan and Australia to Zambia.[45] Local circumstances, however, colored these seemingly universal gripes, giving them a xenophobic hue in countries of immigration, a racist cast in slave or colonial societies, and a bare classist tone in the more homogeneous countries.

In Argentina, xenophobic attitudes toward the predominantly Spanish domestic servants normally took the form of mocking rather than explicit bigotry. The dim-wit *mucama* (maidservant) *gallega* turned into a cultural cliché similar to that of the "Irish biddy" in nineteenth-century North America.[46] The figure became a stock character in popular theater and humor, in newspaper comic strips, and eventually in early Argentine motion pictures. The following joke, sent by a reader to the weekly *Caras y Caretas* (June 9, 1906) for a "humor contest," exemplifies the genre:

The telephone rings and María the maid answers. As soon as she listens to it, she drops the receiver and yells:

"Master! Master!"
"What is it?" he asks, alarmed.
"My cousin just called."
"And that's why you're yelling?"
"It's just that I didn't know the telephone could speak *gallego*."

As is usually the case with ethnic derision, Porteños often portrayed it as innocent and harmless. Some *gallegos* preferred to believe so. But others opted for defiance rather than denial, and, as I shall demonstrate in the last chapter, struck back.

As immigration ceased in the 1930s and foreign-born servants grew older, the *mucama gallega* increasingly became an asexual figure much like the "black nanny" of the southern United States. But in the early part of the century, the youth of the servants, the rapid feminization of the trade, and the predominance of Spaniards in it, seem to have cemented the conceptual connection between Spanish maids and sexuality in Porteño cultural constructions. The apparently casual reference to a cousin in the telephone joke represented a code that few contemporary Argentines could have failed to decipher, and it was common enough to become a formula in popular theater. In a 1910 comedy, for instance, the tenement's Don Juan brags: "I'm off now to the Spanish consulate to sweet-talk a *galleguita* maid with no cousin. . . . Get it?"[47] A decade later, another popular farce again connected the domestic service with ethnic and sexual mocking in the following dialogue:[48]

MAXIMINO [the Argentine-born son in a middle-class Galician immigrant household]: So the maid slept out. . . .
MARIIÑA [the parents' goddaughter]: She left yesterday to spend some time at the *romerías* [Spanish fiestas] and hasn't returned. Something must have happened.
MAXIMINO: What could have happened? That *gaita* [one of the Porteño ethnic epithets for Galicians] must have met some cousin.
MARIIÑA: Oh Jesus!. . . . If Godmother finds out. . . . I don't even want to think about it! She'll fire her at once.
MAXIMINO: Oh no, she won't. It suits the old lady to have a dense *gallega* like Agripina around the house so that her own accent seems less thick.

In more sympathetic terms, an anarchist playwright, in his instructions to the director, described the character of the *gallega* maid as: "A woman of the people. Without prejudices and scruples. Loves just because and as she can, and Nature rewards that genuine and noble freedom with a robust child." He then named the character of the child's father: "'*El Primo,*' one of those innumerable servants' 'cousins.'"[49] At least in this case, the image appears to embody more the maids' bid to engage in "normal" romantic behavior by circumventing their employers' controls than a rebuke of their "promiscuity."

Domestic employment's conceptual association with sexuality, however, went beyond that expressed in the "cousin" stereotype. Contemporaries frequently depicted maids as seductresses and/or seduced—depending on their sympathies and agendas—which, despite the apparent antinomy, represented an analogous figure.[50] That is, whether as flirts or victims, it imaged maids as sexually involved within the household (unlike the "cousin" figure) with the master, the sons, and less often, fellow servants. Others went farther. Many foes of emigration in Spain, as we saw in chapter 1, discerned in domestic service little more than camouflaged white slavery. Less extreme observers portrayed it as a common, if not obligatory, road to prostitution.

Did sexuality permeate the work environment of Spanish maids to such a degree? Undoubtedly, spatial proximity and daily contact between young people who were not blood relatives must have fostered physical and/or amorous relationships. Also, the inequality inherent in master-servant relations, combined with the particular gender composition, lent itself to abuses of power that acquired a sexual dimension. But if immuring and inequality did not exactly nourish chastity, they could hardly efface it in a period that was, after all, presumably more prudish—or virtuous—than ours. The paternalistic discourse of "respectable" heads of household, the mores and jealousy of bourgeois matrons, inherited taboos, and the requirements of work discipline forged a combination too strong to have been totally ineffectual in proscribing sexual affairs or abuse within the home. Of the more than two dozen Spanish ex-maids that I interviewed, only one acknowledged experiencing this form of harassment or any actual liaison with employers, although a few referred to brief and inconsequential fancies. Their main complaints centered on the lack of free time, bossy mistresses, and—less often—the employers' attempts to restrict their romantic lives. The reliability of oral history regarding the theme (particularly given the generational and gender difference) may rightly be questioned; but so can the contrary assumption (that most lied). The image of the loose/abused maid may have been endemic and ingrained in the collective imagination, but that does not make it more accurate than other such figures. It may be as real but as exaggerated as those of the drunken sailor, the ruthless pimp, the corrupt cop, or—in anticlerical Catholic countries—the pedophile priest. It may reveal more about social fears, male fantasies, and fetishes (the combination of sex, power, and uniforms) than about the actual lives of most maids.

Neither did "the service" prove a heavily traveled road to prostitution. Of the 3,432 prostitutes who registered with Buenos Aires' health dispensary between 1913 and 1917, only 8 percent had previously been employed as servants (17 percent if one counts live-out laundresses and ironers), compared with 29 percent who had worked in the needle trades and 45 percent with no previous occupation.[51] Probably, as a contemporary criminologist noted, "the number of clandestine *meretrices* exceeds by infinite proportions those who engage in their trade observing the prescribed regulations."[52] But this should not affect the share who entered the "trade" through domestic service. Indeed, the statistics concur with some Spanish parents' belief that employment "with a good family" actually provided a check on the corrupting influences of the city absent in the more "licentious" conditions of factory work.[53] In terms of nationality, Spaniards—despite their predominance in domestic service—accounted for only 12.5 percent of the 8,486 prostitutes who registered between 1910 and 1923, a slightly higher proportion than Italians (10 percent), but a much lower one, particularly in relation to the size of the respective communities, than the French and Jews (20 percent each).[54]

INTRA-IBERIAN OCCUPATIONAL PATTERNS

Comparisons between immigrants from Spain and those from other nations, particularly Italy, may offer a reliable general perspective but overlook the fact that these were highly heterogeneous countries with gross regional disparities and inequalities. Arguably, Catalans and Piedmontese had more in common with one another than each had with Estremadurans and Calabrians or with Andalusians and Neapolitans, who in turn formed more congruous pairs. Regional origin would thus prove a better predictor of occupational status in the host society than nationality.

Table 36 shows the differences in the occupational distribution of the major Spanish regional or ethnic groups in Buenos Aires in 1855 and in 1888–1910. Some of the findings are hardly surprising. Immigrants from developed Catalonia, the so-called Manchester of Spain, fared much better than immigrants from rural and poor Galicia, often referred to as the Spanish Ireland, just as English Midlanders fared better than the Irish in

Table 36 Occupational distribution of the major Spanish regional groups in Buenos Aires, 1855 and 1888–1910 (in percentages)

Group	N	Unskilled	Semiskilled	Skilled	Low nonmanual	Middle and high nonmanual	Professional
				1855			
Galicians	1,444	39.6	17.1	16.3	21.7	3.9	1.4
Basques	816	37.6	12.0	21.2	21.7	6.3	1.2
Andalusians	435	12.2	11.0	38.2	22.1	11.0	5.5
Catalans	377	9.0	23.1	31.3	22.0	10.6	4.0
Asturians	127	17.3	18.1	14.2	41.7	7.1	1.6
Canary Islanders	124	23.4	37.9	21.1	9.7	2.4	5.6
				1888–1910			
Galicians	6,603	26.5	10.1	20.5	37.6	4.4	0.9
Basques	918	22.3	9.3	14.7	43.1	9.0	1.5
Andalusians	793	9.8	7.9	25.3	47.8	5.9	3.2
Catalans	1,080	8.1	8.0	34.6	37.8	6.5	5.1
Asturians	848	18.2	8.1	13.2	53.1	6.1	1.3
Canary Islanders	83	8.4	1.2	39.8	34.9	10.8	4.8
All Spain	12,572	20.5	8.7	20.2	42.7	6.0	1.9

SOURCES: For 1855, municipal manuscript census returns; for 1888–1910, membership applications for the Asociación Española de Socorros Mutuos de Buenos Aires. Although I had another 5,188 cases from regional associations, I refrained from using them because some of the associations were mutual-aid societies—which recruit members from a wide social background—and others were social clubs—which attract more affluent people. Using these other cases could thus have slanted the sample.

Boston, New York, or Philadelphia.[55] Galicians were four times as likely to work in unskilled or menial positions as Catalans, both in 1855 and at the turn of the century; Catalans were four times as likely to be professionals.

The data in Table 36 also evidence the already stressed fact that the way people came affected the way they adapted. As explained in two previous chapters, most of the Canary Islanders of the midnineteenth century reached Argentina through the auspices of exploitative, semiofficial colonization schemes. By the turn of the century few islanders were choosing Argentina as a destination, but those who did, came individually and spontaneously. This made a tremendous difference. The first arrivals had the highest concentration of all the Iberian groups in low-skilled occupations (61.3 percent); the second, the lowest (9.6 percent).

Other arrivals from provinces with very low emigration rates to Argentina also showed this tendency to do better than average in terms of occupation. In 1855, for example, 20 percent of Spaniards from the twenty provinces with the lowest emigration rates belonged to the top four occupational categories, whereas only 8 percent of the newcomers from the top four emigration provinces did so. During the 1888–1910 period, newcomers from the less migratory half of the peninsula (the twenty-five provinces with the lowest number of cases in the sample) were half as likely to be unskilled and twice as likely to be professionals or wealthy businessmen as were those from the most migratory half (the twenty-four provinces with the highest number of cases). Indeed, in general terms, chances of having a good job in Buenos Aires increased as the number of *paisanos* in the city decreased. This apparent contradiction again demonstrates the impact of the migration pattern on the adaptation process. Obviously, having few friends and relatives in the city could hardly be considered an advantage in the job market. Less obviously but equally certain, their success overseas did not reflect the level of development of their home provinces. On the contrary, as we saw in chapters 1 and 3: the exodus ran thinner precisely in the most backward and isolated provinces. What this indicates is that the social composition of the flow varied according to the stages of its growth curve, with the early phase in the curve containing a disproportional number of better off or more skilled people. In a sense, the lack of knowledge, information, familiarity, and facilities in areas of incipient emigration functioned as sieves through which only the better informed could pass, fences which only the most determined, audacious, or foolhardy could hurdle. Whatever these traits were, they obviously served them well in the new land.[56]

Personal accounts corroborate—or at least illustrate—the quantitative evidence. Two of the four Spaniards who appeared in a fin de siècle bio-graphical collection of Argentina's top forty-two industrialists came from nonemigration provinces.[57] One, Fernando Martí, left Tarragona (a prov-ince with only eleven natives in Buenos Aires in 1855) as an adolescent in 1871 and twenty years later owned the largest shoe factory in South America. The other, Manuel Durán, who arrived in 1870 and founded the largest cigar factory in Argentina, was born in the stony region of Estre-madura, the birthplace of Cortés, Pizarro, and many other sixteen-century conquistadors but of few nineteenth-century immigrants (in 1855 there had been only two Estremadurans in Buenos Aires). Similarly, Carlos Casado del Alisal, a sailor from the province of Palencia who arrived in Buenos Aires in 1857, when not a single *paisano* lived there, became the richest Spaniard in the River Plate. Entrepreneur, banker, explorer, and landowner, in 1878 he became the first exporter of wheat in the coun-try, which prompted President Avellaneda to exclaim that all Argentina needed was "a dozen men like Casado." When a group of English finan-ciers hesitated to grant him a loan of £1 million, he offered as collateral his lands, "which are bigger than the British Isles."[58] And Ramón Santa-marina, who came from Orense in 1843 (a province with only one other native in midcentury Buenos Aires) became one of the richest estancieros in the pampas.

The greater success of arrivals from nonemigration provinces compared with their compatriots from provinces of heavy exodus necessarily reflected both selectivity on one side and commonness on the other. The lack of information, communication, and emigration facilities in provinces of incipient emigration may have prevented the less informed, the impov-erished, and the less resolute from leaving. But as the emigration growth curve ascended toward its saturation phase, the "filter" became increas-ingly porous, the hurdles more easily surmountable. Didn't know enough about Argentina? Immigrant letters, rumors, boasting *indianos* (return-ees), and village gossip and tales would assure a good dose of information mixed with a generous portion of useless, but inciting, hyperbole. No money for the passage? Remittances or a prepaid passage from the ubiqui-tous "uncles" or scores of other kin and friends on the "other side of the pond" could do the trick. If not, the *prestamistas* would always be willing to help. After all, emigration represented these village financiers' bread and butter—and more than that, when they could expropriate the mort-gaged plots of old peasants with forgetful children in the Americas. Not too sure about leaving? The examples of friends and neighbors, the sweet talk of *ganchos* (agents), and even the pressure of kin would help in taking the step.[59] As the composition of the flow became more democratic, emigration ceased to represent the eccentricity of a few trailblazers to become a widespread fever, a massive habit. In some places the "sieve" grew so permeable that perhaps it could only retain—as some critics of emigration complained—middle-aged women, the old, and the infirm.

The Unexpected Contrast between Basques and Andalusians

Emigration patterns—along with a rereading of qualitative sources—can also explain some highly unexpected findings regarding disparities in the occupational status of Basques and Andalusians. Basques enjoyed the highest reputation among all the Iberian ethnic groups in Argentina. In 1905 ex-president Carlos Pellegrini wrote of "the vigor, activity, and endurance that the Basques bring to any task," which earned this "noble, congenial, and strong people" a special place in Argentines' hearts and unlimited success in every sort of commercial, industrial, and professional endeavor.[60] Five years later an Italian writer living in Argentina maintained that just as Argentines, especially the ruling class, preferred northern Europeans to southern Europeans and northern Italians to Neapolitans, they preferred Basques to all other Spaniards because of these immigrants' moral and physical fortitude.[61] And A. Colmo, a professor at Buenos Aires University, wrote in his 1915 book on Latin American history: "The vigor of this youthful race [the Basques] is quite remarkable. They reach our countries with no other capital than their own persons . . . but they triumph and become rich. Their descendants constitute a great nucleus in industry, commerce, the 'aristocracy,' and politics itself, which they often monopolize. . . . It is simply amazing."[62]

Andalusians, on the other hand, suffered one of the worst reputations. A French observer, who agreed that Basques formed "the best of Spanish immigration," described Andalusians as the worst: "mediocre farmers, routinists, lazy, incapable of energetic and prolonged effort." The Argentine consul in Málaga blamed the lack of effort by his government to attract immigrants from that province on the "bad reputation of Andalusians in the River Plate." And another French visitor, the journalist Jules Huret, saw in the "lazy, greasy, and fat" Argentine petty clerks "Andalusians in whom Moorish blood dominates."[63]

Yet, as Table 36 reveals, Andalusians in Buenos Aires proved remarkably more successful than Basques in avoiding low-paid menial jobs and in obtaining desirable ones, both in the mid-1800s and at the turn of the century. In 1855 Andalusians were only one-third as likely as Basques to toil in unskilled or menial occupations but twice as likely to be skilled artisans or affluent business people and five times as likely to be professionals. In the 1888–1910 sample, they continued to outrank Basques in the skilled occupations and professions and to be vastly outnumbered in the unskilled ones.

This gross discrepancy between my findings and the qualitative evidence once again confirms what we encountered in previous chapters: the potential for deception inherent in qualitative sources and the peril of relying solely on this type of material. It validates the need for quantitative methods in social history if its aim is to remain the uncovering of past social realities and not simply—as in literary criticism—the analysis of texts. Qualitative sources, particularly before the advent of mass communication, usually express the point of view of elites—those who can both write and publish—and there were several reasons why the Argentine one should exalt Basques and berate Andalusians.

For one, much of the elite itself was—or claimed to be—of Basque extraction—mostly descendants of late-eighteenth-century merchants and, in lesser numbers, of midnineteenth-century immigrant shepherds and ranchers. The prestige of the claim rested on the presumed racial superiority of this "legendary race of iron and conquistadors" over the Mediterranean stock and the preservation of its purity in the New World. As a proud Argentine oligarch put it, "Basques in the Americas preserved with an intransigent spirit a very noble and lofty concern for the purity of the blood. . . . Hardly ever did they mix with inferior races of Indians, blacks, mulattoes, and *zambos* [people of mixed African and Indian ancestry]. Here is the reason why the most ethnically pure families in America are not those that descend from Andalusians, Galicians, etc., but those that trace their ancestry to Basques."[64]

Basques were also one the few Iberian groups that settled in rural areas. It was they who almost single-handedly erected the fences in the pampas that allowed cattle breeding and cereal farming in the vast estancias of Argentina's agropastoral oligarchy. Understandably, the writings of the ruling group would praise these "muscular and gigantic pioneers, of erect torsos and herculean *brazos* [the ubiquitous and revealing reference to "arms"] who welcome the hard and stimulating endeavors of our grasslands." These "most vigorous of immigrants . . . surely do not bring syphilis and tuberculosis . . . and are [tellingly] the best *peones de estancia*."[65]

Furthermore, unlike the Piedmontese *contadini*, who engaged mainly in agriculture, Basques generally devoted themselves to cattle raising, the most prestigious occupation of the country. It is no coincidence that in 1900 more than one-quarter of the members of the principal elite club in Buenos Aires had Basque surnames, whereas only three bore Italian patronymics—at a time when close to half of the city's population was of Italian birth or ancestry.[66] It may be no coincidence either that in contemporary plays Basque characters, despite their non-Romance linguistic background, normally spoke standard Argentine Castilian—at times even peppered with the idioms of the pampas—whereas Italians more often prated in a ludicrously accented *cocoliche.*[67] In the pre–World War I years, when the social problems of urban growth made many Argentines nostalgic for the less discordant pastoral past, the identification with cattle raising, estancias, and the pampas came in particularly handy. So did the Basque's puritanical Catholicism, renowned sense of loyalty and steadfastness, plus the belief that they came from a rustic and conflict-free society. An Argentine landowner wishfully put it this way: "Basques are superior in adaptability, constancy, and steadfastness to any other immigrant. There is no danger that he will abandon his master. . . . It does not matter how many times his boss, for accidental causes, cannot pay his wages: the Basque will keep on working until better times come!"[68]

By contrast, contemporary elite writers understandably reproved newcomers like the Andalusians (at times referred to as Gypsies), Middle Easterners, and Jews, who, "instead of settling in rural areas, which is precisely where we need *brazos,* cluster in the city to engage in sedentary occupations that do not yield any gain for society. . . . Are these individuals [the so-called Gypsies] capable of engaging in agriculture? [asked this estanciero's scion in his law-school thesis] No way! They are simply idlers who roam the world perpetuating a race that should be exterminated for the good of humanity."[69] Even apparently sympathetic observers questioned the Andalusians' work ethic, identifying them in an airy vein with "jolliness, clamor, music, fun, flowers, bulls, beautiful women, and generous wine." While "the Basque does not go around choosing light, trouble-free occupations," continued the same writer, "Don't talk to the Andalusian of engaging in a hard, steady job."[70]

To others, their sexual habits seemed as disreputable as their work habits (not an uncommon conceptual link). In a 1920 comedy, the playwright described the character of the Andalusian maid as "a flirt, with a tight corset, high heels, and a provocative hair style; often uses her fingers to set her eyebrows and redden her lips, places her hands suggestively on her hips, and walks on and off stage with smooth undulations."[71] The character goes on to seduce the young son of the house and ends up pregnant.

Another farce that opened in the same year questioned the Andalusian manservant's manhood when he gave a transvestite rendition of Salome's slave dance to entertain the master and his young friends. After being physically abused by one of them—appropriately named Macho—the Andalusian masochistically exclaims: "I have become very fond of him. He is a man who seduces by dint of punches."[72] And from a "scientific" rather than a literary perspective, a prominent Argentine professor, Dr. Alejandro Gancedo, "discovered" in his 1910 study *Psicopatía sexual* a high incidence of pederasty among Andalusian prisoners compared with a low rate for the rest of the Spaniards and not a single Basque case.

The other main Andalusian "pathology" was politicoreligious rather than sexual. Depictions of such radical and heretic Andalusians abound in contemporary Porteño literature. In the 1908 comic play *Bachicha*, while the *gallego* character appears as a witless but laborious innkeeper, the Andalusian is a garrulous and idle socialist who addresses everyone as comrade and perpetually sputters fiery oratory against the bourgeoisie and the Church.[73] In the 1917 novel *El conventillo*, the rabble-rouser of the tenement is an Andalusian anarchist christened Pontius Pilate by the other dwellers due to his habit of concluding the tirades against capitalism and religion with the exclamation: "They have to be crucified!"[74] And a similar sacrilegious allusion appears in the classic 1920 farce *Tu cuna fué un conventillo* when the Andalusian character is branded as a "gallego maximalista [Bolshevik] de la madonna!" by the Italian superintendent of the tenement.[75]

Quantitative evidence indicates that in this case there was more to it than literary stereotypes. Indeed, the fact that in a Buenos Aires police file of 661 anarchists in 1902 one-fifth of the Spaniards were Andalusians but there was not a single Basque goes far toward explaining the different reputations of the two groups in qualitative sources.[76]

Yet, the regional groups' success in the host society depended not on their reputation or ill fame, not on whether the dominant classes liked them or not, but on how well their cultural capital matched the structural realities of their new home. It was not that Andalusians came from a more developed region than the Basques. On the contrary, Andalusia constituted (along with Galicia) one of the two most backward corners of the peninsula; and the Basque country (along with Catalonia), one of the two most developed. Nor were they more skillful than the Basques. It was simply that in Buenos Aires their skills fit better, and this reflected diverging emigration patterns.

As we saw in chapters 1 and 3, the dispersed settlements and widespread landownership of the Basque country—and of the Cantabrian sea-board in general—fostered early peasant emigration. The first trait facili-tated the early diffusion of information and emigration fever from the coastal towns to the interior mountains and valleys. The second allowed much of the peasantry to use its land as loan collateral, facilitating financ-ing for the trip, particularly in the early phases of the flow, when remit-tances and prepaid passages had not taken root. So, along with the resi-dents of industrial coastal cities, a large number of rural folk came. In fact, by the turn of the century the hinterland had become the main source of departures.[77] The proverbial laboriousness, reliance, and thrift of these im-migrants, plus their pastoral skills, enabled them to become the most suc-cessful settlers of the pampas and did much to build up their reputation in Argentina. But although patience and consistency may have been a win-ning combination in sheep and cattle raising, its value in the volatile Por-teño economy was definitely more limited.

On the other hand, Andalusia's nucleated settlements and latifundia hindered peasant emigration. The long, uninhabited distances between population centers hampered the diffusion of information about opportu-nities in Argentina from port cities to the hinterland. The inequitable land-tenure system made financing the trip difficult, retarding and re-straining the departure of the mostly landless peasantry. Consequently, coastal cities remained the major source of emigrants throughout the pe-riod. And these loquacious, shrewd, urban Andalusians found a fertile field not in the rich topsoil of Argentina's grasslands but in the streets of its capital, in the expanding commercial economy that the pampas made pos-sible. The official rhetoric of the ruling class may have celebrated stead-fastness, loyalty, and reliance, but the popular worldview exalted *la viveza* (cunning). In the solitary pampas the former virtues may have formed a formidable tool for success, but in the bustling metropolis the latter often came in more handy.

Popular humor provides a window into that worldview that was not re-corded in more conventional sources. The jokes transcribed in Figure 15, published by the leading Porteño weekly between 1904 and 1908, offer a unique social mirror because instead of being written by a staff member, they were sent by readers for contests in which those published received cash prizes. Although still filtered by the editorial office (much like let-ters to the editor), more than one thousand of these were published, and they clearly provide a more faithful reflection of popular culture than do the writings of professional journalists. The number of jokes listed in Fig-ure 15 is large enough to show patterns and collective stereotypes rather

Basque Jokes

1. The druggist—How are you friend? How is your cold? Did the powders I gave you make you fell better? The Basque—Oh! Yes, I'm fine. Powders I swallow easy [sic] but papers gave me a lot of trouble. [he had eaten the powder and the wrapping instead of diluting it in water]
July 21 1906, n. 407.

2. A Basque hears a nightingale singing in a tree and stays listening to it for a while. But all of the sudden he has an idea, goes back, grabs his gun and boom! He has someone fry the bird and when they bring it and he sees that there is little more there than skin and bones, says:
—Yes, Yes..you're nothing but words.
[apparently a reference to Basques's "laconic" nature]
May 2 1908, n. 500.

3. A Basque was taking a nap when a hornet began to buzz in his ear. Seeing it and hurling his beret was one action but with such bad aim that the bug escaped unharmed. As he went back to sleep the buzzing returned, this time a yellow jacket. Off goes the beret again with such an admirable aim now that the "blonde wasp" fell as if struck by lightening. As he sees the victim, the Basque let it have the following explanation: [in broken Spanish]
—You change clothes but you didn't fool me, I recognized your voice
August 31 1907, n. 465.

4. A dentist just extracted a molar from a Basque.
—How much I owe, Doctor? asks he.
—Five pesos, sir.
—What?! Five pesos for one little pull? I spent all day milking cows and don't make five pesos for a pull or even twenty. No, no, not a good deal. Put it back, buddy.
Nov. 30 1907, n. 478.

5. —Hey, Basque, you have made that horse lame. [presumably overburden with milk vats]
—Not a chance!
—Of course he is.
—Don't you know that he is keeping time to the rhythm of zortziko [a Basque dance].
Nov. 26 1904, n. 321.

6. There was a Basque in a gathering who not knowing what to say to approach a young lady he liked, declared his love this way:
He—Well, Well, what a wedding!
She—And who is getting married?
He—Me!
She—And with whom?
He—With you, of course.
Sept. 16, 1905 n. 363.

7. —Have you noticed the analogy that there is between a man's profession and his last words? Napoleon said on his deathbed: "Head of the army" and Mozart, "The Music."
—I wouldn't say so, pal; as he kick the bucket, the Basque from the corner only said "the great bitch." [presumably, instead of "the great cow," alluding to the stereotypical figure of the Basque milkman].
June 9 1906, n. 401.

Andalusian Jokes

A. The food was average the drink worse. The Andalusian tells many jokes during the "banquet". As he is leaving, the host praises his guest's sense of humor.
—Well, this is nothing—answers the Andalusian—you should hear me when I'm regaled with a fine meal.
Feb. 29 1908, n. 491

B. In the train.
—Are you Andalusian?
—No, sir—answers the person questioned.
But on arrival to a station he says as he is departing:
—Yes, sir, I'm . . . but when I'm travelling I don't like to put on airs.
July 21 1906, n. 407.

C. Among Andalusians.
—In my hometown the heat was so intense last summer that even the glass windows melted.
—You don't know what heat is. If you had been in my hometown two years ago, you would have seen that nothing but fried fish came downriver.
Nov. 30 1907, n. 478.

D. Two Andalusians talk:
—I have a maid so tall that she cleans the ceiling without the need of a duster nor a ladder.
—Well, mine is so short that to wash the floor she has to get on top of a chair.
Oct. 1 1904, n. 313

E. An Andalusian gazed admiringly to the moving boulder of Tandil [a tourist attraction south of Buenos Aires]. Someone asked him if he had ever seen such a large rock, to which he answered:
—In my country there is one so enormous that if they had put it on top of Jesus' tomb, I swear, he would have never resurrected.
Nov. 19 1904, n. 320

F. They were talking in a social gathering about the ability of some people to imitate animal calls.
—For that a friend of mine—said an Andalusian—when he starts imitating a rooster in his back yard at night.
—What happens?
—It dawns immediately
June 30 1906, n. 404.

G. The English salesman—The safety box that I sell was placed on slow fire for seven hours, and when the bills were taken out, they were intact.
An Andalusian—Well, that is nothing. The safety box that I sell was placed for seven years on slow fire with a chicken inside . . . And wouldn't you know how the chicken came out?
Everyone—Man! She must have been charred.
The Andalusian—No gentlemen, she was freezing to death.
Jan. 19 1907, 433.

H. An Andalusian receives the news that an aunt he had in Seville had died, and he starts dancing.
—What is it with you that you're so happy?—Asks a friend.
—See here. How do you expect me not to be happy if an aunt has die whom I owed 8 pesetas?
Sept. 1 1906, n. 413

Figure 15. Representations of Basque and Andalusian immigrants in popular humor: Jokes sent by readers to *Caras y Caretas,* Buenos Aires' leading weekly, for contests run between 1904 and 1908. (Date and number of publication listed below each joke)

than an individual's potentially idiosyncratic sense of humor. And the fact that I included all the jokes about Basques or Andalusians published, not simply the ones that illustrated my point, turns them into more systematic evidence than just a few selected and merely illustrative vignettes.

The images and stereotypes that emerge from the jokes contrast sharply with those from more official or elite sources. Basques come out as distinctly asinine (joke 1), or ambiguously so (2 to 5). They swallow the equivalent of an Alka-Seltzer tablet with the wrapping and without water (1), talk and match wits with dead birds and bugs (2 and 3), equate pulling teeth with pulling cows' udders and so want an extracted molar back (4), or court a young woman with the finesse of an ox (6). Andalusians, on the other hand, emerge as charming and humorous (joke A), graciously conceited (B), or hyperbolic in a witty way (C to G). The most offensive joke (H) portrays them as immoral and avaricious but not slow or dense.

Even the Andalusians' "faults" could serve them well. The penchant for prevarication and embellishment alleged in most jokes might not have made them model citizens in the eyes of civic leaders, but it came in handy in the business world. Throughout the period they were the most commercially successful Spaniards, famed for their ice-cubes-to-Eskimos salesmanship (see particularly joke G)—a virtue in the eyes of the average Buenos Airean. As a contemporary put it, "When engaged in commerce, they [the Andalusians] let loose their nervous energy and make the enterprise prosper, monopolizing the best clientele of the barrio to whom they sell with charm merchandise that other store owners cannot get rid of, no matter how hard they try."[78] Another "fault," their reputed avoidance of hard, physical tasks, may have prevented them from becoming wealthy cattlemen, but it also made them eschew unskilled, menial labor in the slaughterhouses and brickyards (two traditional sources of employment for Basques).

In a symbiotic way the prejudice of others, including their compatriots, reinforced this concentration in lighter crafts and white-collar occupations. A Castilian returnee who owned a large business in Buenos Aires in the 1920s recalled in an interview how he would only hire Basques, Galicians, or other "hard-working" northern Spaniards for manual jobs. Andalusian and Madrileño applicants for these positions were rejected outright because they were too "garrulous and lazy, worthless for anything but selling . . . good to have a drink with but not to hire for a man's job." Not without its irony, this type of discrimination probably pushed Andalusians up the occupational hierarchy.

Indeed, underneath the official and manifest exaltation of Basque laboriousness and constancy, one can detect a hidden fascination with Andalusians and what they represented not only in the imagery of popular humor or of creative literature but even in the charges of their detractors. In a city where "un-Spanish," northern Iberians predominated, these southerners came to epitomize, to both Argentines and their compatriots, "postcard" Spain; the Spain of Bizet and Rimsky-Korsakov, of castanets, siestas, matadors, flamenco, and hip-waving señoritas, a Dionysian symbol of freedom in an increasingly materialistic and, to some, soulless milieu.

Intra-Ethnic Contrasts

The Basques' concentration in low-skilled occupations relative to Andalusians reflected, then, the less restricted and less selective nature of their emigration and the fact that it was more representative of the whole region's population than was that of their southern compatriots. Intra-ethnic differences would thus be strongly marked. Table 37 shows how Basques from Biscay (a coastal province that included industrializing areas and the growing mercantile and financial economy of Bilbao) fared significantly better in midnineteenth-century Buenos Aires than did fellow Basques from Navarre (a rich but basically agricultural province with the somnolent administrative capital of Pamplona). In part the difference ensued from the fact that overseas emigration originated in the coastal province and that therefore the Biscayan community in Buenos Aires included a larger number of older, longer-established individuals. After controlling for age and length of residence (by excluding those who were more than forty years old and/or had lived in Argentina for at least ten years), Biscayans, predictably, lost their edge in large business enterprises but continued to outrank Navarrese in the white-collar sector by a gross margin and to be heavily outranked in the unskilled and menial category. By the turn of the century, when the gaps in age and length of residence had disappeared, the Biscayans retained their higher occupational status relative to their fellow Basques from Navarre. In turn, the Navarrese born in Pamplona were half as likely to toil in menial jobs and twice as likely to be professionals as were the arrivals from the rest of the province, both in the midnineteenth century and in the 1888–1910 period.

Similar intra-ethnic patterns were common elsewhere. Catalans from the province of Barcelona (the industrial, commercial, and financial core of the region) were more successful at reaching the middle and top rungs of the occupational ladder, and avoiding the lower ones, than were natives of the other Catalan provinces or the Balearic Islands. Galicians from the

Table 37 Intra-ethnic differences in occupational distribution among Basques from Biscay and Navarre residing in Buenos Aires, 1855 and 1888–1910 (in percentages)

Province	N	Unskilled	Semiskilled	Skilled	Low nonmanual	Middle nonmanual	High nonmanual	Professional
1855								
Biscay	244	23.4	13.1	15.2	31.1	3.7	11.5	2.0
Navarre	245	44.1	10.6	21.2	20.4	1.2	.8	1.6
1855 (immigrants under 40 and in country less than 10 years)[a]								
Biscay	140	30.0	15.7	15.7	36.4	1.4	0	.7
Navarre	162	50.6	11.1	22.2	14.8	1.0	0	.6
1888–1910								
Biscay	244	18.9	4.9	16.0	48.4	8.6	2.0	1.2
Navarre	455	28.4	10.3	14.3	38.0	6.4	1.3	1.3

SOURCES: See Table 36.

a. Because Biscayan emigration to Argentina began before that from Navarre, the Biscayan community in Buenos Aires contained a higher number of older, longer-established immigrants: 25 percent were more than forty years old, compared with 13 percent of the Navarrese; 31 percent had been in Argentina for more than a decade, compared with 24 percent of the Navarrese. Therefore, I controlled here for possible distortion by including only immigrants who were under forty years of age and had been in the country for less than ten years. By the 1888–1910 period this control was not necessary because the two communities were demographically similar.

two more developed Atlantic provinces fared likewise when compared with their compatriots from the two interior provinces. Interestingly, little difference appears between Andalusians from the more urbanized coastal provinces and the small minority from the rural hinterland, suggesting that the thinness of flow from the latifundio region kept the emigration growth curve there in a prolonged incipient phase and that the selectivity associated with this phase made up for the backwardness of the region in terms of the level of skills of the departures. At the local scale, within the same Galician province of La Coruña, those born in Ferrol, a proto-industrial port town, were only half as likely to work in unskilled and menial jobs in midnineteenth-century Buenos Aires as were those born in Santiago de Compostela, an ecclesiastical town famous for the Medieval pilgrimages to the tomb of Saint James (Santiago). In terms of "hacer la América [making it in America]," a previous familiarity with factories, ports, and commercial enterprises was, it seems, more valuable than medieval cathedrals and the good offices of apostles.

Old World geographical origins, therefore, influenced occupational status in the New World city because they denoted differing levels of skills adaptable to an urban environment, something which in turn reflected either the source area's degree of socioeconomic development or the selectivity of its overseas flow—in turn the result of the flow's phase and/or spatial extension. To what degree, then, were the opportunities offered by the host city simply grabbed by those who already possessed the relevant skills? How strong was the continuity between premigratory and postmigratory socio-occupational status?

Data linking 319 immigrants who lived and worked in Buenos Aires during the early decades of this century to their parents in seven Spanish localities point to marked transatlantic and intergenerational persistences (see Table 38). If at the time of one's birth one's father worked in a non-manual occupation in Spain, one's chance of doing the same in Buenos Aires came close to a sure bet (95 percent); if one's father had worked in a manual occupation, it merely surpassed a coin's toss (56 percent).[79] The children of artisans accounted for 18 percent of the total sample but for 33 percent of the artisans; the children of professionals, for 5 percent of the sample and 55 percent of the professionals. The offspring of the peasantry made up 46 percent of the sample but 86 percent of unskilled laborers. Landownership in the Old World apparently helped little in Buenos Aires, for the descendants of peasant-proprietors actually appeared more concentrated in low-skilled occupations than the descendants of landless rural la-

Table 38 Correlation between the occupational status of immigrants in Buenos Aires ca. 1900–1930 and that of their fathers at the time of their birth (in percentages; overrepresentations are underlined)

Immigrant's Job in Buenos Aires

Father's job in Spain at time of future emigrant's birth	N	Unskilled	Semi-skilled	Skilled	Low nonmanual	Middle and high nonmanual	Professional	Total
Rural laborer	76	19.7	15.8	6.6	48.7	9.2	0.0	100
Peasant proprietor	72	29.2	12.5	6.9	37.5	12.5	1.4	100
Sailor/fisherman	13	0.0	23.1	30.8	38.5	7.7	0.0	100
Unskilled urban	14	7.7	7.7	30.8	46.2	7.7	0.0	100
Semiskilled	17	0.0	5.9	29.4	52.9	5.9	5.9	100
Artisan	56	7.1	7.1	21.4	51.8	8.9	3.6	100
Low nonmanual	20	5.0	0.0	0.0	60.0	30.0	5.0	100
Middle and high nonmanual	36	0.0	2.8	0.0	69.4	27.8	0.0	100
Professional	15	0.0	6.3	6.3	31.3	18.8	37.5	100
All	319	13.2	10.0	11.3	48.6	13.5	3.4	100

SOURCES AND METHOD: The information on immigrants and their jobs in Buenos Aires comes from the records of six voluntary associations in the city, including three recreational clubs, which explains the general concentration in the white-collar category. Having the place of birth and age at the time of enrollment, I could link the immigrants to their parents using baptismal records and, preferably, civil birth registers from seven Spanish localities: Corcubión, Finisterre, and Vimianzo in the Galician province of La Coruña; Val de San Lorenzo in León; Pamplona and Tafalla in Navarre; and Mataró in Barcelona. The localities were chosen because they represent a wide spectrum in terms of levels of urbanization, socioeconomic structure, and ethnic composition. Fathers' occupations were used because mothers' were not always listed or were simply listed as "of her house," or the equivalent.

borers. On the other hand, urban or semiurban ancestry by itself did help. The progeny of low-skilled laborers from towns or cities were only one-fourth as likely to work in low-skilled jobs as were the progeny of the peasantry. In this respect, matrilineal urbanism appears particularly relevant. The chances of working in a menial or low-skilled job in Buenos Aires were one in ten if one's mother had been born in a city of more than 20,000 inhabitants; one in five if a town of 2,000 to 20,000 inhabitants was her birthplace; and one in three if she had been born in the countryside. Even among immigrants of otherwise similar conditions—say, of urban birth themselves and working-class origins—those with city-born mothers continued to be significantly less likely to cluster on the lower end of the occupational spectrum. Paternal literacy played a similar role. Among immigrants of urban birth, eight of the forty-seven individuals whose fathers had signed their birth certificates became business owners in Buenos Aires; none of the twenty-one whose fathers scratched an X did.

Heredity—as stored environment if not genetic line—was far from an iron law and surely less binding than in Spain, or in any other country of limited immigration, for that matter.[80] Many children of humble peasants and workers became magnates in Buenos Aires. The Atlantic's waves no doubt eroded ancestral shackles. Yet the majority of those who crossed it continued to follow, for better or worse, in their parents footsteps. Old World inequalities resurfaced on the other shore, inconspicuous in a society that appeared to be either so new and dynamic that it offered an equal starting line or, antithetically, so stratified by colonial legacies and latifundia that it made imported disparities inconsequential. The fact that these disparities offered an insipid subject for political demagoguery and the eventually hegemonic populist discourse further diminished their visibility. Yet these social inequalities shaped Argentina's class formation to a greater degree than did the infamous estanciero oligarchy which, after all, made up an insignificant proportion of the population.

Old Wine and New Bottles: The Interaction of Premigratory Traits and the Host Environment

Old World traits influenced occupational status in a direct way. They also mixed with the host environment to produce a new variable in the adaptation of arrivals: the nature of the immigrant community.

For example, the much higher occupational status in Buenos Aires of immigrants from the municipality of Val de San Lorenzo in the province of León when compared with those from the municipality of Vimianzo in the province of La Coruña (see Table 39) reflected, at the primary level, premigratory conditions. The first municipality—formed by four clusters of terra-cotta dwellings on the wheat-colored Castilian plateau—and the second—a main valley village surrounded by miles of green, rolling hills and scores of brownstone hamlets—are visually dissimilar but seemingly alike economically because they are both agricultural. On paper, the Vimianzo municipal district, with some 8,000 souls in 1900—four times the population of the Leonese municipality—and a higher level of landownership, actually appeared more developed. In reality, it was significantly more rustic, with its population dispersed throughout 11 parishes and 101 medieval-looking hamlets, devoted mostly to subsistence farming, and unable to utter more than a few sentences of broken Spanish. On the other hand, Val's more nucleated and Castilian-speaking population also practiced some commercial agriculture, weaving and marketing of woolen blankets, and mule packing and trade.[81] The fact that one-fifth of the Valense immigrants came from families with some trading experience but that none of their compatriots from Vimianzo did accounts for much of the disparity in Table 39. As in the case of Basques and Andalusians, the applicability or malleability of premigratory skills proved the key element. Although by the time the Valense began to arrive in Argentina textile factories and trains had long since eliminated opportunities for wool weavers and muleteers, they resourcefully adapted their Old World experiences and became successful itinerant, mounted milkmen and dairy- and fabric-store owners.

The more applicable premigratory skills of the Valense, moreover, fostered the formation of a more affluent and organized community in Buenos Aires, which in turn facilitated the adaptation of later arrivals whatever their premigratory skills. The number of Valense business owners capable of employing *paisanos* almost doubled that of Vimianzians. As we saw in the previous chapter, Valense milkmen searching for routes not yet dominated by Basques settled in the modest but up-and-coming district of Palermo, whereas Vimianzians, following in the footsteps of their neighbors from maritime villages, clustered in the declining port zones of La Boca. This unplanned—if not completely accidental—residential choice made Valense home owners look like real-estate wizards compared with their less fortunate Galician compatriots. The Valense founded their own village-based association in Buenos Aires, which by the late 1920s had 140 members, published its own magazine, provided medical and disability

Table 39 Occupational distribution in Buenos Aires of immigrants from Val de San Lorenzo, León, and Vimianzo, La Coruña, ca. 1900–1930 (in percentages)

	N	Unskilled	Semi-skilled	Skilled	Low nonmanual	Medium and high nonmanual
Val de San Lorenzo	87	8.0	6.9	3.4	64.4	17.3
Vimianzo	110	40.9	14.5	10.9	23.6	10.0

SOURCES: Membership records of the Asociación Española de Socorros Mutuos de Buenos Aires; Centro Gallego de Buenos Aires; and Centro Maragato Val de San Lorenzo, Buenos Aires.

insurance, repatriated sick or indigent members, and financed public improvements and education in their hometown. Vimianzians, by contrast, joined a county-based recreational association that included no mutual-aid benefits and was dominated by the natives of the more developed coastal towns of the county. The greater prosperity and organization of this community explains why the offspring of Val's peasantry were twice as likely to procure a nonmanual job in Buenos Aires as were the offspring of Vimianzo's peasantry, despite their similar Old World social origins.

Similar patterns appear among other groups and at other geographical levels. As we saw, Andalusians attained a higher occupational status in Buenos Aires than Basques (see Table 36) because their emigration was less spatially extended, more restricted to coastal cities, and, thus, more selective. Their more adaptable urban skills were reflected in a literacy rate of 75 percent versus 53 percent for Basques in midnineteenth-century Buenos Aires, a gap that was particularly marked among women: 71 percent versus 36 percent, respectively. Andalusians also included a larger proportion of older and longer established immigrants, which forms part of the explanation as to why they were only 32 percent as likely to work in unskilled and menial jobs as were Basques. However, after we control for all of this by including only illiterate males under the age of forty and with fewer than ten years of residence in Argentina, Andalusians still appear only 40 percent as likely to work in unskilled occupations as Basques. The remaining difference resulted in part from the existence of urban—or urban-applicable—skills, such as knowledge of a craft, that were not necessarily measured by literacy. And yet, even if craftsmen are excluded from the control group, Andalusians continued to be only 58 percent as

likely to concentrate at the bottom of the occupational scale as did their
Basque compatriots. The persistent gap reveals a veiled Andalusian skill:
the success of previous arrivals, the greater number of prosperous, well-
connected individuals willing and able to give a hand.

Clearly, then, the intermeshing of Old World attributes and New World
structural realities produced new sets of variables that affected later arrivals. In this case, how well one's friends, kin, and *paisanos* had done in the
new land influenced how well one would fare regardless of one's own
skills, a process that was noticeable even among people from the same region. For example, 7 of the 113 immigrants from the Galician town of
Ferrol who lived in Buenos Aires in 1855 owned a middle-sized or large
business, whereas none of the 43 immigrants from the less-developed
Galician town of Caldas de Reyes did. Juan Saavedra from Ferrol and
Salvador Romero from Caldas de Reyes were both *gallegos*, single, in their
early twenties, literate, and in 1855 had been in Buenos Aires for less than
a year. But Juan possessed an invisible skill: the success of his predecessors
in the migration chain. He was, thus, able to obtain a job as a clerk in an
uncle's store, whereas Salvador had to settle for one as stable groom in the
house of a rich Argentine. Obviously, who they knew was as important as
what they knew.

Other Variables and Occupational Adaptation

The occupational status of immigrants was affected by four variables in
addition to—but not independent of—the adaptability of premigratory
talents and the invisible skills provided by microsocial networks: gender,
marital status, age, and length of residence. In terms of gender, employed
Spanish women were twice as concentrated in unskilled and menial labor
as were their male compatriots during the entire period. They were also
overrepresented in semiskilled jobs. This reflected the limited range of
women's occupational choices. While male job titles numbered in the hundreds, just a few classifications sufficed for the female labor market.

Domestic service alone employed 47 percent of the Spanish women engaged in remunerated work in 1855, a figure that spiraled to 65 percent in
1869 but declined by the turn of the century to 56 percent (see Table 40).
By contemporary world standards, these proportions came close to a median: lower than in frontier regions (e.g., New South Wales, Ontario, and
western Canada) and than in slave or ex-slave cities (Rio de Janeiro, Atlanta, New Orleans, and so forth); similar to those of other bureaucratic-
commercial cities (such as Washington, D.C., Brighton, or York); and

Table 40 Occupational distribution of Spanish immigrant women in remunerated occupations, Buenos Aires, 1855, 1869, and 1894–1910 (percentages of all women working for pay in each occupation)

Occupation	1855	1869	1894–1910
Servants	26.6	34.7	29.2
Cooks	4.6	11.4	13.5
Washerwomen	11.6	14.0	4.3
Ironers	4.0	4.4	9.3
Subtotal, domestic service	46.6	64.6	56.3
Seamstresses	31.5	16.9	14.0
Cigar workers	6.9	8.5	1.6
Shoe binders[a]	2.8	2.9	1.2
Couturiers	0.2	0.4	16.2
Clerks	0.2	0.4	2.6
Merchants	6.4	3.7	3.7
Teachers/nurses	1.0	0.4	1.1
Performing artists	1.2	0.7	0.5
Other jobs	3.2	1.4	2.8
N =	607	306	1,737

SOURCES: For 1855, a statistical universe of all Spaniards in the city, from the municipal manuscript census returns, 1855; for 1869, a one-in-seven random sample of all Spaniards in the city, from the manuscript schedules for the first national census; and for 1894–1910, application forms for the Asociación Española de Socorros Mutuos de Buenos Aires.

a. This occupation consisted of sewing the uppers of shoes.

higher than in industrial cities or countries (see Table 41). By local standards, they surpassed, as we saw, that of all other groups in the city, perhaps with the exception of the small Irish minority. In terms of gender, among Spanish immigrants, and probably in the city as a whole, domestic service became an increasingly feminine affair. Laundresses and ironers had always been female, but in the midnineteenth century fewer than half (47 percent) of the other servants were. By 1869 women already formed a slight majority (53 percent), by 1895 the proportion had risen to two-thirds, and by the first decades of the twentieth century they outnumbered menservants nine to one.[82] The often-mentioned shortage of servants, whether real or perceived, may have accelerated the feminization of

Table 41 Female domestic servants in various groups, cities, regions, and countries, ca. 1850, 1870, and 1900 (in percentages of all women in the labor market, ranked from high to low on the average of the dates)

Group, city, region, country	ca. 1850	ca. 1870	ca. 1900	Average
New South Wales, Australia	84	–	–	84
Ontario, Canada	86	71	–	78
Rio de Janeiro	–	71	–	71
Atlanta	–	74	62	68
Hamilton, Canada West	72	59	–	66
Swedes in the United States	–	–	65	65
New Orleans	–	68	56	62
Irish in the United States	–	–	61	61
Washington, D.C.	–	65	55	60
Brighton, England	–	62	57	59
York, England	59	–	–	59
Japanese in the United States	–	–	57	57
Spaniards in Buenos Aires	47	65	56	56
United States	–	58	48[a]	53
Paris	–	–	45	45
Great Britain[a]	44	47	40	44
London	43	–	–	43
Germans in the United States	–	–	43	43
Boston	–	45	32	39
New York	–	43	33	38
Chicago	–	42	28	35
St. Petersburg	–	33	–	33
Norwich, England	–	36	29	32
Milan	–	32	29	31
Moscow	–	33	25	29
Birmingham, England	–	29	24	26
Japan[a]	–	–	22	22
Italians in the United States	–	–	12	12

SOURCES: New South Wales: Katrina Alford, *Production or Reproduction? An Economic History of Women in Australia, 1788–1850* (Melbourne: Oxford University Press, 1984), 162; Ontario: Marjorie Griffin Cohen, *Women's Work, Markets, and Economic Development in Nineteenth Century Ontario* (Toronto: University of Toronto Press, 1988), 166; Rio de Janeiro: Sandra Lauderdale Graham, *House and Street: The Domestic World of Servants and Masters in Nineteenth Century Rio de Janeiro* (Cambridge, England: Cam-

(continued on next page)

Table 41   (*continued*)

bridge University Press, 1988), 186; Atlanta, the other U.S. cities, and immigrant groups in the United States except Swedes and Japanese: David M Katzman, *Seven Days a Week: Women and Domestic Service in Industrializing America* (New York: Oxford University Press, 1978), 287; Hamilton: Michael Katz, *The People of Hamilton, Canada West: Family and Class in a Mid-Nineteenth Century City* (Cambridge, Mass.: Harvard University Press, 1976), 57; Swedes in the United States: Joy K. Lintelman, "'Our Serving Sisters': Swedish-American Domestic Servants and Their Ethnic Community," *Social Science History* 15, 3 (1991):382; York: Alan Armstrong, *Stability and Change in an English Country Town: A Social Study of York, 1801–1851* (Cambridge, England: Cambridge University Press, 1974), 45; other U.K. cities: Mark Ebery and Brian Preston, *Domestic Service in Late Victorian and Edwardian England, 1871–1914* (Reading, England: University of Reading, 1976), 47; Japanese in the United States: Evelyn Nakano Glenn, "Occupational Ghettoization: Japanese American Women and Domestic Service, 1905–1970," *Ethnicity* 8 (1981):359; Spaniards in Buenos Aires, see Table 40; United States: Elizabeth Faulkner Baker, *Technology and Woman's Work* (New York: Columbia University Press, 1964), 54, 75; Paris: Theresa M. McBride, *The Domestic Revolution: The Modernization of House-hold Service in England and France, 1820–1920* (New York: Holmes & Meier, 1976), 14; Great Britain: calculated from data in Judy Lown, *Women and Industrialization: Gender at Work in Nineteenth Century England* (Cambridge, England: Polity Press, 1990), 20, and in Angela V. John, ed., *Unequal Opportunities: Women's Employment in England 1800–1918* (Oxford: Basil Blackwell, 1986), 37 (Edward Higgs, "Women, Occupation and Work in the Nineteenth Century," *History Workshop: A Journal of Socialist and Feminist Historians* 23 [Spring, 1987]:75, offers lower revised figures for England and Wales of 25 percent in 1851 and 27 percent in 1881, again excluding agricultural workers); London: calculated from figures in Sally Alexander, *Women's Work in Nineteenth-Century London: A Study of the Years 1820–1850* (London: Journeyman Press, 1983), 12, 20–21; St. Petersburg and Moscow: Rose L. Glickman, *Russian Factory Women: Workplace and Society, 1880–1914* (Berkeley: University of California Press, 1984), 60, and Robert E. Johnson, *Peasant and Proletarian: The Working Class of Moscow in the Late Nineteenth Century* (New Brunswick, N.J.: Rutgers University Press, 1979), 56; Milan: calculated from data in Louise A. Tilly, "Urban Growth, Industrialization, and Women's Employment in Milan, Italy, 1881–1911," *Journal of Urban History* 3, 4 (1977):476–78; Japan: computed from data in Konosuke Odaka, "Redundancy Utilized: The Economics of Female Domestic Servants in Pre-War Japan," in *Japanese Women Working*, ed. Janet Hunter (London: Routledge, 1993), 18.

NOTE: Agricultural workers are not included.

the trade. It may have also kept wages up, which in turn would encourage female immigration. A Spanish immigrant in a book written to disparage Argentina admitted that, "for servants, and specially for maids, Argentina is a great country: they are well paid, and shopkeepers delight their ears by calling them señoritas.[83]

Manufacturing followed domestic service as a source of employment for Spanish immigrant women, but opportunities were mostly limited to three sectors. Needlework, by far the most important, absorbed anywhere from one-sixth to one-third of all Spanish women, originally almost exclusively as independent seamstresses, weavers, or embroiderers in their own homes. As the nineteenth century advanced, the popularization of the Singer sewing machines (introduced in 1876) and the industrialization and segmentation of the garment trade increased the specialization of jobs (for example, makers of only ties, trousers, underwear, coats, and so on), the division of tasks, and the number of arrangements (wages or piece-work in factories, sweatshops, and "outwork," in addition to self-employ-ment). The tobacco industry employed 2–8 percent as *cigarreras* (a vague term that can translate as cigar or cigarette makers or workers). In Spain, the feminization of the trade (a process immortalized in Bizet's *Carmen*) reached such a point that women came to predominate in all aspects of production.[84] In Argentina, however, the industry's sexual division of la-bor conformed to a more common pattern found anywhere from Cuba to China, with women engaged mostly as lower-paid strippers—who re-moved the stems from the soft leaf—cigarette packers, and makers of the cheaper stogies.[85] And the shoe industry engaged about 3 percent of the wage-earning Spanish women sewing espadrilles or stitching uppers (shoe-binding), which replaced the fabric but kept the needle, again, the typical, low-paying female task in the trade in other countries.[86] Spaniards' con-centration in these three sectors may have reflected premigratory tradi-tions. But the same could be argued for all other immigrant women since these three industries formed the mainstay of female manufacturing labor almost everywhere. At any rate, the concentration definitely reflected the composition of Buenos Aires' industry and the gender divisions within it. In 1904, textile and garment factories employed 53 of every 100 female industrial workers in the city; the tobacco industry, 16; and footwear shops, 12.[87]

As the century turned, the expansion of private and public enterprises and bureaucracies, plus looser gender roles, created new opportunities in those female white-collar occupations associated with the transition to a mass society: office workers, telephone operators, teachers, and nurses. These jobs, however, were largely dominated by the better-educated na-tives—including the Iberian immigrants' own Argentine-born daughters. Spanish-born women's participation in the nonmanual category was thus mostly confined to their own group's commercial enterprises and to posi-tions such as store clerks, merchants, and, particularly, self-employed dress-makers, or *modistas*—a term that appeared only three times in the 1855 and 1869 census returns but comes up hundreds of times in turn-of-the-century sources. This escalating usage of a word that denotes a higher level of both skills and prestige than *costurera* (the overwhelming title in the earlier sources) suggests one of two things—or perhaps a combination of both: an actual increase in the required skills as women moved into what was once the domain of tailors—the design and fashioning of female garments instead of simply sewing; and/or a linguistic upgrading from a term associated with manual labor and the working class to a euphemism that made it acceptable for the expanding number of lower-middle-class women to engage in it, a mostly decorative uplifting from "seamstress" to "couturiere."[88]

Not only were women relatively concentrated in the lower occupational categories but, even within the same category or particular occupation, they received lower remuneration than men. Female cooks, for example, earned about half of what males co-workers did, in part because while male cooks often worked in restaurants and hotels, females more likely served in private homes. This would also impair women's mobility. Whereas male cooks, if ambitious, skillful, and lucky, could eventually become chefs, no such opportunity existed for women. A similar situation existed between tailors and seamstresses, menservants and nursemaids, dyers and washerwomen, and male and female cigar workers. In 1909, for instance, the top monthly wage in shirt factories was 200 pesos for women but 500 pesos for men; the respective figures for cigar factories were 170 and 500; and book publishers proved, if anything, less enlightened, paying top wages of 80 and 240 pesos, respectively.[89] A woman's chances for mobility were going to be, then, largely dependent on those of her husband. Women listed as merchants or store owners—as opposed to market women or fruit sellers—were more often than not widows, suggesting not a self-propelled ascent into proprietorship but the inheritance of the establishment from their husbands.

The occupational status of immigrant women in the host city depended as much on their parents' Old World social origin as on their husbands' New World success. The daughters of white-collar fathers or city-born mothers were—as Table 42 indicates—highly unlikely to toil as low-paid domestic servants in Buenos Aires, a chance that increased steadily as either the social position of their fathers in Spain or the size of their mother's Iberian birthplace decreased.

A similar interaction between gender and Old World origins can be seen in terms of regional provenance. As Table 43 shows, Andalusians or Catalan immigrant women in Buenos Aires were only between one-fifth and one-half as likely to work in the domestic service as their Galician or Basque sisters. Indeed, they were less likely to work as servants or menial laborers than their Galician or Basque "brothers," showing that the socioeconomic disparities that "came on boats" could surpass the impact of gender-based inequalities.[90] Although Basque and Galician females concentrated on the domestic service as a whole, the former were particularly

Table 42 Occupational status of Spanish immigrant women, by their fathers' occupation in Spain at the time of their birth and by their mothers' birthplace, ca. 1900–1930 (in percentages)

Father's job in Spain at the time of the emigrant's birth	N	Servant	Skilled worker	Nonmanual worker	Did not work for pay
			Daughter's occupation in Buenos Aires		
Landless laborer	19	32	0	10	58
Peasant proprietor	15	27	0	20	53
Urban unskilled or semiskilled	9	11	22	22	44
Skilled	26	11	19	8	62
White collar	13	0	0	23	77
Mother's birthplace[a]					
A village	54	22	0	15	63
A town	18	7	22	17	56
A city	9	0	22	11	67

SOURCES: See Table 38.

[a]A village is defined as a population center with fewer than 2,000 inhabitants; a town, as one with 2,000 to 20,000 inhabitants; and a city, as one with more than 20,000 inhabitants.

likely to be servants, whereas the latter abounded among washerwomen, even after controlling for possible age and marital-status distortions, suggesting a networking process of information, aid, and recruitment. Women from industrial Catalonia predominated among factory workers. Andalusian women accounted for most of the actresses, comediennes, and dancers, reflecting their more urban background, higher literacy, and native (and to many, euphonious) Castilian, as well as the dominance of the supposedly more sensual flamenco over other Iberian musical forms in Buenos Aires' commercial entertainment.

Overall, 53 percent of all Spanish immigrant women over the age of sixteen in 1855, and 54 percent in 1869, engaged in remunerated work; that is, they listed on the census returns an occupation other than housewife or the equivalent. This represents an exceptionally high figure for the time, particularly if one considers that women workers were probably un-

Table 43 Occupational distribution of Spanish immigrant women in Buenos Aires, by regional group, 1855 and 1894–1910 (percentages of all women working for pay from each group in each occupation)

Occupation	Galicians	Basques	Andalusians	Catalans	Canary Islanders
			1855		
Servants	24.8	49.7	7.0	7.1	14.3
Cooks	5.7	8.6	0	0	2.9
Washerwomen	26.2	1.3	2.8	2.4	20.0
Ironers	2.1	5.6	2.8	4.8	8.6
Subtotal, domestic service	58.8	65.2	12.6	14.3	45.8
Seamstresses	24.1	21.2	47.9	57.1	48.6
Cigar workers	7.8	2.6	9.9	4.8	0
Shoe binders	2.8	2.6	2.8	7.1	0
Merchants	5.0	5.3	12.7	9.5	2.9
Teachers/nurses	0.7	0	2.8	4.8	2.9
Performing Artists	0	0	8.5	0	0
Other jobs	0.7	4.0	2.8	2.4	0
N =	141	151	71	42	35
			1894–1910		
Servants	33.3	33.5	3.6	7.9	41.9
Cooks	14.2	16.8	9.0	10.8	14.5
Washerwomen	6.2	3.0	3.6	0.7	1.7
Ironers	9.3	7.8	6.3	11.5	11.1
Subtotal, domestic service	63.0	61.1	22.5	30.9	69.2
Seamstresses	13.0	9.0	33.3	22.3	11.1
Cigar workers	2.5	0.6	0.9	1.4	0
Shoe binders	0.5	1.2	1.8	2.9	1.7
Couturiers	11.7	18.0	31.5	29.5	12.0
Clerks	2.1	3.0	4.5	2.9	2.6
Merchants	3.1	3.6	1.8	3.6	1.7
Teachers/nurses	0.6	0.6	0.9	5.0	0
Performing Artists	0.2	0.6	0.9	0.7	0
Other jobs	3.3	2.4	1.8	0.7	1.8
N =	874	167	111	139	117

SOURCES: See Table 40.

dercounted by census takers (or the informants themselves), who did not always record those who kept boarders, did needlework part time, worked in their parents' or husbands' shops, or engaged in other informal jobs. The figures also seem higher than those for native-born and other immigrant women in Buenos Aires;[91] and than those for immigrant women in contemporary North American cities.[92] By the turn of the century the registers of the main Spanish mutual-aid society show the proportion of women in the labor force as having dropped to 37 percent. The dip, however, may reflect the slightly higher social background of association joiners compared with the general population rather than a real decline. After all, literate women were 10 to 18 percentage points less likely to work for pay than illiterate ones, even controlling for age and marital status.

The latter variable strongly influenced the rate of female participation in the labor force. In 1855, 78 percent of the single female immigrants over the age of sixteen, 73 percent of those separated (listed as married in the census but the husband did not figure in the household), 54 percent of the widows, but only 40 percent of the married women held a remunerated job. The gaps were even wider in 1869 (singles, 83 percent; widows, 66 percent; and marrieds, 37 percent—the random-sampling technique did not allow the identification of separated couples) and in the 1894–1910 period (singles, 65 percent; widows, 42 percent; and marrieds, 24 percent).

Marital status was not the only condition that affected rates of female employment, however. As Table 44 indicates, Galician women were consistently more likely to work for pay than were their Basque compatriots in every one of the seven combinations of marital and educational condition; so were illiterate women in every of the ethnic–marital-status combinations; and celibate ones in every of the ethnic-educational pairs. Clearly, then, the best predictor lay in the meshing of marital status, social background (as measured by literacy), and ethnicity rather than in any one isolated variable. Thus, on the extremes—of both the table and the framework—the chances that a single, illiterate, Galician woman would work for pay were close to certain (96 percent), whereas those of a married, literate, Basque woman did not reach one in three (29 percent).

Similar combinations influenced the particular jobs in which Spanish immigrant women would engage. As Table 45 reveals, the celibacy rate, literacy, and mean age of different women workers varied considerably even within the domestic service. Throughout the whole period, maids were much younger and more literate than other servants and overwhelmingly single, reflecting their live-in situation. The married minority often served as part of husband-wife teams, with their partners working as gar-

Table 44 Adult women (more than sixteen years old) in the labor force of Buenos Aires in 1855, by ethnicity, literacy, and marital status (percentages of all adult women in each category working for pay)

| Marital status | Galicians | | | | Basques | | | |
| | Illiterate | | Literate | | Illiterate | | Literate | |
	Percentage	*N*	*Percentage*	*N*	*Percentage*	*N*	*Percentage*	*N*
Single	28	96	22	77	53	93	29	72
Separated	11	91		–	8	75		–
Widow	11	91	11	55	9	67	13	39
Married	100	49	34	35	99	33	56	29
All	150	64	67	52	169	56	98	43

SOURCE: Municipal manuscript census returns, 1855.

deners, doormen, or chauffeurs. Others, as they grew older and married, became live-out servants. More frequently, for a woman marriage involved a switch from monetarily remunerated work in someone else's house to similar but nonpecuniary work in her own home. Functionally analogous, housework was nevertheless perceived by most contemporary Spanish women as clearly distinct in status and emotional implications from domestic service. Cooks and ironers were older, less literate, and more likely to be married or widowed. Washerwomen surpassed all others in age, widowhood, inability to read or write, were rarely single, and more often than not, were Galician.[93] In the 1890s the construction of Buenos Aires' port, a running-water system, and municipal laundries moved them off the riverbank and eased their task somewhat, but they continued to be among the poorest servants. In manufacturing activities, seamstresses exhibited higher literacy rates than did shoebinders, who in turn surpassed cigarette makers. In commercial activities, clerks—or others dealing with the public—were mostly young and single; market women, middle aged and married; and store owners, older and widowed.

Marital status also affected the occupational distribution of males. Bachelors were consistently overrepresented in menial and unskilled jobs.

Table 45 Mean age, celibacy, and literacy rate of Spanish women workers in Buenos Aires, 1855, 1869, and 1894–1910 (ranked by the mean literacy rate from low to high)

	1855				1869				1894–1910			
	N	Mean age	Percentage single	Percentage literate	N	Mean age	Percentage single	Percentage literate	N	Mean age	Percentage single	Percentage literate
Washerwomen	69	38	14	7	38	35	18	8	75	41	4	9
Cooks	28	36	61	14	31	32	42	10	233	35	31	39
Cigar workers	42	31	12	38	23	38	17	30	27	35	33	31
Ironers	24	30	17	37	12	37	17	33	162	34	37	40
Servants	161	27	76	32	94	25	80	41	508	27	84	52
Shoe binders	17	26	53	41	8	27	37	50	20	31	15	57
Seamstresses	191	31	36	45	46	30	41	56	243	33	32	84
Merchants	39	40	10	51	10	47	20	50	64	34	19	73
Clerks	–	–	–	–	–	–	–	–	46	27	63	82
Couturiers	–	–	–	–	–	–	–	–	281	29	49	87
Teachers/nurses	6	36	17	67	1	26	100	100	20	32	25	100
Performing artists	7	24	43	100	2	30	50	100	9	34	44	83
Housewives	423	35	–	45	184	36	–	53	2,424	35	–	53

Sources: See Table 40.

In part, this resulted from their younger average age. Yet even after controlling for age, they continued to concentrate in the unskilled category. This suggests a reverse causation. That is, they were not poor because they were unmarried, they were unmarried because they were poor. In a city with a shortage of women, where demand exceeded supply, to put it in market terms, poor men found themselves at an evident disadvantage when searching for a mate. After all, Buenos Aires was, according to popular wisdom and many Spanish matriarchs, the place for young women to go if they wanted to marry above their rank. Perhaps not coincidentally, and according to official statistics, it was also the favorite overseas destination of Spanish female emigrants.[94]

Bachelors were also overrepresented in the low-nonmanual category. But here, when separated by age groups, a telling patterns appears: single men under thirty-five tended to concentrate in low-nonmanual occupations, whereas single men over that age tended to concentrate in unskilled and menial jobs. In a sense, the first group was celibate out of choice and was following a traditional socioeconomic strategy, whereas the second group was single out of necessity and had little chance of ever getting married or getting a better job. Among the latter group those still in their thirties and forties could eventually find a mate. But most probably that companion would be a *china*, a lower-class mestiza, instead of a more coveted Spanish woman, and the union would be concubinage rather than marriage. The elderly, unskilled bachelors, however, included the most desolate elements of the immigrant colony. In their efforts to challenge the "pathological" view of immigration, historians have rightly emphasized how most immigrants, using their traditions, responded with relative success to the challenges of the new situation but have, perhaps unintentionally, downplayed the "uprooting" aspects of the process. The response to the new environment by the old, single, illiterate, Spanish peons and day laborers that appear in census returns was anything but successful. More than uprooted, they were ravaged. Their faces seem to surface in the musty manuscripts. Lonely, abandoned, pauperized, they lived in shacks in the outskirts of the city, in asylums, in small *conventillo* rooms, or as *agregados* in the houses of others. There, if fortunate, they would be treated with some deference due to their age; if not, they became *sirvientes*, often treated, whether or not they were senile, with the same respect conferred on servant boys. Forsaken by fate, they seem, nevertheless, to have avoided the mendicant life, perhaps out of an atavistic opprobrium expressed in old Spanish proverbs, such as "El mendigo no tiene amigo [The mendicant has no friend]" or "Quien pide es un apestado y nadie lo quiere al lado [A panhandler is like a person with the plague, whom no-body wants nearby]."[95] Of close to six thousand Spaniards in Buenos Aires around the middle of the century only three ended up as beggars.

On the other hand, many of the young bachelors in the nonmanual category were following a traditional socioeconomic scheme for mobility that had its roots in the colonial past.[96] They formed part of the army of adolescents with "good handwriting and basic arithmetic" who, through the workings of chain migration, came to work in "the store of the uncle," usually his mother's brother, but often a more distant relative, such as a second cousin, who was, at any rate, older and thus called *tío*). The scheme lasted for as long as it did because it benefited every one. Indeed, its equilibrium would have delighted functionalists and exasperated conflict theorists. The *tío* at the same time loved, protected, and exploited the nephew. He received the gratitude of his sister, the blessings of the whole family, cheap labor, and a trustworthy right-hand man in a city where "you couldn't trust anyone." The parents received the famous "remissions from the Indies." The nephew found the chance he had been waiting for to leave the detested limiting ambience of the village, secure employment, a place to live in, and a long-term opportunity to acquire his uncle's store and often even marry his cousin. The *tío*'s Argentine-born sons were liberated from, more than deprived of, the inheritance of a business they perceived as enslavement rather than opportunity, freed to follow their and the family's aspiration to become liberal professionals or government bureaucrats. Whatever tensions arose were tempered by family ties, the respect of elders, and the knowledge that there was light at the end of the tunnel.

The scheme had the added advantage of serving as a sort of preindustrial pension plan. When, after twenty or thirty years "behind the counter," as the Argentine upper class disdainfully put it,[97] the nephew was ready to buy the store, the money would assure the uncle a secure old age and, at times, a chance to cure his *morriña* (a Galician term for homesickness), to return to his native village, where "nothing was as it used to be" and where he would spend his last years longing for the barrios of the great metropolis on the River Plate, where he had dwelled in his golden years. If he lived long enough and was lucky—determined, he usually was—the nephew would one day also cross the Atlantic eastward and achieve that necrophilic but lyrical immigrant dream: "to lay the bones in the land that saw my birth."

Working in the uncle's store offered room and board, a higher status, and brighter perspectives, but less immediate money, than did a job as a skilled manual worker. Therefore, the postponement of marriage became an integral part of the scheme.[98] A job as a smith or even as a stevedore in the port could offer remuneration sufficient to set up house and form a family immediately. It could also mean forfeiting the dream to become occupationally independent, to become a *comerciante*.

Measuring Mobility

But how many fulfilled such dreams? How often and to what extent did the immigrants improve their economic situation in the adopted land? These are old but difficult-to-answer queries in immigration studies. We did see, in the first section of this chapter, that the occupational structure of the Spanish community in Buenos Aires barely changed during the second half of the nineteenth century (see Table 30). But this constancy in overall distribution says little or nothing about mobility. Indeed, it can co-exist, ostensibly, with complete social ascent, descent, none at all, or anything in between.[99] We also saw that from 1869 to the first decade of the twentieth century the proportion of low-skilled laborers declined both in the city's general work force and in samples of Spaniards taken from census returns and voluntary-association records, respectively (see Tables 33 and 36). The change in the general labor market no doubt increased opportunities in skilled and white-collar occupations. Yet it is hypothetically possible, if not likely, that other national groups grabbed most of these and that the decreasing proportion of Spaniards in menial jobs simply reflected biases in the sources (the underrepresentation of the poor among voluntary-association members). Even if we inferred from the two trends an improvement in the job profile of the Spanish community as a whole, it may still say nothing about individual mobility. Again, conceivably, the improvement could have occurred even if all the Spaniards in the original 1869 group had declined in occupational status.

Other sources and methods offer a more appropriate approach to the question of social mobility. One consists in mining the 1855 manuscript census' unusual information on the number of years immigrants had resided in Argentina and cross-tabulating it with their occupational status. The results (see Table 46) reveal a steady and measurable exodus from manual labor in general and from unskilled jobs in particular as length of residence increased and a concomitant ascent into the nonmanual category as a whole and into its higher positions in particular. Other measures of economic success disclose a similar climb. Less than one-half of 1 percent

Table 46 Occupational distribution of Spaniards in Buenos Aires in 1855, by length of residence in the city (in percentages)

Length of residence, in years	N	Unskilled	Semiskilled	Skilled	Cumulative manual	Low nonmanual	Middle and high nonmanual	Professional
0–1	946	36.8	17.2	21.9	76	22.0	0.7	1.4
2–5	1,209	35.4	17.3	21.5	74	22.8	1.4	1.5
6–10	753	28.7	16.3	24.6	70	24.8	4.1	1.4
11–20	992	23.6	17.2	24.8	66	23.5	8.3	2.5
21–39	190	12.1	10.5	12.1	35	19.5	40.6	5.3
40+	192	14.1	6.8	13.5	34	16.1	43.7	5.7

SOURCE: Municipal manuscript census returns, 1855.

of those with fewer than five years in the city could afford domestic servants; one-fifth to one-quarter of those with more than two decades of residence could, and about one-tenth could afford three or more.

Not all of the old-timers' success could be attributed merely to long years of labor and savings. After all, those with more than forty years of residence in the city in 1855 had arrived during the colonial period, when *peninsulares* enjoyed a monopoly on transatlantic trade through their official merchant guild (*consulado*) and other privileges of empire. It is true that the equally successful group with twenty to thirty-nine years of residence had arrived when independence had ended the trade monopoly, both legally and factually, and turned Iberian birth into a handicap rather than an advantage. Yet they also possessed an edge. Their concentration in the professions was probably not the result of longer residence in the city (Buenos Aires had few professional schools at the time, and in those few the native elite youth accounted for most of the enrollment); nor was their higher literacy (77 percent versus 56 percent for those with fewer than twenty years in the city). Most likely, this pioneer group simply included a larger relative number of professionals and better-educated people, a trait that, as I discussed previously, marked the early stages of emigration from a given locality. Their edge rested in their background rather than on Bourbon mercantilism.

Other sources and methods suggest that past imperial privileges and the higher social status associated with the initial stage of emigration provided a head start but did not supplant prolonged and consistent effort. Although other censuses and voluntary-association records rarely specify the immigrants' number of years in the host country, by extrapolating from the few known cases and their mean age of departure I have been able to estimate length of residence for the rest in four large samples covering the whole period from the midnineteenth century to the Great Depression and to correlate that variable with rates of business ownership. The result (see Figure 16) shows that long after independence and the initial stages of the overseas flow, many arrivals continued to climb the economic ladder by spending "their best thirty years behind a store counter." Indeed, after that many years, one or two of every three Spanish immigrants had been able to acquire a business enterprise other than a small artisan shop. If anything, this calculation underestimates the actual increase in ownership (see note to Figure 16). A Spanish ambassador to Argentina in the 1920s described the process this way: "He who begins sweeping the store at the age of fourteen or fifteen can hope to become a

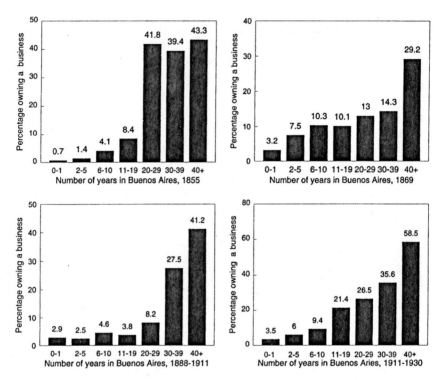

Figure 16. Spaniards owning a business in Buenos Aires, by length of residence, 1855, 1869, 1888–1910, 1911–1930. Small artisan shops are excluded. Length of residence in the last two periods refers to how long the individual had been in the country when he or she joined the association (in any year within each of the two periods). Length of residence in the city was recorded on the census schedules in 1855 but not in 1869. I was able to determine the actual length of residence in 1869 for 49 individuals in the sample because they were traceable to the 1855 census, to passenger lists, or to other sources. Extrapolating from the mean age at the time of arrival for these individuals, I estimated the length of residence for the rest. I used a similar method for the other two periods, extrapolating from 130 and 125 known individuals, respectively. This method may underestimate the escalating numbers of business acquisitions. Had I used it for 1855 instead of the actual number of years of residence in the city, the resulting percentages would have been 0.3 for individuals with less than two years in the city and 2, 3.2, 6.6, 12.5, 16.8, and 29.6 for the other respective time spans. On the other hand, the 1911–1930 sample includes members of recreational associations, which may skew it in favor of businesspeople. These changes in sources and methods hinder comparisons across time. *Sources:* For 1855 (4,396 individuals) and 1869 (1,589 individuals), manuscript census returns; 1888–1910 (3,548 individuals), membership applications of the Asociación Española de Socorros Mutuos de Buenos Aires; 1911–1930 (3,042 individuals), membership applications of the Asociación Española de Socorros Mutuos de Buenos Aires, plus records from five other associations.

clerk before twenty, bookkeeper before thirty, junior partner before forty, and full owner somewhat later."[100]

Another fitting, and more conventional, method of measuring mobility consists of recording the occupations of specific individuals at two points in time.[101] North American social historians have typically done this by tracking individuals from one set of federal census schedules to the next, ten years later. The loss of most Argentine census schedules and the wide gap between the existing ones (1855, 1869, and 1895) obstructed that approach (I tried to trace individuals from the first two, but the extreme attrition rate induced me to abandon the task, and the wider interval to the next census—26 years—dissuaded me from even trying). Fortunately, I was able to locate alternative sources. The remaining membership registers from a Catalan mutual-aid society in Buenos Aires allowed me to trace 274 individuals from 1897 to 1912, 748 from the latter date to 1919, and 182 through all three points. The records from the other voluntary associations used in this book did not permit tracing because they consisted of application forms rather than lists of the entire membership at one point in time. Yet a smaller sample of 69 traceable individuals fortuitously emerged from these sources as I was checking the data sets for duplicates (that is, those who enrolled in more than one association at different times or those who joined, dropped their membership, and later rejoined). Despite its limited size, this sample, which contained Spaniards from all of the localities I had used for microanalysis, provided a useful check against any marked bias in the larger but exclusively Catalan samples. Together, they provide an appropriate and reliable tool for gauging different types of individual occupational mobility.[102]

The most common type was actually "immobility." As shown in Table 47, anywhere from 50 to 83 percent of the individuals traced at different intervals held the same job at the beginning and the end of the period. This career permanency was negatively correlated with the traced interval (that is, it decreased as the latter increased) but could also be affected by external forces. The high persistence rate of the 1912–1919 cohort (83 percent) compared with that of the 1897–1912 group (53 percent) reflected not only the shorter time span but also the fact that the period traversed the World War I depression, whereas the previous interval spanned years of constant economic expansion. With the exception of the World War I sample, and accounting for variation in intervals, the level of career persistence among Spaniards in Buenos Aires did not diverge much from those in other contemporary cities and immigrant groups. If anything, it ranked at the lower end of the international spectrum.[103]

Table 47 Occupational mobility of Spaniards in Buenos Aires, measured by tracing individuals

A. Mobility of members of Montepío de Monserrat,
a Catalan mutual-aid society in Buenos Aires,
from 1897 to 1912 and from 1912 to 1919

	No mobility	Lateral mobility[a]	Upward mobility	Downward mobility	Total	Untraceable
			1897–1912			
Percentage	53	7	32	8	100	
Number	148	18	88	23	277	344
			1912–1919			
Percentage	83	3	10	4	100	
Number	484	20	56	24	584[b]	449

B. Mobility of members of other Spanish immigrant voluntary associations
during the first three decades of the twentieth century, by the length
of the interval over which they were traced (in percentages;
lateral mobility included in None)

		Type of Mobility		
Length of interval	*N*	*None*	*Downward*	*Upward*
Less than 6 years	25	72	8	20
6 to 10 years	34	53	18	29
More than 10 years	10	50	10	40
All (mean years of interval = 7)	69	59	13	28

(*continued on next page*)

Not markedly distinct from occupational persistence, lateral mobility mostly entailed horizontal moves by artisans into closely related jobs—from machinist to toolmaker, gas fitter to plumber, calker to boat carpenter, etc—and accounted for 3 to 7 percent of all traced cases. More frequent was downward mobility, which ranged from 4 to 18 percent. Because the sources did not list any beggars or jobless individuals, this backward movement could not affect those in the bottom unskilled cate-

Table 47 (continued)

C. Percentages of the 182 Montepío de Monserrat members traced from 1897 to
1912 to 1919 falling into each of the nine possible combinations of upward,
downward, and none/lateral mobility during the two intervals

Upward		Erratic		Downward	
Upward and upward	2.7	Upward and downward	3.8	None and downward	3.3
Upward and none	28.0	Downward and upward	1.5	Downward and none	7.7
None and upward	7.7	None and none	45.6	Downward and downward	0.5
Total upward combinations	38.4	Total erratic or static combinations	50.9	Total downward combinations	11.5

SOURCES: A and C, register of the Montepío de Monserrat of Buenos Aires, which listed
the entire membership for the particular years; B, entry or application forms for five other
Spanish voluntary associations. Tracing was only possible for those individuals who discontinued their membership and later rejoined, or who joined other associations, providing
their occupations at two points in time.

[a]Lateral mobility includes people who changed occupations but within the same category
(e.g., carpenter to smith).

[b]Does not include cases traceable to 1919 who had also been members in 1897, to avoid
disproportionate concentrations of older and more established individuals who could have
made the 1912–1919 group less comparable with the 1897–1912 cohort. These are included
in section C.

gory, and it rarely struck those in the next two (semiskilled and skilled laborers) or, on the other extreme, professionals. Occupational downfall
seems to have been almost exclusively the nightmare of the mercantile
classes. It became real for about one-tenth of the low white-collar employees in the samples who tumbled into manual labor and for 30 to 45 percent of the business owners who had to scale down their enterprises or
revert into clerks, indicating a high occurrence of business failure. Those
in high white-collar positions, however, rarely fell to the blue-collar categories.

The allure of Buenos Aires for millions of Spaniards and other immigrants lay not in any security against occupational slippage—a guarantee
more likely to have existed in the villages they left behind—but in its
promise of ascent. For one to four of every ten individuals in the samples
the promise materialized, although again with no guarantee of perma-

nency. Of sixty-three individuals who went up the economic ladder between 1897 and 1912, seven had come back down by 1919. Yet fifty-one
remained up, and five rose even farther. Mobility was neither a one-way
trip nor a fixed one, as the possible nine combination "tours" listed in
Table 47C show. But those who took the upward combinations outnumbered their less fortunate compatriots by more than 3 to 1. Consistently
in all the samples and intervals, those who moved up outnumbered the
backsliders. In the fat 1897–1912 period the ratio reached 4 to 1. During
the leaner 1912–1919 interim it dropped to 2.3 to 1, still not a bad figure
in comparison with other groups in the city and in other cities in the
world. Buenos Aires Jews enjoyed a ratio of 2.2 in a 1895 sample and 1.5
in a 1914 sample; Bostonians had a ratio of 2.5 from 1890 to 1900 and a
negative ratio of 0.9 from 1920 to 1930; in Poughkeepsie, New York, it
was 1.4 from 1870 to 1880; in Eindhoven, Netherlands, 2.2 from 1920 to
1930.[104]

In terms of who moved up, those at the bottom topped all others simply because they had more places to go. But their steps normally reached
only the adjacent rungs of the ladder. The two unskilled laborers in the
sample who became a lawyer and a business tycoon stood out as oddities
among their mobile fellow day laborers who rose to tram conductors,
painters, or at most, store clerks and shopkeepers. In general, occupational
ascent was a gradual affair, with those at the bottom moving to the middle
and those in the middle to the top. Nevertheless, 24 percent of the manual
workers—48 percent if the World War I sample is excluded—rose to the
white-collar class, again a remarkable ascent by contemporary world standards, as the following comparative figures, ranked from high to low, demonstrate:[105]

New York City, Jews (1880–1890, 1905–1915)	38 percent
New York City, Italians (1880–1890, 1905–1915)	30 percent
Birmingham, Alabama (1880–1910 average)	24 percent
Rotterdam (1870–1880)	24 percent
Omaha, Nebraska (1900–1910)	23 percent
Boston (1910–1920)	22 percent
Los Angeles (1910–1920)	16 percent
Hamilton, Canada (1850–1860)	16 percent

Boston (1880–1890)	12 percent
Atlanta (1870–1880)	11 percent
Poughkeepsie, New York, Irish (1850–1880)	11 percent
Graz, Austria (1900–1910)	11 percent
Oskarshamn, Sweden (1890–1900)	10 percent
Norristown, Pennsylvania (1920–1930)	9 percent

Many have debated hard and long whether Gilded Age Argentina embodied an open land of opportunities or a closed oligarchy. The polemic, however, has rarely surpassed the level of vague generalities and unsupported assumptions. The quantification of occupational mobility here arguably presents the most complete analysis of social mobility during the period for any group, immigrant or not, in Argentine historiography.[106] Using two different sources (census returns; mutual-aid society registers or applications) and two different methods (retroactive analysis from a given point in time based on length of residence; tracing) I have obtained roughly similar results. Conditioned by the economic health of the country, a certain length of residency could, in fact, be predicted to produce a determined, and measurable, degree of upward mobility. And that degree compared favorably to most places in the world. I am, thus, confident that the results are a reasonably accurate reflection of what I set out to measure: mobility across occupational categories, degree of business acquisition, and ability to employ domestic servants. I am not as convinced, however, that this is a comprehensive or the only valid measure of social mobility.

The Limits of Quantification

Quantitative methods demonstrated before the perils of relying solely on qualitative sources in the case of Basque and Andalusian occupational success. Now, qualitative sources could reveal the limitations of quantification. In an interview with several members of the Casa de Ribadumia, a Galician village association in Buenos Aires, the old-timers explained to me how almost all of the immigrants from a particular parish near the main village worked at one time or another in the Plaza Hotel as waiters. This in itself illustrates what I have stressed before: the importance of microsocial networks in the adaptation of newcomers. Indeed, the social networks here proved more important than did premigratory work traditions.

Clearly, these people had not been anything remotely resembling waiters in their parish of origin. Of more importance to the present issue, they explained how there had been two routes to mobility: the *gallego* route, in the service occupations of the hotel, and the Italian route, in physical maintenance. Furthermore, within the *gallego* route, these people could enumerate eight distinct steps from bus boy to head waiter. To them each rise in the ladder represented a sign of improvement, and escalation to the top, the epitome of mobility. In the classification scheme used in this chapter (which, by the way, is more discriminating than are blue collar–white collar, or lower-middle-upper-class stratification schemes) they would all have appeared as semiskilled and service. In a macroeconomic analysis the views on mobility of poor *gallego* immigrants may be irrelevant. In a social history of immigrants, not to regard these views is both ahistorical and pedantic, and it denies the richness of a social tapestry.

Farther up the strata, the appearance of the same individual as a merchant, or a similar occupation, at different points in time, may hide a tremendous degree of mobility. For example, Fernando García Cambeiro, an Asturian immigrant who came to Buenos Aires in the first decade of the twentieth century, would always have appeared on any list as a bookdealer. Beyond this apparent lack of mobility lay a tempestuous career in which he bounced more than once from humble kiosk owner to one of the largest bookdealers in the city.[107]

Mobility that did not cross occupational categories was evident in even the lowest categories and was manifested in the Porteño language. The large number of Argentine Castilian terms for servants connotes, for instance, not only different functions but also different statuses. *Criados* (menials) were often no more than children who had been raised in the family or, in the case of Spaniards, "imported" in what detractors called a child-slavery ring and performed the most lowly tasks. The *pinches,* or *peones de cocina,* were also young and played a role in the kitchen subservient to the *cocineros* or *cocineras* (cooks) or to their more elevated cousins, the *chefs de cocina.* Although *amas de leche* (wetnurses) became *nodrizas* in the more prestigious homes, their functions, one would imagine, could not have changed much. Still within the nursery, *niñeras* (nurse girls) ranked just below *ayas* (nursemaids), in a hierarchy that reflected both age and seniority, and way below *institutrices* (governesses),[108] refined young women, ideally French or English born, who took care of the children's higher needs and did not change diapers. Everyone in the nursery, in turn, was, or at least felt they were, above scrubbers and charwomen. One former nursemaid remembered how the masters did not allow "the Spaniards who cleaned the bathroom" to touch the children and added, "It was not cruelty, just divisions."[109] *Mucamos* enjoyed a position higher than that of *criados* and *domésticos* and could advance, in turn, from general menservants or maids-of-all-work to more specialized tasks (footmen, messmen, table maids, chambermaids),[110] to the more genteel positions in personal attendance (valets, waiting maids, companions), or to "management" (*primer mucamos*—maîtres d'hôtel or butlers for Francophile or Anglophile snobs—or head housekeepers). Then there were the servants whose world was wider: doormen, coach drivers, grooms, and "chauffeurs" (a technologically superior version of the coachman). These people, except for the stationary doorman, were mobile in the literal sense of the word. All males, their mobility expanded their horizons. In literature and popular plays they often appear as having a wider network of friends and acquaintances than the other house servants. The facility with which they walked on and off the stage (usually the kitchen) in a way symbolized their greater freedom.[111] Again, most of these people would appear in the same occupational category.

Even the humble *changadores* (Buenos Aires' street porters, often Basque and Galicians), who, according to the Spanish immigrant novelist Francisco Grandmontagne, "represented in the working class the absolute lack of skills," could experience mobility within the "trade."[112] Grandmontagne himself detected three "castes." The "street-corner *changadores,* who idly stood there exchanging jokes whose delicacy could rival a mule's bray, throwing bouquets to the passing maids that would shame the classic bards, and waiting to be called as beast of burden," formed the "dumbest" type. The train-station *changador* was "active and nimble to run after the passengers, and some even ingenious enough to earn their patronage with a clever phrase." And the port *changador* was

> still more alert. Even if he hadn't seen a map in his whole life, he possesses a notable geographical instinct, recognizing in the faces of the passengers the countries they come from. He is too almost a polyglot, dominating in all living languages, and even in the Indo-Asiatic ones, those concepts related to the offering of professional services. He also knows the oscillations of all the world's monetary systems. . . . Lecturing on theoretical finances and duping a few passengers, many have turned into money changers, and it wouldn't be strange if some had proceeded to become bankers.

The rags-to-riches, or *changador*-to-banker myth, ridiculed by the literati and perhaps fomented by the ruling class as a social-control device, formed part, no doubt, of the immigrant worldview. Like most myths, it flourished because it had some basis in reality.[113] In the sixteen years be-

tween 1896 and 1912, at least 3 percent of the sample experienced that
sort of mobility: shoemakers who became industrialists, mailboys who became executives, a day laborer who became a lawyer, and so on. More often than not, however, these self-made men were not the "wretched refuse" of the Iberian shores. Ramón Santamarina, who became one of the
largest estancieros in the pampas, was not a *gallego* peasant boy but the
son of a captain of the Royal Guard. Constantino Bolón, the founder of La
Comercial, the second largest cigar factory in Argentina, came from a *familia acomodada* (a well-to-do family). And Lisardo García Tuñón, an
Asturian telegraphist who, with his five brothers, founded a great shoe industry in the 1880s, had—in addition to a rather odd occupation in 1870s
Spain—a distinguishing characteristic that betrayed his background: the
only remaining brother in the old country belonged to the Parisian
Academy of Inventors.

For most immigrants the rags-to-riches dream was less presumptuous.
It meant going back to the native village dressed in white linen, with a
panama hat and a gold chain watch, to impress kin, friends, and, above all,
local girls and with enough money to lead a life of leisure. In a less puerile way, it formed part of a family strategy and meant the opportunity to
acquire land in the home country. For those who, for a variety of circumstances, became permanent immigrants, it meant the possibility of slowly
improving one's situation and the hope of a better life for one's children. After a few years in Argentina, the notion of an auriferous land, of
"streets paved with gold"—if it ever was regarded seriously—became less
a belief than a butt of jokes. Right before World War I a traveling Englishman heard one about a "Spanish emigrant who had just arrived with
wife and children, and as the group was crossing the Paseo de Julio [the
riverside avenue], the wife spied a silver coin in the gutter. She called to
her husband to pick it up, but he disdainfully answered, 'I have no concern with mere silver money, when I have come here to gather gold!'"[114]

The dream of becoming an Anchorena (the local equivalent of a Rocke-
feller) similarly waxed into a subject of sarcasm, as illustrated in the following lines from the socialist *Almanaque del trabajo de 1920* (p. 190):

> "I began as a peon," said the rich proprietor to his clerk, "and in less than
> five years amassed a fortune."
> "How long were you in jail?" [retorted the clerk].

Epistolary hyperbole received the same fate (see the cartoon ridiculing
immigrants' exaggerations of their accomplishments in letters to Spain,

Figure 17). So did the "wishful" reading of those letters by folks back home, as shown in the following tale in a Basque association's magazine:

> Letter from America. A villager receives a letter from his daughter in Buenos Aires and calls the school teacher–town-hall secretary–church organist–etc.–etc., who begins to read:
> —"Dear father: As you must already know I'm now a mucama [Argemtine term for servant]."
> —En cama? [In bed?] asks the father.
> —No, "mucama," or maybe "muc ama," as if she wanted to say "medio ama" [almost the mistress of the house].[115]

The *gallego* waiters at the Plaza Hotel whom I interviewed would also laugh at the notion that one could go from being a waiter to being waited upon just by washing dishes and saving. The proximity to, and abysmal gap from, the guests of the hotel made the point poignantly clear. With more class rancor and covetousness than humor, one of them described in a 1924 letter to a syndicalist newspaper the "decadent" clientele of the hotel:[116]

> Aristocratic ladies with lavish silk shawls the color of gold; high-class cocottes,[117] well born, resplendent, loaded with jewelery and luxurious transparent dresses, who exhibit themselves in hordes, provoking the satanic lust of the pimps who surround them. Modern young girls with short hairdos and half naked, with their snouts painted and meticulously perfumed, specialize in risqué foot movement and execute tangos in an atmosphere of depravity.... The breasts and the low-cut dresses offer through the light a spectacle as racy as it is tempting. The dance continues and the champagne and sherry pour with no end into fine, Napoleon-style cups. The short-haired girls enter and exit often from reserved saloons accompanied by golden boys ... fatigued, languorous, exhausted, turned into a volcano of fire and feverish carnal desire. Old men with white bald heads partake lecherously in the dance and tightly embrace the slim bodies of the young girls.
> The Plaza Hotel! Beautiful stable of the highest bourgeoisie, of the flower of the great American [meaning Argentine] social parasitism, of *latifundistas*, owners of immense extensions, who can only view their whole estancias through maps, of cocottes and short-haired girls on the arms of their paramours and flesh merchants.

The anarchist writer of the letter, nicknamed *Medio-Kilo* by co-workers for his spasmodic proclamations that half a kilogram of dynamite surpassed the power of a thousand votes in bourgeois elections, never made good on his "explosive" threats and never became rich enough to "join the other side." He neither blew up the Plaza nor tangoed in its ballrooms. But he did advance six steps from dishwasher up to second waiter, raised a family, sent his son to commercial school to become an accountant,

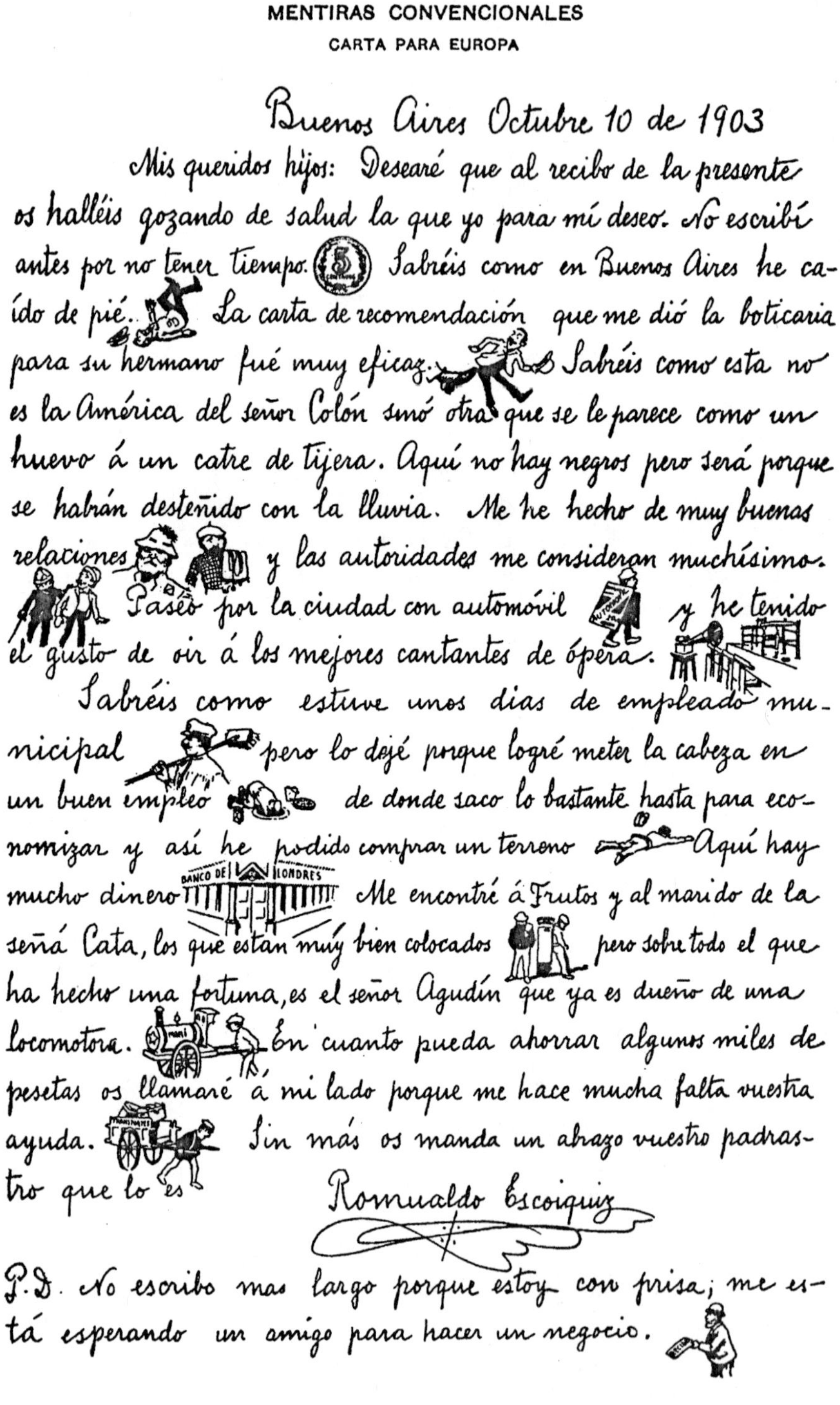

MENTIRAS CONVENCIONALES

CARTA PARA EUROPA

Buenos Aires Octubre 10 de 1903

Mis queridos hijos: Desearé que al recibo de la presente os halléis gozando de salud la que yo para mí deseo. No escribí antes por no tener tiempo. Sabréis como en Buenos Aires he caído de pié. La carta de recomendación que me dió la boticaria para su hermano fué muy eficaz. Sabréis como esta no es la América del señor Colón sinó otra que se le parece como un huevo á un catre de tijera. Aquí no hay negros pero será porque se habrán desteñido con la lluvia. Me he hecho de muy buenas relaciones y las autoridades me consideran muchísimo. Paséo por la ciudad con automóvil y he tenido el gusto de oir á los mejores cantantes de ópera.

Sabréis como estuve unos dias de empleado municipal pero lo dejé porque logré meter la cabeza en un buen empleo de donde saco lo bastante hasta para economizar y así he podido comprar un terreno Aquí hay mucho dinero Me encontré á Frutos y al marido de la señá Cata, los que están múy bien colocados pero sobre todo el que ha hecho una fortuna, es el señor Agudín que ya es dueño de una locomotora. En cuanto pueda ahorrar algunos miles de pesetas os llamaré á mi lado porque me hace mucha falta vuestra ayuda. Sin más os manda un abrazo vuestro padrastro que lo es

Romualdo Escoiquiz

P.D. No escribo mas largo porque estoy con prisa; me está esperando un amigo para hacer un negocio.

Figure 17. "Conventional Lies," a humorous letter from a Spanish immigrant in Argentina to his stepchildren in Spain. *Source: Caras y Caretas* 262 (1903):14.

CONVENTIONAL LIES

A letter to Europe

Buenos Aires, October 10, 1903

My dear children: I wish that as you receive the present you find yourselves in the good health I desire for myself. I did not write earlier because of lack of time [read "money," coin]. You should know that I have landed in Buenos Aires on my right foot [on his ass]. The letter of recommendation that the druggist gave me for her brother proved very effective [in getting him kicked out]. You should know that this is not the America of Mr. Columbus but another one that resembles his the way an egg resembles a folding cot. Here there are no blacks, but it must be because they have discolored with the rain. I move in very selective circles [figures of two street porters or *changadores*], and the authorities consider me highly [a police officer arresting him]. I ride through the city in an automobile [inside an advertising sandwich for automobiles] and have had the pleasure of listening to the best opera singers [on a gramophone in what appears to be the shoe-shining parlor where he works].

You should know that I was a municipal employee [sweeper] for a few days but left it because I was able to stick my head into a better position [the sewer, to clean it] where I make enough to save and that way I have been able to buy a plot of land [drawing of person lying flat, meaning not clear]. Here there is lots of money [in the Bank of London]. I met Frutos and missus Cata's husband; they are both well placed [in street corners as lowly porters], but the one who really has made a fortune is Mr. Agudín, who already owns a locomotive [a peanut-vending cart in the shape of a train locomotive, common at the time]. As soon as I can save a few thousand pesetas, I will call you to my side because I need your help a lot [to carry junk]. With nothing else to add, receive a big hug from your stepfather.

Romualdo Escoiquiz

P.S. I don't write a longer letter because I'm in a hurry; a friend is waiting for me to do some business [a bill collector demanding payment].

From *Caras y Caretas* n. 262 (October 10, 1903), p. 14.

Figure 17. (*continued*)

bought a modest two-family house, and—in a temporal ideological lapse from his egalitarian doctrines—even became vice president, albeit of his village's association in Buenos Aires. If one asks him whether he experienced upward social mobility, he responds that such a thing is impossible under capitalism, an illusion, "opium supplied by those on top." If over a good cup of the sherry he once served to "lascivious estancieros and high-born cocottes" one asks him whether he considers himself a lucky man, he spouts about his achievements with a passion normally reserved for the harangues against priests and adds—in the best Victorian fashion—that every penny he saved came from hard and honest work.

How successful were Spanish immigrants, then, in achieving this long-term, unassuming, and elusive type of mobility that is not reflected in changes across occupational categories? Is it possible to go beyond vague and impressionistic estimates, beyond the simply illustrative anecdotes of a *gallego* waiter? To do so, and to put it in measurable terms, I returned to quantitative methods and compiled a data set with the occupations of European-born and native-born Spanish women who joined the main immigrant mutual-aid society in 1920 and 1930. For the Argentine born, only daughters of Spaniards were included, to assure that this represented the second generation. Women were used precisely because of their dependence on husbands and families for occupational mobility. I wanted to measure how successful Spanish-born men and women had been in achieving their ideal of a better life for themselves and their children in the long run, not just the extent of intergenerational mobility. While sons had greater chances to make it on their own in the world of commerce and industry, opportunity for daughters rested almost totally on their family's capacity to save and to pay for their training and schooling. Self-made, unmarried businesswomen did exist in 1920s Buenos Aires, but without a doubt they were rarae aves.

The data in Table 48 indicate that in their efforts to provide a better life for their children, Spanish immigrants achieved a greater degree of mobility than that implied by changes across occupational categories. This type of mobility may have been from busboy to headwaiter, from kitchen helper to cook, from *sirviente* to valet de chambre or *ama de llaves*, from a shop in the middle of the block to one on the corner (the ambition of every shopkeeper), from a clothing store in the outskirts to one near the center of town, or even from street-corner *changador* to port *changador*. But it was enough to realize one of their primordial goals. If the wives had been servants, the daughters were going to be teachers. Of the Spanish-born women, 43 percent in 1920 and 42 percent in 1930 worked as ser-

Table 48   Occupational distribution of Spanish-born women and
Argentine-born daughters of Spaniards, 1920 and 1930 (in percentages)

	N	Menial[a]	Middle[b]	Professional[c]
			1920	
Spanish-born women	464	43	53	5
Argentine-born daughters	237	13	71	16
			1930	
Spanish-born women	211	42	51	7
Argentine-born daughters	124	9	61	30

SOURCE: Asociasión Española de Socorros Mutuos de Buenos Aires, membership forms
for 1920 and 1930.
[a]Includes servants and unskilled laborers.
[b]Includes seamstresses, clerks, and other low nonmanual employees.
[c]Includes merchants, rentiers, and nurses but consists mostly of school teachers

vants, but only 13 percent and 9 percent of the daughters did. In other
words, some nine-tenths of the Spanish families were able to keep their
daughters from going into domestic service or menial labor. The *gallega*
maid, a stock character in Argentine popular plays and early films, rarely
survived into the second generation. And as Spanish emigration subsided, the upper class would have to look for domestic help from other
sources—the poor interior provinces and Paraguay. By 1930, among the
Spanish born, servants outnumbered teachers six to one. Among the
daughters, teachers outnumbered servants more than three to one.

One afternoon, while strolling through La Recoleta, Buenos Aires' upper-class necropolis, I recognized on the plates of lavish mausoleums the
names of many of the Spanish immigrants whose lives I had been studying. They seemed like poignant diadems for these peoples' triumphs, for
dreams that had begun more than a century ago in Cantabrian mountains
and valleys, in innumerable villages and towns along the periphery of the
Iberian Peninsula. Few of those dreams, to be sure, were ever crowned by
mausoleums. But few ended up in the common graves of the poorhouse.

Few became Anchorenas or tangoed in the Plaza. But many saved some pesos, sent millions in remittances back home, raised families, and became fathers and mothers of teachers and bookkeepers. For the great majority of Spain's inhabitants at the time, that would have counted as upward mobility. For most of the immigrants, that was what "making America" was all about. The rags-to-riches myth never represented much more than a passing fantasy of adolescents, an unimaginative apology for existing inequalities, a favorite straw man for revisionist historians, and a recurrent theme in immigrant humor.

6 Institutional and Social Life

After finding a place and a way to live, the next step in the immigrants' adaptation was to re-create secondary social networks. One of the ways they went about that was to establish and join a plethora of voluntary associations. If, as the truism goes, "Man is a social animal," immigrants surely constitute a particularly associative species of the human fauna. Spanish visitors to the River Plate metropolis consistently expressed amazement at the "associational instinct" of their notoriously unassociative compatriots.[1] Immigrants' adages everywhere emphasize the point: "Two cats form a society," Galicians often say in Buenos Aires; "Two Japanese make an association, and three found a newspaper," goes a saying in southern Brazil; "Put three Germans together and in five minutes you'll have four clubs," proffers a Teutonic version of the idea in Chicago.[2] The same aphorisms have been repeated in numerous other places and languages.

This chapter examines how the Spanish immigrants channeled this associational instinct in Buenos Aires and why their institutional life took the specific form it did. The first section describes the emergence of formal institutions in the midnineteenth century and the patterns they set for the future. Instead of following the tortoiselike evolution of associative life through a sluggish chronological current, the second section leaps ahead sixty years and examines the main institutions and characteristics of the mature organized community. The rest of the chapter tries to answer some main questions: Did localist and parochial tendencies weaken or strengthen the organized community? To what degree did the immigrants' associations reflect a continuation of prearrival practices and to what degree a response to the new setting? What were the sources of conflict and the attenuating elements? And how did the immigrant institutional structure affect assimilation?

THE BIRTH OF A FORMALLY ORGANIZED COMMUNITY

In the early morning of February 4, 1852, Benito Hortelano, a Madrileño printer who had come to Buenos Aires two years earlier, scurried to his bookstore to take down a sign. Meanwhile, Federico de la Llosa, a clerk at the bookstore, nervously dropped bunches of scarlet badges down the back privy. There were two compelling and interrelated reasons for all the fuss. First, the legend on the store sign and badges was, "Long live the Argentine Confederation! Death to the savage unitarians! Death to the madman, traitor, savage unitarian Urquiza!" Second, Urquiza's victorious troops were entering the central plaza, and along with the conquering soldiers—not exemplars of discipline themselves—the vanquished and the suburban rabble were descending on the city to loot it. Five hundred people died that day.[3]

The previous day, a watershed event in Argentine political history had taken place: the defeat of the armies of Juan Manuel de Rosas, governor of Buenos Aires, populist caudillo, and de facto ruler of the country, at the battle of Monte Caseros. The nature of this man and his regime eventually became a leitmotif and, at times, the very crux of Argentine historiography. Liberal and revisionist political historians will probably never agree on the significance of Monte Caseros. Its significance for Spanish immigrants is less disputable. Four events that followed the battle signaled the birth of a formally organized community.

The first was the decree by the conquering Urquiza to exempt Spaniards from conscription in the local militia. Induced by Jaime Cuyas Sampere, a Catalan who acted as his personal banker, General Urquiza had already accorded this privilege to Spaniards in his native province of Entre Ríos. Upon his victorious entry in the capital, he extended the exception to Buenos Aires' Spanish residents—the only foreigners who had been forced to serve in the militia during the Rosas regime. An inconvenience during times of peace, Argentina's numerous civil wars had turned this "civic duty" into a nightmare for Spaniards, many of whom had crossed the ocean to escape military conscription in their homeland. It had also been one of the main impediments to an organized community. The following newspaper advertisement illustrates the point: "Don Manuel Otero informs the public, and his friends in particular, that from now on he will sign using his true name: Ignacio Ramos Otero. In order to avoid misinterpretations, he should explain that on arriving in this country in 1844 he claimed that he was Portuguese instead of Spanish and that his name was Manuel Otero in order to evade the draft."[4] This individual later became a member of the directorate of the Banco Español y del Río de la Plata and of various voluntary associations, and his wife, Emilia, was a founder of the Ladies Commission of the Hospital Español. Obviously, as long as these Spaniards had to deny their nationality and names and to pass for Portuguese or French Basque to evade conscription, the chances of creating a formally organized community were close to nil.[5]

The second event was the creation of a Spanish consular office in Buenos Aires. Because of the impecunious conditions of the nineteenth-century Spanish state, this consular office remained understaffed and less active than those of other European nations. For example, in 1873 the United Kingdom's consulate dispatched thirty-nine petitions to the Buenos Aires police asking for the release of British nationals, the Italian consulate sent thirty-two, and the Spanish one only five. Even the consulates of countries with very few immigrants in Buenos Aires, the Dutch (fourteen dispatches) and the Scandinavian (eight), were more active in defending their nationals' interests.[6] Nevertheless, the consulate provided some official protection for the Crown's subjects in the River Plate, something that Spaniards had eagerly awaited. It could also serve as a channel of communication between family members who had lost touch with each other, as the following newspaper notice illustrates: "Spanish Consulate. The Spanish priests Manuel Marotto and José Colomo, and also Aureliano March, should present themselves at the consulate to provide their families with news about them."[7]

The third event was the appearance of the first Spanish immigrant newspapers in independent Argentina, *El Español*, in July, and *Revista Española*, in November.[8] The first was founded by Benito Hortelano, the man who, on February 4, had dashed to take down the sign from his bookstore and who, on February 5, was printing leaflets giving vivas to "Urquiza the Liberator" and death wishes to the "traitorous, savage federalists." An ardent republican turned pragmatic entrepreneur by his immigration experience, he philosophically characterized this behavior in his memoirs as "a policy fit for the new situation, anathematizing what four days before we had sanctified. . . . That is the way the press is and will always be in every nation."[9]

In the first issue of the newspaper Hortelano ironically advised his countrymen not to meddle in internal Argentine politics. Perhaps he meant to add, "if it will put you in danger but will not produce any benefits." He had learned the lesson that many other immigrants were to learn. His countryman and partner, Antonio Pareja, had refused to adopt "a policy fit for the new situation," claiming that "nothing could prevent him from defending the rights of the people." Hortelano remembered how "the poor devil was to pay dearly for it" and how another Urquiza detractor, Bartolomé Mitre, later president of Argentina, went scot-free because, as *hijo del país*, his friends in power alerted him to police plans for his arrest.[10] The first Spanish immigrant newspaper therefore adopted a policy that the majority, but not all, of later publications followed: "Let's mind our own business and leave Creole politics to the Creoles."[11]

If Argentine policies were considered injurious or insulting to Spaniards, however, the immigrant press could now respond. In the first issue of the *Revista Española*, the second Spanish newspaper to appear in 1852, the front page featured an editorial calling for the removal of a lantern in the national guard's bandstand because it contained an allegorical painting that the Spaniards considered offensive (a woman warrior, representing Argentina, with a lion, representing the defeated metropolis, at her feet). The article infuriated some Argentines, who considered it an affront to a national symbol. But the *Revista Española* was not intimidated. Three days later another article appeared, asking for "the abandonment of the symbols of hatred and old wars."[12]

Advertisements in the newspaper illustrate how it could also serve the more mundane—and most varied—needs of the Spaniards in the city. It could assist:

> Those searching for employment:
>> Clerk or scribe. A youth of 24 offers his services for a commercial establishment, counting house, or office. Good handwriting. Speaks Castilian and Basque. See me in the Spanish inn at the corner of Plaza Monserrat.

> Nursemaid offers her services. Spanish, young, healthy, and robust. 281 Cuyo Street.

> Those seeking employment and a means to keep the family together:
>> Young married couple, no children, recently arrived from Spain, offer their services. The woman as a servant or to sew, the man for any other occupation. The woman sews very well and the man knows how to write a little and can do anything. 23 Tacuarí Street, any time.

Those too weak—or perhaps shrewd—to be employed:
To charitable persons: a poor invalid woman, who for years has been prostrated in bed, implores pious persons for their succor and alms. Lives at 115 Comercio Street.

Those who made their living finding work for others:
Clerks. Spanish youths for groceries or stores. Opportunities at Guerrero Employment Agency.

Those offering and requesting services:
Spanish leeches at three pesos each at 72 Merced Street, barbershop in front of the Catalans' coffeehouse.
Maid needed, preferably Basque or black [*morena*]. Details at the Cigarrería del Toro.

Separated kin and acquaintances:
Wishes to see Elías Valdés or his brother José Valdés, Spaniards from the province of Asturias, to inform them about a matter of interest regarding their parents.

And it could supply official but, I imagine, difficult-to-follow advice: "The Spanish consulate advises its nationals who have taken arms to maintain the public order that it is their duty to maintain the strictest neutrality."[13]

The fourth 1852 event that led to the birth of an organized community was the permission to form an association, granted to Spaniards by the new regime, and the consequent founding of the first Spanish immigrant society in emancipated Argentina, La Sala Española del Comercio.[14] It claimed as its objectives "to foment the spirit of nationality, harmonize the interests of Spaniards . . . and build an asylum of beneficence and hospital to succor poor compatriots."[15] By 1857 this society had vanished, but from its ashes three other institutions emerged: the Club Español, a continuation of the Sala Española that became the elite association of the immigrant colony; La Asociación Española de Socorros Mutuos de Buenos Aires (AESM), a mutual-aid society founded in 1857; and the Sociedad Española de Beneficencia, founded the same year, which by 1877 had built a Spanish hospital.

In its very first year of existence, the organized community already showed some characteristics that would endure for the rest of the period. The first related to the types of immigrants more likely to become actively, rather than passively, involved: merchants, clerks or other non-manual employees, independent artisans, professionals, and the colony's intelligentsia—a mélange of political exiles, journalists, men of letters, coffeehouse philosophers, and anyone bold enough to deliver a resounding speech. The Spanish immigrant novelist Francisco Grandmontagne would mockingly christen the latter type *alborotapueblo,* grandiloquent rabble-rousers who thrived on bombastic oratory at club meetings and on sowing discord among the members.[16]

The second trait was the inevitability of conflict between these groups. On the inaugural day of the Sala Española, right after the tears and emotive words, the clerks and artisans were already complaining about the merchants' plans to impose high entry dues. This, moreover, in part took the form of an intergenerational conflict between "the young crowd [*la muchachada*] of the Spanish commerce" and the older merchants. Meanwhile, the more "enlightened" members complained about the lack of vision of old merchants such as the provisional president, "whom blind Fortuna had loaded with money, even though the dumb ass could hardly read the speech that someone else had written, in which, among other barbarities, he said that we should acclaim 'Doña Isabel dos' [instead of the correct Queen Isabel the Second]."[17]

The third attribute concerned the formation of a leadership network. Benito Hortelano, the newspaper founder, was also the treasurer of the Sala Española. His next-door neighbor and Sala buddy, Felipe Muñoz, brought together some seventy immigrants and, with the assistance of a friend who had founded Spanish mutual-aid societies in Montevideo and in the Argentine towns of Rosario and Santa Fe, established Buenos Aires' first Spanish mutual-help society. Felipe's employer, Enrique Ochoa, who had been an officer in the Sala and in whose house the first assemblies took place, became the treasurer; his brother, Francisco Muñoz, acted as subdirector; Vicente Casares, the first consul, an officer of the Sala and a business associate of Ochoa, became the president; Toribio Ayerza, secretary of the Sala, became the physician; and Juan Arizábalo, a Mexican-born Basque who had served as an officer of the Sala, became the pharmacist.[18]

Unlike the microsocial networks of ordinary immigrants that formed on the basis of localities of origin, the leadership network included Spaniards from different regions of the peninsula who were linked by institutional, commercial, and personal ties. It was also often linked to Argentine elite institutions. Benito Hortelano, for instance, also founded several nonimmigrant newspapers and El Casino Bibliográfico, a bibliophile club which counted as members such distinguished citizens as Rufino Elizalde, minister of the treasury, and Bartolomé Mitre, Argentina's greatest nineteenth-century historian and future president. At least two dozen members of the Sala Española also held positions in local upper-class organizations or were connected to the Porteño elite through business and family ties.[19]

The fourth characteristic of the embryonic organized community of 1852 which enjoyed a long life was interinstitutional feuding. By December the only two newspapers were already at each other's throats over the rights to publish a popular history of Spain. If, as the French philosopher Charles de Rémusat put it, "unanimity is almost always an indication of servitude," Spanish immigrant institutions proved remarkably unservile from their very genesis.

THE MATURE, ORGANIZED COMMUNITY

By the outbreak of World War I the *gran aldea* of 1852 had turned into the grand metropolis of the belle epoque. As Buenos Aires changed from a sleepy town of 90,000 into a city of 1.5 million inhabitants, and as the Spanish colony increased from 6,000 to 312,000, so did the inchoate organizations of 1852 grow into a huge and impressive institutional apparatus.

The modest Sala Española of 1852 had turned into the aristocratic Club Español, which in 1912 built one of the most splendid art nouveau structures in the city (still standing, at 172 B. de Irigoyen Street), with all of the facilities suiting a polite society: a library; chess, billiard, and fencing rooms; and ample salons where it held banquets for visiting *peninsulares*, dances, concerts, movies, billiard contests, and so on. Its monthly dues were as high as those of similar immigrant associations (Circolo Italiano, Club Français, Deutscher Turnverein) and local elite clubs (Jockey Club, Club del Progreso). They were five times higher than the dues of mutual-aid societies and the equivalent of a laborer's weekly salary. In terms of gender, this, and most clubs in the city, fit the caustic definition given by an English clubman: "club—a weapon used by savages to keep white women at a distance."[20] Its elitism made it a favorite target for egalitarian-minded Spaniards. But the club did serve as a converging place for the group from which much of the colony's leadership was to come. In the cozy comfort of its library, or in the more earthy atmosphere of its saloon, the most successful and active immigrants forged personal and institutional ties that functioned as ligaments for the upper levels of the colony's organizational skeleton.[21]

Two years later and five blocks to the south, the Asociación Patriótica Española erected an equally imposing, but more austere, "social palace."

Founded by twenty other associations during the Spanish-American War to channel aid from the immigrant colony to the warring motherland,[22] by 1914 its membership had become very exclusive, and it functioned as an umbrella society that supposedly represented and defended the interests of all Spaniards in the country.[23]

The same building housed the Institución Cultural Española, founded in 1912 to promote Spanish high culture. Many luminaries of the Hispano-Argentine world were to enter its doors: Ortega y Gasset, Menéndez Pidal, Américo Castro, Ramiro de Maeztu, Eugenio D'Ors, García Lorca, Manuel de Falla, Manuel Mujica Láinez, Ernesto Sábato, Ricardo Levene, Claudio Sánchez Albornoz, and Nobel laureates Jacinto Benavente, Juan Ramón Jiménez, Severo Ochoa, and Carlos Saavedra Lamas.[24] Its membership included the social cream of the immigrant colony and more than a few Argentine Hispanophiles from even loftier backgrounds. But apparently this institution's gynephobia matched its Hispanophilia: of the 244 peoples who joined between 1912 and 1920, only one was a woman.[25]

The Cámara Española de Comercio (Chamber of Commerce), founded in 1887, served a less ethereal function. One of the few associations to receive funds from the Spanish government, it basically tried to use the immigrant merchant community to increase the exportation of Iberian products.[26] Like the three above-mentioned institutions, this one heeded not the old Spanish admonition, "Sin una mujer al lado, el hombre es un desdichado [Without a woman by his side, man is a wretch]."

For their part, upper-class Spanish immigrant women founded in 1912, with the assistance of a religious order, an appropriately maternal—despite the title—institution, the Patronato Español, which endeavored to protect young immigrant girls and orphans and claimed that "hundreds of young girls have found in the Patronato a new home full of warmth and affection; they are not abandoned in a strange land and they will not lack the bare necessities of life. Above all, they will never see themselves entrapped by the perils that threaten young girls when away from the protective aegis of the home."[27] Formally, the Patronato (and also the Institución Cultural and the Asociación Patriótica) qualified—in the typology of sociologists C. W. Gordon and N. Babchuk—as an "instrumental" association, that is, one whose aim lay in serving people other than its members.[28] In reality, the function of the organization transcended its stated objectives. Exclusive membership based on prestigious ascriptive qualities acted as a status-conferring mechanism and made the Patronato an "expressive-instrumental" association that expressed or served the social aspirations of the colony's "socialites" as much as the social needs of its clients.

The same was true of the older, larger, and mostly male-run—despite its Ladies Commission—Sociedad Española de Beneficencia. Founded in 1857, by the turn of the next century this beneficent society had become the wealthiest private voluntary association in the country.[29] Its main purpose was to run the Spanish hospital—one of the most important in the city—and to provide free medical care for destitute compatriots. The benefits of membership apparently went beyond the conferring of status. Although its rules and regulations were ambivalent about this, it seems that the institution balanced charity and the need for financial support by providing fee-paying members with certain preferences, such as easier admittance and longer convalescing periods. In 1913 it built an annex facility for the aged and chronically ill on seven city blocks donated by a rich Spaniard in the nearby town of Temperley, which came to fill a gap in its services to the immigrant community.

These six associations reflected the reality of the immigrant class structure. As early as 1880 an immigrant newspaper observed, regarding the increased stratification of associations, that "just as liquids of distinct nature and consistency mix when stirred, so the heterogeneous elements that form society may mix in a moment of enthusiasm or a period of expansion, but once normality returns they, like the liquids, will become divided again in different gradations."[30] The six associations also reflected the sheer growth of the immigrant elite. In relative terms, they may have represented a smaller proportion of the community than in 1850, when much of the old colonial elite was still alive. In absolute terms, however, their members numbered between 6,000 and 10,000 (2–3 percent of the Spaniards); that is, a number greater than all of the Spaniards in Buenos Aires in 1850. The Club Español and the Asociación Patriótica, both elite institutions, boasted more than 1,000 members each in the 1920s. Moreover, unlike the *prominenti* of the southern Italian colonies in North American cities, for instance, the Spanish elite in Buenos Aires was not only truly numerous but truly rich. It included families like the Santamarinas and Menéndezes, who were among the largest estancieros of the country, and others, like the Carides, Casares, and Castells, who belonged to the commercial and industrial top crust. Obviously, then, neither a single multiclass association nor a collection of minute parochial societies could have served the needs of this sector.

A different type of institution, which appeared in the late nineteenth century as the result of the growth of the elite, was the immigrant bank. In the 1870s the Banco Español y del Río de la Plata was founded by a group of immigrant merchants. By 1914 it had become the largest private

bank in South America, flaunted the largest bank advertisement in the entire London *Times* financial section, and had hundreds of branches from
Madrid to Montevideo.[31] Its success rested not only on the deposits of
prosperous merchants but also, as a visiting Spanish sociologist put it, "on
the continuous flow from the small savings of our compatriot immigrants:
servants, milkmen, clerks, coach drivers."[32] To dispute this modest clientele, the Banco Popular Español, a smaller and less successful bank, appeared in 1906. Two others were founded after the War (the Banco de España y América, in 1918, and the Banco Hispano Sudamericano, in 1919).
Monetary regionalism first surfaced in 1906 with the founding of the
Banco de Galicia y Buenos Aires, which would become one of the largest
in the city. Other regional banks soon joined the immigrant financial
scene: the Basko-Asturiano, Santander, Madrid y Buenos Aires, and Castilla y el Río de la Plata.

All of these banks established a reciprocal relationship with the rest of
the organized community. The voluntary associations deposited their cash
in the banks; the banks, in return, donated a small percentage of their
profits to the major associations, arranged mortgages, and provided loans
(at times subsidized) for the expansion of their facilities. They also often
shared the same leadership. For instance, of the eleven members of the directorate of the Banco Español y del Río de la Plata in 1887, seven belonged to the directorate of the Sociedad Española de Beneficencia, the
association that ran the Spanish hospital. Moreover, four of their wives
belonged to the Comisión de Damas del Hospital."[33] Similarly, of 164
leaders of the Instituto Cultural and Asociación Patriótica between 1896
and 1920, 22 were members of the directorates of immigrant banks.[34]

The profusion of banks and their extensive ties to the community may
explain the lack among Buenos Aires' Spaniards of a particularly ubiquitous institution among immigrants elsewhere: rotating credit unions. After all, the many groups who developed these semiformal loans or revolv-
ing credit associations—from the Japanese in Los Angeles to Haitians in
New York and black African migrants in Soweto—explicitly did so not as
a preferable alternative to bank financing but because of the unavailability
or scarcity of financing, and the practice declined as access to the latter increased.[35] Other groups—such as Italians in North American cities—developed "immigrant banks," which the U.S. Senate Commission on Immigration of 1907–1909 described as "privately owned steamship agencies,
labor agencies, real estate offices, groceries and saloons which masquerade
under the name of bank."[36] The early formation and proliferation of bona

fide Spanish banks in Buenos Aires discouraged the emergence of these intermediate arrangements. Spanish immigrants obtained their credit either from formal financial institutions or informally from friends, relatives, or one of the ubiquitous store-owning "uncles," rather than from semiformal schemes like the glorified groceries of Toronto's and New York's Little Italies or the "endless chains" [*Mujin*] of the Angeleno Issei.

Secret societies and/or criminal organizations represented another category absent from the associative spectrum of Buenos Aires' Spaniards. Some Spanish immigrants did form a few small esoteric associations, such as masonic lodges and spiritist circles. But they established nothing remotely similar, either in number or in import, to the secret triads of the Chinese diaspora or to the Cosa Nostra. This may in part follow from the relative lack of such organizations in Spain, or at least in its regions of heavy emigration. After all, the overseas triads and tongs have been shown to descend from the *hui* and *kongsis* of Fujian and Guangdong (the southern provinces that supplied the bulk of Chinese emigrants), and the Cosa Nostra and Black Hand from the Mafia and the Camorra of the Mezzogiorno (the southern source of 80 percent of the Italians who departed for North America).[37] But it may also reflect a greater access to licit organization, power, and status in the host society. After all, the Italians of Buenos Aires (half of whom were southerners) founded no Cosa Nostra.[38]

Spanish immigrant religious associations were more common than secret societies but were actually outnumbered by Spanish banks, which seems to confirm the description of Buenos Aires by visiting Iberians as an impious, materialistic city, and/or the universalist character of the Catholic Church.[39] The 1922 guide *Buenos Aires Católico* boasted about the existence of twenty-three Spanish or Basque "Catholic" entities in the city (pp. 222–26). But this number apparently included any place with a saint's sculpture or a crucifix. Indeed, I visited many of them, and, at least today, they show as many signs of apostolic concern as does a Las Vegas casino or a Communist youth league. In reality only three (one fewer than those formed by Buenos Aires' minuscule Hibernian community) could truly be described as Catholic associations, and they had a combined membership of fewer than 1,000. This dearth of Spanish religious associations may reflect more than the worldliness of the city and the catholicism of the Catholic Church. Unlike the Irish and Polish immigrants in North America, the Church for Spaniards did not embody Old World nationalist redemptions, did not sustain a sense of separate ethnic identity in the host society, and did not supply a significant source of earthly succor and beneficence.[40] In a sense, religion for Spaniards in the River Plate attained (during this period[41]) a more ethereal, nonutilitarian status that, ironically, made it less relevant.[42]

The variety of associations (social, political-patriotic, cultural-academic, business, lady's charitable, beneficent, fraternal, religious) reflected a trend that is well established in the literature on the topic: the transition from premodern, multifunction societies to modern, single-function ones.[43] This trend engendered many other Spanish immigrant associations: choral and musical societies; cyclists', sharpshooters', and other sports associations; amateur theater groups; youth organizations; and political clubs. But another type surpassed all others in wealth and numbers of members: mutual-aid societies.

The AESM was the first and most important of these.[44] From sixty founding members in 1857, it grew into a 33,000-member association by the early 1920s, becoming the largest mutual-aid society of any kind in Argentina, and probably in Latin America. What explained this meteoric ascent?

The association's openness in terms of ethnicity, class, and gender accounts for much of it. As an institution that promoted Spanish unity in the area, the AESM from its inception had fully welcomed all Iberian ethnic groups. In 1870 it had even agreed to accept Portuguese nationals, "in view of the fact that they do not have a mutual-aid society in the city."[45] In their ethnic or regional origins, both leaders and members appear highly typical of the Spanish colony in the city.[46] In their class provenance, the leadership came mostly from the high white-collar and professional sectors, and the membership reflected the entire spectrum, with some underrepresentation of the lowest groups—26 percent of the 579 members who joined in 1895 were unskilled laborers, compared with 35 percent of the Spaniards in Buenos Aires in a sample taken from the manuscript returns for that year's national census. Given the consensus in the literature on voluntary associations that no matter the gauge of socioeconomic stratification employed and no matter the society examined, the lower groups will show significantly lower rates of participation, this level of underrepresentation does not seem notable.[47] In any case, the lower participation of this group may have resulted more from their weaker associative tendencies than from their inability to pay monthly dues, which amounted to no more than three-quarters of the daily wage of an unskilled laborer. As for gender, the AESM restricted enrollment to males for most of the nineteenth century, but, after a failed attempt in 1868, it added a women's wing in 1894, which grew rapidly. Ten years later its female membership surpassed that of all but one of the 288 associations listed in Buenos Aires' municipal census. By the outbreak of World War I its 6,715 women formed 37 percent of the adult affiliation, but were still underrepresented since females accounted for 44 percent of all the Spaniards in the city. By the end of the war the gender gap had disappeared, though only in the membership—the institution's regulations continued to exclude women from positions of leadership.

Another reason for the ascent of the AESM was its ability to overcome what rational-choice theorists have referred to as "the tragedy of the commons" or, more commonly, "the free-rider dilemma."[48] If each member gained the most by minimizing his/her contributions and maximizing his/her benefits, how could the AESM augment, or even preserve, the common fund? As long as it remained a small, tightly knit group, peer pressure seemed enough to prevent freeloading. When it grew into a large, less intimate institution, more formal mechanisms were required to prevent individual greed, abuse, or fraud from depleting its jointly held resources. Some of the first examples appeared in 1864, when the then 1,000-member society required presentation of the monthly-dues receipt for approval of visits to the participating physicians; ordered the latter "to prescribe Russian [steam] baths only in cases of real necessity, in view of the excessive use that some associates make of them"; and expelled some members of the "burial-service committee" for contracting (apparently through graft) an Italian-owned funeral company instead of a Spanish one, as the regulations demanded. A decade later it created a "permanent commission on vigilance" to investigate fraudulent disability claims. Other controls appeared in subsequent years, as the AESM denied entry to applicants over the age of fifty and certain treatments (such as surgery or delivery of babies) to those with less than a specified length of membership.

As the AESM increased its control over individual self-interest and greed, it continued to exercise and benefit from personal and collective altruism. Certain types of pensions and repatriation to Spain were reserved for needy members who could prove their indigence. Although the paid personnel increased from a sole secretary in 1870 to scores of administrative and medical employees as the century turned, the directorate continued to serve without pay. Indeed, administrative costs as a percentage of all expenditures actually declined, with the bulk going to disability payments, medical care, prescriptions, and, in smaller amounts, burial services.[49] Donations by members and immigrant institutions could account for up to one-twentieth of the institution's annual income. Hispano-

Argentine banks provided, in addition to donations, low-interest credit. Real estate bequeathed by departed benefactors added another source of wealth. Spanish ship companies granted a 30 percent discount to the association on the repatriation of their needy members. All sorts of Spanish-owned businesses gave AESM members smaller discounts in what appears to be a form of self-serving altruism.

The AESM's ability to avoid internal ideological or political schisms—if not friction—offers another clue to its steady growth. An official credo that rarely went beyond bland calls for patriotism and solidarity, incapable of offending any but the most susceptible souls, fostered and preserved such harmony. The organization's magazines contained detailed ledgers to allay fiscal suspicions and hundreds of photographic vistas of Spain's natural and cultural monuments carefully selected to please all regional sensibilities, but no article on the ideology of mutualism that could be considered remotely controversial—and that included the then popular, and basically innocuous, writings of the anarchist Prince Pyotr Kropotkin.[50] Old and New World politics received the same quiescent treatment. By comparison, Unione e Benevolenza, the principal Italian mutual-benefit society in the city, which had been founded only a year after the AESM, had by 1914 only one-eighth of the members, principally because monarchical-republican debates had split the society in the 1860s.[51]

Another factor that accounted for the success of the institution was the ingenious policy of reciprocal rights. Several Spanish mutual-aid societies appeared in various neighborhoods of the city in the nineteenth century. The AESM would immediately recognize these small associations as "sister societies," meaning that their members would enjoy the same rights in the AESM as its own members, and vice versa. The statutes of the barrio societies averred this as "a perfect alliance, in no way vassalage or dependency."[52] But, inevitably, the sisters societies soon became "daughter societies," and with time most were simply incorporated into the larger organization.

The reciprocal-rights policy entailed more than a trick to swallow smaller barrio societies, however. By the first decade of the twentieth century such reciprocal agreements had been arranged with more than 200 Spanish mutual-aid societies throughout Argentina and South America. This provided a great benefit to members, for wherever they happened to travel or move they would be protected. Protection in this case meant medical, disability, and life insurance, as well as free medications. In a rather necrophilic way, it also meant the right to be buried in what amounted to a proxy of the motherland, the pantheons of the Spanish societies. Figures from municipal censuses provide a measure of the AESM's success in fending off the challenges of barrio societies and preserving a dominant position throughout the nineteenth century: in 1887 it accounted for 93 percent of all the Spanish mutual-aid-society members in the city, in 1904, for 87 percent.

Ethnic or regional mutual-help associations based on Old World ties would pose a more threatening challenge to the AESM's dominance. The Catalan Montepío de Monserrat, founded the same year as the AESM (1857), represented the only association of this type in the nineteenth century. By the end of the century it had 788 members; by 1930, 1,602. The Centro Asturiano, founded by 200 Asturians in 1914, had 2,400 members by the 1920s. Other regional and provincial groups founded smaller societies, but the toughest competition for the pan-Hispanic AESM came from the Centro Gallego. Founded in 1907, by the outbreak of World War I it had 6,646 members, or 17 percent of all Spaniards who belonged to mutual-aid associations. The AESM, with 22,204 members, still held a 56 percent majority. By 1930 the gap had narrowed: the AESM had 31,000 members; the Centro Gallego, 27,000. From then on, the latter took the lead, with 39,000 members in 1932 and 57,000 in 1938, versus a steady 30,000 in the AESM. These two Spanish immigrant institutions had become the two largest mutual benefit societies in the country.[53]

Regionalism also appeared in other immigrant institutions. Some regional recreational associations had been founded before 1890: Laurak-Bat, a Basque club, in 1877; the Centro Gallego (unrelated to the mutual-aid society founded in 1907), in 1879–1892; and the Centre Catalá, in 1886. Most surfaced in the following two decades and accounted for much of the increase during this period (see Table 49). Journalism did not prove immune to what a visiting Spanish sociologist called "insolidary fractionation." Thirty-two of the seventy immigrant publications catalogued in Table 49 represented Iberian regions, and six of them appeared in a language other than Castilian. As previously discussed, financial institutions also felt the trend, with various regional banks opening in the first two decades of the twentieth century.

With the large waves of newcomers in the decades before and after World War I, the spread of associations acquired a new dimension, campanilism. Arrivals from areas of moderate emigration founded provincial societies, such as Casa Balear (the Balearic Islands), Centro Burgales (Burgos), Centro Montañés (Santander), and Centro Salamanca. But those from zones of heavy emigration, particularly Galicians and Asturians, established organizations based on smaller sociogeographical spheres. The

Table 49 Approximate numbers of Spanish voluntary associations and Spanish immigrant publications founded in Buenos Aires, 1850s–1920s and number in existence in selected years

	Associations		Publications	
Decade	Founded	In existence	Founded	In existence
1850s	4		3	
1860s	6	1864: 8	8	1864: 2
1870s	7		12	
1880s	9	1887: 12	4	1887: 3
1890s	27		14	
1900s	64		15	
1910s	79	1914: 116	11	1914: 13
1920s	76	1925: 237	14	
Total	272		81	

SOURCES: The data on associations were compiled from Argentine censuses, which list only the largest societies, and from notices in immigrants' newspapers and magazines, which often mention smaller ones. Because there were so many immigrant publications and the period covers almost eighty years, only an average of two publications and two years per decade were read. It is almost certain that some associations, particularly those having ephemeral lives, were missed. The 1914 and 1925 figures are probably more complete because they come from association censuses conducted by the Spanish government (Spain, Consejo Superior de Emigración, *La emigración española transoceánica, 1911–1915* [Madrid, 1916], 561–67; and idem, *Boletín de Emigración* 1, [1927]:285–303).

The numbers of newspapers and magazines are based on census information, on books about Argentine journalism, including Juana Lesser, *El periodismo argentino* (Berlin, 1938), and on references in the publications themselves. As with associations, it is certain that some ephemeral publications were not counted. The list includes only the Spanish immigrant press. Spaniards were the foreign group most involved in journalism and during the period also owned or edited close to forty nonimmigrant publications (i.e., those directed to the general public or to sectors such as bankers, estancieros, or merchants). These were not counted. For a list of the immigrant publications, see Jose C. Moya, "Notas sobre las fuentes para el estudio de la inmigración española en Buenos Aires," *Estudios Migratorios Latinoamericanos* 2, 4 (1986):502–3.

former, who accounted for about half of the immigrants, founded the enormous Centro Gallego; several other regional societies (nursing-home, cultural, political, and the like); four social centers (one for each province); and, according to a popular saying, "as many village associations as there are days in the year."

CAMPANILISM: INEFFICIENT FRAGMENTATION
OR FUNCTIONAL PLURALISM?

Immigration historians often disagree on whether associations based on parish or village of origin appeared early in the immigration process or developed later and on whether they typified the predominant associative form of some groups.[54] There is little disagreement, however, over the fact that this institutional campanilism weakened the organizational structure of the group and that it lessened their capacity to act as a united force.

Contemporary Spanish scholars would have agreed. The sociologist Adolfo Posada and the historian Rafael Altamira, who visited Argentina in the years before World War I, expressed amazement at the institutional networks of their proverbially unassociative compatriots. The ubiquity, strength, capital, and membership of the associations elicited from these travelers a volley of admiring words. But "cantonalism," the atavistic attachment to the *patria chica* (the Spanish version of the Italian *paese*) and the proliferation of localist societies that it engendered were blamed for diminishing the efficiency and power of the organized community.[55] As a visiting physician phrased it, "The associative instinct of Spaniards in Buenos Aires is so exuberant that, in practice, it acts as a 'disassociational instinct' that subtracts efficacy from the collective endeavor."[56]

Yet the effect of localist associations on the organized community was one of addition rather than substraction, of multiplication rather than division. And they added rather than subtracted in more than a numerical sense: they added a new, more democratic, or at least inclusive, dimension. To jump from arithmetic to anatomy, they made the organized community more organic; they gave the institutional skeleton, which already had a head (the elite and elite-run institutions), a torso (middle-sized regional associations) and extremities (small provincial and village societies).

The immigrant elite had formed intricate networks based primarily on Old and New World common economic interests and social aspirations—not on Old World village linkages—which served their interests perfectly. These networks enhanced their power and prestige in the immigrant colony and even served as vehicles for crossing over into the world of the local elite. What I noted about the incipient leadership of 1852 was also true of the mature leadership of the twentieth century. Of 164 leaders of the Asociación Patriótica Española and the Institución Cultural Española during the first two decades of the twentieth century, 126 were, or had been, leaders of the AESM; 25, of the Cámara de Comercio; 30, of the

Club Español; 41, of the Sociedad Española de Beneficencia; 36, of the Liga Republicana (an elite association of moderate Spanish republicans); 6 owned Spanish immigrant newspapers; and 22 served in the directorates of Spanish immigrant banks. Moreover, again as in 1852, the linkages crossed into the elite institutions of the host society. Eight were members of the Bolsa de Comercio (the stock market); 10, of the Club del Progreso; an 10, of the Sociedad Rural (the rural oligarchy's society). Ties to the local elite were reinforced, on the other hand, by the fact that Argentine upper-class leaders (like E. Zeballos, R. Saenz Peña, B. Victorica, P. Groussac, L. M. Drago) belonged to the Spanish elite associations.[57]

It is true that although these people had emigrated to "make America" for themselves, they may well have facilitated the road for others. Power and philanthropy are not antithetical. If anything, the latter depends on the former. Without the capital, donations, and organizational skills of the elite, the beneficence hospital, old-age asylums, and large mutual-aid societies would not have been possible. Elite institutions, which primarily served the interests of that class, often benefited ordinary and poor immigrants. The Patronato Español, perhaps founded to nurture the vanity of female socialites, also protected poor immigrant girls and orphans. The Asociación Patriótica Española may have enabled its members to form ties with the local upper class, but it also pressed the Spanish government to enforce hygienic regulations aboard immigrant ships, it helped new arrivals by finding them jobs, providing legal aid, and establishing night schools, and it alleviated the distress of the hopeless by freely repatriating them. Even the "parasitical" Club Español often sent monetary assistance to Spanish regions afflicted by natural calamities and to Spanish overseas communities afflicted by political ones (like those suffered by the *peninsulares* during the Mexican Revolution), or it would collect money among its members for worthy causes in Buenos Aires. Elite-run institutions like the hospital and asylums and the large mutual-aid societies offered an even greater service to ordinary people. If destitute, they could at least be assured of proper, if not optimal, medical care—and this long before the appearance of welfare states. If able and willing to pay a small fee, they could enjoy the disability, pension, and medical services of the large mutual-aid societies and of their extensive networks of sister societies almost everywhere in the country.

On the other hand, not only did elite societies limit admission, but elite-run institutions discouraged active, as opposed to passive, participation. By the 1920s close to 100,000 Spaniards belonged to mutual-aid societies. Indeed, many more working-class immigrants belonged to these associations than to labor unions, a fact that Argentine labor historians have consistently ignored. Belonging and participating were not synonymous, however. The AESM often had a difficult time finding enough delegates for its annual assemblies, even though it required only 1 percent of the membership. Spanish organizations were not the only ones afflicted by this problem: Italian mutual-aid societies experienced similar difficulties.[58] The fact is that it took as much commitment to join a mutual-aid society as it did to buy a life-insurance policy. As early as 1864 B. Victory—a Balearic Islands socialist who, despite his name, never succeeded in his struggles for women's equality, land distribution, a federation of Spanish societies, and against tobacco smoking—accused mutual-aid societies of becoming nothing more than institutional insurance policies: "Today the desire to belong to one of these societies involves no more than a cold calculation: I will pay 60 pesos of entry fee and 20 pesos of monthly dues, and in return when I get sick I will receive 20 pesos daily, will have free doctors and medicines and will enjoy the same benefits in any of the Spanish societies in Buenos Aires, Barracas, San Nicolás [etc.]."[59] Half a century later a less utopian observer, studying mutual-aid societies, reached the same conclusion: "Commonly, the person who joins a mutual-aid society, whether large or small, does it with the exclusive purpose of insuring himself, for a predetermined period, against the risks of illness."[60]

Finding their desire for participation and fraternizing blocked by exclusivist societies and dampened by large, efficient, but impersonal and businesslike elite-run organizations, ordinary immigrants responded by creating hundreds of localist or other small associations. Applied to an early-twentieth-century phenomenon, the term grass-roots movement may sound anachronistic, but it aptly describes the response. More likely than not, the genesis of the associations went back—as had been the case with the first midnineteenth-century organizations—to coffeehouse chats or informal gatherings in a *paisano*'s house. Later, a few townsfolk would decide to pool some money and rent an inexpensive locale that could serve as their home in the new land. They often used precisely that word, or other terms with familial connotations, to name their associations: Casa (House) de Tuy, Hijos (Sons) of the Parroquia (Parish) de San Esteban de Piantón, Hogar (Home) de Rivadumia en Buenos Aires. When the latter formed in 1922, its class inclusiveness appeared in the background of its founders: fourteen of the first thirty-five members were low-skilled workers; eight, skilled workers; seven, low-nonmanual employees; and six, storekeepers.[61]

In addition to being open and representative in terms of occupations, these localist associations affiliated a large portion of their natives in Buenos Aires. For instance, the 1924 manuscript census of Val de San Lorenzo, a village in the province of León, listed 82 of its 958 denizens as "absent in Buenos Aires," and the membership registry of the Centro Val de San Lorenzo de Buenos Aires, founded that same year, included seventy-one (87 percent) of them. Indeed, the association's entire membership (129) exceeded the number of official absentees by 58, because it included individuals born in nearby villages beyond the borders of the municipal district and those whose whole family had emigrated, leaving no one behind to report them as overseas residents.

Membership was not only inclusive but also entailed more active participation than in the large mutual-aid societies. More than half of the members normally attended the general assemblies of the Centro Val de San Lorenzo.[62] The tournament of *bolos* (a lawn-bowling game imported from their region of origin and held in the association's own playing field) attracted around seventy members, almost the entire male contingent. The "grand artistic festivals," held for the benefit of the association's social fund, drew a more gender-balanced—and thus larger—crowd. These Saturday night events consisted of two or three short comic plays (often written for the occasion on Old World themes and performed by semi-amateur companies), followed by regional songs and dances. The summer picnics proved even more popular—a 1925 group picture showed 136 adults, which surpassed the entire membership. The activities included races for men, "young ladies," children, and "fat people," who received a "surprise prize"; games and raffles; folk dances with the traditional piper-drummer; and "modern" ones with The Lovers of the Dry Law (a group playing North American Jazz Age tunes and no-less-trendy local tangos). For sustenance, attendees could count on an array of Spanish *tapas*, a bounteous Argentine barbecue—which never failed to impress villagers from regions where beef remained a luxury—and—the title of the orchestra notwithstanding—ample wine and beer. Despite the musical and culinary cosmopolitanism, the picnics ended with a parochial touch: "heart-felt [and one could imagine, half-drunk] hurrahs for our association and our village," which reached particularly high decibels on the feast day of the town's patron saint. Adding to the allure of the various events—and to the sensation of active participation—the *paisanos* could see themselves in the photographs illustrating the association's yearly magazine—a privilege to which few of the AESM's 30,000-plus members could aspire.

The numerous photographs and portraits from Val de San Lorenzo that appeared in the magazine reveal another goal of localist associations, rarely accomplished by the larger organizations: the maintenance of intimate ties with, and support of, Iberian hometowns. In addition to the photographs, the magazine—like other publications by localist centers—included news, letters, stories, nostalgic poems, and gossip about the old village; a forum for transatlantic personal feuds; and lists of births, baptisms, marriages, and deaths of townsfolk not only in Val and Buenos Aires but elsewhere in the diaspora. The center's directorate appointed five delegates in the village (usually prominent citizens like the schoolteacher, the physician, and successful *americanos* [returnees]) to inform them of local needs and to receive philanthropic remittances. The latter partially financed the village school, provided the pupils with school supplies, succored the indigent, and—appropriately for a campanilist association—paid for a clock in the campanile. Such parochialism vividly incarnated the natural, antediluvian attachment to birthplace expressed by the Galician bagpiper who, on a tour of Madrid, claimed that he was homesick and wanted to go back to "Spain" or, for that matter, by Karl Marx, that champion of universalism who, upon entering the University of Bonn in 1835, joined the student association of his native town of Trier.[63]

A cornucopia of official titles further increased levels and feelings of participation. One-tenth of the Centro Val de San Lorenzo's membership belonged to a directorate that seemed to include a "vice-" and a "pro-" for every rank. A contemporary anecdote, probably apocryphal but nevertheless revealing, told of how one of the presidents of a village association, upon meeting the president of the republic, addressed him as "Dear Colleague." The large number of titles provided people who were generally excluded from positions of leadership in the larger institutions with a feeling of decision making and self-importance. This does not mean that localist associations enjoyed nonhierarchical leaderships. Of the fourteen people in the directorate of 1925, nine were business owners. But stratification reflected the simpler class structure of the village's community in Buenos Aires, rather than that of the Spanish colony as a whole, which allowed modest grocers, clerks, skilled workers, and even loquacious day laborers to reach top elected positions. It also reflected the class structure of the village—rather than the country—of origin, which provided leadership opportunities for newcomers from "respectable" local families who would have lacked a high-enough pedigree to figure prominently in nationally based organizations. The combination of these two factors permitted the bestowal of leadership positions on immigrants of petit bourgeois origins, even if they had achieved little material success in the new land, and on successful sons, even if they lacked the correct lineage.

The heavy use of symbols of authority in these associations—titles, flags, seals, constitutions, coats of arms, assembly minutes, and protocol —further enhanced the sense of participation and self-importance. An immigrant journalist recounted the ceremonious discourse heard at a meeting of one village association:

> "I request the floor, Mr. President."
> "The councilman has the floor."
> "I understand that the honorable Executive Commission should delegate the study of this matter to the Finance Commission."
> "To which matter does the councilman refer?"
> "To the purchase of a minutes book and an inkwell. . . . "
> "The honorable Finance Commission has already issued a dictament on that item. It has accorded that for the time being it can do without the ink-well because the Secretary possesses a stylus and that therefore it should abstain from this superfluous expenditure."
> "Does the council ratify the decision?"
> "Approved!"[64]

The session was then called to a close, and the members headed for the card tables, where, amid gulps of Spanish brandy and Rioja wine, they shouted the most unceremonious obscenities every time someone played a trump. Despite its farcical appearance, the mixture of parliamentary decorum and relaxed conviviality served serious functions. It provided humble arrivals with a vicarious sense of power and dignity and a with real opportunity for camaraderie, normally denied to them by both the host society and the higher spheres of the immigrant community; and it served to regulate and defuse internal conflicts.

If village associations provided easy access to leadership and active participation, the escalating structure of the Spanish organized community supplied ample opportunities for associative ascent. Valenses with broader participatory or leadership desires could "move up" to the provincial center, Centro Región Leonesa, founded in 1916, which had more spacious and elegant quarters, a larger membership, and a higher-status leadership. Villagers with wider identities or ambitions could join the regional Centro Castellano. And those with even wider aspirations could chose from the whole spectrum of Spanish societies described above.

The spread of localist associations, therefore, came to supplement rather than fragment the organized community. It made it more organic, not less.

Indeed, the institutional structure of the Spaniards in Buenos Aires was remarkably functional. It was large where it had to be, and vice versa. Many of the localist associations, including the Centro Val de San Lorenzo, tried to function as mutual-aid societies, but they enjoyed limited success. Mutual-aid societies ran on the same principle that insurance companies did: only the relatively large ones could both provide a broad spectrum of services and survive. Three or four sick members could deplete the social funds of a 100-member society. A minor actuarial miscalculation could similarly wipe out its equity. Small associations could neither accrue the capital nor muster the organizational resources to build hospitals, clinics, and asylums. They could, on the other hand, provide conviviality and companionship, intimate ties with hometowns, and a sphere in which those excluded from the elite and elite-run societies could actively participate. They thus fulfilled both community needs and what sociologists of African American organizations have termed compensatory functions (compensating for exclusion in other realms).[65]

IMMIGRANT ASSOCIATIONS: A CONTINUATION OF OLD WORLD PRACTICES OR A PRODUCT OF THE NEW ENVIRONMENT?

Ever since Alexis de Tocqueville observed in 1831 that "in no country in the world has the principle of association been more successfully used . . . than in America," hundreds of scholars have identified that principle with rationalist, pragmatic individualism and with Anglo-American democratic ideals—attributes that Old World peasants, especially those from the southern and eastern sides of the Continent, presumably lacked.[66] Immigrant associations therefore came to be interpreted fundamentally as the product of the new environment, as evidence of assimilation into what Max Weber called "the association-land par excellence."

In the 1970s, however, a barrage of studies assailed this assimilationist view. Revisionism, like the old wisdom it pretended to supplant, reflected the prevailing ideological milieu. To expanding numbers of North American academics, the United States now represented not a young, dynamic republic but a decadent, racist empire, and individualism not the bedrock of democratic ideals but the embodiment of capitalist greed. The hermeneutic status of "ethnic" and "community" climbed in direct measure to the sinking prestige of "mainstream" and "society." In this atmosphere, immigrant associations began to be interpreted, not surprisingly, as continuations of premigratory ethnic communal practices rather than as the result of an Americanization process.[67] Despite the historiographical trend, the question remains unsettled and the evidence far from conclusive.[68]

In the case of the Spaniards, a British anthropologist studying their twentieth-century expatriate colonies in Mexico and Cuba concluded that Spanish immigrants had founded voluntary associations years before such associations existed in Spain.[69] Such a conclusion is decisively inaccurate. Spanish sodalities and guilds, after all, dated back to the Middle Ages, and masonic lodges and *sociedades de amigos del pais* (private societies that tried to foster the development of the country) to the Bourbon Enlightenment.[70] They were, moreover, particularly numerous in northern Spain, the area of heaviest emigration. Workers' mutual-aid societies existed in Barcelona as early as the 1830s and mushroomed in the following decades with the abolition of guilds.[71] In less-developed Galicia, artisans' unions appeared at least as early as the 1840s. An 1892 Buenos Aires newspaper listed the names and addresses of thirty-four voluntary associations in the Galician town of Ferrol alone, including such diverse types as youth centers, mutual-aid societies, political clubs, cyclists' groups, civic-minded organizations, and trade unions; and a different source shows that one-quarter of the town's population belonged to at least one of these associations.[72]

This Iberian background appears in the recurring and shared traits of Spanish immigrant associations from Tampa to Buenos Aires, São Paulo to Mexico City, and Havana to Montevideo. It materializes most visually in the architecture of these centers, persistently drawn from the styles of the Spanish Golden Age or, less often, from turn-of-the-century Modernism—the Catalan version of art nouveau.[73] It surfaces in the common recreational activities: the omnipresent zarzuelas (Spanish operettas), *sainetes* (picaresque farces), *romerías* (pilgrimage celebrations greatly secularized in the diaspora), picnics, regional dances, dominoes, and *tute* or other Spanish card games. The use of similar language and practices in the statutes of beneficence and mutual-assistance societies and the formation of regional centers offer further testimony to a shared ancestry.[74]

Spanish immigrant associations, however, were not simply transplanted institutions, and their proliferation and characteristics in Buenos Aires obeyed factors other than premigratory antecedents. One was immigration itself, which—everyone seems to agree—invariably boosted associative activity. Southern European visitors to New World cities rarely failed to mention how the ocean crossing turned their erstwhile eremitic compatriots into avid joiners with "a mania for associations."[75] The "mania" seems hardly odd in a situation in which neither traditional institutions—such

as Old World kinship groups and the parish church—nor newer ones
—such as the welfare-state apparatus, insurance companies, and corporations—could satisfy social needs like health care, leisure, and companionship.

Emigration not only accelerated organizational impulses but apparently
also shaped their manifestations. Indeed, certain traits of the Spaniards'
institutional life in Buenos Aires seem like expressions of universal laws
rather than local particularities. Replace the bagpipes with *odon* drums
and the *muiñeira* dance with some *ondo* steps and—phenotypes apart—a
Galician picnic in Parque Palermo in the 1920s will look strikingly like a
Japanese picnic in Los Angeles' Luna Park during the same decade.[76] Make
the corresponding instrumental and choreography changes, and both will
resemble a Filipino picnic in Salinas, five hundred kilometers to the
north.[77] Almost surely the three would have been organized by a hometown association not unlike the Japanese *kenjinkai* that appeared not only
in Los Angeles but also in places as far from each other as São Paulo,
Lima, and Hawaii;[78] or the no less ubiquitous Chinese *hui kuan* of Seattle,
Toronto, Manila, Singapore, and Hong Kong;[79] or the Italian *paese* societies
that mushroomed anywhere from Boston to San Francisco.[80] The phenomenon reached such intensity among Ashkenazi Jews in New York,
Chicago, Philadelphia, Buenos Aires, or, for that matter, Israel that *Landsmanshaftn* became an accepted synonym for village or local-origin associations.[81] They also appeared, under the same German-Yiddish name,
among the Gentile residents of Manhattan's *Kleindeutschland;*[82] and—under different appellations—among such diverse immigrants as the Greeks
of Boston, New Zealand, and Toronto;[83] the Croats of Steelton, Pennsylvania;[84] the Syrians of Cedar Rapids, Iowa;[85] the Ibo of Calabar, Nigeria;[86]
and the Haitians of New York.[87]

The ubiquity of the *Landsmanschaftn*, though striking, does not turn
the process of emigration per se into an all-leveling shaper of associative
activities and universal laws. The practice was surely pervasive but far
from uniform in its expression. For instance, Chinese, Syrian, and Ibo immigrants formed sublocal clan, surname, or blood-tie organizations that
could also be supra-local, because at times they transcended village or
even regional confines, but none of the other groups did. Nor was the
practice universal. One could compile an equally extensive and varied
list of immigrants who did not organize along hometown lines at all.
The Basques of Bakersfield—equidistant from the campanilist Filipinos
of Salinas and Japanese of Los Angeles—and their brethren of Buenos
Aires—neighbors to the parochialist Galicians—formed no hometown as-

sociations; nor did their kinsmen anywhere else in the diaspora.[88] The practice seems equally alien to the overseas English and French,[89] absent among Punjabis in England and Ukrainians in France and Canada,[90] and not particularly common in Irish neighborhoods, Polonias, and Chicano barrios.[91] Tellingly, these groups shared a sharp sense of national or eth-nonational identity, fueled by either imperialist hubris or anti-imperialist grievances that apparently discouraged subethnic formal associations. The size of the immigrant group could play a similar role. Unlike the majority of their compatriots elsewhere, the few Chinese and Spaniards of Detroit imitated their Irish and Polish neighbors and founded pan-ethnic organizations only.[92] But size alone does not seem to be a reliable predictor. After all, the not-significantly-larger Lebanese minority in Detroit fragmented into a constellation of village-based associations, whereas their more numerous countrymen in Montevideo, São Paulo, and West Africa did not, which suggests another important determinant: the nature of the host environment.[93]

In Argentina a combination of institutional underdevelopment and political latitude strongly shaped the associative life of European arrivals. Neither the liberal state nor any other Creole institution had the resources or the inclination to meet many of the newcomers' social needs. At the same time, the government's laissez-faire attitude gave the immigrants enough latitude to establish their own service-providing institutions. That no North American city has a Spanish hospital, bank, large mutual-aid society, and elite club is hardly significant since few Spaniards went there. That, unlike Buenos Aires, none can boast Italian, German, British, French, Jewish, and Arab hospitals, bona fide banks, large mutual-aid societies, and elite clubs, *all at once*, is hardly irrelevant since multiethnicity was more pronounced in North American cities than in Buenos Aires.[94] The tight fiscal behavior of the pre-1930 Argentine state regarding social expenditures clearly inclined immigrant associations toward the direct assistance of their members rather than toward intermediate roles such as referrals to public agencies, demands for entitlements, and lobbying—functions quite common among immigrant associations in post–World War II welfare states.[95] In a similar vein, the inadequacies of Argentine democracy—even after the universal male suffrage law of 1912—plus the related low naturalization rates, discouraged the arrangement of ethnic political clubs for local electoral purposes common in the United States and Canada.[96] On the other hand, the lack of official discrimination against any particular group did not stimulate the formation of ethnic civil-rights movements. At least regarding these features, the nature of the host country seems a more important explanatory variable than does the baggage of the newcomers.

In the case of Buenos Aires' Spaniards, combination variables ensuing from the interaction between Old World cultural traits and New World conditions would distinctly shape their organized community. After all, their compatriots in Cuba founded not one pan-Hispanic hospital but several regional ones, and their foreign neighbors in Buenos Aires did not found a plethora of village associations—something particularly surprising in the case of the notoriously campanilist Italians.[97]

The sociocultural backgrounds of the Spaniards who headed for Cuba and Argentina in the nineteenth century did not exactly match. As noted in the previous chapter, the South American republic, presumably because of its more developed economy, attracted a larger proportion of literate and skilled Spaniards.[98] It is conceivable, thus, that Spaniards in Argentina possessed a more sharply defined sense of nationality in their homeland and that this enabled them to found one large beneficence institution based on national loyalties rather than several based on regional identification, as was the case in Cuba.

Much more important, however, was the way in which prearrival traits accommodated to the realities of the two American countries in the first half of the nineteenth century. In Cuba the Spaniards encountered a colony, an extension of the metropolis where old local distinctions were easily maintained. In Argentina, by contrast, they confronted an independent, and still hostile, republic that branded them as foreigners, or even as enemy aliens. If the mere mark of outsiders exerted a unifying influence—as it normally does on immigrants—the antagonism multiplied it. Moreover, the existence of other large immigrant communities in Buenos Aires (but not in Cuba) highlighted the otherness of the Spaniards. When, in 1852, "after forty years without union, without national relations, without being able to know one another, having to deny our country, pretending to be English [from Gibraltar] or French to evade the persecution of the tyranny," some three hundred tearful founding members gathered to form the first Spanish association in independent Argentina, they longed, not surprisingly, "to foment the spirit of nationality and unite the interests of Spaniards." When five years later the same people gathered to form the AESM they were similarly imbued with the idea that "in unity there is strength." It was, after all, still the time when "we Spaniards were *godos,* poor *godos* [a denigrating term for Spaniards during the Wars of Independence]."[99] Half a century in an inhospitable milieu had done what four centuries of Castilian statesmanship and Castilian repression had been unable to accomplish: turn Basques, Catalans, and Galicians into fervid Spaniards. In the same way that, four centuries before, half-hearted Jews in Spain had turned devout when forced to renounce their faith and become *marranos,* half-hearted Spaniards in Argentina turned patriotic when forced to deny their citizenship in order to avoid induction into local militias.

The Spanishness of midnineteenth-century Iberian ethnic groups in Buenos Aires developed, therefore, from the interaction between their cultural baggage (a weak but prior sense of nationality) and the sociopolitical realities of the host country (an inhospitable but unifying environment and a multinational city that highlighted the Spaniards' separate identity). In other words, Spanishness manifested not a background variable but a combination one. This combination, in turn, engendered another independent variable: an early pan-Hispanic institutional structure whose leaders were not only reluctant to admit diversity but apt to depict it as divisiveness.

As noted in the previous two chapters, the patterns formed in the embryonic stages of the immigrant colony acquired a life of their own and to a large degree shaped later developments. In the associative life of the colony, also, the weight of the past molded the way of the future. The three main pan-Hispanic associations—the Club Español, the Sociedad Española de Beneficencia, and the AESM—had set the tone by the midcentury: strength could only stem from "patriotic" unity; outside the motherland, immigrants could only afford to be Spaniards. Any attempt to form localist organizations was denounced as unpatriotic and harmful to the institutional life of the community because it disassociated and drained its force. Because the leadership of these three associations, and also that of newspapers and later the Banco Español, formed an intricately woven net, its discourse became very efficient.

The large pan-Hispanic societies, therefore, grew on their own efficiency and success and dominated the associative life of the colony throughout the nineteenth century and into the twentieth. It was precisely in this terrain that the *Landsmanschaftn* germinated, as an organic response to both its fertility—in terms of services provided—and its aridity—in terms of opportunities for active and intimate participation. But if the village associations represented a natural and genuine response to the situation, they did not present a challenge. On the contrary, their role vis-à-vis the large institutional infrastructure was supplementary. By increasing the participation of people who were "outside the system," the localist associations increased the organizational potential of the wider community.

For example, Benito Ares, a bakery owner from Val de San Lorenzo, was the vice president and one of the founders of his village society in Buenos Aires. His organization of the townsfolk also benefited the AESM directly. He personally enrolled sixteen of the members of the village association in the large Spanish mutual-aid society.[100] Similarly, Fernando Prado, from Caldas de Reyes in the Galician province of Pontevedra, acted as secretary in his village's association in Buenos Aires. But that was only a voluntary, part-time endeavor, for which he received no pay. His full-time, remunerated job was propaganda agent for the AESM, which may explain why 380 immigrants from that village belonged to it. Village-based societies also helped the finances of the larger ones by renting the latters' halls for their frequent parties, weddings, and other celebrations. Even more than supplemental, the relationship between the large infrastructure and the small localist societies had become symbiotic.

THE FUNCTIONAL BUT CONFLICT-RIDDEN ORGANIZED COMMUNITY

In unreconstructed historical reality, unlike constructed paradigms, antithetical elements coexist without ever reaching a synthesis. Such was the case in the Spanish organized community. It was, as explained, remarkably functional. But it was also conflict ridden. Actually, the very roots of its functionality—the affluence and diversity of organizations—posed a potential, perhaps even intrinsic, source of contention. And a rich array of not completely extramural radical and working-class organizations with heavy Spanish immigrant participation added another explosive element. The roots of conflict, though often intertwined, could be disaggregated into four types: Argentine mainstream politics; radical ideology, particularly anarchism; class divisions; and regionalism or its more extreme variety, ethnonationalism.

Argentine Politics

Argentine mainstream politics arguably represented one of the least divisive issues. In general, later arrivals heeded the hard-learned advice of the first newspaper: "Let's stick to our own concerns and keep out of Creole political imbroglios." The fact that less than 4 percent of Spaniards adopted Argentine citizenship further restricted their participation in local politics. Nevertheless, not all were able or willing to abstain from Creole politics, and some of the conflicts spread to the organized community.

One illustrative case is the clash between various Spanish newspapers in the early 1870's over the Mitrista party.[101] Several times these immigrant newspapers, which insisted on "ignoring their responsibilities as hosts," were shut down by the commissioner of police on orders of President Sarmiento (ironically, the man who became famous for his denunciation of Creole barbarism and for his admiration of European liberalism and civility).[102] This Byzantine conflict showed that the leave-Creole-politics-to-the-Creoles tenet was often only skin deep. One of the newspapers' anonymous editors—widely known to be José Paul y Angulo, an Andalusian ex-seminarian turned republican exile and bon vivant—advised: "Because we cannot aspire to public positions, because we only seek in this land a means to prosper with our constant and modest work, we should care little or nothing about the name of the person who occupies the presidency of the country. As foreigners, it is forbidden for us to militate in any of the conflicting bands, and as merchants, industrialists, artisans, it is simply not in our convenience."[103] The newspaper went on to reassert its independence and endorsed the presidential candidacy of Nicolás Avellaneda.

The other main character in the clash, but not the only one, was Enrique Romero, another Andalusian ex-priest turned radical republican and anticlerical rabble-rouser and a strong supporter of Bartolomé Mitre, Avellaneda's political rival. This flamboyant Malagueño had achieved celebrity in the Spanish colony for a victorious campaign conducted through his newspaper in defense of a Basque maid accused of robbery by her patrons. In a final stroke of political panache, he picked her up from the local jail in a carriage and paraded her through the streets of the city, followed by a swarm of admiring compatriots. A different sort of feat had been his anti-Jesuit instigation, which resulted in the burning of the Colegio del Salvador by a mob in 1875. The two Andalusian apostates were active in the Spanish beneficence association that ran the hospital, where they had often clashed with the more pious Basques, particularly the puritanically Catholic refugees from the Carlist Wars. The mixture of Argentine and immigrant institutional politics proved explosive. During a feast at a Spanish club, the two Andalusians clashed, this time with each other. Romero spat at Paul y Angulo. The latter—who enjoyed fame in the community as a marksman—merely took out his handkerchief, dried his face, and asserted, immutably: "Tomorrow, I will have the pleasure of putting a bullet inside your mouth." He missed his declared target, but not by much, for he fatally severed Romero's carotid in a duel. The next day Justo López de Gomara, a man who would expend much of his energy in a campaign for a federation of Spanish societies and for the naturalization and political participation of his compatriots in Argentina, wrote a short headline in Romero's paper: "ASESINO." Paul y Angulo had to abandon a profitable scheme to take Spanish immigrants to Peru, and, because he could not return to Spain and apparently did not want to go where he wanted to take others, left for France that same day.[104]

Radical Ideologies and Anarchist Organizations

Political ideology was another source of friction. During most of the nineteenth century this had meant confrontation between republicans and monarchists. Dozens of ephemeral immigrant newspapers fought bitter verbal wars over this, which normally degenerated into even more acrid personal feuds. But the immigrant leadership, unlike that of Italians, succeeded in preventing these clashes from splitting the large associations and the principal newspapers. As the century progressed and more radical doctrines came into the picture, even ardent republicanism found itself pushed from the fringes into the middle. The Liga Republicana Española, established in 1903, was anything but combative and an accepted member of the elite organizational clique.[105] Its founder, Rafael Calzada, an Asturian lawyer who had married the daughter of the president of Paraguay, also presided over the Club Español, belonged to the Argentine elite Jockey Club, and—in a role brimming with irony—formed part of the commission to honor the Infanta Doña Isabel de Borbón, the aunt of King Alfonso XIII, on her much-heralded visit to Argentina in 1910.[106] Neither did the socialists, with their emphasis on gradual reform and their orthodox view of capitalism as a higher step in an inevitable historical process, pose an eminent thread to the status quo. In fact, the immigrant press and the large associations' magazines recurrently and triumphantly boasted about the election of Spanish-born Enrique del Valle Iberlucea as the Western Hemisphere's first socialist senator.

Anarchists, on the other hand, were seen as a threat to civilized society and a discredit to the good name of the Spanish community, an anxiety that embodied more than paranoia.[107] If the attention of the international press offers an indication, by the outbreak of World War I Spain and Argentina had become the two main hubs of anarchist activity in the world. Of the eighty-nine articles on the topic that appeared in the London *Times* between 1909 and 1913, thirty-eight dealt with Spain (all but six with Barcelona), and thirteen with Buenos Aires (which surpassed the eleven on France, the five on England, and the four each on Italy and Germany). Buenos Aires' libertarian "silver medal" was not unrelated to Barcelona's first-place finish.[108] A 1902 registry of the Porteño police containing the files of 661 anarchist suspects shows that 149, or 23 percent, were Spaniards, who at the time accounted for 11 percent of the city's population, and that most of them—particularly those termed *exaltados* (zealots) by the authorities—hailed from Barcelona.[109] The "zealots" included a Catalan nihilist and her two sons, who had been expelled from Spain; a twenty-five-year-old baker who, during a strike, had sent legs of lamb stuffed with gunpowder to bakeries; and immigrants suspected of terrorist attacks in Europe. The leadership of the movement also included many Spaniards, among them: Diego Abad de Santillán, by far the greatest anarchist historian in the country;[110] Gregorio Inglán Lafarga, founder of *La Protesta Humana* (1897), for a long time the only anarchist daily in the world;[111] Emilio López Arango, also a long-time editor of *La Protesta* who was murdered in 1929; Antonio *"El Gallego"* Soto, the leader of the Patagonian rebellion of 1920–1921; and José María Borrero, chronicler of that rebellion.[112]

Immigrant anarchists kept close contact with their counterparts on the other side of the Atlantic. Iberian libertarian newspapers circulated so widely in Buenos Aires that when six Spanish anarchists in this city formed the group Los Desheredados (The Disinherited) in 1889, they called for new affiliates by placing an advertisement in Barcelona's *El Productor*.[113] Argentine publications enjoyed comparable popularity in Spain, thanks not only to personal subscriptions but also to a system of institutional exchanges. Buenos Aires' *La Voz de la Mujer: Periódico comunista-anárquico* (1896), perhaps the Western Hemisphere's first radical-feminist newspaper, sent copies to Madrid, Barcelona, Zaragoza, and Tampa's Spanish community, receiving in turn anarchist periodicals from these cities and accepting individual orders for them—a practice also common among *La Voz's* male counterparts.[114] In addition, many Porteño working-class periodicals included a "News of Spain" column as a regular feature, and their pages teemed with all sorts of requests from "the other side": a "persecuted" anarchist lodge in Galicia "humbly begged" for—and received—donations to buy a printing press;[115] a group of Valencian feminists solicited subscriptions, epistolary exchange, and literary contributions for their publication;[116] an author in fin de siècle Madrid sought photographs, letters, personal information, and other relevant sources for a book on the history of anarchism in Spain;[117] a newspaper published by Spanish exiles in London appealed for donations to help compatriots who had been extradited there.[118] From the other shore, labor organizations often beseeched their Spanish counterparts to discourage emigration because capitalists used it to depress wages—a request typically answered with: "We are trying but with limited success because wages are even lower here."[119] From both shores, an array of anonymous characters sent countless—though who knows if critical—cryptic messages back and forth.

A constant transatlantic flow of militants, propaganda, and aid cemented these ties. As Abad de Santillán noted in his memoirs, most deported or relocated radicals from either side simply continued their—at times violent—struggle on the other.[120] Salvador Planas y Virella, a young lithographer who tried to assassinate the Argentine president in 1905, had left his native Catalonia not long before.[121] José Matabosch, a twenty-two-year-old mason, arrived in Argentina from his native Barcelona on May 2, 1909; on May 8 he was already in police custody for organizing a strike, and in October of the same year he planted a bomb in the Spanish consulate to protest the execution of anarchist leader Francisco Ferrer in Barcelona.[122] On the other shore, the terrorist who attempted to take Alfonso XIII's life in 1903 had just spent ten years in Buenos Aires (some in an insane asylum), and his wife and children still lived there.[123] When, a decade earlier, another radical lithographer, Paulino Pallás, hurled two bombs against General Martínez Campo in Barcelona, he had just returned from the Argentine capital.[124] And if the living crossed *in corpus*, the dead crossed in spirit. When, less than a month later, news of Pallás's execution reached the River Plate, he turned into an instant martyr whose death inspired a new organization: Grupo Bomba Pallás.[125] Whether the group made good on its explosive title remains unclear (contemporary newspapers do not mention any bomb attacks in the following months), but it did organize protest rallies, campaigned in support of Pallás's jailed coconspirators, and sent monetary assistance to his widow and three children and to the other prisoners' families—a common practice in immigrant radical circles.[126]

Close ties between Spanish immigrant anarchists and their coreligionists in Spain, however, also transmitted and fostered conflict or conflict-producing cooperation. Buenos Aires' radical press abounded with transatlantic—and not-too-cryptic—brawls about anything from the merits of collectivist versus individualist anarchism and the proper role of theory to petty accusations of embezzlement.[127] Because Old World schisms tended to replicate in the New, these ideological and personal attacks usually ended up being hurled across the street as well as across the ocean and by a number of people that far surpassed those originally involved. Transoceanic sectarian solidarity probably did exceed dissension, both in volume and in intensity, but it often led to equally caustic extramural confrontations. After all, the campaigns of support for jailed comrades in Spain included not only collections for their families but also boycotts against Spanish products and propaganda invectives against the mainstream immigrant newspapers, associations, and businesses deemed "accomplices of the Spanish tyrants' crimes."[128] In January 1897, for example, the anarchist paper *El Oprimido* began printing a supplement in defense of "the prisoners of Montjuich," whose message and title, *La inquisición en España*, affronted the ethnic organizations and newspapers. Already inflamed by the patriotic frenzy sparked by the Cuban insurrection, they denounced the publication as treasonous and urged their members and readers to burn it. Pyromaniac strategies, however, could work both ways, and when, in 1909, a group of Catalan anarchists burned a Spanish flag in Plaza Once in protest against the execution of the libertarian educationist Francisco Ferrer, an indignant Asociación Patriótica Española organized a massive act of repudiation.[129] In response, the anarchists stoned the windows of the association and of the office of a Spanish newspaper.[130]

The anarchist press found various other capital sins in the immigrant "flag-waving" organizations in addition to their lack of concern for Old World prisoners, among them: their support for the motherland's imperialist wars (for example, those in Cuba and Morocco); their inertia regarding the deportation of Spanish anarchists by the Argentine government; their attacks on the Mexican Revolution because of the mistreatment—and murder—of Spaniards, particularly by Pancho Villa; their equivocal position toward Primo de Rivera's fascist regime; and their emphasis on ethnic mutual aid rather than on internationalist struggle. These "iniquities" were castigated in acrid columns that often bestialized the leaders of the Spanish associations as asses full of gold and the affiliates in general as chauvinist hogs, "patrioteer" parrots, and spineless *carneros* (literally rams, but also, in working-class lingo, scabs).[131]

If class ideology posed a source of discord in the Spanish organized community, national loyalties proved an equally contentious issue in the heavily Spanish but multi-ethnic anarchist movement. The problem was particularly exacerbated by international or anticolonial wars, as the following admonition in the August 3, 1895, issue of *El Obrero Panadero* (The Bakery Worker) illustrates: "Truth be told, we cannot understand all the nationalist zeal of our Spanish co-workers, all that enthusiasm to go fight men who feel the hour has come to shake off the yoke of their masters. All workers, whatever their nationality, should see with sympathetic eyes the Cuban revolutionary movement, because for the oppressed, for the exploited, any act of rebellion against an oppressor, against an exploiter, whoever he is, should be a cause for happiness. Think clearly, Spanish comrades!" After a few more exhortations to lucid reflection on the issue, the union's paper apparently shifted strategy, completely avoiding the Cuban question and replacing it with stirring accounts of "our Spanish brothers' ordeal in the dungeons of Montjuich" and other tales of anarchist martyrdom. Other anarchist periodicals followed similar stratagems to avert schisms. On December 12, 1896, for instance, *El Oprimido: Periódico comunista-anárquico* contained a suspiciously innocent three-line note almost hidden in the middle of its third page: "Because of lack of space we cannot publish the original letters received, among them some raising the question of the Cuban war." Continual pressure from readers apparently thwarted this disingenuous attempt to avoid the specter of ethnic divisiveness because, the next issue (January 1, 1897) included a full-page—though no less evasive—editorial claiming that "this is a political struggle of no concern to anarchists . . . if the rebels win you can bet that they will also persecute us . . . therefore we feel that it is not worthy to open a debate on the question since the space can be put to better use."

Editorial silence may have expunged ethnic loyalties and tensions from the pages of anarchist newspapers, but a thorough reading shows them surreptitiously surfacing in the aliases of subscribers. Most, it is true, were properly nihilistic, libertarian, and/or blasphemous:

Nothingness
Zero
Free Love
Nitro Plastique
A stick of dynamite up the bourgeoisie's 7 (Lunfardo for anus)
20 cents . . . for a 20 year-old nun
I wish I could bite the Pope's eyeballs
I give it to the Pope . . . in the ass
One who shits on the Spanish flag
The farce will be ended

But once in a while some evidenced "mixed-up" identities:

An Asturian proletarian
An Andalusian *ácrata* [same root as the English word acrasy, or anti-power]
A shirtless Catalan [*descamisado*, a term later appropriated by Peronist propaganda]
A Spanish atheist

A Piedmontese syndicalist
A German with neither god nor master

Others exhibited the "wrong" consciousness:

Un italiano
Un gallego orgulloso [proud]

Or even an "attitude problem":

Viva Galicia!
Viva Umberto Primo
Arriba España carajo! [Up with Spain, damn it!]

The last two aliases probably expressed a protest against the newspaper's plaudits for the anarchist assassinations of the Italian king Humberto I (1900) and the Spanish prime minister Cánovas del Castillo (1897) or its lack of support for Spain in the Spanish-American War.

Despite their ideological desiderata, pragmatic pressures tended to erode the anarchists' antinationalist and anticapitalist intransigence in the New World's multi-ethnic milieu. Not only did Spanish immigrant anarchists remit their aid to imprisoned comrades in Spain through the Banco Español y del Río de la Plata and the Banco de Galicia y Buenos Aires, but advertisements from these highest emblems of both nationalism and capitalism could be found in the pages of *La Protesta*, right next to strident articles on the evils of these two "isms."[132] After 1912 *La Protesta* became purer and thinner by dropping commercial advertisements, but other less-than-orthodox practices continued to be employed by anarchist organizations that were vying for members with ethnic societies. One consisted of mutual-insurance services based on not entirely altruistic actuarial methods, such as restricting enrollment on the basis of age or health conditions and linking benefits to contributions.[133] A second was the use of alcohol at the previously abstinent anarchist picnics, a change that was fiercely denounced by the more doctrinaire syndicalists.[134] The trend perhaps did not differ in its essence from the tendency of Spanish associations to secularize their *romerías* by emphasizing the feasting in patron-saint feasts, dances over processions, and spirits over the spiritual. As puritanical austerity eroded on both sides, the distinction between their summer outings became increasingly limited to the rhetoric of the speeches, but, according to the confession of an old Andalusian anarchist, the Spanish ones continued to be "much livelier."

Something similar took place with the radical groups' soirees. In the late nineteenth century they seem to have concentrated on ideological lectures and parleys. In the next decades, however, most added social or revolutionary dramas and, later, films—Sergei Eisenstein's *Potemkin* became a favorite choice after the mid-1920s. Others went farther and included comedies, family dances, and lectures on more alluring themes, such as free love and sexuality.[135] In these cases, the difference with the *Landsmanshaftn*'s parties resided mainly in the opening song (a workers' hymn versus the Spanish anthem and/or some regional tunes) and the theme of the plays (working-class struggles and redemption versus homeland or immigrant motifs). But, again, the reminiscences of old militants and the testimony of old photographs assert that the ethnic associations' Saturday night gatherings remained more popular, perhaps because they habitually included comedies and dances and occasionally harangues, whereas the opposite continued to be true for the anarchist, syndicalist, and, later, communist evening functions.

The preference of many newcomers for ethnic organizations over radical labor organizations may reflect more than the relative gaiety of picnics and soirees and the common desire to socialize with one's own kin and hometown friends. If the articles on the working-class press are any indication, the labor movement—perhaps as part of its Argentinization—seems to have adopted a less-welcoming posture toward foreign arrivals after World War I. Even before the war a syndicalist group claimed that "in their bid to placate the warring impulses of the proletariat, the bourgeoisie counts on the cooperation of two invaluable allies: the immigrant flow, whose great majority is made up by very inferior elements from a revolutionary point of view . . . ; and those who deceivingly call themselves 'socialists' and followers of Marx's work."[136] Such feelings became more common in the postwar decade. In 1919 the anarchist FORA (Federación Obrera [Labor] Regional Argentina) expressed itself against immigration.[137] In 1922 the newly formed syndicalist USA (Unión Sindical Argentina) referred to immigrants as "an immense herd of lambs [*carneros*] who will supplant striking workers. . . . For us, the arrival of so many people can never bring any good."[138] The publications of specific labor unions voiced similar opinions;[139] and so did an independent anarchist weekly which, near the end of the decade, claimed that "the ignorance of the newcomers facilitates their exploitation. That is why everywhere workers see in the arriving legions a danger to themselves. The antipathy and lack of solidarity encountered by immigrants has no other origin."[140]

The labor movement's postbellum Argentinization also made it more introversive and factious, and the Primo de Rivera dictatorship (1923–1929) had an analogous effect on the Spanish immigrant organizations. So although intramural quarrels had always exceeded extramural ones (except perhaps at the height of nationalist fervor during the Spanish-American War and right after anarchist executions or assassinations in Spain), in the 1920s both sides turned their bellicosity increasingly inward. The battles among anarchists, syndicalists, communists, and socialists for control over the labor unions, and the no less acrimonious feuds over the Bolshevik Revolution, consumed much of the movement's warring energy, leaving little for the crusades against the immigrant "national chauvinists." On the other side, some of the "patriotic" associations, including the hometown ones, contained—even before the 1920s—their share of eristic political elements. The Unión Radical de Teo, for example, formed before World War I by villagers from that Galician municipality, attacked caciquismo, or the system of corrupt political bosses in Spain, with questionable success but with a truculence that could not help insulting many on both shores of the Atlantic. Various other localist societies with less combative titles did likewise. The Centro Compostelano Pro Laicismo offended even greater numbers with its campaign against religious education in no less than the holiest town in Spain, Santiago de Compostela, site of the tomb of the apostle Saint James. With the increasing polarization injected by Primo de Rivera's coup, twenty-three of these hometown associations banded to form the Marxist-leaning Federación de Sociedades Gallegas. The ferocious onslaught of its newspapers against the fascist dictatorship, the Spanish diplomatic corps in Argentina, and their immigrant sympathizers raised abrasiveness in the overseas colony to levels only matched after 1936.[141]

Class Friction within Spanish Associations

If labor's anti-immigration stance repelled many newcomers during the 1920s, the classist attitudes of some ethnic associations repelled others from the beginning. As I remarked above, on the inauguration day of the first Spanish association friction between the merchants and the clerks and artisans had erupted over high membership dues. The behavior of a few early leaders whose class position rested on the business of emigration no doubt intensified such animosity. In the 1860s, for instance, Fernando Pérez, the Galician-born president of the Casino Español (forerunner of the Club Español), ran newspaper advertisements threatening those who had not yet paid him for their passages with ordering the Spanish *prestamistas* (village moneylenders) to take action and with listing their names in Buenos Aires' Spanish newspapers.[142]

Later in the century the case of Casimiro Gómez, a Galician from Pontevedra who arrived in Buenos Aires in 1864, illustrates a different source of class tension within the community. Casimiro, a self-made man who had begun as an apprentice, came to own a tannery that employed 800 workers. He was a member of most of the large Spanish associations but also the vice president of the Union Industrial Argentina and a member of the stock market and the Sociedad Rural (Casimiro apparently became aware that in Argentina only landownership could confer real status). He enjoyed close ties with *El Eco de Galicia*, and in the mid-1890s this immigrant newspaper often printed proud articles about the great triumphs of its prominent *paisano*, photographs, and even poems such as:

La Labor de Don Casimiro	The Labors of Don Casimiro
No solo ante el altar, llama divina	Not only in front of the altar,
enciende el corazón, que hay un extremo	divine flame does the heart ignite.
aun más allá del ámbito sagrado.	There is another domain beyond the sacred realm.
Porque andamio, taller, fábrica y mena	Because scaffold, workshop, factory, lode
son otros tantos templos, do al Supremo.[143]	are so many other temples to the Supreme Being.

The accompanying photograph of Casimiro's temple to the Almighty indeed showed that more than a third of the beings in it were no bigger than cherubim. Two weeks after the ode the workers declared a strike, with pay rates for child labor as one of the issues. *El Eco*, which had been very sympathetic to the plight of Galician workers in Argentina as long as the exploiters remained faceless capitalists, now portrayed working conditions in the tannery as ideal and the strikers as instigators. In a bout of journalistic sophism, it dismissed the workers' demand for an eight-hour-day as a farce, because everybody there toiled as long as they wanted, thanks to the (exploitative) piecework system, and branded the people involved as external professional agitators rather than as genuine employees of paternal Casimiro.[144]

Other occasions of intra-Spanish class conflict saw the large associations and mainstream immigrant press taking a similar posture. In 1919, for example, when the Banco Español experienced labor clashes, the magazine of the AESM admonished its members that to strike against the bank was unpatriotic. After all, the bank had financed the construction of the association's immense building next to the Congress Palace and contributed one-eighth of 1 percent of its annual profits to the AESM (and 1 percent to the Spanish Hospital)—an amount far from insignificant, coming as it did from the largest private bank in South America.[145]

Such attitudes not only drove many toward anarchist or other labor organizations but also induced others to form national workers' associations. Spanish waiters and cooks, for instance, founded La Unión Española de Mozos y Cocineros as a mutual-aid society in 1893. In addition to providing sick and burial benefits, it endeavored to avoid the exploitative services of employment agencies, and by 1914 it had 360 affiliates. La Unión Obrera Española (The Spanish Workers' Union), another mutual-aid society founded in 1907, proved more successful, at least numerically, for its membership reached 1,553 seven years later. A few other, smaller ethnic-worker groups formed in the early decades of the twentieth century.

Several factors, however, undermined the formation of these ethnic-class associations. One was the relative lack of xenophobia in the general workers' movement, at least before the 1920s. Another was the antagonism of both the proletarian and ethnic leadership who, fearing divisiveness, favored ethnically neutral unions and multiclass mutual-benefit societies, respectively.[146] A third debilitating element was precisely the competition from these last two types of organizations, which, because of their power to strike and their size, respectively, could deliver more benefits. The number of Spanish members in Argentine labor federations dwarfed those in the Unión Obrera Española, which a critic described as "an amalgam of people fighting for different ideals" and whose membership was listed in the 1914 census as composed mainly of white-collar employees instead of manual workers. And there were more waiters and cooks in the AESM or in the Centro Gallego than in the Unión Española de Mozos y Cocineros. Whatever the reasons, these hybrid ethnic-trade associations were much less common in Argentina than in North America.[147]

Not only did the large, multiclass Spanish associations provide a wider and better array of services and facilities than did the Spanish workers' unions, but their very size and anonymity must have also reduced the potential for class conflict and resentment. The actively participating leadership belonged either to the immigrant elite or to aspiring middle classes with similar outlooks, and conflicts among them originated more in personal animosities than in class antagonism. Social contact among the rest of the affiliates was not particularly intimate. Most members simply paid their monthly dues and received their disability pensions at home. If they saw each other, it was more likely than not at the doctor's office. The very stratification of societies played a similar role in attenuating class strife. In the Club Español and other elite societies there could have been sectorial friction (for example, import merchants versus industrialists, who obviously had different views on import tariffs) but very little class conflict, for they all belonged to the same class.

Class clashes posed a less avoidable dilemma for the smaller and more socially mixed provincial and village-based societies. Indeed, the physical propinquity of people of different ranks in not always spacious halls and meetinghouses, the active participation of the general membership, and the intimacy of social contact made class-related friction almost inevitable. In interviews with me, humbler members needed no prodding and minced no words in assailing the *ricachones* (vulgar rich people) who—according to them—tried to dominate the associations, treated others with contempt, and wasted the common funds on useless luxuries instead of helping needy compatriots. One complained about a president who ordered a mahogany desk from Spain and champagne instead of the more plebeian Asturian cider at the parties. Another griped about the same rich people's faces appearing in all of the issues of the association's magazine. More serious charges of embezzlement or malfeasance surfaced less frequently, and—not surprisingly—in informal conversations rather than in taped interviews.

Emigration's perturbation of a previously stable class structure added new elements of potential friction. Many of the interviewed members aimed their sharpest darts toward "the ostentatious *ricachones* who were nobodies back home" and often accompanied the darts with Spanish proverbs, such as: "The monkey even if dressed in silk is still a monkey," or "The rich person who was once poor has a heart of copper" (a metal denoting both hardness and greed). Immigrants from "good families" took pains to distinguish themselves from the nouveau riche of humbler origins if fortune had also smiled on them in Buenos Aires and exhibited a mixture of disdain and envy if it had not. The newly rich villagers, in turn, portrayed those with genteel pretensions as snobs if they had also become rich and as losers forced to rely on the names of their parents rather than on their own accomplishments if they had not, also drawing ammunition from the vast and varied arsenal of Iberian popular aphorisms: "We all come from common folks of few means, more or less, [and] our father Adam went around in the raw," or "Whores, friars nuns, and pages [that is, parasitical or useless people] always claim high birth."

Perhaps some of the same factors that made class friction in the *Landsmanshaftn* unavoidable also attenuated them. The fact that amiable or neutral remembrances outnumbered acrid denunciations in the interviews may suggest more than the tendency of time to soften animosities. The intimacy of relationships and kinship and hometown ties apparently eased some of the class tensions. Admiration for the accomplishments of relatives and friends and the desire to imitate them did likewise. The *ricachones*, after all, tended to be no more than successful shopkeepers and their "triumphs" well within sight of most other members. The truly rich normally found the ambiance of provincial and village-based societies too limiting and moved to larger, elite regional or pan-Hispanic clubs. This self-segregation diminished the possibility of class conflict. The *Landsmanshaftn's* lack of mutual-insurance functions—or tendency to abandon such roles to larger institutions—similarly eliminated another possible source of conflict. Members of these basically recreational entities did not have to fight over the allocation of pensions, medical services, or disability benefits. Indeed, most confrontations in these associations seem to have manifested petty personal feuds rather than clear-cut class clashes.

Ethnic Clashes in a Multi-Ethnic Immigrant Community

Regional and ethnonationalist loyalties would prove more difficult to segregate and control. They insidiously surfaced even in the internationalist—or antinationalist—anarchist movement. An editorial meant to lionize proletarian sobriety and consciousness in the May 10, 1902, issue of *El Rebelde: Periódico anarquista*, for example, betrayed a different sort of consciousness:

> The Catalan is haughty toward the rest of Spain . . . but it is that he knows he is not lazy and the rest of Spaniards are . . . that the Spaniard is given to dissipate his time in bullfights, songs, gambling, and other frivolities . . . that he maintains the rest of Spain. The Catalan is revolutionary . . . the bourgeoisie cannot dupe and play around with the Catalan worker as easily as they can with the Andalusian, Aragonese, Galician, Castilian, and other Spanish characters the product of a very different education and of ethnic conditions which perhaps mold the peculiar personality of each. It is very difficult to dominate conscious beings.

Whether directly influenced by them or not, this putative champion of universalism had invoked a particular Catalan *Volksgeist*, an idea then in vogue among the pioneers of ethnonationalism in Catalonia.[148] A few years earlier another Catalan universalist, the editor of the anarchist classic *La Protesta Humana*, derided the assassinated Spanish prime minister Cánovas del Castillo as "an Andalusian monster" and mocked the wake organized by Buenos Aires' Spanish associations as a gathering of "four *gallegos* of the most brutish race."[149]

The patriotism of the Spanish associations proved even less capable of barring localist loyalties than the universalism of the anarchists, and the regionalist specter would rise there more frontally and threateningly. A Catalan mutual-aid sodality, the Montepío de Monserrat, was founded the same year (1857) as the pioneer AESM.[150] Its proscription of non-Catalans continually insulted patriotic sensibilities. In 1877 a second regionalist association, the Basque Laurak-Bat ("Four in One," a reference to the four Basque provinces of Spain), formed as a protest against the Spanish government's suppression of their traditional liberties following the Second Carlist War.[151] Again, much of the immigrant leadership, imbued with the ideology of pan-Hispanism and class unity, assailed this newcomer for creating divisions in the community, branding it as unpatriotic and exclusivist. But the founders and members defended their action and averred their Spanish patriotism. The next year, on the inauguration day of the Centro Gallego, the members of the Basque association marched down the street with their Galician compatriots, singing folk songs from both regions and defending "Spanish fraternity within diversity."[152] Moderates, who also predominated in this third regional center, maintained that "if there ever was a people on the face of the earth with a right to be regionalist and rebel against the central government, that people must be the Galicians. . . . Yet we will never deny the name of our common mother, Noble Spain. . . . We are not partisans of that rabid regionalism that refuses to speak the national language and to preserve fraternal ties with the Spanish community."[153]

Regional and musical harmony did not always triumph. In an 1899 article entitled "Chistus y Gaitas [Flutes and Bagpipes]," an immigrant writer related the confrontation that broke out at a Spanish association's assembly in a small town outside Buenos Aires over what musician to hire for the annual fiesta.[154] The Galician and Asturian members argued for their traditional bagpipe player; the Basques, for their typical flutist. Amid the chaos and noise of the meeting, one of the latter shouted in broken Spanish:

> The *chistu* is already more national than the bagpipe . . . (as other members laughed and booed) . . . more national of the Basque nation . . . (amid

more catcalls and chuckles). . . . You laugh 'cause you no know *chistu* . . .
and the president no know neither 'cause he's a *gallego* from Galicia.

Asturian! Sir—said the president, who suffered the puerile anxiety of
not wanting to be confused.

Galician . . . Asturian, little difference, same trash . . .

Animal . . . Barbarian—shouted a Galician.

Barbarian?—responded the Basque—you're not even a barbarian . . .
you're a *gallego!*

Meanwhile, the Andalusians screamed for a guitarist and the Catalans for
a *bandurria* (a smaller relative of the guitar common in their region), but
on the final vote sided with the bagpipe to defeat the Basques' flute,
which, they complained, "sounds like a sick bird." The losers did not give
up and ended up paying extra for their own *chistulari* player. At the fiesta's inauguration mass, the priest delivered a patriotic unitarian sermon,
but later he jokingly commented to the writer: "A lost sermon. . . . As
long as bagpipes, *chistus,* and guitars continue to exist, Spain is condemned to perpetual civil war."

At a less popular level, the conflict sometimes shaped up as one between pluralistic-minded intellectuals and conservative business leaders.
The former portrayed the latter as "donkeys full of money" and as vulgar
and intolerant national chauvinists. When, in 1892, Godofredo Coca—a
Galician journalist, cultural regionalist, and president of the Centro Gallego—committed suicide by jumping into the River Plate, the Galician
newspaper for which he wrote blamed the incident on the "bigoted, vulgar, and positivist" milieu of an immigrant community dominated by
narrow-minded shopkeepers.[155] Powerful merchants, on the other hand, attacked the intellectuals for "propagating diabolic ideas that will bring
nothing but hatred and disunity among Spaniards."[156] Their lack of support caused the end of the Centro Gallego in 1893, and no other significant regional association was founded during the remainder of the
nineteenth century.

In the next century not only did other regionalist associations emerge,
but also the regionalism of the non-Castilian ethnic groups acquired a
more militant tone. The accumulating and increasingly intransigent discourse of ethnonationalist thinkers in Spain and the example of the Irish
and Polish people after World War I fueled the trend.

Basques took to it with greater intensity than any other immigrant
Iberian group. Some published separatist periodicals in their native Euskara.[157] Most of the nationalist intelligentsia found it difficult to express
themselves in what had basically become a peasant language, so they en-

gaged in easier and more symbolic forms of linguistic nationalism: using Euskara place-names instead of Castilian ones (Donostia instead of San Sebastián, for example) and replacing *v*s with *b*s, *c*s with *k*s, and *s*s with *z*s in their Spanish prose. During and after World War I, whether writers used *vasco* or *bazko* offered a reliable indication of where they stood on the nationalist issue. The immigrant associations provided a rough ground for the battle between *españolistas* and *bizkaitarras*. In his 1915 history of the Basques in Argentina, the president of the Laurak-Bat defended the former's stance by titling one of the chapters, "The Laurak-Bat Society Is as Spanish as It Is 'Vasca.'"[158] He accused a nationalist clique in the society with enrolling masses of young, radicalized immigrants, who did not intend to become permanent members, right before a critical assembly vote. In response, the more conservative directors on the board raised the entry fee. But the ornery tone of his attacks and the desperate reaction of the directorate suggested a certain despondence. So did a contemporary protest letter from various directors of the Sociedad Vasco-*Española* Laurak-Bat, offering their resignations.[159] By the end of World War I the *bizkaitarras* had taken the reins. A 1922 book by a member of the directorate described the Laurak-Bat as being permeated with "an ambiance of frank, clearly defined, and pure Basquism, without mixtures and compromises" and denounced the *españolistas* as people with mixed-up identities and traitors to the "Euskara race."[160] Sometime in the 1920s the smaller but even more radical Acción Nacionalista Baska was founded.[161] But nationalists seem to have achieved a position of hegemony rather than dominance, and the issue continued to divide the Basque community in Buenos Aires during, and beyond, the 1920s.

Catalans also embraced ethnic nationalism with increasing enthusiasm, but in an apparently less fractious and bellicose way than their Basque compatriots. Possessors of a vernacular that had preserved and/or promoted stronger urban connections and literary vitality than had Euskara, they expressed cultural nationalist aspirations in long-lived and widely read Catalan-language periodicals.[162] The nationalist issue also affected, and often tormented, the two principal Catalan social clubs in the city, the Centre Català and the Casal de Catalunya. Buenos Aires' Catalan mutual-aid society, Montepío de Monserrat, took a dual approach that satisfied both nationalist fervor and the more pedestrian requirements of mutual-insurance economics. It barred Castilian from its assemblies and Catalanized the names of its members, so that the same people who appear as José, Juan, and Francisco in a 1898 roll are listed as Joseph, Joan, and Francesch fifteen years later. On the other hand, in its aim to boost its membership and mutual fund, it became increasingly less restrictive, widening the definition of Catalan to include, first, Balearic Islanders, then, in turn, Valencians, the spouses of members whatever their ethnicity, and Argentines of Catalan ancestry. In a greater insult to nationalist members, the association reverted to the use of Castilian in its records during some years in the 1920s and continued to designate the Spanish ambassador to Argentina as honorary vice president. In 1930 a separatist magazine decried this ambiguity and blasted the Catalan associations for participating in the activities of the Spanish colony, claiming that "la idee de patria Catalana, la idee de patria espanyola son antitetiques. Amb [with] Catalunya o amb Espanya."[163]

This fervid separatism often elicited equally fiery responses, such as the following, from a Valencian *españolista* immigrant, who wrote a choleric book titled *Los biscaitarras* and paid for its publication himself: "The Basque and Catalan separatist societies in Argentine should be foreclosed by the government, stoned by the people, burned by Spaniards; we should apply a pogrom to all separatists."[164]

Galicians, who accounted for half of the Spaniards in Buenos Aires, were less clear on the issue, and their regionalist assertions often arose as a reaction against denigration. Although Basques and Catalans may have felt politically oppressed and economically exploited by Madrid, they also felt culturally or even "racially" superior to the rest of their compatriots, who, after all, came from less-urbanized and less industrially developed regions. One of the main grievances of the above-mentioned Valencian writer was "the insult of *biscaitarras* who call Spain *Maketania*, which in their dialect means *La Marrueca*, alluding to the mixture of Spaniards with Moors from which they claim to be exempt." On the other hand, Galicians, who came from one of the poorest corners of Spain, felt not only subjugated by the central government but also derided by the rest of their fellow citizens.

Such scorn traced its origin to the other side of the Atlantic and to previous migrations. As early as the 1840s, the English visitor Richard Ford noted in his famous travelogue:

> The humbler emigrants ... do the porters' work of Spain and Portugal; hence the term Gallego is synonymous with a boor, 'ganapan,' or a 'hewer of wood and drawer of water,' the biblical expression for the overworked. ....
> The Portuguese, who do not love a neighbour, modestly contend that God first made 'men,' i.e. Portuguese ... and then Galicians, i.e. 'homines' or slaves to wait on them. These white niggers frequently wear wooden shoes,

which, according to Goldsmith's porter when reasoning on Frenchmen's 'Sabots,' is another proof of their being only fit to be beasts of burden.[165]

In a similar vein but from a concerned standpoint, a journalist writing about his coregionalists in Madrid forty years later denounced their victimization by Spaniards and in particular a local quip that depicted the *gallego* as "an animal very similar to man, invented for the respite of the ass."[166] Linguistic bigotry added another element of opprobrium. Ford described the Galician language as "a patois, harsh and uncouth to the ear, quite unintelligible to Spaniards."[167] A 1905 tourist guidebook similarly observed that "their 'language,' or rather patois, is a dialect of the Portuguese, and their lubricous pronunciation of the Spanish, not less than their proverbial naivete . . . has made them the laughing-stock of the more 'cultos' Spaniards."[168] Thus when, half a century after Ford's remarks and an ocean apart, a dispute arose in Buenos Aires' typographers' union, the editor of its paper could easily resort to an old Spanish song to insult a Galician adversary:

Mas vale querer a un perro
que a un gallego protejer
que el perro es agradecido
y el gallego no lo es.[169]

It is better to love a dog
than to protect a *gallego*
for the dog is thankful
and the *gallego* is not.

Argentines' habit of calling all Spaniards *gallegos* stemmed, then, not from faulty nescience or ethnogeny but from awareness. They did it for the same reason that they called all Italians *tanos* (from Neapolitano) or Armenians *turcos:* they knew where it hurt.

In the last third of the nineteenth century, Galicians on both sides of the ocean began to challenge such disdain more openly. From the 1870s on, a literary regionalist movement emerged as Rosalía de Castro and Emelia Pardo Bazán, the foremost Spanish female poets of the century, began to write in their native language.[170] In 1879 Manuel Mugía, the editor of a regional magazine widely read in the diaspora, wrote: "'Tra mor, tra Brythons' as long as the sea remains Breton [the language] will remain, so can we [Galicians] say with the same prophetic spirit."[171] That same year, two Galician periodicals appeared in Buenos Aires (*El Gallego* and *Revista Galaica*). But their contribution to the fulfillment of the prophecy must have been limited, for they were written mostly in Castilian and proved somewhat less eternal than the sea, evaporating in less than two years. In 1892 a group of cultural regionalists founded the slightly more bilingual and much more permanent *El Eco de Galicia,* which lasted until 1919. Soon after its appearance, an enthusiastic Galician priest wrote a letter congratulating the editors on their defense of "the *gallegos,* those beings disdained by the Porteño populace, perhaps because they are the most laborious, the most honest, and the most respectful of the laws of the country."[172] In a similar letter, another writer claimed that:

> the struggle for dignity should continue, a rest can only be taken when Galicia gets rid of repugnant political bosses, when the *paisano gallego* emigrates with professional and industrial training and can present himself in any place, with dignity and the knowledge of his own worth, making obsolete the phrase "I'm going to take a *gallego,*" instead of "I'm going to take a servant", . . . when emigration stops sending us those poor creatures who with a rope on their backs we see in every corner of Buenos Aires like beasts of burden for rent [referring to the porters] . . . when the name *gallego* stops being an insulting and denigrating epithet in Spain and in Buenos Aires.[173]

As the twentieth century dawned, the struggle continued. In 1900 the Unión Gallega was founded to foster mutual help; organize literary contests, cultural conferences, and banquets; inform people back home about Argentina; provide sick and burial benefits and instruction on anything from bookkeeping and grammar to music and fencing; and "reinforce the bonds of the folk."[174] Despite—or perhaps because of—its many goals, the society enjoyed limited success, listing in the 1904 municipal census only 169 members, 45 of them children. A more specialized club, the Círculo Gallego, appeared in 1902. It aimed to attract the more affluent *paisanos* to "a place where we can celebrate our feasts and talk freely and comfortably about the homeland '*na nosa doce fala* [in our sweet tongue].'"[175] Many other regional associations of varying sizes appeared in the following years, but the place of pride went to the Centro Gallego. Founded in 1907, its meteoric rise turned it into the second largest mutual-aid society in Latin America in the 1920s—after the AESM—and the largest by the next decade, with more than 60,000 members. A year after the opening of the Centro Gallego, and in a more literary vein, the first periodical in Argentina written mostly in Galician, the magazine *Aires da Miña Terra,* went to press.

During and after World War I Galician regionalism became increasingly bolder. Various Irmandades da Fala (language brotherhoods) appeared then, aiming to transform Galician from a badge of inferiority to an expression of ethnic awareness and pride. In 1918 the culturally region-alist Casa de Galicia and the autonomist A Terra were founded.[176] Two other unabashedly separatist associations formed soon afterward: the Ir-mandade Nazionalista Galega n'America do Sul (1923), which published five issues of the magazine *Terra;* and the Sociedad Nazionalista Galega Pondal (1925–1936), which published the newspaper *A Fouce.* The lat-ter's members, among other acts of nationalist affirmation, picketed Bue-nos Aires' theaters which showed comedies that ridiculed Galicians, once interrupting a performance of *Doña Quijota de Orense,* by the renowned Argentine playwright Alberto Vacarezza, with shouts of "Out with this garbage. . . . We want a decent national theater. . . . Viva Free Galicia," before being thrown out by the police.[177] Around the same time, two more Galician-language periodicals appeared: *Tempos Novos* (1924), which blended regionalist and anarchist ideology; and the longer-lasting bi-monthly publication *Celtiga* (1924–1932), whose title stressed the pre-sumed Celtic origins of the Galician people, which separated them from the rest of the "Iberian" inhabitants of the peninsula.[178] Whatever its ac-curacy—most ethnographers question it—this division provided the re-gionalist and nationalist movements with the legitimacy of historical, and in this case prehistorical, antecedents that turned *galleguismo* into a Jung-ian archetype.

This putative Celtic origin and a shared history of imperialist oppres-sion induced Galicians to liken their plight to that of the Irish and to be-hold with admiration the latter's Home Movement. Irish independence in 1922, therefore, suggested a possible path for *gallegos.* In its first issue in 1925, the magazine of a Galician village association published, in the na-tive tongue so reviled by the Galicians' neighbors on both sides of the At-lantic, the poem "Coma en Irlanda [As in Ireland]." Some of its lines were very radical indeed:

E Irlanda libre
berra que berra
vence os tiranos
d'Ingalaterra.
Xa non hay foros
nin hay siñores. . . .
Mentras Galicia
cala e otorga.
Na corte os amos
enchen a andorga
Fame e miseria
pr'os labradores!

Festas, banquetes
pr'os seus siñores
Ergue labrego!
Erguete e anda
Coma en Irlanda!
Coma en Irlanda!¹⁷⁹

And free Ireland
bellow after bellow
triumphs over
the English tyrants.
Now there are no lordships
no more seigniors. . . .
Meanwhile Galicia
remains quiet and consents.
In the court the masters
stuff their bellies.
Hunger and misery
for the peasants!
Feasts and banquets
for their seigniors.
Rise, peasant!
Rise up and go,
As in Ireland!
As in Ireland!

Such radical notions, however, failed to transcend the confines of small, intellectual cliques and take root in the general Galician community during this time. The village society that published the poem continued to include articles full of praise for "Mother Spain." Even some of the societies that stressed regional autonomy claimed to do so "within the absolute concept of the Spanish nationality." When moderate autonomists tried to introduce some mild elements of cultural regionalism in the Centro Gallego during the 1920s, the *españolista* majority routinely silenced them, stamping their feet on the floor of the assembly hall and voting to keep the center's apolitical mutual-insurance nature.¹⁸⁰ Nationalist ideologues repeatedly castigated the Galician immigrant masses and their societies for their "antiquated" Spanish patriotism and their predilection for material mutual aid and sybaritic feasts, dances, and card games. Most Galician institutions continued to maintain good and often reciprocal relations with their pan-Hispanic counterparts. In fact, even the Basque and Catalan societies continued to do so. The Laurak-Bat, for example, though ethnonationalist, contributed to the Spanish hospital and to the AESM.

Pan-Hispanic bonds cemented early in the formation of the organized community proved remarkably resistant and durable. The fact that many of the leaders of regionalist societies also led, or at least belonged to, Spanish elite institutions helped to preserve those bonds. So did the lack of separatist leanings among the one-third of the immigrants who came from Castilian-speaking regions and the universality of that language among the educated newcomers who did not—precisely the people who were more active in organizations. Amid a constant cacophony of ideological and political bickering, class friction, and more abundant and Philistine personal quarrels, Buenos Aires' Spaniards managed to construct and maintain a cohesive institutional structure. On the surface, the Spanish Civil War, which is beyond the period of this study, seems to have shattered such equilibrium by cleaving the homeland and the diaspora. But perhaps, beneath the surface, the institutional balancing act continued.

THE ORGANIZED COMMUNITY STRUCTURE
AND ASSIMILATION

Immigration scholars—most of them North Americans—have often posited the relationship between voluntary associations and immigrant assimilation in two opposing ways. The first interpretation contends that the associations provided a mechanism that enabled the newcomers to deal effectively with the challenges of the new setting and that by doing so they eased adaptation to the host country and eventual Americanization.[181] The other propounds that the associations basically maintained and promoted Old World ways and mentalities and a sense of separateness among the arrivals.[182]

Both of these conflicting interpretations partly hold for the Spaniards in Buenos Aires, but the second seems to carry more weight. There is no question, as we have seen, that the associations facilitated the newcomers' adaptation to the host society. They provided a whole spectrum of material services that went from cradle to grave: newborn hospital care; orphanages; young girls' homes; disability, unemployment, medical, and burial insurance; all sorts of banking facilities; job searches; legal aid; ways of locating lost relatives or friends; night schools; repatriation benefits; clinics; old-age asylums; and at the end, pantheons. However, by providing these services the immigrants' institutional structure allowed many of them to prescind from host-society institutions, making the community a more self-sufficient entity. Assimilation, of course, cannot occur without previous adaptation. But perhaps North American scholars have too easily assumed that the latter (which has been the major theme of the last three chapters) is either concomitant with or leads inevitably to the former—an assumption fostered by the tendency to equate immigrant socioeconomic mobility with Americanization. This study—concerned as it is with the immigrant generation—does not go far enough in time to allow a serious examination of assimilation, which should include the second and following generations. But from where we stand in time, the Spaniards' high degree of "institutional completeness" (to use sociologist Raymond Breton's term) seems to have made possible a more independent, if obviously not autarkic, community.[183] Given the relatively low levels—compared with the North American case—of residential and occupational segregation observed in the previous two chapters (and the decline of host-society hostility that will be described in the next), this institutional characteristic played a key role in preserving group coherence and solidarity.

In addition to providing material services, the immigrant institutions sustained a whole range of sociocultural activities that further encouraged the formation of what anthropologists call a subculture—or more appropriately—subcultures.[184] The large associations often organized Spanish festivities, banquets, concerts, patriotic acts, musical and sporting events, cultural conferences, and so on, that brought the immigrants together. The middle-sized and small associations played an even greater, or at least a more immediate, socializing function. Indeed, some of the localist societies, despite their formal constitutions, regulations, statutes, pompous titles and offices, and other paraphernalia of secondary associations, were little more than magnified primary institutions. Their modest *hogares* (literally, homes) re-created the Old World village in the New World metropolis. It was here where the villagers gathered to chat, dance, play, and reminisce, where young, single arrivals overcame loneliness and romances flourished, where older, established immigrants satisfied their leadership ambitions, where revered old matrons concocted marital unions between and among *paisanos* and the new American generations.

Did the localist identities that these societies nourished represent no more than archaic and temporary stepping stones on the road to assimilation, as historian Dino Cinel has argued in his excellent study of San Francisco's Italians? There, he detected a steady process in which the identities and loyalties of this group went from campanilism to regionalism, to Italian nationalism, and finally toward Americanization.[185] Spaniards in Buenos Aires seem to have taken a different path. As we saw, pan-Hispanic nationalism actually anteceded regionalism in the organized community, which in turn predated the appearance of village-based organizations. At one level, Spanish localism resembled that of Italians. The former's attachment to the *patria chica* paralleled the latter's devotion to the *paese:* an organic, rustic, and spontaneous allegiance to the land, to the hometown, to familiar surroundings that evoked nostalgic emotions and memories. On another level, Spanish regionalism (or more specifically, Basque, Catalan, and Galician regionalism) exhibited a trait absent from the Italian variety: an ideological—and often radical—content. In its milder form it expressed itself as autonomist; in its harsher one, as separatist, ethnonationalist. Its style, and sometimes its substance, was liberationist. Cinel maintained that "the Americanization of Italian immigrants should be seen as a chapter in the larger story of declining regional cultures under the impact of modernization."[186] Spanish regionalism, however, was identified by many not with declining peasant cultures but with new currents, with modernity itself.

The *españolista* president of the Laurak-Bat, for example, complained in his 1915 book about the particularly strident Basque nationalism of the Argentine-born members, which he attributed to "the hold that new and radical doctrines usually have on the young."[187] One of the main anti-Spanish leaders in the society and the author of a 1922 history of Basque nationalism was born not in Euskadi (the Basque homeland) but in Buenos Aires.[188] Judging by the marriage patterns of immigrants, Basque identity seemed to have been an equally cohesive force on the parents of the Laurak-Bat's Argentine-born members. As Table 50 indicates, a little more than half of these marital unions represented both national and ethnic endogamy (Spanish Basques marrying each other). However, another one-fifth represented a sort of hidden ethnic endogamy that official censuses, with their stress on citizenship, normally record as exogamy: Spanish Basques who married Argentine or French nationals of Basque ancestry (as indicated by their surnames). This proportion greatly exceeded purely "national" endogamy (those who married their non-Basque Spanish compatriots) and total exogamy (those who married people who were neither Basque nor Spanish). The fact that the data include, but do not differentiate, unions that took place in both the Old and the New World actually underrepresents the degree to which regional ethnicity surpassed citizenship in immigrants' choice of a spouse. After all, unions with non-Basque Spaniards could take place on both sides of the Atlantic but those with Argentine-born Basques normally on only one. Qualitative sources also allude to a high rate of Basque ethnic intramarriage. Indeed, one affronted Spanish immigrant called it, as late as 1961, "one of the two abhorrent practices Basques share with Jews, the other being their pedantry."[189]

Table 50 Marriage patterns of the parents of the 610 Argentine-born members of Buenos Aires' Basque society, Laurak-Bat, who joined between 1910 and 1917

Type of union	N	Percentage
Both partners born in the same village	95	15.6
Both partners born in the same province	126	20.7
Both partners born in the same region	93	15.2
Subtotal, national and ethnic endogamy	314	51.5
One partner born in Argentina, but has a Basque surname	76	12.5
One partner born in France, but has a Basque surname	52	8.5
Subtotal, ethnic but not national endogamy	128	21.0
One partner born in Spain outside Basque country	84	13.8
Subtotal, national but not ethnic endogamy	84	13.8
One partner born in Argentina and has a non-Basque surname	64	10.5
One partner born in another country and has a non-Basque surname	20	3.3
Subtotal, both ethnic and national exogamy	84	13.8
Total	610	100.1

SOURCE: Membership application forms, Laurak-Bat, 1910–1917.

A similar analysis of marriage patterns is difficult to perform for Catalans and Galicians because of their less distinctive patronymics (particularly among the latter). But anecdotal evidence and my own observations suggest that regional loyalties and ethnonationalism also held a powerful, lasting sway over these groups and their Argentine descendants, who at times took to it with the same zeal with which some of their young friends embraced Zionism and others reserved for internationalist, left-wing ideologies. Perhaps the majority (particularly of Galicians, and after the first generation) never heartily espoused these politicized Iberian regionalisms. But for those who did, they would pose not a step on the road to pan-Hispanic national identities and later Argentinization but a barrier against it.

Spanish parochialism, on the other hand, like Italian campanilism, has no ideological base able to capture collective imaginations with that much force. But these hometown loyalties have also proven to be quite durable in their own, less vociferous ways. Rather than being superseded by modern national identities—as propounded by Cinel for San Francisco's Italians—they seem, at times, to have coexisted with them in Buenos Aires. In 1987 I was invited to the Val de San Lorenzo society for the celebration of its sixty-third anniversary. The event embodied the mélange of changes and continuities and the babel of cultural dialogues that characterizes the immigration experience. Almost every one of the hundred or so "villagers" sang the Argentine anthem, but only a few old voices could remember the lyrics of the Spanish one. The banquet included "tripe à la Madrileña" and those thick Argentine steaks that had always impressed Old World arrivals. When the oldest member, the widow of one of the founders, received a commemorative medal, she proudly thanked the congregation in her native tongue, Portuguese. Then there were other Valenses with Castilian-sounding surnames like Rinaldi, Fagen, and Liebermann—called *el rusito* by his *paisanos*. At the same time, second-, third-, fourth-, and even fifth-generation Argentine Valenses danced to the rustic tunes of their ancestral drummer-piper one-man band. This may have been a case of "symbolic ethnicity,"[190] but just the fact that they were there shows an amazing degree of continuity for an identity based on a barren village of 800 souls and an equally impressive quantum of cultural melding, invention, and reproduction.

7 Cousins and Strangers

Spanish immigrants in Argentina, much like the Portuguese in Brazil, the French in Quebec, or the British in Australia, had a dual collective personality. They were children of the Mother Country and foreigners, relatives and outsiders, bestowers of the original culture and uncultured immigrants, cousins and strangers. This dual personality, evidently, represented a cultural construction rather than some pristine essence, and as such it was historically conditioned rather than temporally static. That is, whether one set of attributes or the other was highlighted depended on, and changed with, historical conditions.

This chapter shifts the focus from the socioeconomic and spatial aspects of adaptation (the theme of the previous three) to some of its cultural-cognitive dimensions, to the less concrete, but not less important, realm of perceptions, attitudes, and reputations. Specifically, it examines changes and continuities in the way Spaniards were perceived by their hosts and in the response of the newcomers.

In the search for an explanation for these transformations and persistences, I transferred the analytical framework previously employed to examine emigration and the socioeconomic adaptation of the immigrants to a plane more suitable for the analysis of attitudes and perceptions. Thus the macrostructural has been translated as the general Western intellectual and cultural trends; the microsocial, as the local particularities. The interaction between these global trends and local peculiarities, I argue, provides the most useful framework, at the very least heuristically, to explain the changing nature of Spaniards' dual personality in Argentina and their response to these changes.

INDEPENDENCE AND ITS AFTERMATH

For most of the 3,000 Spaniards in Buenos Aires around 1810 the ordeal of Argentine independence never reached the tragic levels endured by other vanquished groups in contemporary anticolonial wars, such as the French in Haiti or even their compatriots in Venezuela and Mexico. In comparison with these struggles, which occurred in slave or caste societies and often took the form of ruthless class or race wars, Argentine emancipation was a relatively bloodless affair, with most of the fighting taking place not in the capital but in campaigns to "liberate" neighboring countries. Spaniards were neither massacred nor expelled en masse. Family ties to well-placed Creoles acted as a moderating element. So did the desires of the more pragmatic independence leaders to avoid antagonizing the local Iberians in the hope of reversing, neutralizing, or at least reducing their imperial loyalties.

The 1816 play *La libertad civil* offers a histrionic example of these historical attempts. In it, the Creole hero encourages a group of Indians symbolizing America to accept a Spanish character properly attired in "a liberty hat":

Hijos del Mediodía,
Mirad á vuestro hermano,
Tendedle vuestra mano,
Con ansia le estrechad.
Que la filantropía
Con su poder nos ligue,
Y a amarnos nos obligue
Su blanda autoridad.[1]

Children of the South,
Behold your brother,
Extend your hand to him,
And grasp his with eagerness.
Let philanthropy
link us with its power,
and oblige us to love one another
with its tender authority.

Soon afterward, the hero, the heroine, and the Indians embrace the Spaniard as they sing:

Y tú, Español amigo,
Que con murado pecho
Defiendes el derecho

De nuestra Libertad;
Ella te dá su abrigo
Y el suelo americano
Te aclama ciudadano
Y ofrece su amistad.

And you, Spanish friend,
Who, with towering courage,
Defend the right
Of our Liberty;
She gives you her protection
And the American soil
A citizen proclaims you
And offers its friendship.

Not all people or plays were so accepting. The main characters in the anonymous *La acción de Maipú*, written two years later (1818), constantly vow to "wipe out" *godos* (Goths, an insulting epithet for Spaniards)—in prudish editions—or to "make them shit," in the more vulgar and virulent original.[2] Besides thespian threats, Spaniards received real ones from an urban plebe imbued with a mixture of protonationalist and class rancor. Ex-servants accused their former *gallego* masters of real and invented anti-Argentine conspiracies. One denounced a Spanish physician as "one of those *gallegos* who hate us, and one way or another conspire against our existence," for allegedly raising his hand against a young Creole girl who had been teasing and provoking his pregnant wife.[3] Plebeian militiamen often threatened *sarracenos* (Saracens, another Hispanophobic slur of the time) with death for any triviality. In 1812, when seventeen local Spaniards were executed for an antirevolutionary plot, a mob stoned their cadavers. The municipal chief of police thought it expedient to allow this and other venting of anti-Spanish wrath by the urban populace, interfering only to prevent actual lynching.[4] Clearly, limited local warfare, family ties, and the efforts of prudent patriots could reduce but not rescind the hatred and hostility inherent in an anticolonial war.

In addition to spontaneous popular harassment, Spaniards endured the onus of official repression. In the decade following the outbreak of the emancipation struggle in 1810, the new government confiscated their properties, extracted forced loans, prohibited them from forming associations of more than three individuals and even from riding horses, imprisoned or expelled—at times arbitrarily—about four hundred of them, and executed a few dozen loyalists.[5]

Some of the anti-Spanish resentment apparently had less to do with political independence than with sexual politics. Popular contemporary literature insinuates such antagonism. Even before the emancipations wars, a gaucho in the anonymous play *El amor de la estanciera* complained to his wife about the rich Iberian who courted their daughter:

> Mujer, aquestos [*sic*] de España
> son todos medios bellacos;
> más vale un paisano nuestro
> aunque tenga cuatro trapos
>
> Woman, those from Spain
> are all tricky rascals;
> one of our countrymen is worthier
> even if he just has four rags.

The fact that the pretender was actually Portuguese but is identified with Spaniards further implies that they were considered foreigners in the popular mind even though they were not yet legally so. Another anonymous, but postindependence, play expressed a similar idea in the appeal of a man to his wife:

> Solo te pido una cosa:
> Que si acaso quedais viuda
> No te caseis con *gallego*
> Por que son pura basura[6]
>
> I only ask you one thing:
> That if by chance you become a widow
> Do not marry a *gallego* [Spaniard]
> Because they are pure scum.

The rhymes voiced a common resentment against the mostly male Spanish arrivals who increased the competition in—to put it in a materialistic and not necessarily facetious term—the "mate market," particularly against those who, after making some money, courted the "better-looking" or more desirable partners. Here too, action was not limited to rhythmic gripes. Indeed, not without its irony for a movement fighting for freedom from mercantilist controls, some of the new regime's first decrees attempted to monopolize this "market." In 1811 it tried, under the pretext of military security, to confine all single Spaniards in concentration camps.[7] Six years later, again under the pretense of national security, it legally forbade Spaniards from marrying Argentine women, which, given the scarcity of Spanish female immigrants at the time, amounted to enforced bachelorhood.[8] No great amount of Freudian analysis or psychohistorical imagination is required to figure out what kind of security inspired those decrees.

Hispanophobia had a more philosophical side, too, one which could be detected not only in the discourse of the independence warriors but also in that of the civilian leadership that followed, and particularly in that of the four principal liberal intellectuals of the period. In 1818 Bernardino Rivadavia, Argentina's first civilian president, deemed the encouragement of immigration the first priority of the new republic because it was the most efficient, and perhaps the only, method of destroying the decadent Spanish heritage of the country. Litterateur Esteban Echeverría defined Spain as the most backward country in Europe and its bequest to the New World as "routine . . . dogma . . . and superstition."[9] Juan Bautista Alberdi, whose father was actually a Spanish Basque, sarcastically attributed Argentina's entrepreneurial spirit, modern education, parliamentary system, scientific accomplishments, tolerance, social emancipation—in short, every liberal attribute that the country presumably lacked—to "la culta y progresista España [the cultured and progressive Spain]."[10] And in 1841 Domingo Sarmiento, the other prominent liberal thinker of the period who would later serve as president, was still blaming the country's backwardness on the Spanish "love of idleness and industrial incapacity" and advocating its "de-Hispanization."[11]

During this period, then, Spaniards, when not considered enemies, were considered undesirable strangers, their condition as "children of the Mother Country" not often remembered. The aftermath of independence offered a less than enviable situation. Before 1810 they formed a privileged group who monopolized political power, public positions, and transatlantic commerce. Now, Creoles dominated the state, and British and other foreign merchant-adventurers moved into international trade with incremental insistence.

The Spaniards' response, after a few failed antirevolutionary plots, was —not surprisingly—individual, defensive, and rather mute. About one in six responded with their feet, returning to Spain or fleeing to some of the loyal colonies during the first decade of independence. Apparently, the majority were too poor, too rich, or too settled to leave. About one-tenth (276 between 1812 and 1828) took Argentine citizenship out of conviction or, perhaps more often, to avoid harassment and keep public jobs. Some openly repudiated their former nationality in the process. A Galician grocer affirmed in his naturalization papers to have "forgotten that country where fate had me born"; a Catalan baker did not want to be counted anymore among those "nameless monsters who infract the sacred rights of the 'patria'"; another called his ex-compatriots "a pack of stupid beasts who prefer slavery to emancipation."[12] Because the duties of citizenship included the detested militia draft and the Argentine government refused to exempt Spanish nationals from it, an apparently larger number denied their nationality not through naturalization but by camouflaging themselves. Thus, Spanish Basques attempted to pass for French ones; Andalusians, for British subjects (from Gibraltar); and Galicians, for Portuguese (an ironic twist, for in colonial times Portuguese immigrants tried to pass for *gallegos* to avoid expulsion). Those who retained their identity were kept busy trying to prove that they did not form part of a fifth column, and—after the war phobia passed—that Spain was not the most obscurantist country on the planet.

The Hispanophobia of the first half of the nineteenth century in part stemmed from external intellectual movements. English economic liberalism was one of these. Adam Smith's *The Wealth of Nations*, translated into Spanish in 1782, made its way to the River Plate Viceroyalty not long after that. Smith's massive volume offered a bottomless font of anti-Spanish "wisdom" from which Argentine patriots would eagerly drink. It persistently depicted Spain as the most backward and "beggarly" country in Europe—after Poland—and its regime in the Americas as "violent and arbitrary." This regime constrained lands so rich and settlers so energetic that they had thrived in spite of it and would really take off if they could rid themselves of the metropolis. He even used the example of Buenos Aires on several occasions to illustrate his "law of comparative advantage" and the absurdity of banning free international trade.[13] The firebrand revolutionary Mariano Moreno offers, in his Smithian attack on Spanish colonial mercantilism, *Representación de los hacendados* (1809), one of the most explicit examples of this influence.

Early English utilitarianism provided another external source of philosophical Hispanophobia. Jeremy Bentham, whom Rivadavia called "the Newton of legislation ... one destined to be the legislator of mankind," kept up a keen interest in Argentine independence and a copious correspondence with the new republic's first president. In one of his letters to Rivadavia, he disdainfully portrayed Spain as an obscurantist, closed, and censored country that prohibited useful sciences.[14]

The French Enlightenment supplied Argentine patriots with even more abundant intellectual ammunition.[15] Its subversive potential lay not in its anticlericalism, for the Crown itself wished to curb the power of the Church, but in its questioning of traditional authority, antimonarchical tenets, libertarian and egalitarian discourse, and strong anti-Spanish tenor. French encyclopedists and philosophes, after all, had always been fond of portraying Spain and its empire as the quintessence of obscurantism and injustice. Voltaire denounced the conquistadors as cruel fanatics in *Alzire ou les américains* (1736) and painted the Iberian Peninsula as the land of the Inquisition and the Spanish governor of Buenos Aires as a pharisaic fool in *Candide* (1759).[16] Rousseau turned the Caribs into noble savages and the Spaniards into the cruelest of exploiters in his *Discours* of the 1750s.[17] Raynal's *Histoire philosophique des Indes* (1770) added further opprobrium on Spaniards on both sides of the Atlantic. It was through these writings, rather than through the original ones of Bartolomé de Las Casas, that the Black Legend of Spanish colonialism disseminated in Buenos Aires and elsewhere in Latin America.

European intellectual trends, however, acted not in a disembodied manner but mixed with local characteristics to color Argentine Hispanophobia. English economic liberalism found such a fertile soil in the River Plate because the region's economy was already Atlantic oriented but burdened by imperial mercantilism. After all, such doctrines fell mostly on deaf ears in the Pacific colonies of Peru—which actually benefited from colonial restrictions and subsidies—and Chile but found receptive ones in Venezuela, the other Atlantic- and export-oriented colony. Not coincidentally, Buenos Aires and Caracas became not only the first to revolt and secede from the empire but also the foci from which the rest of South America was liberated, even though they were the regions that had thrived the most with the Bourbon Reforms of the late colonial period. Smith's musings about "invisible hands" and "laws of comparative advantage" convinced Porteños so easily because they had already realized that Spain had turned into a useless but expensive intermediary between them and the markets and producers of the North Atlantic, taking a cut on their export profits and hiking the price of imported consumer goods through imperial tariffs. Moreover, the resentment generated by this situation stalked more than just the distant metropolis. The Crown's ban on free trade may have elicited the patriots' cerebral, Smith-inspired assaults, but local Spaniards shouldered the population's daily grumbles. *Peninsulares,* after all, monopolized transatlantic trade through their merchant guild and represented the most direct and visible beneficiaries of the imperial mercantilism that grieved everyone else.

In a similar vein, the French Enlightenment's anti-Spanish notions were eagerly accepted by Porteños not out of some sort of puerile—and servile—Francophilia but because they articulated or served local concerns. The Bourbons' bid to increase royal control of the colonies in the last third of the eighteenth century was accompanied by a swelling army of Spanish bureaucrats, merchants, and plain immigrants who provided an easier target for Creole resentment than did a faraway monarch. In order to cut down on venality, the Crown discontinued the practice of selling public offices and, instead, granted them to these recent arrivals on the assumption that they had less potentially corruptive ties with local society. This accentuated the exclusion of the Argentine born from both public administration and indirect political power, because corruption and venality had previously provided a mechanism for rich Creoles to translate their economic might into political influence.[18] The new peninsular bureaucrats proved relatively efficient, but their very success further alienated settlers. Raising taxes and improving collection pleased the royal treasury but no one else. Quelling illegal contraband did likewise, because smuggling provided Porteños with cheaper consumer goods. Yet the Bourbon Reforms —including the expulsion of the Jesuits from the colonies in 1768—which aimed to secularize and rationalize imperial government, ensued from the principles of enlightened despotism and thus from the same general pool from which patriots drew inspiration for their anti-Spanish orations. Moreover, the Black Legend resurrected by the philosophes denounced not the hardships that Bourbon peninsular bureaucrats and immigrants imposed on the Creoles but those which the ancestors of Creoles had inflicted on Indians. Argentine patriots, therefore, did not simply parrot the French Enlightenment but read it selectively and reconstructed its Hispanophobia to fit their own requirements.

The more radical ideas of the Enlightenment and the French Revolution also combined with local conditions to color attitudes toward Spaniards. Buenos Aires—on the fringe of the empire, lacking an exploited sedentary indigenous mass or a large slave population—had developed from the start along less hierarchical lines than the rest of Ibero-America. The surrounding equestrian culture of the pampas accentuated the frontier environment and what some Argentine historians have called "inorganic democracy." Scores of adjectives have been used to describe the gauchos, but neither foe, friend, nor unconcerned observer has ever used—as far as I know —"submissive." Constant complaints by visitors and residents about the impertinency of the Porteño plebe manifest a relatively fluid ambiance receptive to the egalitarian elements of the French Enlightenment and Revolution.[19] Spaniards, as a "foreign," imperialist, and socially dominant group, presented a perfect target for the ire of a pugnacious populace. Moreover, positions in the imperial administration and high commerce could not accommodate the increasing number of Spanish arrivals, forcing them to seek a living in retail and artisanal trades, where they either directly exploited the native popular sectors or competed with them, adding yet another element of antagonism.[20] And so did the *peninsulares'* feeling of racial superiority, disdain for "native sloth," and the already-mentioned rivalry for available marriage partners. All of these factors combined with the French-inspired propaganda of the more Jacobinian patriots, imbued Hispanophobia during and after independence with a zeal normally found only in more radical liberation movements.

THE POST-ROSAS PERIOD: FROM LIBERALISM TO POSITIVISM

Although the situation had been anything but auspicious during the first half of the nineteenth century, Spaniards, as shown in chapter 3, kept on coming. By 1852, when the caudillo Juan Manuel de Rosas was overthrown, there were some 5,800 Spaniards in the city of Buenos Aires alone. An Argentine scholar correctly identified the main ideological aversions of the new liberal ruling group as "los españoles ('godos'), Rosas, y los caudillos."[21] Yet although the new, modernizing elite may have been more philosophically anti-Spanish than the old nativist caudillo, who at least identified with traditional Hispano-Creole culture, their greater respect for civic rights and liberties allowed Spaniards to organize themselves.

Soon after Rosas' overthrow, the Argentine government acknowledged the right of Spaniards as foreign citizens to be exempted from militia conscription and rescinded the old ban on Spanish associations, allowing them to form their first fraternal organization in independent Argentina.[22] The freer atmosphere also enabled Spaniards to publish their first newspapers and the Spanish government to establish a consular office in Buenos Aires. All of this heralded the transformation of an amorphous collectivity into an organized community.

It did not take long for the organized community to begin defending its good name and that of its country. In its very first issue (November 1852) *La Revista Española* called for the removal, from the national guard's bandstand, of an allegorical painting that the Spaniards considered offensive (a warrior woman, representing Argentina, with a lion, representing the defeated metropolis, at her feet). The sudden display of self-confidence by what many still considered the vanquished enemies of the fatherland took Argentine nationalists by surprise. Some were infuriated by what they deemed an affront to a national symbol and demanded an apology. But the Spanish newspaper stood its ground and did not desist from its petition.

As the immigrant newspapers became increasingly assertive, they targeted not only offensive national symbols but also insulting national leaders. One assailed an Argentine parliamentarian for calling Spain a backward country and comparing her with China on the floor of the national congress. It also denounced President Avellaneda's immigration law and took to task the local chief of police.[23] While condemning the knifing of two Spaniards by a band of gauchos as they yelled "Death to the gringos," it added, "and let the police commissioner come to us now with his idiotic tales about the criminality of Spanish immigrants." Another attacked the Argentine political leaders who formed a commission to aid "the Cuban filibusters," during the island's Ten Years' War (1868–1878) against the Spanish metropolis.[24] A monarchical newspaper blasted a local public figure for "the dastardly insolence of questioning the amorous conduct of our august Queen Isabel II."[25] And another immigrant journalist inveighed against demagogic local politicians who "make a career out of insulting Spain, feeding a popular phobia that has not abated since independence." Mocking the tendency of Argentine liberal intellectuals to equate civilization with non-Iberian European culture, the same writer added: "I thought that the word 'civilization' expressed a complex and relative idea; the Argentine sages have taught me otherwise."[26]

Spokesmen for the community also mounted a campaign to oppose the Black Legend of Spanish colonization.[27] Immigrant and native newspapers would argue about the issue, each defending legends of opposite colors. The most effective Spanish argument seems to have been that of Gil Gelpi, a journalist who published a pamphlet claiming that Bartolomé de Las Casas classified as thieves and murderers the Spaniards who came to the Indies, not those who remained in Spain and that since his ancestors stayed, he would leave it to the descendants of the conquistadors to accept or refute Las Casas' assessment of their forebears.[28] But the immigrant community was not unanimous on the issue. A minority of republican exiles dissented from the more "patriotic" mass. *El Eco Español* (September 7, 1861 and ff.) assailed Miguel García Fernández, a Spanish immigrant "renegade," for his play *La novia del hereje*, which "denigrates the cultural task of the Spanish conquest and colonization in America." The cunning author—the newspaper complained—had "obviously discovered that soiling the name of his country brings carts of flowers and laurels in America."

A different sort of conflict, and one that was to have a long history, arose from the popular *gallego* jokes, in which the Spaniard was assigned the role of the fool. In 1862, for example, a local Argentine daily published the story of a Galician arrival who, getting off the boat, found a

colorful Paraguayan parrot. As he picked it up, the parrot yelled, "Beast"!
The frightened *gallego* placed the parrot back on the ground and, taking
his hat off in deference, said in broken Castilian: "Pardon me, Sir, I am
a foreigner and mistook you for a bird [Ustu perdune caballeru, soy ex-
tranjeru y lu habia tomadu a uste pur pajaru]."[29] The Spanish immigrant
press responded with fire, particularly aimed at the daily's director Carlos
D'Amico, who "with such a name we can be sure that not a drop of noble
Castilian blood runs through his vein." D'Amico, who would later become a minister of government, responded that Spaniards were the most
useless of immigrants because they could not even be counted on to graze
cattle (a reference to their preference for urban areas) and that luckily he
did not have a single drop of Spanish blood.

A similar dispute pitted the Spanish colony against future president
Domingo Sarmiento, an ardent Hispanophobe, who, after a trip to Spain,
had published a book portraying the country as backward and feudal.[30]
Unamuno would, much later, maintain that Sarmiento was "un buen español" because only "a good Spaniard" could be so critical of Spain.[31] The
immigrant colony in Buenos Aires did not see it that way, so it commis-
sioned a Spanish author in Madrid to write a rebuttal to Sarmiento. To the
delight of not only the Spaniards but also of his political enemies, a clever,
mocking booklet, half in prose and half in rhyme, that tore Sarmiento to
pieces was published in Buenos Aires in 1854.[32]

Not one to give up a good fight, Sarmiento continued to attack the
Spanish immigrant leadership and its presumed disrespect for the host
country's symbols and institutions until his death, in 1888. Four years before that, in a letter refuting the charges of the immigrant press, he de-
fiantly wrote: "It is not true that I have said that, in the judgment of the
great modern thinkers, the Spanish race is a decadent one. I said something worse, which I have repeated countless times in my writings: that it
is a race with an atrophied brain and no hopes for improvement. The ir-
reverence and stupidity of the Spanish press here gives ample proof of
this."[33] In an 1882 newspaper article he denounced the "insulting" title of
a local Spanish periodical, *La Colonia Española*—despite the fact that the
term, as in English, also denotes a nonimperialist community of immigrants—and sarcastically alluded to the continuing complaints about the
"lion" in the national emblem from "the 'colonia española,'" which does
not permit the ex-colonized to have symbols that recall their past error of
becoming independent." When, around the same time, the editors of a
Spanish newspaper organized a protest against the police beating of one of
their compatriots, Sarmiento blasted them for their contempt for national

institutions and "shameful presumption that there is a Spain here that they can rule and command at their whim." Even if the abuse took place—added Sarmiento, who doubted it—Spaniards should, like all other citizens, take their complaint to the appropriate Argentine judicial authorities and not, as they usually did, to their own organizations, in blatant disrespect of their host's sovereignty.[34]

Sarmiento was not the only one offended by the Spaniards' disregard for their obligation as "guests." In its June 16, 1864, issue the newspaper *El Nacional* editorialized:

> We have never understood the mission of an immigrant press that occupies itself with the internal politics of a country whose interests it cannot represent. . . . The foreign communities do not have, cannot have, any other interest, than their work and businesses, the material progress of the country, and their newspapers should represent only those needs. Let one criticize any act of the Spanish government, any bad habit of its people, any behavior or product, even if it is just an almanac, and there you have the Spanish immigrant press that through reason or force will call you to order, threatening you otherwise with the furies of hell, and the wrath of their august queen. . . . Stop harassing the people and insulting our sovereignty, and realize, once and for all, your obligations as guests.

The Spanish press failed to comprehend such "obligations" and responded with sardonic attacks on Argentine writers, like the journalists in *El Nacional*, who wanted to "de-Hispanize" themselves. If they wanted to do so, "Let them write in Guarani or Quichua [*sic*] instead of the beautiful tongue of Cervantes and Calderón . . . or commit suicide since, although undeservingly, Spanish blood runs through their veins."[35]

Spanish imperialist adventures during the period exacerbated these frictions. In the 1860s the invasion of Veracruz and Santo Domingo and, closer to home, the bombardment of Valparaíso and the takeover of Peruvian islands by the Spanish Navy produced in Buenos Aires popular outrage against these actions and, thus, against the Spanish immigrant community, which zealously supported Spain's imperialist deeds as acts of self-defense. Crowds attacked the homes of local Spaniards, stoning their doors as they tried to force them open. During the Cuban War of Independence at the end of the century, sympathy for the rebel cause and antipathy toward Spaniards ran high. A series of street fights broke out, and a mob stormed the Club Español, attacking its members.[36]

Urban popular resentment against Spaniards, however, only boiled over during these periods of imperialist imbroglios and wars. In general it took milder forms: animosities toward the *gallego* storekeeper and his practice of hiring only *paisanos;* cavils about some Spaniards' pedantic insistence that the Argentines' language was a bastardized tongue and that the only proper form was peninsular Castilian; and a vague antagonism against the former enemies of the fatherland—an aversion animated by the emphasis of history textbooks on the heroic struggles of national patriots against the Spanish oppressor.[37]

This last particularly disturbed Spaniards. As one complained, "We trust the education of our children to strangers who begin to imbue them, under the pompous name of historical knowledge, with lies offensive to their nation of origin and who do not take long to inoculate in the still innocent heart of the child the virus of antagonism and hatred toward that land that was always a cradle of nobility and honor."[38] The Spaniards, this writer continued, should imitate Italians, Germans, and the English and build their own schools, because "Since, as fate has it, we are 'foreign enemies' in this land, we should at least try not be so in the bosom of our own homes."

His advice bore little fruit. The few attempts to found schools failed from the onset, and generations of Hispano-Argentines grew up with two conflicting views of history: their parents' and the official one. Even if they resented the "lies offensive to their nationality," the expanding public-school system provided the basic instruction that most immigrant parents wanted for their children. The government intended to use public education to Argentinize the second generation and, though not prohibiting them, was ill disposed toward immigrant schools of any nationality. Whatever the reason, foreign schools were already declining by the turn of the century. Moreover, the primary goal of other foreign schools—the preservation of the native language—was not a critical issue for Spaniards, even for those who spoke a native tongue other than Castilian. Like the Yiddish-speaking Ashkenazim, in the Old World they had long been used to a dichotomy in which Castilian represented the official language, the language of schools, courts, administration, and authority and the regional vernacular, the tongue of the family, neighbors, friends, and intimacy. This was particularly so for Galicians, who, like many other subjugated groups in history, had sometimes come to accept the views of the overlord and regarded their own idiom as a rustic, peasant one, while revering Castilian as the language of refinement, power, and status.[39]

This local characteristic (the fact that the community was mostly non-Castilian) again interacted with a general Western ideological trend (liberal republicanism) to color Spaniards' relationships with their hosts. Galicians, Catalans, and Basques made up some four-fifths of the Spanish community in Buenos Aires, and the composition of the leadership reflected this fact. Many of these people—at the very least a sizable minority—viewed Spanish republicanism and liberalism as little more than plots of the centralist Castilian state to take away their traditional liberties. This perception was bolstered by the fact that Catholic conservatives formed the only political group in the peninsula that consistently supported local autonomy and federalism. Basques, especially, arrived in significant number as refugees from the Carlist Wars and thus adhered to a militantly monarchical and Catholic creed. On the other hand, the Argentine intelligentsia in the decades after the overthrow of Rosas was ardently liberal and republican, and its relationship with monarchical Spain and her immigrant defenders necessarily became a stressful one.

The multinational environment of Buenos Aires further complicated this relationship. At the time, the Italian immigrant elite was made up mostly by *Mazziniani*, or exiles who in general supported the Risorgimento, the struggle for a unified, republican Italy. To the exasperation of Spaniards, these Italian liberals began to develop close and harmonious ties with their Argentine correligionists. During the 1860s, for example, *La Tribuna*, Buenos Aires' most liberal newspaper, had kept up a constant feud with the Spanish colony while having nothing but accolades for the "cultured and progressive Italians." It once held that Buenos Aires could not trust its safety to *gallego* night watchmen, who were potential traitors, and suggested that they be replaced with loyal Italians.[40] A Spanish newspaper responded by referring to Italians as "'tutti cuanti farsialeris' [mimicking their language], a crude rabble that we don't know where in the devil it comes from and that are the moth, the termite that will destroy this country if *La Tribuna* keeps up her exaggerated praise of Italians."[41]

Rivalries with Italians indeed dated back to the very birth of the Spanish organized community. In 1852, during one of the many small civil wars the country endured, Buenos Aires' foreign colonies formed voluntary battalions to defend the city from besieging federalist troops. The correspondence of the commanders of these immigrant legions to the minister of war would have provided a good plot for an *opera buffa*. They constantly solicited permission to name more *comandantes*, and the exasperated minister steadily replied that the battalions already contained more officers than soldiers. Their request for war supplies included dozens of pairs of pants, socks, and underwear, never bullets. But a letter from the Spanish commander went further. It complained that the Italian legion had received a new blue velvet winter outfit and the Spaniards had not. The enemy, the letter continued, exploited the incident to create discontent among the troops, and the favoritism shown the Italians offended and de-moralized the soldiers.[42]

These squabbles over trivial velvet outfits do tell us something about the nature of inter-ethnic conflict in Argentina. It was usually over ethnic or national prestige, over status and recognition by the host society, rather than over hard economic issues. As I suggested in the last chapter, the de-velopment of an immigrant associational structure probably delayed Ar-gentinization by providing services that made the community more self-sufficient. But the immigrant colonies had too much internal diversity to be able to form as interest groups. Most of the times that the Spaniards were able to present a united front, the issue was noneconomic, involving, for example, the elimination of a few offensive lines in the Argentine an-them, or support for the homeland during the Spanish-American War. Whenever pragmatic, material interests were at stake, groups that crossed national boundaries were formed. Thus, for instance, industrialists, agri-culturists, tenants, retail merchants, and workers formed associations that included various immigrant groups as well as Argentines in their member-ship. Moreover, the contemporary leftist dogma, especially that of social-ists and anarchists—the most widespread groups in Argentina—construed nationalism as a bourgeois farce. The working class had no nationality. These trends probably served to weaken the Old World national identities of some arrivals, or at least to create new ones based on class or sectorial interests that were related to the host society and thus served as an indi-rect vehicle for the Argentinization of the immigrant population and its descendants.

Overall, the second half of the nineteenth century witnessed a soften-ing of the Hispanophobia related to the independence struggle but a con-tinuation, accentuation, and emergence of other types. Popular resentment lost the zeal of the emancipation war but retained its more innocuous ex-pressions: petty jealousies, accusations of clannishness, offensive humor, and so forth. Indeed, deriding images and jokes about "dumb *gallegos*" seem to have increased as immigration became more massive, and thus more proletarian and peasant in nature, after the middle of the century. External influences continued and evolved as the dominant position of the French Enlightenment in Argentine intellectual circles was inherited by a more general Western liberalism and eventually positivism. Whereas the first movement stressed the obscurantism of Spain, the last two retained anticlericalism and added a whole array of political and economic charges. For the new generations of Argentine liberals, therefore, Spain came to in-carnate not just a land full of priests but, more importantly, social and material backwardness, and the Spanish heritage in their country became an impediment to modernization. Here too, local characteristics molded the interpretation of these general intellectual trends. The extreme underpopulation of the vast country and the increasing arrival of other groups turned the idea that the "stigma" of Hispanic culture could be eradicated through the civilizing influence of non-Iberian immigration into a leitmotif of Argentine anti-Spanish ideology. Northern Europeans could accomplish the task more rapidly and were preferred. But because relatively few northerners came, non-Iberian southerners would do. In his feud with the Spanish immigrant newspapers, Sarmiento delightedly recounted the story told to him by an Italian writer in Argentina of how Rossini loved Spain with a passion because it prevented Italy from being the very last nation of Europe.[43] But now, unlike the aftermath of independence, Spaniards responded to such slights, and even lesser ones, with increasing frequency and confidence. Indeed, the formation of an organized community willing and able to defend its reputation constituted one of the most noticeable changes of this period.

TWENTIETH-CENTURY HISPANISM

In their rivalry with Italians for the recognition and respect of the host society, Spaniards began to gain some ground from the last decades of the century on. By the late 1870s a few members of the Argentine elite were already becoming disenchanted with at least some of the Italian arrivals. One, in a doctoral thesis dated 1877 and directed by Vicente F. López, described those coming from the Mezzogiorno as "ignorant and indigent people used to living in the most complete indolence. To populate our country with such element is to push it backwards, to inject in its new body the degenerated blood of old, corroded societies."[44] However, at the time southerners made up less than one-quarter of the Italian inflow, and the author proposed not to bring Spaniards but, instead, northern Europeans.

Less than a decade later, however, proposals to replace Italians with Spaniards began to surface. In 1885 the Argentine consul general in Barcelona advocated issuing free passages to Spaniards, mentioning "the political convenience of populating the republic with people of our own race ... who could serve as a counterbalance to the influence of the Italian immigration that is becoming stronger by the day."[45] More surprisingly, the Argentine consul in Genoa, a gentleman who, with a surname like Calvari, could not easily hide his Italian ancestry, also mentioned, a year later,

"the necessity of equilibrating the nationalities . . . to avoid in time consequences that if not presenting the extremes of danger, could nevertheless
cause an unpleasant situation."[46] Three years later, in 1889, a commission to protect and foment Spanish immigration (La Sociedad Hispano-
Argentina Protectora de los Inmigrantes Españoles) was formed by members of the Spanish elite and upper-class Porteños, such as Eduardo Wilde,
Estanislao Zeballos, and Manuel Chueco.[47] That same year the Argentine
government subsidized 60,000 passages from Spain to counterbalance the
dangerous preponderance of Italians.[48] The "danger" was often associated
with criminality. The director of the 1887 municipal census found that, in
reality, Italians had one of the lowest rates of apprehension but tellingly
added, "despite the fact that among us they enjoy the worst reputation."[49]
Perceptions seem to have been more powerful than statistics.

As the twentieth century dawned, the trend became more apparent. In
a 1901 school paper, Roberto Bunge, the young heir of one of Argentina's
most prominent families, described Italian immigrants as "full of defects,
some of them capital. . . . The only benefit they bring are their hands, always disposed to the most injurious and servile labor." The Spanish immigrant was "immensely superior to the former; this is the superiority of
the free worker in relation to the servile worker."[50] And in a more "cul-
turalist" vein, one of Bunge's schoolmates depicted Italian arrivals as "illiterate peasant proletariats incapable of contributing to our culture" and
Spanish ones as "a powerful reinforcement to preserve the national spirit
in the face of the dissolving force of other foreign groups."[51]

Bunge's juvenile prejudices did not stop the arrival of 1,372,000 Italians
over the next quarter-century, leading an Argentine journalist to pen in
1924 an alarmist book suggestively titled *La italianización de la Argentina*, which he dedicated to Marcelo T. de Alvear, "President of the Nation, proud descendant of a noble Argentine lineage," with an inscription
that sounded like a call to action: "Carlyle and Cousin have demonstrated
that great men can swerve the course of events, steering the history of a
people."[52] After chastising those who opted for polite platitudes about ethnic fraternity instead of an honest confrontation of a national threat, and
the Argentine elite for "numbing themselves in the Epicureanism of a
Byzantine enrichment while the invasion weaves its snare in the shadows
and in silence," he went on to expose the perilous onslaught. The massive
arrival of crass Italians was obliterating the authentic ethnocultural character of the country, turning it into an amorphous, coarse, and soulless
horde rather than a nation. To sacrifice national identity on the altar of
material progress amounted to spiritual suicide. Only restrictive quotas on

Italian immigration, like those in the United States, could prevent this genocidal "new Conquest." But because the economy required a continual inflow of labor, the government should encourage in every possible way the coming of the old conquerors. Unlike the new invaders, the Spaniards could never harbor imperialist ambitions because "the identity of language, the analogy of feelings, the kinship of habits, the affinity of blood, the common memories . . . make them our brothers." In the "race war" that afflicted the country—the author proceeded—a continual flow of "Iberian blood" would assure its survival and the presence of "Mother Spain." Spaniards, after all, were not "a kindred race but our own race."

The emphasis on race and blood at times revealed a quasi-biological determinism associated with fin-de-siècle social Darwinist writings. In the first sentence of his appositely titled *En la sangre*, of 1887, Eugenio Cambaceres described the purposefully nameless Italian father of the main character in this naturalist novel as "big-headed, with flat features, a hooked nose, a protuberant lower lip; the crooked expression of his small sunken eyes betrayed a vulture's rapacity . . . his gait, the meekness of an ox." The lack of an appellative accentuated the Italian immigrants' condition as "an anonymous mass," a term popularized by another renowned Argentine social Darwinist of the period, the psychologist José María Ramos Mejía. The phenotypical traits conveyed—in the imagery of social Darwinist physiognomists—their social and moral inferiority and their primitive, animalistic nature. And the title underscored the inexorable, perpetual stigma of such inferiority, which the Argentine-born protagonist of the novel carried—despite his efforts to assimilate into the better classes—*In the Blood*.[53] Ramos Mejía himself used even more stereotypical social Darwinist signifiers of inferiority in his 1899 essay *Las multitudes argentinas* to describe Italian arrivals who "land on our shores amorphous and protoplasmatic," an evolutionary or, rather, "paleontological," stage that was: "I would say 'cellular,' in the sense of their complete remoteness from anything resembling progress in the mental organization. It is a slow brain, like that of the ox next to whom they have lived."[54] On the other hand, Ramos Mejía associated the higher elements of the Argentine population with the Spanish heritage; maintained that, unlike the plebe, they had harbored no anti-Spanish hatreds during the Wars of Independence; and defined the populace that supported Rosas and the caudillos as Indian and mestizo rather than Hispanic.[55]

The superiority of the Spanish "blood" and "race" also found less "scientific," but equally "anatomical," expressions in contemporary memoirs and novels. In his 1891 memoirs, raconteur Santiago Calzadilla remembered the beauty of the *"pur sang"* women of his young days, "products of the Spanish race without mixture of gringo or gringa [a term used mostly for Italian immigrants]," mixtures that had enlarged their derrières out of proportion.[56] A nostalgia shared by José Miró in his famous anti-Semitic novel, *La bolsa*, when he alluded to "the onslaught of cosmopolitanism [that] has deformed the Argentine woman, taking from her that vivacious Andalusian stamp that retained the precious heritage of the Spanish blood."[57]

Most Argentine intellectuals, however, found the "precious heritage" of Spain not "in the blood" or in the shape of the feminine figure but in the culture, or as it was often termed by the antipositivist generation forming after the turn of the century, in the "soul." These new groups perceived in social Darwinism part of the materialistic mentality they combatted. For them, blood and race became metaphors for "spiritual" rather than biological bonds, as when Joaquín V. González, the founder of the University of la Plata, enthused about "the salutation of the blood to the blood . . . the jubilant spiritual and emotional reconciliation of two people who once were one";[58] or when, in 1913, the litterateur Manuel Gálvez titled his panegyric to Spanish spirituality and summons to his compatriots to return to it, *El solar de la raza* (The Ancestral Home of Our Race).[59]

By the second decade of the twentieth century a majority of Argentine intellectuals had come to embrace this "unassailable faith in the existence of a transatlantic Hispanic family, community or 'raza'," a movement mostly known as Hispanism.[60] Indeed, by this time a list of the defenders of the country's Spanish legacy against corroding cosmopolitanism would have come close to a who's who of Argentine intellectuals: the abovementioned Manuel Gálvez and Joaquín V. González; Enrique Larreta, whose 1908 epic novel *La gloria de Don Ramiro*, and the neo-Hispanic architecture of his 1916 Buenos Aires mansion, glorified the spirit of Hapsburg Spain; Martín Noel, the designer of Larreta's mansion and best exponent of the architectural expression of Hispanism; Manuel Ugarte, the man of letters who penned innumerable ones advocating pan-Hispanism as an antidote for pan-Americanism, which he identified with Yankee domination;[61] Ricardo Rojas, the preeminent cultural nationalist of the period, who, like Gálvez and Ugarte, wrote an account of his pivotal intellectual pilgrimage to Spain;[62] Estanislao Zeballos—the older parliamentarian, university professor, former foreign minister, and member of the Spanish immigrants' Club Español—who in a 1912 speech asserted: "Only in Spain shall we find the roots of our civilization and the sources of our political, social, and economic progress";[63] Emilio Becher, who, despite his recent Swiss ancestry, urged his compatriots to reaffirm "the indestructible soul or our Hispanic ancestry";[64] and even the Russian-born novelist Alberto Gerchunoff, who fell into the Hispanophilia wave when, in his 1910 *Los gauchos judíos*, he insisted that the Jewish agricultural colonists had adapted to Argentina with so much love because, after centuries of separation, they were reuniting themselves with their Hispanic roots—a historically dubious argument, because most Jews in the country were, like Gerchunoff himself, Ashkenazim rather than Sephardim.[65]

Revising history indeed became part of the *hispanista* trend. The same sources used by previous generations of Clio's disciples to condemn Spanish colonialism were now mustered by Argentine historians, such as Roberto Levellier, Juan Carlos García Santillán, Rómulo Carvia, and José León Suárez, to whitewash the Black Legend.[66] León Suárez turned what used to be "the sacred war against the Spanish oppressors" into an expression of Hispanism in the appropriately titled *Carácter de la revolución americana: Un nuevo punto de vista mas verdadero y justo sobre la independencia hispano-americana* (Character of the American Revolution: A New, Truer, and More Just View of Spanish-American Independence [1916]); and wrote another book proposing that this "new, more accurate, and just" vision be taught in the public schools.[67] Another Buenos Aires University professor, José Antonio Amuchástegui, initiated a similar campaign "to revise the teaching of history in the country's public schools so as to stress that the essence of Argentine life and character came from Spain, not France, Italy, or England."[68] Historian J. Francisco V. Silva blamed a whole generation of Hispanophobic, Gallicized, and "Yankeecizing" liberal "pseudo-historians" for distorting the country's past. Argentina had never been a colony but simply part of the great Spanish Empire; its independence, no more than a civil war; and the philosophical sources of it not the Encyclopédie but Catholic Hispanism. It was after 1810 that it had become a dependency. Echoing nineteenth-century federalism and heralding 1930s "revisionists" and 1960s "dependentists," he condemned Buenos Aires' liberal bourgeoisie for turning the country into an economic colony of Britain and a cultural one of France.[69] The solution lay in halting the "de-Hispanization" of the country, returning to "the Castilian source," and forming a federation with Spain and the rest of the Spanish American republics to counteract Yankee imperialism.

Pro-Spanish historical revisionism was not monopolized by traditionalists. Some liberals also joined the trend. Arturo Capdevila reinvented Rivadavia—that same first liberal president who had wanted to erase the "stigma" of the Spanish legacy—into "el primer amigo de España"; "disproved" the influence of the French Enlightenment and English liberalism on Argentine independence; and reread the struggle against Spain as an expression of the purest Spanish liberalism, in his 1931 *Rivadavia y el españolismo liberal de la revolución argentina* (Rivadavia and the Liberal Hispanism of the Argentine Revolution). Even the inveterately Hispanophobic liberal, Sarmiento, was revamped as "a paradigm of the Spanish psychology" and a lover of Spain. If he did not express that affection clearly, it was due to the contagiousness of the anti-Spanish mania of his days,[70] or because he lacked the soul of an artist.[71]

With an irony that matched that of some of the revisionist works, Hispanophilia reached one of its high peaks during the celebration of the first centennial of independence from Spain in 1910. The visit of the Infanta Doña Isabela, aunt of King Alfonso XIII, turned into the biggest event of the celebration and a Porteño legend. According to contemporary accounts, the infanta outshone Halley's Comet. To the exasperation of an Italian republican, the city, dressed in the red and yellow of the Spanish flag, bowed to the sovereign majesty of the old infanta, a devout Catholic in whose honor the papal flag waved for five days from the tallest point of city hall.[72] In response to this and to the "insult" that the infanta rather than the Italian minister was seated next to the Argentine president, various Italian organizations boycotted the celebrations. Others grumbled about a "Bourbon reconquest." But to the 100,000 Spaniards who paraded along the sumptuous Avenida Alvear to welcome their infanta (among them the leaders of the Centro Republicano!), it was a sign that their time had come.[73]

By now, many Argentines perceived in this army not the enemies of the fatherland but the defenders of its revised and uplifted "Spanish legacy."[74] One, Blanca de los Ríos de Lamperez, proclaimed so in her *Afirmación de la raza ante el centenario de la independencia*.[75] Race had become such a code word in Hispanism that she did not have to specify which *raza*. Spain had in the centennial celebrations—she claimed—"the place of honor, the throne of veneration and respect that mothers deserve at the weddings of their offspring." That the centennial commemorated not a "wedding" but a "bloody divorce" was conveniently forgotten. Gálvez saw it as a turning point and dismissed the remaining "enemies of Spain" as anticlericals, mulattos ("whose hatred for Spain is the hatred of the black for the white"), and "the Italians and their children, who see in her a country rivaling theirs for predominance in Argentina."[76] To a degree, Spaniards had traveled a century-long journey in part of the Argentine collective imagination from enemies, to strangers, to cousins—and, for some, even "brothers."

THE RESPONSE AND ACTION OF THE SPANISH IMMIGRANTS, GOVERNMENT, AND INTELLECTUALS

As attitudes toward them turned less negative, Spaniards' responses became more positive and assertive. In 1900 some still bemoaned "the preponderance of the audacious Italians in Argentina, who double us in size and will not take long to annul us completely."[77] Ten years later they cockily described Argentina's centennial celebration of its independence from their country as "an affirmation of our community's hegemony among all others here resident" and published a book titled *Los españoles en el centenario argentino* to commemorate such ascendancy.[78] In the second half of the nineteenth century they had pleaded for the removal of the humbled Spanish lion from an Argentine national emblem and a few lines they considered offensive from the national anthem. Now, apparently unsatisfied with their success in the removal campaigns, they demanded additions: "Why not also fulfill the sublime idea of perpetuating in the national flag the glorious appellative of the Mother? It should suffice to insert in an angle of the sacred banner, with the best taste possible, a little Spanish flag in miniature."[79]

In the more receptive atmosphere, and aided by a flow of visiting Iberian luminaries around the centennial, the organized immigrant community boosted its efforts to promote Spanish culture in Argentina. With that purpose in mind, they founded, in 1912, the Institución Cultural Española, which affiliated 400 of the richest and most respected Spanish immigrants in Buenos Aires and a handful of Argentine Hispanophiles from even loftier backgrounds. Among other activities, the institution supported a program of academic and cultural exchanges between the two countries that brought to Argentina Spanish intellectuals of the caliber of Ortega y Gasset, Menéndez Pidal, Pérez Galdós, Américo Castro, Eugenio D'Ors, García Lorca, Manuel de Falla, and Nobel laureates Jacinto Benavente, Juan Ramón Jiménez, and Severo Ochoa. Other organizations mounted a campaign against the use of the term Latin America, in favor of Spanish America, perceiving in the former a plot by the Italian colony to take part of the credit for the glorious deeds of the Mother Country.[80] An article by Aurelio Espinosa, a Stanford University professor of Spanish descent, which attacked the use of "Latin" America because "it was Spain who gave her blood to these people, nourished them, and gave them their culture, not France or Italy," was translated, published in the immigrant press, and widely distributed as a pamphlet.[81] Other immigrant associations, like the Club Español and particularly the umbrella organization La Asociación Patriótica Española, subsidized and published works by sympathetic Argentine authors and mounted a campaign to pressure the Argentine government into declaring October 12 a national holiday in honor of Spain.[82]

The attitude of the Spanish government kept pace with the more assertive posture of its overseas subjects' organizations. After its defeat in the Spanish-American War, it showed a growing desire to make up for the loss of the Caribbean colonies by expanding its cultural, diplomatic, and commercial influence in the rest of Spanish America. Argentina, with the richest economy south of the Rio Grande and a Spanish-born population of close to 1 million by the 1920s, naturally attracted the most attention. Various institutions subsidized by the Crown organized a plethora of conferences and colloquia to bolster Hispano-Argentine cultural and trade ties; awarded prizes to books that extolled those ties; increased the quantity and—it was argued—the quality of consular and commercial agents; and granted official status and annuities to the chambers of commerce formed by immigrants in exchange for propaganda campaigns and exhibitions of Spanish products.[83] The Real Academia Española counteracted the attempts by some non-Hispanist nationalists to foster an independent "Argentine national language" with a growing effort to preserve the purity and unity of Castilian and, thus, the linguistic influence of Spain over its old colonies.[84] Language embodied for them a vital and intrinsic force that determined the way people viewed the world and "felt life," a "blood of the spirit," as Unamuno put it, that could preserve the oneness of the Hispanic *raza* even in places, like Argentina, where the physical blood was increasingly non-Hispanic.[85] Semiofficial periodicals appeared in the second decade of the twentieth century addressing the interests of the overseas communities and appealing to their loyalty with slogans such as:

> Spanish emigrants, never forget Spain, the land where you were born.
> Spanish emigrants, raise your children in the cult and love of Spain.
> Spaniards born outside of Spain, love Spain as you love your mother.
> Spanish emigrants, if you love Spain protect its industry by buying Spanish products.[86]

The efficacy of these appeals is difficult to gauge. But the efforts of the Spanish government to turn Hispanism from a cultural movement to a "practical" one by using the overseas communities as a market for its products could not overcome the relative industrial underdevelopment of the country. No matter how numerous and patriotic, there was a limit to how much olive oil and Rioja wine the emigrants could consume. It is true that by 1929 Spanish exports to Argentina doubled in value those to Cuba and equaled those to the rest of Spanish America (including Cuba). But their share of the Argentine market had not grown in the preceding two decades. They still amounted to less than one-tenth of the value of North American exports to Argentina, to less than one-seventh of Britain's, one-fourth of Germany's, one-third of Italy's, one-half of those from France and from Belgium, and they were even surpassed by Brazil's.[87] When it came to commercial influence, the mother country remained a distant relative.[88]

Non-economic Hispanism was not as impotent, and Spanish intellectuals residing in Argentina did much to help the cultural mission of their compatriots' associations and their government. The grammarian Ricardo Monner Sans, who arrived in Argentina in 1889 from his native Barcelona and lived there till his death in 1927, engaged in a lifelong campaign to preserve the purity of Castilian that preceded and complemented that of the Real Academia Española, to which he was admitted a year before his death.[89] He denounced the "anti-Spanish" attempts to declare Argentina's vernacular an independent national language and identified the popularity of lewd French novels and, above all, non-Iberian immigration as the major threats to the purity of Spanish in Argentina.[90] His voluminous Hispanist output included 128 publications, among them: *Dos madres* (1897), a lyric play exalting his dual but unified loyalties; *Mis dos banderas: Poema hispano-argentino* (1912), a poetic variant on the same theme; a book propounding Hispanism as an antidote for Yankee imperialism; another one attacking cosmopolitan materialism and extolling the intrinsic bond between the Castilian language and the Catholic faith; and two volumes advocating a Hispanic curriculum for the secondary schools of his adopted country.[91]

The equally prolific and better-known Basque writer José María Salaverría, who lived in Buenos Aires for three years around 1910, turned the Argentine national epic poem into an expression of the "deepest Hispanism" in his 1918 *El poema de la pampa: 'Martín Fierro' y el criollismo español*. The gaucho, who for the liberal Sarmiento had represented barbarism but had now been elevated by the nationalist Generation of 1910 into *the* national symbol, was—according to Salaverría—"nothing more than a Spaniard transplanted in the Argentine grasslands". Despite his mestizo ancestry, the gaucho embodied the "essence of the conquistadors," the

"Castilian vigor of the *raza*," and felt a virile disdain for non-Spanish servile and effeminate immigrants but a sense of kinship with those from Salaverría's own Basque birthplace.[92] The author also identified the *compadrito*—the "tough guy" of Porteño streets and the urban equivalent of the gaucho in Argentine cultural mythology—with a Spanish character, the *chulo madrileño*, but as a degenerate version because of the harmful and violent influence of southern Italian arrivals.[93] To counteract this influence and the Italianization of the country in general, he urged a forceful reaction from his nation and compatriots.[94]

Another famous Basque essayist, Ramiro de Maeztu, who served as Spain's ambassador to Argentina in the late 1920s, proved to be particularly influential by providing the most philosophical formulation of Hispanism. He titled his classic *Defensa de la Hispanidad* after a neologism coined by a Spanish priest in Buenos Aires to replace the common *raza* and stress the fact that Spanishness represented a spiritual and transatlantic, rather than biological or purely national, essence.[95] This essence was embodied in a humanism that was Spanish, Catholic, and transcendental rather than cosmopolitan, secular, and utilitarian. As such, it was antithetical to liberalism and its left-wing descendants now represented by Yankee and Soviet imperialism. Like other Hispanists, Maeztu depicted Argentine emancipation as "a civil war between Spaniards." But, unlike liberal Hispanists, he found its source not in Spanish liberalism but in the expulsion of the Jesuits by the "Gallicized" Bourbons. His ideal for the Iberian world's renovation indeed evoked pre-Enlightenment Hapsburg paternalism with its emphasis on a hierarchical system based on reciprocal obligations rather than on modern, impersonal, and competitive class relations.

As a contemporary model of this, Maeztu mentioned the commercial system of Spanish immigrants in the Americas, with its combination of "intimacy and hierarchy" that led to a "perfect compatibility of interests and spirit between the owner and his employees." The latter's loyalty emanated from their conviction that sacrifice was justly rewarded with advancement and eventual co- or full ownership. The principle behind it represented nothing more than a modern application of Hapsburg corporativism, of the old hierarchical guilds, and "the quintessence of our 'Siglo de Oro': the firm belief in the possibility (though not the assurance) of salvation for all men on earth."[96] This spiritual superiority explained why Spanish immigrant stores competed successfully with huge Yankee outfits that placed all their hopes in superior capital and wages.

Maeztu's influence on Argentine intellectuals preceded his diplomatic appointment, but during his tenure the Spanish Embassy became a hub for young, right-wing Argentine nationalists intent on ending the "moral corruption" of liberal democracy and replacing it with the Hispanic, Catholic, corporative regime advocated by their famous mentor. This may explain why writer Roberto Arlt, in his play *Severio el cruel,* and through the subterfuge of a mad character, imputed the 1930 coup d'état that ended seven decades of civilian government in Argentina to a fascist colonel and a "bunch of Spanish shopkeepers."[97]

Humbler immigrant "litterateurs" also joined the Hispanist crusade. The obscure poet(aster) V. Serrano Clavero recurred to the same blood and race metaphors, so (ab)used by his better known Spanish and Argentine "colleagues," to title his 1921 book of patriotic rhymes *Sangre y oro: Cancionero de la raza.* The equally unrenowned José Costa Figuera relied on a school tale rather than poetry in his semi-autobiographical novel *La sugestión de América* (1916). In one of its many Hispanist vignettes, Antonio, the Argentine-born son of the Spanish hero, comes home from school furious because the purposefully named "profesor Fianacca" had ordered him to take off from his lapel a pin bearing the Spanish flag: "I became blind with fury, Dad! . . . and told him that the legitimate Argentines were Spaniards, not Italians. I made him see that even he, when wanting to insult students like me, had to do it in our Castilian tongue" (p. 259). In grandiloquent phrases and from a position reminiscent of that of some of the Argentine revisionist historians mentioned before, the precocious child clamored, "Spaniards created Argentine independence. The founders of the republic were dissident Spaniards. They rebelled to make a better and freer Spain. Foreigners want to falsify that noble deed. . . . We have to force these imported cretins in America to respect Spain. . . . Viva España!" And when, a scene later, an Italian character tried to vindicate his language, the father of the young hero dismissed him with, "L'italiano, l'italiano! Bah! L'italiano is here the official language of street sweepers."

Spanish immigrant humanists also found inspiration in another muse and, like their Argentine counterparts, engaged with incremental fervor —and fancy—in the art of historical revisionism. Their glorification of Spain's colonizing genius dated back to the midnineteenth century and continued with volumes such as Salaverría's *Los conquistadores: El origen heroico de América* (1918). Their later attempts to turn Argentine independence into a Spanish saga also kept pace with works such as Monner Sans's *El movimiento de Mayo: Recuerdos históricos* (1920) and *Los catalanes en la Argentina* (1927).[98] But not content with these increasingly passé "scholarly challenges," they took on a more revisionist one. From the end of the nineteenth century, and recurrently in the first decade of the next, the immigrant press carried scores of articles claiming to prove that Columbus was Galician rather than Genoese. In 1914 a Spanish immigrant published a book with the unequivocal title *Colón español,* which provided "nineteen solid arguments" in favor of his thesis.[99] A year later Rafael Calzada, president of Buenos Aires' Club Español, devoted another 257 pages to prove the point.[100] The fights between Spanish and Italian immigrants over Columbus' nationality became a staple of Porteño comedies.[101] We do not know how many were convinced by the Spaniard's iconoclastic argument, but the copy of Calzada's book in the Biblioteca Nacional is dedicated to the highly influential Argentine lawyer Pastor S. Obligado, who belonged to the Spanish club presided over by Calzada. At any rate, the whole crusade for a Spanish Argentina achieved a symbolic triumph in 1917, when October 12 was declared a national holiday, not as Columbus Day but as El Día de la Raza (The Day of the [Hispanic] Race) in honor, according to the decree, of "Spain, mother of nations to whom she, with her brave blood and harmonious language, has given an immortal heritage."

What caused this dramatic transformation in Argentine attitudes toward the previously detested Spaniards and in the Spaniards' responses and actions? Again, the interaction of general Western intellectual trends and local conditions may provide the best answer.

SOURCES AND SHAPING FORCES OF HISPANISM

On a 1923 visit to Argentina, Colombian writer J. M. Vargas Vila claimed that "the Absolute Lack of Originality is the distinction of Buenos Aires, in every aspect, from its Writers . . . to its Revolutionaries, and even its Shoe shiners . . . nothing original, nothing new, nothing its own . . . all imported, all transported, all imitated . . . it's the Patria of Plagiarism."[102] Vargas Vila's exaggerated caricature holds partly true for Argentine Hispanism. Although it formed part of a traditionalist, nationalist, and often xenophobic movement that presented itself as a reaction against cosmopolitanism and foreign (non-Iberian) influences, it was actually—like other, similar movements in Latin America, including Vargas Vila's own country—cosmopolitan and European influenced. After all, the intellectual onslaught against European liberalism was a quintessentially European phenomenon that began and bloomed on the other side of the ocean. During the last decades of the nineteenth century and first few of the next, all sorts of reactionary and nostalgic currents denouncing bourgeois society, its putative individualism, soulless materialism, and vapid rationality, inundated the Old World: Schopenhauer's attacks on liberal reason and celebration of the will; Nietzsche's further exaltation of *The Will to Power* and his implicit racism; the explicit and equally antirationalist one of Chamberlain and Le Bon; the cultural nationalism of Herder and protofascist one of Maurras; the antimodern Christianity of Tolstoy and Menéndez Pelayo; the plays of Strindberg, music of Wagner, and paintings of Klimt; the existential preoccupation with the Spanish soul of the "Generation of '98."

By the end of the century the movement had spread to Latin America. In Nicaragua, Rubén Darío praised "the America that *prays* in Spanish" in his poem "To Roosevelt." Next door to Argentina, José Enrique Rodó, born in Uruguay to Spanish immigrant parents, exalted in his 1900 *Ariel* what positivists were still condemning: Spanish "spirituality," an aristocratic, elitist spirituality in opposition to what he termed the mediocrity of Anglo-Saxon utilitarian democracy. He later blamed non-Iberian immigration for producing a "zoocracy," which exposed the false positivist claim that a cosmopolitan society represented "progress."[103]

Argentine intellectuals drew abundantly from these sources. José María Ramos Mejía appealed to Le Bon's authority on the very first page of his *Las multitudes argentinas* (1899) and continued to do so throughout the work. Manuel Gálvez, the foremost Argentine Hispanophile, described himself at various times as a Tolstoyan and a Nietzschean; compared his crusade to "reclaim the spiritualization of national consciousness" to that championed in Spain by the Generation of '98 ("Ganivet, Macías Picavea, Costa, Unamuno, Pío Baroja, and others"); and was inspired by the antiliberal Catholic Hispanism of Menéndez Pelayo and Ramiro de Maeztu and by the non-Catholic, but equally antiliberal, nationalism of the French political thinker and Hispanist Maurice Barrès.[104] Ricardo Rojas, the founder of cultural nationalism, titled his 1916 book *La argentinidad* after a neologism coined by Unamuno, and in its first sentence thanked the "maestro's" approval plus that of Darío and Rodó.[105] In this and other works, Rojas examined his country's *Volksgeist*, Herder's term for the collective, spiritual force of the *Volk* and adopted the German thinker's concept of *Kulturauftrag*, which assigned to the *Volk* the cultural mission of preserving the national essence.[106] Manuel Ugarte's anti-Yankee Hispano-Americanism betrayed similar influences, and so did Enrique Larreta's literary Hispanism.[107] In general, the Argentine nationalist generation of the second and third decades of the twentieth century displayed in their reaction against positivism and the bourgeois materialist ethos the influence of a full range of similar European currents.

Argentina—as a country experiencing the disruptions of rapid modernization and a rash of immigrant radicalism, strikes, and urban problems—presented a perfect breeding ground for such an antimodernization trend. But the nature of the receiving ground rejected some of the imported seeds, accepted others, modified all, and thus defined the attributes of the resulting fruit.

The first generation to be affected by the European antiliberal reaction, late-nineteenth-century Argentine social Darwinists, among them the influential José María Ramos Mejía, adopted Gustave Le Bon's racism but discarded or ignored his antirationalism. Still imbued with the axioms of positivism, they had little use for the latter, but plenty of use for the former in their efforts to justify and bolster existing social inequalities. In addition, the utilization of Le Bon's doctrines and social Darwinism in general changed with time. Before the massive influx of overseas arrivals in the last quarter of the nineteenth century, they had been employed mostly—as continued to be the case in other Latin American countries with limited immigration—to condemn the "indolence" of the native mestizo masses. But as the Atlantic deluge turned the gauchos into a vanishing minority, social Darwinists and naturalist novelists turned their darts toward the masses of "uncouth" and "pushy" newcomers who, in a way reminiscent of Strindberg's *Miss Julie*, challenged the status of the well bred and refined, particularly those who did not enjoy the security of being in the upper crust. Not only did the target change, but so did the targeted sins. In an impressive volte-face that demonstrates the malleability of imported theories to local circumstances, some of the same people who had decried the lack of economic ambition of the "quixotic" gaucho now denounced the excessive materialistic drive of avaricious arrivals.

Although these charges were hurled against immigrants in general, two factors combined to make Italians the preferred targets: they formed the majority of newcomers (an annual average of 67 percent of the inflow) during the last two decades of the nineteenth century, when the influence of social Darwinism was at its peak; and denigrating them did not pose the potential incongruity that disparaging Spaniards while extolling the superiority of the Spanish-descended native "better classes" did. In this manner social Darwinists, despite the fact that they were not particularly pro-Hispanic, tended to uplift the status of Spanish immigrants by comparison and by default, rather than by design.

These contrasts with other immigrants partly account for some of the changes in attitudes toward Spaniards. Argentina's immigration does not exhibit the sharp division between an old flow from northwestern Europe and a new one after the 1880s from the southern and eastern regions of the Continent that characterizes immigration in the United States. The Italo-Hispanic combination consistently accounted for more than three-quarters of the influx. But behind this apparent continuity, some significant shifts took place. In the Hispanophobic decades following the mid-nineteenth century, besides Spaniards (who made up about a sixth of the stream), the other main immigrant groups were northern Italians, French, and in lesser numbers British and ethnic Germans. In the Hispanophilic second and third decades of the twentieth century, besides Spaniards (who now made up a third of the inflow), the other main groups were southern Italians, eastern European Jews, and Middle Easterners. Clearly, in the ethnic ranking of the Argentine—or for that matter the Western—upper classes, Spaniards compared more favorably with Sicilians, Calabrians, Russian and Polish Jews, and Syrio-Lebanese Muslims and Maronites than with Piedmontese, Ligurians, and northwestern Europeans. It was surely this ranking that led Argentine economist Alejandro Bunge to define in 1925 "the wave of immigration that began in the years before the War" as "of inferior quality to that of the preceding years."[108] The arrival of these "inferior and decaying refuses"—warned Bunge—"endangers the physical and moral conditions of our race . . . and our ethnic type." The same Spaniards who a quarter of a century before had been described by Alejandro's uncle Carlos Octavio as a "race suffering from a collective decadence and degeneration" now seemed to have been cured of that corroding disease by comparison with more "infested" new arrivals.[109] In a sense, the coming of more "exotic" and less "desirable" groups diminished the "otherness" of Spaniards.[110]

The beginning of "undesirable immigrations" in the early twentieth century coincided with a different sort of influence on Argentines' perceptions of Spaniards: the end of Spain's imperialist career. Before the Spanish-American War, the recurrent denunciations by Spanish immigrants of the Yankee menace had fallen mostly on deaf ears. In the memories of most Argentines, imperialism was still associated with their own struggle against the old metropolis. And Spain's continuing adventures, including its repression of Cuba's 1868–1878 revolt and military attacks on neighboring Chile and Peru in the 1860s, did little to put those memories to rest. By comparison, North American expansionism, restricted at the time to its own "backyard," seemed more removed and less threatening. Again, the dominant Western intellectual currents of the time affected these perceptions. To many of the ardent liberal republicans of the period, the U.S. despoilment of Mexico actually represented a dynamic expression of a young, progressive, and enterprising republic's vigor and a reaffirmation of the inferiority of Latin America's Spanish legacy. On the other hand, they detected in Spain's imperialist exploits the incarnation of reactionary forces, the brutish actions of an obscurantist and backward monarchy. The often fierce repression of the 1895 Cuban revolt, reported by the Buenos Aires press to the last gory detail, reinforced those perceptions. Porteño support for the Cuban revolutionaries ran high then, and so did, as previously mentioned, anti-Spanish hysteria. North American involvement, however, began to change some minds. The request to the Iberian Crown for permission to fight on their side by Argentina's great soldier-litterateur, General Lucio Mansilla, illustrates some of these changes: "So long as the Cubans sought their independence we, who had done the same at an earlier time, were with them. But what we cannot accept is that in order to achieve it they have enlisted against the Mother Country the help of a foreign nation that is dangerous both to them and to us.... We will not be able to do anything in our own home without asking permission of North America."[111]

Similar feelings were expressed in an open letter to the Buenos Aires newspaper *El Tiempo* by Professor Calixto Oyhuela, in which he claimed that for Argentines to take the side of the United States was to align themselves against the Hispanic *raza* and community. Others talked of a race war.[112] With the end of Spain's imperialist career and the expansion of that of the United States—which, in the early years of the twentieth century, augmented its previously nil political and economic involvement in Argentina—the immigrant colony's diatribes against *Yankeelandia* began to fall on more receptive ears.

The changed intellectual milieu of the turn of the century prevented Spain's defeat by the Colossus of the North from turning into another reaffirmation of Hispanic inferiority and Anglo-Saxon republican vigor, as had been the case with the Mexican defeat of 1847. The blind faith in liberalism and material progress of the midnineteenth century had given way in the interim to a more critical perception, if not to disillusionment. The United States' victory did not lead to a rash of eulogies for its liberal democracy and its mighty cannons and machinery. It engendered, instead, condemnations of its pedestrian materialism and grossly utilitarian democracy, and exaltations of Spanish dignity and spirituality—Rodó's 1900

Ariel being the best, but far from only, example.[113] The final collapse of Spain's colonial empire turned into a victory for Hispanism. With it, the Hispanophobia of the nineteenth century increasingly gave way to the Yankeephobia of the next, not only in Argentina but in most of Latin America.

Local conditions, however, again channeled the anti-Yankee and anti-positivist currents that flowed in the years following the Spanish-American War. In other Latin American countries of little immigration and strong aboriginal traditions, such as Mexico and Peru, they found expression in a nationalism that was more indigenist than Hispanic. Indeed, indigenism formed there in opposition not only to Europeanization but also to Hispanism, which was often perceived as equally foreign. In Argentina, on the other hand, the lack of a large Indian population and heritage, plus the massive presence of non-Iberian and increasingly "exotic" immigrants, made the Hispanic legacy of the country the closest thing to an autochthonous tradition. Some nationalists, like poet Leopoldo Lugones, did reject Hispanism and located the country's essence in the pampas and the gauchos (much as Turner did with the North American frontier). But if a native landscape combined with ancient aboriginal structures could provide a strong symbolic foundation for indigenism, as it did in, say, Mexico, a physical environment by itself was not likely to do so. Mexican muralists could turn Tenochtitlán on Lake Texcoco and the backdrop of Popocatépetl into a staple of indigenist iconography. Argentine nationalist painters, no matter how imaginative, could hardly do the same with the flat, empty pampas, and the shortcoming was not simply visual.

Gauchos did provide a stronger autochthonous national symbol, but by the second decade of the twentieth century, when cultural nationalism was taking off, they had become—unlike Mexican or Peruvian Indians—a vanishing species. Like their cousins in the American West, the few remaining ones were quickly turning from indomitable cowboys into sedentary cowhands, or as a sarcastic visitor put it, "a hybrid form of 'farmer,' vulgar, pedestrian, and sedentary."[114] The title of Ricardo Güiraldes' nostalgic *gauchesca* novel of 1926, *Don Segundo Sombra* (shadow), suggested this fading process. This by itself did not present a serious obstacle to their glorification. Indeed, it can be argued that it made it easier. Mexican indigenists, after all, found it easier to glamorize the long-gone Aztecs than the masses of poor and still exploited living Indians. But unlike the Indians of Mesoamerica and the Andean region, gauchos did not present a real or symbolic antithesis to Spanishness. Physically, this light mestizo group resembled more Andalusians than they did Araucanians. Culturally, they were never identified, by detractors and glorifiers alike, as communal and submissive—common perceived attributes of the indigenous peoples of the continental highlands. Their virtues were those of the conquistadors: courage, nobility, virility, and a proud and quixotic independence. Their faults were equally "Spanish": arrogance, disdain for manual labor, fierceness, and an archaic and exaggerated sense of honor. With this real or imaginary pedigree, their image could easily coexist with Hispanism or even be appropriated by Hispanophiles—as Salaverría did.

Most Argentine cultural nationalists, therefore, came to agree with historian José León Suárez that "to cultivate Hispanism in our country is the best way to foment Argentinism. . . . Nationalism without Hispanism in our countries of America is an absurdity."[115] Ricardo Rojas, one of the pioneers of the movement, acknowledged the Indian influence and that of the land in the formation of Argentine nationality in his pivotal *La restauración nacionalista* of 1909 and even christened his philosophy *indianismo* in his 1910 *Blasón de plata*. But clearly—though not always admittedly—he emphasized the Hispanic legacy. Tellingly, before he published these manifestos and the 1910 *La argentinidad*, he had written a book whose title alone dispelled any doubts about where the accent lay: *El alma española* (The Spanish Soul, 1908).[116] His extolling account of a 1908 trip to Spain, *Retablo español*, did likewise. Manuel Gálvez, the other "founding father" of cultural nationalism, was so Hispanist that in his *El solar de la raza* (1913) he felt compelled to explain why a nationalist book was so concerned with a foreign country. The paradox—he argued—was only apparent. The book was Argentine to the core precisely because it was so Spanish. To one degree or another, almost all of the nationalists of the first three decades of the twentieth century embraced Hispanism in their revolt against "soulless cosmopolitanism."

Argentina's immigration and the pace and level of its socioeconomic development also set the political tone of Hispanist nationalism. The large foreign presence made the nationalist reaction more xenophobic (as opposed to merely anti-imperialist) than in other Latin American countries. It also made it more right wing because anarchist immigrants had raised left-wing activism to levels unknown in the rest of the continent. Indeed, in most other Latin American countries nationalism not only failed during this time to take strong antiliberal tones but also tended to blend with leftist ideologies—the Mexican revolutionaries and the Peruvian José Carlos Mariátegui being some of the best exponents. In Argentina, nationalists perceived both the old liberal elite and the new immigrant labor activists as cosmopolitan, internationalist foes: the first willing to sacrifice the nation's cultural integrity and spiritual essence in the name of material progress; the second yearning to do so on the altar of godless and global anarchism and, later, communism.

The antimodernization reaction was stronger here precisely because modernization was more rapid and advanced. The process had turned Argentina into the richest country in the region and had spread those riches more widely than in any other place in Latin America with the possible exception of Uruguay—which in demographic and socioeconomic terms was little more than an eastern Argentine province. But along with the riches that immigrant labor made possible came all the problems and frictions inherent to a multi-ethnic, modern mass society. Nationalists acknowledged the accomplishments but concentrated on the problems. And the social mobility that modernization made possible exacerbated—at least in the eyes of the nationalists—those problems. The largest middle class in the region seemed the most pushy and disrespectful of traditional hierarchies, a horde of materialistic and unpatriotic parvenus who successfully competed with the better native classes precisely because they lacked moral scruples and spiritual concerns. The best-paid working class in the region seemed the most contentious, an even more threatening swarm of peddlers with an extreme capitalist ethos and of extremists intent on ending capitalism. The effects ranged from tenement strikes to general ones; from ethnic—and, with the increasing arrival of Jews and Muslims, religious—conflicts to a heightened sense of class struggle; from street beggars to immigrant professionals competing in the university and job market with the scions of déclassé, respectable old families. Not coincidentally, Hispanist cultural nationalism emerged in Buenos Aires, but many of its proponents were provincials from these types of families. Hispanism did more than provide protection from parvenus for the potentially déclassé. With its accent on the past, spiritual values, and an organic society, it came also to be seen by top political leaders as a bulwark against radical change.

Midnineteenth century liberals had dreamed about capitalist modernization. Now that it had come—not as a pure ideal but as a complex and messy reality—nationalists dreamed about an idealized precapitalist and premodern past; about a pastoral, patrician, and patriarchal Argentina where gauchos were loyal and servants knew their place, free of Russian anarchists, French pimps, and Neapolitan thieves. In this atmosphere, the

Spanishness that earlier liberals had wanted to eradicate as an impediment to progress became a nostalgic emblem of that idealized past. Under such circumstances, Hispanism—even if not intrinsically so—could not help becoming traditionalist.

Political trends on both sides of the Atlantic turned Hispanism farther to the right during and after the 1920s. In Argentina the cultural, literary nationalism of the prebellum period gave way to a more political and antiliberal (as opposed to simply antipositivist) force that led to the 1930 military coup d'état. In Spain the fascist regimes of Primo de Rivera, and later Franco, appropriated the cult of Hispanism, imparting to it a falangist tone and an element of cultural imperialism.[117] As these trends evolved and as the influence of Spanish falangism increased in Argentine nationalist circles, the image of Hispanism became increasingly more reactionary. This would pose a dilemma for the majority of Spanish immigrants, who did not perceive Hispanism as the militantly Catholic, corporativist, and antiliberal movement envisioned by right-wing Spaniards and Argentines.

During the course of the nineteenth century the general Western intellectual current had run from the Enlightenment to its maturation, liberalism, to its ossification, positivism, and finally to reaction. During roughly the same period, Argentine history had flowed from an emancipated nation struggling to maintain its newly acquired political independence, to youthful aspirations of progress and modernity, to the materialization of some of these aspirations, and, finally to the formation of a mass society and the conflicts and social problems that this entails. The interaction of these two currents had colored the attitude of the hosts—or at least of the hosts who had the means of expressing their views on paper—toward the Spaniards. In the eyes of many of them, the dominant picture of Spaniards shifted from that of enemies, to that of strangers, to that of children of the Mother Country. The response of the Spanish newcomers also evolved from passivity, to defense, to activism.

CONTINUITIES AND NEW DUALITIES

The road from enemy to stranger to cousin, and its counterpart in the newcomers' response shows only a trend, albeit a clear one. The relationships between Spaniards and their hosts maintained throughout the period a good deal of ambivalence and duality. At the height of Hispanophobia, during the Wars of Independence. there were always a few voices that stressed the fraternal linkages and the commonality of language and culture.[118] At the zenith of Hispanophilia, in the early twentieth century, there were many who still saw them as strangers, or worse.

Spaniards' status in the host society resulted from a complex interaction of changes and continuities in what they represented to Argentines and in how those representations were evaluated. In one of the combinations, the evaluation did not change but what Spaniards represented did. So, for example, anticlerical liberals of the twentieth century held Catholicism in the same negative light as their nineteenth-century counterparts had, but a few of them, imbued with the Hispanophilic atmosphere of their day, now represented the Mother Country not as a bastion of clericalism but as a cauldron of progressive forces. The basic combination included some variants. The new anticlerical liberals could continue to depict Spain as an obscurantist country but its people and emigrants as freethinking champions; or they could simply abstain from using them as representations of clericalism and pick on some other, less popular group, say, southern Italians or mestizos from Argentina's Andean provinces. Most Argentine anticlerical liberals, however, continued both to attack ultramontane Catholicism and to consider Spain as one of its principal exponents. As mentioned before, Manuel Gálvez identified anticlericals as one of the remaining Hispanophobic groups in the country. In this particular combination, neither what Spaniards represented nor the evaluation of it had changed.

What did change were the number and nature of the observers. In the 1910s and 1920s the relative—and maybe even absolute—number of anticlerical liberals among the Argentine intelligentsia paled by comparison with what it had been in the heyday of the nineteenth century. In addition, the still numerous—perhaps majority—liberals had either abandoned or considerably softened their previous anticlericalism. The attempts to secularize education, cemeteries, birth registries, and other vestiges of the Church's temporal powers had been largely accomplished by 1900. Spanish regimes had done likewise. This, plus its overall success and aging, had blunted the radical edge of liberalism. Most of its now moderate exponents simply left the old Hispanophobic harangues about obscurantist friars and nuns to the more iconoclastic freethinkers and anarchists. Many liberals, among them President Yrigoyen, shared the Krausism of their Spanish counterparts in their attempt to harmonize material development with natural religion.[119] Krausist or not, they applauded any sign of the Mother Country's scientific and material progress, such as Ramón y Cajal's 1906 Nobel Prize for medicine or the expansion of Catalan industry. Even those liberals who continued to regard France and England as their model, and who continued to consider Spain and its people as backward and listless, usually did so with more sympathy and less disdain than had their nineteenth-century coreligionists.

Although often hidden by florid rhetoric and semiotic duality, the most important combination involved a continuity in the perceived essence of Spaniards with changing assessments of that essence. In the European worldview, and largely due to its influence, in the Argentine, Spaniards had mostly represented all throughout the period the polarity—if not necessarily the opposition—of western European modernization and its attachments. As the evaluation of modernization changed, however, so did the description of this unchanging "essence." So, for example, accurately or not, both the anticlerical liberals of the nineteenth century and the nationalists of the next imaged Spaniards as preservers of a nonmodern, antisecular religiosity. But the first group termed them obscurantists and dogmatic and the second, spiritual and transcendental. Similarly, the representation of Spaniards as the antipode of capitalism and liberal tolerance continued, but the adjectives describing this trait tended to change from impractical to visionary, stubborn to tenacious, and vain to proud or even arrogant. These shifts in terminology, or in connotations, cloaked the high degree of substantive persistence. The more drastic change again resided in the number and nature of the observers. Nationalists made up an insignificant, and not particularly articulate, group in the decades following the fall of Rosas. But in the years following the 1910 centennial, they formed the most vibrant, vocal, and fastest-growing sector of the Argentine intelligentsia. In addition, not only had most embraced Hispanism, but also, in a not unrelated trend, a good number had rediscovered their Catholicism, at times with the fervor of militancy.

In addition to continuities from the past, attitudes toward Spaniards in the twentieth century evidenced new or transformed ambivalence and dualities. One lay in contrasting attitudes toward the abstract concept of Hispanism and Spanish immigration in general and toward actual Spanish immigrants. In a 1921 speech to the Institución Cultural Española of Buenos Aires, replete with acclamatory remarks about the "indelible bonds of language, blood, and religion of the Hispanic race," Argentine Hispanophile Joaquín González welcomed what he termed "the good emigration" but admonished the Mother Country for sending "what the English and Americans of the North call 'undesirable' immigration [which] alienates the sympathy and cooperation of receiving countries. It is not a good policy to get rid of those unwanted elements, under the pretext of contributing emigrants to the nations that welcome them; it is an injustice, an attempt against international conviviality, a useless or harmful burden that is dumped on a neighbor against all laws of hygiene and friendship."[120] Another Argentine nationalist, in a book titled *Nuestra raza* voiced the Hispanists' concern for the purity of the Castilian language but felt the mostly Galician, Basque, and Catalan immigrants were no more help than the Italians because most actually learned that language in Argentina.[121] A young lawyer, in his 1916 graduate thesis, did deem Spanish immigration the best medium for preserving Argentina's "homogeneity, character, and nobility" but found in the newcomers a critical defect: their tendency to concentrate in urban centers and unwillingness to settle on the pampas, where their "arms [were] needed."[122] Three years later another defender of the country's Hispanic heritage against soulless cosmopolitanism elaborated on the same point, describing those who stayed in the city as "the most fanatical champions of exaggerated demands for social improvements, the most frightening exemplars regarding subversion and violence."[123] And another Argentine nationalist disparaged not only their lack of agricultural aptitudes and radical leanings but also "the Spanish immigrant with certain education, professional training, and economic resources [because he] thinks he can impose himself on our society, is pretentious, and demands too many considerations."[124]

Spanish intellectuals residing in Argentina were themselves not exempt from these ambivalent attitudes. The champion of Hispanism José María Salaverría complained that "in Spain, it is an article of faith that rural laborers are the ones who should emigrate, and not middle-class youths, engineers, and capitalists."[125] This exodus saddled all Spaniards with a poor reputation in the host country, and unless Spain started sending more urban and educated immigrants, it would concede cultural hegemony in Argentina to other European countries. (Ironically, Italian intellectuals often expressed the same complaints about their own compatriots.[126])

A version of this duality took the form of what could be called a conquistador-versus-immigrant conceptual dichotomy. The same Salaverría who derided his immigrant compatriots wrote *Los conquistadores: El origen heroico de América* (1918), which, as the title indicates, lauded those earlier arrivals. This dichotomy appealed even more to Argentine nationalists because it glorified the nobility and legacy of their presumed ancestors but either ignored or disdained the larger mass of Spanish newcomers. In his 1910 *Blasón de plata*, subtitled "Meditations and Evocations of Ricardo Rojas on the Lineage of the Argentines," Rojas exalted the Spanish soul and lionized all sorts of conquistadors but wrote not a single line about any Spaniard who arrived during the national period—apparently they did not form part of the Argentine "lineage." His 1908 *El alma española* was dedicated not to the hundreds of thousands of Spaniards then landing in his country but "to the memory of the first conquistadors of America." Similarly, Enrique Larreta's 1908 masterpiece, *La gloria de Don Ramiro* and his 1934 play *Santa María del Buen Aire* glorified Hapsburg Spain and the spirit of the conquerors, not the modern immigrants. Indeed, even during a homage given to him by the immigrants' Club Español, Larreta devoted his speech to extolling not his hosts but Medieval Avila, "home of saints, knights and conquistadors."[127] None of the Argentine authors, as far as I know, reached the sophism of their next-door neighbor Nicolás Palacio, who, in a bizarre version of Le Bon's racial principles, argued in his 1904 *La raza chilena* that whereas the Chilean people were descendants of two advanced races—the tall, aboriginal Araucanians and the equally gigantic Visigoth conquistadors from northern Spain—-the newcomers were southern Spaniards of inferior Mediterranean stock. The twist of history had been as bizarre. For whatever it is worth, the conquistadors actually came from southern Spain and the immigrants, as we have seen, mostly from the northern seaboard.

Another related dual scheme—with its roots in Old World attitudes but magnified in the River Plate—rested on intra-Spanish divisions. Not all children of the Mother Country were alike. In the best tradition of dual Spain, Argentine litterateurs often divided Spaniards into Quixotes and Sancho Panzas, assigning the first role to Castilians and Basques. Larreta revered his "noble Basque ancestry" and found eternal Spain in the Castilian plateau, "where one is closer to God."[128] Gálvez detected in Castile the moral and spiritual heart of Spain and of his own country and found Basques, "the 'pioneers' of our grasslands," Castilian to the core.[129] The same traits that had made Basques unpopular among nineteenth-century liberals now turned them into the favorite ethnic group in nationalist circles. Their putative puritanical Catholicism, Carlist leanings, and opposition to secular political centralism matched the ultramontane and federalist proclivity of many Argentine nationalists.[130] Their tendency to engage in livestock raising and to settle in the pampas fit perfectly with a nostalgic, neoromantic, and antimodernist ideology that derided the materialistic cosmopolitan city and celebrated the traditions of the pastoral past. And the notions of Castilian nobility (*hidalguía*), mysticism, and austerity suited the nationalists' perennial denunciations of Anglo-Saxon utilitarianism and of the shallowness of French rationalist culture.

Other Iberian groups with less appropriate cultural "characters" came

to play the other persona of dual Spain, the Sancho Panza. The Andalusians' presumed gaiety, anticlericalism, political radicalism, and tendency to
engage in urban, mercantile occupations earned them few accolades from
Argentine traditionalists. Gálvez termed Andalusia "African Spain" and
found it far removed from the Argentine soul, which was quintessentially
Castilian.[131] Other Argentine writers, as discussed in chapter 5, often portrayed Andalusian immigrants as guitar-strumming, lazy, garrulous, or
even effeminate charlatans and as blasphemous anarchists. Catalans suffered from the opposite ailment. These "Spanish Jews" were too sober,
materialistic, and stingy; too close to the soulless utilitarianism that traditionalists decried.[132] But they shared one of the Andalusian defects: heavy
participation in the anarchist movement, of which Barcelona was then the
world capital. The Andalusian or Catalan anarchist became a stock character in Argentine theater.[133] Quantitative sources indicate they were as numerous in police archives. Of the 149 Spanish anarchists included in a
1902 file, a quarter were Andalusian, and more than half, Catalan.[134] During the labor riots and right-wing reaction of the Semana Trágica (Tragic
Week] of January 1919, Catalans became, along with Jews, the main targets of nativist vigilantes, who shortly afterward formed the first combat-
ively nationalist association in the country, the Liga Patriótica Argentina.[135] Clearly, not all the children of the Mother Country were perceived
by nationalists as preservers of Argentina's Hispanic soul.

Galicians, who accounted for more than half of the Spanish immigrants
in Buenos Aires, made an even better Sancho Panza because they did not
share the threatening traits of Andalusians and Catalans. Lacking the presumed nobility, gravity, and spirituality of Castilians and Basques, they
attracted little attention from the apostles of cultural nationalism. On
their pilgrimages to ancestral Spain, neither Gálvez nor Rojas, Ugarte, or
Larreta bothered to visit Galicia.[136] In contemporary literature, Galicians
normally appeared as hard working but dense. Indeed, as I have shown,
the term *gallego* often functioned as a synonym for dumb.[137] A particularly abundant character was that of the *gallego* servant. It surfaced in the
persona of "Ramona," a popular comic strip of the 1930s, in the first Argentine movies of Nini Marshall, such as *Cándida* (1937), in short stories
and novels, and in innumerable *sainetes* (the short, popular plays of the
day). Of the eighty-one plays that opened in Buenos Aires during the
1921 season, nineteen included at least one *gallego* servant in the plot.[138]
The stereotypical one was sometimes vivacious, most often dull, but almost always loyal, a loyalty which denied the social conflict that so dis-
tressed the upper and middle classes. Maximalism, anarchism, and other

undesirable "isms" could be discarded as alien diseases. The loyal *gallego* servant seemed to attest to the existence of a patriarchal Argentina where the master was paternal and the servant, filial.[139] All Galicians were offended by the "dumb" images, but some perspicacious ones also resented the praise about loyalty. When, in a speech to a Galician immigrant association, the Hispanophile Argentine historian José León Suárez praised their hard work, humbleness, loyalty, and constancy, most of the audience applauded. But an immigrant journalist interrupted the speech, observed that these were the same qualities normally used to describe asses, and went on to list, with sarcasm and a certain pride, all sorts of "less loyal" Galicians: sly bank robbers, cunning gangsters, and slippery outlaws who outwitted the Argentine police.[140]

Feuerbach's famous materialistic dictum, "Man ist was er isst" could have served as the basis of another, more mundane—and popular—version of the conquistador—immigrant dichotomy. The beef of the pampas, many claimed, had made natives superior to Spanish newcomers (and immigrants in general). The country's carnivorous diet was a sign of its richness for many Argentines, who proudly compared it with the "potatoes-and-garlic" fare of European peasant arrivals. "One is what one eats" had, thus, certain social implications. In a 1921 play, the Argentine-born children view the "stinking" Galician meals of their immigrant parents as evidence of their cultural crudeness.[141] In another play, *Mi Buenos Aires de ayer*, a streetwise Porteña mockingly describes the pedigree of a recent Spanish arrival as "three generations of Galician tuna pies."

The reference to generations betrayed a related popular view, or better, a popular version of an elite concept. The first decades of the twentieth century witnessed an obsession with genealogy on the part of the upper classes. Books on surnames and their presumed noble origins appeared by the dozen, and the idealization of old, traditional family names took a leap. Surely this functioned as a mechanism to prevent "pushy" and materially successful foreigners from entering the world of the native elite. It was also, perhaps, a sign of the maturation (or decadence?) of a class that had achieved present power and now sought past glories. Whatever the case, the idea that one's social standing could be partially measured by the number of generations in the land easily took root in an immigrant society and, often translated into years rather than generations, found expression in an old-timers–greenhorn dichotomy.

The gap appeared particularly wide between the second generation, or those who had come when they were very young, and the recent arrivals. The native popular classes of Buenos Aires in, say, 1850, had been born in an unimpressive midsized town and were to a significant degree a mestizo people disdained by the white elites and even by some of the poorer arrivals. Their counterparts in the early twentieth century, on the other hand, had been born in a grand metropolis (the second largest on the Atlantic seaboard) and were as European looking as the arrivals. They were also better fed, usually taller, definitely "better" dressed, more literate, familiar with urban ways, and natives of a young country that still brimmed with pride about its present and sanguinity about its future. Not surprisingly, these new, urban Creoles were going to have a hard time perceiving the peasant arrivals as carriers of superior European culture. By the early decades of the century, there was little question in the popular mind as to which formed the top half in the native–immigrant or old-timer–greenhorn dichotomy. Only urban, middle-class newcomers could be part of the top half from the time of their arrival. The rest, the Spanish *labradores* and the Italian *contadini* who arrived en masse in the decade prior to and after World War I, became the *gaitas* and *yoyegas* (slurs for the former), and the *tanos*, *nápoles*, and *bachichas* (slurs for the latter), of Buenos Aires' ethnic world and nomenclature.

Postbellum popular theater offers a window into this world and evidence of the low status of newcomers on its prestige scale.[142] Professional and white-collar positions, "education," bourgeois manners, and other indications of upper- and middle-class sociocultural—as opposed to purely economic—status were clearly identified in the plays—and likely in the popular mind—with the Argentine born or raised. Only in 3 of the 308 dramas and comedies that opened in Buenos Aires between 1919 and 1922, were recent arrivals portrayed as refined and classy leading characters.[143] Many, on the other hand, referred to the embarrassment that Argentine-born children felt for the coarse manners of their Italian, Spanish, or Russian parents, whether poor or nouveau riche—an observation often found also in travelers' accounts.[144] Some of the plays actually characterized the new generation as spoiled brats, unappreciative of their parents' honest hard work and sacrifice. But these sympathetic portrayals actually make the plays a more credible representation of social reality. They indicate that the authors were less motivated by xenophobia than by a desire to use a common situation with which the public could easily identify. This situation may explain the assertion of writer Raúl Scalabrini Ortíz that "paternal authority is a myth in Buenos Aires when the parent is European. The one who exercises real authority and tutelage is the son";[145] or the more drastic grievance of a Spanish immigrant, that "the Argentine children of immigrated Spaniards brag about their contempt for

Spain. Their first hatred is their own father, whose humble past they know; their contempt for Spain is a prolongation of this hatred, fertilized with the anti-Spanish education they receive in school."[146]

The children of the immigrants were probably less affected by school propaganda than by their desire to identify with local adolescent subculture. But what in more culturally homogeneous, nonimmigrant societies expresses itself simply as juvenile rebelliousness here also took the form of rejection of Old World habits. In one of the plays the children are ashamed when their Galician parents talk in "that ugly language that here only porters and domestics speak" and compel them to have their Galician music parties in the back room, so that neighbors would think the parties were the servants' rather than the family's.[147] The younger generation wanted to dance not to the tunes of Old World tarantelas and fandangos but to the beat of the trendy tango. In another *sainete,* a young *gallego* taking a few awkward tango steps responds to a surprised older relative: "Esto es criollada pura. . . . Vos eres gaita. . . . No te has enterao [This is pure, native dynamite. . . . You are a *gallego* greenhorn. . . . You don't get it]."[148] His language alone—Argentine slang as imperfectly awkward as his tango steps—was revealing. In many of the plays, youngsters disdained the *cocoliche* (a mocking term for the broken Spanish of Italian immigrants) or the heavily Galician or Yiddish accented speech of their parents. They wanted to use—depending on their age and social aspirations—either properly bourgeois Spanish or *el habla criolla* the "cool," streetwise, Lunfardo-peppered lingo of the *compadritos,* those tough but suave dandies of Buenos Aires' barrios. To make it even more unintelligible to the uninitiated mass of newcomers, they freely employed the Lunfardo habit of inverting syllables. So Spaniards, whom Argentines had long ago turned—with intentional malice—into *gallegos* and, later, *gaitas* (bagpipes, a traditional Galician instrument), now became *tagais.*

Because of their "clumsy" speech, music, dress, habits, and dull image, *tagais* and other greenhorns lacked perhaps the most esteemed attribute in adolescent subculture: sexual appeal. The failed efforts of immigrant parents to keep their daughters away from native-born dandies and marry them to older countrymen formed a staple of Argentine humor and theater. Some *gaitas* and *tanos* did try to imitate the mannerisms of the *compadritos.* But their mimicked tango steps and tough walk came out clumsy rather than "cool." Their Lunfardo betrayed awkward accents. They could not contain "uncool" romantic insecurities or their petty-merchant instinct; as a *sainete* character claimed, "An Italian who's not jealous is like a Jew who doesn't know how to multiply."[149] In another play, a young *ga-*

llega leaves her virtuous but jealous and timorous countryman for a racy but sweet-talking *compadrito*. The *gaita otario* (Galician fool) did not know "how to talk backwards like a good Creole," lacked class, did not make her shiver and feel "nasty," and had no hopes of doing so, as she told him in faulty Lunfardo:

> Tu no puedes ¡jaita misio!
> Hay que saber, pues es fama
> que la vida del cafísio
> nunca se aprende; se mama.[150]

> You cannot, poor Galician devil!
> One has to know, 'cause it's clear
> that the life of a tough lover
> it's never learned; it's sucked.

Compadritos could "suckle" their sensual allure from mothers of any ethnic background, and did not have to be born in the new country. But such appeal required intimacy with the adolescent subculture of Buenos Aires' barrios, familiarity with its quirks and codes, and it was denied to gringos and *gaitas* fresh off the boat.

Clearly, the Hispanist discourse of Argentine nationalist literati did not always make it down to Buenos Aires' barrios. There, Spanishness was less associated with Don Quixote, Loyola, El Cid, and other icons of Iberian spirituality and nobility than with the "backward" habits of *gallego* neighbors. As a Spanish immigrant complained:

> Argentines know full well that in Spain there are Castilians, Catalans, Andalusians, etc. But they intentionally and maliciously make *gallegos* of us all. The name itself is not injurious, as the Argentines would desire. But the malicious intention and incessant repetition are. And so we won't have a shadow of a doubt about their intention, when they call us *gayegos* (they don't even call us *gallegos* [a reference to Argentines' use of the *y* sound in place of the Castilian *ll*]), they often append the alias with another qualifier to fully express all the hatred and disdain they have for us. Sometimes we are called *gayegos patas sucias* (filthy-footed Galicians) and others, "shitty *gayegos*."[151]

He went on to blame his own rural compatriots, "who had come to know shoes, socks, and shirts in Argentina," for such perceptions. Buenos Aires, which they could only compare with their own villages, awed them. Their acknowledgment that "Spain (which was always their hamlet) lacked cities, comforts, and riches, provided Argentines with plenty of merriment."[152] Whether this immigrant's complaints were exaggerated or not, it is clear that by the 1920s most people in Buenos Aires, locals and newcomers alike, considered its urban culture more modern, prestigious, and praiseworthy than the "rustic" ways of newcomers from Spanish *aldeas,* Italian *communi,* and eastern European *shtetlach.*

Many immigrants responded with loud claims about their own culture's superiority. The above writer argued that if Spaniards were "shitty *gayegos,*" Argentines, as their descendants, were "shit of *gayegos.*"[153] Others scorned everything about their hosts, from their "corrupt politics" and socioeconomic "backwardness" to their "immorality" and "anti-aesthetic capital." In the mouths of some of the newcomers from urban middle-class background or from "advanced" countries, such assertions carried the pedantic tone of real conceit. But on the lips of the majority the claims often sounded like those of contemporary Italian, Polish, or other discriminated immigrants in the United States: not like arrogant or even confident assertions of superiority but like defensive reactions in the face of constant derision by the dominant culture and, at times, their own children. They echoed—to use an inapplicable but illustrative comparison —not the hubris of colonizers but the self-doubt of the colonized. Such hubris had been possible—except vis-à-vis the elite—in the nineteenth century, when the country was still an undeveloped backwater, the city an overgrown village, and the immigrants "the carriers of progress" in the hegemonic discourse. But it rang hollow in the 1920s, when the country was the eighth richest in the world, the capital a metropolis larger than Rome or Madrid, its inhabitants richer and more literate, and the newcomers little more than *brazos* in the eyes of the now "civilized" Porteños.

THE IMPACT OF HISPANISM ON SPANISH IMMIGRANTS' ADAPTATION AND ASSIMILATION

It is in such a context of existential experiences and everyday barrio life, rather than simply in the writings of cultural nationalists and revisionist historians, that the meaning of Hispanism for the mass of Spanish immigrants can be understood. To begin with, this intellectual trend had limited impact on the demographic, socioeconomic, geographical, and organizational aspects of immigration and adaptation examined in the previous six chapters. In this regard, Spaniards behaved not like cousins, not like strangers, but like immigrants. Indeed, in some respects, the patterns of their emigration resembled less those of other ex-colonizers, like the French in Quebec or the English in the United States, than those of other southern and eastern European groups, like the Italians in Buenos Aires or the Poles in Chicago. Like the latter, their exodus peaked in the early twentieth century, not because of Hispanism but because of the interaction of the forces analyzed in the first three chapters of this book. Their settlement in the host city, choices of employment, and organizational structure similarly obeyed the forces examined in the previous three chapters rather than intellectual or literary trends.

In addition, Hispanism, as an intellectual trend, meant a different thing to the mass of Spanish arrivals than it did to the Argentine nationalist intelligentsia, to the Spanish government, and even to the Spanish immigrant leadership. In the hands of Argentine nationalists—even semiliberal ones—Hispanism acquired a basically conservative, and often reactionary, texture. Neoromantic thinkers would use it to condemn what they perceived as a positivist, materialistic, and cosmopolitan milieu and call for *Kulturauftrag*, a nationalist spiritual revival. The established elite would find in it a useful idea to stress tradition and social harmony, to glorify its past, to bolster a hierarchical society, and to preserve the old status quo. The less secure gentry would wield it to differentiate itself from pecuniarily successful *nouveau arrivés*. For the Spanish government it entailed a way to expand its influence in the old colonies and to counteract that of the Colossus of the North. Some hoped it would grow into a pragmatic movement and increase exports and commercial influence. Others, in an ironic sense more pragmatic, seemed content with stressing the cultural bonds of the transatlantic Hispanic *raza* and with the vicariousness of "spiritual" imperialism, as its more tangible, economic variety continued to be a basically Anglo or Yankee affair. For the Spanish immigrant leadership, Hispanism provided a medium for heightening its prestige, stressing social harmony and unity in the immigrant community, and controlling the "disassociative" forces of regionalism, ethnonationalism, and class ideologies. Obviously, for the nonelite immigrant masses Hispanism could not represent a tool of social control. For them it represented a means of upholding their self-esteem in a society that often scoffed them. It played a role similar to that of fascism in the Little Italies of North America. It was an amalgam of vague and often contradictory ideas that, nevertheless, influenced their collective identity and sustained a sense of self-dignity.

In this function Hispanism, despite its basic conservatism, did not represent for Spanish immigrants a concept incompatible with ideologies of change. The nature of the existing historiography hinders an assessment of the degree to which this was true. The numerous studies of the anarchist movement in Argentina emphasize the role of foreign-born workers in it, yet none presents any solid data on the nationality of these workers.

Table 51   Relative participation of Spaniards and other nativity groups in Buenos Aires' anarchist movement, 1902

	A	B	C	D
			Each group as a percentage	Degree of over- or
			of all males aged 20 to 49	underrepresentation in the anarchist
Nativity group	Number listed in a 1902 police file	Percentage of total listed in the file	in the city[a]	movement of each group (B/C)
Spaniards	149	22.5	18.5	1.22
Italians	389	58.8	38.3	1.53
French	21	3.2	3.3	0.96
Argentines	87	13.2	31.4	0.42
Other foreigners	15	2.3	8.5	0.27
Total	661	100.0	100.0	

SOURCES: For column A, Archivo de la Policía, Buenos Aires, "División Investigación Orden Social, Antecedentes de Anarquistas, 1902, No. 1" (a file of 661 suspected anarchists in the city). For column C, Buenos Aires, Dirección General de Estadística Municipal, Censo general de población, edificación, comercio e industrias de la ciudad de Buenos Aires, 1904 (Buenos Aires: Compañía Sud-Americana de Billetes de Banco, 1906), 30–54. Columns B and D are computed from data in columns A and C.

[a]I used males aged 20 to 49 to measure degree of representation because all but three of the individuals in the file were male and all but twenty-four were between those ages. Using the general population would have exaggerated the participation of foreigners. Spaniards, for instance, accounted for 10 percent of the city's total inhabitants, and their degree of overrepresentation would thus have appeared as 2.3, almost double the more accurate 1.22.

Table 52   Comparative enrollment of Spanish and Italian immigrants in La Fraternidad, the Argentine socialist railroad-workers' union, 1904 and 1914–1916

	(A)	(B)	(C)	(D)	(E)	(F)
Spaniards	71			150		
Italians	179			105		
Ratio		40	41		143	82

SOURCES: For union members, application forms for La Fraternidad; for the male population, Argentina, Comisión Directiva del Censo, *Segundo censo de la República Argentina, 1895*, 3 vols. (Buenos Aires: Taller Tip. de la Penitenciaria Nacional, 1898), and Argentina, Comisión Nacional del Censo, *Tercer censo nacional, 1914*, 10 vols. (Buenos Aires: Talleres Gráficos de L. J. Russo, 1916–1919).

NOTE: Column headings are as follows: (A) Numbers enrolled in 1904; (B) Spanish-to-Italian ratio among union members; (C) Spanish-to-Italian ratio in the male population of Argentina in 1895 census; (D) Numbers enrolled in 1914–1916; (E) Spanish-to-Italian ratio among union members; (F) Spanish-to-Italian ratio in the male population of Argentina in 1914.

The Spanish and Italian male populations of Argentina as a whole were used to compare enrollment in unions because members joined all over the country, not just in the capital.

Data from a 1902 file of 661 suspected anarchists that I was able to locate in Buenos Aires' police archives, however, indicate that Spaniards' participation in this movement was not random. Even after controlling for possible gender and age distortions, they emerge—along with the Italians—as the only nativity groups overrepresented in the file (see Table 51). Moreover, various of the suspects also appear in the lists I compiled from membership records of Spanish immigrant associations. For them, anarchism and patriotism did not seem incompatible.

A similar historiographical situation exists in regard to labor unions: many publications but few data on the particular nationality of the joiners. By mere coincidence (I happened to stay in their hotel for a few days and casually asked the main clerk there), I located the manuscript enrollment forms of La Fraternidad, the socialist railroad workers' union. This is only one labor union, and it may or may not be representative of other unions. But the data offer a measurable indication of Spaniard's relative participation in a socialist association, the other important working-class movement in the country. Using the other main immigrant group in Argentina as a point of comparison, Table 52 shows that the Spanish–Italian ratio among those who joined in 1904 was 40. That is, there were 40 of the former for every 100 of the latter. The Spanish male–Italian male ratio in Argentina in 1895 (the closest national census to 1904) was 41, which means that the relative participation of the two groups in the union was about the same. By 1914 both the Spanish population and Hispanism had risen. In that year there were 82 Spanish males for every 100 Italian males in the country. But among the union members who joined in the 1914–1916 period, there were 143 Spaniards for every 100 Italians. In other words, the relative participation of Spaniards in this union equaled that of Italians in 1904 but surpassed it in 1914–1916, precisely at the time when the expansion of the conservative concept of Hispanism was reaching a peak.

Clearly then, Hispanism did not prevent Spanish immigrants from engaging in anarchist and socialist activities. What in the discourse of Argentine intellectuals was a traditionalist concept, the arriving masses did not perceive as antithetical to ideologies of change. In Spain, internationalist convictions and nationalist loyalties rarely coexisted. In the new country, a multi-ethnic milieu where one's nationality stood out in contrast to others' and competed with them, they often did. Novelist Luis Pascarella described this duality in the character of an Andalusian anarchist: "Neither country nor religion, he repeated with a sententious tone, and got excited to the point of frenzied tears when anyone dared to question the military power of Spain, thundering against 'swines' who with no right meddled in Spanish things."[154] Anarchism articulated the immigrants' class interests and longings. Hispanism voiced their national pride and served to uphold it in the face of derision by competing ethnic groups. Contradictory or not, their personalities as children of the Mother Country and workers led not to schizophrenia but to synthesis. Like most of us, they had many personalities out of which each individual managed, more or less successfully, to construct one person.

In the end, Hispanism probably retarded the Spanish immigrants' Argentinization, or at least gave it a form different from that of the Italians. Because the immigration of the latter had reached massive dimensions somewhat earlier than the former's, by the first decade of the twentieth century they outnumbered Spaniards among old-timers and Argentines of Italian immigrant stock outnumbered those of recent Spanish immigrant stock among natives. In their competition for recognition and prestige, the children of the Adriatic peninsula would thus often portray themselves as the top half of the old-timer–greenhorn and native–immigrant dichotomies; the true Porteños as opposed to the un-Argentine *gallego* arrivals, who of course were also the old enemies of "our fatherland." Some of the

Spaniards who had lived in the city for a long time naturally vied for those positions. But, by glorifying the Spanish legacy of Argentina and fomenting national pride among the Spaniards, Hispanism offered an alternative claim to others, particularly to newcomers. They did not have to portray themselves—went the argument—as the "true" Argentines because they were the progenitors of the country, the endowers of its language and its culture, the source of what was best in it. The Hispanophilic discourse of Argentine cultural nationalists, constantly repeated in the immigrant press and often out of context for hyperbolic effect, convinced many of the newcomers that more than cousins, or even brothers, they were now founding fathers.

Immigrant perceptions attest to these differing assimilation strategies. An old *gallega* immigrant distrusted Argentines because they all seemed to have Italian parents.[155] In more colorful language, another one termed them *pichones de italianos* (Italians' baby pigeons). A Spanish writer felt that his compatriots' pride, obstinacy, and integrity clashed with similar traits among Hispano-Creoles and prevented them from assimilating to the new country as rapidly as the pliant Italians, with their "crafty undulating psychology," and the "oily and servile shrewdness of their race."[156] The danger lay in that as they Argentinized themselves they also Italianized Argentina. No wonder that the tango—a music he claimed de-Hispanized the country—was "almost always sung by voices of Italian extraction."[157] Another Spanish immigrant complained, in verse, about the Italian linguistic and culinary influence:

> Del italiano no hablemos
> pues no hay dialecto italiano
> que en la Argentina ignoremos;
> se barre en napolitano
> y en siciliano bebemos.
> Va la lengua castellana
> tan mezclada a la italiana,
> que grandes y chiquitines
> · parecemos Cherubines,
> de el dúo de La Africana,
> pues decimos "ma" por pero,
> *farabuti* (hombre grocero),
> y en las fondas y figones
> remplazan los macarrones
> al archiespañol puchero.[158]

> Of Italian let's not talk,
> for there is no Italian dialect
> unknown to us in Argentina.

Sweeping is done in Neapolitan,
and drinking in Sicilian.
The Castilian language goes
so mixed with the Italian
that old and young alike
sound like Cherubim
from the duet of L'Africaine,
for we say "ma" for but,
farabuti (vulgar man),
and in the inns and taverns
the macaroni replaces
the arch-Spanish stew.

On the other hand, Italians, in a different tone but a similar argument, liked to portray Spaniards as inflexible and inept at assimilating and to stress the persistence of old animosities with Argentines from the independence struggles. One wrote: "The Italians are the ones who more easily familiarize themselves with the Argentines. The Spanish, on the contrary, prefer to keep to themselves. In Buenos Aires in particular, there are numerous cafés frequented exclusively by them."[159] He attributed that segregation to the Argentines' perception of the them as the descendants of the old enemies of their country. In language reminiscent of Hispanism, but with an Adriatic twist, an Italo-Argentine claimed in his Buenos Aires law-school dissertation that "the state should foster the immigration of those people who belong to our race and resemble us in religion, language, and character. None fit these qualities better than Italians."[160] And a recent Argentine scholar agreed that "the Italian 'Argentinized' himself more agreeably than the Spaniard did."[161]

Popular theater stereotypes, residential segregation, and marriage patterns point in the same direction. The figure of the "Creolized Italian" (*italiano acriollado*) permeated the Porteño thespian scene. He imitated and adopted the speech, habits, and mannerisms of Porteño popular culture more frequently and with more enthusiasm than did any of the other immigrants portrayed in the plays. As shown in chapter 4, throughout the period Spaniards consistently exhibited higher rates of residential segregation than did Italians. Moreover, the gap in the segregation indexes of the two groups was particularly wide in relation to the native population. Since the late nineteenth century the endogamy rates of both Spanish males and females have surpassed those of their Italian counterparts.[162] Finally, as I demonstrated in chapter 6, regionalism among the Spaniards had often an ideological, ethnonationalist dimension absent from the Italian variety, which elicited stronger loyalties, loyalties that served as a bulwark against Argentinization. By themselves, none of these indicators is conclusive. But all together, they forcefully suggest that the "children of the Mother Country" actually assimilated to the new land more slowly and more reluctantly than did the "alien" Italians whose "foreignness" Argentine cultural nationalists so often attacked. In the process, both had transformed the country to which they were assimilating.

Whether a defined Argentine national culture had developed by the 1920s or not—as most contemporaries lamented—remains unclear. What does seem clear is that, unless the imagination of scores of not particularly imaginative playwrights was so lush that they could invent a vivid reality ex nihilo, a Porteño culture had. It was not the Parisian milieu that some cosmopolitan liberals still dreamed of—although in part it echoed it. It was not the Adriatic colony the Italian government had once envisioned—although, as the joke went, Argentines became "Italians who speak Spanish and think they are British." It was not "Madrid," as Spanish immigrants, most of whom had never been there, insisted—although it had much of it. Nor was it the traditional Hispano-Creole culture that nostalgic nationalists wanted to revive—although it retained much of that heritage. It may have been—as visiting Colombian writer Vargas Vila put it—the "Patria del Plagiarismo." But perhaps Vargas Vila never saw a sainete, met a compadrito or heard a tango. By the 1920s Buenos Aires' eclectic atmosphere had definitely produced one of the most distinct and vibrant urban cultures in the world. And the Porteños' perpetual complaints (or boasts) about their lack of an autochthonous culture became itself an idiosyncratic mark of it.

Spanish immigrants in their many personalities had helped to shape that culture and were shaped by it. As immigrants (the subject of chapters 4–6) they went about finding housing, jobs, ways of improving their material conditions and forming ethnic and working-class associations. In the process, by mere numbers, labor, and enterprise, they helped transform Buenos Aires into a grand metropolis and Argentina into a mass society. As children of the Mother Country, sometimes by their mere presence and at other times by design, they proved instrumental in preserving the Hispanic inheritance of the country and thus set a perimeter to its cultural metamorphosis. But more than preserving the idealized, static, and archaic Castilian heritage envisioned by many Argentine Hispanists, they delivered a vital and varied Iberian smorgasbord that included anything from Galician dishes and idioms to Catalan anarchism and accents. Nevertheless, and not without irony, their presence probably allayed the Creole elite's growing fear of cultural genocide, giving this ruling group enough confidence in the survival of Argentina's "Hispanic heritage" to permit immigration to continue and, thus, the transformation of the country to proceed.

Eventually, Spaniards ended up eating the macaroni they once feared would supplant the "arch-Spanish *puchero*," speaking the "bastardized and Italianized" tongue they had railed against, and mixing with the "imported foreigners" who had "threatened Argentina's Spanish character." But the other "imported" ones and their descendants ended up eating *pucheros*, speaking "the noble Castilian language," and playing Basque handball. In retrospect, the clashes between *gaitas*, gringos, and Creoles seem to have manifested both the impossibility of frictionless ethnic relations and the possibility of ethnic coexistence. Indeed, in a world beset with ethnic genocide, they appear as examples of realistic—rather than romanticized—ethnic pluralism and conviviality.

Conclusion

Elisa Carmen María Sánchez, a schoolteacher from Corcubión County, on the northwestern tip of the Iberian Peninsula, and her friend Consuelo Gracia emigrated to Argentina for personal reasons. Dropping her first two names, altering the third to Mario, and passing for a male, Elisa had married Consuelo in 1900. When the scheme was discovered soon afterward, these "love birds of the same feather"—as the *paisanos* called them —fled to Buenos Aires, where they attempted to marry again.[1] Ten years later and on the other extreme of the peninsula, Ramón Frances left Corella, Navarre, also for personal reasons: not with his lover but after her. His girlfriend had emigrated to Argentina with her parents, and desolate Ramón followed her to what was actually his native land (he had been born in Rosario and taken to Navarre as an infant by his returnee parents).[2] Farther north in the same province, in the Pyrenean Baztán Valley, Fermín Mendiberri also left for personal, albeit less romantic, motives: to evade the draft, or—as his daughter claimed—because his aunt had advised him to do so. When I asked an immigrant in Buenos Aires' Centro de Val de San Lorenzo (León) why he had come to Argentina in the 1920s, his reason was also personal: poverty and hunger. Then, when his townsfolk reminded him that his family had two cows and a wool spinner, he dropped hunger as a reason and began to wonder about poverty. Others mentioned lack of opportunities, making money to buy land back home, higher wages, boredom with village life, whims, nasty stepmothers, the insistence of a parent, the call of relatives, and a rather telling reason: caught in the wave.

Personal decisions may indeed have been innumerable and thus, by themselves, unyielding to scholarly analysis. A list of reasons why people emigrated would run into an epistemological abyss. Categorizing them into economic, political, psychological, and so forth—a favorite procedure of some migration scholars, particularly in Spain—forms no more than a pseudoscientific approach that organizes more than explains. The mechanical scheme of turning them into a dual magnetic field may provide a useful heuristic device, but little more. As I argued in the first chapter, a lengthy list of so-called push and pull factors could be easily compiled for countries and regions that neither sent nor received immigrants.

But history is not, as Emerson maintained, "only biography." And what makes innumerable biographies and personal decisions susceptible to scholarly examination is the fact that they do not take place in a vacuum. Individual agency normally exists within the boundaries of, and interacts with, historical structures and forces. Had the Corcubionese lesbian couple married in 1850 instead of 1900 they would not have fled to Buenos Aires. Only seven Corcubionese lived there then, all of them male, and none related to their families or even from the same village or area of the county. The Valense who fled from what he called poverty and hunger in the 1920s would have stayed put, poor and hungry, in 1850. The first person from Val de San Lorenzo to come to Argentina did so in 1864, and the bulk arrived after 1900.[3] The broken-hearted Navarrese and his girlfriend would not have gone either. Emigration fever had not yet reached their part of Navarre and would not for a few more decades. There was not a single soul from the area in Buenos Aires in 1855. Most of these people did not even know such a place existed 7,000 miles and a whole ocean away, and if some geography buffs did, they had not the slightest idea of how to get there other than on a map. Yet draft-dodging Fermín Mendiberri from the Baztán Valley, 55 miles to the north, could have headed for Buenos Aires in 1850 as easily as he did in 1910, even if he had never seen a map in his life. Indeed, that same year another Fermín Mendiberri—probably an ancestor—and scores of his neighbors had done so. Most had left at draft age, through the French port of Bayonne, and without any papers.

The immediate reasons why the two pairs of lovers, the "hungry" Valense, draft-dodging Fermín, and millions of other Spaniards emigrated may have been personal and even intimate. The larger reason lay elsewhere. Mass emigration was more than the accumulation of millions of individual decisions. It resulted from the interaction of macrostructural and microsocial forces, from the alloy of global trends and locally based networks analyzed in the first part of this book.

A grosso modo, emigration resulted from, and formed part of, a process of global modernization. This concept fell into disrepute during the 1960s and 1970s, particularly among Latin American scholars who often associated it with modernization theory. To the *dependentistas* of the period, the theory—and by default the concept—represented little more than an apology from North American academics for liberal capitalism and U.S. imperialist domination; a self-serving or naive view of progress as a linear movement that would diffuse from the industrialized core to the underdeveloped periphery; and a recipe for policies that stressed economic growth over distribution and social welfare. But whatever the merits of such interpretation—and it had many—modernization represents an undeniable historical process that should not be confused with a theory, or its advocacy. Whether one views it as progress, as decline, or as neither, such a thing as demographic modernization—the transition from a system of high birth and death rates to one of low fertility and mortality—did take place in Europe and is taking place in much of the world. This transition produced—as mortality fell faster than fertility—the first sustained population explosion in human history. European mass emigration took place neither during the static demographic system of *l'ancien régime* nor during the equally static one of post–World War II Europe but during the transition from one to the other.

This demographic revolution represented a key force behind transatlantic crossings but not the only, or a sufficient, one. Indeed, if nineteenth-century censuses offer a reliable indication, population expansion in Spain, and on the other end of the continent, in Russia, was not immediately followed by mass departures. It was when other aspects of modernization gained enough momentum that Spanish emigration took off: when the commercialization of agriculture disrupted the countryside and, along with population growth, increased competition for land, expelled many peasants from it, and awakened previously infeasible ambitions in others; when industrialization displaced rural artisans, weakened the ties of country folks to their birthplaces, and created new consumption demands and desires; when railroads crossed the peninsula and steamers the ocean; when liberalism made freedom of movement an individual right and material acquisitiveness a virtue. Again, mass emigration took place neither during the subsistence agricultural system of the seignorial past nor during the recent period of agribusinesses and a mostly urban population but during the stage between one and the other; not during the preindustrial past nor the fully industrial or postindustrial era but during the extended and often arduous road from the former to the latter. The fact that Spain (and southern and eastern Europe in general) embarked on this road later than its northwestern neighbors explains why the first Europeans to cross the Atlantic were also among the last to cross it en masse, why emigration represented a viable option for the broken-hearted or needy of 1900 but not for those of 1850. Emigration, often viewed as a symptom of Spain's backwardness and poverty by national politicians, was instead fostered by, and an evidence of, change.

Capitalist modernization did impoverish many, but its link to emigration lay elsewhere. The tendency of contemporary observers to blame poverty for pushing people to abandon their homes may have echoed genuine sympathy for the less fortunate or, on a more cerebral plane, the ostensible logic of the push-pull concept. But it was misplaced. As shown in chapter 1, the exodus originated not from the most impoverished and inegalitarian areas but from the relatively better off and more economically democratic ones, and within these areas not among the poorer folk but among their more fortunate neighbors. The "hungry" Valense, as his friends observed and my quantitative analysis corroborated, belonged to the latter group. Those who left Val de San Lorenzo, including the individual in question, were more literate, more likely to own land and larger parcels, and more likely to own wool-weaving workshops than were those who stayed behind. Similar analyses of other villages produced the same results. The poorer inhabitants tended to stay or to move internally. For those who "crossed the puddle," the popular metaphor for emigrating overseas, the disruption, opportunity, dissatisfaction, and ambition that capitalism engendered proved to be more causal than did its poverty. Despite the omnipresent pitiful images of emigrants, most of these people confronted the imperatives of a changing system with diligence and vigor—a point that many other recent studies have stressed.[4]

On the other side of the ocean, some of the same global forces made Argentina a country of immigrants. At the most primary level, this movement reflected demographic-ecological phenomena. The surplus of the European "Malthusian devil" did not simply flee haphazardly to new continents. More than 95 percent of the 56 million Europeans who left their homeland between 1820 and 1930 moved, in a clear direction, to areas that shared a particular ecology: temperate, European-like climates; fertile, cereal-producing plains; and scant, or scattered, aboriginal populations (in 1820 London had four times as many inhabitants as all of Argentina, a country the size of continental Europe). At this level, Argentine immigration represented a biological movement of European flora and fauna—including everything from weeds and germs to cattle and humans—to what Alfred Crosby aptly termed "Neo-Europes" (the River Plate region from southern Brazil to eastern Argentina; North America, north of the Rio Grande; Australia–New Zealand; and parts of South Africa). Besides nourishing emigration directly, the European population explosion also increased the demand for the temperate agropastoral commodities of Argentina (and the other "Neo-Europes"), which in turn fostered immigration because, as shown in chapter 2, the country's economy became increasingly labor intensive.

In a similar symbiotic way, the same industrial revolution that fostered mobility—including across the ocean—in the Old World made possible the international division of labor on which Argentine expansion and its demand for immigrant labor rested. The urbanization of the Old World that uprooted people from the land and often served as a stepping-stone for overseas movement also increased the number of Europeans who did not grow their own food, expanding the demand for Argentina's agricultural production and thus the need for more immigrants. The same steamers that carried millions to the River Plate—including the harvesters of the pampa's crop—hauled that crop in the other direction. The same railroads that expanded the emigration pool by taking the inhabitants of the European hinterland to the port made possible Argentina's cereal economy by taking the grain of the riverless plains to the coast. And the same liberal revolution that crashed the exit doors in the Old World opened the entry gates in the New.

The Argentine ruling class viewed immigration as essential for the country's development and for a while even as a civilizing agent. This has been interpreted by various historians as a key cause of the inflow. But, as I showed in chapter 2, ruling classes from Bolivia to Mexico expressed similar views and enacted similar policies with little success. The Argentine elite preferred Anglo-Saxon and Germanic immigrants, yet Mediterraneans, eastern Europeans, and Middle Easterners accounted for more than nine-tenths of the newcomers. By the 1920s the Argentine upper classes had turned increasingly nativist and even xenophobic. But six times as many foreigners settled in the country during that decade as in the three decades following the overthrow of Rosas in 1852, when xenophilia and the political discourse of immigration as civilization reached a peak. Clearly the mass-immigration process obeyed laws other than those enacted by Argentine legislators. The only important government legislation was simply to keep the borders open. Other than that, political rhetoric and official policies proved superstructural and even superfluous. When receiving countries began to restrict entries around 1930, the mass-emigration period came to an end. And only such restrictions prevent today's Third World emigration from dwarfing yesterday's great European exodus.

Modernization's global revolutions in a sense set the stage for a popular revolution of equally mighty dimensions. Mass emigration came to embody an expression of popular will that overshadowed—in numbers, participation, and the way it changed people's lives—most prepolitical or political revolts and revolutions. Never before in human history had so many common peasants and workers taken so many decisions that altered their personal lives and the world in which they lived so drastically. They created gigantic new countries and changed the outlook of tiny old villages. Railroads, steamers, the mail system, the telegraph, the photograph, deepwater ports, and macadamized roads provided the essential paths for people and information to move. But it was common travelers, the famous "American letters," the alluring portraits of immigrants in their Sunday best, the tales and songs about their adventures, the boasting of returnees and local emigration agents, the remittances of relatives, the gossip and stories passed from one Spanish town to another, and idioms such as *Amerika hemen aurkitu*—defined in a Basque dictionary as "to become rich" but literally "to find America here"—that filled those paths. They carried the information, dreams, and assistance that made the emigration of the six characters mentioned in the opening paragraph, and of millions like them, possible.

At this level, emigration represents a popular diffusion of information and behaviors that was global in its dimensions but locally based. As shown in chapter 3, emigration began in a few particular points with access to overseas information and from there spread, at varying speeds, to other places. The forces of modernization aided the process. The expanding apparatus of the liberal state improved the mail and transport system and relocated schoolteachers, bureaucrats, national guards, and draftees, facilitating the spread of news across the peninsula. The agricultural and industrial revolutions took peasants to markets and salesmen to villages; connected countryside and towns; and increased internal mobility. But again, it was word of mouth, family letters and photographs, and popular tales that disseminated and augmented information about Buenos Aires. People became not simply aware of the city but also, and more importantly, increasingly knowledgeable about where to go, how to get there, who to go to for assistance, where to stay, how to find a job, and so on. Eventually, even people who had never been there could describe particular neighborhoods, streets, and sights, at times with amazing details. No wonder that the Corcubionese lesbian couple fled to Argentina's capital rather than to their own country's or even their own province's. This diffusion of information explains the recurrent appearance of the emigration fever metaphor anywhere from Scotland to Hungary and Finland to Spain. Not only did it spread geographically in a form resembling that of communicable diseases, it also possessed the psychological contagiousness that the term implies.

Immigrants, like most people, think of their actions as personal, individual, idiosyncratic. During my interviews with them, many portrayed their emigration as a pioneer, lone adventure. The lists I had compiled from archival sources, however, often showed that scores of people from their villages had already settled in Buenos Aires when they came, and dozens with their same surnames. Instead of questioning their version, I asked them to describe their trip and landing. Normally, memories of numerous kin at the dock, of spending the first weeks at one of their houses, and the like came to mind then. Besides showing the unreliability of oral history when employed by itself, this betrays the existence of a wider tendency to stress or overstate the individual's role in the immigration experience. Perhaps this reflects the high value placed on individual exploits and personal independence by Spanish, masculine, and liberal capitalist culture, a value embodied in the figures of El Cid, the conquistadors, and the self-made man. Perhaps people just do not like to feel that they simply follow the pack. Whatever the case, most emigrated as part of social networks rather than as isolated individuals. As information about the New World grew, in many localities of origin emigration became not a pioneer venture or even a common practice but expected behavior or, as contemporaries often put it, a habit, a mania. Despite the innumerable personal motives, many were, as one of the Valense immigrants admitted, simply caught in the wave.

The nature of emigration as a diffusion process also adds some insight into why the first Europeans to cross the Atlantic were among the last to cross it en masse. The square, massive shape of the peninsula, its mountainous topography, and the slow modernization of its communication and transportation infrastructure retarded the geographical spread of emigration fever from the original foci to the hinterland. In 1850 there were already places, like the Baztán Valley of draft-dodging Fermín Mendiberri, where the intensity of the exodus surpassed that of most Irish counties. But whereas the rest of the Iberian Peninsula did not participate then, the entire Emerald Isle contributed to the overseas flow at the time. The geographical spread of the phenomenon, more than its intensity per se, made Ireland a pioneer of emigration and Spain a latecomer.

This study uncovered other characteristics of local social networks that help illuminate the process of emigration. One is what I called the phenomenon of the dormant chain. Transoceanic microsocial networks could survive prolonged periods when wars, lack of transportation, restrictive legislation, or other macrostructural conditions obstructed emigration and direct contact. The chain then became less active and carried occasional information or simply preserved family memories. But once the general situation became less adverse, it reactivated itself and began to convey larger flows of information and, eventually, assistance and people. In addition, the previous economic success of the immigrants usually determined how long the chain could survive in a dormant stage—apparently, rich uncles were easier to remember. If inauspicious conditions persisted for more than four or five decades, however, the chain normally broke or the flow headed in other directions. This phenomenon seems worth exploring in the relationship between pre–Great Depression and post–World War II emigration to Argentina, Canada, and the United States.

Another key characteristic of chain migration uncovered in this study relates to its multiplier effect. Although the metaphor is useful, chain migration resembled more webs or unending branches than a chain. Links did not simply attach sequentially to one another but joined in every direction. Forward, they connected to younger relatives and new generations that preserved and enhanced the temporal dimension of the process. Laterally, they branched out to increasingly distant relatives, to cousins of cousins of cousins, who would in turn become trunks and ramify even farther. Moreover, because internal migration in the country of origin often meant that the overseas emigrants had relatives and friends in towns and provinces other than their native ones, this lateral branching also served as a key mechanism for disseminating emigration fever across the Iberian Peninsula. It often explained why the fever did not always spread uniformly but vaulted into new areas, creating seemingly isolated foci. This tendency of network-based emigration to branch out allowed the process to spread and multiply with self-generating force. Emigration thus developed an autonomous, self-perpetuating dynamic, which explains why people kept on arriving during the receiving country's worst economic depressions or after wages had actually dropped to a level lower than that in the home country—an aspect consistently overlooked in economic studies of population movements. But the independence of this force had its temporal limits and could not stand consistently adverse structural conditions. It is true that after long years, during which the World Depression, the Spanish Civil War, and World War II halted Spanish emigration, the dormant chain resuscitated with vigor in the late 1940s. But when Argentina's stagnation became seemingly permanent in the next decades, Spaniards began to stay home or to shun the River Plate for less familiar places despite the existence of long-established primary networks. Indeed, as the Spanish "economic miracle" gained momentum in the 1980s, some of the descendants of the immigrants even began to use the old networks to cross the Atlantic in the opposite direction, toward the land their parents and grandparents once left.

The self-generating nature of chain migration also tended to give the process a definite life span. In most localities of origin the flow resembled a growth curve, with an early phase of initiation, followed by a period of growth, a phase of saturation, and eventual regression and cessation. The shape of the curve varied. In some localities, like Mataró, it was rather flat and long; that is, people came in small numbers and over a long period of time. In others, like Vimianzo (La Coruña), villagers arrived in larger numbers and concentrated on a few decades. As previously stressed, the way people came influenced the way they adapted. In this case, the first shape induced a more successful adaptation to the new country than did the second. The phases also influenced the composition of the flow. In the initiation or pioneer phase, literate males of higher social origin predominated. As the growth curve moved toward its saturation phase, the flow became more inclusive, in terms of both gender and social class. This again influenced the adaptation of new arrivals to the host society. The composition of the flow also varied among different localities in terms of the family position of the emigrants. For reasons examined in chapter 3, fathers who departed by themselves made up a high proportion of the emigration from Corcubión County in Galicia but an insignificant one in the flow from the Baztán Valley in Navarre.

This study uncovered, however, not an infinity of unique local cases but particular local patterns. It revealed not the epistemological quagmire of limitless variety but the intellectual challenge of finite diversity. It is true that local peculiarities impeded a generalized characterization of Spanish emigration. Yet these peculiarities represent types of emigration, rather than singular instances, types that were compared to similar ones in other places. Indeed, by exposing the universal nature of local patterns, this macro-micro approach brings us closer to a general understanding of population movement than does any, presumably broader, national-level perspective. The nation-state may offer the optimal unit of analysis to study emigration and immigration policy, but a faulty one for examining the actual process. Here, conventional wisdom to the contrary, the vantage point lies not in the middle but in the extremes or, more precisely, the intersection of the extremes: of global modernization and local particularities, of transcontinental revolutions and kinship networks, of the world and the village.

This dialectical macro-micro approach (expanded to include Buenos Aires' physical and class structures in the first set and the immigrants' social networks and cultural background in the second) also provided the best framework to analyze the theme of the second part of the book: the adaptation of the arrivals in the host city.

This analytical framework, for example, provided us with a remarkable capacity for predicting where the Corcubionese lesbian couple settled when they arrived in Buenos Aires as the twentieth century dawned. To begin with, we could assert that their chances of settling in La Boca, where about one-third of their *paisanos* lived, were just about nil.

This enclave, oddly situated in the heart of the city's traditional Genoese neighborhood, had begun in the 1850s when a group of sailors from the maritime head village of the county (Corcubión) settled—not unnaturally—in the shipping quarters along La Boca (the mouth) of the Riachuelo River. During the next half-century the interaction of global and local forces on both sides of the ocean transformed the situation. The transportation revolution and the expansion of Atlantic trade provided the maritime town of Corcubión with a flourishing business of supplying coal to passing steamers and with a growing mercantile and artisan class. The growth of the liberal Spanish state and its bureaucracy also helped make the social structure of the administrative head of the county quasi-urban, despite its population of less than 1,700. As the petite bourgeoisie of the small town grew, its emigration reflected the trend.

On the other side of the ocean, the growth of the Atlantic economy had the opposite effect on La Boca. As the country's international trade grew and a deepwater port was built on the central and northern shores of the city to accommodate the swelling volume, La Boca's previous maritime prosperity dwindled. The ward turned increasingly into a lower-class bastion, hardly the place to attract the offspring of merchants, schoolteachers, scribes, clerks, and bureaucrats from Corcubión County's developing head town.

In that long interim, the ramification and diffusion processes mentioned before had taken emigration fever from its original foci (the maritime towns of Corcubión and Finisterre) to the rural hinterland of the county. These new peasant immigrants reached La Boca pulled by the self-propelling momentum of this process rather than by the area's nautical activities. They simply trailed acquaintances who in turn had followed those sailors from the county's coastal villages who had settled there two or three generations before. By the twentieth century the newcomers from the rural interior formed a majority of the immigrants from Corcubión County in the area, which was now inhabited by mostly male day laborers. The direct "descendants" of the original settlers from the county seat, on the other hand, dodged the neighborhood and settled mostly in another enclave a few blocks southwest of the city's central plaza. It was here that the majority of Corcubionese females of middle-class background lived. And unless the particular sexual orientation of Elisa and her lover directed them toward some other, unexpected place, the chances that they lived here were better than four in five.

The analytical framework that enables such accurate predictions surpasses urban-ecological approaches (such as that of the Chicago school), which only take into account social class and ethnicity. Had we known only that Elisa was a schoolteacher the chances of pinpointing where she resided in the city would have been little better than finding the proverbial needle. All we could have done, perhaps, would be to eliminate the poorest slums. Had we known only that she was Spanish, we could not have done even that. As shown in chapter 4, Buenos Aires had one of the lowest ethnic segregation indexes in the world. Spaniards did concentrate in certain wards, but they lived in large numbers in all the wards of the city, and there was nothing remotely resembling an ethnic ghetto.

Chain migration approaches, with their emphasis on locality of origin, could have done better. Had we known only that Elisa was from Corcubión County and not known her sex, the chances of finding the ward where she resided would have been about one in three. But in this particular case, the prediction would have been wrong because her gender and class background would have made it so. Here lies the key weakness of traditional chain-migration approaches: their disregard for social class and gender, their tendency to view arrivals from a particular village as equally poor peasants. As demonstrated in this study, chains were not class blind, and "urban villagers" formed not homogeneous communities but internally divided ones.

This example illustrates, in a nutshell, the necessity for combining ecological and chain-migration approaches to fully understand the process of immigrant-neighborhood formation. It demonstrates that only by examining Old and New World trends, global and local forces, migration patterns and urban ecology, class and ethnicity, can we gain a fuller understanding. In addition, the interaction of these elements produced early molds that in turn became independent variables and influenced future formations. These early patterns infused the communities, and the city, with a marked historical continuity. As I argued in chapter 4, the huge Spanish community of 1910 represented in many respects (here spatially) just an amplified copy of the tiny one of 1850. The example therefore also indicates the necessity of studying immigrant communities from their early formation. Had I not begun my study in 1850, the presence in 1900 of Spanish peasants in an Italian and maritime neighborhood would have seemed just a quirk, another example of social science's futility in the face of chance. Instead, it seemed to confirm novelist Rémy de Gourmont's contention that "Chance is a mask, and it is precisely the historian's duty to lift it or tear it away."

This approach—by elucidating how immigrants form neighborhoods and why they settle in and move to some places and not others—also illuminates how and why the city developed as it did. As demonstrated in chapter 4, the timing and nature of immigration to Argentina does much to explain why Buenos Aires—contrary to the arguments of various scholars who examined it only at the macrolevel—did not develop along the lines suggested by the Chicago school model; why a process of "invasion and succession" did not take place; why—unlike North American cities—the urban center preserved its status as the periphery expanded; why the River Plate metropolis exhibited one of the lowest ethnic segregation indexes in the world. The capacity of this macro-micro framework to illuminate both the residential decisions of "little people" and the formation of a giant metropolis offers the best response to those who feel they can understand one without the other.

The interplay of macro- and microforces and Old and New World realities, and the molds it created along the way, also determined how (and how successfully) the newcomers made a living in the host city. The analysis of this synergetic process explained why immigrants from certain regions and villages fared better than others. It explicated apparent paradoxes. It offered an insight into why Andalusians (who came from one of Spain's poorest and most inegalitarian regions and were often branded by their hosts as indolent and unreliable) fared better economically than Basques (who came from one of the peninsula's most developed and economically democratic corners and formed the most prestigious ethnic group in Argentina). In this case, the way in which emigration fever diffused in the sending society affected the types of emigrants and their adaptation in the receiving one. Similar insights gained from the analysis of emigration patterns as a growth curve explained the equally puzzling fact that immigrants who had few townsfolk in Buenos Aires (that is, those who came during the initial phase of the curve) normally fared better than did those with many *paisanos* and relatives.

The analysis in chapter 5 also demonstrated that—contrary to the argument of various revisionist studies and despite the enrichment of the oligarchy—Buenos Aires offered ample opportunities for upward socioeconomic mobility. Different measuring methods relying on thousands of cases extracted from manuscript censuses and immigrant-association sources, and comparisons with dozens of cities in North America and Europe, indicated that Spaniards in the city enjoyed relatively high rates of occupational ascent. Oral interviews, immigrant letters, literature, and humor suggested that the concept of upward mobility—or, in the immigrants' own words, "making America"—rarely meant for them the rags-to-riches myth so easily ridiculed by facile revisionism. And an alternative method for measuring the type of less visible mobility they had in mind showed that Spanish families proved remarkably competent at improving their material lives and those of their children.

At the same time, my investigation revealed hidden continuities in this upward ascent. The comparison of the occupational status of parents in Spain with that of their children in Buenos Aires demonstrated that those who took advantage of the opportunities the city offered were not the "wretched refuse" of Iberian shores. Many children of humble peasants and workers did become Porteño magnates. But the majority, despite the crossing of an ocean, continued to follow, socioeconomically, in their parents' footsteps.

At times, Old World inequalities resurfaced on the other shore inconspicuously. Even among immigrants of similar social background (say, of urban birth and working-class origin), the chances of owning a business or finding a white-collar job in Buenos Aires increased in direct relation to the size of their mothers' birthplace in Spain. The veiled skill that they possessed must resemble what sociologist Pierre Bourdieu called cultural capital: the ability of parents (in this case urban-born mothers) to transmit attitudes and codes useful in a competitive situation that go beyond formal education and skills.[5]

These inequalities were reinforced in the New World by a different sort of invisible skill. Immigrants whose hometown communities in Buenos Aires were more prosperous fared better than did those who belonged

[margin note: Who you know, rather than what you knew]

to less successful immigrant networks, even if their level of skills, age, gender, and length of residence in the new country were identical. Their invisible skill lay in the success of the townsfolk who had preceded them in the chain, in belonging to a network that included more business owners or other influential people who could lend them a hand, in who they knew rather than what they knew.

Again, by uncovering mechanisms like these, this approach furthers not only our understanding of immigrant adaptation but also that of wider processes—in this case that of Argentine social-class formation. Depending on the period and on how sanguine or disgruntled they feel about their country, Argentine scholars have taken opposite views on this process, but none has bothered to take a look across the Atlantic. For some, the freshness and dynamism of the new country offered an equal starting line, at least for newcomers, that presumably—it was rarely spelled out—made the imported inequalities of the arriving masses inconsequential. For others, colonial legacies and latifundia had made the country's social structure so stratified, so ossified, that—again presumably—it made these inequalities equally irrelevant. The fact that the prearrival disparities among immigrants offered an inapplicable, or at least insipid, subject for political demagoguery and for the eventually hegemonic populist discourse of Peronism further diminished their visibility. Yet these social inequalities, which "arrived on boats" and en masse and were reinforced in the new land by invisible skills, shaped Argentina's class formation to a greater extent than did the (in)famous, omnipresent—and seemingly omnipotent—estanciero oligarchs who, after all—and whatever their power—made up an infinitesimal proportion of the population.

[margin note: Concl. ✗]

Indeed, the relevance of these findings goes beyond the issue of Argentine class formation. They show how continuity and change, disparities and opportunities easily coexisted and illuminate the process by which social inequalities were reproduced in immigrant societies. They expose the limits of meritocracy even in societies that arguably were more open and fluid than those of the Old World. And, for those who value social equality over economic growth, these findings confirm the unavoidability of redistributive "social engineering" even in countries of opportunity.

The Spaniards' associations, on the other hand, could be interpreted as evidence of the "superiority" of private—albeit collective—enterprises. Long before the appearance of the welfare state, these (and other) immigrants had formed an impressive institutional network that provided cradle-to-grave services. Mutual-aid societies flourished, finding a way to avert what rational-choice theorists have termed the free-rider dilemma with a combination of peer pressure, calls to patriotic altruism, and actuarial controls. By the 1920s the Asociación Española de Socorros Mutuos and the Centro Gallego of Buenos Aires formed the two largest mutual-benefit associations in the country (and probably in Latin America).

Spanish immigrants, unlike, for example, Italians in New York or Poles in Chicago, formed a truly multiclass community. Though underrepresented at the top, they could be found throughout the Porteño social hierarchy. The immigrant elite was both numerous and truly rich; the middle class, naturally, larger; and the working-class majority, well organized and often militant. Reflecting this diversity, they founded various elite social clubs and societies, more numerous and less exclusive ones for those of lesser means, and labor organizations—a few explicitly Spanish, but the rest cosmopolitan in nature.

Reflecting what some critics derided as "dissociative cantonalism" but what this study found to be an expression of grass-roots energy and a complementary source of vitality and strength, they established numerous regional and provincial associations and a plethora of hometown societies. It was here—in their gatherings, picnics, and dances—where many greenhorns "learned" about their new home from old-timers who reminisced about the homeland, where young, single arrivals overcame loneliness and romances flourished, where revered old matrons concocted marital unions between and among fellow villagers and the new American generations. These associations both facilitated adaptation to the new land and—particularly given the low ethnic spatial segregation of Buenos Aires—played a critical role in preserving Old World cultures and loyalties.

Other voluntary associations common in immigrant communities elsewhere failed to develop in Buenos Aires. The early formation and proliferation of Spanish immigrant bona fide banks (including two of the largest in Latin America) discouraged the development of ROSCAS, those semiformal rotating saving and credit associations so ubiquitous among migrant populations all over the world. Perhaps reflecting the existence of greater legal opportunities in the host country, secret semicriminal societies—like the Chinese tongs and the Cosa Nostra—also failed to appear in the Spanish immigrants' associative spectrum. Catholic associations did appear, but they were few and insignificant. Unlike the case of, say, Irish and Polish immigrants in North America, the Church for Spaniards did not embody Old World nationalist redemptions, did not sustain a sense of separate ethnic identity in the host country, and did not supply a significant source of earthly succor and beneficence. In a sense, religion for Spaniards in the River Plate attained a more ethereal, nonutilitarian state that, ironically, made it less relevant.

As shown in chapter 6, prearrival traits and the host environment, plus the variables that their interaction produced, shaped the organized life of the immigrants. The societies were neither imported institutions nor rootless products of the new environment. The emigrating experience itself raised associative activity to levels unknown in Spain and influenced its nature. The conflicts that riddled the organized community were often imported but also molded by the new situation. Regionalist and ethnonationalist frictions took new forms as previously geographically separated groups came to live side by side. The fact that more than three-quarters of the arrivals were non-Castilian minorities (Galicians, Basques, and Catalans) accentuated cultural and linguistic distinctiveness and created a multi-ethnic community in a multi-ethnic city.

Class friction was similarly complicated. To old contentions, new ones were added: conflicts between immigrants of different class background in Spain, between those of different class status in Buenos Aires, between immigrants from "good families" who had not made it in the new land and those who had made it but lacked the proper "pedigree," between both of these and immigrants who had neither pedigree nor money. The combinations could be numerous and were further fueled by conflict ideologies. The leadership of the ethnic associations denounced the "unpatriotic" offenses of their anarchist compatriots. Anarchists, in return, found all sorts of sins in their fellow citizens' "flag-waving" associations, denouncing the leaders as asses full of gold and the affiliates in general as chauvinist hogs, "patrioteer parrots," and spineless scabs.

Yet several factors attenuated these conflicts. Ethnically, the relative absence of Castilians—a group presumably more intransigent concerning expressions of "un-Spanish" ethnic loyalties—may have promoted a more tolerant and pluralistic atmosphere. At the same time, their condition as outsiders, the pan-Hispanic discourse of the leadership, the lack of separatist leanings among the Galician majority, and the belief that strength lay in unity fostered the concept that "outside Spain, we're all Spaniards." In most cases, Spanishness represented a New World invention, a cultural construction that used both prearrival and local materials. The very stratification of the institutional structure, admiration for the accomplishments of rich *paisanos* (which were often modest enough to be within sight), and other factors previously discussed tended to attenuate class conflicts. So did the fact that anarchists spent more time fighting with each other than with their "flag-waving" compatriots. Indeed, the emigration experience, the insulting *gallego* jokes, and rivalry with other national groups often softened the Spanish anarchists' internationalist fervor and antipatriotic postures in the new land.

In the end, the very profusion and diversity of associations that made frictions inevitable also provided tremendous vitality. The organized community was both conflict ridden and functional. Institutions were large and impersonal precisely where such traits represented an advantage: in beneficent societies that required capital and organizational skills to build and run hospitals, clinics, asylums, and so forth, and in mutual-aid societies, where large numbers and actuarial expertise prevented the mutual fund from being depleted by a few sick or dishonest members and where a large equity allowed a broad spectrum of services. Institutions were small and familiar where it counted: in the *landsmanshaftn* that provided conviviality and companionship, intimate ties to hometowns, and a sphere where those who were excluded from the elite and elite-run societies could participate actively. Despite the constant complaints of the defenders of "unity," the relationship between the two types became, as demonstrated in chapter 6, complementary, even symbiotic. Amid a constant cacophony of regionalist and ideological bickering, class friction, and more abundant and philistine personal quarrels, the Spaniards of Buenos Aires were able to construct and maintain a cohesive and remarkably functional institutional structure.

In addition to material aid and sociability, the immigrants' institutions, including a lively press, also served to defend and promote their reputation and good name in a country that did not always honor them. Argentine attitudes toward Spaniards were always characterized by ambivalence and duality. They were, after all, the "charter group," the bestowers of the original culture, but also "uncultured" new arrivals, immigrants, foreigners. Their dual personality, however, represented not a static essence but a cultural construction that remained in a continual process of definition.

A macro-micro approach—in this case the analysis of the interaction between general Western intellectual trends and local conditions—again offered the optimal perspective from which to elucidate such a process. During the course of the nineteenth century the hegemonic position of the Enlightenment gave way to general Western liberalism, later to positivism, and eventually to antiliberal reaction. During roughly the same period, Argentina evolved from a recently emancipated nation, to a youthful country full of illusions about liberal progress, to one obsessed with material advancement, and eventually to a cosmopolitan mass society with all the complexities this entailed. As explained in chapter 7, the combination of the two trends transformed the dominant representation of Spaniards in the discourse of the Argentine elite from enemies, to subjects of an obscurantist, monarchical, and backward nation, to defenders of the then reevaluated Hispanic legacy of the country in the face of cosmopolitan and soulless materialism.

Although the change was marked, continuities carried into the twentieth century, and new or transformed dualities emerged. Some liberals softened their previous Hispanophobia, but others continued to regard Spain as the antithesis of Western European modernization. The increasingly dominant cultural nationalists did reject that modernization as arid and overly utilitarian and glorified, instead, the traditional Hispanic heritage of their country, the spirituality and dignity of mother Spain, and the nobility and valor of their conquistador ancestors. But they often ignored or even scorned the masses of new arrivals. Moreover, not all Iberian groups were regarded equally. In the nostalgic and neo-Romantic writings of the literary elite, Castilians came to embody the austerity of Hapsburg Spain, of El Cid, Quixote, and Cortés; and Basques, the pioneers of the pampas and the progenitors of Argentina's aristocracy. But other groups received few accolades. In novels and plays, Catalans often appeared as stingy and anarchist; Andalusians, as garrulous, blasphemous, and equally anarchist; and Galicians, as harmless but dull.

In addition, the Hispanophilic discourse of nationalist litterateurs did not always filter down to Buenos Aires barrios. By the 1920s Porteños inhabited not the overgrown village of the midnineteenth century but a grand metropolis, the second largest in the Atlantic seaboard after New York, or as they liked to put it—the second largest Latin city, the "Paris of South America." Their wages were a quarter higher than in the real Paris. Their country was no longer an empty backland but the eighth richest in the world. They were better educated, dressed, fed, and usually taller than the arrivals and their own European-born parents. They found it difficult, therefore, to view the mostly peasant newcomers from Italy and eastern Europe as carriers of superior European civilization (the old dogma of some nineteenth-century liberals regarding non-Iberian immigration). But they also failed to behold the equally rural arrivals from the Iberian Peninsula as upholders of a glorified Hispanic legacy (as some Hispanophile nationalists now claimed). Unlike the ex-colonizing English in North America, the ex-colonizing Spaniards in Argentina were not among the most materially successful or prestigious immigrants (see chapter 5).

Despite the swelling tide of Hispanism among the intelligentsia, for most Porteños the dominant figure of Spaniards continued to be not El Cid, Loyola, or Quixote, but Sancho Panza—the *gallego* servant, the Basque milkman, the Catalan shopkeeper. The hatreds of the postindependence period were mostly gone, but only to be replaced by a certain resentment against the "educated" minority who bragged about the purity of their Castilian language and culture vis-à-vis the "hybrid" Argentine versions and by a more common disdain toward the mass of "uneducated" greenhorns. This never reached the point of institutionalized discrimination or deep-seated enmity—although some Spaniards and other immigrants claimed that it did. But it is possible that as the Porteño population became more affluent and "civilized," its contempt of newcomers in general increased.

It is in this context that the meaning of Hispanism for the mass of Spanish arrivals can be understood. For them Hispanism represented not the traditionalist concept wielded by the Argentine elite to romanticize its past but a means of defending their reputation in the face of popular derision. Immigrant newspapers constantly reprinted or commented on, it seems, every paragraph favorable to Spain or its emigrants written by Argentine intellectuals. Spanish elite institutions regaled every prominent Argentine Hispanophile who was willing to be feted. Immigrant "historians" penned numerous books "proving beyond any doubt" that Columbus was Galician instead of Genoese, and lay *gallegos* fought with their Italians neighbors about it. Learned and lay alike denounced the term "Latin" America as a French and Italian conspiracy to take credit for the glorious deeds of Spain. They became rabid defenders of Argentina's "true Hispanic character and soul," and by mere numbers and tenacity, plus the help of Argentine traditionalists, they were partially successful in their crusade.

Yet the exaltation of the Hispanic legacy of Argentina by cultural nationalists may actually have helped to slow down the "nationalization" of the Spanish immigrants. The newcomers read this discourse as further evidence that more than cousins, or even brothers, they were founding fathers. Why should parents assimilate to the way of their children? Spaniards' most common method of asserting their self-worth, particularly in their endemic competition with Italian immigrants, lay in claiming not that they were rightful and genuine Argentines—as the latter often did—but in insisting that true Argentines could only be Spanish. Of course, Argentines had ceased to be merely transplanted Spaniards centuries ago, and they were so even less now that more than half of them traced their ancestry to places other than the Iberian Peninsula. They were no more transplanted Spaniards than North Americans were transplanted Englishmen. The Spanish cousins, therefore, ended up assimilating to the new land more slowly and more reluctantly than did the "alien" Italians whose alterity Argentine cultural nationalists so ardently attacked.

In this, and other, regards, this book provides, I feel, significant contributions to the existing scholarly literature and some suggestions for future researchers. At the most primary level, it has offered a thorough examination of a previously unstudied but important immigrant colony. Buenos Aires' Spaniards, after all, formed one of the largest urban immigrant communities in the world. Given the "dual personality" of the Spaniards, it may also provide an original and suitable model for comparisons with the experiences of the Portuguese in Brazil, the English in the United States, and perhaps even the French in Quebec.[6] Although studies of these groups do exist, none—that I know of—traces the changes and continuities in their relationships with their hosts and with other immigrants. The Spaniards' diversity, and the comparative approach toward it that I have taken, makes it also a model study of a multi-ethnic national group in a multinational city. The insight gained from the contrasts between the different Iberian ethnic and local groups should encourage this type of approach in Spain, where the majority of emigration studies have centered on one or other particular region or province, rarely comparing them. It could be equally applicable for the study of British emigrants (whose ethnic diversity resembles that of Spaniards) in the multi-ethnic cities of North America.

Despite their dual personality, Spaniards behaved, in terms of their emigration and adaptation (as opposed to cultural assimilation), not like cousins or strangers but like immigrants. Indeed, I was often struck by the analogies I found with the experiences of groups as diverse as the Swedes in Chicago and the Chinese in Manila and have noted these, as well as divergences, throughout the text. In this context, the findings of this book may enhance our understanding of the immigrant experience in general, not just that of Spaniards or in Argentina.

A theoretical comprehension of this universal experience, I maintained, can be advanced only by a dialectical and comparative framework that analyzes the interaction between the Old World background (wherever that happens to be) and the new environment, macroforces and microsocial networks, global trends and local realities. Approaches that do not, will likely fail to further our understanding of a phenomenon that has shaped the world and will continue to do so, in blatant disregard of political barriers and border patrols.

Methodologically, I endeavored to demonstrate that the study of immigration requires the use of both quantitative and qualitative sources; documents in national archives and in the institutions, villages, and homes of the immigrants; demographic material and creative literature and oral history. Studies that do not, run the risk of giving a partial or even distorted picture. As I found on various occasions, the most productive and accurate analysis emerged from contrasting different types of sources, and using only one of them would have led to fallacious conclusions. This book has also confirmed the effectiveness of the nominative method; that is, the construction of collective biographies culled from a variety of sources and organized as computer databases (see the appendix). During the past decade, postmodernist historiography has down played or impugned this method because of its presumed positivist assumptions. But—trendy terminology notwithstanding—this antiempiricist challenge has actually revived old idealist approaches that sought verification from impressionistic evidence or abstract argumentation rather than from concrete data. If sociocultural history is to remain an inquiry into real people's lived experiences rather than literary criticism of reified "texts," we cannot afford to abandon what arguably represents the most important methodological innovation in modern historiography.

This book aimed to explain the experiences of Spanish immigrants in Buenos Aires rather than the historical formation of modern Argentina, but by doing the former it automatically shed light on the latter. As James Scobie observed when he subtitled his pioneer social history of Argentina *A City and a Nation*, the capital epitomizes the country, and not simply because one-third of its people live there. By examining the residential patterns of immigrants, this study necessarily elucidated the changes and continuities in the social ecology of a city where they formed a majority. The theoretical models employed in chapter 4, the data mustered to test them, and the comparisons with other world cities explained much about Buenos Aires' sociospatial development during its crucial metamorphosis from *gran aldea* to grand metropolis. Similarly, while analyzing the occupational structure and mobility of immigrants, this study illuminated wider and related issues: the comparative level of economic opportunities in the city, the process of Argentine class formation, the reproduction of social inequality, the domestic service, women's work, and so forth. This refutes the endemic gripes about academic specialization and the notion that microhistory can only generate minuscule snapshots that are unable to illuminate, by themselves, the much larger puzzle. Social histories of specific groups—if embedded in a macro-micro framework—may indeed provide a picture of large social processes that is sharper—and not necessarily narrower—than that afforded by presumably more holistic—and definitely fuzzier—surveys.

Finally, the search for historical patterns in this book is not blind to the fact that much of life may not fit any. Spaniards may have reached the River Plate shores in waves, but those waves actually consisted of hundreds of thousands of individual, distinct—sometimes antithetical—drops: midwives and morticians, anarchists and priests, prostitutes and nuns, grammarians and illiterates, peasants and proletarians, broken-hearted lovers and lone lovers of adventure. Their experiences in the new land, like their reasons for coming, included the ends of any spectrum. José Buedo, a Galician immigrant, never rose above the category of a landless peon, and remainders of his existence are found only in dusty manuscript census returns and old graveyard lists;[7] his *paisano* Ramón Santamarina became the largest landowner in a country of large landowners, and his name appears in every who's who in the country. Isidora Sánchez lived in the local beggars' asylum; her countryman Marcos Muñoa, in the finest mansion in midnineteenth century Buenos Aires.[8] In 1912 Dolores Campo, who never read a newspaper in her life and could barely scratch an *X* as her signature, dwelled at 611 Alsina Street, the very same spot where sixty years earlier her compatriot Benito Hortelano had founded the first Spanish immigrant newspaper in Argentina.[9] Antonio Castro and Antonio Soto both arrived in Buenos Aires in 1912 from their native Galician town of Ferrol and settled in the same block of Juncal Street. But a decade later the first Antonio was leading an obscure life as a sexton, while the second Antonio, imbued with atheist anarchist principles, was leading the largest labor revolt in Argentine history, a feat later immortalized in several books and a popular film.[10]

This diversity of experience has reminded me during the past decade that what I set out to understand was indeed difficult to schematize. It has had a humbling effect by revealing that much was simply unfathomable. On a more revitalizing facet, it has often brought to mind the words Goethe once placed on Mephistopheles' lips: "Gray, my friend, all theory is gray—Green the golden tree of life."

Yet the fundamental assumption in this work has been that to let diversity and greenness deny pattern is tantamount to intellectual nihilism. To Goethe's sage comment I added two bits of wisdom from the antipositivist Kierkegaard: "Life must be lived forward, but can only be understood backward"; and "Repetition is reality." The approach in this book betrays, then, not theoretical hubris or blind empiricism but simply a recognition that only in historical patterns can we hope to fathom the greenness of the golden tree of life.

APPENDIX

SOURCES AND METHODOLOGY

PUBLISHED GOVERNMENT DOCUMENTS

The Argentine government conducted three national censuses during the period that this study covered (1869, 1895 [3 volumes], and 1914 [10 volumes]), and the municipality of Buenos Aires conducted four (1887 [2 volumes], 1904, 1909 [3 volumes], and 1936 [4 volumes]). No Latin American city, and few anywhere, can boast such coverage during the time, and the quality of the material compares favorably with contemporary censuses elsewhere. Together with the *Registro Estadístico del Estado* [*Provincia* after 1862] *de Buenos Aires*, 1854–1880, the *Boletín de Estadística Municipal*, 1887–1894, and the *Anuario Estadístico de la Ciudad de Buenos Aires*, 1891–1923, they offer a wealth of information on the spatial, infrastructural, demographic, and socioeconomic evolution of the Argentine capital. Except for the 1869 national census, and unlike many U.S. censuses, they also specify the district of residence of each nativity group, allowing a steady (though not entirely comparable, because the district boundaries were changed in 1904) analysis of ethnic segregation. The 1887 and 1895 censuses specify both the nationality and the literacy of the population in each district, permitting a rough comparison of ethnic and class segregation. But the others do not, and the 1904 and 1909 censuses do not even indicate literacy by district, making it impossible to determine whether Buenos Aires became more or less segregated in terms of class. They do, however, offer other indicators that can be used to reconstruct the social ecology of the city (see Tables 18 and 19). The published censuses normally specify the nationality of home owners and proprietors of commercial and industrial enterprises, but, at best, they classify the city's labor force only under the broad rubric of "native" and "foreigner," a critical shortcoming for a study of immigration.

Other official published sources employed in this study include:

A. Argentina, Comisión Nacional de Educación, *Censo escolar nacional, 1883–84*, 3 vols., and Comisión Nacional de Educación, *Censo general de educación, 1909*, 3 vols., for schooling of the native population and the various immigrant groups (I have not found the manuscript schedules on which these published censuses are based, but I urge other scholars to join the search because the schedules would make a wonderful source, including, as they do, the name, sex, birthplace, and date of birth of the students, their literacy, and where they learned to read, plus the name, nationality, and address of their parents).

B. The *Memorias de la Dirección* [*Departamento* after 1888] *General de Inmigración, 1869–1926*. I have not located a complete collection, but the Biblioteca Tornquist in Buenos Aires (call number M.28), with twenty-nine volumes, comes closest to it. Unlike the censuses, the quality of the *Memorias* is significantly inferior to that of similar publications in the United States, and the Dirección General de Inmigración, *Resumen estadístico del movimiento migratorio en la República Argentina, 1857–1924*, is too brief to be of any use. Rather laconic when it comes to the social history of the immigrants, the *Memorias* have much to say about the institutional evolution of the official immigration agency, policy, and politics.

C. The *Boletín del Departamento Nacional del Trabajo*, published since 1907, contains large amounts of tedious minutiae on labor legislation but also illuminating inquiries into working conditions in particular industries.

D. Argentina, Ministerio de Relaciones Exteriores, *Memoria del Ministerio Presentada al Honorable Congreso Nacional*, published from 1859 to 1905 and again after 1910, plus a *Boletín Mensual*, published from 1884 to 1891 and, under the new title of *Documentos Diplomáticos y Consulares*, from 1903 on. The library of the Ministry of Foreign Relations at the Palacio San Martín holds the most complete collection. Though plagued with diplomatic formalities, the consular reports, particularly those from smaller Spanish and Italian towns, afford much information on the changing local conditions in areas of emigration.

Spanish official emigration statistics began with the Dirección General del Instituto Geográfico y Estadístico, *Estadística de la Emigración e Inmigración de España en los Años de 1882 a 1890* and continued with volumes for the years 1891–1895, 1896–1900, 1901–1902, 1903–1906, 1907–1908, and 1909–1911. After this, the Consejo Superior de Emigración published *La Emigración Española Transoceánica: Memoria 1911–1915* and annual reports until 1924; and the Dirección General del Trabajo issued annual reports from 1925 until, at least, 1930. Not only did emigration statistics begin later in Spain than in other European countries, they were also less thorough. Among the main shortcomings is the lack of information on the provincial origin of the exodus to Argentina, except for 1885–1895 and the post–World War I years. The other two principal Spanish statistical series are the national censuses (1857, 1877, 1887, 1900, 1910, 1920, 1930) and the Instituto Nacional de Estadística, *Anuario Estadístico de España*, published since 1858.

MANUSCRIPT CENSUS RETURNS

Published censuses, statistical annuals, and other similar materials, though valuable, offer only aggregate data—and often not the data that are needed. The nature of the data makes it impossible to examine the relationship between variables such as ethnicity, gender, age, class, birthplace, and residence. Only manuscript sources with information on individuals can allow such analysis.

In this regard, early in my research I learned that Argentine demographer Alfredo Lattes had directed a team that had taken a one-in-ten random sample from the manuscript returns of an unpublished city census of 1855. Buenos Aires had a population of 93,000 at the time, of whom 5,700 were Spaniards To my delight, the data had been stored on magnetic tape. Dr. Lattes graciously offered me the tape, which had not been used by other researchers.[1] Unfortunately, his team had failed to record the very variable that was most important to me: locality of birth. For a microhistorical approach, of course, the country of birth—which had been recorded—was not enough. Thus my wife Paula, more than graciously, ended up spending weeks in the Archivo General de la Nación entering data on the universe of all Spaniards in the city into a portable computer.

Similar sources for later periods were not so rich. The returns for 1855 were exceptional in that they included not only region or locality of birth for about three-quarters of the cases but also length of residence in Argentina. The manuscript schedules for the 1869 and 1895 national censuses did not. And those for the other municipal and national censuses have been lost, probably irreparably so.

I tried to link the individuals in the 1855 sample to those in the 1869 census returns, but the preliminary results were disappointing. Four main problems plagued the effort: misspelled or barely legible names on the returns; the time span between the two dates (North American traces from federal schedules span only a decade, and when state censuses are available, even a quinquennium); the fact that Argentine sources (unlike Spanish documents and the immigrants' own records) include the paternal but not the maternal surname of the individual; and the fact that jobs, addresses, marital status, and so forth often changed and thus did not offer reliable identifiers. Having only the first and last names and the age of the persons to go by, I found it difficult, at times, to determine whether someone with a common name was actually the same individual in the two years. Many people, of course, had either died or left the city. I tried to use cemetery records, ship-departure registers, and city directories, but again the results were disappointing. I finally settled for a one-in-seven random sample (2,080) of the Spaniards residing in the city, which allowed individual-level analysis of the community at that point in time and comparisons with that of 1855.

The 1895 census schedules contain two critical shortcomings: they do not specify the province or town of birth, except for a few isolated cases in which census takers misunderstood the question and recorded that instead of the native country; and they do not indicate clearly street addresses and household boundaries. On the good side, they (and the other Argentine returns) offer more accurate and detailed information about women's occupations than do U.S. census schedules.

From the 1895 census schedules, I compiled a sample of 8,923 cases drawn from three different districts, selected to be as representative as possible of the city as a whole. Rather than a random sample, I included every working adult in those districts because my main purpose was to compare the occupational distribution of Spaniards with that of the other nativity groups in the city (Table 34 includes an analysis of the method and source). In addition to this sample, I was also able to use a sample of about 5,000 adults from a Buenos Aires upper-class neighborhood, kindly facilitated by Professor Stephanie Bower, who had compiled it for her study of the provincial elite living in the city. Its class bias made it unusable for most purposes, but it was a plus for my study of servants in chapter 5.

The other important manuscript source with individual-level information found in official archives was a file of 661 suspected anarchists located in the police archive (Chacabuco Street), which had never before been used by historians and may never be used again, for on a recent research trip to buenos Aires, I was told by the archivist that it had been lost. I also located a perfect counterpart to the anarchist file in the enrollment records (1,529 cases) of La Fraternidad, the socialist railroad workers' union for various years between 1904 and 1916. Besides a rich picture of the people involved (particularly in the police file), these two documents were invaluable in assessing Spanish participation in the particular movements. Although the historiography on anarchism and labor unions in Argentina is copious and consistently emphasizes the role of immigrants, few works—if any—contain information about their actual nationalities. Police files and labor-union initiation forms cannot, however, offer representative information on the majority of immigrants.

RECORDS OF IMMIGRANTS' VOLUNTARY ASSOCIATIONS

The records of the immigrants' own institutions offer more representative data and, fortunately, become abundant after the last decade of the nineteenth century, precisely when the availability of census returns ceases.

My first experience at the Asociación Española de Socorros Mutuos de Buenos Aires, once the largest mutual-aid society in the country but then on the brink of default, proved a fiasco. Understandably under the circumstances, the administrators refused to believe that my *investigación* was historical rather than fiscal. With a letter from the cultural attaché of the Spanish embassy certifying me as harmless, and after a few days of roaming around, I found (in a bathroom closet, of all places) what proved to be, despite its humble surroundings, a gold mine: individual enrollment forms from at least the 1880s, with the name of the applicant (including the maternal surname), age, locality and province of birth, sex, marital status, occupation, address, names and addresses of the two members who served as sponsors, transfer papers if they had belonged to other Spanish mutual-aid societies in South America, and their signatures or Xs, which served as a proxy for literacy. I recorded all variables except names and addresses for the 16,119 members who joined up to 1910; and complete information for immigrants from the specific localities I had selected for microhistorical analysis who joined between 1900 (when the forms began to specify hometown as well as province of birth) and 1930 (3,546 cases).

What made the mine even more auriferous was the representativeness of the data. As a pan-Hispanic institution, its membership was open to all Iberian groups, and it presented a very accurate reflection of the provincial makeup of Spaniards in the city. In terms of gender, women were underrepresented during the nineteenth century but achieved almost total relative balance by the first decade of the next. In terms of class, 20 percent of the membership held unskilled and menial jobs at a time when 26 percent of the immigrants in the city did so, a remarkably low level of underrepresentation considering that studies all over the world have demonstrated the lower participation of the poor in voluntary associations (see chapter 6). At any rate, I used this source for comparisons between different Iberian groups and not to represent the class constitution of the whole Spanish colony in the city.

Data sets with the names and information of immigrants from the areas I selected for microhistorical analysis were also constructed from the membership lists or application forms of the following regional, provincial and village associations (records existed only for the dates listed):

1. Centro Gallego: 1,281 cases between 1907 and 1930 of immigrants from five specific Galician localities included in the selected group. In addition to the list of incoming members, the center kept in a different "archive" old personal medical files that can be located via the member's number. Checking both sources, I determined the member's address, job, marital status, and the like, when he or she joined, and subsequent doctor visits or hospital stays, which allowed tracing. The problem, besides the dust and the rodents, lay in the fact that most of the records were missing but the cardboard files holding them were not, so one had to search in some fourteen files to find one record. Four days of manual labor produced fewer than a hundred traceable cases. But the method may prove productive for other urban and immigration historians.

2. Centro Navarro: 1,312 cases of natives of Navarre who joined the association between 1919 and 1930. Along with other sources dating back to the 1840s, this source was useful in the analysis of the diffusion of emigration from that province. That is, using New World sources I was able to show how the local origins of the immigrants from Navarre changed over almost a century.

3. Laurak-Bat (a Basque association): 128 cases of Navarrese immigrants who were members in 1878, and 1,110 who joined between 1901 and 1930 (526 of the latter included the names and birthplaces of their parents, which allowed some basic inter-generational and transatlantic tracing)

4. Centro Val de San Lorenzo (a village of 800 inhabitants in the province of León: 116 members between 1924 and 1930.

5. Montepío de Monserrat (a Catalan mutual-aid society): the entire membership for the following years: 1897 (709 members), 1912 (1,553), 1919 (1,357), and 1922 (1,613). Unlike the other sources, this one did not include information on birthplace (other that they were from Catalonia) and thus could not be used for microhistorical analysis. What made these

documents valuable was that—unlike those from the other associations, which consisted of lists of incoming members or their application forms —they listed the entire membership at the end of the year. I thus recorded all names, addresses, and occupations and was able to trace changes and measure spatial and occupational mobility and the relationship between the two.

From the various manuscript sources discussed above, I was able to construct data sets that, together, included information on more than 50,000 individuals (not counting information from Spanish documents). In addition to a solid empirical base, a data set of this size allowed an impressive level of analytical refinement. After all, when one begins to control for certain variables, the size of the sample can shrink amazingly fast. The large numbers therefore permit, for example, an examination of the impact of age and marital status on the occupations of women from a particular ethnic group, or at times even a village, at a level that is still statistically significant.

ORAL INTERVIEWS

The biographical data in the computer files were completed or augmented for the selected areas with information gathered through oral interviews and other sources. A procedure that proved helpful in this regard was taking lists of the immigrants from a particular area to community gathering places and events and to villages in Spain. By adding not only more information on the people I already had on the lists but also new names I could, in some cases, eliminate the problem of representativeness. At times the lists included more than nine-tenths of the immigrants from a particular locality in Buenos Aires.

Forty-nine taped interviews and innumerable (and often collective) chats in bars, cafés, and homes on both sides of the ocean also offered a wealth of information that could not be codified precisely because of its complexity and richness. The lists, however, not only served to awaken memories but also to double check their veracity. Some immigrants (normally males) displayed a proclivity to portray their journeys as pioneering adventures and their lives in the new land as great conquests. Perhaps this reflects the high value placed on personal independence and individual exploits by the Spanish, masculine, and capitalist culture; perhaps just plain bragging. Whatever the case, the lists often showed scores of people from their same village and dozens with the same surnames (at times both paternal and maternal) already settled in Buenos Aires when they arrived and that they held menial, low-paying jobs. Instead of confronting their versions directly, I merely asked them to describe their landing and their daily work life. Normally, memories of numerous relatives at the dock, of spending the first days at an uncle's house, of hard chores and nasty bosses came to mind. This demonstrates the risk of relying on only one type of source or method, in this case personal interviews and oral history but, as I showed in the text, also quantitative analysis.

SPANISH BAPTISMAL RECORDS AND CIVIL BIRTH REGISTRIES

The lists compiled from manuscript sources in Buenos Aires also allowed me to link information on immigrants there with that on their parents in Spain. Baptismal records offered a way of doing this, and before the appearance of the Spanish civil registry in 1871, the only one. But it is a laborious and inefficient way. For one thing, baptismal records only record births in a specific parish, and a single municipality can have several of them, sending the researcher into a forced tour of local chapels.[2] In addition, some immigrants listed the main village rather than the specific hamlet as their birthplace, making tracing in this manner extremely difficult. The information also varied considerably. Some priests recorded the occupation and birthplace of the parents and grandparents; others did not. For these reasons, the civil birth registries of the municipalities offer a more reliable source, and I used baptismal records only when unavoidable and in some specific case studies of illegitimacy. Using mostly the civil registries, I was able to link 405 immigrants from the following localities: Corcubión (41 cases), Finisterre (31), and Vimianzo (76), in the province of La Coruña, Galicia; Val de San Lorenzo, León (76); Pamplona (79) and Tafalla (59), Navarre; and Mataró, Barcelona (43). The linked data served to measure the degree and type of internal geographical mobility in the Old World (by comparing the birthplace of the immigrants to that of their parents) and its relationship to overseas emigration. It also permitted the analysis of transatlantic changes and continuities in social status.

I also worked with baptismal and marriage records from Buenos Aires parishes with large Spanish immigrant populations, using information on witnesses and their addresses to determine the importance of local neighborhood relations in comparison with Old World links. But the attempt was not productive because the documents do not specify the locality of birth of those involved (only the country, except, of course, for the christened child), which also made it difficult to link the information culled from these sources to the other data sets.

Municipal *padrones de vecindad* provided another useful source in Spain. These municipal manuscript censuses listed the names of all inhabitants of the locality, their age, birthplace, marital status, occupation, literacy, length of residence in the locality, whether they resided there at the time, and (in some cases) where the absentees were and how long they had been gone.[3] A welcome feature of these local registries is that they were taken often, even in years when no national census was conducted. But many have been lost, and for some localities, none has been preserved. In this regard, the fact that I had collected data on the Buenos Aires diasporas of dozens of Iberian communities (including various counties and the entire province of Navarre) increased the chances of finding *padrones* for specific municipalities. Using the remaining ones from six municipal districts from all over the peninsula (Corcubión, Finisterre, and Zas in Galicia; Val de San Lorenzo in León; the Baztán Valley in Navarre; and Mataró in Barcelona) and covering various years between 1847 and 1940, I was able to compile several data sets totaling just over 5,000 individual cases. The data allowed me to compare the emigrants with those who stayed behind in terms of the variables listed and in terms of their position in the household (which was not always listed but could be determined from the other information). Because the data came from six different districts, they also permitted a comparison of the composition of the population and the emigrants in the various localities (see notes to Table 8 for methodological issues regarding the use of the *padrones*).

In Arizkun, a small village on the piedmont of the Navarrese Pyrenees, the local priest provided a card file with the addresses of the 356 emigrants (scattered from Idaho to Chile) who received the parish newsletter around the 1960s. Although somewhat late for this study, this type of source could be particularly helpful for historians of more recent flows.

The correspondence from the Spanish embassy and consulate in Buenos Aires to the Spanish Ministry of Foreign Relations (kept in its archives in Madrid) offers another useful source. The reports concentrate mostly on political and commercial issues, but they also describe the situation of the Spanish community there. Among the correspondence, I also found a list of the 998 Spanish males who entered Argentina in 1861, with name, birthplace, age, marital status, occupation, and intended occupation in the new land (Archivo del Ministerio de Relaciones Exteriores (Madrid), "Correspondencia embajada Argentina," Legajo 1348). The comparison of the last two variables would have been interesting but proved useless because the clerk had rarely recorded both at the same time. Nevertheless, given the fact that Spanish emigration statistics begin only in 1882 and even after that are some of the worst in Europe, the document provided a way of locating the geographical origins of early emigrants. Other than this, I have had to rely on Argentine sources to establish the local origins of the immigrants.

The procedure of adding information from interviews and various sources to the computer files turned quantitative data into "semiqualitative" material. The files containing data on the parents had 32 fields (including "comments," with sundry information not suitable for quantitative analysis) and basically provided short biographies of the immigrants. In addition to this and oral interviews, I also relied on a wide range of more standard qualitative sources, which included:

IMMIGRANTS' NEWSPAPERS AND MAGAZINES

I was able to identify eighty-one of these by title but could locate only forty-two. The rest are not likely to have been preserved, for I searched almost every Buenos Aires library, including those of the immigrants' associations. (For a list of these publications see Jose C. Moya, "Notas sobre las fuentes para el estudio de la inmigración española en Buenos Aires," *Estudios Migratorios Latinoamericanos* 2, 4 [1986]:502–3.) They were particularly useful for information on community affairs and conflicts. Indeed, relying on this source alone would have led one to believe that the immigrants lived only to fight each other. I also located ephemeral publications from hometown associations in Buenos Aires that have only been preserved in people's homes. They filled many empty fields in the data sets and shed much light on community life at a more intimate and, I believe, meaningful level. Of the Spanish areas of origin selected for microanalysis, Mataró, Barcelona, was one of the few that was urban enough to have had newspapers then, and I used several from the second half of the nineteenth century that were held in the town library. The fact that they made few allusions to emigration was in itself, as we saw, meaningful.

ANARCHIST AND OTHER WORKING-CLASS PERIODICALS

I found the most complete collection of these in Amsterdam's Internationaal Instituut voor Sociale Geschiedenis, but most of the ones I used came from a surprisingly rich collection at the University of California, Los Angeles. These newspapers are plagued by long and repetitious editorials on doctrine, but the shorter articles and notices provided a means of examining the relationships and conflicts between and among Spanish immigrant anarchists and the rest of their compatriots in chapter 6. They also offer many insights into the links between immigrant anarchists in Buenos Aires and their coreligionists in Spain (although these connections cannot be fully understood without reading Spanish anarchist periodicals, which, to my surprise, I could not find, either in the Spanish national library or the national archive).

Except for *Caras y Caretas* (Buenos Aires' leading magazine of the period), I only read specific issues of Argentine mainstream newspapers to look for particular events.

LAW-SCHOOL THESES

I read twenty-four doctoral dissertations related to emigration, hoping to find in them a reflection of the Argentine elite's view on the subject. The task, besides tedious, proved futile. With four or five exceptions, they were circumspect and bland, full of platitudes and even plagiarism. For a catalogue of the theses, see: Revista de la Universidad de Buenos Aires, *Bibliografía doctoral de la Universidad de Buenos Aires y catálogo cronológico de las tesis en su primer centenario, 1821–1920* (Buenos Aires, 1920).

CONTEMPORARY SPANISH BOOKS AND ARTICLES
ON EMIGRATION

About thirty of these books, and a larger number of articles, were located. They are more open than the Argentine theses and reveal the Spanish elite's views on the subject but not much more. Town and village annals by local amateur historians proved particularly useful in the few cases they were available.

TRAVELERS' ACCOUNTS, TOURIST GUIDES, AND MEMOIRS

I used more than sixty travelers' accounts on both Spain and Buenos Aires, but mostly on the latter. Unlike the theses, these accounts tend to be candid and full of anecdotal evidence. Indeed, by using a large number of them, they can be turned into more than anecdotal evidence. When the same observations are repeated by scores of visitors one must assume either their accuracy or some form of collective self-delusion. Tourist guides are less numerous but also useful, particularly in their descriptions of Spanish villages on which there is little information. Memoirs (seven by Spanish immigrant leaders, and the rest by upper-class Argentines) give an elite version of matters. But perhaps because their authors are usually at an advanced age, they tend to be rather uninhibited and do offer valuable descriptions of city life.

POPULAR PLAYS

I used 334 of these dramas and comedies (or *sainetes*). Except for eleven from Spain, the rest were Argentine. Three hundred and eight opened between 1919 and 1922 and were published in Buenos Aires' theater bi-weekly *La Escena: Revista teatral.* I chose to concentrate on only a few years in order to be able to examine large numbers of contemporary plays and diminish the risk that they could reflect authorial idiosyncrasies rather than those of the genre. Using a bibliographical program (Notebook), a database was created from the eighty-one that alluded to immigration and ethnicity, copying the relevant lines or references into fields such as "portrayals of . . . " (*gallegos*, Italians, servants, and so forth). This allowed me to locate references speedily, but little else (in retrospect, I should have used a more powerful text-analysis program). At any rate, the plays provided a revealing window into Porteño attitudes and worldview. Attendance ran in the millions, making this form of entertainment more representative of mass culture than other literary forms. At the same time, competition was fierce, forcing playwrights to connect with the public. Plots, obviously, could not replicate the detailed monotony of everyday life. But they had to "make sense" to a massive audience, to speak a comprehensible language (in more than the linguistic sense), and to reflect easily identifiable social realities. The plays were not particularly creative, not to say experimental or audacious. But their mundane naturalism enhanced, I believe, their reliability as social-history sources.

In terms of films, early Argentine features (beginning in 1908) dealt mostly with early-nineteenth-century historical epics rather than with contemporary realities and immigration. The most useful in terms of portrayals of Spanish immigrants come in the 1930s, with a series in which the actress Nini Marshall plays the role of Cándida, a Galician servant, in the 1937 movie of the same name and in others.

POPULAR HUMOR

I collected more than 1,000 jokes sent by readers to *Caras y Caretas* for contests conducted between 1904 and 1908, in which those that were published received small cash prizes. Although filtered by the editorial office (much like letters to the editor), the fact that they manifested the views of more than 1,000 people rather than those of a staff writer made the jokes a more reliable reflector of popular opinions. The large numbers also turned them into a body of data that could reveal patterns rather than just anecdotal evidence. They were used to explore representations of two Iberian groups (Basques and Andalusians) and of servants in popular humor and to contrast these with portrayals in more conventional (and thus elite) sources.

CREATIVE LITERATURE

I used fiction and essays by Argentine litterateurs mostly in the last chapter and only to appraise the attitudes of the intelligentsia toward Spaniards and immigrants in general. Fiction by Spanish immigrants is more difficult to find with the exception of the novels and stories of the better-known Francisco de Grandmontagne. But I was able to locate some novels, stories, poems, and so forth in the libraries of the immigrant associations and in the immigrant press.

Notes

INTRODUCTION

1. Because the unevenness of national immigration statistics, the receiving countries' share of the Spanish overseas flow is difficult to determine. However, the following figures on Spanish residents in the principal host countries at about the time of World War I provide an approximate comparative picture:

Country	Year	Population	Foreigners	A	Spaniards	B	C
Argentina	1914	7,885,980	2,357,952	29.9	829,701	10.5	35.2
Cuba	1919	2,889,004	339,082	11.7	245,644	8.5	72.4
Brazil	1920	30,635,605	1,565,961	5.1	219,142	0.7	14.0
Uruguay	1911				50,000		
United States	1920	105,710,620	13,920,692	13.2	49,535	.05	0.4
Mexico	1910				30,000		
Chile	1920	3,753,799	120,436	3.2	25,962	0.7	21.6

A: Foreigners as a percentage of total population
B: Spaniards as a percentage of total population
C: Spaniards as a percentage of foreign-born population
SOURCES: Argentina, Comisión Nacional del Censo, *Tercer censo nacional* (Buenos Aires: Talleres Gráficos de L. J. Rosso, 1916–1919), vol. 2, 109, 396; Chile, Dirección General de Estadística, *Censo de población de la República de Chile levantado el 15 de diciembre de 1920* (Santiago: Soc. Imp. y Litografía Universo, 1925), 276, 289; Cuba, Dirección General del Censo, *Census of the Republic of Cuba 1919* (Havana: Maza, Arroyo y Caso, [1920?]), 310; for Mexico, Mariano Gonzalez-Rothvos y Gil, *La emigración española a Iberoamérica* (Madrid: Instituto Balmes de Sociología, 1949), 111; United States, Bureau of the Census, *Fourteenth Census of the United States Taken in the Year 1920* (Washington, D.C.: Government Printing Office, 1921–1923), vol. 2, 693; Brazil, Directoria Geral de Estatistica, *Recenseamento do Brazil realizado em 1 de setembro de 1920* (Rio de Janeiro: Typ. da Estatistica, 1922–1930), vol. 1, iv, 302–3, 316–17; for Uruguay, Spain, Consejo Superior de Emigración, *La emigración española transoceánica, 1911–1915* (Madrid: Hijos de T. Minuesa, 1916), 219.

2. Some 450,000 Spaniards are estimated to have come to the New World before 1650 (Peter Boyd-Bowman, "Patterns of Spanish Emigration to the Indies until 1600," *Hispanic American Historical Review* 56, 4 [1976]:580–604). Few data are available for the following 150 years, but rough estimates rarely exceed half a million.

3. Dedier Norberto Marquiequi, *La inmigración española de masas en Buenos Aires* (Buenos Aires: Centro Editor de América Latina, 1993), despite the title, deals not with the city of Buenos Aires but with the small Spanish community in the town of Luján in the province of Buenos Aires. Blanca Sánchez Alonso, *La inmigración española en Argentina: Siglos XIX y XX* (Gijón, Spain: Ediciones Jucar, 1992), deals with the country in general but offers much useful information on Buenos Aires. See also my review of this book in *Revista de Historia Económica* (Madrid) 11, 1 (1993):238–40. Hebe Clementi, ed., *Inmigración española en la Argentina (Seminario 1990)* (Buenos Aires: Oficina Cultural de la Embajada de España, 1991), also contains some chapters on Buenos Aires. And several of the many books on emigration published in Spain during the 1992 quincentenary touch on the exodus of one or another Iberian regional group to Argentina. None, however, offers, a monographic study of the Spanish community in Buenos Aires.

4. T. J. McMahon, "The Spanish Immigrant Community in Mexico City during the Porfiriato, 1876–1911" (Ph.D. diss., University of Notre Dame, 1978); and Michael Kenny, "The Integration of Spanish Expatriates in Ibero-America and Their Influence on Their Communities of Origin" (D.Phil. diss., University of Oxford, 1967), which deals with Mexico and Cuba. The only two books published by North American scholars on Spaniards in postindependence Latin America deal also with Mexico but not with mass migration. On one temporal extreme is Harold D. Sims, *La expulsión de los españoles de México, 1821–1828* (Mexico City: Fondo de Cultura Económica, 1974); on the other, Patricia Fagen, *Exiles and Citizens: Spanish Republican Exiles in Mexico* (Austin: University of Texas Press, 1973). William A. Douglass and Jon Bilbao, *Amerikanuak: Basques in the New World* (Reno: University of Nevada Press, 1975), deal mostly with the United States but include a fine chapter on Basque immigration in South America (chap. 3).

5. As an indication of the studies published on each country I used the electronic database WorldCat, which contains catalogues more than 30 million volumes in libraries worldwide, using the subject heading of emigration or immigration and the particular country.

6. I searched under the subject headings "Spaniards in Argentina," "Italians in Argentina," and so forth in WorldCat and then went through the list, noting those by Argentine scholars.

7. Charlotte Erickson, *Invisible Immigrants: The Adaptation of English and Scottish Immigrants in Nineteenth-Century America* (Coral Gables, Fla.: University of Miami Press, 1972).

8. The argument that one cannot understand immigrants' experiences without examining where they came from has been brilliantly demonstrated in a few but fine Latin American studies: Ida Altam's prize-winning study of emigration from Cáceres and Trujillo in northern Estremadura, *Emigrants and Soci-*

ety: Extremadura and Spanish America in the Sixteenth Century (Berkeley: University of California Press, 1989); and Samuel Baily's forthcoming book on Italians in Buenos Aires and New York, the manuscript of which the author kindly shared with me. Of Baily's several articles on the topic, "The Adjustment of Italian Immigrants in Buenos Aires and New York, 1870–1914," *American Historical Review* 88, 2 (1983):281–305 provides the best example of the overall approach of the book. William A. Douglass, *Emigration in a South Italian Town: An Anthropological History* (New Brunswick, N.J.: Rutgers University Press, 1984), which contains a chapter on immigrants from the town of Agnone in Buenos Aires, also offers a splendid example of how a microhistorical examination of the place of origin can illuminate the migration process.

9. Some of the best examples are: Dino Cinel, *From Italy to San Francisco: The Immigrant Experience* (Stanford, Calif.: Stanford University Press, 1982); and Ewa T. Morawska, *For Bread with Butter: The Life-Worlds of East Central Europeans in Johnstown, Pennsylvania, 1890–1940* (Cambridge, England: Cambridge University Press, 1985).

10. In addition to my own initial empirical findings, reading Ulf Beijbom's *Swedes in Chicago: A Demographic and Social Study of the 1846–1880 Immigration* (Uppsala: Studia Historica Upsaliensia, 1971) also encouraged me to begin my study at an earlier date. This book had a shortcoming: it ended before the Swedes began to arrive in Chicago in massive numbers, before the community had reached middle age. It also had a great virtue: by analyzing the immigrant community from its infancy it showed how some of its adult features originated.

11. Some of the classic studies on assimilation are: Milton M. Gordon, *Assimilation in American Life: The Role of Race, Religion, and National Origins* (New York: Oxford University Press, 1964); S. N. Eisenstadt, *The Absorption of Immigrants* (London: Routledge & Paul, 1954); and Charles Price, "The Study of Assimilation," in *Migration*, ed. J. A. Jackson (London: Cambridge University Press, 1969), 181–237.

1. FIVE GLOBAL REVOLUTIONS

1. Argentina, Ministerio de Relaciones Exteriores, *Memoria del ministerio presentada al Honorable Congreso Nacional en el año de 1882* (Buenos Aires, 1883), 140. (This and all other translations in the book are mind.) The library of the Ministry of Foreign Affairs (Palacio San Martín) in Buenos Aires has a complete collection of these Memorias, published between 1859 and 1905, and again after 1910, plus a *Boletín Mensual del Ministerio de Relaciones Exteriores*, published from 1884 to 1891, and, under the new title of *Documentos Diplomáticos y Consulares*, from 1903 on. While working there, I organized the volumes in chronological order and found them, though plagued with diplomatic formalities, to be a good qualitative source, particularly the consular reports from smaller towns, for information on the changing local conditions in areas of emigration.

2. Although overly mechanistic, some of the early systematizations of the push-pull scheme were anything but simplistic. In the pioneer works of Harry

Jerome and Dorothy S. Thomas, for example, the scheme appeared not as a heuristic device but as a developed model. Harry Jerome, in *Migration and Business Cycles* (New York, 1926), argued that fluctuations in the rate of immigration to the United States followed, sometimes with a lag of a year or two, cycles in the American economy. Moreover, to prove the primacy of the U.S. "pull," he asserted that business cycles were broadly synchronous on both sides of the Atlantic and that, therefore, immigrants were attracted by the upswings in the North American economy despite simultaneous prosperity in the Old World. On the other hand, Dorothy S. Thomas, in *Social and Economic Aspects of Swedish Population Movements 1750–1933* (New York, 1941), found that although American economic cycles had a clear impact on the rate of Swedish emigration, expansion in the Scandinavian industrial sector and the subsequent increase in internal rural–urban migration could significantly reduce the transatlantic flow. In the past two decades or so many demographers and cliometricians have used the push-pull approach in econometric studies in an effort to account for fluctuations in the flow and to reach a level of predictability. For an intelligent analysis of this literature, see J. D. Gould, "European Inter-Continental Emigration 1815–1914: Patterns and Causes," *Journal of European Economic History* 8 (Winter 1979):593–679. This trend has been running counter to the "human-centered" emphasis of social histories of immigration.

3. Asian emigration was actually greater than this figure, but movements, often seasonal, to neighboring countries accounted for much of it. According to Kingsley Davis (*The Population of India and Pakistan* [Princeton, N.J.: Princeton University Press, 1951], 13–14, 99), 30 million people left India between 1834 and 1932. Although a significant number went to the British Caribbean or South Africa, most were seasonal migrants to nearby Burma or Ceylon and the net emigration was only 6 million. Similarly, of 9 million Chinese who were overseas in about 1920, more than 90 percent lived in Southeast Asia (Siam, Malaya, the Dutch East Indies, French Indo-China, and so forth) (Victor Purcell, *The Chinese in Southeast Asia* [London: Oxford University Press, 1951], 43, 85, 175, 360, 386, 497). In the New World, Cuba became their most important destination (if we do not include Hawaii). See Duvon C. Corbitt, *A Study of the Chinese in Cuba, 1847–1947* (Wilmore, Ky.: Asbury College, 1971). The Japanese, on the other hand, preferred intercontinental to intra-Asiatic migration. Of the 776,000 who left their home islands between 1868 and 1941, 620,000 went to the Americas (Alcides Parejas Moreno, *Colonias japonesas en Bolivia* [La Paz, 1981], 37–38). Most Filipinos headed for the United States, where they were not barred by immigration quotas. See Antonio J. A. Pido, *The Pilipinos in America* (New York: Center for Migration Studies, 1986).

4. Although intercontinental migration (including that from Mexico to the United States and an estimate of illegal flows) has been increasing since the end of World War II, and particularly since 1980, it has not come close to the levels of the early part of this century, in either absolute or relative terms. In 1900 the world had 1.55 billion inhabitants and in the next decade 14.8 million people emigrated from their native continents. By 1980 the world population had tripled, to 4.48 billion, but the number of people leaving their native continents in the next decade had fallen by more than half, to 7.1 million. In absolute num-

bers the early-twentieth-century movement was thus two times larger than that of the 1980s; in terms of proportion to world population, six times larger. Calculated from data in Imre Ferenczi and Walter F. Willcox, *International Migrations* vol. 1 (New York, 1929); Maurice R. Davie, *World Immigration* (New York, 1936); and Fred Arnold, *Revised Estimates and Projections of International Migration 1980–2000* (Washington, D.C.: World Bank, Population and Human Resources Department, 1989).

5. Brinley Thomas' seminal *Migration and Economic Growth* (Cambridge, England: Cambridge University Press, 1954) was the first serious attempt to go beyond immediate symptoms by analyzing migration in terms of long, global trends. Key to Thomas' center-periphery model is the concept of a world, or at least an Atlantic, capitalist economy. Malthusian crises and disturbing technical innovations in the stratified and industrialized "center" (Britain) act as the original motivating factors for the population movement toward the fluid, underpopulated, and developing "periphery" (the United States). Increased migration is followed in the receiving country by increments in domestic investment, in imports of capital and goods, and in building and railroad construction and in the sending country by the opposite effects (what he called the minor secular cycle of eighteen to twenty years, in contrast to Jerome's synchronous business cycles). Then lower demographic pressure, a revitalized export economy, and surpluses in the balance of payments in the sending country eventually bring the other part of the cycle (characterized by low emigration and capital export and by high internal migration, domestic investment, and production). Over time, however, Thomas argued that the transfer of labor and capital narrowed the gap between the center and the periphery and brought migration to an end (this in contrast to orthodox dependency theories, in which the continuous relationship between center and periphery is thought to widen the gap). Like most ambitious paradigms, this one has received its share of criticism. At any rate, it does little to explain population movements from Spain to Argentina, both peripheral zones in the world economy, where the only significant transfer of capital was a reversed one—in the form of immigrant remittances—from the receiving country to the sending one.

6. K. F. Helleiner, "The Population of Europe from the Black Death to the Eve of the Vital Revolution," in *Cambridge Economic History of Europe*, vol. 4, ed. E. E. Rich and C. H. Wilson (Cambridge, England: Cambridge University Press, 1967), 1–95.

7. Herbert Moller, "Introduction," in *Population Movements in Modern European History*, ed. Herbert Moller (New York: Macmillan, 1964), 5–7. J. N. Biraben offers a different estimate: that the European population increased from 146 million in 1750 to 422 million in 1900, with its share of the world population going from 19 to 26 percent ("Essai sur l'évolution du nombre des hommes," *Population* 34, 1 [1979]:13–25). The twentieth century has witnessed a reversal of the trend. As the century ends, Europe holds less than one-tenth of the world's population. With the exception of Ireland, none of the twelve member states of the European Community have birthrates high enough to keep the population growing or even stable. The continent of the great nineteenth-century exodus is rapidly becoming a receptacle for Third World emigrants.

8. Michael W. Flinn, *The European Demographic System, 1500–1820* (Baltimore, Md.: Johns Hopkins University Press, 1985), esp. chaps. 1 ("The Revolution in Historical Demography"), 2 ("The Demographic System of the 'Ancien Régime'"), and 6 ("Breaking Out of the System").

9. This is not an uncontested argument. Two classic books published the same year—G. T. Griffith, *Population Problems in the Age of Malthus* (Cambridge, England, 1926); and M. C. Buer, *Health, Wealth and Population in the Early Days of the Industrial Revolution* (London, 1926)—presented the first modern elaborations of the traditional argument that the European population explosion had been due primarily to a marked decline in the death rate, in turn the result of declines in the number and severity of famines and plagues, reduction of war mortality, and improvements in agricultural technology, food supplies, and midwifery.

This view went largely uncontested until after World War II, when some revisionist scholars began to claim that improvements in sanitary and alimentary conditions had not been remarkable and that the demographic explosion had more to do with rising fertility than with declining death rates. See, for example, William Langer, "Europe's Initial Population Explosion," *American Historical Review* 69, 1 (1963):1–17.

More recent studies, however, have tended to vindicate the traditional analyses of Griffith and Buer. In a thorough study of seven European countries (including Spain), for example, Michael Flinn concluded that "[T]here is generally very little evidence to support the view that the European acceleration in the rate of population growth may be explained in terms of rising fertility: there is indeed more evidence of the reverse happening." "In most parts fertility either remained constant or actually declined. . . . The acceleration has to be explained in terms of mortality falling fast enough both to compensate for declining fertility and to produce a real increase in the rate of population growth" (Flinn, *European Demographic System*, 90, 100–101).

10. Jaime Vicens Vives, *An Economic History of Spain* (Princeton, N.J.: Princeton University Press, 1969), 179–81, 242–44 (for the demographic depression of the fifteenth century), 330–32 (for the expansion of the sixteenth century), 412–16 (for the seventeenth century's losses), 483–87, 617–21 (for the increase during the eighteenth and nineteenth centuries, respectively); Jordi Nadal, *La población española (siglos XVI a XX)* (Barcelona: Ariel, 1973); and Pedro Romero de Solís, *La población española en los siglos XVIII y XIX* (Madrid: Siglo XXII, 1973).

11. The linguist Peter Boyd-Bowman has compiled a list of 55,000 sixteenth-century Spanish emigrants to the Americas in five volumes published since 1964. For a summary of his findings on the regional origin of the settlers, see his "Patterns of Spanish Emigration to the Indies until 1600," *Hispanic American Historical Review* 56, 4 (1976):580–604. The calculation of population distribution in sixteenth-century Spain is based on figures contained in Javier Ruiz Almanza, *Población de Galicia: 1500–1945* (Madrid, 1948).

12. David A. Brading, *Miners and Merchants in Bourbon Mexico, 1763–1810* (Cambridge, England: Cambridge University Press, 1971), 106; also idem, "Los españoles en México hacia 1792," *Historia Mexicana* 23, 1 (1973):126–44; and

Susan Midgen Socolow, *The Merchants of Buenos Aires 1778–1810* (Cambridge, England: Cambridge University Press, 1978), 18–19, 186.

13. British writers often referred to Galicia as the Ireland of Spain because of its Celtic origins, its land-tenure and inheritance systems, its demographic growth, its "greenness," and its high emigration rates. See, for instance, John Lomas, ed., *O'Shea's Guide to Spain and Portugal* (London: Adam & Charles Black, 1905), 146–47; Annette M. B. Meakin, *Galicia: The Switzerland of Spain* (London: Methuen & Co., 1909), 51, 173, 177; Martin Hume, "Introduction" to Walter Wood, *A Corner of Spain* (London: Eveleigh Nash, 1910), 18–19; and Raymond Carr, *Spain, 1808–1939* (Oxford: Clarendon Press, 1970), 8, 421.

14. Antonio Pérez Prado, *Los gallegos y Buenos Aires* (Buenos Aires: Ediciones La Bastilla, 1973), 164. In an April 3, 1860, letter to the Spanish Ministry of Foreign Relations, the consul in Buenos Aires claimed that "the system of denigrating Spaniards by designating them with the disparaging name—among the local inhabitants—of 'Gallegos,' dates, my Lord, from the regime of General Rosas, who made of them the most despised beings in this society." But the practice of calling Spaniards *gallegos* appears also in early-nineteenth-century documents. See Archivo del Ministerio de Relaciones Exteriores (Madrid), "Correspondencia embajada Argentina," Legajo 1348, no. 44.

15. William Nimmo, *Random Sketches of Buenos Aires* (Edinburgh, 1868), translated into Spanish as *Estampas informales de Buenos Aires*, commentary by C. Moncaut (City Bell, Argentina: Editorial El Aljibe, 1983), 67. A quarter of a century later, another Scotch traveler also compared Basques to "old Scotch clans," this time because of their unwillingness to "mix much with Spaniards or natives, or, indeed, with any other nationality" (C. E. Akers, *Argentine, Patagonian, and Chilian Sketches, With a Few Notes on Uruguay* [London: Harrinson & Sons, 1893], 53).

16. Nadal, *Población española*, 192.

17. Ibid., 143; Romero de Solís, 232. The relative growth between 1750 and 1850 was also higher for Spain than for most other countries on the continent (Massimo Livi-Bacci, *Population and Nutrition: An Essay on European Demographic History* [Cambridge, England: Cambridge University Press, 1991], 6).

18. Vicente Pérez Moreda, "Spain's Demographic Modernization, 1800–1930," in *The Economic Modernization of Spain, 1830–1930*, ed. Nicolás Sánchez-Albornoz (New York: New York University Press, 1987), 13–41, questions the reliability of pre-1857 censuses, arguing that "The term 'population explosion'—frequently used to describe modern demography—cannot be applied to the Spanish case prior to 1900," but agrees with the other scholars cited in that "growth occurred most vigorously in the first half of the century, especially between 1815 and 1860; slackened in the second half; then resurged after 1900" (p. 13). Similarly, Adrian Shubert maintains that Spain made the transition to modern demographics (low death rates and birthrates) later than did western European countries but that Spanish population growth "from 1800 to 1850 equalled the European rate, from 1850 to 1900 . . . was below and from 1900 to 1950 . . . was above it" (*A Social History of Modern Spain* [London: Unwin Hyman, 1990], 24–32).

19. From a base of 100 in 1750, Russia's population had increased to 143 by

1800, 245 by 1850, and 451 by 1900. This rate of early expansion is comparable only to that of Great Britain: 100, 142, 281, and 500 for the respective years.

20. The French, Dutch, Swedes, and other Europeans had also come to the New World. But only the immigration of the four national groups mentioned reached significant proportions in the eighteenth century. See R. J. Dickson, *Ulster Emigration to Colonial America, 1718–1785* (Belfast: Ulster Historical Foundation, 1976); and A. G. Roeber, *Palatines, Liberty, and Property: German Lutherans in Colonial British America* (Baltimore, Md.: Johns Hopkins University Press, 1993). I do not know of any study of eighteenth-century Portuguese emigration to Brazil, but the economist Celso Furtado, *The Economic Growth of Brazil: A Survey from Colonial to Modern Times* (Berkeley: University of California Press, 1963), 80–81, considered this migration the most important factor in the development of the country during that century, of greater relevance than the discovery of gold and diamonds, which ended up in English coffers. The general studies of Joel Serrão, *Emigração portuguesa, sondagem histórica* (Lisbon: Livros Horizonte, [1971]), 55, 62; and Eduardo Sousa Ferreira, *Origens e formas da emigração* (Lisbon: Iniciativas Editoriais, 1976), 33, mention the predominance of the Portuguese Northeast in the eighteenth-century exodus. The same was true a century later, as shown by Ann M. Pescatello, "Both Ends of the Journey: An Historical Study of Migration and Change in Brazil and Portugal, 1889–1914" (Ph.D. diss., University of California, Los Angeles, 1970), 49–51.

21. For the increase in migration restrictions in the twentieth century, see Alan Dowty, *Closed Borders: The Contemporary Assault on Freedom of Movement* (New Haven, Conn.: Yale University Press, 1987). Of the twenty-one countries with the greatest emigration restrictions during the 1980s "all [were] ideologically doctrinaire one-party states, and, except for Burma, Iraq, and Somalia, define themselves as Marxist-Leninist" (p. 185). With the collapse of the Socialist block, the constraints are now mostly limited to immigration controls in capitalist countries, "quasi-Liberal" insofar as they favor, at least officially, the unconstrained circulation of goods, capital, technology, and ideas but constrain the free inflow of people.

22. For the population theories of these classical economists and demographers, see J. Overbeek, *History of Population Theories* (Rotterdam: Rotterdam University Press, 1974), 35–50. For the continuing populationist positions of Spanish officials during the first half of the nineteenth century and their rejection of Malthusian doctrine, see Robert S. Smith, "The Reception of Malthus' Essay on Population in Spain," *Rivista Internazionale di Scienze Economiche e Commerciali* 16, 6 (1969):550–65.

23. For the role of local authorities, see Marcus Lee Hansen, *The Atlantic Migration, 1607–1860* (Cambridge, Mass.: Harvard University Press, 1940), chap. 1; and Kristian Hvidt, *Flight to America: The Social Background of 300,000 Danish Emigrants* (New York: Academic Press, 1975), chap. 2. The role of local authorities at times surpassed mere encouragement. In the 1870s, for example, several Swiss cantons used emigration systematically to get rid of not only the poor but also the invalid, sick, old, and criminal. In Spain the third article in the "Royal decree of 16 September, 1853" instructed local authorities to

issue passports and licenses gratis to paupers, but I found no instance in which the authorities paid for the fares of undesirables; and neither did a U.S. correspondent traveling through the country in the 1920s: "I saw more beggary in Spain than in any other country, possibly excepting Portugal. There is no evidence, however, of any definite attempt to send their destitute out of the country to America, North or South, or to Cuba" (Fred H. Rindge Jr., "Spain and Her Emigrants," *Current History* 19 [1923]:481–82). The practice did not seem prevalent in the Nordic countries, either. See Hans Norman and Harald Runblom, *Transatlantic Connections: Nordic Migration to the New World after 1800* (Oslo: Norwegian University Press, 1988), 122.

24. For the changing emigration policies of different European countries, see: H. J. M. Johnston, *British Emigration Policy* (New York: Oxford University Press, 1973); Hvidt, *Flight to America*, chap. 2 (for Denmark); Ann-Sofie Kalvemark, "Swedish Emigration Policy in an International Perspective, 1840–1925," in *From Sweden to America*, ed. Harold Runblom and Hans Norman (Minneapolis: University of Minnesota Press and Uppsala: Acta Univesitatis Upsaliensis, 1976), 94–113; Miriam Halpern Pereira, *A politica portuguesa de emigração (1850–1930)* (Lisbon: A Regra do Jogo, 1981), 48–58; and Benjamin P. Murdzek, *Emigration in Polish Socio-Political Thought, 1870–1914* (Boulder, Colo.: East European Quarterly, 1977).

25. A list of the principal legislative measures on emigration in the nineteenth century can be found in Javier Vales Failde, *La emigración gallega* (Madrid, 1902), 143–226.

26. Moisés Llorden Miñambres, "Posicionamientos del estado y de la opinión pública ante la emigración española ultramarina a lo largo del siglo XIX," *Estudios Migratorios Latinoamericanos* 21 (August 1992):275–90, concludes that the main concern of Spanish authorities regarding emigration was to prevent draft evasion.

27. The local census (or *padrón*) listed both actual residents and those absent from the municipality, their ages, and how long they had been absent, allowing me to identify all males who had emigrated between the ages of eighteen and twenty-three. I then compared this list with the notarial registers of permits for draft-age emigrants between 1840 and 1865 compiled by Carlos Idoate Ezquieta in his *Emigración navarra del Valle de Baztán a América en el siglo XIX: Inventario de documentos* (Pamplona: Gobierno de Navarra, [1988?]).

28. See for example, Meakin, *Galicia*, 172–73; Spain, Congreso de los Diputados, *Diario de las sesiones de cortes*, Legislatura de 1887–88, Tomo II, num. 16, pg. 347; Argentina, *Memorias del Ministerio de Relaciones Exteriores*, 1898, 178.

29. Luis de Larra and Mauricio Gullón, *Los emigrantes: Sainete lírico en un acto y tres cuadros en prosa* (Madrid, 1889).

30. Antonio Conrado y Asprer, *Cartas sobre emigración y colonias* (Madrid: Imprenta de D. A. Pérez Dubrull, 1881), 61. See José Colá y Goiti, *La emigración vasco-navarra* (Vitoria, Spain: Establecimiento Tipográfico de la Viuda e Hijos de Iturre, 1883) for another contemporary work expressing similar antiemigration views.

31. Miguel López Martínez, *Emigración y colonización* (Madrid, 1881), 3, 29.

32. Antonio Correa Fernández, *Historia de fin de siglo: Descripción histórica-geográfica de la provincia de Lugo* (Lugo, Spain, 1900), 98; idem, *Ensayo de topografía médica de la provincia de Lugo* (Lugo, Spain, 1891), 86–88; and Miguel Gil Casares, *La herencia y el contagio de la tuberculosis pulmonar y de la lepra en Galicia* (Santiago, Spain, 1912), 5–6, 9–10.

33. Wenceslao Fernández-Flórez, *La casa de la lluvia; Luz de luna; La familia Gomar* (Madrid: Renacimiento, 1931), 135, 147, 166.

34. Cited in Juan Díaz-Caneja, *Apuntes sobre la emigración castellana* (Palencia, Spain: Imprenta y Librería de Gutiérrez, Liter y Herrero, 1909), 8.

35. Benito Pérez Galdós, *El tacaño Salomón* (Madrid: Librería de los Sucesores de Hernando, 1916). Buenos Aires' Spaniards found the play offensive, and one of their leaders, Félix Ortiz y San Pelayo, wrote a book vindicating them against this and other attacks by their peninsular compatriots (*Vindicación de los españoles en las naciones del Plata* [Buenos Aires: Librería La Facultad, 1917]). In fairness to Pérez Galdós, one can argue that the representation of emigrants and returnees in his opus was more often than not sympathetic, or at least more so than the norm in contemporary Spanish literature. The character of Agustín Caballero in his 1884 novel *Tormento*, for example, is frank, industrious, dignified, and, unlike most other *indianos* [rich returnees] in Spanish literature, does not flaunt his wealth. Similarly, José María Cruz, the *indiano* in his 1892 *La loca de la casa*, appears as an energetic agent of progress and modernity favorably contrasted to the other characters' lethargy, an almost Darwinian force essential for the regeneration of an ossified society. Even the persona of José Salomón that so insulted the immigrants in Buenos Aires ends up teaching some useful lessons in frugality to the prodigal protagonist back home.

36. Ramón Bullón Fernández, *El problema de la emigración y los crímenes de ella* (Barcelona, 1914). Other examples of writings entitled "El problema" are: Ricardo Mella y Cea, *El problema de la emigración en Galicia* (Barcelona, 1885); Cristóbal Botella, *El problema de la emigración* (Madrid, 1888); Francisco Serrano de la Pedrosa, *El problema de la emigración* (Madrid, 1900); J. Amengual Oliver, *El problema de la emigración* (Palma de Mallorca, 1905); Marquéz de la Fuensanta de Palma, *El problema migratorio* (Madrid, 1905); Práxedes Zancada, "El problema de la emigración," *Nuestro Tiempo* (Madrid), February 10, 1906; Luis Otero Pimentel, *En honor a Galicia: Estudios sobre los problemas de la emigración* (Cádiz, 1907); Aguilera (el Licenciado), "El problema de la emigración," *Vida Marítima* (Madrid), February 28, 1907; Eduardo Calvet, *El problema de la emigración* (Barcelona, 1913); and Francisco Arderius, *Política hispano-americana: Problemas de la emigración* (Madrid, 1915).

37. Blanca Sánchez Alonso, "La visión contemporánea de la emigración española," *Estudios Migratorios Latinoamericanos* 13 (December 1989):439–66, also noticed the persistence and predominance of anti-emigration discourses throughout the mass-exodus period.

38. Rafael M. Liern, *Americanos de rega: Juguete cómico-lírico en un acto* (Madrid, 1873).

39. Colá y Goiti, *La emigración vasco-navarra*, 79.

40. Cited in Díaz-Caneja, *Apuntes sobre la emigración castellana*, 8.

41. This semipornographic novelette dissembled as a naturalist novel was

written in Buenos Aires by the Spaniard Eduardo López Bayo in 1891. It tells the story of a respectable and refined orphan from Madrid who emigrates to Buenos Aires expecting to find work as a governess and is deceived by an Argentine madam and seduced by her son.

42. Fernando Fernández Rosete, *La emigración: Comedia en dos actos* (Cangas de Onís, Asturias, Spain, 1913).

43. See Spain, Patronato Real para la Represión de la Trata de Blancas, *Recueil des lois et ordonnances en vigeur pour la . . .* (Madrid, 1913).

44. Spain, Consejo Superior de Emigración, *La emigración española transoceánica, 1911–1915* (Madrid, 1916), 403. Legally, at that time married women were required to have their husband's authorization to emigrate alone and single women under the age of twenty-five, that of their parents. All other women simply required a personal identification card, as did men.

45. Conrado y Asprer, *Cartas sobre emigración y colonias*, 35.

46. López Martínez, *Emigración y colonización*, 25.

47.. Luis Palomo, *La emigración española a América* (Madrid, 1911), 17.

48. For the treatment of emigration in the creative literature of other European countries during the same period, see: Pasquino Crupi, *Letteratura ed emigrazione* (Reggio di Calabria, Italy: Casa del Libro Editrice, 1979), a study of the theme in the works of eight Italian authors and of its relative absence from Italian poetry; Fernanda Silva-Brummel, *"E todos, todos se vão": Emigration und emigranten in der portugiesischen literatur* (Frankfurt: Haag & Herchen, 1987), 29–35, 118–40, for the views of Portuguese intellectuals and for literary portrayals of emigrants and *brasileiros* [returnees, the equivalent of Spain's *indianos*]; Hans-Georg Stalder, *Anglo-Irish Peasant Drama: The Motifs of Land and Emigration* (Bern: Peter Lang, 1978), 76–148, for the themes of emigration and return in four dramas about rural life written in English by Irish playwrights; and Mary Lowe-Evans, *Crimes against Fecundity: Joyce and Population Control* (Syracuse, N.Y.: Syracuse University Press, 1989), 31–50, for Joyce's defense of emigration and attack on the Catholic Church for causing the exodus and then opposing it.

49. Fernández Rosete, *La emigración*, 5–7. Four decades earlier, another Asturian dramatist, Saturio Alvarez Montequín, had also denounced emigration in his *La emigración a la Habana: Drama original en un acto y en verso* (Oviedo, 1874) but defended "the liberty that we all should have to fix our residence in any corner of the world."

50. From Manuel Curros Enríquez's poem, "A Emigración" (written in the 1880s), *Obras completas* (Madrid: Aguilar, 1979), 111–13.

51. See, for example, the following parliamentary sessions: Spain, Congreso de los Diputados, *Diario de las sesiones de cortes*, Legislatura de 1887–1888, vol. 1, no. 10, 200–201, and vol. 2, no. 13, 279.

52. José Lago, interview by author, tape recording, Finisterre, Galicia, Spain, August 22, 1989. Interestingly, his concept of individual freedom of movement related only to emigration restrictions. When I asked him about Argentine immigration restrictions after the 1930s, he felt that "it is their country and they have the right to do what they want."

53. The Andalusian rhyme is a common one that I have heard in many

places; the Galician one is a local song from the Rianxo, a sea inlet in the south of the province of La Coruña, transcribed in J. A. Duran, *Historia de caciques bandos e ideologías en la Galicia no urbana: Rianxo, 1910–1914* (Madrid: Siglo XXI, 1972), 144.

54. The practice of enclosure dated back to Tudor times but only became widespread in the eighteenth century. See J. D. Chambers and G. E. Mingay, *The Agricultural Revolution, 1750–1880* (London: B. T. Batsford, 1966), chap. 4; J. A. Yelling, *Common Field and Enclosure in England, 1450–1850* (London: Macmillan, 1977); and Robert Allen, *Enclosure and the Yeoman* (New York: Oxford University Press, 1992).

55. Leslie Page Moch, *Moving Europeans: Migration in Western Europe since 1650* (Bloomington: Indiana University Press, 1992), 149; Philip E. Ogden and Paul E. White, eds., *Migrants in Modern France: Population Mobility in the Later Nineteenth and Twentieth Centuries* (London: Unwin Hyman, 1989), 7, 34–38; and G. Noiriel, "L'Immigration en France: Une histoire en friche," *Annales: Économies, Sociétés, Civilisations* 41 (1986):751–69.

56. Josep Fontana, "Transformaciones agrarias y crecimiento económico en la España contemporánea," in *Cambio económico y actitudes políticas en la España del siglo XIX*, ed. Josep Fontana (Barcelona: Ariel, 1973), 149–96.

57. J. Harrison, *An Economic History of Modern Spain* (New York: Holmes & Meier, 1978), 26–39.

58. Angel García Sanz, "Crisis de la agricultura tradicional y revolución liberal (1800–1850)," in *Historia agraria de la España contemporánea*, vol. 1, ed. Angel García Sanz and Ramón Garrabou (Barcelona: Editorial Crítica, 1985), 30. See also Francisco Simón Segura, *La desamortización española del siglo XIX* (Madrid: Instituto de Estudios Fiscales, 1973).

59. Jaime Vicens Vives maintained that disentailment "in the end benefitted only the rich; that is, those who had money to buy the lands which were being disentailed" (*Economic History of Spain*, 625). Raymond Carr agrees in that "sales inevitably benefitted the more prosperous proprietors who could withstand bad years and buy out his less fortunate neighbors" (*Spain, 1808–1939*, 625). Angel García Sanz sees the liberal revolution as an alliance between the bourgeoisie, the nobility, and prosperous peasants against the Church and the majority of the peasantry ("Crisis de la agricultura tradicional," 9–17). And Joseph Harrison claims that "Spain provides us with an example of the French revolution of 1789 in reverse: agrarian reform was carried out at the expense of the peasantry" (*Economic History of Modern Spain*, 25).

60. Díaz-Caneja, *Apuntes sobre la emigración castellana*, 69–72. For a recent effort to link emigration and agrarian crisis, see Ricardo Robledo, "Crisis agraria y éxodo rural: emigración española a ultramar, 1880–1920," in *La crisis agraria de fines del siglo XIX*, ed. Ramón Garrabou et al. (Barcelona: Editorial Crítica, 1988), 212–44.

61. For the mild effects of disentailment in Galicia, see Jesús García Fernández, *Organización del espacio y economía rural en la España atlántica* (Madrid: Siglo Veintiuno, 1975), 143–44.

62. The findings of Spanish historian Antonio M. Bernal for the early decades of the twentieth century concur with my data on the nineteenth century.

He found little relationship between Andalusian rural poverty and emigration and concluded that most overseas emigrants originated not from the areas of latifundia but from those of widespread landownership ("La emigración de Andalucía," in *Españoles hacia América: La emigración en masa, 1880–1930*, comp. Nicolás Sánchez-Albornoz [Madrid: Alianza Editorial, 1988], 154–60). The same inverse relationship between latifundia and emigration has been found in Portugal, Italy, and Germany. See Fernando E. da Silva, *Emigração portuguesa* (Coimbra: Franca & Armenio, 1917), 153–59, 331; Pino Arlacchi, *Mafia, Peasants and Great Estates: Society in Traditional Calabria*, trans. Jonathan Steinberg (Cambridge, England: Cambridge University Press, 1983), 185; and Takenori Inoki, "Aspects of German Peasant Emigration to the United States, 1815–1914: A Reexamination of Some Behavioral Hypotheses in Migration Theory" (Ph.D. diss., Massachusetts Institute of Technology, 1974), 243–44.

63. Rafael Gómez Chaparro, *La desamortización civil en Navarra* (Pamplona: Ediciones Universidad de Navarra, 1967), 170–71.

64. Rachel Bard, *Navarra: The Durable Kingdom* (Reno: University of Nevada Press, 1982), 175.

65. Pedro de Madrazo, *Navarra y Logroño*, vol. 18, no. 2, *España, sus monumentos y artes, su naturaleza e historia* (Barcelona, 1886), 94, 110–11.

66. Combining municipal census lists for 1855 and the notarial records for 1851–1855, I calculated the average annual emigration from the municipality of Baztán (a 275-square-kilometer area with 9,732 inhabitants disseminated across fifteen main villages and hundreds of farmsteads which occupies the eastern half of the Bidasoa Valley in Navarre) to be 27.7 per thousand for the quinquennium 1851–1855. The comparative figure for Ireland for the same period is 22.8 per thousand. Of the thirty-two Irish counties only the six counties in Munster Province and two others surpassed the northern Navarrese figure. See Kerby A. Miller, *Emigrants and Exiles: Ireland and the Irish Exodus to North America* (New York: Oxford University Press, 1985), 576.

67. Zas, a municipal district of 132 square kilometers and a population of 5,760 in 1897, is dispersed over 17 parishes and 108 villages and hamlets, only two of which had more than 300 inhabitants. The literacy figures for males aged fifteen to forty include all emigrants in that cohort (53) and nonemigrants in the same cohort (98) from a one-in-ten random sample of the rest of the population.

68. In 1905 the municipal district of Corcubión consisted of a maritime town of 1,328 surrounded by five agricultural hamlets with a combined population of 280. The literacy rates for male peasants aged fifteen to forty were 63 percent for emigrants (N = 19) and 53 percent for nonemigrants (N = 32). For young males from the town, the rates were 81 and 72 percent, respectively. The figures are based on a universe of all adults (aged thirteen and over) listed in the 1905 *padrón*. The figures for Val de San Lorenzo, León, a village of 958 inhabitants in 1924, are drawn from all emigrants and a one-in-five sample of the rest of the population. Here, 98 percent of young emigrant males (N = 46) knew how to read and write, compared with 91 percent of their counterparts who stayed home (N = 24). The high overall figures reflect the facts that this

region traditionally enjoyed higher literacy rates than Galicia and that the sample comes from a more recent date, when the educational system had expanded.

69. Argentina, *Boletín mensual del Ministerio de Relaciones Exteriores*, May 1884, 96. A quarter of a century later, Spanish officials would employ a logic similar to that of their Argentine counterparts to explain the exodus from the nearby town of Sanlúcar de Barrameda. They could not understand why so many left for Argentina from a town that seemed thriving and prosperous, so they blamed an old phylloxera attack on the grapevines of the surrounding countryside (Spain, *Boletín del Consejo Superior de Emigración*, 1909, 569–70).

70. This link between relative prosperity and emigration has been noticed in other places and from different angles. In terms of employment, Monika Glettler found "many examples in Eastern and Western Slovakia showing that, especially in the poorer regions, no, or almost no, emigration took place. Conversely, in areas where it was easy to work during the whole year, the Slovak population left to make money in the U.S. ("The Hungarian Government Position on Slovak Emigration, 1885–1914," in *Overseas Migration from East-Central and Southeastern Europe, 1880–1940*, ed. Julianna Puskas [Budapest: Akademiai Kiado, 1990], 117). In terms of collective prosperity, Julianna Puskas observed that in multi-ethnic Hungary the most prosperous group, the Germans, were the first to emigrate overseas ("Some Results from my Research on the Transatlantic Emigration from Hungary on the Basis of Macro- and Micro-Analysis," in *ibid.*, 50, 237). Within Calabria, Italy, sociologist Pino Arlacchi found that the "most wretched and oppressed communities" had the lowest rates of emigration, and vice versa (*Mafia, Peasants and Great Estates*, 175–76, 183–87). From a temporal angle, Rudolph M. Bell, in his trailblazing study of four Italian communities, found a strong correlation between "good times" and peasant emigration during the nineteenth century (*Fate and Honor, Family and Village: Demographic and Cultural Change in Rural Italy since 1800* [Chicago: University of Chicago Press, 1979], 187). For Germany, Takenori Inoki concluded that most overseas rural emigrants were peasant proprietors from the more egalitarian southwestern states (Baden, Wurttemberg, the Rhenish Palatinate and the Rhine Province). Moreover, those who originated from the East Elbian regions dominated by Junkers and their large estates were primarily "landless contract-bounded agricultural workers, a segment of rural society that was far from being the lowest category within the rural economic hierarchy" ("Aspects of German Peasant Emigration," 243–48).

` Yda Saueressig-Schreuder, on the other hand, claims that among Dutch Catholics "emigration was related to poverty and most emigrants were drawn from the lower classes of rural society." Yet her own data seem to prove otherwise. Of the 215 emigrants listed in Table 8 of her article, only 22 percent are categorized as "needy," the majority (65 percent) appear in the middle category of *mingegoed* or "less well-to-do," and 14 percent appear as "well-to-do." She admits that those "with some landed property of their own [rather than the landless] . . . formed the bulk of the emigrant population" ("Dutch Catholic Emigration in the Mid-Nineteenth Century: Noord-Brabant, 1847–1871," *Journal of Historical Geography* 11, 1 [1985]:50, 64–67).

71. Shubert, *Social History of Modern Spain*, 78. For the only empirical study of remittances, mostly related to Asturias, see José R. García López, *Las remesas de los emigrantes españoles en América, siglos XIX y XX* (Colombres, Spain: Ediciones Jucar, 1992).

72. Idoate Ezquieta, *Emigración navarra*, 26.

73. See for example, Julio Caro Baroja, *La hora navarra del siglo XVIII* (Pamplona: Institución Príncipe de Viana, 1969), 21–22.

74. Alejandro Arizcun Cela, *Economía y sociedad en un valle pirenaico del Antiguo Régimen: Baztán, 1600–1841* (Pamplona: Gobierno de Navarra, Departamento de Educación y Cultura, 1988), 63, shows that 53 of the 115 landowning households in the northern Navarrese village of Irurita in 1851, and 26 of the 88 landless ones, were extended families.

75. A. Meijide Pardo, *La emigración gallega intrapeninsular en el siglo XVIII* (Madrid: Instituto Balmes de Sociología, 1960), 8, 65–66; Germán Ojeda and José L. San Miguel, *Campesinos, emigrantes, indianos: Emigración y economía en Asturias, 1830–1930* (Gijón, Spain: Ayalga, 1985), 19.

76. Benito de Cabo Ares, interviewed by author, tape recording, Val de San Lorenzo, León, Spain, August 17, 1989.

77. For example, the literacy rate of the sixty people from Zas who had emigrated overseas by 1897 was 70 percent; that of the eighty who had moved to Portugal and Madrid, 51 percent, about the same as the cohort who stayed home (Zas, "Padrón de 1897" in the municipal archive). Similarly, better-off Irish peasants crossed the Atlantic while their poorer neighbors crossed the Irish Sea to Britain (Cecil J. Houston and William J. Smyth, *Irish Emigration and Canadian Settlement: Patterns, Links, and Letters* [Toronto: University of Toronto Press, 1990], 21). Poorer peasants were also overrepresented among internal migrants in the German, Austro-Hungarian and Russian empires (Walter Nugent, *Crossings: The Great Transatlantic Migrations, 1870–1914* [Bloomington: Indiana University Press, 1992], 68, 87). Even among internal migrants, some English works suggest that "long-distance migrants had more skill or education than short-distance migrants" (D. B. Grigg, "Ravenstein and the 'Laws of Migration,'" *Journal of Historical Geography* 3, 1 [1977]: 48).

78. W. W. Rostow noticed that the flow of emigration coincided with industrialization in Japan, Russia, Sweden, and Germany in his classic *The Stages of Economic Growth* (Cambridge, England: Cambridge University Press, 1960), xi. Seventy years earlier, E. G. Ravenstein had turned such observation into one of his laws of migration: "Migration increases in volume as industries and commerce develop" ("The Laws of Migration," *Journal of the Royal Statistical Society* 52 [1889]: 286).

79. There are numerous studies of industrialization in Catalonia. Two of the most thorough ones are: Pierre Vilar, *La Catalogne dans l'Espagne moderne: Recherches sur les fondements économiques des structures nationales* (Paris: S.E.V.P.E.N., 1962), 3 vols; and J. Carrera Pujal, *La economía de Cataluña en el siglo XIX* (Barcelona: Bosch, 1961), 4 vols.

80. Felipe Gallego, *Los comienzos de la industrialización en España* (Madrid: Ediciones de la Torre, 1979), 14–15.

81. Jordi Nadal, "The Failure of the Industrial Revolution in Spain, 1830–1914," in *The Fontana Economic History of Europe*, vol. 4, no. 2, ed. C. M. Cipolla (London: Collins/Fontana, 1973), 608.

82. In addition to proto-industrial towns, the sources of early emigration were small islands and mountain valleys near the coast, in our case the Canary and Balearic islands and the Cantabrian and Pyrenean foothills. Apparently, people inhabiting these types of geographies joined the flow not only earlier but also with greater force. In her superb synthesis *Moving Europeans*, Moch found that "the provinces of western Europe that sent the greatest proportion of their people abroad were mountainous regions and small islands" (p. 149).

83. Vicens Vives, *Economic History of Spain*, 623.

84. Spain, Dirección General del Instituto Geográfico y Estadístico, *Reseña geográfica y estadística de España* (Madrid, 1912), vol. 2, 127. The statistics may contain some distortion because they included all overseas passengers, not just emigrants.

85. Carr, *Spain, 1808–1939*, 268.

86. Ibid, 54, 206.

87. Jaime Vicens Vives, *Cataluña en el siglo XIX*, trans. from the Catalan by E. Borrás Cubells (Madrid: Rialp, 1961), 44.

88. A recent attempt to deal with the issue is Robert Kleiner, Tom Sorensen, Odd Dalgard, Torbjorn Moum, and Dale Drews, "International Migration and Internal Migration: A Comprehensive Theoretical Approach," in *Migration across Time and Nations*, ed. Ira A. Glazier and Luigi De Rosa (New York: Holmes & Meier, 1986). Despite the subtitle, however, the approach is anything but comprehensive, for it deals only with the differences between in-migration and emigration in terms of the decision-making process of the prospective migrant. The questions of relative timing and causation are not posed.

89. This was one of the basic arguments in Dorothy Thomas' pioneer work *Social and Economic Aspects of Swedish Population Movements*. Similarly, Walter Nugent found, in his recent synthesis *Crossings*, that in Germany, Sweden, and England "areas around large industrializing cities were underrepresented in the overseas migration because they absorbed the potential labor force nearby" (p. 66).

90. Brinley Thomas, *Migration and Economic Growth*. See note 5 for an explanation of his model.

91. For a similar case, see Franco Ramella, "Emigration from an Area of Intense Industrial Development: The Case of Northwestern Italy," in *A Century of European Migrations, 1830–1930*, ed. Rudolph J. Vecoli and Suzanne M. Sinke (Urbana: University of Illinois Press, 1991), 261–62.

92. Ramón Castro López, *La emigración en Galicia* [1912] (La Coruña: Tipografía El Noroeste, 1923), 66–68.

93. Fernández Rosete, *La emigración*.

94. Manuel Gil de Oto, *La Argentina que yo he visto* (Barcelona: B. Bauzá, 1914), 66.

95. Hansen, *Atlantic Migration*. Chapter 8 contains a very perceptive analysis of the relationship between emigration and trade routes in the years up to 1860.

96. Some of the key mechanical inventions actually took place decades before the midnineteenth century, but their use became widespread much later. For example, thirty-seven years separated James Watt's steam engine (1770) and Robert Fulton's successful use of it in a steamboat (1807); and three more decades went by before Samuel Cunard founded the first transatlantic steamship line (1840). Similarly, the introduction of iron hulls (1818), the screw propeller (1836), steel hulls (1870), the triple expansion engine (1874), internal combustion engine (1886), compound steam turbine (1884), and diesel engine (1895) and their widespread use was often separated by decades. See K. T. Rowland, *Steam at Sea: A History of Steam Navigation* (New York: Praeger, 1970).

97. James E. Vance Jr., *Capturing the Horizon: The Historical Geography of Transportation since the Sixteenth Century* (Baltimore, Md.: Johns Hopkins University Press, 1990), 456–75.

98. N. R. P. Bonsor, *South Atlantic Seaway: An Illustrated History of the Passenger Lines and Liners from Europe to Brazil, Uruguay and Argentina* (Jersey Channel Islands: Brookside Publications, 1983), catalogs sixty-four major companies serving those routes between 1851 and 1930, of which only three flew the Spanish flag.

99. The Argentine consul in Vigo, Galicia, reported in 1877: "Until two or three years ago the emigrant traffic was in the hands of three Spanish vessels dedicated solely to that trade, but the steamers of the Pacific Steam Navigation Company, which make monthly stops here, have snatched the whole business" (Argentina, *Memorias del Ministerio de Relaciones Exteriores*, 1878, 123). A decade later the British Foreign Office also noted the business that the "increasing Spanish emigration to Argentina [represents] for the British shipping trade." Great Britain, Foreign Office, *Miscellaneous Series, n. 123; Reports on Subjects of General and Commercial Interest; Notes on Emigration to the Argentina Republic, 1857–88* (London: Her Majesty's Stationery Office, 1889), 1.

100. A British traveler wrote in 1909, "I do not think I entered a single town in Galicia upon the walls of which I did not see placards denoting the speedy departure of [Hamburg-American] liners from Europe to South America" (Meakin, *Galicia*, 153).

101. Recent studies have found that conditions on ships were not as dismal as once thought. For example, Helen R. Woolcock, *Rights of Passage: Emigration to Australia in the Nineteenth Century* (London: Tavistock Publications, 1986), xvii–xviii, maintained that "it became clear that travel conditions, contrary to popular impressions of 19th century migration, were far from 'frightful,'" especially after 1850, when "life at sea was, on the whole, a safe, healthy and tolerable experience."

102. Eugenio de la Riva, "La Argentina y Europa," *La Argentina: Revista mensual, órgano de la Sociedad Juventud Argentina* (Barcelona) 1, 1 (1915):4.

103. Gould, "European Inter-Continental Emigration," 611 ff.

104. A similar rise took place in Norway at the time: foreign steamship companies charged U.S.$30 in 1869 for a one-way ticket to North America, "whereas the fare in sailing ship was about $14 with an addition of approximately $8 for provisions which the emigrants had to cater for themselves." Despite the price increase, steamers augmented their share of Norwegian overseas

passengers from 10 to 67 percent between 1866 and 1871. See Lauritz Pettersen, "From Sail to Steam in Norwegian Emigration," in *Maritime Aspects of Migration*, ed. Klaus Friedland (Cologne: Bohlau, 1989), 125–26.

105. By comparison, the average sailing time from northern Europe to New York in 1867 was forty-four days. The trip took fourteen days by steamer, a duration that went down to ten days by the 1880s and a week after 1900 (Moch, *Moving Europeans*, 152).

106. Santos Madrazo, *El sistema de transportes en España, 1750–1850*, vol. 1 (Madrid: Colegio de Ingenieros de Caminos, Canales y Puertos, 1984), 17.

107. See ibid., vol. 1, chap. 3, for the expansion of the road network in the century following 1750; and vol. 1, chap. 4, for a detailed description of contemporary methods of road construction.

108. David Ringrose, *Transportation and Economic Stagnation in Spain, 1750–1850* (Durham: Duke University Press, 1970).

109. Santos Madrazo, *El sistema de transportes*, vol. 2, chap. 5.

110. Gonzalo Menéndez Pidal, *Los caminos en la historia de España* (Madrid: Ediciones Cultura Hispánica, 1951), 6, 136; *Enciclopedia Universal Ilustrada* (Madrid: Espasa-Calpe S.A., 1923), vol. 21, 292–93.

111. Francisco Wais, *Historia de los ferrocarriles españoles*, 3d ed., vol. 1 (Madrid: Fundación de los Ferrocarriles Españoles, 1987), 75–76.

112. Calculated from information in Santos Madrazo, *El sistema de transportes*, vol. 2, 544–60 and in Vicente Castañeda, *Los primeros ferrocarriles españoles* (Madrid: Viuda de E. Maestre, 1946), 42–46.

113. For maps showing the geographical spread of the railroad by quinquennium, see Miguel Artola et al., *Los ferrocarriles en España, 1844–1943*, vol. 1 (Madrid: Servicio de Estudios del Banco de España, 1978), 245–56.

114. Ibid., vol. 1, 324–25, 333–35, and vol. 2, 370; Anibal Casares Alonso, *Estudio histórico-económico de las construcciones ferroviarias españolas en el siglo XIX* (Madrid: Estudios del Instituto de Desarrollo Económico, 1973), 112–13, 205; and George L. Boag, *The Railways of Spain* (London: The Railway Gazette, 1923), 65–67.

115. Transcribed in Wais, *Historia de los ferrocarriles* vol. 2, 50.

116. Calculated from data in Santos Madrazo, *El sistema de transportes*, vol. 2, 548–60, and Artola, *Los ferrocarriles*, vol. 1, 334–35, 397.

117. In 1887 the Argentine consul in Barcelona reported that fares from Spanish ports, which were three days closer to Buenos Aires, were 20 percent higher than those from French and Italian harbors. He attributed this paradox to "the unmeasured ambition of the companies that seem to have agreed not to compete and lower prices." Three decades later the national Spanish Emigration Commission complained that "all the companies that serve the northern ports have syndicated into a 'Pull' [pool] that assigns a fixed price for tickets and a quota of passengers" (Spain, Consejo Superior de Emigración, *La emigración española transoceánica*, 290–91). Berit Brattne and Sune Akerman have noticed similar practices in Sweden, where in the 1880s fares varied according to the volume of emigration, actually rising during peak emigration years in part due to monopolistic arrangements among shipping companies ("The Importance of

the Transport Sector for Mass Emigration," in *From Sweden to America*, 186–89).

118. Spain, Consejo Superior de Emigración, *La Emigración Española Transoceánica*, 291.

119. Compiled from membership lists and other papers of the Centro Navarro de Buenos Aires, from interviews with some of its members, and from civil birth registries of Tafalla, Navarre.

120. Transcribed in José M. Iribarren, *Batiburrillo navarro: Segunda parte de retablo de curiosidades* (Zaragoza: Imprenta Heraldo de Aragón, 1943), 19.

121. Mafalda Díaz Melián, "Emigración española hacia la Argentina en la década del 80," *Boletín del Instituto de Historia Argentina y Americana "Dr. Emilio Ravignani"* (Buenos Aires) 26 (1980):118.

2. ARGENTINA BECOMES A COUNTRY OF IMMIGRANTS

1. The other two are the North American Great Plains (including the Canadian prairies) and the Ukrainian *chernozem*, or black earth of the steppes; with the smaller South African veld and Australian downs, they comprise the planet's temperate grasslands, now mostly turned into farmland.

2. The *World Almanac and Book of Facts, 1996*, lists the white population of these countries as follows: United States, 83 percent of the total; Canada, 97 percent; Argentina, 85 percent (in the eastern part of the country the proportion is closer to 95 percent); Uruguay, 88 percent; Brazil, 55 percent (south of São Paulo the proportion has been estimated at between 85 and 95 percent); Australia, 95 percent; New Zealand, 88 percent; and South Africa, 18 percent.

3. Alfred Crosby, *Ecological Imperialism: The Biological Expansion of Europe, 900–1900* (Cambridge, England: Cambridge University Press, 1986).

4. Cited in ibid., 160.

5. It was easier for non-Spaniards to enter the peripheral viceroyalty of the Río de la Plata than the central viceroyalties of New Spain and Peru. Nevertheless, foreigners, many of them Portuguese trying to pass for Spaniards, never amounted to more than 1 percent of the population. Fernando Bidabehere, *El problema inmigratorio: Sus características en la República Argentina* (Buenos Aires: El Ateneo, 1940), 14.

6. Rubén H. Zorrilla, *Cambio social y población en el pensamiento de Mayo, 1810–1830* (Buenos Aires: Editorial Belgrano, 1978), 44–46.

7. Ibid., 45.

8. J. B. Alberdi, "Bases y puntos de partida para la organización política de la República Argentina" [first published in 1852], in *Obras completas de J. B. Alberdi* (Buenos Aires, 1886–1887), 3 (1886), 422.

9. Ibid., 427–28. See also Orlando Lázaro, "Alberdi, Avellaneda y la inmigración," in *La inmigración en la Argentina*, ed. Universidad Nacional de Tucumán, Facultad de Filosofía y Letras (Tucumán, Argentina, 1979), 73–80.

10. Sarmiento to Victorino Lastarria, Santiago, Chile, January 18, 1853, in *Correspondencia entre Sarmiento y Lastarria, 1844–1888*, ed. María L. del Pino de Carbone (Buenos Aires, 1954), 28, cited in Donald S. Castro, "The Develop-

ment of Argentine Immigration Policy, 1852–1914" (Ph.D. diss., University of California, Los Angeles, 1970), 14. Later in life, both Sarmiento and Alberdi would temper their enthusiasm for immigration and look at the rural native population with kinder eyes. See Abelardo Jorge Soneira, *La inmigración y el projecto liberal* (Buenos Aires: Centro Editor Argentino, 1981), 30, 32.

11. David R. Ochs, "A History of Argentine Immigration, 1853–1924" (Ph.D. diss., University of Illinois, 1939), 23.

12. Ibid.

13. Soneira, *La inmigración y el projecto liberal*, 12–13. See also Irene García de Saltor, "Antecedentes de la política inmigratoria: Bernardino Rivadavia," in *La inmigración en la argentina*, 25–40.

14. Juan A. Alsina, *La inmigración europea en la Argentina* (Buenos Aires: Imprenta Felipe S. Alsina, 1898), 24–35.

15. Foreigners' civil rights did not entail voting in national elections but did include exemption from military conscription, an immensely more valuable prerogative if one remembers that during the nineteenth century elections were few and corrupt (universal male suffrage came only in 1912) and that wars were many and bloody. The decline of the Argentine colored population, for example, has often been blamed—albeit with limited evidence—on their high war mortality.

16. In 1869 the Sarmiento government organized the Comisión Central de Inmigración in the Ministry of the Interior, which published annual *Informes* until 1874. In 1875 the commission was changed to the Departamento General de Inmigración, which submitted its annual *Memorias* to the minister of the interior until 1886 and to the minister of foreign affairs from 1887 to 1892. In 1898 the department was changed to the Dirección General de Inmigración, which submitted its annual *Memorias* to the newly created Ministry of Agriculture until at least the 1920s.

17. David Rock, *Argentina, 1516–1987: From Spanish Colonization to Alfonsín* (Berkeley: University of California Press, 1987), 137.

18. Argentina, Departamento General de Inmigración, *Memorias del, . . . correspondiente al año 1889* (Buenos Aires: Imprenta M. Biedma, 1890), 65; and Alejandro Gancedo, *La Argentina: su evolución* (Buenos Aires: García Dasso, 1913), 32.

19. Studies and books advocating immigration in Peru were so numerous that an author in 1906 began his book with "Something else on immigration? . . . I imagine people exclaiming, with a skeptic shrug of the shoulders, as they see a new volume appearing on such a battered theme" (Luis Pesce, *Indígenas e inmigrantes en el Perú* [Lima: Imprenta de la Opinión Nacional, 1906], 1). At least since 1875, an official immigration agency ran a hostel, paid for the ship fare of 92 percent of the 916 Europeans who came to Peru that year, and granted many of them lands. See P. Aurelio Penegri, *Memoria que presenta a la Sociedad de Inmigración Europea su presidente P. Aurelio Penegri* (Lima, 1876). For other works advocating European immigration at various periods, see Juan de Arona [pseud. of Pedro Paz Soldán y Unánue], *La inmigración en el Perú* (Lima, 1891); Perú, Ministerio de Fomento, *Guía del inmigrante en el Perú*

(Lima, 1902); Juan Angulo, *Inmigración y medios de adquirirla* (Lima, 1907); Mario E. del Río, *La inmigración y su desarrollo en el Perú* (Lima, 1929); and "Peru Extends Offer of Free Passage to Would-Be European and American Immigrants," *New York Times*, January 5, 1907, 14.

20. From its independence in 1824 until 1930, Peru received about 30,000 European immigrants (Giovanni Bonfiglio Volpe, "Introducción al estudio de la inmigración europea en el Perú," in *Primer seminario sobre poblaciones inmigrantes*, eds. Wilfredo Kapsoli et al. [Lima: Consejo Nacional de Ciencia y Tecnología, 1987], vol. 1, 34, 39). Argentina received more than twice that number during December 1912 (Roberto Cortés Conde, *El progreso argentino, 1880–1914* [Buenos Aires: Editorial Sudamericana, 1979], 195). In the last week of March 1907, Ellis Island (which accommodated 78 percent of the 1,285,349 immigrants who entered the United States that year) admitted more than 40,000 arrivals (*New York Times*, March 28, 1907, 10:4). On an average day it received 5,000 newcomers (Ann Novotny, *Strangers at the Door: Ellis Island, Castle Garden and the Great Migration to America* [Riverside, Conn.: Chatham Press, 1971], 11).

21. Gran Colombia passed legislation to foster immigration and contracted an agent in London even before the new republic had been recognized by Great Britain ("Primer congreso constitucional" [June 18, 1823] [document at the Bancroft Library xff f2251.c73 no. 19], and Francis Hall, *Colombia: Its Present State . . . and Inducements to Immigration* [London, 1824]). In 1825, when Costa Rica was still part of the chaotic and disunited United Provinces of Central America, the (technically provincial) government contracted with a John Hale to bring English colonists to the country (Alberto Quijano Quesada, *Costa Rica ayer y hoy, 1800–1939* [San José, 1939], 8–10). For later attempts to bring German and Belgian immigrants, see Costa Rica, Sociedad Itineraria del Norte, Cartago, *Estatuto de la compañía alemana de colonización para Centro America* (Cartago, Costa Rica, 1852); and Edouard Pougin, *L'État de Costa Rica et ce qu'on pourrait y faire dans l'interest . . . de l'émigration belges* (Anvers, 1863). For a general call for European immigration, see Manuel M. Peralta, *La republique de Costa Rica (Amérique Centrale): Appel a l'émigration européene* (Geneva, 1871). For the other countries, see: Nicaragua, *Datos relativos a la projectada inmigración al país, presentados por las comisiones nombradas con este fin por el supremo gobierno de la república de Nicaragua* (Managua: Imprenta del Gobierno, 1868); Honduras, *Contrata para una empresa . . . de colonización en Honduras firmada por el gobierno y Don Otto Zurcher* (Tegucigalpa: Tipografía Nacional, 1895); Honduras, *Ley de inmigración* (Tegucigalpa, 1906); Guatemala, *Law of Immigration of the Republic of Guatemala, Central America, Published by the Consulate General at New York* (New York, 1879); and M. T. de la Fuente, *Agricultura e inmigración: Bases para el fomento de la agricultura en Guatemala* (Guatemala City, 1897). For the attempts of the Central American republics to attract European immigrants in the 1870s, see Joseph Laferrière, "De la colonisation au Centre-Amérique," in his *De Paris a Guatémala: Notes de voyages au Centre-Amérique, 1866–1875* (Paris: Garnier Frères, 1877), 383–404.

22. Soneira, *La inmigración y el projecto liberal*, 12–14; and Lázaro Schallman, "Proceso histórico de la colonización agrícola," in *Inmigración y nacionalidad*, eds. Dardo Cúneo et al. (Buenos Aires: Paidós, 1967), 155–57.

23. See Benito Díaz, *Inmigración y agricultura en la época de Rosas* (Buenos Aires: Editorial El Coloquio, 1975)

24. Argentina, Departamento General de Inmigración, *Memorias del, ... correspondiente al año 1890* (Buenos Aires: Imprenta de Pablo E. Coni e Hijos, 1891), 53–56.

25. During the two decades following the subsidized passages of 1888–1889, law students at the University of Buenos Aires submitted twenty-three dissertations on the topic of immigration for what at the time was a doctoral degree. In contrast, only four dissertations on the topic were submitted between 1821, when the university was founded, and 1888. In general, these theses followed a similar format and, at times, plagiarized each other—what seemed to be popular paragraphs were often repeated without citations. For a catalogue of these doctoral dissertations, see Universidad de Buenos Aires, *Bibliografía doctoral de la Universidad de Buenos Aires y catálogo cronológico de las tesis en su primer centenario, 1821–1920* (Buenos Aires, 1920).

26. For example, Vicenzo Misuriello, *Política de la inmigración en la Argentina, 1853–1970* (Tucumán, Argentina: Universidad de Tucumán, 1993), chap. 2; Soneira, *La inmigración y el proyecto liberal*; most of the articles in Argentina, Ministerio de Educación y Justicia, Secretaría de Cultura, *Primeras jornadas nacionales de estudios sobre inmigración en Argentina* (Buenos Aires: Ministerio de Cultura y Educación, 1985); and James Foreman-Peck, "A Political Economy of International Migration, 1815–1914," *The Manchester School* 10, 4 (1992):366.

27. Castro, "Development of Argentine Immigration Policy," ix–x. Castro, however, abandoned this thesis in his book, *The Development and Politics of Argentine Immigration Policy 1852–1914: To Govern Is to Populate* (San Francisco: Mellen Research University Press, 1991), which became a rich politico-institutional history of nineteenth-century Argentina rather than an attempt to explain immigration (see also my preface to Castro's book).

28. Cited in Domingo Borea, *La colonización oficial y particular en la República Argentina* (Buenos Aires, 1923), 30–31.

29. For an economic history of this period, see Miron Burgin, *The Economic Aspects of Argentine Federalism, 1820–1852* (Cambridge, Mass.: Harvard University Press, 1946; reprint, New York: Russell & Russell, 1971).

30. James R. Scobie, *Argentina: A City and a Nation* (New York: Oxford University Press, 1971), 66, 83.

31. *The Brazil and River Plate Mail*, November 22, 1865, cited in Hilda Sabato, *Agrarian Capitalism and the World Market: Buenos Aires in the Pastoral Age, 1840–1890* (Albuquerque: University of New Mexico Press, 1990), 1.

32. Sabato, *Agrarian Capitalism*, 155; Argentina, Comisión Directiva del Censo, *Segundo censo de la República Argentina, 1895*, 3 vols. (Buenos Aires: Taller Tip. de la Penitenciaria Nacional, 1898), vol. 3, lxxxviii; and *Revista de Economía Argentina* 22, 132 (1929):461. Rock, *Argentina, 1516–1987*, 133, gives the sheep population in 1888 as 87 million, outnumbering people 30 to 1,

a figure much higher than the 67 million given by other sources based on a provincial census.

33. Scobie, *Argentina: A City and a Nation*, 83; and Sabato, *Agrarian Capitalism*, 194–200.

34. Horacio Giberti, *Historia económica de la ganadería argentina* (Buenos Aires: Solar, 1961), 184.

35. Recorded in David J. R. Watson, *Los criollos y los gringos: Escombros acumulados al levantar la estructura ganadera-frigorífica, 1882–1940* (Buenos Aires: J. Suárez, 1941), 16. For the predominance of immigrants in sheep raising, see Sabato, *Agrarian Capitalism*, 89–92.

36. Ricardo M. Ortiz, *Historia económica de la Argentina* (Buenos Aires: Plus Ultra, 1987), 344.

37. Alfredo J. Montoya, *Historia de los saladeros argentinos* (Buenos Aires: Editorial Raigal, 1956), 100.

38. Argentina, *Segundo censo*, vol. 3, xxxi; and Argentina, Comisión Nacional del Censo, *Tercer censo nacional, 1914*, 10 vols. (Buenos Aires: Talleres Gráficos de L. J. Rosso, 1916–1919), vol. 5, xiii.

39. Rock, *Argentina, 1516–1987*, 172.

40. José L. Bacigalupo, "Proceso de urbanización en la Argentina," in *La urbanización en América Latina*, ed. Jorge Hardoy and Carlos Tobar (Buenos Aires: Editorial del Instituto, 1969), 410.

41. Quoted in Eric Rhode, *A History of the Cinema from Its Origins to 1970* (New York: Hill and Wang, 1976), 4.

42. Adolfo Dorfman, *Historia de la industria argentina* (Buenos Aires: Solar/Hachette, 1970), 73, 208, 285. I estimated the national figures for 1853 based on data for the city of Buenos Aires, which that year had 106 factories and 746 workshops. Because Buenos Aires contained about one-fifth of all Argentine manufacturing establishments in 1914 but one-third in 1895, I figured that the proportion in 1853 must have been closer to this earlier date and that the national number could not have exceeded 3,000 around the middle of the nineteenth century.

43. Ibid., 285.

44. In 1914, for example, the thirteen *frigoríficos* in Argentina were an infinitesimal proportion of the 48,800 industrial establishments but accounted for 9.4 percent of capital invested, 21.6 percent of energy consumed, and 4.9 percent of workers employed in the secondary sector (Dorfman, *Historia de la industria argentina*, 316).

45. A 1914 industrial census of Buenos Aires listed 203 different types of establishments (Argentina, Ministerio de Agricultura, Dirección General de Comercio e Industria, *Censo industrial y comercial de la República Argentina, 1908–1914*, Boletín no. 20 [Buenos Aires, 1915], 39–63).

46. From figures in Vicente Vázquez-Presedo, "La evolución industrial (Argentina, 1880–1910," in *La Argentina del Ochenta al Centenario*, comp. Gustavo Ferrari and Ezequiel Gallo (Buenos Aires: Editorial Sudamericana, 1980), 408.

47. Emilio Coni, *El urbanismo en Argentina* (Buenos Aires: 1919), 12–13. Population centers of 2,000 or more inhabitants were considered towns.

48. Xesús Montero, *Cantigas sociales recollidas do pobo* (Vigo, Spain: Ediciones Castrelos, 1969), 10.

49. Colin M. Lewis, *British Railways in Argentina, 1857–1914: A Case Study of Foreign Investment* (London: University of London Institute of Latin American Studies, 1983), xii, 68, 196; Ortiz, *Historia económica de la Argentina,* 244, 583.

50. *Revista de Economía Argentina* 22, 132 (1929):461.

51. Arsenio Isabelle, cited in Eduardo H. Pinasco, *El puerto de Buenos Aires el los relatos de veinte viajeros* (Buenos Aires, 1947), 122–23.

52. William Hadfield, cited in ibid., 146.

53. James R. Scobie, *Buenos Aires: Plaza to Suburb, 1870–1910* (New York: Oxford University Press, 1974), 70–91.

54. George J. Mills, *Argentina: Physical Features, Natural Resources, Means of Communication, Manufactures and Industrial Development* (New York: D. Appleton & Company, 1914), 107–8.

3. WEAVING THE NET

1. See Juan B. Vilar, *Emigración española a Argelia (1830–1900)* (Madrid: Instituto de Estudios Africanos, 1975); and Jean-Jacques Jordi, *Le espagnol en Oranie, 1830–1914: Histoire d'une emigration* (Montpellier: Africa Nostra, 1986).

2. Javier Rubio, *La emigración española a Francia* (Barcelona: Ariel, 1974); see pp. 111 and 119 for provincial origins of emigrants.

3. Timothy Hatton and Jeffrey Williamson, *Late-Comers to Mass Emigration: The Latin Experience,* NBER Working Paper 47 (Cambridge, Mass.: National Bureau of Economic Research, 1993), table 1, show that real wages in Spain amounted to 30 percent of those in the United States in 1870, 34 percent in 1890, and 30 percent in 1913, in comparison to 57 percent, 86 percent, and 54 percent of those in Argentina during the respective years.

4. Of these, only Cuba received a significant number of Mataronese. Colonial status, however, does not seem to have been the determining variable. After all, more Spaniards (728,000) went to Cuba in the two decades following the island's independence from Spain in 1900 than in the last two decades of colonial rule (522,000)—a gap that was probably larger in reality if one considers that the last figure contains a large number of soldiers in addition to regular immigrants. Dutch emigrants provide another example of the limited relevance of colonial status: they preferred the United States over their own colonies by a ratio of more than six to one (calculated from statistics in Imre Ferenczi and Walter Willcox, *International Migrations,* vol. 1 [New York, 1929], 742–43 [Dutch], 850–55 [Spanish]). Similarly, historian Walter Nugent, in his recent synthesis *Crossings: The Great Transatlantic Migrations, 1870–1914* (Bloomington: Indiana University Press, 1992), 105, noticed that "colonies proved no better a sponge of excess population for Portugal than they did for Germany and Italy."

5. Santos Fernández Arlaud, "La emigración española a America durante el reinado de Isabel II," *Cuadernos de Historia* (Madrid) 4 (1973):464, cites the

case of an Argentine consular office in the Canary Islands that was even involved in a fraudulent and exploitative emigration scheme.

6. The cases that follow come from a list of thirty-nine Mataronese immigrants in Buenos Aires during the eighteenth and early nineteenth centuries that I compiled from the following sources: Francisco Avella, "Los catalanes en Buenos Aires durante el siglo XVIII," *Saitabi* (Valencia, Spain) 19 (1969):75–117, which includes a list of Catalans in the city collected from Church records; Ricardo Monner Sanz, "Los catalanes en la Argentina," *Humanidades* (La Plata, Argentina) 16 (1927):123–205; Museu Comarcal del Maresme, *L'aventura americana del Maresme* (Mataró, 1986); Ramón Salas i Oliveras, *Presencia Mataronina al Rio de la Plata a les darreries del segle XVIII i primera meitat del XIX* (Mataró: Caixa D'estalvies Laietana, Editorial Rafael Dalmau, 1977); and Henry Vogel, "Elements of Nationbuilding in Argentina: Buenos Aires 1810–1828" (Ph.D. diss., University of Florida, 1987), which contains three Mataronese in a list of Spaniards who became Argentine nationals during that period. Josep Delgado Ribas, "La emigración española a America Latina durante la época del Comercio Libre (1765–1820): El ejemplo catalan," *Boletín Americanista* (Barcelona) 26, 32 (1982):115–137, found twenty-two Mataronese merchants in Buenos Aires (12 percent of the Catalan merchants in the city) and twenty-five in Montevideo, but he did not list their names.

7. For the Mataronese connection to the Americas through Cádiz during the middle of the eighteenth century, see Carlos Martínez Shaw, *Cataluña en la carrera de Indias, 1680–1756* (Barcelona: Editorial Crítica, 1981), 29, 107–8, 111–12, 116–19. Before the Casa de Contratación (the House of Trade, which controlled commerce with the Indies) moved to Cádiz in 1717, Seville had played a similar role of entrepôt in the movement of Spaniards to the colonies. See Ida Altman, *Emigrants and Society: Extremadura and America in the Sixteenth Century* (Berkeley: University of California Press, 1989), 205–8.

8. Federico Rahola y Trémols, *Comercio de Cataluña con América en el siglo XVIII* (Barcelona: Artes Gráficas, 1931), 155–56.

9. Another Mataronese immigrant, unknown to schoolchildren but deservedly acclaimed by scholars, is Juan Bialet Massé, who arrived in Argentina in 1876 and in 1904 wrote *El estado de las clases obreras argentinas a comienzos del siglo*, a massive and perceptive study of the working class in the interior of the country.

10. Rubén H. Zorrilla, *Cambio social y población en el pensamiento de mayo, 1810–1830* (Buenos Aires: Editorial de Belgrano, 1978), 87–88.

11. *L'aventura americana del Maresme.*

12. For the diplomatic conflicts over the question of nationality, see Mario Belgrano, *La cuestión de la nacionalidad y el tratado con España de 1863* (Buenos Aires, 1942).

13. I was able to find this connection through an obituary for José Riera Canals that appeared in the local newspaper *El Mataronés* on April 24, 1881, and listed Lázaro Carrau as his son-in-law. Mr. Riera, in turn, appears in the Buenos Aires manuscript census of 1855 as a dry-goods-store owner. The June 4, 1882, issue of the local weekly *El Mataroné: semanario popular de la presente ciudad y su partido* carried an advertisement for the "grand opening of Carrau &

Brothers drugstore and 'herbaristeria,' with wonderful connections to overseas suppliers."

14. *Americano* remained the most common term for the successful returnee for most of the mass-emigration period. The older *indiano* of colonial times had been widely used by Golden Age authors (see Alfonso Urtiaga, *El indiano en la dramática de Tirso de Molina* [Madrid: Revista Estudios, 1965]; and Jaime Martínez Tolentino, *El indiano en las comedias de Lope de Vega* [Kassel: Edition Reichenberger, 1991]) and was revived and made increasingly popular by late-nineteenth- and early-twentieth-century writers, who often portrayed him as a greedy and stingy old man. See Dionisio Scarlatti de Aldama, *El indiano y la planchadora: Zarzuela en un acto en verso* (Madrid: Imprenta de G. Alhambra, 1871); Enrique Segovia Rocaberti, *El indiano: Comedia en un acto y en verso* (Madrid: José Rodríguez, 1887); R. D. de la Cortina, *El indiano* (New York: R. D. Cortina, 1893), a bilingual Spanish-English updated version of García de la Vega's play in which the old returnee wants to marry the young daughter of a déclassé aristocratic family, although at the end he generously allows her to marry her lover and pays for their wedding; Eva Canel, *El indiano: Comedia en tres actos y prosa* (Havana: Universal, 1894); Emilio Soldevilla Banchs, *El indiano: Boceto dramático* (Aranjuez: El Heraldo de la Rivera, 1900?); Gustavo Morales, *El indiano de Valdella* (Barcelona: Juan Gili, 1909); Santiago Rusiñol, *El indiano* (Madrid: Renacimiento, 1912); Benito Pérez Gáldos, *El tacaño Salomon* [Solomon the Miser] (Madrid: Sucesores de Hernando, 1916); Francisco Fernández Zorrilla, *Un indiano: Como se gana el dinero en América* (Madrid: Renacimiento, 1923); and "Los indianos," *La Protesta: Suplemento semanal,* July 24, 1922, 3, by the Spanish anarchist in Buenos Aires, Emilio López Arango, who portrays them as "bloodsuckers who enjoy in Spain the riches stolen from the Americas and motivate those insulting words in the mouths of the Creoles: Gallego, Godo, Gachupín!" Tellingly, a play that opened in Buenos Aires in 1901 (Xavier Santero, *El indiano: Zarzuela en un acto* [Buenos Aires: Imprenta Hispania, 1905]) is one of the few that portray the returnee as a young, attractive, and even semiheroic figure. For a study of the *indiano* theme in Spanish naturalist novels, see Guadalupe Gómez-Ferrer Morant, "El indiano en la novela realista," *Cuadernos Hispanoamericanos* 466 (April 1989):25–49.

15. Antoni Cuyas Sampere, *Apuntes históricos sobre la provincia de Entre Ríos de la República Argentina* (Mataró: Establecimiento Tipográfico de Feliciano Horta, 1888).

16. A good example is Manuel Miñones, who became Argentine vice consul in Corcubión in 1928 but had served for years as the representative in the village of his paisanos' association in Buenos Aires and had acted for decades as the main entrepreneur in the local emigration business. This small banker had profited since the end of the nineteenth century by loaning money for passages, collecting fees from shipping companies, maintaining an inn in the port city of La Coruña, where Corcubionese emigrants stayed while waiting for the ship's departure, maintaining a network of subagents in the smaller villages of the hinterland, and charging fees for remittances and benefiting from the deposits

they represented (*Alborada, organo de la Asociación Benéfica Cultural del Partido de Corcubión* [Buenos Aires], January 1928; and Paco Teijeira Lopez, interview by author, tape recording, Corcubión, Spain, August 7, 1989.

17. Similarly, Lars Ljungmark, *For Sale—Minnesota: Organized Promotion of Scandinavian Immigration, 1866–1873* (Göteborg, Sweden: Laromedelsforl, 1971), found that the recruitment of Swedish immigrants in the colonization districts of that state owed their success to the previous presence of townsmen rather than the activities of the agents themselves.

18. Argentina, Archivo General de la Nación (hereafter referred to as AGN), Marina, entrada de pasajeros, Sala X, 36–8–17 to Sala X, 36–8–40.

19. Given the lack of an emigration register, it is impossible to determine the destination of the Mataronese with exactitude. I have used proxy sources and methods to reach an approximation. One method consisted of counting the destination of the letters detained by the local post office for insufficient postage, incomplete addresses, and so forth during 1867 and 68 and listed in the local weekly *Crónica Mataronesa*. The destination of the eighty-four overseas letters detained was the following: Cuba, thirty-nine; Argentina, eighteen; Uruguay, nine; Puerto Rico, seven; the Philippines, five; other, six.

Another alternative source is the "Bajas de Vecinos, 1883–1907" and "Bajas de Domicilio, 1908–1916," two manuscript volumes held in the Mataró municipal archive, which presumably list all those who moved from Mataró between those dates but appears very incomplete, with long periods when the town clerk registered few or none of the people leaving the town. This source shows that by the 1880s Argentina had replaced Cuba as the main destination, attracting 76 percent of the seventy-eight emigrants listed. Complete information only reappears for 1909–1910. Of the ninety-seven people who moved overseas then, fifty-six went to Argentina.

20. "Bajas de domicilio," 1908–1916, in Mataró's municipal archive.

21. The Salvador family story is based on information in Mataró's *padrones*, or manuscript censuses, of 1900 and 1920.

22. In addition to these thirty-three Argentine sons and daughters of returnees, the overseas-born population in 1920 included twenty-four Cubans, nine Filipinos, and five Puerto Ricans, most of them older people who had returned from the colonies with their parents in the nineteenth century.

23. The publications and years checked were: *Revista Mataronesa* (weekly), 1864–1866; *Crónica Mataronesa* (weekly), 1866–1868; *El Mataronés* 1876–1880; *El Mataroné: Semanario popular de la presente ciudad y su partido*, 1881–1887; *El Nuevo Ideal: Periódico republicano democrático federal*, 1887–1890; *Semanario de Mataró*, 1891–1894; *Vida Nueva: Periódico socialista revolucionario de Mataró*, 1911–1913; and *Mataró en Broma*, 1915.

24. Argentina, *Memorias del Ministerio de Relaciones Exteriores*, 1882.

25. Of the 5,319 settlers listed in Peter Boyd-Bowman, *Indice geobiográfico de más de 56 pobladores de la América hispánica I. 1493–1519* (Mexico City: Fondo de Cultura Económica, 1985), only two are from Ferrol and seven from Bilbao.

26. Manoel Lelo Bellotto, *Correio marítimo hispano-americano: A carreira*

de Buenos Aires, 1767–1779 (Assis, Brazil: Faculdade de Filosofia, Ciencias e Letras de Assis, 1971), esp. 99, 246–47, 255.

27. For the unsuccessful petitions and attempts to establish direct commerce between Bilbao and Buenos Aires, see José M. Mariluz Urquijo, *Bilbao y Buenos Aires: Projectos dieciochescos de compañías de comercio* (Buenos Aires: Universidad de Buenos Aires, 1981). For their fulfillment after 1788, see Román Basurto Larrañaga, *Comercio y burguesía mercantil de Bilbao en la segunda mitad del siglo XVIII* (Bilbao: Servicio Editorial Universidad del Pais Vasco, 1983), 82, 97–100, 117–18. For Ferrol, see Luis Alonso Alvarez, *Comercio colonial y crisis del antiguo régimen en Galicia, 1778–1818* (La Coruña: Xunta de Galicia, Conselleria da Presidencia, 1986), 72. For the volume and origin of the traffic between Spain and Buenos Aires during the last decade of the eighteenth century, see Emanuel S. da Veiga Garcia, *O comércio ultramarino espanhol no Prata* (São Paulo: Editora Perspectiva, 1982), 93–101.

28. The Cuban exile communities present an amazing modern example of the ability of immigrant groups to sustain linkages with their localities of origin in the face of structural obstacles. Through three decades of a formal North American blockade of Cuba, they have been able to maintain not only family connections but also an informal, illegal, and elaborate currency-exchange system in which money never crosses an international frontier and rates even fluctuate. Based on mutual trust, an exile would give U.S. dollars or some other currency to another exile, usually from the same Cuban town. A relative or friend of the latter in Cuba would then give the equivalent in pesos (determined by demand and supply in this informal market) to the former's relative or friend on the island.

29. For example, many of the migration chains from Estremadura and New Castile to the Indies in the sixteenth and seventeenth centuries apparently just dwindled and expired. When those regions began to send emigrants overseas again in the late nineteenth century, these were new movements, not connected to the previous ones. Similarly, Finnish settlement in Delaware during the seventeenth century did not lead to sustained immigration, and the flow of Finns to North America in the nineteenth century represented not a resurgence but a new movement (A. William Hoglund, *Finnish Immigrants in America, 1880–1920* [Madison: University of Wisconsin Press, 1960], 7).

30. In John and Leatrice Macdonald's scheme of chain migration, the early stages were dominated by *padroni*, or labor bosses, rather than by kinship ("Chain Migration, Ethnic Neighborhood Formation and Social Networks," *Milbank Memorial Fund Quarterly* 13, 42 [1964], 84–87). In a sense, some of the Spanish immigration during this period was, as seen by the linkages, a continuation of a movement that had started in colonial times; this could explain the early role of kinship. But the Argentine historian Fernando Devoto also found that in the case of early Italian immigration to Buenos Aires, the family, rather than *padroni*, played the most important role and that movements under the auspices of labor bosses actually took place at a later stage ("Las cadenas migratorias italianas: Algunas reflexiones a la luz del caso argentino," *Estudios Migratorios Latinoamericanos* 3, 8 (1988):119–20.

31. My interviews of immigrants from the village of Val de San Lorenzo in

the province of León indicate that the role of women as "middle links" probably became even more common in later stages of migration during the twentieth century. For example, Amalia Cuesta came to Buenos Aires in the early 1920s to live with an uncle (actually a cousin of her mother), and after a year of working as a cook's helper she paid the passage of a younger sister, who also obtained a job in domestic service. A year later they brought over their third-oldest sister and a female cousin. In three more steps, two more sisters, three brothers, the mother, the father (who had actually been in Buenos Aires before World War I), and four relatives came (taped interviews by author with José Valle Pollan, Buenos Aires, May 24, 1987; Rosa Rodríguez de Andrés, Buenos Aires, May 24, 1987; and Amalia Cuesta, Buenos Aires, August 26, 1987).

32. An interesting later case is that of Antonio J. C., from a Galician village. His father left for Buenos Aires in 1903, when Antonio was four, returned in 1912, stayed in Galicia for less than a year (enough to sire another son), and departed again for Buenos Aires, this time for a thirty-year absence. In 1923 Antonio left his wife in the village and came to Buenos Aires, hoping to be assisted by his father—the passage being paid with money loaned by his father-in-law. He found his father living in concubinage with an Argentine woman, with whom he had a daughter, and not happy at all at the surprise arrival of his son. Unable to obtain assistance from his father, Antonio ended up living for three weeks in the *conventillo* (tenement house) room of a cousin of his wife, her "saintly" Italian husband, and her four children (interview with Antonio J. C., Buenos Aires, August 22, 1987).

33. Apparently, emigration soon ceased to be an issue in Málaga unless it could be exploited for other purposes. For example, in an October 1889 speech to the National Congress on the "problem of emigration," a Malagueño deputy spent one minute on the presumed subject of the oration and half an hour urging the minister of finance to extend the government monopoly on tobacco cultivation to his province in order to prevent future departures (Spain, Cortes, *Diario de las sesiones de Cortes, Congreso de los Diputados, legislatura de 1889–90*, vol. 3, no. 31, 924–27).

34. A similar case can be found in the contrast between Spanish emigration to New York and to Hawaii during the first decade of the twentieth century. The inflow into New York, like that from Pontevedra to Buenos Aires, represented a spontaneous movement of hundreds, and later thousands, of people that became self-propelled and sustainable. On the other hand, the arrival of 2,250 Andalusian peasants in Hawaii in 1907, like that from Málaga in Argentina in 1889, was concocted by agents, in this case of the islands' planters, and failed to pave the way for any sustained immigration—even most of those who came soon left the tropical plantations and ended up in California. See Beverly Lozano, "The Andalucia–Hawaii–California Migration: A Study in Macrostructure and Microhistory," *Comparative Studies in Society and History* 26, 2 (1984):305–24; and German Rueda Hernanz, "The Life and Misadventures of Eight Thousand Spaniards in Hawaii during the First Decades of the Twentieth Century," *Anglo-American Studies* (Spain) 5, 1 (1985):55–70. For a comparison with other groups, see Alan Takeo Moriyama, *Imingaisha: Japanese Emigration Companies and Hawaii, 1894–1908* (Honolulu: University of Hawaii Press,

1985); and Tadeusz Gasinski, "Polish Contract Labor in Hawaii, 1896–1899," *Polish American Studies* 39 (1982):14–27.

35. AGN, "Emigrados Canarios," División Gobierno Nacional, Sala X, 25.2.6.

36. Ibid., for stipulations in several contracts.

37. The original ship's passenger list is in AGN, Sala X, 25.2.6; the Buenos Aires manuscript census returns of 1855, also in the AGN, include an *"instituciones"* section that lists people in hospitals, convents, asylums, and so forth. The records of poor and insane asylums and the cemetery (which includes the name of the deceased, age, marital status, country of birth, at times region of birth, cause of death, and place of death) were also examined in the following documents in the Archivo de la Municipalidad de Buenos Aires (with a day's notice the documents can be transferred to the more comfortable Biblioteca de la Municipalidad de Buenos Aires): "Hospital de hombres, asilo de mendigos," Legajo "Salud Pública," year 1859, box 7; "Lista de enterrados en el cementerio del norte," Legajo "Gobierno," years 1859 box 5, 1861 box 5, 1862 box 8.

38. "Diary of Ramón Mayo"; I am indebted to the historians Samuel Baily and Carlos Mayo for this manuscript. A February 28, 1910, letter from a Spanish coach driver in Buenos Aires to his trade union's publication (*El latigo del carrero* [The Whip of the Coachdriver], p. 3, col. 2) provides another example of the returnees' role in the formation of village tales and emigration. The writer recounts the allegedly true story of Mister Juan, an emigrant to Argentina who returned to the village, rich and enlightened, after a twelve-year absence. The free-thinking *americano* married the most beautiful maiden in the district without a religious ceremony, earning the enmity of the parish priest and other "obscurantist bats and buzzards." Sometime later, while on a hunting trip, Mister Juan fell from a boulder and, after a few weeks in a coma, "returned his tribute to Nature." The priest's claim that the devil was coming for the deceased's body frightened the family into leaving the village and hiring three local lads to keep wake. In the middle of that night, and with much commotion, the devil was fatally shot while taking the corpse. After being unmasked, he turned out to be the parish's sexton. The returnee in the tale represented an image not only of economic and romantic success (returning rich and marrying the village beauty) but also of personal and collective intellectual liberation, a hero who unmasked pharisaic propaganda, a figure worthy of emulation.

39. *La Emigración Española: Vida española en el extranjero, revista quincenal de emigración y colonias,* May 15, 1917, 78; Julio Hernández García, *La emigración de las Islas Canarias en el siglo XIX* (Las Palmas, Spain: Cabildo Insular de Gran Canaria, 1981), 177, 183 ff.

40. Archivo del Ministerio de Relaciones Exteriores (Madrid), "Correspondencia embajada Argentina, 1852–1866," Legajo 1348, no. 18.

41. This abundance of official documents on recruited emigration in turn distorts representations in contemporary works. For example, a 1987 Buenos Aires television documentary on the Spanish presence in Argentina, *La otra tierra,* devoted more time to the Canarian expedition and the Llavallol agents than to the hundred-times-thicker spontaneous, kinship-organized flow. Miguel Angel de Marco, *Argentinos y españoles* (Rosario: Fundación Complejo Cultural

Parque de España, 1988), includes a chapter on the Canarian expedition and various chapters on particular personalities, but none on Spanish immigration in Argentina.

42. This exaggerated attention to recruited immigration is not limited to Spain and Argentina. For instance, an examination of the *New York Times* index for 1907 revealed 115 articles on the recruitment of Japanese to faraway Hawaii and California (a hot political and diplomatic issue) but only 7 on immigration from Italy, Austria-Hungary, and Russia, which, combined, accounted for 69 percent of the U.S. total that year and represented a veritable deluge on the *Times* own hometown. Similarly, the sole article on Greek immigration dealt with allegations that the Greek consul in Boston had recruited laborers from his homeland; and the two on French immigration, with the recruitment of weavers to work in Paterson, New Jersey, and how this violated U.S. laws.

43. The accounts of family emigration from the Baztán Valley in the following paragraphs come from a data set I compiled using the following sources: the Baztán Valley municipal *padrones* for 1847, 1853, 1863, and 1897; Carlos Idoate Ezquieta, *Emigración navarra del Valle de Baztán a América en el siglo XIX: Inventario de documentos* (Pamplona: Gobierno de Navarra, Departamento de Educación y Cultura, [1987]), a list of 1,903 notarial records related to emigration from 1801 to 1879; baptismal and marriage records from various parishes in the valley; the manuscript schedules for the unpublished 1855 census of Buenos Aires in the AGN; and Argentine manuscript passenger list from 1840 to 1860, AGN, Sala X, 36.8.17 to Sala X, 36.8.40.

44. Although the Guerra Grande ended in 1851, its aftermath marred Uruguay through the 1850s. In *Between the Economy and the Polity in the River Plate: Uruguay, 1811–1890* (London: University of London, Institute of Latin American Studies, 1993), 32–33, Fernando López-Alves found contemporary assessments of that decade "overwhelmingly consensual" in depicting an appalling economic condition that drove thousands to the other side of the River Plate. He cites a Spanish consular report of February 2, 1854, that mentions the crossing of 15,000 individuals in "a very short period of time." The hundreds of Spaniards residing in Buenos Aires in 1855 with Uruguayan-born children offer further evidence of the phenomenon.

45. Space prevented me from including all offshoots and the sources from going beyond 1870; I also excluded from the figure friends and likely kin whose specific relation could not be determined from the documents.

46. Sixty-two percent of the passenger traffic out of Bordeaux between 1865 and 1920 headed for Argentina; Spaniards (mostly Basques), accounted for about half of the 202,000 people who embarked at this Aquitainean port for Buenos Aires during the period (estimated from data in Philippe Roudié, "Long-Distance Emigration from the Port of Bordeaux, 1865–1920," *Journal of Historical Geography* 11, 3 [1985]:270–71, 277–78).

47. Idoate Ezquieta, *Emigración navarra*, 227, record 759.

48. For a disparaging literary portrayal of emigration agents, see Wenceslao Fernández Flórez's novel *Luz de luna*, in *La casa de la lluvia; Luz de Luna; La familia Gomar* (Madrid: Renacimiento, 1931), 129–213.

49. In 1868 a French tourist guidebook listed "Fonda de Estevan Fort" as

the place to stay in Elizondo. It also noted that "aujourd'hui les Basques de la vallée émigrent en grand nombre pour la Plata. Un agent d'émigration réside a Elizondo" (A. Joanne, *Itinéraire de la France: Les Pyrénées* [Paris, 1868], 78).

50. For example, Hans Norman observed that in Scandinavian countries the agents "were often local merchants, inn or tavern keepers, elementary school teachers, or employees of the post office or railway ... and 'Yankees,' [successful returnees]" and that the recruitment and propaganda efforts of shipping companies had little effect on rates of emigration (Hans Norman and Harald Runblom, *Transatlantic Connections: Nordic Migration to the New World after 1800* [Oslo: Norwegian University Press, 1987], 120). Similarly, Carole Marks, in an article on the northward movement of blacks out of the southern United States during World War I, concluded that only a minuscule part of the flow was attributable to labor or migration agents ("Lines of Communication, Recruitment Mechanisms, and the Great Migration of 1916–1918," *Social Problems* 31, 1 [1983]:76). And Franc Sturino, in his thorough study of emigration from the district of Rende in Calabria, maintained that "though often subsumed under the epithet 'agenti' by nationalists of the time, the local intermediaries were far from shady steamship agents inciting innocent peasants to emigrate. Indeed, those profiting from the 'commerce of migration' were often part of the middle-class backbone of the local community. Notaries, merchants, teachers, pharmacists, postmen, and the like all came to rely to some degree on the emigration trade as ticket-sellers, letter-writers and readers, money-lenders, advisers, and contacts to important officials." Furthermore, their relation with the peasant emigrants was characterized more by a sense of mutual obligation than by unscrupulous business practices (*Forging the Chain: A Case Study of Italian Migration to North America, 1880–1930* [Toronto: Multicultural History Society of Ontario, 1990], 76–77).

51. Idoate Ezquieta, *Emigración navarra*, 153, record 379.

52. Interestingly, in the early 1850s, when the shift from Uruguay to Argentina was taking place, a number of unflattering folk poems about Uruguay, including some with titles such as "Eskualdun Baten Bihotzminak Montevideo-Rat Joanez" [The Sorrows of a Basque Emigrant in Montevideo], appeared in the region. See the "Chants de Montevideo," transcribed in Francisque Michel, *Les Pays basque: Sa population, sa langue, ses moeurs, sa littérature et sa musique* (Paris: Librairie de Firmin Didot Frères, Fils et Cie., 1857), 339–352.

53. For an analysis of the changing destinations from a southern Italian village during the same period, see Samuel L. Baily, "The Village Outward Approach to the Study of Social Networks: A Case Study of the Agnonesi Diaspora Abroad, 1885–1989," *Studi Emigrazione* 29 (March 1992):43–68.

54. For the role of the Jáuregui family in Peru and New Spain, see Barbara H. and Stanley J. Stein, "1808: Spain and New Spain between Crisis and 'Revolution.' A New View of the Collapse of an Old Empire" (paper presented at Rutgers University, February 19, 1988), 21–23. For the effort of Baztanese to procure Peruvian inheritances, Idoate Ezquieta, *Emigración navarra*, documents 92, 734.

55. For a wonderful depiction of this expedition, see German filmmaker Werner Herzog's movie *Aguirre, the Wrath of God.*

56. All of the nine immigrants from Corcubión County that I was able to identify in the 1855 manuscript census of Buenos Aires came from the maritime villages of Finisterre and Corcubión, and seven lived in the La Boca–Barracas neighborhood. These two villages also provided all of the eight immigrants from Corcubión county who came to Argentina in 1860 and the first half of 1861 (Archivo del Ministerio de Relaciones Exteriores [Madrid], "Estado demostrativo de la emigración española en Buenos Aires desde Enero de 1860 a fin de Junio de 1861; Correspondencia embajada Argentina," Legajo 1348, no. 44 [a list compiled by the Spanish consul in Buenos Aires and sent to the Spanish Foreign Ministry]). For an analogous case of Norwegians who settled Manhattan's port areas in the 1830s because "their cultural heritage had given them the tools whereby they were able to elicit meaning and value from this particular environment" (p. 39), see Christen Jonassen, "Cultural Variables in the Ecology of an Ethnic Group," *American Sociological Review* 14, 1 (1949):32–41.

57. Francisco Santiago Lago (also known as Paco Peru), interview by author, tape recording, Corcubión, Spain, August 10, 1989.

58. Some Basques did go to North Queensland, but they originated from areas other than the Baztán Valley (apparently mostly from the seaside town of Lequetio, Biscay), arrived only after World War I, and engaged in the sugarcane industry rather than shepherding (Al Grassby, *The Spanish in Australia* [Melbourne: AE Press, 1983], 51–52).

59. Some cliometricians have tried to quantify the pull effect of the immigrant stock already settled in the host country on emigration flows. The phrase "immigrant stock" is, of course, a synonym for the size of the social network, or better yet, for the number and extension of networks, because these were local rather than national. Most of these studies focus on Scandinavian countries ecause of the excellence of local demographic sources there. See, for example, J. M. Quigley, "An Econometric Model of Swedish Emigration," *Quarterly Journal of Economics* 86, 1 (1972):111–26; T. Moe, "Some Economic Aspects of Norwegian Population Movements: An Econometric Study," *Journal of Economic History* 30, 1 (1970):257–70; and J. D. Gould, "European Inter-Continental Emigration 1815–1914: Patterns and Causes," *Journal of European Economic History* 8, 3 (1979):593–679, particularly pp. 622 ff., for a review of this literature.

60. The reconstruction of this family's history is based on my taped interviews with twelve family members (including four who were visiting from overseas) in Finisterre on August 10–14, 1988, on parish baptismal and marriage records, on manuscript censuses in Finisterre and Buenos Aires, and on the records of several voluntary associations records in Buenos Aires.

61. A team of anthropologists found that in the mid-1960s the peasantry in Corcubión County tended to emigrate to Germany and Switzerland and the coastal people to Scandinavia, both in search of "strong currencies" (J. M. Gómez-Tabanera et al., *Migración y sociedad en la Galicia contemporánea* [Madrid: Ediciones Guadarrama, 1967], 215).

62. The habit of drinking mate led to this early-twentieth-century Finisterre carnival song:

Hace tiempo que en el pueblo
se ha desarrollado una gran aficción
la de tomar yerba mate,
pero sobre todo la de Napoleón.
Y mate toman aquí,
y mate toman allá,
hay quien le toma para dormir
y al levantarse vuelve a recuncar.

For quite some time in this town
a strong habit has developed
of drinking yerba mate,
particularly the Napoleon brand.
And they drink mate here,
and they drink mate there,
some drink it to sleep
and once again when they wake up.

Miguel González Fernández, *Tradicións e costumes populares da Fisterra* (Corcubión, Spain: Concello de Corcubión, 1989), 43.

63. Transcribed in Angel García-Sanz Marcotegui, "La emigración navarra
a América a través de la publicística, 1877–1915," in *Historia general de la emigración española a Iberoamérica*, vol. 2 (Madrid: Ministerio de Trabajo y
Seguridad Social, Dirección General de Migraciones, 1992), 418–19.

64. Rosalía de Castro, *Obras completas* (Madrid, 1880), vol. 2, *Follas Novas*, 246.

65. Transcribed in González Fernández, *Tradicións e costumes*, 14–15.

66. Dolores Marcote Marcote, interview by author, tape recording, Finisterre, Spain, August 7, 1989.

67. For the same practice in neighboring Portugal, see Caroline B. Brettell,
*Men Who Migrate, Women Who Wait: Population History in a Portuguese Par-
ish* (Princeton, N.J.: Princeton University Press, 1986).

68. Javier Vales Failde, *La emigración gallega* (Madrid: Est. Tip. a cargo de
Antonio Haro, 1902). For his comments to the visiting Briton, see Annette M. B.
Meakin, *Galicia: The Switzerland of Spain* (London: Methuen & Co., 1909),
181. Another Galician priest, Ramón Castro López, also blamed the region's
presumed high illegitimacy for the exodus, in *La emigración en Galicia* (La Coruña: Tipografía el Noroeste, 1923), 46. In a comparable way, Donna Gabaccia,
the foremost student of Sicilian emigration, found that "Sambucesi of illegitimate birth showed an especially strong propensity to migrate. At least three-
quarters of the children born to unmarried or unknown mothers in the years
after 1871 went to the United States" (*Militants and Migrants: Rural Sicilians
Become American Workers* [New Brunswick, N.J.: Rutgers University Press,
1988], 79).

69. This was similar to the general Spanish illegitimacy rate of 4.9 percent
of all live births between 1896 and 1900, a rate that ranked on the low end of

the European spectrum, as the following figures, for the same period, show: Austria 14.1, Portugal 12.1, Sweden 11.3, Denmark 9.6, Hungary 9.0, Germany 9.0, France 8.8, Belgium 8.0, Norway 7.4, Scotland 6.8, Finland 6.6, Italy 6.2, Poland 6.1, Switzerland 4.5, England 4.1, Russia 2.7, and The Netherlands 2.7 (Shirley Foster Hartley, *Illegitimacy* [Berkeley: University of California Press, 1975], 36–39).

70. Landownership, combined with primogeniture, seems to have played a larger role in determining which offspring would leave than in the emigration of parents. The data from the Baztán municipal census list of 1897 show that among landowning families the firstborn accounted for a smaller proportion (39 percent) of all emigrating sons and daughters than was the case among landless families (51 percent). Moreover, when the second-oldest offspring of landowning families emigrated, they were usually not following their older sibling, who, in 84 percent of the cases, stayed home. In contrast, the majority (63 percent) of emigrating second-oldest children from landless families were following their older brother or sister.

71. See, for example, Manuel Curros Enríquez, "A emigración," in *Obras completas* (Madrid: Aguilar, 1979), 111; and various poems by Rosalía de Castro transcribed in Nidia A. Díaz, *La protesta social en la obra de Rosalía de Castro* (Vigo, Spain: Editorial Galaxia, 1976), 40–49.

72. Seventy-three percent of the 812 Baztanese emigrants who expressed a motive for leaving in nineteenth-century notarial records listed "mejorar fortuna," which has the dual connotation of "improving one's fortune" and "increasing one's wealth." Sixty-one percent of the 162 absentees listed in the Finisterre census of 1897 gave "seeking sustenance," sometimes proceeded by "for his family," as the reason they were overseas.

73. Notice, for example, the literacy rates of emigrant and nonemigrant males from the municipal district of Corcubión in 1905, when broken down by age cohort: (in percentage, numbers in parentheses)

| Age cohort | Emigrants | | Nonemigrants | |
	Number	Percentage literate	Number	Percentage literate
13–30	36	81	147	64
30–39	33	79	54	63
40–49	26	58	57	74
50+	13	38	83	66

Interestingly, these findings concur with Kristian Hvidt's assertion that in the Danish case, love of adventure presented a more important motive than did economic distress for younger emigrants, and vice versa for those over the age of forty (*Flight to America: The Social Background of 300,000 Danish Emigrants* [New York: Academic Press, 1975], chap. 7).

74. The perception that emigrating at an advanced age betrayed personal

failure appears poignantly in a 1914 drama in which a rich Argentine, on returning from Europe, tells of an old *gallego* emigrant on the ship who daily intoned a sad ballad entitled "The Song of the Vagabond" and who one day, after kneeling in prayer, committed suicide by jumping overboard. A cynical friend then asserts: "He did the right thing . . . because a man who in his old age has to travel in third class has no right to live." Francisco Collazo and Evaristo Arias, "Piadosas mentiras," in *La Escena: Revista teatral*, suppl. 39, May 30, 1921, scene 1.

75. For a discussion, in English, of the importance of the *echea*, see William A. Douglas, *Death in Murelaga: Funerary Ritual in a Spanish Basque Village* (Seattle: University of Washington Press, 1969), chap. 3. For a much longer, illustrated study, see Julio Caro Baroja, *La casa en Navarra*, 4 vols. (Pamplona: Casa de Ahorro de Navarra, 1982).

76. Richard Ford, *A Hand-Book for Travellers in Spain and Readers at Home* [originally published in 1845] (London: Centaur Press, 1966), vol. 3, 1491.

77. The Baztán municipal *padrones*, for example, consistently listed the name of the house. The identification with the *casa* seems to have been less strong among emigrants. Of the fifty-seven who appear in a manuscript list of departures from Baztán in 1909, twenty-three simply mentioned their hometown.

78. Unlike baptismal records, which include only the specific parish, the civil registry encompasses not only the main town of Vimianzo but the entire municipal district. This allowed me to trace even those who were born in smaller villages but had listed the main town as their birthplace.

79. Gregorio González Lago, interview by author, tape recording, Corcubión, Spain, July 24, 1989.

80. Members of the Asociación de Hijos de Ribadumia en Buenos Aires, interview by author, tape recording, Buenos Aires, August 22, 1987.

81. "Galicia obscura, Finisterre vivo," 2, memoir of Manuel Domínguez López (1899–1986), transcribed from an interview by his grandnephew Luis Lamela García and kindly provided by the Domínguez Insúa family of Finisterre, Spain.

82. Waldo A. Insúa, "La emigración en general," in *Congreso social y económico hispano-americano, reunido en Madrid el año 1900*, vol. 2 (Madrid, 1902), 161, 167.

83. An English woman living in Galicia in the early twentieth century noted that the most common local explanation for emigration was "the spirit of adventure inherent in their Celtic blood" (Meakin, *Galicia*, 178–79). Some years later the Galician writer Julio Camba noted the same in his "El Celta migratorio," *Obras completas* (Madrid: Plus Ultra, 1948), vol. 1, 497.

84. Cited in Eric Richards, "Varieties of Scottish Emigration in the Nineteenth Century," *Historical Studies* 21, 85 (1985):475.

85. Guglielmo Godio, *Nuovi Orizzonti: L'America ne suoi primi fattori; La colonizzazione e l'emigrazione* (Florence, 1893), 99.

86. Leopoldo Alas, in the prologue to Eduardo González Velasco, *Tipos y bocetos de la emigración asturiana* (Madrid, 1880), 2.

87. Francesco Cordasco, ed., *Dictionary of American Immigration History* (Metuchen, N.J.: Scarecrow Press, 1990), 226.

88. Briant Lindsay Lowell, *Scandinavian Exodus: Demography and Social Development of 19th-Century Rural Communities* (Boulder, Colo.: Westview Press, 1987), 130.

89. Kerby A. Miller, *Emigrants and Exiles: Ireland and the Irish Exodus to North America* (New York: Oxford University Press, 1985), 193.

90. Marcin Kula, "El Brasil y la Polonia de fines del siglo XIX en las cartas de los campesinos emigrados," *Jahrbuch für Geschichte von Staat, Wirtschaft und Gesellschaft Lateinamerikas* 13 (1976):38–55. For the general use of fever motives in Poland, see Benjamin P. Murdzek, *Emigration in Polish Social-Political Thought, 1870–1914* (Boulder, Colo.: East European Quarterly, 1977), 55, 61.

91. Julianna Puskas, ed., *Overseas Migration from East-Central and Southeastern Europe, 1880–1940* (Budapest: Akademiai Kiado, 1990), 53, 208, 237.

92. The study of the process by which knowledge and innovations diffuse has such a long pedigree in the social sciences that it has turned into an "ism." Emerging in the early twentieth century as a reaction to nineteenth-century evolutionist dogmas, diffusionism maintained that the spectrum of human culture resulted from the dissemination, through contacts or migrations, of a few original cultures rather than from independent invention and evolution in many places. In Germany it was associated with the *Kulturkreis* school of anthropogeography; in the United States, with the work of Edward Sapir and Franz Boas. Both on the continent and in the Anglo-American world, it dominated anthropology and archeology until the midtwentieth century. In a less imperious and more eclectic way, it continues to influence those two disciplines, as well as geography, sociology, management, and marketing.

I encountered four main obstacles when I tried to borrow from this corpus and adapt its frameworks to a historical study of how the idea—and reality—of overseas emigration spread in nineteenth-century Spain. First, most diffusion studies deal either with prehistoric periods and premodern people or, on the other extreme, with present-day institutions, corporations, and consumers. Second, when they deal with the time period after writing but before computers, the focus tends to be on the spread of artifacts and technologies rather than of ideas and behaviors. Third, their interest in migration centers on its role as a carrier of innovations, not on how migratory behavior disseminates (see, for example, P. G. Duke et al., *Diffusion and Migration: Their Roles in Cultural Development* [Calgary, Canada: University of Calgary, Archeological Association, 1978]). Fourth, the cumulative effect of innovation adoptions and of emigration decisions differ in a critical way. In the span of x years the inhabitants of a region may increasingly adopt a new technology or fashion or convert to a new religion, until the practices become universal. If the same happens with the practice of emigration, the region will have a decreasing number of people, instead of an increasing number of "converts," and will eventually cease to exist as a human entity. Despite its limited direct applicability, however, I found this literature a source of valuable ideas and opportunities for comparison.

For a cross section of the innovation diffusion literature, see the following works. Torsten Hägerstrand, *Innovation Diffusion as a Spatial Process* (Chicago: University of Chicago Press, 1967) is a classic study of a few Swedish parishes in the post–World War II years first published in 1953. The first part of chapter 7 deals with short-distance migration, but there is nothing on overseas emigration except an acknowledgment that it must have expanded private information (p. 241). Lawrence A. Brown, *Innovation Diffusion: A New Perspective* (London: Methuen, 1981), emphasizes the role of the diffusion of technological innovations in economic development. Peter J. Hugill and D. Bruce Dickson, *The Transfer and Transformation of Ideas and Material Culture* (College Station: Texas A&M University Press, 1988), is a collection of articles, mostly by geographers. Cristiano Antonelli et al., *The Economics of Industrial Modernization* (London: Academic Press, 1992), uses econometric models to study the diffusion of technological innovations in cotton manufacturing. For the use of the concept by historians in a basically descriptive way, see Andrew M. Watson, *Agricultural Innovation in the Early Islamic World: The Diffusion of Crops and Farming Techniques, 700–1100* (Cambridge, England: Cambridge University Press, 1983); and John V. Pickstone, ed., *Medical Innovations in Historical Perspective* (New York: St. Martin's Press, 1992). For a limited attempt to use the "innovation diffusion" concept in the study of emigration, see Sune Akerman, "Theories and Methods of Migration Research," in *From Sweden to America*, ed. H. Runblom and H. Norman (Minneapolis: University of Minnesota Press, 1976), esp. 27–32; and J. D. Gould, "European Inter-Continental Emigration: The Role of 'Diffusion' and 'Feedback,'" *Journal of European Economic History* 9, 2 (1980):310.

93. Of the eleven immigrants from the interior provinces shown on Map 3A, six were soldiers or clerics who had come through national institutions that recruited or enlisted their members from all over the peninsula or, for that matter, the empire. Another three were born in Orense to an Andalusian military officer stationed there but moved with the family to Cádiz early in life and had little, if any, connection with their birthplace. With the end of the empire these institutional relocations ceased to be a source of newcomers to the Americas, so the geographical origins of immigrants narrowed to the places where private links with American localities had existed and survived.

94. Joanne, *Itinéraire de la France*, 78.

95. For the Catalan connection, see L. Alonso Alvarez, *Industrialización y conflictos sociales en la Galicia del Antiguo Régimen, 1750–1830* (Madrid, Akal Editor, 1976).

96. Argentina, AGN, Sala X, 4.6.1.

97. Alejandro Arizcun Cela, *Economía y sociedad en un valle pirenaico del Antiguo Régimen, Baztán 1600–1841* (Pamplona: Gobierno de Navarra, Departamento de Educación y Cultura, 1988), 302–4. For the role of trade in spreading information about internal migration opportunities, see Torsten Hägerstrand, "Migration and Area: Survey of a Sample of Swedish Migration Fields and Hypothetical Considerations on Their Genesis," in *Migration in Sweden: A Symposium*, ed. David Hannerberg et al. (Lund: C. W. K. Gleerup, 1957), 27–158.

98. See Charles L. Freeston, *The Passes of the Pyrenees: A Practical Guide to the Mountain Roads of the Franco-Spanish Frontier* (New York: Charles Scribner's Sons, 1912), chap. 13 for the passes and roads connecting Navarre and France, and the folding map following p. 188 for the contour of the Pyrenees.

99. José M. Iribarren, *Batiburrillo navarro* (Pamplona: Editorial Gómez, 1957), 175; and Ford, *Hand-Book for Travellers*, vol. 3, 1476.

100. Contraband was so common that the subject appears in scores of local folk tunes. See the *kontrebandistaren Kantuak* (contrabandist songs) recorded in Michel, *Les Pays basque*, 361–63. Michel also devotes a chapter to "Les Contrebandiers Basques" and several pages to Basque emigration to South America (pp. 113–27, 193–98).

101. This case was compiled from the Buenos Aires 1855 census return; the Argentine passenger lists; the list of Spanish men who entered Argentina in 1860–1861, sent to the Spanish Ministry of Foreign Relations by the consul in Buenos Aires; and the baptismal and marriage records in the parish of Aoiz.

102. The Zas municipal *padrón* of 1897 lists only 2 women among the 60 overseas emigrants and 10 among the 59 internal migrants; the Corcubión 1930 *padrón* lists 18 women (17 percent) among the 107 emigrants and 5 (33 percent) among the 15 migrants. This preference of women for shorter-distance internal migration was also noted in nineteenth-century England by E. G. Ravenstein, who then turned the observation into one of his famous "laws" ("The Laws of Migration," *Journal of the Royal Statistical Society* 52 [1889]:287).

103. J. M. de Arratia, ed., *Cancionero popular del país vasco* (San Sebastián: Editorial Auñamendi, 1968), vol. 1, 76.

104. Xesús Alonso Montero, *Cantigas sociales recollidas do pobo* (Vigo: Ediciones Castrelos, 1969), 43.

105. A Galician essayist, for example, observed that, in the early decades of this century, "for each magazine from Madrid that reaches Galicia there are five or six from Argentina" (Julio Camba, *La rana viajera* [Madrid: Calpe, 1920], 96).

106. Cited in Blanca Sánchez Alonso, "La visión contemporánea de la emigración española," *Estudios Migratorios Latinoamericanos* 13 (December 1989):456.

107. Part of a longer poem, this appeared in *Messager de Bayonne*, October 6, 1853, and was transcribed in Michel, *Les Pays basque*, 342–45.

108. José Costa Figueiras, *La sugestión de America* (Buenos Aires, 1917), 206.

109. Cited in William A. Douglass, *Emigration in a South Italian Town: An Anthropological History* (New Brunswick, N.J.: Rutgers University Press, 1984), 95, 107, who also includes an early-twentieth-century description of emigration as "a sport, a custom, a mania, a fever."

110. The case of China, a country of even more delayed and incomplete economic development than Spain, illustrates how late modernization can slow the geographical spread of emigration. In 1822 just four *hsien* (the equivalent of U.S. counties) in coastal Fukien Province furnished 93 percent of the emigrants to Manila. Seventy years later the same four *hsien* still accounted for 88 per-

cent of those heading for the Spanish colony (D. F. Doeppers, "Destination, Selection and Turnover among Chinese Migrants to Philippine Cities in the Nineteenth Century," *Journal of Historical Geography* 12, 4 (1986):385.

111. From the end of the Napoleonic Wars to the start of the Great Famine, about a million Irish from all over the island emigrated to North America (Miller, *Emigrants and Exiles*, 193, 199–200).

112. For contemporary descriptions of Irish shepherds from Wexford and Westmeath counties in the Buenos Aires pampas, see William MacCann, *Two Thousand Miles' Ride through the Argentine Provinces* (London: Smith, Elder & Co., 1853), vol. 1, chaps. 3, 4; and Thomas J. Hutchinson, *Buenos Ayres and Argentine Gleanings* (London: E. Stanford, 1865), 252.

113. Emigrants from urban Ulster and the English Midlands shared with the Mataronese, and others from the Catalan and Basque industrial belts, the fact that they had old, established ties with the host country, that they emigrated in moderate numbers over a long period of time, their skilled background, and that often they sought occupational independence rather than higher wages (Miller, *Emigrants and Exiles*, 137, 197; Rowland Tappan Berthoff, *British Immigrants in Industrial America* [Cambridge, Mass.: Harvard University Press, 1953], 20–29; and Charlotte Erickson, *The Invisible Immigrants* [Coral Gables, Fla.: University of Miami Press, 1972], 27–28, 233–36).

4. SETTLING IN THE CITY

1. These two cases were reconstructed from the membership lists of the Asociación Española de Socorros Mutuos, the Centro Gallego, and the Sociedad Agraria y Cultural Hijos del Partido de Corcubión, all in Buenos Aires; *Alborada*, the monthly magazine published since 1925 by the Sociedad Agraria y Cultural Hijos del Partido de Corcubión; *Finisterre*, the monthly magazine published by the Sociedad Finisterre en America, a society formed by immigrants from a municipality in Corcubión County, in the second half of the 1920s; the civil birth registry in the municipalities of origin; and interviews with various people from the area, in both Spain and Buenos Aires.

2. Robert Harney and J. Vicenza Scarpaci, eds., *Little Italies in North America* (Toronto: Multicultural History Society of Ontario, 1981), 3–4, for example, cite the description by the visiting political analyst Luigi Villari of Little Italies in North America at the turn of the century as "amorphous and incomplete societies, lacking many of the elements that constitute a normal social organism . . . an army without officers, commanded by corporals and sergeants." The authors view these attitudes and the use of pejorative terms such as *Italietta* and *bas Italia* as evidence that Old World scholars perceived these settlements as a source of embarrassment and thus avoided serious study of them.

3. See Roy Lubove, *The Progressives and the Slums: Tenement House Reform in New York City, 1890–1917* (Pittsburgh: University of Pittsburgh Press, 1962).

4. Among the classic works of the Chicago sociologists are: William I. Thomas and Florian Znaniecki, *The Polish Peasant in Europe and America*, 5 vols. (Boston: Gorham Press, 1918–1920); Robert E. Park, *Race and Culture* (Glen-

coe, Ill.: Free Press, 1950), where most of Park's articles on ethnic topics are reprinted; Robert Park and Herbert Miller, *Old World Traits Transplanted* (New York: Harper & Brothers, 1921); Louis Wirth, *The Ghetto* (Chicago: University of Chicago Press, 1928); and Harvey Warren Zorbaugh, *The Gold Coast and the Slum* (Chicago: University of Chicago Press, 1929) (the former being "the home of Chicago's 'Four Hundred'" and the latter, "Little Sicily, also known as 'Tenement Town' and 'Little Hell'" (pp. 46, 159). For recent works on the Chicago school, see Stow Persons, *Ethnic Studies at Chicago, 1905–45* (Urbana: University of Illinois Press, 1987); and Barbara Ballis Lal, *The Romance of Culture in an Urban Civilization: Robert E. Park on Race and Ethnic Relations in the Cities* (London: Routledge, 1990).

5. See Thomas and Znaniecki, *Polish Peasant,* vol. 4, part 1, chap. 1, "The Concept of Social Disorganization"; vol. 5, part 2, chap. 1, "Disorganization and the Immigrant"; and vol. 2, part 2, chap. 1, "Demoralization"; Park, *Race and Culture,* part 4, "The Marginal Man"; and Park and Miller, *Old World Traits Transplanted,* chap. 5, "Immigrant Demoralization." The Chicago sociologists were not, however, the first to portray immigrant settlements in terms of social pathology. From what many would consider an opposite ideological pole, Engels, in the midnineteenth century, described the Irish immigrants in London as "sunk in the whirlpool of moral ruin which surrounds them, sinking daily deeper, losing daily more and more of their power to resist the demoralizing influence of want, filth, and evil surroundings" and the inhabitants of Manchester's Little Ireland as "creatures who . . . must surely have sunk to the lowest level of humanity" (Friedrich Engels, *The Condition of the Working-Class in England* [Moscow: Progress Publishers, 1973], 67–68, 81, and passim.

6. Oscar Handlin, *Boston's Immigrants, 1790–1865* (Cambridge, Mass.: Harvard University Press, 1941); and idem, *The Uprooted: The Migrations That Made the American People* (Boston: Little, Brown, 1951), in which the chapter on residence is significantly titled "Ghettoes."

7. See Sam Bass Warner Jr. and Colin B. Burke, "Cultural Change and the Ghetto," *Journal of Contemporary History* 4 (October 1969):173–87, for one of the earliest criticisms of the social dimensions of the Chicago school model; and David Ward, *Poverty, Ethnicity, and the American City, 1840–1925: Changing Conceptions of the Slum and the Ghetto* (Cambridge, England: Cambridge University Press, 1989), for one of the latest.

8. For example, Irving Cutler, "The Jews of Chicago: From Shtetl to Suburb," in *Ethnic Chicago,* ed. Peter Jones and Melvin Holli (Grand Rapids, Mich.: W. B. Eerdmans, 1984), 69–108, maintains that the move to the suburbs did not imply an abandonment of ethnic culture.

9. Even in Donald Tricarico, *The Italians of Greenwich Village* (Staten Island, N.Y.: Center for Migration Studies, 1984), a work whose main thesis is that the Italian enclave in the South Village changed but did not disappear, the author has to admit that "the old neighborhood is in eclipse" and that ethnic life has taken on a more suburban aspect (p. 165). Indeed, today New York's Little Italy is little more than two blocks of restaurants and a tourist attraction. David Ward, *Cities and Immigrants: A Geography of Change in Nineteenth-Century America* (New York: Oxford University Press, 1971), 105–21, is an-

other work that tries to question the Chicago school's model but ends up concurring with much of it.

10. See, for example, John W. Briggs, *An Italian Passage: Immigrants in Three American Cities, 1890–1930* (New Haven, Conn.: Yale University Press, 1978), 118–19; and Dino Cinel, *From Italy to San Francisco* (Stanford, Calif.: Stanford University Press, 1982) one of whose sections on residence is precisely titled "Settlements, Not Ghettoes" (p. 106 ff).

11. Some scholars have found isolated cases in which the areas of first settlement developed outside the city's central wards. See Dominic Candeloro, "Suburban Italians: Chicago Heights, 1890–1975," in *Ethnic Chicago*, 239–68. For a case in which secondary-settlement areas also attracted immigrants straight from the Old World "who brought their own outlook and made their demands in a 'primary-settlement way,'" see Thomas Kessner, *The Golden Door: Italians and Jewish Mobility in New York City, 1880–1915* (New York: Oxford University Press, 1977), 157–60, quotation on p. 159. Lynn H. Less noticed a "pattern of movement from place to place within a small area" plus "a current of reverse migration" from the suburban areas to the older ethnic quarters in the inner city in "Patterns of Lower-Class Life: Irish Slum Communities in Nineteenth-Century London," in *Nineteenth-Century Cities: Essays in the New Urban History*, ed. S. Thernstrom and R. Sennett (New Haven, Conn.: Yale University Press, 1969), 359–85.

12. For example, in one of the most comprehensive urban historical studies of the last decade, Olivier Zunz concluded that Detroit's spatial arrangement around 1920 fit the Chicago school's model (*The Changing Face of Inequality: Urbanization, Industrial Development, and Immigrants in Detroit, 1880–1920* [Chicago: University of Chicago Press, 1982], 327–28, 348–49).

13. For Argentina, see Eugene F. Sofer, *From Pale to Pampa: A Social History of the Jews of Buenos Aires* (New York: Holmes & Meier, 1982), 66–85, who detected four stages "in the history of Jewish ghettoization": arrival and the search for spatial stability, "ghettoization and unity," "ghettoization and the westward movement," and "dispersion and the fragmentation of the community." Charles S. Sargent, *The Spatial Evolution of Greater Buenos Aires, 1870–1930* (Tempe: Arizona State University, Center for Latin American Studies, 1974), 30–31, 65, 82, 119, maintained that by 1900 Buenos Aires fit the Burgess concentric model of income segregation, with impoverished immigrants entrapped in the center while the more successful white-collar employees moved to the periphery. Among other scholars who make the same argument are: James R. Scobie, *Buenos Aires: From Plaza to Suburb, 1870–1910* (New York: Oxford University Press, 1974), 135, 146, 160; Richard J. Walter, *Politics and Urban Growth in Buenos Aires, 1910–1942* (Cambridge, England: Cambridge University Press, 1993), 9; Nora Clichevsky, "Condiciones de vida y transporte: El caso del subterráneo de Buenos Aires, 1900–1945," *Revista Latinoamericana de Estudios Urbano Regionales* 14, 42 (1988):99, 101; Horacio Torres, "Evolución de los procesos de estructuración espacial urbana: El caso de la ciudad de Buenos Aires," *Desarrollo Económico* 15, 58 (1975):281–306; and Sandra Lauderdale Graham, *House and Street: The Domestic World of Servants and Masters in Nineteenth Century Rio de Janeiro* (Cambridge, England: Cam-

bridge University Press, 1988), 26. For a survey of seven sociological studies of Latin American cities that have employed the Burgess hypothesis, see Leo F. Schnore, "On the Spatial Structure of Cities in the Two Americas," in *The Study of Urbanization*, ed. Philip M. Hauser and Leo F. Schnore (New York: John Wiley & Sons, 1965), 347–98.

14. The post–World War II Australian scholars who developed the concept of chain migration emphasized its importance for settlement patterns. In fact, the title of the article by John and Leatrice MacDonald that popularized the concept in North American scholarly circles explicitly referred to the topic: "Chain Migration, Ethnic Neighborhood Formation and Social Networks," *Milbank Memorial Fund Quarterly* 13, 42 (1964), 82–95.

15. A partial exception may be Rudolph J. Vecoli, "The Formation of Chicago's 'Little Italies,'" in *Migration across Time and Nations: Population Mobility in Historical Contexts*, ed. Ira A. Glazier and Luigi De Rosa (New York: Holmes & Meier, 1986), 287–301, who argues that *paesani* migration chains and time of arrival played a more significant role in settlement patterns than did the city's concentric arrangement or its industrial ecology.

16. Herbert J. Gans, *The Urban Villagers: Group and Class in the Life of Italian-Americans* (1962; reprint, New York: Free Press, 1982). Gans, however, was a sociologist and city planner, and in this study of Boston's West End he concluded that class was a more important concept than ethnicity in understanding the way of life of Italo-Americans there. Nevertheless, like many historians of chain migration, he perceived the immigrants as members of a homogeneous class. He then argued that this "functional working-class subculture" should be understood on its own terms and advised middle-class "caretakers" not to impose their own values on it (pp. 296, 310).

17. Sargent, *Spatial Evolution of Greater Buenos Aires*, 119.

18. Woodbine Parish, *Buenos Ayres and the Provinces of the Rio de la Plata* (London: John Murray, 1852), 101.

19. Arsenio Isabelle, *Voyage a Buenos Aires et a Porto Alegre pour la Banda Oriental, les Missions d'Uruguay el la Province de Rio Grande do Sul, de 1830 à 1834* (Le Havre, 1835), 110.

20. Benito Hortelano, *Memorias* (Madrid: Espasa-Calpe, 1936), 187–90. For other travelers' descriptions of the port Buenos Aires between 1690 and 1912, see Eduardo H. Pinasco, *El puerto de Buenos Aires en los relatos de veinte viajeros* (Buenos Aires: Talleres Gráficos de El Ejército de Salvación, 1947).

21. At the time the largest black neighborhood was the barrio of Monserrat, scornfully referred to as *barrio del mondongo* (barrio of the paunch) (Francisco L. Romay, *El Barrio de Monserrat* [Buenos Aires, 1952]). The manuscript returns for the 1855 municipal census are a superb source for the study of this population because they often include the "tribal" or ethnic affiliation of the African-born and the year of arrival in Argentina. Unfortunately, George Reid Andrews seems to have overlooked this source in his pioneering *The Afro-Argentines of Buenos Aires, 1800–1900* (Madison: University of Wisconsin Press, 1980), and so have later historians of this population.

22. The term *gran aldea* (large village) was used with some nostalgia by belle-epoque Buenos Aireans for the city of the mid-1800s; it also provided

the title for Vicente Fidel López's semiautobiographical novel. Interestingly, the same sobriquet of "big village" became "the most recurrent image of late-nineteenth-century Moscow" (Joseph Bradley, *Muzhik and Muscovite: Urbanization in Late Imperial Russia* [Berkeley: University of California Press, 1985], 62).

23. William MacCann, *Two Thousand Miles' Ride through the Argentine Provinces* (London: Smith, Elder & Co., 1853), vol. 1, 168–69.

24. Isaac B. Strain, *Sketches of a Journey in Chili, and the Argentine Provinces, in 1849* (New York: Horace H. Moore, 1853), 271.

25. Xavier Mamier, *Buenos Aires y Montevideo en 1850* (Buenos Aires: Ferrari, 1948), cited in María Sáenz Quesada, *El estado rebelde: Buenos Aires entre 1850–1860* (Buenos Aires: Editorial Belgrano, 1982), 18. The description does not differ much from that of an English mining engineer, F. B. Head, *Rough Notes Taken during Some Rapid Journeys across the Pampas and among the Andes* (London: John Murray, 1826), 30.

26. Benjamín Vicuña Mackenna, *La Argentina en el año 1855* (Buenos Aires: La Revista Americana, 1936), 28.

27. Richard Darwin Keynes, ed., *Charles Darwin's Beagle Diary* (Cambridge, England: Cambridge University Press, 1988), entry for November 3, 1832, 113. For other comments on the chessboard layout, see Parish, *Buenos Ayres*, 101; MacCann, *Two Thousand Miles' Ride*, vol. 1, 169; C. S. Stewart, *Brazil and La Plata: The Personal Record of a Cruise* (New York: Putnam, 1856), 193; and C. B. Mansfield, *Paraguay, Brazil, and the Plate: Letters Written in 1852–1853* (Cambridge, England: MacMillan, 1856), 137–38. Although the gridiron plan obeyed Spanish royal ordinances (see Zelia Nuttall's translation of the 1573 document, "Royal Ordinances Concerning the Laying Out of New Towns," *Hispanic American Historical Review* 5 [1922]:249–54), it also characterized colonial towns in English America (see John W. Reps, *The Making of Urban America: A History of City Planning in the United States* [Princeton, N.J.: Princeton University Press, 1965], chap. 11, "Gridiron Cities and Checkerboard Plans").

28. On changing architectural styles in the nineteenth century, see Mario Buschiazzo, *La arquitectura en la Republica Argentina, 1810–1930*, 2 vols. (Buenos Aires: Mac Gaul, 1971); Instituto de Arte Americano, Facultad de Arquitectura y Urbanismo, *La arquitectura en Buenos Aires, 1850–1880* (Buenos Aires, 1965); José X. Martini and José M. Peña, *La ornamentación en la arquitectura de Buenos Aires*, vol. 1, 1800–1900, vol. 2, 1900–1940 (Buenos Aires, 1966–1967); and Federico Ortiz et al., *La arquitectura del liberalismo en la Argentina* (Buenos Aires: Editorial Sudamericana, 1968).

29. The introduction of these new technologies was not devoid of tragic and comic incidents. In his memoir, Manuel Bilbao relates how "the simple folk could not understand how by just turning the key on the pipe and lighting a match a light as bright as day could appear. Many used to turn the light off by blowing on the flame and this provoked explosions or the deaths of those who were sleeping" (*Tradiciones y recuerdos de Buenos Aires* [Buenos Aires: Ferrari, 1934], 320). On the trial run of the first train, the city's prominent citizens who were riding in it became so enthusiastic that they asked the conductor to increase the speed beyond 25 miles per hour, causing a derailment. Panicking,

the Basque merchant Bernardo Larroudé is said to have "jumped on the first horse he found, and blessing the traditional mode of transportation, he galloped to his home where he almost rode into the kitchen" (Sáenz Quesada, *El estado rebelde,* 161).

30. The Spanish population in the capital of the Río de la Plata viceroyalty apparently reached a peak toward the end of the colonial period. Surviving census schedules for fourteen of the twenty districts into which the city was divided in 1810 list 1,669 Spaniards (1,570 men and 99 women), 5.9 percent of the total. It is not clear, however, whether this group includes only *peninsulares,* because 48 people in it are listed as *de color,* and it seems unlikely that European-born individuals, even if swarthy, would be classified as colored. Taking this into consideration and extrapolating to the most reliable approximations of the city's total population (45,000), I estimated the Spanish-born population in 1810 at 2,565. For the information on the 1810 census and the estimates of the city's total population, see Alberto B. Martínez, *Estudio topográfico e historia demográfica de la ciudad de Buenos Aires* (Buenos Aires: Compañía Sud-Americana de Billetes de Banco, 1889), 238–42.

31. Santiago Calzadilla, in his 1891 memoirs *Las beldades de mi tiempo,* recalled that in the 1830s and 1840s the quarters south of the central plaza were still "the Saint-Germain of the Porteño aristocracy" (pp. 12, 34).

32. Unless otherwise indicated, data for this section come from my analysis of the manuscript schedules for the unpublished Buenos Aires census of 1855 at the Archivo General de la Nación. In addition to creating a data set with all Spaniards in the city (except those in precinct [*cuartel*] 2, for which the schedules are missing), I recorded the number of Italians, French, and Argentines and the total population, their gender, and their literacy, for every block in the city using the summaries written in the back of each census booklet.

33. Carl Skogman, *Viaje de la fragata sueca "Eugenia," 1851–1853* (first published in Stockholm, 1855), trans. Kjell Henrichsen (Buenos Aires: Solar, 1942), 71–72.

34. Cited in Enrique Horacio Puccia, *Barracas: Su historia y sus tradiciones, 1536–1936* (Buenos Aires: n.p., 1968), 46; and MacCann, *Two Thousand Miles' Ride,* vol. 1, 4.

35. Black indexes of segregation in U.S. cities during the post–World War II period frequently range from 80 to over 90; those of South Asians and West Indians in English cities usually surpass 50 (Joe T. Darden, "Black Residential Segregation since the 1948 'Shelly v. Kraemer' Decision" *Journal of Black Studies* 25, 6 [1995]:680–91; Vaughan Robinson, "The Development of South Asian Settlement in Britain and the Myth of Return," in *Ethnic Segregation in Cities,* ed. Ceri Peach, Vaughan Robinson, and Susan Smith [Athens: University of Georgia Press, 1981], 158–60; and Kenneth Prandy, "Residential Segregation and Ethnic Distance in English Cities," *Ethnicity* 7 [1980]: 372). The segregation of "new" immigrants in the United States is treated later in the chapter.

36. Zunz, *Changing Face of Inequality,* 41–42, discussed the general consensus among historians that, in North American cities, "social divisions did not readily translate into spatial divisions through most of the nineteenth century." In a similar vein, sociologist Douglas Massey wrote in a recent review article:

"Preindustrial cities display little variation in social, family, or ethnic status, and what variation there is not spatially patterned" ("Ethnic Residential Segregation: A Theoretical Synthesis and Empirical Review," *Sociology and Social Research* 69, 3 [1985]:317). And English geographer David Ward, alluding to nineteenth-century North American cities, referred to "weak levels of residential differentiation and a rather high degree of interspersal of both occupational and ethnic groups" ("Victorian Cities: How Modern?" *Journal of Historical Geography* 1, 2 [1975]:137). In the case of British cities, L. D. Schwarz, "Social Class and Social Geography: The Middle Classes in London at the End of the Eighteenth Century," *Social History* 7, 1 (1982):178, maintained that spatial class mixing was the norm; and G. Gordon, "The Status Areas of Early to Mid-Victorian Edinburgh," *Transactions of the Institute of British Geographers* 4, 2 (1979):168–91, found the rich and the destitute in well-delimited, small areas but the groups in between evenly dispersed throughout the city. Other English geographers disputed the level and type of residential segregation in their Victorian cities. See, for instance, H. Cater and S. Wheatley, "Residential Segregation in Nineteenth-Century Cities," *Area* 12, 1 (1980):57–62; the critique by Mark Shaw in *Area* 12, 4 (1980):318–20; and Carter and Wheatley's reply on pp. 320–21. On the other hand, Gideon Sjoberg, in his pioneering *The Preindustrial City: Past and Present* (New York: Free Press, 1960), chap. 5 and p. 323, presented social-class—and ethnic—residential segregation as one of the distinguishing marks of preindustrial urban centers, which otherwise exhibited little differentiation in land use.

37. For a comparison with another South American city at about the same time, see Armando de Ramón, "Santiago de Chile, 1850–1900: Límites urbanos y segregación espacial según estratos," *Revista Paraguaya de Sociología* 15, 42–43 (1978): 253–76, whose evidence, though limited, also indicates high levels of spatial separation among social strata.

38. Stuart Blumin also detected a large gap, this time in the accumulated wealth, between clerks and laborers in 1860 Philadelphia: that of a clerk was $1,410; of a laborer, $180 ("Mobility and Change in Ante-Bellum Philadelphia," in *Nineteenth-Century Cities*, 169). Sam Bass Warner found, for the same city and year, that clerks concentrated in the central districts and laborers in the periphery ("If All the World Were Philadelphia: A Scaffolding for Urban History, 1774–1930" *American Historical Review* 74 [1968]:182–95).

39. A good example is E. Franklin Frazier, "The Negro Family in Chicago" in *Urban Sociology*, ed. Ernest Burgess and Donald Bogue (Chicago: University of Chicago Press, 1967), 224–38. He divided the black neighborhood in that city into seven zones, each progressively farther from the downtown area. As one moved outward from zone to zone, literacy and occupational status consistently increased.

40. M. G. Mulhall, *Handbook of the River Plate* (Buenos Aires: The Standard, 1869), 16.

41. For example, Stuart Blumin argued that as late as 1860 Philadelphia represented the reversal of Burgess' pattern, with "the interior zone the most affluent, the surrounding ring middle-class, and the urban poor located in the periphery." He went on to use centripetal movement as indication of upward

mobility and vice versa ("Mobility and Change in Ante-Bellum Philadelphia," in *Nineteenth-Century Cities*, 188ff). Sam Bass Warner Jr. also posited that the social geography of the city in 1860 was almost the reverse of the "core of poverty and ring of affluence," which he dates from the late nineteenth century; he held the same for Boston (*The Private City: Philadelphia in Three Periods of its Growth* [Philadelphia: University of Pennsylvania Press, 1968], 55–56, and *Streetcar Suburbs: The Process of Growth in Boston, 1870–1900* [Cambridge, Mass.: Harvard University Press, 1962], 15–34). On the other hand, Oscar Handlin, referring to 1850s Boston, wrote of a "centrifugal movement [that] winnowed the well-to-do from the impoverished, and consequently segregated the great mass of Irish within the narrow limits of old Boston (*Boston's Immigrants*, 94). And Kenneth Jackson criticized Stuart Blumin's equating outward movement with downward socioeconomic mobility in Philadelphia, claiming that, at least since 1850, "the precise opposite was true" ("Urban Deconcentration in the Nineteenth Century: A Statistical Inquiry," in *The New Urban History: Quantitative Explorations by American Historians*, ed. Leo F. Schnore and Eric E. Lampard [Princeton, N.J.: Princeton University Press, 1975], 129–32). For Detroit, Olivier Zunz found that as late as 1880 the upper and middle classes tended to concentrate in the central quarters (*Changing Face of Inequality*, 61–67).

42. Walter Nugent, *Crossings: The Great Transatlantic Migrations, 1870–1914* (Bloomington: Indiana University Press, 1992), 106.

43. E. J. Hobsbawm, *Primitive Rebels* (New York, 1959); J. S. MacDonald, "Agricultural Organization, Migration and Labour Militancy in Rural Italy," *Economic History Review*, 2d ser., 16, 1 (1963):61–75. Donna Gabaccia, "Neither Padrone Slaves nor Primitive Rebels: Sicilians on Two Continents," in *Struggle a Hard Battle: Essays on Working-Class Immigrants*, ed. Dirk Hoerder (DeKalb: Northern Illinois Press, 1986), 95–117, challenges some of these views, particularly the implication that southern Italians had no tradition of organized labor militancy (as opposed to spontaneous rebellion). Nevertheless, she shows that militancy was higher and rates of emigration lower in areas characterized by *latifondi*. See also her *Militants and Migrants: Rural Sicilians Become American Workers* (New Brunswick, N.J.: Rutgers University Press, 1988), esp. chap. 4.

44. Agustín Millares Torres, *Historia general de las Islas Canarias* (Las Palmas, Spain, 1893–95), vol. 17, 142–43.

45. AGN, "Emigrados Canarios," División Gobierno Nacional, Sala X, 25.2.6.

46. Class here is used in the broader sense of socioeconomic or occupational status. In the Marxist sense of relation to the means of production, all but four of the Ferroleans belonged to the same class of "have-nots." Regardless of the validity of such a scheme for macroanalysis, at this level it obviously oversimplifies this group's realities. For an interesting and comparable case of class-divided chains, see Gabaccia, *Militants and Migrants*, esp. chaps. 5–7. Gabaccia found that 91 percent of the emigrants from the Sicilian town of Sambuca to Louisiana were poorer peasants who went to work—often seasonally and under the auspices of *padroni*—in the sugarcane fields. On the other hand, 55 percent

of those who headed for New York City were artisans and 9 percent members of Sambuca's elite, and they migrated under the auspices of family and friends, rather than of *padroni*, from the beginning. The class makeup of the emigrants to Chicago and Tampa occupied a middle ground between these two cases. Moreover, the class background of the emigrants also influenced in which of the various Sambucesi enclaves within New York City they would settle.

47. Félix Basterra, *El crepúsculo de los gauchos: Estado actual de la República Argentina* (Paris, 1903), 111–12.

48. Richard E. Boyer and Keith A. Davies, *Urbanization in 19th Century Latin America: Statistics and Sources* (Los Angeles: University of California at Los Angeles, Latin American Center, 1973), 7, 23, 25, 42, 59–60; and Nicolás Sánchez-Albornoz, *The Population of Latin America: A History* (Berkeley: University of California Press, 1974), 179. For Santiago the source is Chile, Oficina Central de Estadística, *Censo jeneral [sic] de la república de Chile levantado en abril de 1854* (Santiago: Imprenta del Ferrocarril, 1858), 18.

49. The eighteen cities on the Atlantic seaboard that surpassed Buenos Aires in population during the middle of the nineteenth century were (population in thousands): New York (516), Liverpool (422), Dublin (263), Lisbon (257), Amsterdam (225), Edinburgh (194), Hamburg (193), Rio de Janeiro (181), Baltimore (169), Bristol (150), Salvador do Bahia (150), Bordeaux (142), Brooklyn (139), Boston (137), New Orleans (116), Seville (112), Newcastle (111), and Ghent (108). The populations of Latin American cities are taken from Boyer and Davies, *Urbanization*, 7, 23, 25; of U.S. cities, from Edward K. Spann, *The New Metropolis: New York City, 1840–1857* (New York: Columbia University Press, 1981), 430; of Seville, from Spain, Junta General de Estadística, *Censo de la población de España según el recuento verificado el 21 de mayo de 1857* (Madrid: Imprenta Nacional, 1857), 863; and of other European cities, from Paul M. Hohenberg and Lynn Hollen Lees, *The Making of Urban Europe, 1000–1950* (Cambridge, Mass.: Harvard University Press, 1985), 227.

50. For the fin-de-siècle transformation of Buenos Aires, Scobie, *Buenos Aires*, remains the best overall work. José Juan Maroni, *Breve historia física de Buenos Aires* (Buenos Aires: Municipalidad de la Ciudad de Buenos Aires, 1969) includes much on the physical transformation during this period. Stanley Ross and Thomas F. McGann, eds., *Buenos Aires: 400 Years* (Austin: University of Texas Press, 1982), a collection of papers presented at a Library of Congress symposium in celebration of the fourth centennial of Buenos Aires' foundation, contains articles by James Scobie and Mark Szuchman on the nineteenth century. Delfin L. Garasa, *La otra Buenos Aires* (Buenos Aires: Sudamericana-Planeta, 1987) examines the city as it appears in Argentine literature and includes many vignettes on the turn-of-the-century period, and García de D'Agostino, *Imagen de Buenos Aires a través de los viajeros, 1870–1910* (Buenos Aires: Universidad de Buenos Aires, 1981) shows the city as seen through the eyes of travelers. Walter, *Politics and Urban Growth*, takes up where Scobie left off and, as the title indicates, focuses on municipal politics.

51. Pablo Mantegazza, *Viajes por el Río de la Plata y el interior de la confederación argentina* [translation by Juan Heller of chapters from *Río de la Plata y Tenerife*, 3d ed., Milan, 1876] (Buenos Aires: Coni, 1916), 47.

52. Georges Clemenceau, *South America To-Day: A Study of Conditions, Social, Political, and Commercial in Argentina, Uruguay and Brazil* (New York: G. P. Putnam's Sons, 1911), 30–31.

53. Buenos Aires, Dirección General de Estadística Municipal, *Censo general de población, edificación, comercio e industrias de la ciudad de Buenos Aires, 1909*, 3 vols. (Buenos Aires: Compañía Sud-Americana de Billetes de Banco, 1910), vol. 3, 571–73, contains a graph showing the increase in the number of blocks from 1757 to 1909 and a map showing the physical growth of the city over the same period. Sargent, *Spatial Evolution of Greater Buenos Aires*, xvi–xvii, xxii–xxvii, 11, 13, 21, 87, also has excellent maps showing the physical expansion of the city during that period.

54. Francisco Rahola, *Sangre nueva: Impresiones de un viaje a la América del Sud* (Barcelona: La Académica, 1905), 82.

55. Clemenceau, *South America To-Day*, 30.

56. Le Corbusier, *Proposición de un plan director para Buenos Aires* (Buenos Aires, 1947), 24–25.

57. Donald M'Corquodale, *The Argentine Revisited, 1881 & 1906* (Glasgow: W. & R. Holmes, n.d.), 30.

58. Woodbine Parish wrote in 1852: "It will hardly be credited that water is an expensive article within fifty yards of the Plata; but so it is" (*Buenos Ayres*, 105).

59. Cited in Enrique G. Herz, *Historia del agua en Buenos Aires* (Buenos Aires: Municipalidad de la Ciudad de Buenos Aires, 1979), 29–30. See also José A. Wilde's famous memoirs *Buenos Aires desde 70 años atrás* (Buenos Aires, 1881), chap. 23.

60. Martínez, *Estudio topográfico*, 83; chapter 7 describes the evolution of the water and sewer system.

61. Buenos Aires, Dirección General de Estadística Municipal, *Censo general de población, edificación, comercio e industrias de la ciudad de Buenos Aires, 1904* (Buenos Aires: Compañía Sud-Americana de Billetes de Banco, 1906), 349. For a description of the development of public works in general during the period, see Olga N. Bordi de Ragucci, "Las obras de salubridad en el desarrollo urbano de la ciudad de Buenos Aires, 1870–1900," in Municipalidad de la Ciudad de Buenos Aires, Secretaría de Cultura, *Primeras jornadas de historia de la ciudad de Buenos Aires* (Buenos Aires, 1985): 61–74.

62. The escalating per capita consumption reflected expansion of service rather than increased use by those who already enjoyed it. By 1904 57 percent of the city's buildings and 72 percent of its inhabitants enjoyed running water; by 1920 it had become almost universal (Buenos Aires, *Censo general, 1904*, 349; Guy Bourdé, *Urbanisation et immigration en Amérique Latine: Buenos Aires, XIX et XX Siècles* [Paris: Aubier, 1974], 140–41; and Sargent, *Spatial Evolution of Greater Buenos Aires*, 102).

63. Buenos Aires, *Censo general, 1904*, 349; and Martínez, *Estudio topográfico*, 72. In 1924 a visiting Philadelphia engineer expressed surprise at finding Buenos Aires' waterworks as good as the best in the United States and better than most, with first-rate pumping plants and laboratories employing a large number of chemists, biologists, and physicists (J. W. Ledoux, "The Modern

Water-Works of Buenos Aires, Argentina," *The American City Magazine* 31, 1 [1924]:43).

64. E. J. M. Clemens, *La Plata Countries of South America* (Philadelphia: J. B. Lippincott Co., 1886), 99.

65. Thomas A. Turner, *Argentina and the Argentines: Notes and Impressions of a Five Years' Sojourn in the Argentine Republic, 1885–1890* (London: S. Sonnenschein & Co., 1892), 18.

66. M. Castilla Portugal, *La República Argentina: Su historia, geografía, industria y costumbres* (Barcelona, 1897), 23.

67. Edmundo de Amicis, *Impresiones sobre la Argentina* (Buenos Aires: Emecé Editores, 1944), 46–47. Thomas A. Turner, an English resident of Buenos Aires between 1885 and 1890, described the same scene and noted that "these puddles are utilized as a sort of natural washtubs by the scores of Italian women, children and men who gain a living at this unsavory business" (*Argentina and the Argentines*, 16). Two decades earlier, visitors and residents alike had consistently described the washerwomen as mostly black or mulatto.

68. *Caras y Caretas* 56 (1899):9.

69. Rahola, *Sangre nueva*, 91. Similarly, "the pristine streets and the regularity and frequency of the cleaning services" reminded the French journalist Jules Huret of German cities (*En Argentine: De Buenos Aires au Gran Chaco* [Paris: Bibliothèque Charpertier, 1913], 25), and his compatriot Paul Walle found the street-cleaning service much better than Paris' (*L'Argentine telle qu'elle est* [Paris: Librairie Orientale & Americaine (1913)], 19–20).

70. Sargent, *Spatial Evolution of Greater Buenos Aires*, 87.

71. Martínez, *Estudio topográfico*, 175, lists twenty specific dumps that by 1889 had become squares or public spaces. See also Buenos Aires, *Censo general, 1904*, 344.

72. Buenos Aires, *Censo general, 1904*, 345.

73. José M. Salaverría, *Paisajes argentinos* (Barcelona: Gustavo Gili, 1918), 136–39.

74. Mansfield, *Paraguay, Brazil, and the Plate*, 128.

75. May Crommelin, *Over the Andes: From the Argentine to Chili and Peru* (London: Bentley and Son, 1896), 45.

76. See, for example, Mantegazza, *Viajes por el Río de la Plata*, 44–45; Walle, *L'Argentine*, 20; and James Bryce, *South America: Observations and Impressions* (New York: Macmillan Co., 1913), 317, for visitors' remarks on the fact that Buenos Aires deserved its name.

77. Edward A. Ross, *South of Panama* (New York: Century Co., 1921), 119.

78. José Vasconcelos, *La raza cósmica: Misión de la raza iberoamericana, Argentina y Brazil* (Mexico City: Espasa-Calpe Mexicana, 1948), 150. Vasconcelos' remarks referred to his 1924 trip.

79. Rahola, *Sangre nueva*, 83.

80. Vicente Blasco Ibáñez, *La Argentina y sus grandezas* (Buenos Aires, 1910), 484–85. For other visitors' comments on the clean and prosperous aspect of pedestrians, see Huret, *En Argentine*, 24–25; Bryce, *South America*, 318; and Harry A. Franck, *Working North from Patagonia* (New York: Century Co., 1921), 10, 16.

81. Infectious-disease mortality declined from 44.8 per 10,000 inhabitants in the 1870s to 10.7 by the first decade of the twentieth century, and infant mortality declined from 23.5 percent of all live births to 9.9 during the same period (Buenos Aires, *Censo general, 1909*, vol. 2, xii–xvi).

82. Ibid., xi.

83. Ibid.

84. Huret, *En Argentine*, 46. The Brazilian tourist Arthur Dias, *Do Rio a Buenos Aires: Episodios e impressões d'uma viagem* (Rio de Janeiro: Impresa Nacional, 1901), 119, expressed similar amazement at the profusion of electric lights on the streets of the "magestosa princeza do Plata."

85. Javier Bueno, *Mi viaje a América* (Paris: Garnier Hermanos, [1911]), 148.

86. J. A. Hammerton, *The Real Argentine: Notes and Impressions of a Year in the Argentine and Uruguay* (New York: Dodd, Mead & Co., 1915), 59–60.

87. Martínez, *Estudio topográfico*, 194. Ironically, the source of the city's wealth, the thick and porous topsoil of the pampas, was also the origin of its notoriously poor roads and infamously deep potholes. But this cannot wholly account for the omnibus' failure. According to Sam Bass Warner Jr., the omnibus also proved unsuccessful in Boston because "it moved slowly, held relatively few passengers, and cost a lot" (*Streetcar Suburbs*, 16. John P. McKay, *Tramways and Trolleys: The Rise of Urban Mass Transport in Europe* (Princeton, N.J.: Princeton University Press, 1976), 10–13, 239, concurs that these "infrequent, uncomfortable, and expensive coaches . . . at an average speed of five miles per hour beat walking, but not by much." The omnibus appeared in Buenos Aires (1852) later than in Paris (1828), London (1829), New York (1831), and Berlin (1844) but earlier than in Leipzig (1860) and Munich (1861).

88. McKay, *Tramways and Trolleys*, 8, found the same for Europe: "Of crucial importance in moving goods and passengers long distances *between* cities, railroads were nonetheless of very little significance in moving people *within* cities.".

89. Will Payne and Chas. T. Wilson, *Missionary Pioneering in Bolivia, With Some Account of Work in Argentina* (London: H. A. Raymond, [1906]), 5–6.

90. *The [London] Times South American Supplement*, August 30, 1910, 10.

91. Albert B. Martínez, *Baedeker of the Argentine Republic* (Barcelona: R. Sopena, 1910), 100. Rahola, *Sangre nueva*, 86, also mentioned the City of Tramways sobriquet in 1905, and so had another Spanish visitor in 1896: Castilla Portugal, *La República Argentina*, 20.

92. W. A. Hirst, *Argentina* (London: T. Fisher Unwin, 1910), 147.

93. McKay, *Tramways and Trolleys*, 194–97; Charles W. Cheape, *Moving the Masses: Urban Public Transit in New York, Boston, and Philadelphia, 1880–1912* (Cambridge, Mass.: Harvard University Press, 1980), 214.

94. In 1938 Buenos Aires' 558 rides per capita were surpassed only by Paris' 637. The figures for other major cities were: London, 430; New York, 393; Boston, 353; and São Paulo, 332. The data are from Federico G. Schindler, "Evolución del transporte urbano de pasajeros en la ciudad de Buenos Aires," *Revista de Economía Argentina* 42, 300 (1943):287.

95. Rahola, *Sangre nueva*, 85–86. A Brazilian visitor in 1901 agreed that no

American city, except New York and Chicago, had as many carriages as Buenos Aires (Dias, *Do Rio a Buenos Aires*, 104–5).

96. Buenos Aires, Dirección General de Estadística Municipal, *Anuario estadístico de la ciudad de Buenos Aires* 15 (1905), 80; 22 (1912), 215; and 25 (1915/1923), 216.

97. Ibid., 25 (1915/1923), 216.

98. Ibid.

99. Bueno, *Mi viaje a América* 147.

100. See respectively, Huret, *En Argentine*, 46; L. E. Elliot, *The Argentine of Today* (London: Hurst & Blackett, [1925]), 13; John Foster Fraser, *The Amazing Argentine* (New York: Cassell & Co., 1914), 25; and E. Gómez Carrillo, *El encanto de Buenos Aires* (Madrid: Mundo Latino, 1921), 51.

101. Fraser, *Amazing Argentine*, 34.

102. Jose Costa Figueiras, *España en ultramar: La sugestión de América*, 2 vols. (Barcelona, [1917]), vol. 1, 220.

103. The common assumption is that class segregation in general (not simply the isolation of the upper crust) increases with urban modernization. I tried to test this hypothesis by using literacy as a proxy for social class and calculating the dissimilarity index between the literate and illiterate populations. The indexes for 1887 and 1895 actually show a decline from 18.0 to 13.5, indicating less rather than more class segregation; but the census districts for the two years changed and therefore the figures are not entirely comparable. Other censuses do not specify the literacy rate in each city district and do not offer any other alternative way of measuring class segregation.

104. Scobie, *Buenos Aires*, 19; Huret, *En Argentine*, 53–55; and Karen Mead, "Oligarchs, Doctors and Nuns: Public Health and Beneficence in Buenos Aires, 1880–1914" (Ph.D. diss., University of California, Santa Barbara, 1994), chap. 6.

105. Scobie, *Buenos Aires*, 196.

106. Buenos Aires had 8,119 industrial establishments and 93,163 workers in 1909; New York City, with its numerous textile shops (one-third of the total), had 25,938 establishments and 680,510 employees; and Chicago, where large meatpackers and foundries predominated, had 9,656 plants and 356,954 workers. An industrial census of 1913 lists 11,132 industrial establishments in Buenos Aires employing 145,902 workers, or an average of 13 per establishment, still about one-half and one-third of New York's and Chicago's, respectively. Data are from Buenos Aires, *Censo general, 1909*, vol. 1, 151–55; Argentina, Ministerio de Agricultura, Dirección General de Comercio e Industria, *Censo industrial y comercial de la República Argentina, 1908–1914* (Buenos Aires, 1915), *Boletín no. 20*, 60–61; and United States, Department of Commerce and Labor, Bureau of the Census, *Thirteenth Census of the United States Taken in the Year 1910*, Vol. 9, Manufactures, 1909 (Washington, D.C.: Government Printing Office, 1912), 285–88 (Chicago), 858–63 (New York).

107. Michael Johns and Fernando Rocchi, "The Industrial Capital and Urban Geography of a Primate City: Buenos Aires at the Turn of the Century" (unpublished paper, 1991), 34–35.

108. The number of Spaniards per hundred Italians in the city during its

census years was: 1855, 56; 1869, 33; 1887, 29; 1895, 44; 1904, 46; 1909, 63; 1914, 98; and 1936, 109.

109. Spaniards were also highly centralized, even more than the French, in Córdoba (Mark D. Szuchman, *Mobility and Integration in Urban Argentina: Córdoba in the Liberal Era* [Austin: University of Texas Press, 1980], 94–95).

110. See, for example, Guillermo Rawson, *Estudio sobre las casas de inquilinato en Buenos Aires* (Buenos Aires, 1885); Eduardo Wilde, *Curso de higiene pública* (Buenos Aires, 1883); Samuel Gache, *Les logements ouvriers à Buenos Aires* (Paris, 1900); F. R. Cibils, "La decentralización urbana en la ciudad de Buenos Aires," *Boletín del Departamento Nacional del Trabajo* 16 (March 1911):88; and Luis Pascarella, *Miserias porteñas (llagas sociales); El conventillo, novela de costumbres bonarenses,* 3d ed. (Buenos Aires: Taller Gráfico "La Lectura", 1917).

111. Sargent, *Spatial Evolution of Greater Buenos Aires,* 30–31, 65, 82, 119.

112. James R. Scobie, "Changing Urban Patterns: The Porteño Case (1880–1910)," in *Urbanization in the Americas from its Beginnings to the Present,* ed. Richard P. Schaedel et al. (The Hague: Mouton Publishers, 1978), 433. See also Scobie, *Buenos Aires,* 135, 146, 160.

113. See note 13 above.

114. The measurement of crowded living conditions used—inhabitants per room—is not unequivocal, because mansions with many rooms misleadingly decrease the average number of people per room in an area. Yet this measurement is far more accurate than is inhabitants per hectare—an indicator so biased against densely built, high-rise areas that it will reveal New York's sumptuous Park Avenue and Fifth Avenue as slums.

115. The northward shift of the better-off is often dated to the 1871 yellow fever epidemic and the consequent flight from the lower lands of the area south of the central plaza. But, as Map 7 shows, by 1855 the literacy rate of the wards just north of the plaza already surpassed those immediately south of it, a pattern than continued into the twentieth century.

116. Hohenberg and Lees, *Making of Urban Europe,* 306, found that compared to the North American case, the well-to-do in European cities did not abandon the central zones, and the periphery was thus settled, on the average, by poorer people, leading to higher densities. Bradley, *Muzhik and Muscovite,* 54–59, reached similar conclusions for Moscow. The exception in Europe seems to be Britain. Indeed, geographer Peter Hall wondered whether "the inner city problem is a uniquely British—or, more accurately, an Anglo-American—problem" (*The Inner City in Context* [London: Heinemann, 1981], 64–70).

117. Among them Hall, *The Inner City,* 64.

118. Obviously, if we designate, say, the inner 100 blocks of a 500-block city as the "center" at x point in time, and ten years later define the "center" again as the central 100 blocks of a 1,000-block city and continue the same procedure of fixed "centers" in a physically growing entity, the "center" will surely appear to be losing people to the "periphery" even if there was actually a population inflow. The statically defined center simply became a smaller portion of an expanding Buenos Aires, holding a smaller proportion of the city's dwellings and, naturally, a smaller proportion of its inhabitants. In fact, between the census

years of 1904 and 1909 the drop in the percentage of all city dwellings located in the center (Districts 10–14 and 20) was sharper than the drop in the percentage of all city inhabitants residing in it, indicating that although there may have been a great deal of back-and-forth movement, a real population outflow, relative to living space, did not take place (calculated from figures in Buenos Aires, *Censo general, 1904,* cix, and in Buenos Aires, *Censo general, 1909,* vol. 1, 171.) In absolute numbers, the center continued to grow, naturally at a much slower pace than the rest of the city because only vertical physical expansion was possible, until at least 1924. See the tables in Marino Jalikis, *Historia de los medios de transporte y de su influencia en el desarrollo urbano de la ciudad de Buenos Aires* (Buenos Aires: Compañía de Tranvías Anglo Argentina, 1925), 18, 22, 33, 36, 40.

119. James Scobie, "Buenos Aires as a Commercial-Bureaucratic City, 1880–1910: Characteristics of a City's Orientation," *American Historical Review* 77, 4 (1972):1045.

120. Buenos Aires, Dirección General de Estadística Municipal, *Censo general de población, edificación, comercio e industrias de la ciudad de Buenos Aires, 1887,* 2 vols. (Buenos Aires: Compañía Sud-Americana de Billetes de Banco, 1889), which Scobie used, shows the percentage of inhabitants living in *conventillos* in the four central districts (1–4) as 28, 36, 24, and 26, respectively, whereas in the northern district 13 it reached 49 percent; in La Boca, 40 percent; and in the semi-peripheral districts 8, 14, and 16, 30 percent each.

121. In 1914, 29 percent of Middle Eastern immigrants lived in the central wards, 20 percent on the semi-periphery, and 51 percent on the periphery, compared with 39 percent, 22 percent, and 39 percent, respectively, of French immigrants.

122. See, for example, Victor Gálvez (nom de plume of Vicente G. Quesada), *Memorias de un viejo,* 3 vols. (Buenos Aires: Jacobo Peuser, Editor, 1889), vol. 2, 216–28; and José Wilde, *Buenos Aires,* 122–28, 133–34.

123. A good example is Jorge Luis Borges and Adolfo Bioy Casares' motives for writing *Los orilleros* (1951; reprint, Buenos Aires: Editorial Losada, 1955): "Los orilleros expressed a yearning to hail, in some way, certain *arrabales* [suburbs], certain nights and twilights, the oral mythology of courage" (p. 9). In the poems "Las calles" and "Arrabal," from his 1923 book *Fervor de Buenos Aires,* and "El tango," all in *Obra poética, 1923–1964* (Buenos Aires: Emecé Editores, 1964), 17, 38–39, 173–75, Borges found Buenos Aires' cultural "entrails" not in its "energetic streets harassed by haste and hustle" but in the back streets of its *arrabales* and located the true tango there, in a mythological underworld of haughty, knife-wielding toughs and masculine bravado. This identification of the city's outskirts with genuine Porteño culture and folklorized delinquency or poverty appears in countless other contemporary poems, plays, and novels. See Miguel D. Etchebarne, *La influencia del arrabal en la poesía argentina culta* (Buenos Aires: Editorial Guillermo Kraft, 1955).

124. The following excerpt from Eduardo Wilde, *Curso de higiene pública,* 39, is a good example of the vivid and bleak contemporary descriptions that succeeding scholars are inclined to select and reproduce:

A room in a *conventillo,* as these train-shaped houses which accommodate from beggars to small industrialists are called, has a door to the patio and a window at most, measures four square meters, and serves all the following purposes: bedroom for the husband, wife, and the brood [*cría*], as they say in their expressive language—the brood being five or six duly dirty kids; also dining room, kitchen, pantry, patio for the kids to play in, place to deposit excrement—at least temporarily, garbage deposit, storeroom for dirty laundry and clean clothes—if there are any, dog and cat house, deposit for water and combustible liquids . . . in short, each of these rooms is a pandemonium where four, five or more persons breathe against all hygienic precepts, all the laws of common sense and good taste, and even against the exigencies of the body itself.

The passage is quoted in Buenos Aires, *Censo general, 1904,* cxxiv; in Bourdé, *Urbanisation et immigration,* 250–51; and in Leandro Gutiérrez, "Condiciones de la vida material de los sectores populares en Buenos Aires, 1880–1914," *Revista de Indias* 41, 163–64 (1981):178.

125. The same photographs of *conventillos* appear in Sargent, *Spatial Evolution of Greater Buenos Aires,* 57; Scobie, *Buenos Aires,* 147, 149, 151; and Jorge Páez, *El conventillo* (Buenos Aires: Centro Editor de América Latina, 1970), 62. One photograph (in Scobie, *Buenos Aires,* 151, and in Páez, *El conventillo,* 62) shows six children and a dog crowded into a tenement room; yet an 1890 tenement census shows not a single building in which the density was seven dwellers per room and only six, or 0.2 percent, of the 2,246 tenements in the city in which the density was six (Buenos Aires, *Anuario estadístico de la ciudad de Buenos Aires* 1 [1891], 634). Official statistics may rightly be questioned, but a picture is not always worth a thousand words, particularly when the positivist reformers who ordered the tenement census did so not to minimize the crowded conditions of *conventillos* but to support their denunciations of it.

126. Scobie, *Buenos Aires,* 147. Only on pp. 180–81 does Scobie discuss lower-class housing in the periphery.

127. Oscar Yujnovsky, "Políticas de vivienda en la ciudad de Buenos Aires," *Desarrollo Económico* 14, 54 (1974), 357.

128. For the quality of housing stock and land and property values, see Buenos Aires, *Censo general, 1909,* vol. 1, 171, 177–79; and Buenos Aires, *Anuario estadístico de la ciudad de Buenos Aires* 20–21 (1910/1911), 285.

129. Buenos Aires, *Censo general, 1904,* 64, 96–97.

130. Regarding Italians' ideal of home ownership, see Donna Gabaccia, *From Sicily to Elizabeth Street: Housing and Social Change among Italian Immigrants, 1880–1930* (Albany: State University of New York Press, 1984), chap. 1.

131. Gary R. Mormino and George E. Pozzetta, *The Immigrant World of Ybor City: Italians and Their Latin Neighbors in Tampa, 1885–1985* (Urbana: University of Illinois Press, 1987), 243–44, 266–71.

132. There were 916 Spaniards in La Boca, of whom 98 (or 11 percent) were home owners; there were 5,096 in District 2, immediately south of the central plaza, of whom only 44 (0.9 percent) were home owners (Buenos Aires, *Censo general, 1887,* vol. 2, 62, 142).

133. Both groups' ownership was higher in the peripheral districts, so the

fact that Italians predominated there gave them a higher overall rate. To check the weight of this variable, I multiplied the percentage of all Italians over the age of eight (the only age breakdown the data allowed) residing in each census district by the total number of Spaniards in the same age group living in the city. The products represented the numbers of Spaniards who should have resided in each particular district had their distribution been the same as that of the Italians. I then multiplied each of these results by the actual home-ownership rate of the Spaniards in each corresponding district. The results represented the number of Spanish owners that should have existed in each district; and the sum of all, the number of Spanish owners that should have existed in the entire city if their residential distribution had been the same as that of the Italians.

134. Mario C. Nascimbene, *Historia de los italianos en la Argentina, 1835–1920* (Buenos Aires: Centro de Estudios Migratorios Latinoamericanos, 1986), 110–13.

135. Calculated from data in Buenos Aires, *Censo general, 1904,* 119–20; and Buenos Aires, *Censo general, 1909,* vol. 1, 96–101.

136. Calculated from data in Jalikis, *Historia de los medios de transporte,* map at end of book.

137. Salaverría, *Paisajes argentinos,* 153–57; and Yujnovsky, "Política de Vivienda," 353, 362–63.

138. Unlike the Catalan Montepío's registers used to compile Table 25, which list the entire membership at the end of the year, the records I found in the main Spanish and Galician mutual-aid societies were either lists of incoming members or their application forms and medical records, which makes tracing virtually impossible. I traced 103 cases over an average span of seven years and a period covering the first three decades of this century when I checked for duplicates in the database on the immigrants from the localities I chose for microhistorical analysis. Some of these people dropped their memberships in voluntary associations and later rejoined or joined other societies. Because I perused hundreds of thousands of admission forms or lists from various associations and recorded all of the individuals from particular localities, many appeared in the database more than once, allowing their tracking. The Centro Gallego's records offered a different method of tracing: checking lists of incoming members with medical records, which, given the fact that the latter were often lost, produced less than a hundred traceable cases.

139. In his superb synthesis *America Becomes Urban: The Development of U.S. Cities and Towns, 1780–1980* (Berkeley: University of California Press, 1988), 196, Eric Monkkonen concluded that "people who stayed in the same house, apartment, or room [in the early twentieth century] were the exception, not the rule."

140. See ibid., 194–97.

141. Scobie, *Buenos Aires,* 146, 159.

142. Although the term was coined to describe a current process of gentrification or polarization whereby the rich and the poor come to dominate some North American inner cities, Richard Harris demonstrates in a recent article that "Manhattan was 'Manhattanized' in the early-twentieth century"

("Industry and Residence: The Decentralization of New York City, 1900–1940," *Journal of Historical Geography* 19, 2 (1993):170.

143. This was particularly true of the Spanish areas in the central districts (13 and 14), because by the first decades of the twentieth century oligarchical mansions were mostly built in the Barrio Norte in District 20. Because of the Middle Eastern slums in the southern fringes of this last district, the contrast between wealth and poverty there was the sharpest in the city.

144. See Buenos Aires, *Censo general, 1909*, vol. 1, 177–79.

145. It is interesting to note how similar are the pictures and descriptions of working-class housing in Anthony Jackson, *A Place Called Home: A History of Low-Cost Housing in Manhattan* (Cambridge, Mass.: MIT Press, 1976), 8, 13, 36; Oscar Handlin, *Boston's Immigrants*, 110–11; James Borchert, *Alley Life in Washington: Family, Community, Religion, and Folklife in the City, 1850–1970* (Urbana: University of Illinois Press, 1980) (which also includes pictures of London and Philadelphia alleys), 109–15, 171, 227–33; S. Martin Gaskell, ed., *Slums* (Leicester, England: Leicester University Press, 1990), 39, 197 (for Birmingham and London); George J. Sánchez, "Becoming Mexican American: Ethnicity and Acculturation in Chicano Los Angeles, 1900–1943" (Ph.D. diss., Stanford University, 1989), 106–109; June E. Hahner, *Poverty and Politics: The Urban Poor in Brazil, 1870–1920* (Albuquerque: University of New Mexico Press, 1986), 25; Gabaccia, *From Sicily to Elizabeth Street*, 16–17; Hohenberg and Lees, *Making of Urban Europe*, 309 (for a plan and description of a workers' apartment house in Vienna); and Scobie, *Buenos Aires*, 148–49. The only noticeable difference is that in Los Angeles, Rio de Janeiro, Buenos Aires, and Sicily the rectangular corridor took the form of an uncovered, internal patio that was part of the building, whereas in the northern cities it formed an external alley.

146. See Gabaccia, *From Sicily to Elizabeth Street*, 66–74, Hahner, *Poverty and Politics*, 29, 166–67; and Irwin Press, *The City as Context: Urbanism and Behavioral Constraints in Seville* (Urbana: University of Illinois Press, 1979), 45, for how New Yorkers, Cariocas, and Sevillians made a distinction between these types of multifamily working-class housing that was similar to that made by Porteños between *conventillos* and *casas de inquilinato*.

147. Buenos Aires, *Censo general, 1909*, vol. 1, 171–79.

148. According to data provided to me by the historian James A. Baer, Spaniards were overrepresented among the participants in the 1907 tenement rent strike. See also his "Tenant Mobilization and the 1907 Rent Strike in Buenos Aires," *Americas* 49, 3 (1993):343–68.

149. By 1914, for example, 9 and 10 percent of the Spaniards residing in the central districts 13 and 14, respectively, were home owners. In the peripheral districts 1, 15, and 16, the percentages ranged from 12 to 15.

150. More than three decades ago, sociologists Otis Duncan and Stanley Lieberson wrote of cities like Chicago, Philadelphia, and Los Angeles, where "the foreign born generally had higher home ownership rates than the second generation who, in turn, had larger proportions owning homes than did the native whites of native parentage ("Ethnic Segregation and Assimilation," *American Journal of Sociology* 64 [1959]:364–74). For similar conclusions in terms of

both nativity and class, see Carolyn Tyirin Kirk and Gordon W. Kirk Jr., "The Impact of the City on Home Ownership: A Comparison of Immigrants and Native Whites at the Turn of the Century," *Journal of Urban History* 7, 4 (1981):471–97; Zunz, *Changing Face of Inequality*, 152; and Robert Burchell, *The San Francisco Irish, 1848–1880* (Berkeley: University of California Press, 1980), 62.

151. Stephan Thernstrom, *Poverty and Progress: Social Mobility in a Nineteenth Century City* (Cambridge, Mass.: Harvard University Press, 1964), 201.

152. Daniel Luria, "Wealth, Capital, and Power: The Social Meaning of Home Ownership," *Journal of Interdisciplinary History* 7 (1976):274.

153. Proverb cited in Gabaccia, *From Sicily to Elizabeth Street*, 12.

154. Buenos Aires' rate was calculated from data in Buenos Aires, *Censo general, 1909*, vol. 1, 179; the rest, from data in Monkkonen, *America Becomes Urban*, 184.

155. For a history of the avenue, see Ricardo M. Llanes, *La Avenida de Mayo* (Buenos Aires, 1955); and Manrique Zago et al., *La Avenida de Mayo: Progreso, modernidad, urbanismo* (Buenos Aires: Manrique Zago Ediciones, 1988).

156. Clemenceau, *South America To-Day*, 28.

157. Happily, the Avenida is being renovated. See Joe Goldman, "Argentine Renaissance," *Architectural Record* 181, 1 (1993):44–46.

158. See Michael Banton, "Social Distance: A New Appreciation," *Sociological Review* 8 (1960):169–83; T. R. Balakrishnan, "Changing Patterns of Ethnic Residential Segregation in the Metropolitan Areas of Canada," *Canadian Review of Sociology and Anthropology* 19, 1 (1982):92–110, who found that during the 1960s and 1970s the ethnic groups' segregation increased in proportion to their "social distance" from Anglo- or French Canadian culture, irrespective of socioeconomic status; and Kenneth Prandy, "Residential Segregation and Ethnic Distance in English Cities," *Ethnicity* 7 (1980):367–89, who found the same pattern in the 1960s, with Scots and Welsh at the bottom of the segregation scale, followed by Irish, then Italians and Poles, and on the other extreme Pakistanis, Indians, and West Indians.

159. For example, in Philadelphia, the only northern city with a significant Afro-American population (5.4 percent of the total in 1910), their index of segregation (45.7) was lower than the Russians' (56.0) or the Italians (59.8). The census did not list Poles till 1930, when their index of dissimilarity (vis-à-vis native whites) reached 55.6. However, while white ethnics' residential segregation in U.S. cities has been decreasing since 1910, that of blacks' has been increasing. See the classic work by Karl E. Taeuber and Alma F. Taeuber, *Negroes in Cities: Residential Segregation and Neighborhood Change* (Chicago: Aldine, 1965); and Darden, "Black Residential Segregation."

160. This strong correlation between sociocultural distance and spatial separation, irrespective of socioeconomic class, also appeared in Australian cities during the post–World War II period as the origins of arrivals to the island continent diversified. F. L. Jones, "Ethnic Concentration and Assimilation: An Australian Case Study," *Social Forces* 43, 3 (1967):412–23, found immigrants from the British Isles and New Zealand highly dispersed throughout Melbourne,

those from The Netherlands and Poland considerably less so, and those from Greece, Yugoslavia, Italy, and Malta strongly concentrated. I. H. Burnley observed the same rank order not only in Melbourne but also in Sidney, in "Southern European Populations in the Residential Structure of Melbourne, 1947–1971," *Australian Geographical Studies* 16 (1976):116–32, and in "European Immigration and Settlement Patterns in Metropolitan Sidney, 1947–1966," *Australian Geographical Studies* 10 (1972):61–78. Ian McAllister and Rhonda Moore, "Social Distance among Australian Ethnic Groups," *Sociology and Social Research* 75, 2 (1991):95–100, used survey data to measure social distance with results that ranked the groups in the same order as the previous studies of spatial separation. On the other hand, Seamus Grimes, "Residential Segregation in Australian Cities: A Literature Review," *International Migration Review* 27, 1 (1993):103–20, castigates these studies for their "assimilationist ideology," for their assumption that segregation from the host society is negative and for their failure to discern that immigrant adaptation goes beyond residential patterns and that upward economic mobility has occurred among the spatially concentrated, but he does not question their actual findings.

161. See Stanley Lieberson, *Ethnic Patterns in American Cities* (New York: Free Press of Glencoe, 1963), chaps. 3, 4, 6, for the relationship between time of arrival, occupational status, and residential segregation; Douglas S. Massey, "Social Class and Ethnic Segregation: A Reconsideration of Methods and Conclusions," *American Sociological Review* 46 (October 1981):641–50, who uses both direct standardization and cross-sectional correlation methods to show a strong relationship between social class and ethnic segregation in the 1970s; and Sharon E. Bleda, "Intergenerational Differences in Patterns and Bases of Ethnic Residential Dissimilarity," *Ethnicity* 5, 2 (1978):91–107, who indirectly demonstrates the importance of length of residence in the host country in decreasing spatial segregation by showing that the second generation of each of the twelve national groups studied in fifteen U.S. metropolitan areas in 1970 consistently exhibited significantly lower dissimilarity indexes than did the first generation.

162. Barbara J. Flint, "Zoning and Residential Segregation: A Social and Physical History, 1910–1940" (Ph.D. diss., University of Chicago, 1977), esp. chaps. 1, 6; and Monkkonen, *America Becomes Urban*, 202–5.

163. Even the high segregation indexes of Buenos Aires' Jews (48 in 1909 and 40 in 1936) and Middle Easterners (50 and 30, respectively) are significantly lower than those for southern and eastern European immigrants in North American cities:

	New York	Boston		Philadelphia		New Haven		Rochester		Kansas
	1910	1910	1930	1910	1930	1900	1930	1910	1920	1920
Russians	54	45	65	56	56	71	73			
Italians	48	64	54	60	59	65	69	59	57	67
Poles					54				67	

SOURCES: Computed from raw data in United States, Bureau of the Census, *Thirteenth*

Census of the United States Taken in the Year 1910, vol. 2, 890 (Boston), vol. 3, 235 (New York City), vol. 3, 605 (Philadelphia). The remaining data were taken from Stephan Thernstrom, *The Other Bostonians: Poverty and Progress in the American Metropolis, 1880–1970* (Cambridge, Mass.: Harvard University Press, 1973), 209; Theodore Hershberg et al., "A Tale of Three Cities: Blacks, Immigrants, and Opportunity in Philadelphia, 1850–1880, 1930, 1970," in *Philadelphia: Work, Space, Family, and Group Experience in the Nineteenth Century*, ed. T. Hershberg (New York: Oxford University Press, 1981), 468; Ceri Peach, "Ethnic Segregation and Ethnic Intermarriage: A Re-Examination of Kennedy's Triple Melting Pot in New Haven, 1900–1950," in *Ethnic Segregation in Cities*, 208–9; and Briggs, *Italian Passage*, 97.

164. Howard R. Marrano, "Italians in New York during the First Half of the Nineteenth Century," *New York History* 26, 3 (1945):280; and Robert Ernst, *Immigrant Life in New York City: 1825–1863* (New York: King's Crown Press, 1949), 193–96, 213.

165. Most social scientists agree that ethnic segregation tends to drop over time, so that the indexes of dissimilarities of earlier arrivals naturally begin to decline earlier. In Buenos Aires, as Table 24 shows, this was the general trend. For one of the few dissenting views, see Nathan Kantrowitz, *Ethnic and Racial Segregation in the New York Metropolis* (New York: Praeger Publishers, 1973), in which he argues that white ethnic segregation in that city persisted into the 1960s. He later attacked the academic establishment's consensus on the diminishing relevance of ethnic segregation, maintaining that it had actually increased in New York City between 1960 and 1980 (Nathan Kantrowitz, "Ethnic Segregation: Social Reality and Academic Myth," in *Ethnic Segregation in Cities*, 43–57. See also Peter Jackson, "Paradoxes of Puerto Rican Segregation," in *Ethnic Segregation in Cities*, 109–26, esp. 112, which shows that segregation increased for most white ethnic groups in New York City between 1960 and 1970.

166. From an Afro-Argentine carnival song of 1876. See Andrews, *Afro-Argentines of Buenos Aires*, 180–88. Another carnival song transcribed in Horacio Jorge Becco, *Negros y morenos en el cancionero rioplatense* (Buenos Aires?: Sociedad Argentina de Americanistas, 1953), 33, is:

Ya no hay negros botelleros
ni tampoco changador,
ni negro que vende fruta,
mucho menos pescador;
porque esos napolitanos
hasta pasteleros son,
y ya nos quieren quitar
el oficio de blanqueador
    Coro
Ya no hay sirviente
de mi color
porque bachichas
toditos son;
dentro de poco,
¡Jesus, por Dios!
bailaran samba
con el tambor.

> There are no longer black bottle makers
> no more porter,
> no black selling fruits,
> not to speak of fisherman;
> because those Neapolitans
> even pastry makers have become,
> and now they want to take from us
> our bleaching jobs
>   Chorus
> There are no servants
> of my color no more
> because bachichas
> they've all become;
> pretty soon,
> Jesus, by God!
> they will dance the samba
> to the drum.

All of the jobs mentioned were traditional Afro-Argentine trades, but pastry making was particularly so; thus the emphasis in the song. *Bachichas,* presumably from the Genoese *Baciccia* (Baptist, a common Christian name in Liguria), was a disparaging nineteenth-century term for Italian immigrants.

167. In fact, already by 1855 only one-tenth of the Italian population of the city lived in La Boca. Fernando Devoto, "The Origins of an Italian Neighborhood in Buenos Aires in the Mid XIX Century: La Boca," *Journal of European Economic History* 18, 1 (1989):37–64, shows the limited occupational opportunities of the area: most of its inhabitants were either sailors or worked in related occupations, such as boat carpenters or calkers.

168. For examples of the sociological literature on ethnic segregation see notes 158, 160, 161, and 165 above, plus: Lieberson, *Ethnic Patterns in American Cities,* chaps. 3–5; Michael J. White, "Racial and Ethnic Succession in Four Cities," *Urban Affairs Quarterly* 20, 2 (1984):165–83; Ronald M. Pavalko, "The Spatial Dimension of Ethnicity," *Ethnic Groups* 3, 2 (1981):111–23; William L. Yancey et al., "The Structure of Pluralism: 'We're All Italian Around Here, Aren't We, Mrs. O'Brien," *Ethnic and Racial Studies* 8, 1 (1985):94–116, which offers a conceptual analysis of assimilation, cultural pluralism, and ethnogenesis as creative as the title and also a section on the ecology of residential segregation in Philadelphia between 1850 and 1980; Edward E. Telles, "Residential Segregation by Skin Color in Brazil," *American Sociological Review* 57, 2 (1992):187–97, who examines the segregation levels of whites, blacks, and mulattoes by social class in the thirty-five largest metropolitan areas using the 1980 Brazilian census; and Dudley L. Poston Jr. and Michael Micklin, "Spatial Segregation and Social Differentiation of the Minority Nationalities from the Han Majority in the People's Republic of China," *Sociological Inquiry* 63, 2 (1993):150–65, who employs the index of dissimilarity, in an unusual way, to measure spatial differentiation between a country's counties rather than a city's districts.

169. Midnineteenth-century Buenos Aires was the equivalent of districts 2–4, 8–14, and 19–20 of the twentieth-century city. In 1855, 75 (65 percent) of

the 116 Ferroleans in the city lived in the area between the riverbank on the east, the streets of Entre Ríos and Callao on the west, Córdoba on the north, and Garay on the south; that is, the equivalent of districts 12–14 after 1904. In about 1920, the 65 Ferroleans living in districts 12–14 represented 56 percent of the total identified (123) but 64 percent of those (102) living in the area comparable to the midnineteenth-century city.

170. Argentine data that include village of birth are scarce for most of the nineteenth century (with the exception of 1855), but information on province of birth can be obtained from the membership records of Spanish associations in Buenos Aires for the last two decades of the century. I therefore recorded all of the cases of immigrants from the province of León who joined Spanish associations during this period and later compared the names with those of Val de San Lorenzo's immigrants in the twentieth century. The comparison suggests that very few of the immigrants from the province of León in the 1880s and 1890s came from Val de San Lorenzo. What makes the comparison trustworthy is the fact that only a few surnames (e.g., Andrés, Arce, Geijo, Navedo) appear among the immigrants from the village. Actually, fewer than a dozen surnames suffice to name more than nine-tenths of the immigrants with both paternal and maternal surnames. Similarly, documents in the village's church and town hall are rather laconic on nineteenth-century population movements, but a manuscript census for 1900 lists fewer than a dozen people overseas.

171. The following reconstruction of Valense settlement in Buenos Aires is based on fourteen oral interviews conducted on both sides of the Atlantic; the data file from immigrant voluntary associations, including the Centro Val de San Lorenzo de Buenos Aires; the magazine of this last society (published biyearly, but not consistently, since 1926); the manuscript returns of the 1895 Argentine national census; Ricardo García Escudero, *Por tierras maragatas* (Valdespino, León, 1953), a historical and contemporary description of the Leonese district where the village is located, written by the local schoolteacher and sponsored by the village's association in Buenos Aires; and manuscript censuses and the civil birth registry in Val de San Lorenzo.

172. For a similar case of latecomers (Poles) who settled in newer and peripheral sections of the city (Philadelphia), see Caroline Golab, *Immigrant Destinations* (Philadelphia: Temple University Press, 1977), 112–17.

173. Recounted in García Escudero, *Por tierras maragatas*, 288–89.

174. For example, immigrants from the county of Corcubión in the Galician province of La Coruña formed a satellite colony in Avellaneda, a working-class town just south of the Federal District. Those from Peralta, a town of 3,000 inhabitants in the province of Navarre, created a satellite colony in Villa Ballester, six kilometers northwest of the Federal District. Seventeen of the forty-two Peraltenses in the sample lived there. Most other Navarrese localities formed secondary (in some cases primary) settlements all over the Buenos Aires pampas, where they eventually gained a virtual monopoly of dairy farms and turned the Basque jai alai court into an ubiquitous site.

175. Amalia Navedo, interview by author, tape recording, Buenos Aires, August 26, 1987.

176. Carmen Urtasún, interview by author, tape recording, Buenos Aires, May 14, 1987.

177. The analysis of a sample of 118 successful Basques compiled from ethnic newspapers and contemporary hagiographic books produced corresponding results. Of the 66 whose geographical and economic mobility could be linked and traced, 32 (48 percent) had moved from the province into the city after making their fortunes; 6 (9 percent) had become prosperous in the city and moved out; and 14 (21 percent) had moved out to the province as poor immigrants, became affluent, and stayed there. See Jose R. Uriarte, ed., *Los bascos en la nación argentina* (Buenos Aires: Editorial La Baskonia, 1916); J. Giralt, *Los vascos en América. Tomo I, Chile, Argentina, Uruguay* (Santiago, Chile: Editorial Athalonia, 1937); *La Vasconia*, a weekly newspaper that was published between 1893 and 1937.

The flow into the city was also common among the second generation. Of a sample of 122 American-born Navarrese who resided in the Federal District in the first decades of the twentieth century, 38 had been born in Buenos Aires Province, 14 in other provinces and 3 in Uruguay. The sample (made up of those who joined the Laurak-Bat association between 1906 and 1911, 1917 and 1922, and 1928 and 1930) is slanted toward nonmanual employees or merchants. But this bias, if anything, implies again that it was precisely the more successful who more often moved into the city. The tendency for the more successful among the second generation to move into the capital was also noted by Hilda Sabato and Juan Carlos Korol in their study of Irish immigrants in the nineteenth century: the sons of shepherds would often move into Buenos Aires and become white-collar employees (*Así fué la inmigración irlandesa en la Argentina* [Buenos Aires: Plus Ultra, 1981]).

178. The following section on Corcubionese settlement in Buenos Aires is based on nineteen oral interviews conducted on both sides of the Atlantic; the data file from immigrant voluntary associations; *Alborada*, the monthly magazine of the Corcubión County immigrant association in Buenos Aires, 1924–1932; *Finisterre*, the magazine of the native-place association in Buenos Aires of this municipality in Corcubión County (published monthly since 1924, although I was able to locate only a few issues kept by old returnees in Finisterre); the manuscript returns of the 1895 Argentine national census; and manuscript censuses, the civil birth registry, and parish baptismal certificates in four of the eight municipalities that make up the County of Corcubión (Corcubión, Finisterre, Vimianzo, and Zas).

179. These include 26 people from the data file plus 72 whom I counted from monthly lists published in *Alborada*. These lists only include the names of new members and their village of birth.

180. This at times created legal problems for the immigrants. In the archives of mutual-aid societies I found four different letters by illegitimate children who, apparently for inheritance purposes, asked that one of the surnames be dropped from their files because the mother had spuriously given them a second surname "to keep up appearances."

181. This concentration in La Boca and Barracas (the district immediately

to the west) influenced the location of the Corcubionese satellite colony. As early as the 1880s some immigrants began to cross the Riachuelo River and settle in Avellaneda, a working-class industrial town just south of the Federal District. Of the sample of 640 from the Spanish and Galician mutual-aid societies of Buenos Aires, fewer than a dozen lived in Avellaneda. But this is totally misleading, because those who lived in Avellaneda would most probably join the Spanish mutual-aid society there. The membership records of the Corcubión County social association would have provided a better sense of the immigrants' distribution in greater Buenos Aires, but only a few have survived. Of the thirty-eight members whose addresses in the late 1920s I was able to identify from scattered membership cards, fourteen lived in Avellaneda.

182. This tendency to re-create the settlement patterns of the area of origin in the receiving city was also noticed by Cinel, *From Italy to San Francisco,* 116–21.

183. My data for the twentieth century—drawn from Spanish community sources because Argentine census returns have been lost—do not allow an analysis of residential mixing between Iberian townspeople and other groups, and data from published censuses allow comparisons only at the national and ward levels. However, using Samuel Baily's pioneering studies "Chain Migration of Italians to Argentina: Cases Studies of the Agnonesi and the Sirolesi," *Studi Emigrazione* 19, 65 (1982):73–91, and "Patrones de residencia de los italianos en Buenos Aires y Nueva York: 1880–1914," *Estudios Migratorios Latinoamericanos* 1, 1 (1985):8–47, I was able to compare the spatial distribution of Iberian and Italian villagers at the city-block level. In the three small clusters of Italian villagers Baily located in ward 14, I was able to locate an even greater number of Navarrese and Ferroleans, interspersed in the same city blocks. As in the midnineteenth century, the heavily Spanish area in what became ward 14 was confined mostly to three or four blocks north of Rivadavia Street, which divided that ward from ward 13 to the south. But as it diffused into the adjacent blocks it overlapped with old Italian settlements.

184. Two of the best-known attacks on the melting-pot concept, both based on marriage patterns, are Mark D. Szuchman, "The Limits of the Melting Pot in Urban Argentina: Marriage and Integration in Córdoba, 1869–1909," *Hispanic American Historical Review* 57, 1 (1977):24–50; and Samuel L. Baily, "Marriage Patterns and Immigrant Assimilation in Buenos Aires, 1882–1923," *Hispanic American Historical Review* 60, 1 (1980):32–48.

185. In addition to the 2,566 cases from 17 towns or villages in Table 28, the data file contains 1,901 cases of individuals from another 438 villages and hamlets with addresses in Buenos Aires which were not included in the table because separately the numbers were not statistically significant. Immigrants from these small villages often clustered with those from the same *comarca,* a Spanish term for district as a natural, sociogeographical space where people have face-to-face contact rather than as a politico-administrative entity. Only 209 (or 11 percent) of the 1,901 resided more than five blocks away from another immigrant from the same *comarca.*

186. Some of the invasion-succession phenomena occurred from the 1960s on, when European immigration subsided and migrants from the interior prov-

inces and bordering countries began to move into the Spanish and Italian neighborhoods on the south side of the city and the previous residents began to move out.

187. "Buenos Aires es un porvenir, una carrera, y hasta una religion" (Julio Camba, "El oro de America," in *Obras completas* [Madrid: Plus Ultra, 1948] vol. 1, 267).

5. MAKING A LIVING AND "MAKING AMERICA"

1. Letter, José María Rojas to Juan Manuel de Rosas, February 7, 1869, reproduced in Arturo E. Sampay, *Las ideas políticas de Juan Manuel de Rosas* (Buenos Aires: Juárez, 1972), 159.

2. The inadequacy of a two-class model becomes apparent in Mark D. Szuchman, *Order, Family, and Community in Buenos Aires, 1810–1860* (Stanford, Calif.: Stanford University Press, 1988), 83: in a sample of 2,287 women drawn from census returns, those classified as high status actually outnumber those in the low-status category. Because the sample was meant to be representative of the general population and because—by definition—the elite cannot outnumber the masses, the only explanation for this oddity is that the majority of people classified as high status belong to a middle category.

3. Mark D. Szuchman and Eugene F. Sofer, "The State of Occupational Stratification Studies in Argentina: A Classificatory Scheme," *Latin American Research Review* 11, 1 (1976):159–71; also an unpublished list of occupations devised by the authors. Another compatible element is that the sources used in the authors' pioneer studies of social mobility in Córdoba and Buenos Aires (census returns and voluntary-association records) resemble those used in this chapter.

4. Stephan Thernstrom, *The Other Bostonians: Poverty and Progress in the American Metropolis, 1880–1970* (Cambridge, Mass.: Harvard University Press, 1973), app. B; and Alba M. Edwards, "A Social Economic Grouping of the Gainful Workers of the United States," *Journal of the American Statistical Association* 27 (1933):377–87. See also Michael Katz, "Occupational Classifications in History," *Journal of Interdisciplinary History* 3 (1972):63–68; Clyde Griffen, "The Study of Occupational Mobility in Nineteenth-Century America: Problems and Possibilities," *Journal of Social History* 5 (1972):310–30; and Patrick M. Horan, "Occupational Mobility and Historical Social Structure," *Social Science History* 9, 1 (1985):25–47.

5. *La Tribuna*, January 2, 1855. A Spanish immigrant who arrived in Buenos Aires in 1855 complained to his government that it should "prohibit a type of emigration that affects no other nation, that of children with no trade or experience" (Gil Gelpi, *Españoles en América* [Buenos Aires, 1862]), 16.

6. Bakers, tailors, shoemakers, and the rest of the craftsmen who owned a shop and employed one or two persons were classified with small shopkeepers in general in the low-nonmanual category.

7. Julio Mafud, *La vida obrera en la Argentina* (Buenos Aires: Editorial Proyección, 1976), 131.

8. Lucio V. López, "Holiday in Buenos Aires" [from his classic *La gran*

aldea], in *Tales from the Argentine*, ed. Waldo Frank (New York: Farrar & Rinehart, 1930), 109.

9. The Spanish immigrant novelist Francisco Grandmontagne mocked this type of supercilious lower-middle-class immigrant in "El bachiller," *Caras y Caretas* 28 (1899):6–7, and in "Juancho y los bachilleres, o el éxito en América," in *Los inmigrantes prósperos* (Madrid: M. Aguilar, 1933), 19–27.

10. Conversation with the Italian historian Romulo Gandolfo; and Guiglielmo Godo, *Nuovi orizzonti: L'America né suoi primi fattori, la colonizzazione e l'emigrazione* (Florence, 1893), 391–92, for a mocking description of one of the many *immigranti di buona famiglia* who, unable to obtain a position in Buenos Aires' commercial houses, refused any other "dishonoring" manual job.

11. Ronald C. Newton, *German Buenos Aires, 1900–1933: Social Change and Cultural Crisis* (Austin: University of Texas Press, 1977), 106–7.

12. Information on this and other Spaniards was gathered from the 1855 census returns and two contemporary city directories: *Almanaque comercial y guía de forasteros para el Estado de Buenos Aires, año de 1855* (Buenos Aires: Imprenta de la Tribuna, 1855); and Alejandro Bernheim, *Anuario del comercio, de la industria, de la magistratura y de la administración de Buenos Aires, 1854–1855* (Buenos Aires, 1855).

13. List of members of the Jockey Club, 1923.

14. For a history of the Noel family and their industry, see Telmo Manacorda, *La gesta callada: Biografía de una industria* (Buenos Aires, 1947).

15. Vicente Osvaldo Cutolo, *Nuevo diccionario biográfico argentino, 1750–1930* (Buenos Aires: Editorial Elche, 1968–1985), vol. 6, 663–64.

16. Other sources are either inadequate or inappropriate for determining the occupational structure of Spaniards—or any other immigrant group—in Buenos Aires. Published Argentine censuses, at best, classified the city's labor force only under the broad rubric of "native" or "foreigner." Alternative sources, such as voluntary-association membership lists, useful for comparisons of the various Iberian regional or local groups, do not provide a representative sample of all Spaniards in the city in terms of occupation. Even in an open voluntary association, such as the Asociación Española de Socorros Mutuos, the main Spanish mutual-aid society in the city, low-skilled workers were underrepresented. Of 12,455 gainfully employed new members during the first decade of this century, 19.3 percent were unskilled and 8.4 percent semiskilled. In 1914, by comparison, 26.1 percent and 12.7 percent of all immigrant workers in the city were respectively so. And this is actually a relatively low level of underrepresentation. Countless studies have shown that, no matter what gauge of socioeconomic stratification is used, those in lower-class positions tend to exhibit lower rates of participation in voluntary associations (see chapter 6).

17. For examples of plays in which the Argentine-born are embarrassed by the lower-class and Old World culture of their parents, see, for Italians, Armando Discépolo and R. J. de Rosa, "El guarda 323" (scene 3), *La Escena: Revista teatral*, suppl. 17, November 15, 1920 (the play opened on May 18, 1915); for Galicians, Alberto T. Weisbach, "Farruco," *La Escena: Revista teatral*, no. 145, April 7, 1921; and for Jews, Emilio Sánchez, "El jarrón de Sevres," *La Escena: Revista teatral*, no. 160, July 21, 1921.

18. In 1914 only 1.4 percent of all foreigners in Argentina were naturalized, in comparison with 47 percent in Canada and 52 percent in the United States (Carl E. Solberg, *The Prairies and the Pampas: Agrarian Policy in Canada and Argentina, 1880–1930* [Stanford, Calif.: Stanford University Press, 1987], 29). Torcuato Di Tella, "El impacto inmigratorio sobre el sistema político argentino," *Estudio Migratorios Latinoamericanos* 12 (August 1989):211–30, attributes the immigrants' disinclination to adopt Argentine citizenship to their sense of superiority vis-à-vis the host country. Whether or not such an attitude of superiority prevailed among the arrivals (I argue otherwise in chapter 7), a more convincing explanation for the low rate of naturalization is simply the lack of incentives for doing so. Foreigners had all of the rights of citizens (except the right to vote in national elections—a dubious advantage, given Argentina's oligarchical political system, particularly before the Saenz Peña law of 1912 established universal male suffrage and the secret ballot) but were exempted from the most cumbersome civic obligation: military service. In the United States, on the other hand, the vote, particularly in ward politics, offered more tangible benefits; many government jobs—including municipal street cleaning, an important occupation among Italians—required citizenship; and the military draft did not exempt foreigners. In Canada, the Dominion Land Law restricted homestead grants to native or naturalized citizens. See Walter Nugent, *Crossings: The Great Transatlantic Migrations, 1870–1914* (Bloomington: Indiana University Press, 1992), 148.

19. In 1909, of the 3,861 members of the municipal police force, only 78 were foreign-born. For a history of the police force from colonial times to the twentieth century, see Francisco L. Romay, *Historia de la Policía Federal Argentina*, 5 vols. (Buenos Aires: Biblioteca Policial, 1963–1966).

20. The first labor strike in Buenos Aires occurred in 1878; in 1895 there were 16 strikes; from 1907 to 1913 the yearly average of strikes was 154 (Hobart Spalding, *La clase trabajadora argentina* [Buenos Aires: Editorial Galena, 1970], 18, 87–88).

21. E. P. Thompson, *The Making of the English Working-Class* (New York: Vintage, 1963); and Harry Braverman, *Labor and Monopoly: The Degradation of Work in the Twentieth Century*, foreword by Paul M Sweezy (New York: Monthly Review Press, 1975). See also Stephen Wood, ed., *The Degradation of Work? Skill, Deskilling and the Labour Process* (London: Hutchinson, 1982).

22. In Boston, by comparison, the trend was the opposite of Buenos Aires', with the proportion of low-skilled workers in its labor force rising from 32 percent in 1880 to 43 percent in 1910 (Thernstrom, *Other Bostonians*, 50).

23. For the role of Taylorism in deskilling, see, in addition to Braverman, *Labor and Monopoly Capital*, Anthony Elger and B. Schwarz, "Monopoly Capitalism and the Impact of Taylorism: Notes on Lenin, Gramsci, Braverman and Sohn-Rethel," in *Capital and Labour: A Marxist Primer*, ed. Theo Nichols (London: Fontana, 1980), 358–69. For Argentina, see Mirta Z. Lobato, *El "taylorismo" en la gran industria exportadora argentina, 1907–1945* (Buenos Aires: Centro Editor de América Latina, 1988), a thirty-page booklet that concentrates on the meatpacking industry.

24. For example, both Samuel Baily, "The Adjustment of Italian Immigrants

in Buenos Aires and New York, 1870–1914," *American Historical Review* 88, 2 (1983):281–305, and Herbert Klein, "La integración de italianos en la Argentina y los Estados Unidos: Un análsis comparativo," *Desarrollo Económico* 21, 81 (1981):3–27 [a revised version of which appeared in the same journal and issue as Baily's article] agree that Italian immigrants fared much better economically in Argentina than in the United States. On the other hand, Eugene Sofer, *From Pale to Pampa: A Social History of the Jews of Buenos Aires* (New York: Holmes and Meier, 1982), 128, concluded that "until 1945, at least, Jews did not experience in Argentina the same degree of mobility that Jews are assumed to have enjoyed in the United States" and attributed this precisely to the fact that "the Argentine economy was not sufficiently industrialized to generate those opportunities that stimulate mobility." There are, however, two potentially weak spots in the road taken by Sofer to reach this conclusion. One relates to the methodology and sources used: changes of occupation listed for individuals in the rolls of immigrant voluntary associations. As I point out later, such a method may underestimate mobility. The other has to do with the fact that the author did not systematically compare the Buenos Aires Jewish community with those in North American cities. It is thus possible that the different degree of mobility—if indeed it existed—may reflect not so much the different levels of industrialization in the two receiving societies but the fact that, whereas in Argentina Jewish immigration was basically an eastern European and twentieth-century phenomenon (as late as 1887, according to Buenos Aires, Dirección General de Estadística Municipal, *Censo general de población, edificación, comercio e industrias de la ciudad de Buenos Aires, 1887*, 2 vols. [Buenos Aires: Compañía Sud-Americana de Billetes de Banco, 1889], vol. 2, 22, there were only 289 Jews in Buenos Aires), in the United States there was an important nineteenth-century inflow of mostly German Jews who by the years before World War I had already achieved a significant measure of worldly success.

25. According to Baily, "Adjustment of Italian Immigrants," 295–96, 25 percent of the Italians who emigrated to the United States between 1899 and 1910 and 40 percent of those who headed for Argentina were listed as skilled or white-collar workers. Spanish emigration statistics for the same period do not specify the occupations of emigrants, providing instead categories, such as commerce and transportation, that are too aggregated to determine level of skills; and Cuban statistics suffer from the same deficiency. However, an analysis of the few years when the actual occupations of the emigrants are listed in Instituto Geográfico y Estadístico, *Estadística de la emigración e inmigración de España* (1915, 1919, and 1920), shows that those heading for Argentina were more than twice as likely to belong to the skilled and white-collar categories (an average of 12.7 percent for the three years, compared with an average of 5.7 percent of those going to Cuba).

26. The nature of competing groups, not simply the structure of the economy, also delimited opportunities in the countryside. Unlike in the urban economy, here the lack of preexisting latifundia and the passing of more generous homestead laws provided greater opportunities for immigrants in North America than in South America. Carl Solberg found that in Argentina the monopoly of political power by a landed elite made landownership for the "average

immigrant . . . a dream, an unattainable goal," but that in Canada—with an economy also characterized by agro-export and external dependency—the policies of the merchant-financier political ruling class fostered the formation of a large rural middle sector (*Prairies and the Pampas*, esp. chaps. 4–5).

Yet although there were thousands of Italian landowners on the pampas there was not a single Italian landowner on the Prairies, even though Italians formed a significant colony in Canada (42,000 by 1931; ibid., 84–85, 87, 91). In the same vein, Basques in Argentina became remarkably successful at cattle, sheep, and dairy farming, while their compatriots in the northwestern United States showed a relative lack of ability to rise from shepherd to landowner. See William Douglass and Jon Bilbao, *Amerikanuak: Basques in the New World* (Reno: University of Nevada Press, 1975). This may, in part, be due to the fact that both Italians and Basques arrived in Argentina before they arrived in North America (that is, when presumably both places were still frontier societies and land more easily available). But time of arrival does not fully explain the difference. After all, as Walter Nugent has shown, homesteads in Canada were basically a twentieth-century phenomenon, with most allocated in the 1920s and many to Poles, Ukrainians, and other non-Anglos. As for the United States, "It is not often realized that more homesteads began after 1900 than before" (*Crossings*, 145–48, 153). (It is also not often realized that a significant number of Spaniards had arrived in the United States by 1860—16,248—more than Russians and Italians combined—15,167.)

This shows that the economic structures of, or even the relative opportunities offered by, receiving societies cannot by themselves determine how well a given immigrant group will do. The nature and skills of the particular group and of competing groups also play a role. Immigrants in general may have done better in the rural areas of North America because homestead acts there offered them greater opportunities to become landholders, but Italians and Basques did better in Argentina because the groups with whom they competed were less skilled than were those in North America. In Argentina the opportunities were fewer but in the competition for land plots the seminomadic, impoverished gauchos and peons who inhabited the pampas proved no match for the thrifty Italians and Basques. In the Prairies and the Great Plains the opportunities were greater, but thrift proved insufficient to compete with a native rural middle class, British yeomen, and Scandinavian immigrants, all of whom were experienced in temperate-zone farming, had the necessary skills and cultural predisposition, and were already settled in the land.

27. After World War II the increased migration, first of native mestizos from the northwest (disdainfully referred to as *cabezitas negras* by middle-class Porteños) and later of Bolivian and Paraguayan workers, created a situation similar to that of the mid-nineteenth century, in which people of Amerindian origins came to occupy the lower rungs in the socioeconomic structure.

28. Buenos Aires, Dirección General de Estadística Municipal, *Censo general de población, edificación, comercio e industrias de la ciudad de Buenos Aires, 1909*, 3 vols. (Buenos Aires: Compañía Sud-Americana de Billetes de Banco, 1910), vol. 1, 17, 35, 38, 132. I compared the number of commercial establishment owners with the number of males over the age of twenty in each group

rather than with the total group. Because the native-born population contained a greater proportion of women and minors (that is, persons highly unlikely to own a commercial enterprise), comparisons based on the entire population are highly misleading, making the immigrants seem more successful than they actually were. Had I used the ratio of owners to the total members of the group, for instance, the Spaniards would have appeared as five (rather than two) times as likely to own a commercial establishment as Argentines.

29. Somewhat surprisingly, although the British were twice as concentrated in the low-nonmanual category as the others, they were not particularly overrepresented in the middle and high nonmanual categories. This coincides, however, with an observation made by Santiago Calzadilla four years before the census: "The majority of these [the arrivals of the 1820s] came from England to run powerful merchant houses, and not like now, when only the clerks come and the owners stay there" (*Las beldades de mi tiempo* [Buenos Aires, 1891], 19).

30. Based on information on the 827 import and export houses of the city in the Buenos Aires, *Censo general, 1887*, vol. 2, 306.

31. Buenos Aires, *Censo general, 1909*, vol. 1, 17, 35–44, 132.

32. There was an upsurge of German migration in the early decades of the twentieth century. However, according to the foremost historian of the group, these latecomers found it increasingly difficult to compete with the "patient, endlessly industrious, self-denying Italians, Basques, and Galicians" (Newton, *German Buenos Aires*, 42, 98, 104, 106).

33. Of those entering the country with declared occupations between 1876 and 1895, 74 percent of the French, 77 percent of the Spaniards, and 89 percent of the Italians were classified as rural workers or laborers. On the other hand, 10 percent, 8 percent, and 5 percent, respectively, were classified as skilled workers, and 6 percent, 4 percent, and 2 percent as merchants or liberal-arts professionals. Argentina, Comisión Directiva del Censo, *Segundo censo de la República Argentina, 1895*, 3 vols. (Buenos Aires: Taller Tip. de la Penitenciaria Nacional, 1898), vol. 1, 651.

34. Aníbal Latino, *Los factores del progreso de la República Argentina*, 2d ed. (Buenos Aires: Librería Nacional, 1910), 80.

35. Census data show that 18.2 percent of the Spaniards and 9.2 percent of the Italians worked in the city's commerce (Buenos Aires, *Censo general, 1887*, vol. 2, 11, 306 [for ownership of medium or large commercial houses, also]).

36. In 1912, Spaniards owned one-tenth of the 795 newspapers in the country and three-tenths of the 661 cigar factories—the highest proportion in both cases among foreigners (Argentina, Ministerio de Agricultura, Dirección General de Comercio e Industrias, *Censo industrial y comercial de la República Argentina, 1908–1914*, Boletín no. 14, *La prensa periódica* [Buenos Aires, 1912], 13; and idem, *Censo industrial y comercial de la República Argentina, 1908–1914*, Boletín no. 15, *Manufactura de tabacos* [Buenos Aires, 1914], 9). Similarly, in 1909, Spaniards owned 244 (36 percent) of the 674 bookstores in Buenos Aires, a much higher proportion than that owned by the more numerous Argentines and Italians (28 percent and 13 percent, respectively [Buenos Aires, *Censo general, 1909*, vol. 1, 131]).

37. In 1887, for example, 3.05 percent of the Italians and 2.24 percent of the

Spaniards were owners of manufacturing shops or industries (Buenos Aires, *Censo general, 1887*, vol. 2, 11, 346). In 1895, Italians were also slightly more successful than Spaniards when it came to ownership of manufacturing shops (Romulo Gandolfo, "The Italian Mutual Aid Societies of Buenos Aires: Issues of Class and Ethnicity within an Immigrant Community [1880–1920]" [unpublished paper presented at the Fifth Latin American Labor Conference, Princeton University, April 1988]).

38. Transcribed in Isabel Laura Cárdenas, *Ramona y el robot: El servicio doméstico en barrios prestigiosos de Buenos Aires, 1895–1985* (Buenos Aires: Ediciones Búsquedas, 1986), 82–84.

39. The limited role of language in explaining concentration in domestic service also appears in the United States, where Swedish women were more likely to work as servants than were Irish women, and German women more than English women (Stephen Gross, "Domestic Labor as a Life-Course Event: The Effects of Ethnicity in Turn-of-the-Century America," *Social Science History* 15, 3 [1991]:400).

40. French servants were also highly regarded as a mark of prestige in Great Britain (E. S. Turner, *What the Butler Saw: Two Hundred and Fifty Years of the Servant Problem* [New York: St Martin's Press, 1962], 26, 123, 153–55).

41. *La Prensa*, January 16 and February 6, 1910. Of the 292 persons who offered their services, 42 indicated that they were Spaniards and 35 that they were Italians. That is, Spaniards outnumbered Italians here 1.2 to 1, whereas in the city's population as a whole the latter outnumbered the former by 1.6 to 1. Moreover, 20 of the Spanish advertisements but only 3 of the Italian ones were from single women offering themselves as live-in maids.

42. In her classic, *Family and Community: Italian Immigrants in Buffalo, 1880–1930* (Ithaca N.Y.: Cornell University Press, 1977), 53, 205–11, Virginia Yans-McLaughlin found that Italian women were less likely to work outside the home or to engage in domestic service than their Polish counterparts, restricting their employment to "positions that permitted strict sexual and familial controls," such as homework, taking care of boarders, and cannery work, where the large number of Italian women of various ages functioned as a control mechanism. For similar findings, see John W. Briggs, *An Italian Passage: Immigrants to Three American Cities, 1890–1930* (New Haven, Conn.: Yale University Press, 1978), 115–18, for Rochester, Utica, and Kansas City; Miriam Cohen, *Workshop to Office: Two Generations of Italian Women in New York City, 1900–1950* (Ithaca, N.Y.: Cornell University Press, 1992), 53; Donna Gabaccia, *Militants and Migrants: Rural Sicilians Become American Workers* (New Brunswick, N.J.: Rutgers University Press, 1988), 113, 115, 135–36, for Tampa and Brooklyn; Barbara Klaczynska, "Why Women Work: A Comparison of Various Ethnic Groups, Philadelphia, 1910–1930," *Labor History* 17 (Winter 1976):73–87; and Franc Sturino, *Forging the Chain: A Case Study of Italian Migration to North America, 1880–1930* (Toronto: Multicultural History Society of Ontario, 1990), 191–93, for Toronto. For an unconvincing attack on Yans-McLaughlin's cultural argument, see Stephen Steinberg, "Why Irish Became Domestics and Italians and Jews Did Not," chapter 6 of his *The Ethnic Myth: Race, Ethnicity, and Class in America* (Boston: Beacon Press, 1989).

43. A similar situation was found by Konosuke Odaka for Japan. Tradition and familiarity made domestic service more acceptable to women than industrial work, forcing factory owners to increase wages in order to counteract this preference ("Redundancy Utilized: The Economics of Female Domestic Servants in Pre-War Japan," in *Japanese Women Working*, ed. Janet Hunter [London: Routledge, 1993], 18–24). In the case of the United States, the evidence regarding the preference of domestic or factory work during the nineteenth century seems more ambiguous. See David M. Katzman, *Seven Days a Week: Women and Domestic Service in Industrializing America* (New York: Oxford University Press, 1978), 29–32; and Alice Kessler-Harris, *Out to Work: A History of Wage-Earning Women in the United States* (New York: Oxford University Press, 1982), 135.

44. The musical "El pibe del corralón," written by Estevanez and Vergara and printed in *La Escena: Revista teatral*, suppl. 14, October 18, 1920, 7, includes a tune sung by upper-class characters complaining about servants' insolence. Another, less common, complaint centered on servants' criminality (Alejandro Gancedo, *La Argentina: su evolución* [Buenos Aires: García y Dasso Editores, 1913], 357–58).

45. For complaints about the indolence, immorality, and insolence of servants in various countries, see, in alphabetical order (full citations are in the note that accompanies Table 41 or in other notes): Argentina: Cárdenas, *Ramona y el robot*; Australia: Alford, *Production or Reproduction?*, 175; Brazil: Graham, *House and Street*, chap. 5; Britain: Turner, *What the Butler Saw*, McBride, *The Domestic Revolution*, 19, 99, 106; Canada: Claudette Lacelle, *Urban Domestic Servants in 19th Century Canada* (Ottawa: Environment Canada–Parks, 1987), 125–27, and Cohen, *Women's Work*, 86; France: Pierre Guiral and Guy Thuillier, *La vie quotidienne des domestiques en France au XIX siècle* (Paris: Hachette, 1978), 132–44; Germany: K. Schlegel, "Mistress and Servant in 19th-Century Hamburg: Employer-Employee Relationships in Domestic Service, 1880–1914," *History Workshop: A Journal of Socialist and Feminist Historians* 15 (1983):60–77; Italy: Margherita Di Fazio Alberti, *Il servo nella narrativa italiana della prima metà dell'Ottocento* (Naples: Liguori, 1982); Japan: Gary P. Leupp, *Servants, Shophands, and Laborers in the Cities of Tokugawa Japan* (Princeton, N.J.: Princeton University Press, 1992), 108–11, 121–22; Southern Africa: Cecile Swaisland, *Servants and Gentlewomen to the Golden Land: The Emigration of Single Women from Britain to Southern Africa, 1820–1939* (Oxford: Berg, 1993), 91–93; and United States: C. Lasser, "The Domestic Balance of Power: Relations Between Mistress and Maid in 19th-Century New-England," *Labor History* 20, 1 (1987):5–22, Christine Stansell, *City of Women: Sex and Class in New York, 1789–1860* (Urbana: University of Illinois Press, 1987), 155–68, Faye E. Dudden, *Serving Women: Household Service in Nineteenth Century America* (Middletown, Conn.: Wesleyan University Press, 1983), 3–4, 59–62, Katzman, *Seven Days a Week*, chap. 6; and Karen Tranberg Hansen, *Distant Companions: Servants and Employers in Zambia, 1900–1985* (Ithaca, N.Y.: Cornell University Press, 1989), 2, 50–51.

46. The "Irish biddy" stereotype, however, contained an element of religious bigotry absent in the *mucama gallega* figure (Dudden, *Serving Women*, 65–71).

47. Alberto Novión, "Los primeros fríos," *La Escena: Revista teatral*, no. 125, November 18, 1920, 3 (the play opened on June 22, 1910).

48. Alberto T. Weisbach, "Farruco, comedia en tres actos, de ambiente gallego," ibid., April 7, 1921, 3.

49. Juan González Castillo, "El mayor prejuicio," ibid., September 19, 1918, 4.

50. The topic forms a leitmotif in contemporary theater. Federico Mertens' 1920 play "Mama Clara," ibid., January 13, 1921, portrays maids as both flirtatious and seduced in the main character and in that of Soledad. In Roberto Cayol, "La casa donde no entró el amor," ibid., suppl. 10, September 20, 1920, scene 6, a lecherous old man lectures his young friends on how to seduce a maid. Julio F. Escobar, "Palabra de casamiento," ibid., suppl. 8, August 23, 1920, scene 1, deals with flirting between servants. Turner, *What the Butler Saw*, chap. 6, examines similar links between domestic service and sexual morality in eighteenth- and nineteenth-century English literature.

51. Argentina, Departamento Nacional del Trabajo, *Boletín del Departamento Nacional del Trabajo* 42 (1919):168. One can assume that not all prostitutes in the city registered in the health dispensary, but this should not affect the proportion who had been servants before. By comparison, in the United States, "nineteenth-century investigators of prostitution found that former domestics constituted by far the largest group of recruits to prostitution, disproportionately outnumbering women who had worked as seamstresses, or clerks, or any other line of work" (Dudden, *Serving Women*, 213). Donna J. Guy, *Sex & Danger in Buenos Aires: Prostitution, Family, and Nation in Argentina* (Lincoln: University of Nebraska Press, 1991), 65, 72, found that in an 1893 report, of the 368 prostitutes registered, 32 percent held no jobs before, 22 percent had been maids, and 23 percent seamstresses or dressmakers; from this she deduced that "unemployment and poorly paid domestic service, rather than employment outside the home, drove women into prostitution." She later concluded from a 1910 report on prostitutes which listed smaller proportions of ex-servants that "domestic service had been either unattractive or unavailable to these women compared with those who registered in 1893."

52. Eusebio Gómez, *La mala vida en Buenos Aires* (Buenos Aires: Editor Juan Roldán, 1908), 127.

53. Amable Rivas Canosa, interview by author, tape recording, Finisterre, La Coruña, Spain, August 9, 1989; Mercedes Fernández de Cabo, interview by author, tape recording, Val de San Lorenzo, León, Spain, August 16, 1989; and Juana Echenique, interview by author, tape recording, Irurita, Navarre, Spain, August 23, 1989.

54. Victor A. Mirelman, *En búsqueda de una identidad: Los inmigrantes judíos en Buenos Aires, 1890–1930* (Buenos Aires: Editorial Milá, 1988), 349. Frenchmen and Jews also predominated, to an apparently even greater extent, among pimps, with the former forming the "aristocracy" and the latter organizing their own mutual-aid society, synagogues, and a cemetery (pp. 344–52). See also Guy, *Sex & Danger*, 107, 120–29. The association of Buenos Aires and white slavery in French popular culture must have been common enough for film director Jacques Demy to remember boyhood tales of a local house where

women entered and vanished because they were sold to "harems in Argentina"; told in the biographical film *Jacquot*, made by his wife Agnes Varda in 1991.

55. According to Thernstrom, *Other Bostonians*, 131, 65 percent of the Irish but only 31 percent of the English in Boston in 1890, for example, were employed in low manual occupations (the equivalent of our two lowest categories, to which 58 percent of the Galicians but 32 percent of the Catalans in Buenos Aires in 1855 belonged).

56. The tendency for first arrivals to be better educated reached such a degree in the case of Swedes in Chicago that Ulf Beijbom subtitled his chapter on the pioneers "The Upper Class Immigrants" (*Swedes in Chicago: A Demographic and Social Study of the 1846–1880 Immigration* [Uppsala, Sweden, 1971]). The same tendency was noted by Humbert Nelli for a different group in the same city (*Italians in Chicago 1880–1930: A Study in Ethnic Mobility* [New York: Oxford University Press, 1970], 4–5, 22–23). And in Buenos Aires the major conflict within the German community pitted the old resident's *Geld-Aristokratie* against late-arriving workers y(Newton, *German Buenos Aires*, chap. 1).

57. Manuel Chueco, *Los pioneros de la industria argentina* (Buenos Aires, 1886, 1896).

58. Manrique Zago, *Los españoles de la Argentina* (Buenos Aires: Ediciones Manrique Zago, 1985), 57.

59. For example, Amalia C., from the village of Val de San Lorenzo in the province of León, one of eleven siblings and a girl of fourteen in 1930, explained in an interview how her mother had pressured her to come to Buenos Aires to join a sister, threatening that if Amalia was so selfish that she could not think of the family's situation and did not have "enough guts," she herself would emigrate, leaving the children with the father (interview by author, tape recording, Buenos Aires, May 24, 1987).

60. Pierre Lhande, *L'Émigration basque, preface de Carlos Pellegrini ancien president de la République Argentine* (Paris: Nouvelle Librairie Nationale, 1910), vii–xv. (Pellegrini's preface was a speech given in 1905 in the Basque association Euskal-Echea).

61. Latino, *Factores del Progreso*, 79–80, 171–72.

62. A. Colmo, *Los paises de América Latina* (Madrid, 1915), 46.

63. Pierre Berne, *L'Immigration européenne en Argentine* (Paris: Marcel Rivière & Cie., 1915), 87, 89; Argentina, Ministerio del Exterior, *Memorias del Ministerio del Exterior*, 1886; and Jules Huret, *En Argentine: De Buenos Aires au Gran Chaco* (Paris: Bibliothèque Charpentier, 1913), 87.

64. Lucas Ayarragaray, in *Los baskos en la nación argentina*, ed. José R. de Uriarte (Buenos Aires: La Baskonia, 1916), 442. These racial myths merged with the Argentine oligarchy's blue-blooded cravings to make searching for a Basque noble lineage a genealogical pastime of upper-class Porteños in the early decades of this century. (The hobby apparently was not limited to Argentina, as the title of Rafael Nieto's *Los Villa-Urrutia: Un linaje vasco en México y la Habana* [Havana, 1952] suggests). The immigrant novelist Francisco Grandmontagne would mockingly christen them *la aristocracia del tarro* (an Argentine term for a tin milk container and an allusion to descent from the Basque milk-

men who monopolized the trade in Buenos Aires; "La dinastia de los Goitzeko-Yzarra," *Caras y Caretas* 92 [1900]:10–11).

65. The description of Francisco A. Sicardi in *Los baskos en la nación argentina,* 446.

66. List of members of the Jockey Club, Buenos Aires, 1900. One of the three members of Italian ancestry was Carlos Pellegrini, son of a French-speaking Saboyan engineer and ex-president of the nation, who, while ambling along the boardwalk of the Spanish seaside resort of San Sebastián with his wife, was amazed to read on the beach cubicles the names of his club buddies. He remembered: "Arana, Aguirre, Iturraspe, Irigoyen, Elortondo, Iraola, Anchorena, Urquiza, Alzaga, Iriondo, Larrazábal, Unzué . . . and many others; it seemed as if done on purpose; we thought we were in Mar del Plata [an Argentine beach resort] surrounded by the most distinguished Porteño society"; and he came to the conclusion that Argentina's high society was "essentially Basque" ("Los vascos y la Argentina, palabras pronunciadas en la Sociedad Euskal-Echea de Buenos Aires, por el doctor Pellegrini el 17 de diciembre de 1905" [loose leafs in the library of the Laurak-Bat society, Buenos Aires]). Moreover, reaching the social crest proved a slow process for Italians: in 1923 no more than 1 percent of Jockey Club members bore Italians surnames.

67. Some good examples are Carlos M. Pacheco's plays *Los disfrazados* (1906) and *Las romerías* (1909) (reprint, Buenos Aires: Editorial Universitaria de Buenos Aires, 1964); and Vicente R. Pecci and Rafael Cabrera, "Corrida de Toros," *La Escena: Revista teatral,* no. 205, June 1, 1922. For a recent study, see Ana Cara-Walker, "Cocoliche: The Art of Assimilation and Dissimulation among Italians and Argentines," *Latin American Research Review* 22, 3 (1987):37–67.

68. José Pio Sagastume, *La inmigración: Su influencia en el país* (La Plata, Argentina, 1916), 51. In a similar but more disdainful way, Horace Rumbold described Basques in Argentina as "a simple and somewhat dull race of men, of frugal habits and few wants, who have a marked capacity for patient toil of all kinds" (*The Great River of Silver* [London: John Murray, 1890], 122).

69. Saul Escobar, *Inmigración (tesis)* (Buenos Aires, 1907), 69, 74. Although numerous, Gypsies represented a minority in Andalusia, and, even though there are no data on the subject, it seems highly unlikely that they would form a disproportionately large sector of Andalusian immigrants. For a similar attack on immigrants who settle in cities, see Mauro Freire, *La inmigración en la República Argentina (tesis)* (Buenos Aires, 1899); and José A. Wilde, *Buenos Aires desde setenta años atrás* (Buenos Aires, 1881), 95, who praised Basques' sobriety, pastoral inclination, probity, and industriousness and assailed "the drifting immigrants who seek employment in the cities, who consume but do not produce."

70. Sagastume, *La inmigración,* 50, 56. A similar view of Andalusian immigrants seems to have existed in Cuba. A narrator in Sara Gómez's 1974 film *De Cierta Manera* describes them as "sailors recruited from the marginal sectors of Cádiz and Seville as indentured workers who brought to our budding capital their code of violence, male chauvinism, knifing and female worship."

71. Mertens, "Mama Clara" (the play opened on July 10, 1920).

72. Francisco E. Collazo and Torcuato Insausti, "La chica del gorro verde," *La Escena: Revista teatral*, no. 120, October 14, 1920, 14, 19, 24.

73. Agustín Fontanella, *Bachicha: Sainete cómico lírico dramático, en un acto y 3 cuadros* (Buenos Aires, 1908). Similarly, in Carlos M. Pacheco's 1908 comedy "Las romerías" (reprinted in *Los disfrazados y otros sainetes* [Buenos Aires: Editorial Universitaria de Buenos Aires, 1964]), the Basque character appears as a respectable hotel owner, a bulwark of the community, and the Andalusian one as a brigand trailed by the police for extradition to Spain.

74. Luis Pascarella, *El conventillo: Novela de costumbres bonaerenses* 3d ed. (Buenos Aires: Talleres Gráficos La Lectura, 1917), 33–34.

75. Alberto Vacarezza, *Tu cuna fué un conventillo*, in *El sainete criollo*, ed. Tulio Carella (Buenos Aires: Librería Hachette, [1957]), 357–58.

76. "División Investigación Orden Social, Antecedentes de Anarquistas, 1902, No. 1" the list is in the Buenos Aires police archives on Chacabuco Street. Andalusia (along with Catalonia) constituted the principal foci of anarchist activity in the Iberian Peninsula. See Temma Kaplan's classic *The Anarchists of Andalusia* (Princeton, N.J.: Princeton University Press, 1978) and J. R. Corbin, *The Anarchist Passion: Class Conflict in Southern Spain, 1810–1965* (Aldershot, England: Avebury, 1993).

77. Almost half (429) of the 873 Basque immigrants in the Asociación Española 1888–1910 sample were from the interior and mostly rural province of Navarre.

78. Sagastume, *La inmigración*, 51.

79. The odds were probably lower, because the sample is drawn from voluntary-association members; that is, people more likely to belong to the white-collar category than the norm. See note 16 in this chapter.

80. See for instance, Michael Hout, *Following in Father's Footsteps: Social Mobility in Ireland* (Cambridge, Mass.: Harvard University Press, 1989), which traces the persistence of inherited inequality between 1959 and 1979 in both the Republic of Ireland and Northern Ireland.

81. Their commercial proclivity earned the people of the district where Val is located the sobriquet of *Maragatos* [derived from *mercader*, or merchant], presumed Semitic origins, and the stigma of a "cursed race" from more traditional peasants. See José M. Miner Otamendi, *Los pueblos malditos* (Madrid: Espasa-Calpe, 1978), 114–15. For illustrations of everyday life and economic activities in Val de San Lorenzo, see Concepción Casado Lobato, *Imágenes maragatas* (Valladolid: Junta de Castilla y León, 1986), a collection of photographs and watercolors by a group of artists who visited the area in 1926.

82. This trend toward feminization occurred in other places at similar or earlier times. In French Canada, women made up only one-half of all servants in Quebec City and one-third in Montreal in about 1818–1825 but by 1871 accounted for nine-tenths—compared with the 53 percent of Buenos Aires' Spaniards in 1869 (Lacelle, *Urban Domestic Servants*, 75). In four Japanese cities the proportion of maidservants went up from 19–36 percent in the eighteenth century to 35–51 percent in the 1860s (Leupp, *Servants, Shophands, and Laborers*, 62. Theresa M. McBride, *The Domestic Revolution: The Modernization of Household Service in England and France, 1820–1920* (New York: Holmes &

Meier, 1976), 9, 34, 39, 45, also refers to the "feminisation [*sic*] of service" in these two countries from the eighteenth to the midnineteenth century. She offers no figures for that period but shows that the trend continued: the male proportion of all servants declined from 31.7 percent in 1851 to 17.1 percent in 1911 in France and from 10.1 percent to 7.9 percent in England.

83. Manuel Gil de Oto, *La Argentina que yo he visto* (Barcelona, 1914), 65–66.

84. Rosa M. Capel Martínez, *El trabajo y la educación de la mujer en España, 1900–1930* (Madrid: Ministerio de Cultura, 1982), 150–59. Female tobacco workers earned considerably more than did other female workers, leading the author to title this section of her book "La cigarrera: Elite del proletariado femenino español."

85. In Cuba, women were often employed as ringers (who placed the band around the cigar), cigarette packers, but above all as tobacco strippers or stemmers since at least the 1870s (Jean Stubbs, *Tobacco on the Periphery: A Case Study in Cuban Labour History, 1860–1958* [Cambridge, England: Cambridge University Press, 1985], 71). The same was true in Bristol, England (Anna Pollert, *Girls, Wives, Factory Lives* [London: Macmillan Press, 1981], 29–33); and among Tampa's Italians (Gary R. Mormino and George E. Pozzetta, *The Immigrant World of Ybor City: Italians and Their Latin Neighbors in Tampa, 1885–1985* [Urbana: University of Illinois Press, 1987], 107). Rose L. Glickman, *Russian Factory Women: Workplace and Society, 1880–1914* (Berkeley: University of California Press, 1984), 75–77, mentions the high female participation in the tobacco industry, and although she does not explain the sexual division of labor in it, a photograph on page 66 shows women stemming leaves in a factory. The same is true in Sherman Cochran, *Big Business in China: Sino-Foreign Rivalry in the Cigarette Industry, 1890–1930* (Cambridge, Mass.: Harvard University Press, 1980), 25, 57, and photographs of women strippers and packers on p. 156. In Durham, North Carolina, the task also formed part of the trade's racial division of labor, with stemming done mostly by black women, and most black women in the trade (more than 80 percent) engaged in this task (Dolores E. Janiewski, *Sisterhood Denied: Race, Gender, and Class in a New South Community* [Philadelphia: Temple University Press, 1985], 100–3). See also Nannie M. Tilley, *The R. J. Reynolds Tobacco Company* (Chapel Hill: University of North Carolina Press, 1985), 36–37, 248, 266–69; and Patricia A. Cooper, *Once a Cigar Maker: Men, Women, and Work Culture in American Cigar Factories, 1900–1919* (Urbana: University of Illinois Press, 1987), 15–18, for women's concentration in stemming and the manufacturing of cheaper "five-cent cigars" and stogies.

I have not found a historical study of tobacco workers in Argentina. Cristina M. Sonsogni, *Evolución de la actividad tabacalera en Corrientes y en Misiones, 1870–1940* (Corrientes, Argentina: Conicet, 1983), deals with cultivation only and has little on labor. But partial evidence for the early twentieth century points to a gender division of labor in the trade similar to that in the other places mentioned. Issues of the *Boletín* of the Departamento Nacional del Trabajo show that women made up 59 percent of the tobacco industry's workforce in 1907 (no. 3, pp. 342–44) and 75 percent ten years later (no. 42, pp. 32–33).

The 1907 issue does not provide any gender breakdown but consistently uses the feminine form *empaquetadoras* and *despalilladoras* when referring to packers and stemmers. It also explains that women predominated among makers of cheaper leaf cigars [referred to as *trabuquillos* and likely the equivalent of North American stogies] in small shops or at home. The 1917 issue shows 51 percent of the 2,432 women tobacco workers as packers, 33 percent as makers but below the "master" category, and 8 percent as strippers. Also, a graphic report on Buenos Aires' industry by the weekly *Caras y Caretas*, May 25, 1910, contains photographs of a cigarette-packing room and of cigarette-gluing machines, in which all workers are women. For a description of female tobacco workers in midnineteenth-century Buenos Aires, see Wilde's memoir, *Buenos Aires*, chap. 19.

86. For women's concentration in shoebinding, see Elizabeth Faulkner Baker's pioneer *Technology and Woman's Work* (New York: Columbia University Press, 1964), 27–30; Mary H. Blewett, "The Sexual Division of Labor and the Artisan Tradition in Early Industrial Capitalism: The Case of New England Shoemaking, 1780–1860," in *To Toil the Livelong Day: America's Women at Work, 1780–1980*, ed. Carol Groneman and Mary Beth Norton (Ithaca, N.Y.: Cornell University Press, 1987), 37–38; and Nancy Grey Osterud, "Gender Divisions and the Organization of Work in the Leicester Hosiery Industry," in *Unequal Opportunities: Women's Employment in England 1800–1918*, ed. Angela V. John (Oxford: Basil Blackwell, 1986), 46.

87. Computed from desegregated figures in Buenos Aires, *Censo general, 1904* (Buenos Aires: Compañía Sud-Americana de Billetes de Banco, 1906), 192–201. In addition to the three sectors mentioned, mechanized or hand laundries employed 4 percent of the 7,835 women working in industrial establishments, match factories, 3 percent, and the remaining 10 percent mostly engaged in food processing or bookbinding.

88. Glickman, *Russian Factory Women*, 50, 61–63, found a similar division among women garment workers between "those who did plain sewing, *beloshveiki* [which must be close to the Spanish *costurera*], a female occupation, and those who could do the more skilled tailoring, which employed men and women." She also noticed an increase in the relative number of women among the latter type, similar to what I found in Buenos Aires.

89. Buenos Aires, *Censo general, 1909*, vol. 1, 164–68. By way of comparison, a similar gap existed in contemporary Brazilian and Russian cities, where women received two-thirds and one-half of average male wages, respectively (June E. Hahner, *Poverty and Politics: The Urban Poor in Brazil, 1870–1920* [Albuquerque: University of New Mexico Press, 1986], 199–200); and S. A. Smith, *Red Petrograd: Revolution in the Factories, 1917–1918* (London: Cambridge University Press, 1983), 47. Women's lower wages may have reflected, in part, their limited participation in labor unions and strikes. Of the 4,762 strikers listed in Buenos Aires, *Censo general, 1909*, vol. 2, 379, only 14 were women.

90. Of all Andalusian women over the age of fourteen who worked for pay in midnineteenth-century Buenos Aires, 13 percent labored in unskilled and menial occupations, mostly as servants; the respective figures were 15.4 percent for Catalan women, 36.9 percent for Galician men, and 33.7 percent for Basque

men. The gap was even wider if one counts all adults instead of only the working population. Indeed, women from the two Mediterranean regions were less likely to work as servants than were Galician males in 1855. Similar gaps also appeared in the 1894–1910 sample.

91. The following sample from the 1895 census schedules for an upper-class district in Buenos Aires (see the note to Table 35 for description), likely exaggerates the proportion of women in remunerated work because of the large number of servants, but it gives an idea of different rates of participation by nativity.

Women over the age of twelve			Married women under the age of forty		
Birthplace	N[a]	Percentage working for pay	Birthplace	N[a]	Percentage working for pay
Ireland	14	85.7	Spain	92	50.0
Spain	344	77.3	France	79	45.6
France	269	62.5	Italy	235	37.0
England	54	57.4	Germany	30	30.0
Argentina[b]	467	52.7	Argentina[b]	77	24.7
Italy	600	52.2	Buenos Aires Province[c]	211	21.3
Germany	71	52.1	Latin America[d]	58	13.8
Switzerland	31	48.4	Buenos Aires city[e]	171	11.1
Austria	19	47.4			
Buenos Aires Province[c]	1,099	40.9			
Latin America[d]	235	40.9			
Buenos Aires city[e]	714	29.6			
All	4,044	47.2			

[a]Groups numbering ten or fewer are not included.
[b]Born in Argentina outside Buenos Aires Province.
[c]Born in Buenos Aires Province outside the city of Buenos Aires.
[d]More than three-quarters of the Latin Americans are Uruguayans.
[e]Born in the city of Buenos Aires.

92. For example, Stanley Nadel, *Little Germany: Ethnicity, Religion, and Class in New York City, 1845–80* (Urbana: University of Illinois Press, 1990), 75, found that census takers recorded only 17–20 percent of German women (adult, one guesses) as gainfully employed but estimated the correct figure as closer to 35–40 percent (still 14–19 points lower than Buenos Aires' Spaniards). Thomas Kessner, *The Golden Door: Italian and Jewish Immigrant Mobility in New York City, 1880–1915* (New York: Oxford University Press, 1977), 72–77, also maintained that census takers underenumerated women working for pay when he found only 7 percent of the Italian wives (rather than adults in general) in 1880 and 2 percent of the Jewish ones "working outside the home"

(perhaps a synonym for gainfully employed, since U.S. census schedules do not specify work addresses). Thus, unless Argentine census takers registered women's employment with an accuracy absent in their North American colleagues—an unexpected but possible occurrence—the proportions of Spanish wives working for pay in Buenos Aires (40 percent in 1855 and 37 percent in 1869) greatly surpassed those of their New York counterparts.

93. A similar situation existed among German washerwomen in New York, who were older and poorer than other workers (Nadel, *Little Germany,* 75). Judging by novelist Francisco Grandmontagne's description of an immigrant's mother as "a poor woman, the last in the social hierarchy—the village's laundress—(one cannot be less)," the same was true in late nineteenth-century Spain (*Los inmigrantes prósperos,* 19).

94. Spanish emigrants in general favored Argentina over any other destination, but women demonstrated a particularly strong predilection for it. As a yearly average, 36 percent of the Spaniards who departed for Argentina during the peak 1901–1914 period were women. The comparable percentages for other countries are: Uruguay, 33; Brazil, 32; Chile, 31; Mexico, 22; Cuba, 19; the United States, 14. Computed from data in Spain, Dirección General del Instituto Geográfico y Estadístico, *Estadística de la emigración e inmigración de España 1901–1902* (1904), *1903–1906* (1907), *1907–1908* (1910), and *1909–1911* (1912); and Spain, Consejo Superior de Emigración, *La emigración española transoceánica, 1911–1915* (Madrid: Hijos de T. Minuesa, 1916), 69–71. Data on gender composition are not available for Uruguay, Chile, or the United States for 1901–1908, so their averages are based on 1911–1914 data.

The gender composition of the Spanish immigrants settled in New World countries point in the same direction. Thirty-eight percent of the 830,000 Spaniards living in Argentina in 1914 were women. The comparable figures for other countries and years are: 34 percent of the 26,000 living in Chile in 1920; 26 percent of the 50,000 living in the United States in 1920; and about 25 percent of the 246,000 living in Cuba in 1919 (the census does not specify sex by nationality, only for "foreign whites"; Spaniards accounted for 90 percent of these). Argentina, Comisión Nacional del Censo, *Tercer censo nacional, 1914,* 10 vols. (Buenos Aires: Talleres Gráficos de L. J. Rosso, 1916–1919), vol. 2, 396; Chile, Dirección General de Estadística, *Censo de población de la República de Chile levantado el 15 de diciembre de 1920* (Santiago: Soc. Imp. y Litografía Universo, 1925), 276; Cuba, Dirección General del Censo, *Census of the Republic of Cuba 1919* (Havana: Maza, Arroyo y Caso, [1920?]), 310; and United States, Bureau of the Census, *Fourteenth Census of the United States Taken in the Year 1920* (Washington, D.C.: Government Printing Office, 1921–1923), vol. 2, 693.

95. Luis Iscla Rovira, *Spanish Proverbs: A Survey of Spanish Culture and Civilization* (Lanham, Md.: University Press of America, 1984), 173, 262.

96. See Susan Socolow, *The Merchants of Buenos Aires, 1778–1810: Family and Commerce* (Cambridge, England: Cambridge University Press, 1978).

97. For instance, Hector Varela, the owner of Buenos Aires' principal daily during the mid-nineteenth century, in a dispute with a Spanish theater impresario, sarcastically remarked, "It suits him to sit behind a grocery-store coun-

ter and not engage in debates with respectable people" (*La Tribuna*, April 5, 1855, 1).

98. In 1862 a Spanish writer who had spent seven years in Buenos Aires described this type of immigrant as it had developed from late colonial times: "hardworking but of limited political vision and culture, leading a Spartan life, spending their best thirty years in a store, *marrying late*, and thinking only of making money" (Gelpi, *Españoles en América*, 32).

99. To give a hypothetical example, let us say that in 1850 there were 65 poor Spaniards and 35 rich Spaniards in the city and that twenty years later the number had doubled but the proportion had remained constant; that is, 130 poor Spaniards and 70 rich Spaniards. This continuity in social structure could involve complete upward mobility (for example, 30 of the original rich had gone back or died in the interim and all 65 of the original poor had enriched themselves, or any similar combination), complete decline (all the originally affluent had lost all of their wealth and had been replaced by affluent newcomers), no mobility (all of the original population remained in their respective classes), and so forth. Whatever the reality, little can be inferred about individual mobility from continuities or changes in the overall occupational distribution of the community from one point in time to another.

100. Ramiro de Maeztu, *Defensa de la hispanidad* (edition authorized by the author's widow for America and the Philippines; Buenos Aires: Editorial Poblet, 1941), 137.

101. The other widely used method, particularly among European scholars, consists in measuring intergenerational mobility by comparing the occupations of parents (usually fathers) and their children (again, normally sons). See Andrew Miles and David Vincent, eds., *Building European Society: Occupational Change and Social Mobility in Europe, 1840–1940* (Manchester, England: Manchester University Press, 1993). Ostensibly, the key distinction between North American and European students of social mobility lies in the former's conceptual emphasis on status and the latter's, on class. I have found this contrast exaggerated and mostly semantic. Both assess social position (whatever the term) by the job of the individual, and the Europeans' bourgeoisie in occupational composition mirrors the North Americans' white-collar or nonmanual sector. I found the Old World scholars' preference for intergenerational mobility studies a more pronounced distinction and the outcome not of philosophical principles but of more pedestrian matters: European marriage registers include information on the occupations of both the couple and their parents, eliminating the need to use several sources and the difficult process of tracing involved in intragenerational analysis. For obvious reasons, such sources are of little use for an emigrant population. (For my analysis, through other source material, of the relationship between fathers' occupations in Spain and their children's occupations in Buenos Aires, see Table 38).

102. Another way to check the validity of the traced sample is to compare its occupational distribution with that of all of the original group. Because the persisters usually tend to be more settled and better off than the rest, the question seems to be one of degree (that is, what level of deviation invalidates the traced sample). Obviously, there is no cutting line, but a comparison with the

samples used by Kessner in his classic *Golden Door* can provide a frame of reference.

Kessner considered the overrepresentation of the traced group in the white-collar categories (4–8 percentage points higher than in the original samples) "sufficiently slight to avoid a situation where white-collar workers are traced, most laborers are ignored, and the findings passed off as a study of mobility" (p. 113). The slant in my sample (3 percentage points higher) is less marked, its size larger, and the percentage traced higher, which makes its validity comparatively high. In my view, the principal drawback of the tracing method lies not in ignoring the pattern of mobility of the individuals who could not be traced but in not knowing whether the traced ones were recent arrivals or old residents at the starting point. This makes it advisable to combine this method with that based on length of residence whenever possible.

103. Rates of career persistence for various cities and groups ranked from low to high are:

City, group, date	Persistence (in percentages)
New York, Italians, 1880–1890 and 1905–1915	51[a]
Buenos Aires, Spaniards, ca. 1910, average 7 years' span	59
Buenos Aires, Catalans, 1897–1912	60[b]
New York, Jews, 1880–1990 and 1905–1915	66
Boston, 1910–1920	69
Rotterdam, 1870–1880	71
Hamilton, Canada, 1850–1860	71
Boston, 1880–1890	74
Norristown, Pennsylvania, 1910–1920	76
Newburyport, Massachusetts, 1870–1880	79
Graz, Austria, 1900–1910	79
Poughkeepsie, New York, 1870–1880	82
Buenos Aires, Catalans, 1912–1919	86
Eindhoven, Netherlands, 1890–1900	86

SOURCES: For New York, Kessner, *Golden Door*, 113; for Buenos Aires, see Table 47; for Boston, Thernstrom, *Other Bostonians*, 53; for the Netherlands, Henk van Dijk, Joop Visser, and Emmy Wolst, "Regional Differences in Social Mobility Patterns in the Netherlands between 1830 and 1940," *Journal of Social History* 17, 3 (1984):445; for Hamilton, Michael Katz, *The People of Hamilton, Canada West: Family and Class in a Mid-Nineteenth Century City* (Cambridge, Mass.: Harvard University Press, 1976), 177; for Norristown, Sidney Goldstein, *Patterns of Mobility, 1910–1950: The Norristown Study* (Philadelphia: University of Pennsylvania Press, 1958), 169; for Newburyport, Thernstrom, *Poverty and Progress*, 96; for Graz, William H. Hubbard, "Social Mobility and Social Structure in Graz, 1875–1910," *Journal of Social History* 17, 3 (1985):456; for Poughkeepsie, Clyde Griffen and Sally Griffen, *Natives and Newcomers: The Ordering of Opportunity in Mid-Nineteenth Century Poughkeepsie* (Cambridge, Mass.: Harvard University Press, 1978), 60.

[a]"A bit over half."

[b]I included mobility to jobs within the same category as persistence in order to facilitate comparisons because most other works do.

104. Sofer, *From Pale to Pampa*, 95–96; Thernstrom, *Other Bostonians*, 60; Griffen and Griffen, *Natives and Newcomers*, 58; van Dijk, Visser, and Wolst, "Regional Differences," 445.

105. New York: Kessner, *Golden Door*, 117; Birmingham, and Oskarshamn: Hartmut Kaelble, *Historical Research on Social Mobility: Western Europe and the USA in the Nineteenth and Twentieth Centuries* (New York: Columbia University Press, 1981), 37; Rotterdam: van Dijk, Visser, and Wolst, "Regional Differences," 445; Omaha, Boston, Los Angeles, and Norristown: Thernstrom, *Other Bostonians*, 234; Graz: computed from data in Hubbard, "Social Mobility," 456; Hamilton: M. Katz, *People of Hamilton*, 144; and Poughkeepsie: Griffen and Griffen, *Natives and Newcomers*, 68.

106. Mark D. Szuchman, *Mobility and Integration in Urban Argentina: Córdoba in the Liberal Era* (Austin: University of Texas Press, 1980) and Sofer, *From Pale to Pampa*, who questioned the extent of upward social mobility during the period, significantly lifted the scholarly level of debate. The analysis in this book is more complete only in that it employs a wider variety of sources, methods, and measures of mobility and much larger samples. It also covers a longer period and compares mobility rates to those in dozens of other cities in the Americas and Europe. In terms of local groups, Szuchman's examination is actually more thorough, because it includes the French and Spaniards.

107. Conversation with Fernando García Gambeiro (son), Buenos Aires, March 18, 1987.

108. According to McBride, *Domestic Revolution*, 12, "The instructress's title in France implied a level of education which placed her above the servant class," whereas "in England, the status of the governess was more ambiguous." In this respect, the Argentine *institutriz* resembled more the former than the latter.

109. Servant interview transcribed in Cárdenas, *Ramona y el robot*, 92.

110. In her book manuscript, "Gender, Ethnicity, and Kinship in the Urban African Diaspora: Salvador, Brazil, 1808–1888" (1994), chap. 1, pp. 31–32, Mieko Nishida found among domestic slaves "a hierarchy, with special maids called 'mucamas' (*mucumbos*) at the top. The 'mucamas', who were often mulattoes, and might be mistresses or common-law wives of the owners, served as supervisors of other slaves, washerwomen, cooks, housekeepers, and wet-nurses for the owners' legitimate children."

111. See in particular, Armando Discepolo, *Babilonia: Una hora entre criados*, a one-act comic play written in 1925 (several editions).

112. "El Changador," *Caras y Caretas* 41 (1899):6.

113. For an attack on the rags-to-riches myth, see Robert E. Shipley, "On the Outside Looking in: A Social History of the Porteño Worker During the 'Golden Age' of Argentine Development 1914–1930" (Ph.D. diss., Rutgers—The State University, 1977).

114. J. A. Hammerton, *The Real Argentine: Notes and Impressions of a Year in the Argentine and Uruguay* (New York: Dodd, Mead & Co., 1915), 289.

115. *Laurak-Bat: Revista de la Sociedad Vasco-Española de Buenos Aires*, May 1879. The habit of sending home photographs showing off material possessions and fancy New World garments also received its share of mocking, as

shown in the following lines from a 1914 farce: "Old immigrant matron—[to the photographer who is taking a family picture to send back home] Does the house come out well? Does it show that we pay 250 pesos [of rent]? . . . [to her husband] Hide those shoes, Joaquín, or else when your *paisanos* see the photograph they're gonna think we wear tree trunks here [perhaps alluding to worn-out boots]" (Rafael J. De Rosa and Armando Discepolo, "Mi mujer se aburre," *La Escena: Revista teatral*, no. 136, February 3, 1921 [the play opened on August 13, 1914]).

116. *Bandera Proletaria: Organo de la Unión Sindical Argentina*, November 8, 1924, 4.

117. The term used in the letter, *cocotes*, is a French loanword in Lunfardo, the turn-of-the-century argot of Buenos Aires' underworld, but does not exist in standard Spanish. Unlike the French and English equivalents, which the dictionaries define as a "loose" or "sexually promiscuous" woman, José Gobello, *Diccionario Lunfardo* (Buenos Aires: Peña Lillo Editor, 1975) adds, "One who mingles in high social circles."

6. INSTITUTIONAL AND SOCIAL LIFE

1. Federico Rahola, *Sangre nueva* (Barcelona, 1905), 125–31; Manuel Menacho, *Un viaje a la Argentina* (Barcelona, 1911), 206–15; and Carlos M. Santigosa, *El Río de la Plata, Montevideo, Buenos Aires (recuerdos de viaje)* (Seville, 1906), 166–69. The immigrants' gregariousness has also been noted by visitors of other nationalities and in different places—for example, Giovanni Schiavo, *The Italians in Chicago* (Chicago, 1928), 55, "Among the Italians in the United States the desire to form mutual-benefit societies turned into a veritable mania"—and by present-day scholars—Stanley Nadel, *Little Germany: Ethnicity, Religion, and Class in New York City, 1845–80* (Urbana: University of Illinois Press, 1990), 110–11, refers to "their mania for forming *Vereine*"; and Alixa Naff, *Becoming American: The Early Arab Immigrant Experience* (Carbondale: Southern Illinois University Press, 1985), 305, observed that the previously unassociative Syrians took to organizing in the United States "with a vengeance. . . . At any given time the number of organizations was out of all proportion to [their] numbers in America."

2. Takashi Maeyama, "Ethnicity, Secret Societies, and Associations: The Japanese in Brazil," *Comparative Studies in Society and History* 21, 4 (1979):589; and Rudolf Hofmeister, *The Germans of Chicago* (Champaign, Ill.: Stipes, 1976), 114.

3. Benito Hortelano, *Memorias* (Madrid: Espasa-Calpe, 1936), 209–12. Hortelano remembered how, after North American soldiers who were on guard at the consulate shot and killed two looters, the foreign merchants of the city found the courage to arm themselves and defend their stores.

4. *El Imparcial Español* (Buenos Aires), February 24, 1864.

5. In 1855 this effort to deny Spanish nationality was still visible. Fifty-seven immigrants in the census returns who claimed to be French or Portuguese nationals betrayed their true nationality when they gave Spanish villages as their place of birth. Although possible, it is highly unlikely that these mid-

nineteenth-century villagers had gone through the bureaucratic procedures of foreign naturalization. Most, if not all, had clearly been trying to avoid militia service by simply denying their true nationality. Another suspicious point is the high number of immigrants (116) who claimed Gibraltarian birth and, therefore, British nationality.

6. Argentina, Archivo General de la Nación, "Policía," 1873, legajo 238, Sala X, 35.4.1. An active consular office, however, could be a mixed blessing. Along with the letters requesting the release of nationals, there were various soliciting the incarceration of defecting sailors.

7. *La Tribuna*, January 2, 1855.

8. A Spanish newspaper, *El Español Patriota en Buenos-Ayres* (*sic*), had been founded in 1818, but it was written by recent liberal exiles with few or no connections to the immigrant community, and only two issues were published.

9. Hortelano, *Memorias*, 212.

10. Ibid., 215–16.

11. *El Español*, July 18, 1852, 1.

12. *Revista Española: Diario de intereses españoles y argentinos*, November 2 and November 4, 1852.

13. Ibid., November 2, 1852, to January 29, 1853.

14. In 1821 Spanish liberal exiles had founded two Masonic lodges, Aurora and Libertad. Like the first newspaper (founded in 1818), however, these esoteric associations favored Argentine emancipation, represented only a few expatriated ideologues, did not have the organization of Spaniards in Buenos Aires as one of their goals, and had ephemeral lives.

15. *El Español*, July 25, 1852, 1.

16. "El Bachiller," *Caras y Caretas* 28 (1899):7.

17. Hortelano, *Memorias*, 229–30.

18. Joaquín Pesqueira, "Historia de la Asociación Española de Socorros Mutuos de Buenos Aires," published in monthly installments in the association's magazine, *Revista Mensual de la Asociación Española de Socorros Mutuos de Buenos Aires* 8, 82–90 (1919).

19. Information on the institutional, business, and family links between the members of the Spanish association and the local elite was culled from the manuscript census returns of 1855, from contemporary newspapers, and from the following city guides: *Almanaque comercial y guía de forasteros para el Estado de Buenos Aires, año de 1855* (Buenos Aires, Imprenta de la Tribuna, 1855); and Alejandro Bernheim, *Anuario del comercio, de la industria, de la magistratura y de la administración de Buenos Aires, 1854–1855* (Buenos Aires, 1855).

20. Cited in Jack C. Ross, *An Assembly of Good Fellows: Voluntary Associations in History* (Westport, Conn.: Greenwood Press, 1976), 5.

21. Of the first ten presidents of the club, for example, two were to serve in the same position in the Sociedad Española de Beneficencia, which ran the Spanish hospital; three, in the Asociación Española de Socorros Mutuos, the largest Spanish mutual-aid association; one, in the largest Basque society; and one in the two most important Catalan associations. For a history of this association, see Emilio F. de Villegas, *Club Español: Su Historia y evolución* (Buenos

Aires, 1912). The club's library also maintains a scrapbook of newspaper articles related to the institution.

22. Interestingly, the contemporary Boer War created a similar movement toward unity among the different British ethnic groups in North America (Rowland Berthoff, *British Immigrants in Industrial America* [Cambridge, Mass.: Harvard University Press, 1953], 203–8).

23. Felix Ortiz y San Pelayo, *Estudio sobre la Asociación Patriótica Española* (Buenos Aires: El Correo Español, 1899); idem, *Boceto histórico de la Asociación Patriótica Española* (Buenos Aires: La Facultad, 1914). From 1903 on the association also published a magazine, *España* (renamed *Hispania* in 1911). Articles by Unamuno, Pérez Galdós, Juan Ramón Jiménez, and Blasco Ibáñez and by Argentine intellectuals such as Estanislao Zeballos and Miguel Cané often appeared in its pages.

24. Braulio Díaz Sal, *Guía de los españoles en la Argentina* (Madrid: Ediciones Iberoamericanas, 1975), 85–88. For a scholarly analysis of this association, see Alejandro Fernández, "Patria y cultura: Aspectos de la acción de la elite española de Buenos Aires (1890–1920)," *Estudios Migratorios Latinoamericanos* 2 (August–December 1987):291–307.

25. Institución Cultural Española, *Anales*, vol. 1 (1912–1920) (Buenos Aires, 1947), list of members on pp. 9–11.

26. Manuel Gaitero, "La Cámara Española de Comercio," *Revista Mensual de la Asociación Española de Socorros Mutuos de Buenos Aires*, January 1916. The Chamber of Commerce also published a *Boletín Oficial de la Cámara de Comercio Española*, which it sent gratis to Spanish merchants in Argentina.

27. "El patronato español," *Revista Mensual de la Asociación Española de Socorros Mutuos de Buenos Aires*, January 1916.

28. C. Wayne Gordon and Nicholas Babchuk, "A Typology of Voluntary Associations," *American Sociological Review* 24 (February 1959):22–29. The authors divided voluntary associations according to expressed function into "instrumental" (which assisted people outside the organization) and "expressive" (which served the needs of the membership).

29. Buenos Aires, Dirección General de Estadística Municipal, *Censo general de población, edificación, comercio e industrias de la ciudad de Buenos Aires, 1904* (Buenos Aires: Compañía Sud-Americana de Billetes de Banco, 1906), 212–35. The Sociedad Española de Beneficencia's income of 286,000 pesos in its "last fiscal report" surpassed that of all 288 associations listed in this census, with its Italian counterpart running a close second (260,800 pesos). The main Argentine beneficent society, Sociedad de Beneficencia de la Capital, had a higher income, but 86 percent of it came from the state (p. 236). For a history of this society, see Cynthia Little, "The Beneficent Society of Argentina" (Ph.D. diss., Temple University, 1980); and Karen Mead, "Oligarchs, Doctors and Nuns: Public Health and Beneficence in Buenos Aires, 1880–1914" (Ph.D. diss., University of California, Santa Barbara, 1994).

30. *Laurak-Bat: Revista de la Sociedad Vasco-Navarra de Buenos Aires*, April 1880. In the previous monthly issue of the magazine (p. 1) the same idea had been expressed: "The recreative associations, the Spanish club as much as the French, Italian, and English, began as relatively open and democratic institu-

tions, but as the communities grew and became more heterogeneous in terms of socio-economic gradations, these associations began to lose their original democratic character and to become more exclusive; acquiring luxuries that can not be maintained by small monthly dues, they begin to raise them and thus to eliminate the less wealthy."

31. See *The Times (London)*, April 7, 1911, first page of the Finance, Commerce and Shipping Section, for an example of the Banco Español del Río de la Plata's advertisement; *Caras y Caretas* 483 (1908), for a ten-page illustrated article on the bank; and Buenos Aires, Dirección General de Estadística Municipal, *Censo general de población, edificación, comercio e industrias de la ciudad de Buenos Aires, 1909,* 3 vols. (Buenos Aires: Compañía Sud-Americana de Billetes de Banco, 1910), vol. 3, 168, 177, for data on deposits and loans between 1887 and 1909.

32. Adolfo Posada, *La república argentina: Impresiones y comentarios* (Madrid: Victoriano Suárez, 1912), 214.

33. Banco Español y del Río de la Plata, *Memoria*, 1887; and Sociedad Española de Beneficencia, *Memorias y reglamentos*, 1880–1887.

34. Fernández, "Patria y Cultura," 291–307.

35. Fumiko Fukuoka, "Mutual Life and Aid among the Japanese in Southern California with Special Reference to Los Angeles" (M.A. thesis, University of Southern California, 1937), 31–35. Michel S. Laguerre, *American Odyssey: Haitians in New York City* (Ithaca, N.Y.: Cornell University Press, 1984), 99–102, observed that rotating credit associations or *sangues* have a high risk of default and are mostly popular among undocumented immigrants who do not have access to formal banking facilities because they lack a social security number. Shelly Tenenbaum, *A Credit to Their Community: Jewish Loan Societies in the United States, 1880–1945* (Detroit, Mich.: Wayne State University Press, 1993), 140, 158–59, noted the diminishing popularity of these societies as access to bank credit increased. Lizabeth Cohen, *Making a New Deal: Industrial Workers in Chicago, 1919–1939* (Cambridge, England: Cambridge University Press, 1990), 276, stressed that, when the option was available, workers preferred to do business with larger banks rather than with their own ethnic credit associations. Similarly, Timothy Besley et al., "The Economics of Rotating Savings and Credit Associations," *American Economic Review* 83, 4 (1993):792–811, show these "ROSCAS" suffer high rates of failure and represent not a preference but a worldwide response by social groups, particularly immigrants, to exclusion from credit markets. For the high rates of participation (one-third of the population) of a nonimmigrant excluded group, see Julian Y. Kramer, "Self Help in Soweto: Mutual Aid Societies in a South African City" (M.A. thesis, University of Bergen, Norway, [1975?]), 31–53. For a comparison of rotating-credit associations and banking among three ethnic groups in American cities, see Ivan H. Light, *Ethnic Enterprise in America: Business and Welfare among Chinese, Japanese, and Blacks* (Berkeley: University of California Press, 1972), chaps. 2, 3.

36. Cited in John E. Zucchi, *Italians in Toronto: Development of a National Identity, 1875–1935* (Kingston, Ont.: McGill-Queen's University Press, 1988), 104–5.

37. Martin Booth, *The Triads: The Growing Global Threat from the Chinese*

Criminal Societies (New York: St. Martin's Press, 1991); Jean Chesneaux, ed., *Popular Movements and Secret Societies in China, 1840–1950* (Stanford, Calif.: Stanford University Press, 1972), particularly F. Wakeman, Jr., "The Secret Societies of Kwangtung, 1800–1856," 29–47; David Ownby and Mary Somers Heidhues, eds., *Secret Societies Reconsidered: Perspectives on the Social History of Modern South China and Southeast Asia* (Armonk, N.Y.: M. E. Sharpe, 1993); Stanford M. Lyman, "Forerunners of Overseas Chinese Community Organization," in his *Chinese Americans* (New York: Random House, 1974), 8–28; Humbert S. Nelli, *The Business of Crime: Italians and Syndicate Crime in the United States* (New York: Oxford University Press, 1976); and Pino Arlacchi, *Mafia, Peasants and Great States: Society in Traditional Calabria*, trans. Jonathan Steinberg (Cambridge, England: Cambridge University Press, 1983), 62–63, 111–21.

38. Carlos Cúneo and Abel González, *La delicuencia* (Buenos Aires: Centro Editor de América Latina, 1971), 93–105, do mention the formation of a mafia by Sicilians in Argentina during the 1920s and 1930s, but the organization remained small and mostly circumscribed to the city of Rosario. For the United States, Nelli, *Business of Crime*, acknowledges Italian influences, particularly on the pre-1920s "Black Hand," but posits the American environment as the key influence on Italo-American organized crime.

39. Visiting Spaniards rarely failed to mention the "materialistic" culture of Buenos Aires. The Catalan writer and painter Santiago Rusiñol, *Un viaje al Plata* (Madrid: V. Prieto, 1911) titled one of his chapters "El Dios 'Peso'"; E. Gómez Carrillo, *El encanto de Buenos Aires* [1914] (Madrid: Mundo Latino, 1921) titled one of his "La fiebre del oro"; the Basque litterateur José M. Salaverría, *Tierra Argentina* (Barcelona: Gustavo Gil, 1918) went for the more direct "Materialismo"; and Manuel Gil de Oto, *La Argentina que yo he visto* (Barcelona: B. Bauzá, 1914), 100–2, took the lyrical route with his poem "Deus americanus," in which the god was the "golden calf." For the views of an Argentine monseigneur on the work of the Church on behalf of immigrants, see Albino Mensa, "L'Émigration vue du pays de l'immigration," *Social Compass* 3, 5–6 (1955):125–30.

40. For the central role of the Church among Irish and Polish immigrants both in the formation of nationalist ideology and in the organization of social support and charity, see: Joan M. Donohoe, *The Irish Catholic Benevolent Union* (Washington, D.C.: Catholic University of America, 1953); Thomas N. Brown, *Irish-American Nationalism, 1870–1900* (Philadelphia: Lippincott, 1966), 1–2, 34–39, 136–50 and passim; Donna Merwick, *Boston Priests, 1848–1910: A Study of Social and Intellectual Change* (Cambridge, Mass.: Harvard University Press, 1973), which analyzes the clash between the moderate Catholicism of the Yankee clergymen who administered the diocese for most of the century and that of the Irish immigrant majority which was "Jansenistic, tied to a village way of life, nationalistic, and militantly anti-Protestant" (p. x); Jay P. Dolan, *The Immigrant Church: New York Irish and German Catholics, 1815–1865* (Baltimore, Md.: John Hopkins University Press, 1975), esp. chaps. 1, 3; Brian P. Clarke, *Piety and Nationalism: Lay Voluntary Associations in the Creation of an Irish-Catholic Community in Toronto, 1850–1895* (Montreal: McGill-

Queen's University Press, 1993); William J. Galush, "Faith and Fatherland: Dimensions of Polish-American Ethnoreligion, 1875–1975," in *Immigrants and Religion in Urban America,* ed. Randall M. Miller and Thomas D. Marzik (Philadelphia: Temple University Press, 1977); Victor Greene, *For God and Country: The Rise of Polish and Lithuanian Ethnic Consciousness in America* (Madison: State Historical Society of Wisconsin, 1975); Joseph S. Parot, *Polish Catholics in Chicago, 1850–1920: A Religious History* (DeKalb: Northern Illinois University Press, 1981); and Anthony J. Kuzniewski, *Faith and Fatherland: The Polish Church War in Wisconsin, 1886–1918* (Notre Dame, Ind.: University of Notre Dame Press, 1980), which examines the struggle of Polish immigrants to gain access to the Irish- and German-controlled hierarchy. The Poles' cynical description of the American Catholic Church as "One, Holy, *Irish*, and Apostolic" (p. ix), and their proverb "As long as the world continues whole, a German will not be a brother to a Pole" (p. 7), hint at the acidity of the conflict. For a perspective from the "South," see Frederick C. Luebke, *Germans in Brazil: A Comparative History of Cultural Conflict during World War I* (Baton Rouge: Louisiana State University Press, 1987), 35–47, who concludes that "immigrant churches quickly became the most important institutions among German Brazilians" (p. 61).

41. The fratricidal eruption of 1936 (which is beyond the scope of this study) would change this, revitalizing the faith with a supracelestial force that surpassed nineteenth-century Carlism, or for that matter, the Catholic Anglophobia and Russophobia of the Irish and the Poles. Wedded to Falangist nationalism, Catholic militancy sprouted then with a zeal previously unknown in the polarized Spanish community of Buenos Aires.

42. The articles in a special issue of *Estudios Migratorios Latinoamericanos* 5 (April 1990) devoted to religion and immigration suggest that the Church also played a less than primary role among Italians in Argentina. Nestor T. Auza, "La iglesia argentina y la evangelización de la inmigración" (pp. 105–37) contrasts their apostolic apathy with the fervor and activism of the Irish immigrants in Argentina. Daniel J. Santamaría, "Estado, iglesia e inmigración en la Argentina moderna" (pp. 139–81) makes a similar observation and describes how the pastoral efforts of the Church were hindered by the secular or anticlerical sectors that dominated most of the Italian immigrants' institutions. Fernando Devoto, "Catolicismo y anticlericalismo en un barrio italiano de Buenos Aires (La Boca) en la segunda mitad del siglo XIX" (pp. 182–211) questions the habitual equation of Italian immigrants with anticlericalism, but only to produce a more nuanced portrayal that concedes the Church's limited influence in the institutional life of the community. These findings concur with Virginia Yans-McLaughlin, *Family and Community: Italian Immigrants in Buffalo, 1880–1930* (Ithaca, N.Y.: Cornell University Press, 1977), 119–20, who held that, contrary to the case of the Irish, the Church played a feeble role in the lives of the Italians, and with Samuel L. Baily's forthcoming book comparing Italians in Buenos Aires and New York, and contradict Silvano M. Tomasi, *Piety and Power: The Role of Italian Parishes in the New York Metropolitan Area* (New York: Center for Migration Studies, 1975), who pictures the Church as "the most relevant institution" in the lives of Italian immigrants there.

43. See, for example, Ross, *Assembly of Good Fellows,* and Constance Smith and Anne Freedman, *Voluntary Associations: Perspectives on the Literature* (Cambridge, Mass.: Harvard University Press, 1972).

44. The following description of the AESM is based on the magazine of the association, published between 1916 and 1932 (see note 18 above), on minutes of meetings and accounting records found in the AESM's archive, and on a database I compiled with the 16,119 members who joined between 1888 and 1910. For a recent study of this association, see Alejandro Fernández, "El mutualismo español en Buenos Aires, 1890–1920: Un estudio de caso," *Cuadernos de Historia Regional* 3, 8 (1987):36–71.

45. Luso-Hispanic unity did not last long. Eight years later (1878), the Portuguese founded their own mutual-benefit society, the Sociedad Portuguesa de Socorros Mutuos (José Mendes Pereira and José Dias Rato, *Historia del Club Portugués de Buenos Aires* [Buenos Aires: Impresor Sur, 1969], 21).

46. All major regional areas of emigration were more or less evenly represented in the leadership. Of the nineteen presidents between 1857 and 1918, eight were Galicians, four Asturians, three Basques, two Catalans, one Andalusian, and one Castilian. Similarly, of the 14,165 Spanish-born new members between 1888 and 1910, 51 percent were Galicians, 7 percent Asturians, 8 percent Basques, 8 percent Catalans, 7 percent Andalusians, and 7 percent Castilians.

47. For example, Murray Hausknecht, *The Joiners: A Sociological Description of Voluntary Association Membership in the United States* (New York: Bedminster Press, 1962), 17, 111–125, found that as education, income, and white-collar employment levels decreased, so did membership in voluntary associations. Smith and Freedman, *Voluntary Associations, Perspectives on the Literature,* 115–54, and John Hart Lane Jr., *Voluntary Associations among Mexican Americans in San Antonio, Texas* (New York: Arno Press, 1976), 181–82, reached similar conclusions. Even within working-class organizations, P. H. Gosden, *Self-Help: Voluntary Associations in 19th-Century Britain* (New York: Harper & Row, 1974), 13, 46, and Mary Ann Clawson, *Constructing Brotherhood: Class, Gender, and Fraternalism* (Princeton, N.J.: Princeton University Press, 1989), 95–107, found that skilled, better-paid workers were much more likely to join English friendly societies and North American fraternal orders than were unskilled, low-paid workers. On the other hand, Ross, *Assembly of Good Fellows,* 100, maintained that in ancient China and Rome voluntary associations were prevalent among the lower classes. But his claim that this fragmentary and impressionistic evidence from antiquity "may be taken as a general invalidation of what is widely accepted as the best-grounded universal empirical generalization in the research area, that higher class is correlated with more memberships," seems farfetched.

48. See G. Hardin, "The Tragedy of the Commons," *Science* 162 (1968):1243–48; Bonnie J. McCay and James Acheson, eds., *The Question of the Commons* (Tucson: University of Arizona Press, 1987); Michael Hechter, Debra Friedman, and Malka Appelbaum, "A Theory of Ethnic Collective Action," *International Migration Review* 16, 2 (1982):412–32; and Michael Hechter, *Principles of Group Solidarity* (Berkeley: University of California Press, 1987).

49. The AESM's ledgers indicate that administrative costs accounted for 20

percent of total expenditures in the 1870s, 34–36 percent in the 1890s, but only 9–17 percent during the first three decades of the twentieth century.

50. Contrary to Bakunin, Kropotkin stressed rationality and theory rather than violent struggle, and his writings on mutual aid—penned mostly in the 1890s and collected in *Mutual Aid: A Factor of Evolution*, rev. ed. (New York: McClure Phillips, 1904), form basically a critique of social Darwinism rather than of capitalism per se. For a recent interpretation, see Stephen J. Gould, "Kropotkin Was No Crackpot," *Natural History* 7 (1988):12–21.

51. Fernando J. Devoto, "Elementi per un'analisi delle ideologie e dei conflitti nella comunità italiana d'Argentina, 1860–1910," *Storia Contemporanea* 27, 2 (1986):281.

52. *Nuevo Reglamento de la Asociación Española de Socorros Mutuos de Barracas, 1865* (Buenos Aires, 1865).

53. C. Niklison, *Contribución al estudio del mutualismo en la República Argentina* (Santa Fe, Argentina: Instituto Social de la Universidad Nacional del Litoral, 1938), 5.

54. See Samuel Baily, "Las sociedades de ayuda mutua y el desarrollo de una comunidad italiana en Buenos Aires, 1858–1918," *Desarrollo Económico* 21 (January-March 1982):486–514, for an overview of the debate regarding the associative practices of Italian immigrants.

55. Posada, *La República Argentina* (Madrid, 1912), 440–44; and Rafael Altamira, *España y el programa americanista* (Madrid, 1917), 29–30. The disdain for localist associations could be expressed through silence instead of open denunciation. For example, Michinari Fujita, a Japanese national writing a master's thesis at Northwestern University in 1928 on "The History of the Japanese Associations in America," devoted 152 pages to praise *the* Japanese Association—a semiofficial institution supported by the Japanese government—and its branches and not a single sentence to the more numerous *kenjinkai* or localist "people's clubs" based on prefecture or village of origin.

56. Menacho, *Viaje a la Argentina*, 207. Similarly, historian John E. Zucchi noted that "Italian bureaucrats, philanthropists, clerics, or journalists who visited Canadian and American 'colonies' at the turn of the century were struck by the hopeless provincialism of their conationals in the North American urban centers" (*Italians in Toronto*, 5).

57. Fernández, "Patria y Cultura."

58. Fernando Devoto, "Participación y conflicto en las sociedades italianas de socorro mutuo," in Fernando Devoto and Gianfausto Rosoli, *La inmigración italiana en la Argentina* (Buenos Aires: Editorial Biblos, 1985), 141–64.

59. *El Imparcial Español*, May 5, 1864. B. Victory y Suárez, born in the Balearic island of Mahon in 1833, emigrated to Buenos Aires at the age of thirteen. He became the editor of several Spanish and Argentine newspapers (*El Artesano, La Crónica del Progreso, El Pueblo Español, La Iberia*) and translated Etienne Cabet's *Credo comuniste* to the Spanish. A collection of his articles appeared in *Cuestiones de interés público* (Buenos Aires, 1873).

60. D. Borea, "La mutualidad y el cooperativismo en la República Argentina" in Argentina, Comisión Nacional del Censo, *Tercer censo nacional, 1914*, 10 vols. (Buenos Aires: Talleres Gráficos de L. J. Rosso, 1916–1919), vol. 10, 91.

61. I found a ledger in this village association that had just the names of the first fifty-one members. Thirty-five of these, however, were also members of the AESM or the Centro Gallego, and the membership lists of these two associations provided me with information on their jobs, age, marital status, addresses, and so forth.

62. The following information comes from the association's remaining minutes and registries; the *Revista del Centro Val de San Lorenzo*, a magazine published sporadically, usually every year or two, since 1926 (I thank Amalia Navedo for making available to me what surely must be one of the few remaining collections); oral interviews; manuscript censuses and enumerations of emigrants held in Val de San Lorenzo's town hall; and Ricardo García Escudero, *Por tierras maragatas* (Valdespino de Somoza, León, Spain, 1953), a local history of the district surrounding Val de San Lorenzo that includes details on the diaspora.

63. Michael R. Weisser, *A Brotherhood of Memory: Jewish Landsmanshaftn in the New World* (Ithaca, N.Y.: Cornell University Press, 1985), 14.

64. José L. Lence, *Memorias de un periodista* (Buenos Aires: Talleres "The Standard," 1945), 146.

65. North American sociologists have employed two competing approaches to explain the relatively high levels of black participation in voluntary associations: the "ethnic community perspective" (which emphasizes group consciousness and solidarity), and "compensatory theory" (which views it as an attempt to compensate for exclusion from "mainstream organized life"). Although the first perspective is the more applicable to Spanish institutional activity in Buenos Aires, compensatory theory also offers some insight into the formation of the localist associations insofar as these compensated for the lack of opportunity for active participation in elite or elite-run societies. What do not apply to Spaniards (and most sociologists now doubt apply to blacks) are some neo-Freudian perspectives at times attached to the theory that view participation as compensatory for the low self-esteem of groups with subordinate status. If anything, most studies have shown a positive correlation between self-esteem and participation in voluntary associations. See A. M. Orum, "A Reappraisal of the Social and Political Participation of Negroes," *American Journal of Sociology* 72 (1966):682–97, for one of the first elaborations of compensatory theory; and Bruce London and Michael Giles, "Black Participation: Compensation or Ethnic Identification?" *Journal of Black Studies* 18 (1987):20–44, and Christopher Ellison and Bruce London, "The Social and Political Participation of Black Americans: Compensatory and Ethnic Community Perspectives Revisited," *Social Forces* 70 (March 1992):681–701, for an evaluation of the literature and an analysis that supports the ethnic community perspective.

66. Alexis de Tocqueville, *Democracy in America*, 2 vols. (New York: Vintage Books, 1954), vol. 1, 198.

67. See, for example, John W. Briggs, *An Italian Passage: Immigrants to Three American Cities, 1890–1930* (New Haven, Conn.: Yale University Press, 1978), esp. chap. 2; and Gary R. Mormino and George E. Pozzetta, *The Immigrant World of Ybor City: Italians and Their Latin Neighbors in Tampa, 1885–1985* (Urbana: University of Illinois Press, 1987), 175–76.

68. For a review of the issue, see John Bodnar, "Ethnic Fraternal Benefit Associations: Their Historical Development, Character, and Significance," in *Records of Ethnic Fraternal Benefit Associations in the United States: Essays and Inventories,* ed. Susan H. Shreve and Rudolph J. Vecoli (St. Paul: Immigration History Research Center, University of Minnesota, 1981), 5–6.

69. Michael Kenny, "Twentieth Century Spanish Expatriates in Cuba: A Subculture?" *Anthropological Quarterly* 34 (1961):85–93; and idem, "Twentieth Century Spanish Expatriates in Mexico: An Urban Subculture," *Anthropological Quarterly* 35 (1962):169–80.

70. Antonio Rumeu de Armas, *Historia de la previsión social en España: gremios, hermandades, montepíos* (Madrid: Editorial Revista de Derecho Privado, 1949); George M. Foster, "Cofradía and Compadrazgo in Spain and Spanish America, " *Southwestern Journal of Anthropology* 9, 1 (1953):1–26; and Emilio Novoa, *Las sociedades económicas de amigos del país: Su influencia en la emancipación colonial americana* (Madrid: Talleres Prensa Española, [1955]).

71. Jaime Vicens Vives, *Cataluña en el siglo XIX* (Madrid: Riale, 1961), 231–60.

72. F. Estrada Catoira, *Contribución a la historia de la Coruña* (La Coruña, Spain, 1930); *El Eco de Galicia,* December 20, 1893; and Jesús M. Palomares Ibáñez and María del Carmen Fernández Casanova, *La Comisión de Reformas Sociales y la cuestión social en Ferrol, 1884–1903* (Santiago de Compostela, Spain: Universidad de Santiago de Compostela, 1984), 53.

73. Personal observation. See also the photographs in Moisés Llordén Miñambres, "Las asociaciones españolas de emigrantes," and María Cruz Morales Saro, "El centro asturiano de Buenos Aires y la arquitectura neoespañola en el Plata," both in *Arte, cultura y sociedad en la emigración española a América,* ed. Moisés Llordén Miñambres and María Cruz Morales Saro (Gijón, Spain: Universidad de Oviedo, 1992).

74. For the common traits of Spanish organizations, see: Llordén Miñambres and Morales Saro, *Arte, cultura y sociedad;* Carlos Badia Malagrida, *Ideario de la colonia española: Su organización y su programa* (Mexico City: Don Quijote, 1921); Manuel Peláez Cebrián, *Historia de la beneficencia española en Mexico, D.F.* (Mexico City: Oficina Cultural de la Embajada de España en Mexico, 1990); Sociedad Española de Beneficencia de Panamá, *España en Panamá* (Panama City: Editorial Chen, 1986); Durward Long, "An Immigrant Co-Operative Medicine Program in the South, 1887–1963," *Journal of Southern History* 31 (October 1965):417–34, on Tampa's Spanish mutual-aid societies; Antônio Jordão, "O imigrante espanhol em São Paulo: Principais conclusões de uma pesquisa," *Sociologia* [São Paulo] 26, 2 (1964):249–52; and Carlos Zubillaga Barrera, *Los gallegos en el Uruguay* (Montevideo: Ediciones Banco de Galicia, 1966), chap. 10.

75. See Note 1 above.

76. Fukuoka, "Mutual Life and Aid," 19–23; and John Modell, "The Japanese of Los Angeles: A Study in Growth and Accommodation, 1900–1946" (Ph.D. diss., Columbia University, 1969).

77. Edwin B. Almirol, "Filipino Voluntary Associations: Balancing Social Pressures and Ethnic Images," *Ethnic Groups* 2, 1 (1978):74.

78. *Ken* means prefecture and *jinkai*, people's club or organization. Japanese immigrants also organized four types of subprefecture clubs: *shijinkai* (based on a district with more than 30,000 inhabitants); *chojinkai* and *sonjinkai* (based on less-populated, less-urbanized districts); and *azajinkai*, whose members came from the same ancestral hamlet. See Yukiko Kimura, "Locality Clubs as Basic Units of the Social Organization of Okinawans in Hawaii," in *Uchinanchu: A History of Okinawans in Hawaii*, ed. Ethnic Studies Oral History Project, United Okinawan Association of Hawaii (Honolulu: University of Hawaii at Manoa, 1981), 283–90 (six other short articles on various aspects of Okinawan associations follow on pp. 291–351); Takashi Maeyama, "Ethnicity, Secret Societies, and Associations: The Japanese in Brazil," *Comparative Studies in Society and History* 21, 4 (1979):604; and Amelia Morimoto, *Los inmigrantes japoneses en el Perú* (Lima: Universidad Nacional Agraria, 1979), 76.

79. Lyman, *Chinese Americans*, 17–22 (on the *hui kuan* Chinese antecedents), 32–37 (on their formation in North American Chinatowns); Paul Wong, Steven Applewhite, and Michael J. Daley, "From Despotism to Pluralism: The Evolution of Voluntary Organizations in Chinese American Communities," *Ethnic Groups* 8, 4 (1990):216–18; W. E. Wilmott, "Chinese Clan Associations in Vancouver," *Man* 64 (1964):33–37; Richard H. Thompson, *Toronto's Chinatown: The Changing Social Organization of an Ethnic Community* (New York: AMS Press, 1989), 71–83; Antonio S. Tan, *The Chinese in the Philippines, 1898–1935: A Study of Their National Awakening* (Quezon City: R. P. Garcia Publishing, 1972), 203–6; Ownby and Heidhues, *Secret Societies Reconsidered*, 82–85, 121, 137; Mak Lau Song, *The Locality and Non-Locality Organizing Principles: A Taxonomy of Chinese Voluntary Associations in the 19th Century Straits Settlements* (Singapore: National University of Singapore, Department of Sociology, [1986]), the twenty-seven pages of which concentrate on the role of birthplace and dialect in the formation of the associations; and Graham E. Johnson, "Natives, Migrants and Voluntary Associations in a Colonial Chinese Setting" (Ph.D. diss., Cornell University, 1971), 106–20, for the native-village associations of Chinese migrants in 1960s Hong Kong.

80. See William M. De Marco, *Ethnic and Enclaves: Boston's Italian North End* (Ann Arbor, Mich.: UMI Research Press, 1981), 66–68, 114; Yans-McLaughlin, *Family and Community*, 110–11, 130–31; Zucchi, *Italians in Toronto*, 92–94, 159; Franc Sturino, *Forging the Chain: A Case Study of Italian Migration to North America, 1880–1930* (Toronto: Multicultural History Society of Ontario, 1990), 133–35 (for Chicago and Toronto); Briggs, *Italian Passage*, 146, 161 (on Kansas City, Missouri, and Utica and Rochester, New York); Donna Gabaccia, *Militants and Migrants: Rural Sicilians Become American Workers* (New Brunswick, N.J.: Rutgers University Press, 1988), 111, 136–38 (for Louisiana and Brooklyn); and Donald Tricarico, *The Italians of Greenwich Village: The Social Structure and Transformation of an Ethnic Community* (Staten Island, N.Y.: Center for Migration Studies, 1984), 7–8 (for Southern Italian campanilism in that Manhattan district).

81. Steven M. Lowenstein, *Frankfurt on the Hudson: The German-Jewish Community of Washington Heights, 1933–1983, Its Structure and Culture* (Detroit: Wayne State University Press, 1989), 105–6, 254; Hannah Kliger, ed., *Jew-*

ish Hometown Associations and Family Circles in New York (The WPA Yiddish Writers' Group Study) (Bloomington: Indiana University Press, 1992), which includes the original 1938–1939 study plus an introduction and afterword by the editor; Weisser, *Brotherhood of Memory;* Michael N. Dobkowski, "Refugee Landsmanshaftn," in *Jewish American Voluntary Associations,* ed. Michael N. Dobkowski (New York: Greenwood Press, 1986), 603–11; Víctor A. Mirelman, *En búsqueda de una identidad: Los inmigrantes judíos en Buenos Aires, 1890–1930* (Buenos Aires: Editorial Milá, 1988), 314, 334–36; and Hannah Kliger, "Ethnic Voluntary Associations in Israel," *Jewish Journal of Sociology* 31, 2 (1989):109–19, which examines six Polish *landsmanshaftn* in present-day Israel. Unlike the pre–World War II period, they no longer maintain ties with the hometowns, because the Jewish population in Poland was virtually exterminated, but they do keep some links with townsfolk elsewhere in the diaspora. The practice is not restricted to Ashkenazi immigrants: see Walter P. Zenner, "Sephardic Communal Organizations in Israel," *Middle East Journal* 21, 2 (1967):173–86. On the other hand, Josef Korazim, "Immigrant Associations in Israel," in *Ethnic Associations and the Welfare State: Services to Immigrants in Five Countries,* ed. Shirley Jenkins (New York: Columbia University Press, 1988) does not mention a single localist society but concentrates instead on the large national or even "continental" associations like that of Latin American immigrants, with 75,000 members. One has to wonder in how many other cases village-based associations were abundant and simply overlooked by scholars.

82. Nadel, *Little Germany,* 110–11, 116–17, 159.

83. Mary Bosworth Treudley, "Formal Organization and the Americanization Process, With Special Reference to the Greeks of Boston," *American Sociological Review* 14 (1949):49; I. H. Burnley, "The Greeks," in *Immigrants in New Zealand,* ed. K. W. Thompson and A. D. Trlin (Palmerston North, New Zealand: Massey University, 1970), 121–22; and Lia Douramakou-Petroleka, "The Elusive Community: Greek Settlement in Toronto, 1900–1939," in *Gathering Places: Peoples and Neighbourhoods of Toronto, 1834–1945,* ed. Robert F. Harney (Toronto: Multicultural History Society of Ontario, 1985), 267.

84. John Bodnar, *Immigration and Industrialization: Ethnicity in an American Mill Town, 1870–1940* (Pittsburgh, Pa.: University of Pittsburgh Press, 1977), 111.

85. Naff, *Becoming American,* 308.

86. W. T. Morrill, "Immigrants and Associations: The Ibo in Twentieth Century Calabar," *Comparative Studies in Society and History* 5 (July 1963):424–48. See also Joel D. Barkan, Michael L. McNulty, and M. A. O. Ayeni, "'Hometown' Voluntary Associations, Local Development, and the Emergence of Civil Society in Western Nigeria," *Journal of Modern African Studies* 29, 3 (1991):457–80, for an analysis of three localist societies founded by internal migrants.

87. Laguerre, *American Odyssey,* 63. On the other hand, Saskia Sassen-Koob, "Formal and Informal Associations: Dominican and Colombians in New York," *International Migration Review* 13, 2 (1979):314–31, mentions no localist associations among the Haitian Caribbean and West Side neighbors.

88. Mary Grace Paquette, *Basques to Bakersfield* (Bakersfield, Calif.: Kern

County Historical Society, 1982). The most complete study of Basques in the Western Hemisphere, William A. Douglass and Jon Bilbao, *Amerikanuak: Basques in the New World* (Reno: University of Nevada Press, 1975), 339, 384–86, mentions animosities between French and Spanish Basques but no village-based associations. In Argentina, French and Spanish Basques did form separate clubs, and immigrants from the province of Navarre, which is not wholly Basque, did form a provincial association, but no hometown societies were founded.

89. Students of these two emigrant groups do not specify that they did not form village-based associations but consistently fail to mention them. For example, David G. Green and Lawrence G. Cromwell, *Mutual Aid or Welfare State: Australia's Friendly Societies* (Sydney: G. Allen & Unwin, 1984), mentions scores of English and Irish fraternals but none based on county or village of origin. In Charlotte Erickson's *Invisible Immigrants: The Adaptation of English and Scottish Immigrants in Nineteenth-Century America* (Coral Gables, Fla.: University of Miami Press, 1972), localist associations are more invisible than the immigrants of the title. In Andrew Graham-Yooll, *The Forgotten Colony: A History of the English Speaking Communities in Argentina* (London: Hutchinson, 1981) they are as forgotten as the colony, probably because they did not exist. The same is true of famed sociologist Gilberto Freyre's *Ingleses no Brasil: Aspectos da influencia britânica sobre a vida, a paisagem e a cultura do Brasil* (Rio de Janeiro: José Olympio, 1948); of Josefina Plá, *The British in Paraguay, 1850–1870* (Richmond, England: Richmond Publishing Co., 1976); and of Brenda Harriman, *The British in Peru* (Lima: Editorial Gráfica Pacific Press, 1984). Anny P. Stuer, *The French in Australia* (Canberra: Australian National University, Department of Demography, 1982), 129, 148–49, 222–23, mentions only broadly based societies that even welcomed Francophone Canadians, Belgians, and Swiss; Mark D. Szuchman, "La colonia francesa en la ciudad de Córdoba: La 'Société Française de Secours Mutuels,'" *Revista de Historia* (Buenos Aires) 6 (1980):207–17, deals with the only French society there, a nationally based one; Manrique Zago, ed., *Los franceses en la Argentina* (Buenos Aires: Manrique Zago Ediciones, 1986), mentions and richly illustrates the French Club and other institutions but no localist society except for a few large French Basque organizations; and Henri Pitaud, *Les français au Paraguay* (Bordeaux: Editions Bière, 1955), mentions no localist group.

90. DeWitt John Jr., *Indian Workers' Associations in Britain* (London: Oxford University Press, 1969), 116–17, notes the lack of village associations among Punjabi immigrants in England and attributes this to their strong national identity. Robert T. and Gallatin Anderson, "Voluntary Associations among Ukrainians in France," *Anthropological Quarterly* 35, 4 (1962):158–68, mention nothing more restricted than some East-West divisions; and Zoriana Yaworsky Sokolsky, "The Beginnings of Ukrainian Settlement in Toronto, 1891–1939," in *Gathering Places*, 279–302, alludes to religious separation of Jews and Orthodox but actually found a merging trend between Ukrainian Byzantine and Latin rite Catholics, fervid nationalist associations, and no village-based ones.

91. Hasia R. Diner, *Erin's Daughters in America: Irish Immigrant Women in the Nineteenth Century* (Baltimore, Md.: John Hopkins University Press, 1983), 121, alludes in one sentence to " . . . 'county-based clubs' (what Yiddish-speaking immigrants would later dub 'Landsmanshaftn')." Robert Ernst, *Immigrant Life in New York City, 1825–1863* (New York: Columbia University Press, 1949), 122, also refers to "the most ignorant Irishmen [who] clan together in secret societies representing . . . counties." But the 300-plus pages of Michael F. Funchon, ed., *Irish American Voluntary Organizations* (Westport, Conn.: Greenwood Press, 1983), contain no mention of any of these county-based clubs or secret societies; nor do most of the various books on the Irish diaspora that I have read. This lack of attention seems to indicate their rarity rather than their presumed esoteric nature. After all, barrels of ink have been devoted to the surely more clandestine Chinese secret societies.

Helena Znaniecki Lopata, "The Function of Voluntary Associations in and Ethnic Community: 'Polonia,'" in *Urban Sociology,* ed. Ernest W. Burgess and Donald J. Bogue (Chicago: University of Chicago Press, 1967), 117–37, makes no reference to localist associations; nor does Dominic A. Pacyga, *Polish Immigrants and Industrial Chicago: Workers on the South Side, 1880–1922* (Columbus: Ohio State University Press, 1991), who otherwise describes communal life in minute detail. The same is true of Danuta Lukasz, "Las asociaciones polacas en Misiones [Argentina], 1898–1938," *Estudios Latinoamericanos* (Warsaw) 8 (1981):169–88; of Paul H. Price, "The Polish Immigrant in Brazil: A Study of Immigration, Assimilation and Acculturation" (Ph.D. diss., Vanderbilt University, 1951); of Marian Kaluski, *The Poles in Australia* (Melbourne: AE Press, 1985), 63–83 (of 175 societies, none seemed to be a *landsmanshaft*); and of I. H. Burnley, "The Poles," in *Immigrants in New Zealand,* 147–49, who mentions only nationally based organizations and an omnipresent Church.

Richard Griswold del Castillo, *The Los Angeles Barrio, 1850–1890: A Social History* (Berkeley: University of California Press, 1979), 136–38, includes a table with fifteen organizations, none of them localist. José Amaro Hernández, *Mutual Aid for Survival: The Case of the Mexican American* (Malabar, Fla.: R. E. Krieger, 1983), mentions no village- or even province-based associations; nor does John H. Lane Jr., "Voluntary Associations among Mexican Americans in San Antonio, Texas: Organizational and Leadership Characteristics" (Ph.D. diss., University of Texas at Austin, 1968), although he lists 162 societies, or Nina L. Nixon, "Mexican-American Voluntary Associations in Omaha, Nebraska," *Journal of the West* 28, 3 (1989):73–85.

Swedes are another immigrant group that seems not to have formed hometown associations—at least the various authors in Philip J. Anderson and Dag Blanck, eds., *Swedish-American Life in Chicago: Cultural and Urban Aspects of an Immigrant People, 1850–1930* (Urbana: University of Illinois Press, 1992) do not mention any; nor do any of the other books and articles about this group that I have read.

92. John Amos Brown, "Voluntary Associations among Ethnic Minority Groups in Detroit, Michigan: A Comparative Study" (Ph.D. diss., University of California, Berkeley, 1975), 27–43, 52–81, and 93–100, which describes the or-

ganizations of the Irish, the Poles, and the Chinese during the first quarter of the twentieth century; and Germán Rueda, *La emigración contemporánea de españoles a Estados Unidos, 1820–1950* (Madrid: Mapfre, 1993), 98, 233–34.

93. Naff, *Becoming American*, 307–8. Antonio D. Seluja Cecín, *Los libaneses en el Uruguay* (Montevideo: personal edition, 1989), 154–91, which mentions only one village association among the eleven founded in Montevideo; Oswaldo Truzzi, "Etnicidade e diferenciação entre imigrantes síriolibaneses em São Paulo," *Estudios Migratorios Latinoamericanos* 9 (April 1994):7–46, which stresses the immigrants' localism but identifies only two hometown associations among the score Truzzi names; and the various articles in Albert Hourani and Nadim Shehade, eds., *The Lebanese in the World: A Century of Emigration* (London: Centre for Lebanese Studies, 1992), do not mention any hometown associations among the Lebanese in Montreal (pp. 227–42), Tucumán, Argentina (pp. 323–24), Colombia (pp. 361–78), or Mexico (pp. 379–92) but do mention 50–130 of these village societies in Melbourne (p. 480) and "a proliferation" of them in Sidney (pp. 460–64). R. Bayley Winder, "The Lebanese in West Africa," in *Immigrants and Associations*, ed. L. A. Fallers (The Hague: Mouton, 1967), 103–53, and Said Boumedouha, "Adjustment to West African Realities: The Lebanese in Senegal," *Africa* (London) 60, 4 (1990):538–49, mention Shi'a, Sunni, and Maronite associations but none based on hometowns.

94. By comparison, in New York, the largest immigrant city in North America, only two of the seven groups mentioned seem to have founded their own hospitals: the Germans (now Lenox Hill Hospital; Nadel, *Little Germany*, 84); and the Jews, who by 1927 had a total of twenty-five, most of them sanatoria and convalescent homes rather than hospitals (Harry S. Linfield, *The Communal Organization of the Jews in the United States, 1927* [New York: The American Jewish Committee, 1930], 99). Italian religious orders, rather than the immigrant community, founded some hospitals in New York (personal communication from historian Samuel L. Baily). Ernst, *Immigrant Life*, specifies that the Irish did not establish a hospital (p. 56) and does not mention one for the other groups except the Germans and Jews. He also mentions that only the Irish and the Germans established banks (p. 133), although Jews and Italians did so later in the century. Naff, *Becoming American*, mentions no Arab hospital or bank in New York; nor does Rueda, *La emigración contemporánea*, for the Spaniards.

95. See Jenkins, *Ethnic Associations*, which contains articles on New York, Britain, Israel, the Netherlands, and Australia.

96. Samuel L. Baily, in his book manuscript comparing Italians in Buenos Aires and New York (chaps. 8, 9), observes that although those in the Argentine capital proved more successful in forging an institutional structure in general, their compatriots in New York began to form political clubs earlier and at a faster pace, due to the importance of elections and political machines in the northern metropolis. For a general overview of immigrants' involvement in North American politics, see Oscar Handlin's Pulitzer Prize–winning classic *The Uprooted*, 2d ed., enl. (1951; Boston: Little, Brown, 1973), chap. 8. For Canada, see Raymond Breton, *The Governance of Ethnic Communities:*

Political Structures and Processes in Canada (New York: Greenwood Press, 1991).

97. Italians, who in New York City founded almost two thousand village associations (Nathan Glazer and Daniel Moynihan, *Beyond the Melting Pot* [Cambridge, Mass.: M.I.T. Press, 1970], 192–94), seem to have founded few village (as opposed to regional) societies in Buenos Aires. In his pioneer study Samuel Baily mentioned only one society, which seemed to have begun as a village association but soon lost that character ("Las sociedades de ayuda mutua," 496, 499–500. Of the dozens of articles on Italian associations in Argentina that have appeared in Devoto and Rosoli, *La inmigración italiana*, in F. Devoto and E. Miguez, eds., *Asociacionismo, trabajo e indentidad étnica: Los italianos en América Latina en una perspectiva comparada* (Buenos Aires: CEMLA, 1992), and in the journal *Estudios Migratorios Latinoamericanos*, only Alicia Bernasconi, "Cofradías religiosas e identidad en la inmigración italiana en Argentina," in *Estudios Migratorios Latinoamericanos* 5 (April 1990):211–24, mentions numerous village associations, most of which were founded after War World II.

98. At least, as was noted in chapter 3, this was the case from the 1880s on. It is impossible to determine whether this was also the case before that period because statistics were not kept.

99. That was the way the historian of the AESM put it sixty years later (*Revista mensual de la Asociación Española de Socorros Mutuos de Buenos Aires* 8, 82 (1919).

100. This information emerged from the AESM's practice of requiring the name and signature of one, and later two, sponsors for the new member on application forms.

101. Six Spanish immigrant newspapers were involved: *El Correo Español*, first published in July 1872, was shut down by the authorities several times, but lasted until 1905; *El Español*, which lasted only two years, 1874–1875; *Fray Gerundio*, with the amusing subtitle of "Periódico político y literario, serio-jocoso, crítico-burlesco dedicado a las niñas porteñas y españolas residentes en el Plata," edited by a Spanish republican who had conspired against Narvaes in 1848, lasted only three months during 1876; *El Correo de España*, only nine issues in 1874; *La Revista Española*, 1876; and *Antón Perulero*, 1876. The details of the clash come from these newspapers.

102. Censorship also extended to zarzuela (Spanish operetta) performances. The zarzuela "Receta contra la crisis" [Recipe against the Crisis] of the Spanish writer Casimiro Prieto Valdés, who had a column in *La Nación*, the opposition newspaper owned by future president Mitre, was banned by the municipal government for political reasons.

103. *El Correo de España*, October 10, 1874.

104. *El Correo Español*, August 27, 1876, had criticized Paul y Angulo's plan to take Spanish immigrants to Peru because "it is a country where there are no guarantees; the complaints of Italian and Oriental settlers there have been answered with bullets; there is too much anti-Spanish feeling, and no Spanish diplomatic representative." For a short biography of Paul y Angulo, see Hugo E. Biagini ed., *Redescubriendo un continente: La inteligencia española en*

el París americano en las postrimerías del XVIII (Seville: Diputación Provincial, 1993), 267–79.

105. Emilio Villegas, *Bosquejo histórico de la Liga Republicana Española en la Argentina* (Buenos Aires, 1907).

106. See his autobiography: Rafael Calzada, *Cincuenta años de América: notas autobiográficas*, 2 vols. (Buenos Aires: Editorial Jesús Menéndez, 1926).

107. The diverging attitudes toward socialism and anarchism of the Spanish immigrant elite mirrored those of their Argentine counterparts. A professor at Buenos Aires Law School, for example, contrasted Marx with Bakunin in these terms: "The former is the man of science, the thinker who delves into the depth of social problems to solve them on the basis of rationality; the latter, the reckless agitator simply aiming to shatter whatever exists; one is the theoretician of the grand constructions, the other the blind fury of the hurricane. . . . Marx struggles within the bourgeois state; Bakunin longs to exterminate everyone in power. . . . One organized labor parties that have evolved into the socialism of today, the other destroys and founds anarchism (Juan P. Ramos, "Prologue," in Julio Herrera, *Anarquismo y defensa social: Estudio de la ley de defensa social n. 7029 precedido de una exposición general sobre el anarquismo* [Buenos Aires: Librería e Imprenta Europea de M. A. Rosas, 1917], viii).

108. Iaacov Oved, author of perhaps the most thorough study of late-nineteenth-century anarchism in Argentina, *El anarquismo y el movimiento obrero en Argentina* (Mexico City: Siglo XXI, 1978), maintains that during this period Spanish immigrants played such a critical role in the formation of the Argentine movement that their influence surpassed that of the more numerous Italian newcomers (Iaacov Oved, "Influencia del anarquismo español sobre la formación del anarquismo argentino," *Estudios interdisciplinarios de América Latina y el Caribe* [Tel Aviv] 2, 1 [1991]:5, 8).

109. "División Investigación Orden Social, Antecedentes de Anarquistas, 1902, No. 1," in the Buenos Aires police archives on Chacabuco Street. For the image of the Catalan anarchist in popular Argentine theater, see Mario Flores, "Cruz Diablo," *La Escena: Revista teatral*, no. 152, May 26, 1921.

110. Among Diego Abad de Santillán's works are: *El movimiento anarquista en la Argentina* (Buenos Aires: Argonauta, 1930); *La FORA* (Buenos Aires: Nervio, 1933), a history of the anarchist labor federation; and the multivolume *Historia argentina* (Buenos Aires: Tea, 1965–1971).

111. First published in 1897, *La protesta humana* began to appear daily in 1904, dropping *humana* from its title, and continued, apparently uninterrupted, until the September 1930 coup d'état, surfacing sporadically after that. From 1922 to 1930 it also published a weekly supplement that was reprinted (at least in 1922, vol. 1) as *La Protesta. Suplemento* (Vaduz, Liechtenstein: Cabildo, 1975).

112. José María Borrero, *La Patagonia trágica* (Buenos Aires, 1928). For an exhaustive study of the rebellion, see Osvaldo Bayer, *Los vengadores de la Patagonia trágica*, 3 vols. (Buenos Aires: Editorial Galerna, 1972–74); and for a cinematic version, Hector Olivera's *La Patagonia rebelde* (1974).

113. Oved, "Influencia del anarquismo español," 8.

114. I found eight issues of this newspaper, edited by Josefa Calvo, from

January 8 to November 14, 1896, in the Special Collection Archives of the University of California, Los Angeles, but there may have been three more. The July 15, 1897, issue of *La Protesta Humana* included a list of donation-subscriptions for the eleventh issue of *La Voz de la Mujer* and also a letter from its editors dated July 1: "After a long absence of five months the paper now disappears, but we will repeat it: Without women's emancipation nothing will be durable, all will be fictitious. As we retire, only one phrase, a mixture of impotence and rancor, bursts from our lips: Long live the emancipation of women! Martyr of sorrow, woman of today, till soon!" Surprisingly, this seminal newspaper is mentioned in a sentence in Marifran Carlson, *Feminismo!: The Woman's Movement in Argentina from Its Beginnings to Eva Perón* (Chicago: Academy, 1988), 127. For an article on this publication, see Maxine Molyneux, "No God, No Boss, No Husband: Anarchist Feminism in Nineteenth-Century Argentina," *Latin American Perspectives* 48 (Winter 1986):119–45, who stresses "the paper's affiliation with Spanish Anarchism and with the Spanish immigrant community."

115. From the editors of *El Corsario* in La Coruña to the readers of *La Revolución Social: Organo comunista-anárquico*, August 15, 1896, 4. Similarly, *El Libertario: Decenario anarquista*, April 3, 1923, 4, included a list of forty-one people from the Grupo Espártaco who had donated money in support of Barcelona's anarchist paper *Tierra y Libertad*.

116. The letter, addressed to "our sisters overseas," *El Rebelde: Periódico anarquista*, January 31, 1901, 4, came from the Valencian feminist periodical *La Humanidad Libre*, edited by Rosa Lidón.

117. *El Rebelde: Periódico anarquista*, May 7, 1899, 3. The author, Federico Urales (nom de plume—or perhaps de guerre—of Juan Montseny y Carret), asked that any relevant source be sent to *La Revista Blanca*, Ponzano 8, Madrid (the main anarchist newspaper of the Spanish capital). Urales wrote several plays, novels, and a two-volume history of Spanish philosophy (in 1934), but the book in question must have been *La anarquía*, a thirty-two-page pamphlet published by the newspaper in 1900 (a microfilm of which I found in the library of Columbia University).

118. *La Montaña: Periódico socialista revolucionario*, September 15, 1897, 6. This newspaper was edited by José Ingenieros (who would later become the preeminent Argentine sociologist) and Leopoldo Lugones (who would later become "the" national poet and a right-wing nationalist). The contributions were to be sent to the editors of *El Siglo*, 53 Fleet Street, London.

119. See for example, *El Gráfico: Periódico mensual*, April 1906, 4, and *La Acción Socialista: Periódico sindicalista revolucionario*, August 30, 1910.

120. Diego Abad de Santillán, *Memorias, 1897–1936* (Barcelona: Editorial Planeta, 1977), 52.

121. Herrera, *Anarquismo y defensa social*, 93; Oved, "Influencia del anarquismo español," 15.

122. *La Prensa* (Buenos Aires), October 17, 1909, 9.

123. "El atentado contra Alfonso XIII; José Collar Feito y su familia," *Caras y Caretas* 224 (1903):2. Also in November 1902, Alfonso García Mata, a twenty-five-year-old Argentine of Spanish parents, arrived in Spain to assasi-

nate the king, although he gave up his mission because of lack of cooperation by his Galician comrades (Joaquín Romero Maura, "Terrorism in Barcelona, 1904–1909," *Past and Present* 41 [December 1968]:134.

124. Diego Abad de Santillán, *Contribución a la historia del movimiento obrero español, desde sus orígenes hasta 1905* (Puebla, Mexico: Cajica, 1962), 432–33.

125. *El Perseguido: Periódico comunista-anárquico*, (Buenos Aires), October 22, 1893. The execution of another anarchist typographer, the Italian Michele Angiolillo, who assassinated Spanish Prime Minister Cánovas del Castillo on August 8, 1897, had a similar posthumous influence. On his way to the scaffold, Angiolillo said only one word: "Germinal"—the title of Émile Zola's novel about striking mine workers. On November 14 a new publication appeared in Buenos Aires: *Germinal: Periódico anarquista*.

126. The practice was also common among Spanish anarchists elsewhere in the diaspora. New York's *El Despertar: Periódico quincenal anarquista*, June 1, 1894, 4, published a letter from Angela Vallés, widow of Pallás, telling of the birth of her posthumous son—whom she "hoped would imitate his father and avenge the crime of the bourgeoisie"—and thanking them for the 1,025 pesetas they had sent.

127. For some examples of quarrels between Spanish radicals in Argentina and their comrades at home, see: *El Perseguido: Periódico comunista-anárquico* (the subtitle of the first eleven issues was *voz de los explotados*), January 20, 1893, and later issues, and December 8, 1895, 2–3; *Germinal: Periódico anarquista*, December 12, 1897; *La Antorcha*, January 5, 1923; and *Antecedentes: Periódico de Batalla*, July 17, 1923. In the 1890s the principal altercations pitted *organizadores* (or anarcho-collectivists) against *anti-organizadores* (or anarcho-communists); in the 1920s, attitudes toward the Bolshevik Revolution seem to have become the main point of contention.

128. For example, *La Acción Socialista: Periódico sindicalista revolucionario*, February 19, 1910, and later issues, included this large announcement: "BOYCOTT! Workers, do not consume Spanish products as long as the prisoners of Montjuich are not set free. War on all Spanish products!"; *La Protesta* of the same dates carried a boycott campaign against *El Diario Español*, the principal immigrant newspaper; and *La Antorcha*, May 16, 1924, not only called for a boycott of Spanish products but also held the Spanish associations and commercial firms in Argentina "responsible for the crimes of the Spanish dictatorship."

129. *La Prensa*, October 15, 1909, 10, October 16, 1909, 8, and October 17, 1909, 9, for the anarchist general strike, demonstrations, and the burning of the Spanish flag; *La Prensa*, October 21, 1909, 11, for the Spanish associations' counterdemonstration. Contemporary anarchists and Spanish historians—except for a few conservative ones—considered Ferrer innocent of the charges and his execution an attempt by the government to silence his propagation of modern educational principles. However, Romero Maura, "Terrorism in Barcelona," 139, 141–46, uncovered new material which shows that he did indeed mastermind the 1905 and 1906 attempts against King Alfonso XIII's life.

130. Lence, *Memorias*, 13.

131. *El Perseguido: Periódico comunista-anárquico*, September 8, 1895, 1–2;

Caserio: Periódico comunista-anárquico, April 18, 1896; *La Revolución Social: Organo comunista-anárquico,* November 12, 1896, 3; *Germinal: Periódico anarquista,* November 14, 1897, and later issues, January 16, 1898, and later issues, and July 3, 1898; *El Rebelde: Periódico anarquista,* June 10, 1900, 1; *La Protesta,* July 4, 1905, 2, May 5, 1914, 1–2, June 11, 1915, 2, and March 27, 1924, 2. For similar polemics in the Spanish immigrant community of Brazil and Uruguay, see *El Grito del Pueblo: Defensor de los intereses proletarios,* October 28, 1899, 3, a newspaper of Spanish socialists in São Paulo; and *El Derecho a la Vida: Periódico anarquista* (Montevideo), January 7, 1894, 3.

132. *La Protesta,* April 24, 1910, and later issues.

133. In 1895, for example, the anarchist bakers' mutual-aid society already charged different quotas according to age, limited admission to people under the age of fifty, and competed for members by allowing those who left the trades to retain their membership as long they paid dues (*El Obrero Panadero,* March 14, 1895, 4).

134. *Bandera Proletaria: Organo de la Unión Sindical Argentina,* December 12, 1922, 1.

135. The program for the December 1, 1906, soiree of the Agrupación Socialista Sindicalista, appearing in *La Acción Socialista: Periódico sindicalista revolucionario,* illustrates the format:

1st. Workers' anthem by the orchestra
2nd. Conference by the comrade Luis Bernard
3rd. The interesting social drama "The Bread of the Poor," condensed in two acts and two scenes by José A. Paonesa with the title "Redemption"
4th. The hilarious comic play in one act and prose titled "The Colonel's Assistant"
5th. Family dance
Tickets one peso . . . Ladies and young girls free.

136. *La Acción Socialista: Periódico sindicalista revolucionario,* August 30, 1910.

137. *La Organización Obrera: Organo de la FORA,* December 27, 1919, 4.

138. *Bandera Proletaria: Organo de la Unión Sindical Argentina,* December 9, 1922; and also the article by Alejandro Priotti, "La emigración y los emigrantes," *Bandera Proletaria: Organo de la Unión Sindical Argentina,* December 14, 1922, 4.

139. *Acción Obrera: Organo del Sindicato Obrero de la Industria del Mueble,* June 1927; and *El Carpintero y Aserrador,* July 1922.

140. *La Antorcha,* May 26, 1928, 4. See also June 19, 1925, 1, and October 30, 1925, 4.

141. *El Despertar Gallego,* 1922–1930 (in 1930 it changed its title to *Galicia*).

142. *La Tribuna,* March 3, 1866.

143. *El Eco de Galicia,* October 30, 1895.

144. Ibid., October–December 1895.

145. *Revista Mensual de la Asociación Española de Socorros Mutuos de Buenos Aires,* January 1919.

146. A good example of this disapproval of ethnic unionism appeared in the

Acción Obrera, the monthly publication of the Furniture Makers' Union. In the January 1926 issue its syndicalist leaders bragged effusively about how this "false consciousness" had withered away in the face of proletarian unity. In the next issue they assailed the Jewish Committee of the union for acting too independently, holding its own assemblies, and spending common funds on its own library and publication. The following month they questioned its right to exist: "We can understand the need for an Israelite bakers' union like the one that exists here in Buenos Aires because there is a particularly Jewish way of making bread . . . but on what grounds can you explain the existence of a separate furniture-makers' group?"

147. Ethnic-trade associations seem to have been common in the United States. Ernst, *Immigrant Life,* devoted an entire chapter (10) to the Germans' trade *Vereine* and labor unions and also referred to their existence in Philadelphia, Baltimore, Cincinnati, St. Louis, Chicago, and Milwaukee. Almirol, "Filipino Voluntary Associations," 75–78, included "occupational groups and labor unions" as one of the principal types of Filipino associations in Salinas, California; so did Light, *Ethnic Enterprise,* 68–72, 90–95, for the Japanese and Chinese in various U.S. cities. Weisser, *Brotherhood of Memory,* 151, noted that despite their strong participation in general labor unions, New York Jews also formed their own trade organizations, "embracing nearly every type of industrial and commercial activity in which Jews were employed." John, *Indian Workers' Associations,* examines the formation of these IWAs by Punjabi immigrants in England and their relationship with labor unions.

148. See Josep R. Llobera, "The Idea of 'Volksgeist' in the Formation of Catalan Nationalist Ideology," *Ethnic and Racial Studies* 6, 3 (1983):332–50.

149. *La Protesta Humana,* August 19, 1897, 1, and September 2, 1897, 2–3.

150. In 1886 another Catalan association was founded, the recreational club Centre Català, which appears with 368 members in Buenos Aires, *Censo general, 1904,* 216.

151. *Centenario Laurak-Bat, 1877–1977,* a sixty-four-page booklet published by the association for its centennial.

152. *Laurak-Bat: Revista de la Sociedad Vasco-Navarra de Buenos Aires,* May 1879.

153. *El Eco de Galicia,* May 15, 1892.

154. Francisco de Grandmontagne, "Chistus y Gaitas," *Caras y Caretas* 38, 1899, 9–10. The story also appeared in modified form in his *Los inmigrantes prósperos* (Madrid: M. Aguilar, 1933), 73–82.

155. *El Eco de Galicia,* October 13, 1893; and Alberto Vilanova Rodríguez, *Los gallegos en la Argentina,* 2 vols. (Buenos Aires: Ediciones Galicia, 1966), vol. 2, 941–42.

156. *El Eco de Galicia,* February 21, 1893.

157. *Aberu-Eguna,* published between 1932 and 1933.

158. Felix Ortiz y San Pelayo, *Los Vascos en América* (Buenos Aires, 1915), 85.

159. Ibid., 89–103.

160. Tomás Otaegui, *Nacionalismo Basko: Su carácter actual* (Buenos Aires, 1922), 16–35. For an account of the contemporary European side, see William

A. Douglass and Milton da Silva, "Basque Nationalism," in *The Limits of Integration: Ethnicity and Nationalism in Modern Europe*, ed. Oriol Pi-Sunyer (Amherst: Department of Anthropology, University of Massachusetts, 1971), 147–80.

161. José Uriarte, *¿Quiénes son los baskos?* (Buenos Aires, 1930), 121.

162. *L'aurenata*, 1871–76; *Ressorgument*, 1916–1949; *Anuari dels Catalan*, 1923–?; and *Catalunya*, 1930–1945. I found the best, though incomplete, collection of these periodicals in the library of the Casal de Cataluña, one of the two main Catalan social clubs in Buenos Aires.

163. *Ressorgiment* 15, 162 (January 1930):2619.

164. Jacinto Zaragozi, *Los biscaitarras* (Santa Fe, Argentina: personal edition, 1961). The author had arrived in Argentina in 1915 as a nineteen-year-old youth.

165. Richard Ford, *A Hand-Book for Travellers in Spain, and Readers at Home*, 2 vols. (London: Centaur Press, 1966 [1845?]), vol. 2, 964.

166. Ibid., 149.

167. Ibid., 966.

168. *O'Shea's Guide to Spain and Portugal*, 13th ed. (London: Adam & Charles Black, 1905), 146.

169. *La Voz del Arte*, January 28, 1894.

170. For the regionalism of Galician intellectuals during this period, see José Castelos Paredes, "La mentalidad nacionalista: El caso de la 'Intelligentsia' Gallega, 1875–1900" (doctoral diss., Universidad de Barcelona, 1987).

171. *La Ilustración Gallega y Asturiana* (1879), 251.

172. *El Eco de Galicia*, August 10, 1893.

173. Ibid., October 10, 1892.

174. Vilanova Rodríguez, *Los gallegos*, vol. 2, 961.

175. Ibid., 962.

176. Xosé Manoel Nuñez Seixas, "Emigración y nacionalismo gallego en Argentina, 1879–1936," *Estudios Migratorios Latinoamericanos* 5 (August–December 1990):379–406.

177. *Crítica*, April 19, 22, and 23, 1934; and *El Mundo*, April 20 and 21, 1934.

178. The library of the Centro Gallego de Buenos Aires has the best, and perhaps only, collection of these publications. At least eight other Galician periodicals appeared during the first three decades of the twentieth century, but most of them were written in Castilian.

179. *Alborada: Organo de la Sociedad Agraria y Cultural Hijos del Partido de Corcubión* (Buenos Aires), August 1925.

180. Lence, *Memorias*, 141–42.

181. See, for example, Hechter, *Principles of Group Solidarity*, 115.

182. See, for example, Weisser, *Brotherhood of Memory*, 82–86.

183. Raymond Breton, "Institutional Completeness of Ethnic Communities and the Personal Relations of Immigrants," *American Journal of Sociology* 70 (September 1964):193–205. Breton, using Montreal as a case study, postulated that the higher the degree to which an ethnic community's formal organizations satisfied the needs of its members, the more their social relationships

would stay within the community's boundaries. "Institutional completeness," however, is rarely "complete." Spanish immigrants, after all, relied mostly on Argentine institutions when it came to educational, religious, and professional matters (that is, public schools, the Church, and unions).

184. The British anthropologist Michael Kenny concluded, on the basis of their associative practices, that the Spaniards in Cuba and Mexico formed a "sub-culture." He did not explain the exact meaning of the term, but it seems to be similar to what a historian would call, with no more precision, an unassimilated group. See note 69 of this chapter.

185. Dino Cinel, *From Italy to San Francisco, The Immigrant Experience* (Stanford, Calif.: Stanford University Press, 1982), chaps. 9–10.

186. Ibid., 255.

187. Felix Ortiz y San Pelayo, *Los vascos en América*, 106.

188. Otaegui, *Nacionalismo Basko*.

189. Zaragozi, *Los biscaitarras*, 16.

190. For a recent use of the concept, see Mary C. Waters, "The Construction of a Symbolic Ethnicity: Suburban White Ethnics in the 1980s," in *Immigration and Ethnicity: American Society—"Melting Pot" or "Salad Bowl"?*, ed. Michael D'Innocenzo and Josef P. Sirefman (Westport, Conn.: Greenwood Press, 1992), 75–90.

7. COUSINS AND STRANGERS

1. Anonymous play attributed to Esteban de Luca, reprinted in Universidad de Buenos Aires, Facultad de Filosofía y Letras, Instituto de Literatura Argentina, *Sección de documentos* vol. 1, 3 (1924):61–72.

2. Ibid., vol. 1, 2 (1924):21–55.

3. Henry Vogel, "Elements of Nationbuilding in Argentina: Buenos Aires, 1810–1828" (Ph.D. diss., University of Florida, 1987), 222–30.

4. Hugo Raúl Galmarini, "Los españoles de Buenos Aires después de la Revolución de Mayo: La suerte de una minoría desposeída del poder," *Revista de Indias* 46, 178 (1986):577. See also idem, "La situación de los comerciantes españoles en Buenos Aires después de 1810," *Revista de Indias* 44, 173 (1984):273–90.

5. Rubén H. Zorrilla, *Cambio social y población en el Pensamiento de Mayo, 1810–1830* (Buenos Aires: Editorial Belgrano, 1978), 87–88. The *Memorias del Ministerio de Relaciones Exteriores Argentino* show that as late as 1873, Spaniards or their inheritors were still demanding compensation from the Argentine government for the forced loans and properties confiscated during the War of Independence, and that, at least at this late time, most of the demands were rejected.

6. "La acción de Maipú" (1818), in Universidad de Buenos Aires, *Sección de documentos*, vol. 1, 3 (1924):51.

7. Galmarini, "Los españoles," 578–79.

8. The decree went into effect on April 4, 1817, and was revoked on August 3, 1821. Argentina, *Registro Nacional de la República Argentina que comprende los documentos desde 1810 hasta 1891*, 14 vols. (Buenos Aires,

1879–1891), vol. 1, 1810–1821. The title of the first three volumes is "Registro Oficial."

9. Esteban Echeverría, *Obras completas* (Buenos Aires: Zamora, 1951), 249–50.

10. Juan Bautista Alberdi, "Qué nos hace la España" (1838), reprinted in *El Plata Científico y Literario* (Buenos Aires), 5 (March 1855).

11. Tulio Halperin Donghi, "¿Para qué la inmigración? Ideología y política inmigratoria y aceleración del progreso modernizador: El caso argentino (1810–1914)," *Jahrbuch Für Geschichte von Staat, Wirtschaft und Gesellschaft Lateinamerikas* 13 (1976):446.

12. Argentina, Archivo General de la Nación, "Emigrados Canarios," División Gobierno Nacional, Sala X, 9.6.2; and Galmarini, "Los españoles," 589.

13. Adam Smith, *The Wealth of Nations* [1776] (New York: Alfred A. Knopf, 1991), vol. 1, 134–35, 184–86, 211, 220, vol. 2, 62–67 and passim.

14. Miriam Williford, *Jeremy Bentham on Spanish America: An Account of His Letters and Proposals to the New World* (Baton Rouge: Louisiana State University Press, 1980), 114–21, 128.

15. Roland D. Hussey, "Traces of the French Enlightenment in Colonial Hispanic America," in *Latin America and the Enlightenment*, ed. Arthur P. Whitaker (Ithaca, N.Y.: Cornell University Press, 1961), 23–51, examined book inventories of private libraries in the principal colonial cities and showed that they contained the whole spectrum of Enlightenment writings, including those forbidden by the Inquisition.

16. See also Manuel Moreno Alonso, "América española en el pensamiento de Voltaire," *Anuario de Estudios Americanos* 38 (1981):57–100.

17. Jean Jacques Rousseau, *Discourse on the Origin and Basis of Inequality among Men*, 148–52, 168; and *Discourse on the Arts and Sciences*, 228, both in *The Essential Rousseau*, trans. Lowell Bair (New York: Mentor, 1974). For his influence in Argentina's independence movement, see J. A. Doerig, "Suárez y Rousseau como precursores espirituales de la independencia hispanoamericana," *Humboldt* 11, 41 (1970):54–56.

18. Susan Midgen Socolow, *The Bureaucrats of Buenos Aires, 1769–1810: Amor al Real Servicio* (Durham, N.C.: Duke University Press, 1987), 132, 227–28, 260–64, shows that of all of the high-ranking officials appointed between the creation of the Viceroyalty of the Río de la Plata in 1776 and the declaration of independence in 1810, fifty-six had been born in Spain and only six in Buenos Aires. She also concludes that royal officials became less likely to marry local women during this period and that the imperial bureaucracy became more powerful, independent, and isolated from local society.

19. The visitor Francisco Milla, *Descripción de la Provincia del Río de la Plata* (Buenos Aires: Espasa-Calpe, 1947), 42–44, described Buenos Aires in the 1770s as "one of the towns in the Americas more populated by whites [*gente española*]. . . . No large fortunes exist here, but the number of middle ones is high. . . . Even among poor people, indigence is not known due to the low cost of food that allows them to save and afford some decent clothing." Fifty years later, an English visitor noted, in addition to the "impertinence of commoners," a high degree of social mingling in public places (F. B. Head, *Rough Notes Taken*

during Some Rapid Journeys across the Pampas and among the Andes, 2d ed. [London: John Murray, 1826], 31).

20. David Rock, *Argentina, 1516–1987: From Colonization to Alfonsín* (Berkeley: University of California Press, 1987), 65, attributed the rapid growth of guilds in Buenos Aires after the 1780s to the increasing immigration of Spaniards and their "attempt to monopolize the crafts, expelling from them servile or caste groups."

21. Gladys Onega, *La inmigración en la literatura Argentina* (Buenos Aires: Editorial Galerna, 1969), 19.

22. The decree excepting Spaniards from militia conscription came on February 16, 1852, just two days after the overthrow of Rosas (*Revista Oficial de la Provincia de Buenos Aires de 1852*, 13, document 2011.

23. *Anton Perulero,* August and September, 1876.

24. *El Correo Español,* August 1, 1872 and later issues.

25. *El Imparcial Español,* July 1, 1864.

26. Gil Gelpi, writing about 1862, quoted in José León Suárez, *Carácter de la revolución americana* (Buenos Aires: La Facultad, 1917), 23, 25.

27. Similar polemics engaged the Spanish immigrant community in Mexico. See: *Polémica entre el diario oficial y la colonia española sobre la administración virreinal en Nueva España y la colonización de Mexico,* 2 vols. (Mexico City: Imprenta Poliglota, 1875).

28. Gil Gelpi, *Españoles en América* (Buenos Aires, 1862).

29. *El Nacional,* July 23, 1862.

30. José Ingenieros, Argentina's most prominent turn-of-the-century sociologist, described Hispanophobia as the main element in Sarmiento's ideology in his prologue to a posthumous edition of the latter's *Conflicto y armonías de razas en América* (Buenos Aires: La Cultura Argentina, 1915), 19, 25, 37.

31. Miguel de Unamuno, *Algunas consideraciones sobre la literatura hispanoamericana,* 3d ed. (Madrid: Espasa-Calpe, 1968), 77. See also Dardo Cúneo, *Sarmiento y Unamuno,* 4th ed. (Buenos Aires: Editorial Belgrano, 1981), 21–21. The Argentine writer Ricardo Rojas recounted an anecdote that Unamuno once told him about reading Sarmiento's diatribes against Spain to a blind friend who abhorred foreigners who took such liberties. When the blind man did not react indignantly but, on the contrary, seemed to relish it, Unamuno inquired about the unexpected tolerance. His friend responded, "It is that that American bad-mouths Spain as we do, not like a foreigner" (*Retablo español* [Buenos Aires: Editorial Losada, 1938], 257).

32. J. M. Villergas, *El Sarmenticidio, o al mal Sarmiento buena podadera* (Buenos Aires: Imprenta de la Revista, 1854).

33. Domingo Sarmiento, letter dated January 6, 1884, included in the collection of his writings, *Condición del extranjero en América* (Buenos Aires: La Facultad, 1928), 240–43.

34. Ibid., 162, 169–70, 172–74.

35. *El Imparcial Español,* July 9, 1864.

36. Rafael Calzada, *Cincuenta años de América: Notas autobiográficas,* 2 vols. (Buenos Aires: Librería de Jesús Menéndez, 1926), vol. 2, 18–19.

37. Estanislao Zeballos, a prominent Argentine writer and statesman, remembered how in the late 1870s his history teacher always referred to Spaniards with the denigrating term *godos*. When Zeballos argued that *españoles* was a more appropriate and polite term, the infuriated teacher commanded him to write *los Godos* ("Conferencia pronunciada en el Ateneo Hispano Americano," *Revista de Derecho, Historia y Letras* (Buenos Aires) 43 (1912):579.

38. *Laurak-Bat: Revista de la Sociedad Vasco-Española de Buenos Aires*, November 1878.

39. There had always been, however, a few ardent defenders of the language, and in the past decades Galicia, like other regions of the Continent, has experienced a regional cultural-linguistic revival. One encounters, as I did in 1987, the spectacle of a middle-class ethnonationalist intellectual speaking in Galician to a peasant, who, showing the bonds of the past, responded in broken Castilian, as if to show his "culture."

40. *La Tribuna*, June 22, 1864.

41. *La España*, June 24, 1864.

42. Argentina, Archivo General de la Nación, "Emigrados Canarios," División Gobierno Nacional, Sala X, 18.8.2.

43. Sarmiento, *Condición del extranjero*, 243.

44. Abraham Echazú, *Inmigración y colonización en la República Argentina* (Buenos Aires, 1877), 17.

45. Argentina, *Boletín Mensual del Ministerio de Relaciones Exteriores* 2, 2 (1885):897.

46. Ibid., 3, 1 (1886):705.

47. Ibid., 6 (February 1889).

48. Argentina, *Memoria del Departamento General de Inmigración correspondiente al año 1890* (Buenos Aires: Imprenta de P. Coni & Hijos, 1891), 51. The other principal receivers of free passages were the French (45,500) and the Belgians (10,524); Italians received only 6,272, despite the fact that they were the principal immigrant group in the country.

49. Buenos Aires, Dirección General de Estadística Municipal, *Censo general de población, edificación, comercio e industrias de la ciudad de Buenos Aires, 1887*, 2 vols. (Buenos Aires: Compañía Sud-Americana de Billetes de Banco, 1889), vol. 2, 556; also in M. A. Lancelotti, *La criminalidad en Buenos Aires: Al margen de la estadística, 1887–1912* (Buenos Aires: V. Abeledo, 1914), 43–44.

50. Roberto Bunge, *Emigración e inmigración: Trabajo de clase del estudiante* (Buenos Aires, 1901).

51. Clodomiro Cordero, *El problema nacional* (Buenos Aires, 1911), 18, 38.

52. Carlos Nestor Maciel, *La italianización de la Argentina: Tras las huellas de nuestros antepasados* (Buenos Aires: Librería de Jesús Menéndez e Hijo, 1924), 4.

53. For a study of Italian immigrants' portrayal in the novels of the 1880s, see Luciano Rusich, *El inmigrante italiano en la novela del 80* (Madrid: Playor, 1974).

54. José María Ramos Mejía, *Las multitudes argentinas* [1899] (Buenos Aires: J. Lajouane, 1912), 261, 264.

55. Ibid., 64–67, 251–52.

56. Santiago Calzadilla, *Las beldades de mi tiempo* [1891] (Buenos Aires: Centro Editor de América Latina, 1982), 58.

57. José Miró [nom de plume of Julián Martel], *La Bolsa* [1891] (Buenos Aires: Plus Ultra, 1975), 247–48.

58. Cited in Anibal Latino, *Los factores del progreso de la República Argentina*, 2d ed. (Buenos Aires, 1910), 67–8. Significantly, González titled three talks that he gave in three different Spanish immigrant institutions in Buenos Aires between 1916 and 1919: "Spain in America," "The Problem of the Race," and "Race and Patriotism." In all three he referred to a cultural rather than a physical concept of race (*Anales de la Institución Cultural Española* 2 (1921–1925), part 1:77–109.

59. Myron I. Lichtblau, *Manuel Gálvez* (New York: Twayne Publishers, 1972), 23–24, considers this book Gálvez's first commercial success and one of his most acclaimed. Gálvez was nominated for the Nobel Prize in Literature in 1932, 1933, and 1951, but he never won. See also Mónica Quijada, *Manuel Gálvez: 60 años de pensamiento nacionalista* (Buenos Aires: Centro Editor de América Latina, 1985), esp. 84–89, on his pro-Spanish ideology.

60. A description of Hispanism by its foremost student, Frederick B. Pike, *Hispanismo, 1898–1930: Spanish Conservatives and Liberals and Their Relations with Spanish America* (Notre Dame, Ind.: University of Notre Dame Press, 1971), 1. The movement was also often referred to as Hispanoamericanism or pan-Hispanism.

61. These writings were collected in Manuel Ugarte, *La patria grande* (Madrid: Editora Internacional, 1924). See also his *El porvenir de la América española* [1911] (Valencia: Prometeo, 1920), esp. chap. 3, on the Spanish legacy; and his account of an influential trip to Spain, *Visiones de España: Apuntes de un viajero argentino* (Valencia: Prometeo, n.d.)

62. Rojas wrote of his 1908 trip to Spain, "My Spanish soul and heart burned with the anxiety of seeing the land of my ancestors" (*Amigos y maestros de mi juventud* [Buenos Aires: Hachette, 1961], 214). He considered the trip decisive in the formation of his cultural nationalist ideology, which he voiced in the next two years in *La restauración nacionalista* (Buenos Aires, 1909), perhaps the most influential Argentine book published during the first two decades of the century, in which he forewarned that immigration and the cosmopolitan materialistic ethos it engendered could destroy the country's cultural roots and identity and advocated nationalist education to prevent this; and in *Blasón de plata: Meditaciones y evocaciones sobre el abolengo de los argentinos* (written in 1910 and published two years later in Buenos Aires), a historical search into the nation's cultural roots. Rojas did not publish his notes on the trip to Spain in one place until thirty years later, in *Retablo español;* he dedicated the work to "my compatriots, and the Spaniards living in our country, whom I have never considered foreigners here, as I was not considered foreigner in Spain" (pp. 7–8).

63. Zeballos, "Conferencia," 577. His pro-Spanish attitude was extolled by the Catalan immigrant educator Ricardo Monner Sans in the pamphlet *El*

hispanismo de Estanislao S. Zeballos (Buenos Aires, n.d.). Zeballos wrote a glowing introduction to Monner Sans's defense of the purity of the Castilian language in the face of the "degenerating impact of cheap French novels and immigration," *Notas al castellano en la Argentina, con un prólogo del Dr. Estanislao S. Zeballos* [1903], 2d ed. (Buenos Aires: Agencia General de Librería y Publicaciones, 1924).

64. Cited in David Rock, *Authoritarian Argentina: The Nationalist Movement, Its History and Its Impact* (Berkeley: University of California Press, 1993), 41.

65. Alberto Gerchunoff, *Los gauchos judíos* [1910] (Buenos Aires: M. Gleizer, 1936), 21–22, 81–82, 121–23, 156, 159–63, 170–72.

66. Pike, *Hispanismo*, 193, 207–8, 415.

67. José León Suárez, *Enseñanza secundaria* (Buenos Aires, 1909).

68. Pike, *Hispanismo*, 193.

69. J. Francisco V. Silva, *Reparto de América Española y pan-hispanismo* (Madrid: F. Beltrán, 1918), and *Argentina bajo la opresión de Buenos Aires desde 1810* (Madrid, 1918). Indeed, "La leyenda del progreso," a chapter in the latter work, foreshadowed the arguments made sixty years later by North American historian E. Bradford Burns in his similarly titled *The Poverty of Progress: Latin America in the Nineteenth Century* (Berkeley: University of California Press, 1980). Inebriated with the "myth of progress" and motivated by shortsighted self-interest, the nineteenth-century liberal elites had tragically imitated the constitutional traditions of the United States, emulated the habits of non-Iberian Western Europe, and disdained their own people and heritage.

70. León Suárez, *Carácter de la revolución americana*, 15–16.

71. Manuel Gálvez, *El solar de la raza* [1913], 5th ed. (Madrid: Editorial Saturnino Calleja, 1920), 40. Apparently the author felt that turning Sarmiento into a Hispanophile stretched reality a bit too thin because he eliminated the passage after this or the next edition. See the 7th edition, published in 1943 and reissued by Ediciones Dictio (Buenos Aires), 1980, 32.

72. *Il Maldicente*, May 29, 1910, quoted in Hebe Clementi, *El miedo a la inmigración* (Buenos Aires: Editorial Leviatan, 1984), 82–83.

73. An exultant Valle Inclán, covering the centennial celebrations for the Madrid newspaper *El Mundo*, June 12, 1910, 1, wrote: "The Spanish Indies, as my grandmother used to say long ago and it is so gratifying for me to keep on saying, came again to be called by that voice of marvel and adventure". . . . "The good Spanish boors who close their stores during these days are delighted and relate to the maids, when they take them in their arms to see the fireworks, all the glories of the popular Infanta" (Juan Antonio Hormigón, *Valle Inclán: Cronología, escritos dispersos, epistolario* (Madrid: Fundación Banco Exterior, 1987), 306–7.

74. Zeballos, "Conferencia," 579; Ugarte, *El porvenir*, 36; Joaquín V. González, *La Argentina y sus amigos*, in *Obras Completas*, vol. 9 (Buenos Aires, 1906–1910), 189.

75. Blanca de los Ríos de Lamperez, *Afirmación de la raza ante el centenario de la independencia* (Madrid, 1910).

76. Gálvez, *El solar de la raza*, 53.

77. Francisco Camba and Juan Mas y Pi, *Los españoles en el centenario argentino* (Buenos Aires: Imprenta Mestres, 1910).

78. *Congreso Social y Económico Hispano-americano, reunido en Madrid en el año de 1900* (Madrid: Hijos de M. G. Fernández, 1902), vol. 2, 191–92, 201.

79. The proponent of the idea was Pedro García Cogolludo, who also wrote a poem, "Las dos banderas. El apellido" [The Two Flags. The Family Name], to promote it (*La Argentina: Revista mensual, órgano de la Sociedad Juventud Argentina* (Barcelona) 2, 14 (1916):4.

80. Juan García Caminero, *El problema hispano-americano* (Madrid, 1926), 84–85.

81. The article, which originally appeared in *Hispania* (the organ of the American Association of Teachers of Spanish) 3 (1918), was also published in *Revista de Derecho, Historia y Letras* (Buenos Aires), 64 (1919):54–64.

82. As part of their long campaign to make October 12 a national holiday, the Asociación Patriótica Española organized annual gatherings and celebrations on that date and published the speech given by Argentine sociologist and Renaissance man Ernesto Quesada, *Nuestra raza* (Buenos Aires: Librería Bredahl, 1900); and idem, *El día de la raza y su significado en Hispano-América* (Buenos Aires: Araujo Hermanos, 1918). It also published the fourth edition (16,000 copies) of León Suárez, *Carácter de la revolución americana*, in 1917, with a long appendix including all the letters the author had received supporting his pro-Spanish argument. The first edition (1916) does not seem to have been published by the association, and I did not find the next two editions.

83. For a list of the principal Spanish institutions fostering transatlantic Hispanism and the subsidies they received from the Spanish government, see José A. de Sangróniz, *La expansión cultural de España en el extranjero y principalmente en Hispano-America* (Madrid: Editorial Hercules, 1925), 88; and Emilio Zurano, *Alianza Hispano-Americana* (Madrid: J. Pueyo, 1926).

84. Luciano Abeille, *Idioma nacional de los argentinos* (Paris: Librairie Émile Bouillon, 1900) offered the best-known defense of Argentine Spanish as not simply Castilian, or even a dialect, but a new language in the making. The French-born author identified Spaniards as the principal enemies of the concept (pp. 39–41, 64–65) and French as the main external influence on the formation of the new Argentine language (pp. 282–89). Whatever the qualms of the purists at the Real Academia Española, the author continued, this process was irreversible, fit the reality of a new immigrant country, and reflected linguistically the "political independence Argentines so valiantly earned" (pp. 402–28). The principal attack on this position came from Ernesto Quesada, Argentine member of the Real Academia Española, in *El problema del idioma nacional* (Buenos Aires: Revista Nacional, 1900), who questioned the capacity of a Frenchman to comprehend the nuances of Argentine Spanish, "even if he has resided among us for a long time," and defended the purity and unity of "the glorious mother language" and the dignity of Spain, "who will always be for us our generous alma mater" (pp. iv–vii, 8).

85. Pike, *Hispanismo*, 134–37.

86. *La Emigración Española: Vida española en el extranjero, revista quince-nal de emigración y colonias* (Madrid), April 15, 1916, 61, 62; June 15, 1916, 93; August 30, 1916, 138; and November 15, 1918, 164. This magazine was pub-lished from 1912 until at least 1920. The other magazine was *El Emigrante Español: Organo oficial de la Bolsa del Trabajo Internacional y de las colonias españolas en el extranjero*, published in Madrid from June 1918 until at least June 1921.

87. *Revista de Economía Argentina* 27, 161 (1931):369.

88. Domingo Quiroga, *El mito del hispanoamericanismo* (n.p., 1927?) ar-gued in this booklet that Hispanism was little more than a dream, too "spiri-tual for a century so materialistic," and that given Spain's economic under-development, it could not be otherwise.

89. Ricardo Monner Sans's works on the subject include dozens of articles, listed in his *Mi labor en el Plata* (Buenos Aires, 1922), 35–74, and the books *Notas al castellano* and *Barbaridades que se nos escapan al hablar* (Buenos Aires, 1924).

90. Monner Sans, *Notas al castellano*, 46, 52–53.

91. Ricardo Monner Sans, *España y Norte América: Antecedentes y consi-deraciones* (Buenos Aires: Imprenta A. Monkes, 1898), *La religión en el idioma español: ensayo paremiológico* (Buenos Aires: F. Lajouane, 1899), *Apuntes e ideas sobre educación a propósito de la enseñanza secundaria* (Buenos Aires: F. Lajouane, 1896), and *Antología escolar hispano-argentina para enseñanza se-cundaria y normal* (Buenos Aires: A. Estrada y Cía., 1920).

92. José María Salaverría, *El poema de la pampa: 'Martín Fierro' y el crio-llismo español* (Madrid: Calleja, 1918), 11, 14, 34–35, 124, and *Tierra argentina: Psicología, tipos, costumbres, valores de la República del Plata* (Madrid: Librería de Fernando Fe, 1910), 165–67.

93. Salaverría, *El poema de la pampa*, 18–19, 72–73.

94. Salaverría, *Tierra argentina*, 174–84.

95. Ramiro de Maeztu, *Defensa de la hispanidad* (Buenos Aires: Poblet, 1942), 137–38. The book first appeared in 1934, the year in which Maeztu was executed by a republican firing squad, but it contained many of his earlier writ-ings.

96. Ibid.

97. Roberto Arlt, *Obras completas*, 2 vols. (Buenos Aires: C. Lohlé, 1981), vol. 2, 453.

98. In the first half of *Los catalanes* Monner Sans concentrated on their roles in repelling the British invasions of Buenos Aires in 1806–1807. This pre-sented a favorite and safe historical theme for Spanish immigrant writers, be-cause it placed Argentines and Spaniards in fraternal unity against foreign in-vaders, and it had the added attraction of fueling Anglophobia. The immigrant colony, like Spaniards in the peninsula, resented the English occupation of Gi-braltar, had formed numerous leagues against it, and often likened their claims to those of Argentines over the Falkland Islands. In the second part of the book, however, the author takes on the more challenging task of turning the anti-Spanish wars of emancipation into an expression of Hispanism.

99. Celso García del Riega, *Colón español* (Buenos Aires, 1914).

100. Rafael Calzada, *La patria de Colón* (Buenos Aires, 1920) [based on a 1915 conference].

101. See, for example, José M. Casais, "Lala Marieta," *La Escena: Revista teatral*, no. 165, August 25, 1921, 2–3. Manuel Romero and Domingo Parra, "Don Jaime el conquistador," *La Escena: Revista teatral*, no. 159, July 14, 1921, 10, ridicule intra-Spanish feuds over the issue. A Catalan immigrant brags that Columbus was from Barcelona. When an Argentine replies, "But they say he was *gallego*," he begins to whine about how the "envious *gallegos*" wanted to steal this glory from Catalonia and adds all sorts of famous names, from Lenin to Juan de Garay (a Basque conquistador in Argentina) to his list of Catalan natives.

102. J. M. Vargas Vila, *Odisea romántica: Diario de viaje a la República Argentina* (Madrid: Biblioteca Nueva, [1927]), 139 (capitals are in the original).

103. Rock, *Authoritarian Argentina*, 41.

104. Ibid., 42; and Gálvez, *El solar de la raza*, 15–16, 44.

105. Rojas, *Obras completas*, vol. 3; and idem, *La argentinidad*, 2d ed. (Buenos Aires: La Facultad, 1922), 7.

106. Earl T. Glauert, "Ricardo Rojas and the Emergence of Argentine Cultural Nationalism," *Hispanic American Historical Review* 43, 1 (1963):1–13.

107. Ugarte called Maeztu "mi amigo, el excelente escritor" and kept up a copious correspondence with him (*Visiones de españa*, 134 ff). For the European influences on Larreta, see André Jansen, *Enrique Larreta: Novelista Hispano-Argentino, 1873–1961* (Madrid: Ediciones Cultura Hispánica, 1967).

108. Alejandro Bunge, "La raza argentina," *Revista de Economía Argentina* 14, 81 (1925):198. The article was written under the pseudonym Vieytes.

109. Carlos Octavio Bunge, *Nuestra América: Ensayo de psicología social* [1903], 7th ed. (Madrid: Espasa-Calpe, 1926). The first part of the book is devoted to a "scientific analysis" of the Spanish character, and chapters 7 and 9 are titled, respectively, "Physiological Consequences of Spanish Arrogance in the Modern Age: The Collective Degeneration," and "Decadent Forms of Spanish Arrogance: Indolence and Ferocity."

110. Jews and Middle Easterners did indeed provide a favorite target for twentieth-century xenophobic writers. Saul Escobar, in his law-school thesis *La inmigración* (Buenos Aires, 1907), 68–69, called them "corrupted oriental races" and, paraphrasing Alberdi's dictum of "To govern is to populate," added, "To populate with such vipers is not to govern but to make government impossible." Ernesto M. Aráoz, *La inmigración en la Argentina y sus vinculaciones con la cuestión social* (Salta, Argentina: Imprenta Pascual y Baleirón de las Llanas, 1919), 48, also argued for the exclusion of "these people that can shatter the homogeneity of our race," on the grounds that the constitutional right of all Europeans to immigrate to Argentina did not apply to them. The writers of the 1853 constitution had not explicitly excluded them simply because Turkey and the Eastern European countries were not politically significant then and had few relations with Argentina. José Pio Sagastume, *La inmigración: Su influencia en el país* (La Plata, Argentina, 1916), 134–46, referred to the *turcos* (the Argentine popular term for Middle Eastern immigrants in general) as unproduc-

tive and stingy peddlers; and to *rusos* (the equivalent term for Jews) as filthy, backward, dishonest petty traders but "submissive and respectful of authorities." To Francisco Stach, *La defensa social y la inmigración* (Buenos Aires, 1916), 26–28, "the so-called Rusos" represented "the most undesirable element, full of anarchists, pimps, and prostitutes all capable of criminal acts," and so did the "Turk, Syrian, and other similar immigrations."

On the other hand, the ex-Minister of Agriculture, Damián M. Torino, *El problema del inmigrante y el problema agrario en la Argentina* (Buenos Aires, 1912), 30–31, found "much good" in Jewish immigrants except for the anarchists and revolutionaries, adding: "The Jew is dangerous or damaging only in poor and lethargic countries. It is a microbe that harms weak and tired organisms but adapts well to potent and virile ones. His laborious intelligence and commercial instinct strains the social fabric of weak peoples who see in them a whip. Among peoples who, on the contrary, are endowed with similar aptitudes, or even superior ones to that of the Jew, he competes with equal rivals, and his arrival yields in these prosperous environments nothing but extra vitality." He considered Argentina such an environment and said similar things about Middle Easterners.

111. Pike, *Hispanismo*, 65.

112. Ibid.

113. In terms similar to Rodó's, Gálvez, *El solar de la raza*, 60, defined North American energy as "barbarous and automatic" compared with the "harmony, elegance, and intelligence of Latin energy." Quesada, *Nuestra raza* (1900) and the contemporary works of Rubén Darío and Manuel Ugarte expressed similar views.

114. Salaverría, *El poema de la pampa*, 15. He also called them "suburban cowboys" (p. 18).

115. In prologue to Eugenio Capdevila Romero, *Labor Hispano-Argentina: Conferencias patrias* (Buenos Aires, 1919).

116. Published in Valencia by F. Sempere y Cía., this little-known book was dedicated to "the memory of the first conquistadors of America and the new Spanish writers," whose work it examined.

117. For example, Argentine intellectual Alberto Zum Felde, *El problema de la cultura americana* (Buenos Aires: Editorial Lozada, 1943), 48–53, strongly rejected Hispanism as a form of Spanish hegemony. He added that the greatest danger lay not in the pretensions of Spanish imperialists but in the power of the numerous Argentine Hispanophiles and found no difference between them and the old liberals who wanted to turn Argentina into a cultural colony of France.

118. Juan Baustista Alberdi's impressions of a trip to Spain in 1843 offer a good example of a friendly voice during a period when few were raised. Softening his previous Hispanophobia and infatuation with French and English models, he wrote:

> We have already said all the bad things possible about our race; it is time to start looking at the other side. . . . We have already acclaimed those of 1810 [the heroes of independence]; let us take things to a higher plane and acclaim those of 1492; those who invented half of the earthly orb, depopulated it of barbarous races, a sort of human underbrush, to populate it with the most beauti-

ful race of Europe, the noble Spanish race. . . . Let us not attack the Spanish race, because we are it; its work, because it is the world we inhabit; its domination, because it embraces all of our existence except the last eighth; its legacy, because it still governs us in the largest part, and it must not have been that bad when it gave us the aptitude to emancipate ourselves when the opportunity came. Let us study Spain, then, to know ourselves.

He then described the War of Independence as nothing more than a civil conflict between Spaniards. Alberdi perhaps became the first important liberal thinker to reassess the Hispanic legacy and Creole culture. The above arguments precede by seventy years those made by José León Suárez, Manuel Gálvez, and other twentieth-century champions of Hispanism (*Viajes y descripciones*, "Grandes Escritores Argentinos" series, vol. 12 [Buenos Aires: W. M. Jackson, n.d.], 212–15).

119. For the role of Spanish Krausists in Argentina, see Hugo E. Biagini, ed., *Redescubriendo un continente: La inteligencia española en el París americano en las postrimerías del XVIII* (Seville: Diputación Provincial, 1993), 281–91, which, despite the title, deals with the late-nineteenth and twentieth centuries.

120. *Anales de la Institución Cultural Española* 2 (1921–1925), part 1:107.

121. Manuel A. Zuloaga, *Nuestra raza: Condición del extranjero en la Argentina* (Buenos Aires: Ferrari Hermanos, 1931), 81.

122. Antonio Fernández, *Población e inmigración: Tesis escrita en julio de 1916* (Buenos Aires, 1917), 66–69.

123. Clodomiro Zavalía, *Defensa social de la nación* (Buenos Aires, 1919), 44.

124. Stach, *La defensa social*, 24.

125. Salaverría, *Tierra argentina*, 173–77; "Quienes deben emigrar," *A B C* (Madrid), December 20, 1909. See also Beatrice Ramos Petriz, "A Biographical and Critical Introduction to José María Salaverría" (Ph.D. diss., University of California, Los Angeles, 1956), 157–70.

126. Cesarina Lupati Guelfi, *Vida argentina* (Barcelona: Maucci, 1910), 248, 256, lamented that Italy sent "pauperism" instead of capital to Argentina and that Argentines unfairly gauged Italy by its emigration. Bartolomeo Bossim, *Noblesse oblige* (Genoa, 1886), lived in Argentina for fifty years and found his immigrant compatriots a source of shame rather than pride. He thus ridiculed the Italian government's imperialist dreams that the immigrant colony would eventually evolve into a real one or, as Guelfi had put it: "not Italians in America, [that is, Argentina] but Italy in America."

127. Enrique Larreta, "Palabras pronunciadas en el Club Español . . . Buenos Aires, 1933," in *Obras completas* (Madrid: Editorial Plenitud, 1949), 898–99.

128. Jansen, *Enrique Larreta*, 53, 192.

129. Gálvez, *El solar de la raza*, 39, 42–43, 59, 79, 221–25; and *España y algunos españoles* (Buenos Aires: Editorial Huarpes, 1945), 20, 74–75. In this last book, Gálvez also includes a panegyric to the Jesuit order (pp. 265–72).

130. Rock, *Authoritarian Argentina*, 2–3, observed that "the opposition of the Nationalists to what they called centralized despotism and their quest for a church free of subjection to the state recalled Spanish Carlism." One of the ear-

liest examples is Silva, *Reparto de América Española* (1918). This proud son of "Córdoba del Tucumán, the true historic capital of Argentina," accused the "atheist, centralist, liberal bourgeoisie" of Buenos Aires of denationalizing and de-Hispanizing the country and turning it into a foreign colony. Foreshadowing the "historical revisionism" of the 1930s and 1940s, he revaluated old federalist caudillos, particularly Facundo Quiroga, whom Sarmiento had made the incarnation of barbarism in his famous *Facundo: Civilización y barbarie* (Santiago, Chile, 1845).

131. Gálvez, *El solar de la raza*, 181.

132. In his 1891 novel *La bolsa*, 214–16, Julián Martel, despite his real Catalan surname (José Miró), portrays an unnamed Catalan character as an ungrateful miser who refuses to loan some money to his ex-benefactor, who now is broke. Tellingly, the miser in the next scene is a Jew.

133. For portrayals of Catalan and Andalusian anarchists in Argentine theater, see Carlos M. Pacheco, "Los fuertes" [1906?], *Bambalinas* 200 (1922); Agustín Fontanella, *Bachicha: Sainete cómico lírico dramático, en un acto y 3 cuadros* (Buenos Aires, 1908); Alberto Vacarezza, "Tu cuna fué un conventillo" [1920], reprinted in *El sainete criollo*, ed. Tulio Carella (Buenos Aires: Librería Hachette, 1957); and Mario Flores, "Cruz Diablo," *La Escena: Revista teatral*, no. 152, May 26, 1921.

134. "División Investigación Orden Social, Antecedentes de Anarquistas, 1902, No. 1," Buenos Aires Police Archive.

135. María Inés Barbero and Fernando Devoto, *Los nacionalistas, 1910–1932* (Buenos Aires: Centro Editor de América Latina, 1983), 40. For a fine history of the Liga Patriótica Argentina, see Sandra McGee Deutsch, *Counterrevolution in Argentina, 1900–1932: The Argentine Patriotic League* (Lincoln: University of Nebraska Press, 1986).

136. Rojas visited Vigo and La Coruña, but only because the steamer made stops there (*Retablo español*, 142).

137. For examples of plays where *gallego* is used as a synonym for dumb, see: José M. Bosch, "La gallega" [opened in 1917], *La Escena: Revista teatral*, no. 135, January 27, 1921, 6; Pedro Benjamín Aquino, "La carrera de charrua," *La Escena: Revista teatral*, no. 147, April 21, 1921, 5; and Julio C. Traversa and J. Luque Lobos, "El taita de Triunvirato," *La Escena: Revista teatral*, no. 197, April 6, 1922, 2.

138. The plays were published in the biweekly theater magazine, *La Escena: Revista teatral*, usually a week or two after their opening.

139. Real Galician servants seem to have been less compliant and disinterested than their theatrical representations. An Argentine employer asserted in 1916 that: "In the majority of the large Porteño newspapers one can read advertisements for domestics which specifically exclude *gallegos*. This is due to the fact that these servants have not lowered their [monetary] expectations of better times and do not compete with people of other nationalities, more adaptable, refined, humble, and with less pretensions. If they do not want to lose their positions in the service, they will have to accommodate to the present circumstances, which have changed much in the last years, and abandon their immoderate pretensions" (José Pío Sagastume, *La inmigración*, 47).

140. Lence, *Memorias,* 124–25.

141. Alberto T. Weisbach, "Farruco," *La Escena: Revista teatral,* no. 145, April 7, 1921, 11.

142. For an examination of this theater by a historian, see Judith Evans, "Setting the Stage for Struggle: Popular Theater in Buenos Aires, 1890–1914," *Radical History Review* 21 (Fall 1979):49–61, which includes an English translation of Nemesio Trejo's "Los Inquilinos" on pp. 62–83.

143. Bosch, "La gallega," deals with a love affair between an upper-class Creole youth and the leading character, who is not a real *gallega* but a refined, beautiful Spanish señorita just arrived from Valladolid, in the heart of Old Castile. In Casais, "Lala Marieta," the title character is an earthly Genoese matron, but her nephew Rafael is an urbane, attractive young man who has lived in Madrid for several years, speaks flawless, elegant Spanish, and has come to Buenos Aires as an attaché to the Italian embassy. And Romero and Parra, "Don Jaime el conquistador," includes another cultured, recently arrived nephew, this one from Barcelona.

144. For examples of plays in which the Argentine-born children express embarrassment at their parents' Old World ways, see the following, all of which appeared in *La Escena: Revista teatral:* Weisbach, "Farruco," no. 145, April 7, 1921 (for Galicians); Federico Mertens, "Mama Clara," no. 133, January 13, 1921 (for Catalans); idem, "Mi abuela Graciana," no. 203, May 18, 1922 (for French Basques); Emilio Sánchez, "El jarrón de Sevres," no. 161, July 21, 1921; Carlos M. Pacheco, "Ropa vieja," July 23, 1923, suppl. 84 (for Jews); Alberto and Mario Rada, "¡Criollos, gringos y judíos!" no. 180, December 8, 1921 (for Italians and Jews); and the following, for Italians: Augusto Vaccari, "The Equatorial," no. 121, October 21, 1920; Armando Discépolo and R. J. de la Rosa, "El guarda 323," November 15, 1921, suppl. 17, scene 3; Carlos C. Sanguinetti, "La medalla," December 20, 1920, suppl. 21; and José González Castillo and Juan Comorera, "Puerto Madero," July 9, 1923, suppl. 82.

145. Cited in Miguel D. Etchebarne, *La influencia del arrabal en la poesía argentina culta* (Buenos Aires: G. Kraft, 1955), 79.

146. Manuel Gil de Oto, *La Argentina que yo he visto* (Barcelona, 1914), 68.

147. Weisbach, "Farruco."

148. Pacheco, "Ropa vieja," 11.

149. Julio F. Escobar, "Flor de lys," *La Escena: Revista teatral,* January 10, 1921, suppl. 22, 9.

150. Carlos Schaefer Gallo, "Canciones populares," *La Escena: Revista teatral,* October 11, 1920, suppl. 13, 9.

151. Gil de Oto, *La Argentina,* 264–65.

152. Ibid., 64.

153. Ibid., 265.

154. Luis Pascarella, *El conventillo: Costumbres bonaerenses* (Buenos Aires: La Lectural, 1917), 34.

155. Antonio Pérez-Prado, *Los gallegos y Buenos Aires* (Buenos Aires: La Bastilla, 1973), 86.

156. Salaverría, *Tierra argentina,* 161–65, 175.

157. Salaverría, cited in Etchebarne, *La influencia del arrabal,* 87.

158. Gil de Oto, *La Argentina*, 88–89.

159. Angel Bonetti, *De la República Argentina y sus detractores* (Buenos Aires, 1910), 210.

160. Antonio Cafferato, *Apuntes sobre inmigración y colonización*, Tesis (Buenos Aires, 1898), 53–54. To an Italian visitor in the same decade, some of his compatriots' *argentinismo* represented not a virtue but a chagrin that often reached "the ridiculous extreme of disavowing their own names, of Hispanizing them as to hide their true origin" (Fernando Resasco, *En las riveras del Plata*, trans. Antonio Sánchez Pérez [Madrid, 1891], 309–10).

161. Domingo F. Casadevall, *Buenos Aires: Arrabal, sainete, tango* (Buenos Aires: Compañía General Fabril, 1968), 38.

162. Ruth F. de Seefeld, "La integración social de extranjeros en Buenos Aires según sus pautas matrimoniales: ¿Pluralismo cultural o crizol de razas? (1860–1923)," *Estudios Migratorios Latinoamericanos* 1, 2 (1986):213.

CONCLUSION

1. *Alborada: Organo de la Asociación Benéfica Cultural del Partido de Corcubión* (Buenos Aires) 5 (December 1929):53.

2. The information on this and the following people comes from the membership records of the various immigrant associations in Buenos Aires used in this study, from interviews with their members and with people in the Spanish villages and towns, and from other sources mentioned in the preceding chapters.

3. Val de San Lorenzo claims, as do most towns and villages in Spain, it seems, both conquistadors and colonizers. Whatever the merit of those claims, in the national period they began to arrive in significant numbers only after 1900.

4. See note 70 of chapter 1.

5. Pierre Bourdieu and Jean-Claude Passeron, *Reproduction in Education, Society and Culture* (London: Sage Publications, 1977). Bourdieu used the cultural-capital concept to express the tendency of the late-twentieth-century bourgeoisie (or of the bureaucratic elite in communist countries) to maintain its position not so much by transferring material property to its children but by transmitting certain values and attitudes that gave the latter an edge in the educational and economic system. My findings suggest that a similar process was taking place at the beginning of the twentieth century and among people of humbler origins. Immigrants from nonpropertied but urban or semiurban families fared better economically in Buenos Aires than did those from propertied but rural families.

6. Numerical predominance, sharp differences with the indigenous population, and/or colonial status seem to make the English in Australia, New Zealand, Canada, and South Africa and the French in Algeria less suitable cases for comparison with Argentina's Spaniards.

7. Manuscript census returns of the Buenos Aires municipal census of 1855, kept in the Archivo General de la Nación; "Lista de enterrados en el Cementerio del Norte," Legajo Gobierno, caja 5, 1861, kept in the Archivo Histórico de la Municipalidad de la Ciudad de Buenos Aires.

8. "Nomina de asilados en el Asilo de Mendigos," Legajo Salud Pública, Caja 7, 1859, kept in the Archivo Histórico de la Municipalidad de la Ciudad de Buenos Aires; and María Sáenz Quesada, *El estado rebelde: Buenos Aires entre 1850–1860* (Buenos Aires: Editorial Belgrano, 1982), 130.

9. Membership application forms of the Asociación Española de Socorros Mutuos de Buenos Aires, 1912; and *El Español: Periódico de intereses españoles,* July 18, 1852.

10. Antonio "*El Gallego*" Soto, a stagehand in a Spanish traveling theater company, arrived in the Patagonian province of Santa Cruz in 1920 at the age of twenty-three. Elected a year later as secretary general of the local labor federation, he led a widespread workers' insurrection that was put down only after an army-led massacre of 1,500 rebels. Jose María Borrero, a Spanish immigrant lawyer who participated in the events on the side of the workers, wrote the first book on the revolt, *La Patagonia trágica* (Buenos Aires, 1928). More recently, the Argentine historian Osvaldo Bayer published a three-volume study of the topic, *Los vengadores de la Patagonia trágica* (Buenos Aires: Editorial Galerna, 1972–1974); and cineast Hector Olivera directed the popular motion picture *La Patagonia rebelde* (1974).

APPENDIX

1. The manuscripts themselves have been used by Fernando Devoto, "The Origins of an Italian Neighborhood in Buenos Aires in the Mid XIX Century: La Boca," *Journal of European Economic History* 18, 1 (1989):37–64, and by Mark D. Szuchman in his excellent study of family life and social controls, *Order, Family, and Community in Buenos Aires, 1810–1860* (Stanford, Calif.: Stanford University Press, 1989).

2. The Historical Department of the Church of Jesus Christ of Latter-day Saints in Salt Lake City contains a vast collection of parish and other demographic records from all over the world that can be borrowed by researchers through family-history centers in the local temples of most U.S. cities. Unfortunately, records from the parishes in which I was interested are not included.

3. At times, the *padrones* do not specify where the absentees live, listing only "America," a problem that also plagues similar Italian population registries. See Donna Gabaccia, *Militants and Migrants: Rural Sicilians Become American Workers* (New Brunswick, N.J.: Rutgers University Press, 1988), 177–78.

Index